"Based on a superb mastery of the archival sources and the secondary literature, Browning leads his readers through the step-by-step radicalization of Nazi policies in the critical months after the outbreak of WWII. . . . This book is sure to become the standard work on the emergence of the Holocaust."—*Publishers Weekly* starred review

"The more Nazi leaders talked of radical solutions, fundamental solutions, total solutions, eradication, total liquidation and final solutions, the more obvious it became what finality would consist of. Browning takes us there, step by step, false lead by false lead, with never-failing intellectual mastery. It is difficult to see this work being superseded in the foreseeable future."—*Times Literary Supplement*

"[*Origins of the Final Solution*] is clearly structured, well-written, and free of intentionalist determinism. Its strength lies in the author's remarkable precision and eye for detail."—*American Historical Review*

"This book is Browning's most comprehensive work—a blend of careful analysis of primary sources, broad geographical coverage, and civilized historiographical dialogue carried out in the text and notes. It deserves to be read and studied for many years. . . . Faced with difficult problems of interpretation, good scholars examine the relevant documentation carefully, consider the alternatives, and set forth clearly why they have reached their views. Browning and Mattäus have both done this and more in this splendid volume."—Richard Breitman, *Central European History*

"With his characteristically meticulous research and reasoning, Browning has written what will quickly become a classic in Holocaust studies."—*Journal of Interdisciplinary History*

"Browning's account of the evolution of the Nazi genocide is the most comprehensive that has yet appeared."—William D. Rubinstein, *First Things*

"Browning's *Origins* illustrates the complexities of the decision-making process. This is an important book and to date marks the only comprehensive analysis of the origins of the Final Solution. For this reason it should be read by anyone serious about this subject. Scholars and graduate students alike will find it illuminating."—*H-Net Book Reviews H-German*

"Browning's volume is essential reading for all students of the Shoah."—*Library Journal*

"The prodigious scholarship and comprehensive bibliography that inform this volume makes it indispensable for understanding the origins of the Final Solution."—*Choice*

"Browning recounts the sequence of events that led from 'ethnic cleansing' to the mass murder of Europe's Jews. . . . It is the most detailed examination of this aspect of the Holocaust yet published."—*Booklist*

"[Browning's] sources strikingly reveal just how far and deep scholars have delved into the subject. The accumulated wealth of such detailed studies contributes equally with primary sources to produce this comprehensive overview."—George C. Browder, *Holocaust and Genocide Studies*

"Browning has turned up a rich mine of information which provides nuance to, and enhances our understanding of, the various stages which accompanied Nazi Germany's thinking about the disposition of the Jewish communities it found under its control after the conquest of Poland."—Arnold Ages, *Chicago Jewish Star*

"Effective and powerful. . . . Not a cheerful book but one of the most profound meditations, however indirect, on the character of human wickedness in the 20th century. Read it and weep."—Charles T. Mathewes, *Virginia Quarterly Review*

The Comprehensive History of the Holocaust

Yad Vashem initiated the Comprehensive History of the Holocaust project together with historians from a number of universities and research institutes. The project seeks to summarize research findings on the Holocaust during the generations following the war.

THE ORIGINS OF THE FINAL SOLUTION

THE EVOLUTION OF NAZI JEWISH POLICY,

SEPTEMBER 1939–MARCH 1942

CHRISTOPHER R. BROWNING

With contributions by Jürgen Matthäus

Published by the

UNIVERSITY OF NEBRASKA PRESS, *Lincoln,*

and YAD VASHEM, *Jerusalem*

Library of Congress
Cataloging-in-Publication Data
Browning, Christopher R.
The origins of the Final Solution : the
evolution of Nazi Jewish policy, September
1939–March 1942 / Christopher Browning ;
with contributions by Jürgen Matthäus.
   p. cm. — (Comprehensive history of the
Holocaust)
Includes bibliographical references and index.
ISBN 0-8032-1327-1 (cl : alk. paper)
1. Holocaust, Jewish (1939–1945).
2. Holocaust, Jewish (1939–1945)—Causes.
3. Jews—Government policy—Germany—
History—20th century. 4. Germany—Politics
and government—1933–1945. 5. Germany—
Ethnic relations. I. Matthäus, Jürgen, 1959–
II. Title. III. Series.
D804.3.B773 2004
940.53'1811—dc22   2003060813
ISBN-13: 978-0-8032-5979-9 (pa : alk. paper)
ISBN-10: 0-8032-5979-4 (pa : alk. paper)

The publication of this series was

made possible by the generous gift of the

Ike and Roz Friedman Family Foundation,

in loving memory of

Ike Friedman and Janis Friedman Yale

and all those who perished in the Holocaust.

Contents

Illustrations

Preface

This book on the origins of the Final Solution is part of a wider project for a multivolume comprehensive history of the Holocaust. This role shapes its conception and format in three fundamental ways. First, within this wider project as conceived of by Yad Vashem, it is just one of three volumes devoted to an examination of the development of Nazi Jewish policy. Since it will follow a volume on the prewar years, September 1939 is the clear starting point for this volume, and it makes no attempt to cover the earlier years beyond brief background references. It will precede a volume on the implementation of the Final Solution, and here there is no clear and unambiguous temporal dividing line between origins and implementation that would be valid for all regions of Europe under German occupation. We have chosen March 1942, the point when the Germans were poised to liquidate the Polish ghettos and gas Jews in Belzec, to receive the initial transports from France and Slovakia, to renew deportations from the Reich, and to launch the second wave of killing on occupied Soviet territory. In our opinion this cluster of fateful events marks the most reasonable dividing point between the origins and implementation of the Final Solution and the one best suited to our interpretational framework.

Second, while this volume was one of three specifically commissioned to focus on Nazi policy making, most of the remaining volumes of the series cover the histories of each national Jewish community in Europe under the impact of the Holocaust. Thus, in contrast to some recent works that have ambitiously sought to synthesize the history of the perpetrators and victims into a single narrative, this volume makes no such attempt to include the perspective and experience of the victims other than where the initiatives and tactics of Jewish leaders, particularly Rumkowski in Lodz and Czerniakow in Warsaw, played an important role in shaping Nazi policy. It does not seek to do superficially and redundantly what most of the other volumes in the series will do in great detail.

Third, when this wider multivolume project was originally conceived, it was immediately recognized that no project involving so many authors either could or should aspire to interpretational uniformity. It was accepted that different scholars would have different perspectives, approaches, and emphases, and that this pluralism inherent in the world of scholarship should be on display in the series. Discerning readers will note that the two authors of this volume articulate interpretations that differ in some small ways. We have made no attempt to force our views into a single mold but rather, in the spirit of the wider project, have let each interpretation speak for itself.

The authors are grateful to a number of institutions whose help has been indispensable. For their generous financial support for research, Christopher Browning would like to express his thanks for fellowships from the DAAD, the Alexander von Humboldt Foundation, the Institute for Advanced Study in Princeton, and the Institute for Advanced Study on the campus of Hebrew University of Jerusalem, for the J. B. and Maurice C. Shapiro and Ina Levine Scholar in Residence Awards from the Center for Advanced Holocaust Studies of the U.S. Holocaust Memorial Museum, and for the sabbatical and Regency Advancement Award programs of Pacific Lutheran University, a Fulbright research fellowship, and a W. R. Kenan, Jr., Leave from the University of North Carolina at Chapel Hill. He is also grateful for the cooperation and support of the archivists and staffs at the Yad Vashem Archives, the Archives of the U.S. Holocaust Memorial Museum, the Politisches Archiv des Auswärtigen Amtes formerly in Bonn, the Bundesarchiv in Koblenz and Berlin, the Bundesarchiv-Militärchiv in Freiburg, the Zentrale Stelle des Landesjustizverwaltungen in Ludwigsburg, the Berlin Document Center, the U.S. National Archives, the Archivum Panstwowe in Warsaw, the Jewish Historical Museum in Belgrade, and the Landgerichten of Nürnberg-Fürth, Bonn, Hanover, Cologne, and Konstanz.

Jürgen Matthäus thanks the archivists at the Bundesarchiv Berlin, the U.S. Holocaust Memorial Museum, and the Zentrum für Antisemitismusforschung Berlin. While the opinions contained in the relevant parts of the book are his own and do not reflect the opinions of the U.S. Holocaust Memorial Museum, he is grateful for the permission of the museum's International Archival Programs Division and its Center for Advanced Holocaust Studies to pursue this project outside his official functions as museum historian.

Over the years numerous colleagues have generously shared their critical insights and provided valued support for our work. We would like specifically to thank Raul Hilberg, Michael Marrus, Yehuda Bauer, Saul Friedländer, Peter Hayes, Jonathan Steinberg, Eberhard Jäckel, Ulrich Herbert, Dina Porat, Richard Cohen, Israel Gutman, Dov Kulka, George Mosse, Yaacov Lozowick, Henry Friedlander, Gerhard Weinberg, Helmut Krausnick, Karl Schleunes, Thomas Sandkühler, Konrad Kwiet, Dieter Pohl, Jürgen Förster, Christian Gerlach, Hans Mommsen, Nechama Tec, and Klaus-Michael Mallmann. For the shortcomings and deficiencies that remain, we are of course fully responsible.

Christopher R. Browning
Jürgen Matthäus

THE
ORIGINS
OF THE
FINAL
SOLUTION

I

Background

In a brief two years between the autumn of 1939 and the autumn of 1941, Nazi Jewish policy escalated rapidly from the prewar policy of forced emigration to the Final Solution as it is now understood—the systematic attempt to murder every last Jew within the German grasp. The mass murder of Soviet Jewry had already begun in the late summer of 1941, and only one-half year later the Nazi regime was ready to begin implementing this policy throughout the rest of its European empire and sphere of influence. The study of these 30 months—from September 1939 through March 1942—is crucial for understanding the genesis of the Final Solution and constitutes the core of this book. At this time the Nazi regime stood on the brink of a true watershed event in history. But why, after two millennia of Christian-Jewish antagonism and one millennium of a singular European anti-Semitism, did this watershed event occur in Germany in the middle of the 20th century?

Christians and Jews had lived in an adversarial relationship since the first century of the common era, when the early followers of Jesus failed to persuade significant numbers of their fellow Jews that he was the Messiah. They then gradually solidified their identity as a new religion rather than a reforming Jewish sect. First, Pauline Christianity took the step of seeking converts not just among Jews but also among the pagan populations of the Roman Empire. Second, the Gospel writers—some 40 to 60 years after the death of Jesus—sought to placate the Roman authorities and at the same time to stigmatize their rivals by increasingly portraying the Jews rather than the Roman authorities in Palestine as responsible for the crucifixion—the scriptural origin of the fateful "Christ-killer" libel. Finally, the Jewish rebellion in Palestine and the destruction of the Second Temple motivated early Christians not only to disassociate themselves completely from the Jews but to see the Jewish catastrophe as a deserved punishment for the stubborn refusal to accept Jesus as the Messiah and as a divine vindication of their own beliefs. Christians and Jews, two small sects that had much more in common with one another by virtue of their monotheism and scriptures than either had with the rest of the tolerant, syncretic, polytheistic pagan Roman world, developed an implacable hostility to one another.

This hostility became historically significant in the course of the fourth century when, following the conversion of the Emperor Constantine, Christianity became first the favored and then the official religion of the Roman Empire. The religious quarrel between two small and relatively powerless sects, both at odds with the pagan world in which they lived, was suddenly transformed into an unequal relationship between a triumphant state religion and a beleaguered religious minority. Even so, the Jews fared better than the pagans. Triumphant Christians destroyed paganism and tore down its temples; but the synagogues were left standing, and Judaism remained as the sole legally permitted religion outside Christianity. Without this double standard of intolerance—paganism destroyed and Judaism despised but permitted—there would have been no further history of Christian-Jewish relations.

Seemingly triumphant Christianity soon faced its own centuries-long string of disasters. As demographic and economic decline eroded the strength of the Christianized Roman Empire from within, the western provinces fragmented and collapsed under the impact of the numerically rather small Germanic invasions from the north. The later invasion of the Huns from the east dissipated, but not so the subsequent Muslim invasion, which stormed out of the Arabian Peninsula and conquered half the old Roman world by the end of the seventh century. In the area destined to become western Europe, cities—along with urban culture and a money economy—disappeared almost entirely. A vastly shrunken population—illiterate, impoverished, and huddled in isolated villages scraping out a precarious living from a primitive, subsistence agriculture—reeled under the impact of yet further devastating invasions of Vikings from Scandinavia and Magyars from central Asia in the ninth and tenth centuries. Neither the Christian majority nor the Jewish minority of western Europe could find much solace in these centuries of affliction and decline.

The great recovery—demographic, economic, cultural, and political—began shortly before the millennium. Population exploded, cities grew up, wealth multiplied, centralizing monarchies began to triumph over feudal anarchy, universities were invented, cultural treasures of the classical world were recovered, and the borders of western Christendom began to expand.

But the great transformation did not bring equal benefits to all. Europe's first great "modernization crisis," like any such profound transformation, had its "social losers." A surplus of disgruntled mounted warriors—Europe's feudal elite—faced constricted opportunities and outlets. A new money economy and urban society eroded traditional manorial relationships. Expanding literacy and university education, coupled with an intoxicating discovery of Aristotelian rationalism, posed a potential and unsettling threat to traditional Christian faith. Growth, prosperity, and religious enthusiasm were accompanied by bewilderment, frustration, and doubt.

For all that was new and unsettling, incomprehensible and threatening, in this modernization crisis, the Jewish minority provided an apt symbol. The anti-Judaism (and "teaching of contempt") of Christian theologians that characterized the first millennium of Christian-Jewish antagonism was rapidly superseded by what Gavin Langmuir has termed "xenophobic" anti-Semitism—a widely held negative stereotype made up of various assertions that did not describe the real Jewish minority but rather symbolized various threats and menaces that the Christian majority could not and did not want to understand.[1] A cluster of anti-Jewish incidents at the end of the first decade of the 11th century signaled a change that became more fully apparent with the murderous pogroms perpetrated by roving gangs of knights on their way to the First Crusade.[2] In the words of Langmuir, "These groups seem to have been made up of people whose sense of identity had been seriously undermined by rapidly changing social conditions that they could not control or understand and to which they could not adapt successfully."[3]

Urban, commercial, nonmilitary, and above all nonbelievers, the Jews were subjected both to the immediate threat of Europe's first pogroms and to the long-term threat of an intensifying negative stereotype. Barred from the honorable professions of fighting and landowning, often also barred from the prestigious economic activities controlled through guilds by the Christian majority, the Jewish minority was branded not only as unbelievers but now also as cowards, parasites, and usurers. Religiously driven anti-Semitism took on economic, social, and political dimensions.

In the following centuries the negative stereotype of xenophobic anti-Semitism was intensified and overlaid by fantastical and demented accusations, such as the alleged practices of ritual murder and torturing the Host. Such accusations seem to have originated in the actions of disturbed individuals finding ways to cope with their own psychological problems in socially acceptable ways.[4] In the fertile soil of xenophobic anti-Semitism, such chimeras multiplied and spread, and were ultimately embraced and legitimized by the authorities. As the Jews were increasingly dehumanized and demonized, the anti-Semitism of the medieval period culminated in the expulsions and the widespread massacres that accompanied the Black Death.

Anti-Semitism in western Europe was now so deeply and pervasively embedded in Christian culture that the absence of real Jews had no effect on society's widespread hostility toward them. In Spain, the land of the last and greatest expulsion of Jews, even conversion was increasingly felt to be inadequate to overcome what was now deemed to be innate Jewish evil. The Marranos were subjected to ongoing persecution and expulsion, and notions of pure-blooded Christians—eerily foreshadowing developments 500 years later—were articulated.

Europe's Jews survived this escalating torrent of persecution because the Church, while sanctioning it, also set limits to it.[5] And permeable boundaries allowed expelled Jews to escape and settle elsewhere. (The 20th century, in contrast, would not feature such permeable boundaries and effective religious limits.) The eventual slow decline in the virulence of anti-Semitism was due not so much to the relative absence of Jews in many parts of western Europe but rather to the gradual secularization of early modern European society—Renaissance humanism, the fracturing of religious unity in the Reformation, the scientific discoveries of Galileo and Newton in the 17th century, and the Enlightenment. Western Europe was no longer a Christian commonwealth with religion at the core of its culture and identity.

During this relative respite, Jews filtered back into some areas of western Europe from which they had previously been expelled. However, the demographic center of European Jewry was now clearly anchored in the east. Jews had begun settling in eastern Europe in the medieval period, often welcomed by local rulers for the complementary economic functions they performed, and by the 18th century there had been a veritable Jewish population explosion. All Europeans—Jews and non-Jews—were profoundly affected by the "Dual Revolution" of the late 18th and early 19th centuries. The French Revolution signaled the emergence of liberalism and nationalism; the Industrial Revolution set in motion a profound economic and social transformation.

Initially the Dual Revolution seemed a great boon to Europe's Jews. With liberalism came "Jewish emancipation." In a few brief decades, the centuries-long accumulation of discriminatory, anti-Jewish measures gave way to the liberal doctrines of equality before the law and freedom of conscience—not just in England and France but even in the autocratic German and Austro-Hungarian empires. And the Industrial Revolution opened up unprecedented economic opportunities for a mobile, educated, adaptable minority with few ties to and little nostalgia for a declining traditional economy and society in which they had been so restricted and marginalized.

But ultimately Europe's second great "modernization crisis" was fraught with even greater danger for the Jews than the first, nearly a millennium earlier.[6]

Once again the "social losers" of the modernization crisis—traditional elites and small-scale producers in particular—could find in the Jews a convenient symbol for their anguish. If the Jews were benefiting from the changes that were destroying Europe's traditional way of life, in the minds of many it seemed plausible that they had to be the cause of these changes. But in the far more secular and scientific world of the 19th century, religious beliefs provided less explanatory power. For many, Jewish behavior was to be understood instead as caused by allegedly immutable characteristics of the Jewish race.[7] The implications of *racial* anti-Semitism posed a different kind of threat. If previously the Christian majority pressured Jews to convert and more recently to assimilate, racial anti-Semitism provided no behavioral escape. Jews as a race could not change their ancestors. They could only disappear.

If race rather than religion now provided the rationale for anti-Semitism, the various elements of the negative anti-Semitic stereotype that had accumulated during the second half of the Middle Ages were taken over almost in their entirety and needed little updating. The only significant addition was the accusation that Jews were responsible for the threat of Marxist revolution. With little regard for logical consistency, the old negative image of Jews as parasitical usurers (updated as rapacious capitalists) was supplemented with a new image of Jews as subversive revolutionaries out to destroy private property and capitalism and overturn the social order. After 1917 the notion of menacing "Judeo-Bolshevism" became as entrenched among Europe's conservatives as the notion of Jews as "Christ-killers" had been among Europe's Christians.

These developments in the history of anti-Semitism transcended national boundaries and were pan-European. Why then did the Germans, among the peoples of Europe, come to play such a fateful role in the murderous climax that was reached in the middle of the 20th century? Scholars have offered a number of interpretations of Germany's "special path" or *Sonderweg*, with England and France usually being the standard or norm against which German difference is measured. One approach emphasizes Germany's cultural/ideological development. Resentment and reaction against conquest and change imposed by revolutionary and Napoleonic France heightened Germany's distorted and incomplete embrace of the Enlightenment and "western" liberal and democratic ideals. The antiwesternism of many German intellectuals and their despair for an increasingly endangered and dissolving traditional world led to a continuing rejection of liberal-democratic values on the one hand and a selective reconciliation with aspects of modernity (such as modern technology and ends-means rationality) on the other, producing what Jeffrey Herf terms a peculiarly German "reactionary modernism."[8]

According to another, social/structural approach, Germany's prolonged political disunity and fragmentation—in contrast to England and France—provided an environment less conducive to economic development and the rise of a healthy middle class. The failed liberal-national revolution of 1848 put an end to Germany's attempt to develop along the lines of, much less catch up with, France and England in concurrent political and economic modernization. Thereafter, the precapitalist German elites maintained their privileges in an autocratic political system, while the unnerved middle class was both gratified by national unification through Prussian military might, something they had been unable to achieve through their own revolutionary efforts, and bought off by the ensuing prosperity of rapid economic modernization that this unification unleashed. Fearful of rising socialism and manipulated by an escalating "social imperialism," the German middle class never became the mainstay of a strong liberal-democratic center as it did in the political culture of England and France.[9] Germany became a "schizophrenic" nation—an increasingly modern society and economy ruled by an autocratic monarchy and traditional elites—incapable of gradual democratic reform.

A third approach asserts a German *Sonderweg* in terms of the singular breadth, centrality, and virulence of anti-Semitism in Germany. According to Daniel Goldhagen, "No other country's antisemitism was at once so widespread as to have been a cultural axiom. . . . German antisemitism was *sui generis*," and it "more or less governed the ideational life of civil society" in pre-Nazi Germany.[10] Painting with a less broad brush, John Weiss is careful to place the late 19th-century loci of German anti-Semitism in populist movements and among the political and academic elites.[11]

Shulamit Volkov's interpretation of late 19th-century German anti-Semitism as a "cultural code" constitutes an admirable synthesis of major elements of these different, though not mutually exclusive, notions of a German *Sonderweg*. German conservatives, dominating an illiberal political system but feeling their leading role increasingly imperiled by the changes unleashed by modernization, associated Jews with everything they felt threatened by—liberalism, democracy, socialism, internationalism, capitalism, and cultural experimentation. To be a self-proclaimed anti-Semite in Germany was also to be authoritarian, nationalist, imperialist, protectionist, corporative, and culturally traditional. Volkov concludes, "Antisemitism was by then strongly associated with everything the conservatives stood for. It became increasingly inseparable from their anti-modernism."[12] As Uriel Tal has noted, German conservatives made their peace with modern nationalism and the modern state by understanding them in terms of a traditional German "Christian state" and traditional values that were seen as the distinct antithesis of the values identified with modern, emancipated, relatively assimilated Jews rather than traditional, religiously observant Orthodox Jews—rationalism, liberalism, "Manchesterism," and socialism.[13] The result was a strange amalgam of religious and cultural but for the most part not yet racial anti-Semitism.

By the turn of the century German anti-Semitism had become an integral part of the conservative political platform and had penetrated deeply into the universities. It had become more politicized and institutionalized than in the western democracies of France, England, and the United States. But this does not mean that late 19th-century German anti-Semitism dominated either politics or ideational life. The conservatives and single-issue anti-Semitic parties together constituted only a minority. While majorities could be found in the Prussian Landtag to pass discriminatory legislation against Catholics in the 1870s and in the Reichstag against socialists in the 1880s, the emancipation of Germany's Jews, who constituted less than 1% of the population and were scarcely capable of defending themselves against a Germany united against them, was not revoked. And at the other end of the political spectrum stood Germany's SPD, which was Europe's largest Marxist party and consistently won the largest popular vote in German elections between 1890 and 1930.

In comparison with western Europe, one might conclude that Germany's right was more anti-Semitic, its center weaker, its left stronger, its liberalism more anemic, and its political culture more authoritarian. Its Jews were also more prominent. This prominence (to be sure, in those areas of life not dominated by the old elites, such as the professions and business, as opposed to the officer corps and civil service), the deep attachment of German Jews to German culture, and a relatively high rate of intermarriage indicate a German milieu in which Jews did not face universal hostility but in fact thrived. Anti-Semitism may have been strong in influential pockets, especially in comparison to the west, but it was not so pervasive or strident as in territories to the east, from which beleaguered east European Jews looked to Germany as a land of golden opportunity. And this image, it should be noted, was *not* shattered by the behavior of German troops in eastern Europe during the First World War.

The turn-of-the-century anti-Semitism of German conservatives fits well Langmuir's notion of "xenophobic" anti-Semitism. For them the Jewish issue was but one among many, neither their top priority nor source of greatest fear. As Langmuir notes, however, xenophobic anti-Semitism provides fertile soil for the growth of fantastic or "chimeric" anti-Semitism—or what Saul Friedländer has recently dubbed "redemptionist" anti-Semitism.[14] If Germany's xenophobic anti-Semitism was an important piece of the political platform of an important segment of the political spectrum, the "redemptionist" anti-Semites with their "chimeric" accusations—from Jewish poisoning of pure Aryan blood to a secret Jewish world conspiracy behind the twin threats of Marxist revolution and plutocratic democracy—were a group for whom the Jews (perceived above all as a racial threat) were the major preoccupation and obsession. However, at this time what Tal dubs the "anti-Christian racial" anti-Semites were still a fringe phenomenon. "In the period of the Second Reich . . . the vast majority of voters still disassociated themselves from the non-Christian and anti-Christian attitude of modern anti-Semitism."[15] Or as Richard Levy concludes, "One of the greatest failings of the anti-Semitic parties of the empire was their inability to recruit the German right to their own brand of 'sincere' anti-Semitism."[16]

The succession of traumatic experiences in Germany between 1912 and 1929—loss of control of the Reichstag by the Right, a terrible war concluded in military defeat and revolution, runaway inflation, and economic collapse—transformed German politics. Germany's divided and traumatized society did not provide a propitious base on which to establish a moderate, stable, functioning democracy. The right grew at the expense of the center, and within the former the radicals or New Right grew at the expense of the traditionalists or Old Right. "Chimeric" and racial anti-Semitism grew commensurately from a fringe phenomenon to the core idea of a movement that became Germany's largest political party in the summer of 1932 and its ruling party six months later. That fact alone makes the history of Germany and German anti-Semitism different from that of any other country in Europe.

But this singular event must be kept in perspective. The Nazis never gained more than 37% of the vote in a free election, less than the combined socialist-communist vote. In a highly divided Germany there was only one consensus. Over half the electorate (the combined Nazi-communist vote) did support some form of totalitarian dictatorship to replace the paralyzed Weimar democracy. The Nazis offered many messages to many voters. Germans voted for them out of frustration over political chaos and economic collapse, fear of the Left, and aggrieved nationalism, not just because of their anti-Semitic commitment. On the other hand, of course, those millions of Germans who voted for the Nazis for other reasons were not deterred by Nazi anti-Semitism either. The anti-Semitism of German conservatism and the German universities had made it politically and intellectually respectable.

Thus Hitler's coming to power would not only "unleash" the Nazis and their right-wing allies—the longtime carriers of anti-Semitism in Germany—to harm the Jews, but would do so with the tacit support of millions of Germans for whom the fate of the Jews weighed lightly or not at all on the scales in comparison with their other concerns, and increasingly with the active support of millions of other Germans eager to catch the political tide. (As William Sheridan Allen has succinctly concluded, many people "were drawn to anti-Semitism because they were drawn to Nazism, not the other way around.")[17] At the same time, with staggering speed, the political parties and labor unions were abolished, and the civil service, education system, state and local government, and virtually all associational and cultural life were "coordinated." Germany ceased to be a pluralistic society, and there were no significant "countervailing" forces outside the alliance of Nazis and conservative nationalists on which the regime rested.

Hitler's conservative allies favored deemancipation and segregation of the Jews as part of the counterrevolution and movement of national renewal. They strove to end the allegedly "inordinate" Jewish influence on German life, although this was scarcely a priority equal to dismantling the labor unions, the Marxist parties, and parliamentary democracy, and initiating rearmament and the restoration of Germany's Great Power status. It is most unlikely that the conservatives on their own would have proceeded beyond the initial discriminatory measures of 1933–34 that drove the Jews out of the civil and military services, the professions, and cultural life.

But what the conservatives conceived of as sufficient measures were for the Nazis scarcely the first steps. The Nazis understood far better than the conservatives the distance that separated them. As complicitous in the first anti-Jewish measures as they were in the wrecking of democracy, however, the conservatives could no more oppose radicalization of the persecution of the Jews than they could demand for themselves rights they had denied others. And while they may have lamented their own increasing loss of privilege and power at the hands of the Nazis they had helped into power, with strikingly few exceptions they had no remorse or regret for the fate of the Jews. To argue that the Nazis' conservative allies were not of one mind with Hitler does not deny that their behavior was despicable and their responsibility considerable. As before, xenophobic anti-Semitism provided fertile soil for the chimeric anti-Semites.

What can be said of the German people at large in the 1930s? Was the bulk of the population swept along by the Nazis' anti-Semitic tide? Only in part, according to the detailed research of historians like Ian Kershaw, Otto Dov Kulka, and David Bankier, who have reached a surprising degree of consensus on this issue.[18] For the 1933–39 period, these historians distinguish between a minority of activists, for whom anti-Semitism was an urgent priority, and the bulk of the population, for whom it was not. Apart from the activists, the majority did not clamor or press for anti-Semitic measures. But the majority of "ordinary" Germans—whom Saul Friedländer describes as "onlookers" in contrast to "activists"[19]—nonetheless accepted the legal measures of the regime, which ended emancipation and drove the Jews from public positions in 1933, socially ostracized them in 1935, and completed the expropriation of their property in 1938–39. Yet this majority was critical of the hooliganistic violence of activists. The boycott of 1933, the vandalistic outbreaks of 1935, and the Kristallnacht pogrom of November 1938 did not have a positive reception among most of the German population.[20]

More important, however, a gulf had opened up between the Jewish minority and the general population. The latter, while not mobilized around strident and violent anti-Semitism, was increasingly "apathetic," "passive," and "indifferent" to the fate of the former. Many Germans who were indifferent or even hostile toward Jews were not indifferent to the public flouting of deeply ingrained values concerning the preservation of order, propriety, and property. But anti-Semitic measures carried out in an orderly and legal manner were widely accepted, for two main reasons. Such measures sustained the hope of curbing the violence most Germans found so distasteful, and most Germans now accepted the goal of limiting, and even ending, the role of Jews in German society. This was a major accomplishment for the regime, but it still did not offer the prospect that most ordinary Germans would approve of, much less participate in, the mass murder of European Jewry, that the onlookers of 1938 would become the genocidal killers of 1941–42.

If neither the conservative elites nor the German public were committed to a further radicalization and escalation of Jewish persecution, the same cannot be said of Hitler, the Nazi leadership, the party, and the bureaucracy. Hitler's anti-Semitism was both obsessive and central to his political outlook.[21] For him the "Jewish question" was the key to all other problems and hence the ultimate problem. Hitler's anti-Semitism created an ideological imperative that required an escalating search for an ultimate or final solution.

The emotional and ideological priority of Hitler's anti-Semitism and the wider understanding of history as racial struggle in which it was embedded were shared by much of the Nazi leadership and party. They defined and gave meaning to the politics of the Third Reich. They also provided the regime with a spur and a direction for ceaseless dynamism and movement. Within the polycratic regime, Hitler did not have to devise a blueprint, timetable, or grand design for solving the "Jewish question." He merely had to proclaim its continuing existence and reward those who vied in bringing forth various solutions. Given the dynamics of the Nazi political system, a ratchetlike decision-making process permitted bursts of radicalization periodically alternating with tactical pauses but never moderation or retreat. In the end "final solutions" would become the only ones worthy of submission to Hitler. As Göring announced on Hitler's behalf following the Kristallnacht pogrom in November 1938, the "Jewish question" had to be solved "one way or another." And in the case of the war that Hitler both intended and prophesied in January 1939 (thus setting a new level of expectation for his followers), an acceptable final solution would result in "the destruction of the Jewish race in Europe." Thus the combination of Hitler's anti-Semitism as ideological imperative and the competitive polycracy of the Nazi regime created immense pressures for the escalation of Nazi Jewish policy even without broad public support in that direction.

By the late 1930s, the escalation and radicalization of Nazi Jewish policy were also furthered by a process of "bureaucratic momentum." Within months of the Nazi assumption of power almost every branch and agency of the German government had appointed lower-echelon civil servants—some of whom were longtime party faithful, some recent converts, some adaptable and ambitious careerists—to a "Jewish desk" (*Judenreferat*) to handle all matters related to Jewish policy that impinged on their jurisdictions. No ministry affected by Nazi Jewish policy could afford to be without experts to advise it about the impact of Jewish legislation emanating from other sources, to participate in various inter-ministerial conferences to defend the ministry's point of view, and of course to prepare the ministry's own measures. As this corps of "Jewish experts" (*Juden-sachbearbeiter*) proliferated and became institutionalized, the impact of their cumulative activities added up. The existence of the career itself ensured that the Jewish experts would keep up the flow of discriminatory measures. Even as German Jews were being deported to ghettos and death camps in the east in 1942, for instance, the bureaucracy was still producing decrees that prohibited them from having pets, getting their hair cut by Aryan barbers, or receiving the Reich sports badge![22] Such a bureaucratic "machinery of destruction" was poised and eager to meet the professional challenge and solve the myriad problems created by an escalating Nazi Jewish policy. In Raul Hilberg's memorable phrase, the German bureaucrat "beckoned to his Faustian fate."[23] Not just for Hitler and the party faithful but also for the professional experts of the German bureaucracy, the outbreak of war in September 1939 and the ensuing victories would offer the opportunity and obligation to solve the "Jewish question" and make history.

2

Poland, Laboratory
of Racial Policy

The German invasion and conquest of Poland in September 1939 was an event of decisive importance in the evolution of Nazi Jewish policy toward the Final Solution. Over 2 million Polish Jews fell into German hands, and some 1.7-1.8 million remained at the end of the year when the border between the German and Russian zones was closed.[1] Until then, the Nazis' search for a solution to the Jewish question had been undertaken in reference to German Jews, and despite the addition of the Jews of Austria, the Sudetenland, and the Protectorate, the prospect of a solution through emigration and piecemeal expulsion remained feasible. Such a solution still offered the hope of a Germany ultimately "free of Jews" (*judenfrei*). But the outbreak of war now threatened to constrict even further the already fast diminishing avenues of emigration, while the conquest of Poland swamped Germany with additional Jews on an unprecedented scale. Once on a path of imperialistic expansion, the Nazis could no longer view the Jewish question primarily within a German framework. The Jewish question would not be completely solved until the territories within the German spheres of occupation and influence, growing steadily until 1942, were likewise "cleansed" or "purified" of their Jews. The fragile solution of emigration could not begin to cope with the staggering numbers now involved. Thus the conquest of Poland inevitably set in motion a search for a new kind of solution to the Nazis' Jewish problem.

The change was not just quantitative, however, for this search would take place within drastically altered circumstances. Germany was now at war. While this was not accompanied by the waves of hypernationalistic euphoria that had marked August 1914, nonetheless it did free the Nazi leadership from various restraints and inhibitions under which it had labored for the past six years.[2] For some time Nazi propaganda had branded the Jew as the enemy of Germany; if war came, it would be through the machinations of "international" Jewry. The

Jew was an integral part, indeed the quintessence, of the Nazi *Feindbild* or stereotyped image of the enemy.[3] Now that Germany was at war, harsh measures against the "enemy," including "potential enemies" (noncombatant civilians, women, children), seemed self-evident and justified by national interest. The German people were much readier to accept and rationalize away the most brutal and horrendous of these measures as "excesses" inevitably accompanying the realities of war. And foreign reaction could easily be dismissed as a repetition of the allegedly shameless and false atrocity propaganda that had besmirched Germany's honor and reputation in World War I.

If Nazi propaganda had not succeeded in turning many Germans into rabid anti-Semites in Hitler's own image, Nazi policies had succeeded in isolating German Jewry from the rest of society. The Jews had increasingly become an abstract phenomenon to whose fate Germans could be indifferent, not fellow citizens and human beings with whom Germans could identify and empathize. The German encounter with Poland gave new credibility to the Nazi message. Easy victory over Poland seemed to confirm the Germans as a *Herrenvolk* or "master race" deserving and destined to rule over inferior Slavs in eastern Europe. And now many young German soldiers for the first time saw the strange *Ostjuden* or Jews of eastern Europe, so different from assimilated German Jews and hitherto known primarily through the caricatures of Nazi propaganda. Moreover, they were encountered in numbers that lent plausibility to the claim that they were the biological and spiritual sources of an alien people who were the antithesis of everything German.[4]

If the state of war and the conquest of Poland released Hitler and the Nazi regime from many of the constraints of the past six years, and shattered the old framework within which a solution to the "Jewish problem" had been sought, they also reignited the radical tendencies within the party so precariously contained since 1933. Six years of relative calm and stability had followed the giddy adventure of the *Machtergreifung* or initial seizure of power. Now the radicals, like their Führer, were freed from past restraints. Unlike the riots of Kristallnacht, which had been played out before the shocked sensibilities of German burghers, Poland offered a field of activity at a conveniently discreet distance from direct observation. The descent upon Poland thus offered party radicals their second great chance for "National Socialist self-realization."[5] In Poland, furthermore, they encountered ethnic German minorities (*Volksdeutsche*) who had lived under Polish rule for twenty years and experienced a harrowing ordeal in the period of growing tension before the invasion and in the week immediately following. Now suddenly thrust into the position of masters and intoxicated by the opportunity to brutalize, plunder, drive off, or murder their Polish and Jewish neighbors with impunity, the *Volksdeutsche* became another "grassroots" source of radicalization behind Nazi racial policy in Poland.

The conquest of Poland affected the Nazi search for a solution to its self-imposed "Jewish question" in another way as well. Just as anti-Semitism had long antecedents in European history, so did imperialism. For the past five centuries, European conquest of territories inhabited by what were alleged to be "backward" and "uncivilized" peoples had often resulted in horrific population decimation and on occasion even total or near total extinction. By the late 19th century such population decimations were increasingly understood and justified in social Darwinist and racial terms, that is, as the inevitable triumph of the superior "white race" over inferior "dark races" whose defeat, subjugation, and even extinction were inherent in the natural process by which mankind progressed. Hitler's belief in the need for German *Lebensraum* implied that the Nazis would construct an empire in eastern Europe analogous to what other European imperial powers had constructed overseas. Not surprisingly, this also meant that the Nazi regime stood ready to impose on conquered populations in Europe, especially Slavs in the east, the methods of rule and policies of population decimation that Europeans had hitherto inflicted only on conquered populations overseas.[6]

Poland was thus destined to become a "laboratory" for Nazi experiments in racial imperialism, an area where they tried to turn into reality ideological slogans such as *Lebensraum* (living space), *Volkstumskampf* (ethnic or racial struggle), *Flurbereinigung* (a basic or comprehensive cleansing), and *Endlösung der Judenfrage* (Final Solution to the Jewish question). This would involve much trial and error, for the slogans were not explicit, their meanings were not self-evident, and often the need to choose priorities and make pragmatic compromises forced delays and modifications in the Nazis' "realization of Utopia."[7]

Not only did the Nazis have to experiment in their policies, but they also had to construct the instruments of power to carry them out. Indeed, the story begins with the early failure of the German Wehrmacht to preserve its position as the initial holder of "executive power" in Poland, its feeble resistance to even the earliest manifestations of mass murder, and the resulting division of spoils between Heinrich Himmler's ss on the one hand and the party satraps on the other—a political defeat ultimately as stunning and fateful as the Wehrmacht's concurrent military victory.

The conquest of Poland and the ensuing population and racial policies that Germany carried out there were decided upon by Hitler only during the course of events in 1939. While the Slavic populations of eastern Europe undoubtedly inhabited a rather low rung in his racial hierarchy, this never prohibited Hitler from allying with Slavic nations when it suited him. For example, having helped facilitate the disintegration of Czechoslovakia, the Slovaks were rewarded with a "model" vassal state. Poland's earlier pressure on Czechoslovakia, through its demands for Teschen during the Munich crisis, had led Hitler to envisage a similar relationship with that country. If Poland accepted territorial adjustments along the German border, then it would be well compensated with Ukrainian territory in the east. It was only Poland's failure to take up this offer and the subsequent British guarantee of Poland in March 1939 that led Hitler in April to order his military to be prepared for an invasion of Poland no later than the following September. With Foreign Minister Joachim von Ribbentrop in Moscow to sign the Nazi-Soviet Non-Aggression Pact, rendering Poland's position helpless, Hitler summoned his leading generals to the Berghof on August 22 for a long exposition, interrupted only by a break for lunch, of his views on the strategic situation and the future of Poland. His hatred of the Poles was now given free rein. One secretive note taker recorded his remarks as follows: "Destruction of Poland in the foreground. The aim is elimination of living forces, not the arrival at a certain line. Even if the war should break out in the west, the destruction of Poland shall be the primary objective. . . . Have no pity. Brutal attitude. Eighty million people shall get what is their right. Their existence has to be secured. The strongest has the right. Greatest severity."[8]

While Hitler portrayed the postwar fate of Poland in ominous terms and exhorted his generals to brutality, the army prepared for the occupation of Poland on a business-as-usual basis. The army would assume "executive power" in occupied Polish territory. The guidelines for troop behavior allowed for the use of force against not only armed resistance but also strikes, sabotage, and passive resistance. Irregulars, like spies, were to be brought before a court-martial and sentenced to death. However, a reassuring statement was issued that "the Wehrmacht does not see the population as its enemy. All provisions of international law will be observed. The economy . . . will be restored."[9]

Even left to itself, however, the army that invaded Poland carried with it a set of attitudes common to both officers and ordinary soldiers that would militate against compliance with its own assurances. The very existence of Poland, created in part out of pre-1919 German territory, was a symbol of the humiliating defeat of World War I and the hated Versailles Treaty. The population, both Poles and *Ostjuden*, were looked down upon as primitive and inferior, fit for colonial rule by a German master race. They were viewed, moreover, as inherently treacherous and anti-German and hence threats to security against which German occupation personnel had to be permanently on guard. Such an attitudinal climate would prove to be highly conducive to the harsh treatment of the civilian population in Poland and the committing of atrocities.[10]

Moreover, the army was not acting alone. ss units known as Einsatzgruppen der Sicherheitspolizei (special task forces of the Security Police) were also to participate in the occupation and pacification of Poland. Initially, five Einsatzgruppen were formed, with one assigned to each of the invading armies. Subsequently, two more Einsatzgruppen and a separate Einsatzkommando 16 from Danzig were added. Together they totaled over 3,000 men.[11] The men were drawn from the Gestapo, Security Service (SD), and Criminal Police (Kripo), and in the case of the seventh Einsatzgruppe formed—that of Udo von Woyrsch—a detachment of Order Police (Orpo). Many of the leaders were from the stable of Nazi intellectuals recruited by Himmler's deputy Reinhard Heydrich. Of the 25 Einsatzgruppen and Einsatzkommando leaders, 15 carried the *Doktortitel*, most of them as doctors of jurisprudence or philosophy.[12]

Negotiations between the military and the ss concerning the role of these units began early. An agreement of July 31, 1939, defined their task as the "combating of all anti-German elements in hostile country behind the troops in combat." Heydrich was very concerned to avoid complications. His commanders and liaison men were to be held "personally responsible" for "frictionless" relations with the army and civil administration. The men were to be "resolute but correct." The goals of the Einsatzgruppen were "to be reached in such a way that complaints were avoided as much as possible."[13] The most important task assigned by Heydrich to the Einsatzgruppen was the sweeping arrest of potential enemies—all "who oppose the measures of the German authorities, or obviously want and are able to stir up unrest owing to their position and stature."[14] The ss-army negotiations were concluded on August 29, when Heydrich and Dr. Werner Best met with the quartermaster general of the Wehrmacht High Command (Oberkommando der Wehrmacht, OKW), Eduard Wagner. Despite finding the "notorious" Heydrich "especially unsympathetic" and learning that the Einsatzgruppen had lists of 30,000 people to be arrested and sent to concentration camps, Wagner reported that quick agreement was reached.[15]

If Germany's highest military leaders still had any doubt before the outbreak of the war that its promise to abide by international law was going to be massively violated, such doubts were certainly dispelled in the first two weeks of the war. Revelations of Polish atrocities against ethnic Germans in Poland during the first week of the war, in particular the notorious "Bloody Sunday" in Bydgoszcz (Bromberg), as well as the continuing resistance of Polish troops cut off behind the fast-advancing German lines—which was difficult to distinguish from partisan war—raised temperatures on the German side and occasioned a revealing outburst by Heydrich against the army. Though 200 executions took place daily, he complained that the courts-martial were much too slow. "The people must be shot or hanged immediately without trial. The little people we want to spare, but the nobles, priests, and Jews must be killed."[16]

Military leaders were aware that such a statement was not just a fit of pique by Heydrich, for they attributed similar sentiments to Hitler as well. On September 9 the army's chief of the general staff, Franz Halder, revealed to Major Helmuth Groscurth that "it was the intention of the Führer and Göring to destroy and exterminate the Polish people."[17] When Admiral Canaris, the head of military intelligence (Abwehr), pointed out to the chief of the OKW, Wilhelm Keitel, that he "knew that extensive executions were planned in Poland and that particularly the nobility and the clergy were to be exterminated," Keitel answered that "the Führer had already decided on this matter." Hitler had "made it clear" that "if the Wehrmacht did not want any part of these occurrences, it would have to accept the SS and Gestapo as rivals" and the "ethnic extermination" (*volkstümliche Ausrottung*) would be left in the hands of civilians.[18]

Ironically, while the earliest atrocities in Poland confirmed top military leaders' understanding of Nazi intentions to carry out extensive executions, systematic mass murder had in fact not yet begun. The early German atrocities in Poland were perpetuated by three different groups: vigilante bands of ethnic Germans; military personnel, mostly but not exclusively in Waffen-SS units; and of course the Einsatzgruppen. If the Volksdeutsche vigilantes acted in areas remote from the center of military attention, and the various massacres by Waffen-SS men could be dismissed as regrettable but understandable lapses of discipline,[19] the behavior of the Einsatzgruppen presented military leaders with a challenge to their authority that could not lightly be ignored. Hitler's specific orders for Einsatzgruppe IV to take reprisals in Bydgoszcz had led the Army High Command (Oberkommando der Heeres, OKH) to order the army there not to intervene, and there is certainly no indication that the army was unsympathetic in this particular case.[20] But events surrounding Einsatzgruppe II of Emanuel Schäfer and the special Einsatzgruppe of Udo von Woyrsch finally did move the army to take some action.

In southern Poland Einsatzgruppe II had already carried out executions that ran into the hundreds when on September 12 the intelligence officer of Army Group South, Major Rudolf Langhäuser, heard of plans to shoot 180 Polish civilians in a camp just turned over from the army to the SS. He promptly returned the camp to army control. The following day he refused the SS demand to turn over the prisoners, and confronted the Einsatzgruppe commander, Emanuel Schäfer, in Czestochowa. The latter justified his actions by referring to an order from Himmler, unknown to the army, that all members of insurgent bands were to be shot. Further inquiry confirmed that an order to shoot insurgents without trial had been issued from the "Führer's train" directly to the police. Schäfer also noted that such executions had already been carried out in Tarnow and Katowice (Kattowitz), where Woyrsch's Einsatzgruppe operated.[21]

Schäfer's intimation that Woyrsch's unit was ahead of his own in executions was soon confirmed when the intelligence officer of the 14th Army reported to Abwehr chief Canaris on September 20 on "the unrest that has arisen in the army's area of jurisdiction through partially illegal measures of Einsatzgruppe Woyrsch (mass shootings, especially of Jews). The troops are especially vexed over the fact that young men, instead of fighting at the front, test their courage on defenseless people."[22]

After discussions with the army's commander in chief, Walther von Brauchitsch, and his chief of staff Halder on September 18, the military's negotiator concerning the Einsatzgruppen, Quartermaster General Wagner, went to Berlin to meet with Heydrich for a "very important, necessary, and outspoken" conversation.[23] Indeed, the conversation must have been very frank. Wagner insisted that the army be informed of the Einsatzgruppen's tasks, which Heydrich did in no uncertain terms: "Fundamental cleansing [*Flurbereinigung*]: Jews, intelligentsia, clergy, nobles." Wagner countered with the demand that this "cleansing" take place only "after the withdrawal of the army and the transfer to a stable civilian administration. Early December."[24] Wagner then left to prepare Brauchitsch for a meeting with Hitler the following day.[25] Meanwhile Heydrich summarized the results to his staff: "In this meeting it was established that the commanders of the Einsatzgruppen are subordinate to the army commanders, but receive direct instructions from the Chief of the Security Police. The entire conversation must be characterized as a very propitious result in terms of our cooperation with the military."[26]

On September 20 Brauchitsch met with Hitler, who assured the army commander in chief that he would be informed of all decisions affecting the army's executive power in Poland taken by the Führer himself, Himmler, Heydrich, and the Einsatzgruppen commanders. As with Heydrich vis-à-vis Wagner the day before, Hitler then treated Brauchitsch to a preview of what was intended in

Poland. Poles were going to be cleared out of the pre-1918 German territories. Other possible mass movements of population were also being considered. In any case, such operations would not be undertaken as long as transportation was needed for the troops. "The general idea of ghettos exists [*Ghetto-Gedanke besteht im grossen*], though the details were not yet cleared up. Consideration of economic interests from the beginning." Ominously, Hitler noted that Himmler would be consulted about the possibility of setting up his own police courts. As Wagner had requested of Heydrich the day before, the civil administration and not the army would be in charge of "cleansing." In reply Brauchitsch said that he hoped that nothing would occur "that would create the possibility abroad of making atrocity propaganda out of these events." He also expressed a special concern regarding the persecution of Catholic clergy.[27]

Brauchitsch partially informed his army commanders of the upshot of this conversation, telling them that the Einsatzgruppen had received orders from Hitler to carry out "certain ethnic tasks" (*gewisse volkspolitische Aufgaben*) in occupied Poland. The execution of these orders was incumbent upon the Einsatzgruppen commanders and "lay outside the responsibility" of the army commanders. The nature of these ethnic policies Brauchitsch chose not to elaborate.[28]

Two days later, on September 22, both Brauchitsch and Wagner met with Heydrich to finalize ss accommodation to the army's desires: "a) Orientation of the army over all orders of the ss. b) By order of the Führer economic interests must have precedence for the moment in all measures. Thus no too rapid removal of the Jews, etc. c) Ethnic movements only after the end of operations. d) No measures that can have disadvantageous effects abroad." Brauchitsch was apparently far less intimidated by Heydrich than by Hitler, and a hot discussion ensued. Heydrich promised that orders of the ss would be made known to the army. While criticizing the army courts as too slow, Heydrich admitted that the order to shoot insurgents without trial had been rescinded. Alongside army courts, however, police courts would now be set up with appeal only through police channels, not to the army. Concerning economic interests, Heydrich was adamant that "no consideration could be given to nobles, clergy, teachers, and legionnaires. They were not many, only a few thousand. These had to be immediately arrested and sent to a concentration camp."[29]

After Brauchitsch left, Wagner remained to discuss various details and succeeded in extracting from Heydrich the assurance that the notorious Woyrsch Einsatzgruppe would be withdrawn from Poland.[30] Afterward, in contrast to his first meeting with Wagner on September 19, Heydrich declared himself very unsatisfied.[31] Wagner, on the other hand, was jubilant. He wrote to his wife that he had gained "much, much influence over the course of political matters in Poland" and that "this time I have delivered a great blow to invisible forces."[32]

But Heydrich's initial dissatisfaction and Wagner's glee must not obscure the significance of what had happened. First of all, faced with clear knowledge of the criminal nature of the Nazi plans for Poland, including mass arrests, vast population transfers, and the wholesale murder of targeted groups of people, the top military leadership (in this case, Keitel, Brauchitsch, Halder, and Wagner) had made no objection *on principle*. Indeed, they did not so much oppose these measures on principle as they feared the ss challenge to army authority and the potential taint to their professional reputation abroad. *Flurbereinigung* and *Ausrottung* were not contested for what they were—a massive assault upon basic human rights, in violation of international law, made possible by the army's conquest of Poland. And the contribution of the Einsatzgruppen to counter the presumed behind-the-lines security threat posed by despised Poles and Jews was too useful to renounce entirely, even if occasional atrocities and "excesses" were regretted.[33] Having failed to draw the line in Poland, the army became an "accomplice" of the regime and was never again capable of taking a principled stand against Nazi crimes even as its military conquests fed ever more victims to the Nazi Moloch.[34]

The second fatal decision of the top military leadership was not to share their knowledge of Nazi intentions with their fellow officers. The criminal nature of the regime was now incontrovertible, but the evidence to this effect was not disseminated beyond the very narrow circle of Keitel, Brauchitsch, Halder, and Wagner. As the continuing shock and protest of local commanders in Poland over the events they were witnessing demonstrated, the officer corps was still capable of moral indignation. Many among the officer corps were not yet morally numbed. They had not yet learned how to turn a blind eye to mass murder. But shock and indignation could only be used to mobilize the officer corps in a united front against the crimes of the regime if the officers were made fully aware that they were witnessing, not local excesses committed by individual members of the ss acting on their own, but rather local manifestations of sweeping government policies authorized by Hitler himself. Only Admiral Canaris of the Abwehr systematically informed a trusted group of intelligence officers, who were later to form the heart of the military resistance to Hitler; the rest fostered a "conspiracy of silence." Unwilling themselves to realize that they could no longer be "good Germans" in the traditional sense—that is, loyal both to the government of their country and to the moral norms of their profession and culture—they did their best to shield the officer corps from the awareness that such a choice was inevitable. But if such a choice were not made consciously, it would be made by default in favor of complicity with National Socialism.

In failing to make a stand on principle and in fostering a conspiracy of silence, the army leaders were of course behaving no differently from other elites in German society. Even the churches sought accommodation with National Socialism and balked at posing to their adherents the stark choice between Christian morality and loyalty to their country's regime. The officer corps was, after all, part of German society. The tragedy was that if the military had only distinguished itself from other institutions in Germany in its response to National Socialism, it could have made a difference.[35]

Instead of confrontation, Brauchitsch, Halder, and Wagner decided in mid-September on a far more cautious, three-pronged policy: (1) contesting the ss on only the narrowest issues, (2) erecting some administrative framework in Poland that might obstruct the worst Nazi "excesses," and (3) buying time to extract the army from Poland with its hands still clean. They won some early skirmishes on the narrow issues. Himmler's order to the Einsatzgruppen to shoot insurgents without trial was temporarily rescinded, assurance was given that other orders of the kind would not be issued without informing the army, and the notorious Woyrsch Einsatzgruppe was withdrawn.[36] Likewise there was agreement to Brauchitsch's request that the "cleansing" not take place until the army had withdrawn and authority had been transferred to a stable civil administration. However, this made it all the more imperative for Hitler that the emerging German administration be an instrument of, not an obstacle to, Nazi policy and that the army's executive power in Poland be terminated soon. Wagner's hope of leaving behind a stable civil administration capable of preventing the worst was naive delusion.

When the Germans were preparing for the invasion of Poland, each army was assigned not only an Einsatzgruppe but also a chief of military administration. The German armies swept forward so fast that no real administration could be established, and within days the borderland Nazi Gauleiter or regional party leaders swept in to grab their spoils. The military attempted to give some system to the division of spoils. On September 7 Wagner met with Brauchitsch and prepared proposals for dividing Poland into military districts. Since a distinction was made between the former German territories of Danzig–West Prussia, Poznan (Posen), and Upper Silesia on the one hand and the proposed districts of Lodz and Cracow on the other, Wagner was in no doubt that this constituted a "fourth partition" of Poland. Each military district was to have both a military commander and a chief of military administration. Hitler "accepted everything as proposed"[37] and promptly confirmed as the respective chiefs of administration Albert Forster, the party leader or Gauleiter of Danzig, in Danzig–West Prussia; Arthur Greiser, the Danzig Senate president, in Poznan; and Gauleiter Josef Wagner of Upper Silesia for the corresponding Polish district. By September 15 Hitler's lawyer and minister without portfolio Hans Frank had been named chief of military administration for all of Poland as well as for the Lodz district. He was assured that his temporary subordination to the military commander would be ended as soon as possible.[38]

Thus even as Wagner turned to the task of establishing a "stable" administrative framework in Poland, capable of containing Nazi radicalism, the ex-German borderlands were already in the hands of Nazi satraps who were filling administrative positions with their followers, the Hitler loyalist Frank had been nominated as the overall chief of military administration in Poland, and Hitler had decided to end military governance as quickly as possible after the cessation of hostilities. Nonetheless, Wagner and his staff worked feverishly to complete regulations for the military administration in Poland which provided for appointment of civilian officials only through the army commander, established the Reich Ministry of the Interior as the coordinating center through which all other government and party agencies had to pursue their own interests in Poland, and forbade the granting to third parties of special powers that infringed upon the ultimate responsibility of the army. Hitler hurriedly signed the decree while sitting in his car waiting to depart after a quick visit to Warsaw. Wagner was elated, thinking that he had secured the military administration in Poland on a long-term basis. The military occupation authorities were requested to prepare a budget through the end of March 1940. But events were soon to show that Hitler had signed the decree without quibbling precisely because it was to be an interim solution of only one month's duration.[39]

Hans Frank paid a cursory visit to his newly appointed superior, General von Rundstedt, at the military headquarters at Spala outside Lodz on September 29 before leaving for Berlin. Inquiries to Frank's deputy revealed that important decisions were being awaited in Berlin, and Frank would not return until they had been made.[40] The key decisions were indeed made in the two weeks following Hitler's signature on Wagner's decree. On September 28 the final demarcation line between the Russian and German occupation zones was settled, which also provided for the return of ethnic Germans from the Soviet sphere. The following day Hitler was presented with the first draft of a decree empowering Himmler to handle their return and resettlement as well as other matters relating to the "strengthening of Germandom" in the east. The final decree was signed on October 7. Himmler thereupon created the Reich Commissariat for the Strengthening of Germandom (Reichskommissariat für die Festigung deutschen Volkstums or RKFDV), which now gave him a second power base, in addition to the police, in Polish territory.[41] Also on September 28 Göring secured for himself the right to coordinate economic exploitation in the occupied territories, and on October 19 he established his own agency for the confiscation of Polish and Jewish property, the Haupttreuhandstelle Ost (Main Trusteeship Office East or HTO.)[42] The ink was thus not dry on Wagner's decree prohibiting the granting of special powers to third parties before it was hopelessly compromised.

That was just the beginning. On October 5, when Forster complained that the army failed to understand the racial measures being taken in West Prussia, Hitler removed this territory from military administration and placed it under Forster as Reichskommissar. The following day Hitler decided to forgo halfway measures and ordered the preparation of a decree for the incorporation of the military districts of Danzig–West Prussia, Poznan, and East Upper Silesia into the Third Reich; the decree was signed on October 8 to go into effect on November 1, 1939.[43] Not to be left out, the Gauleiter of East Prussia, Erich Koch, got his share of the spoils in the region between East Prussia and Warsaw known as Zichenau and now referred to as Southeast Prussia.[44]

At the same time, work was begun on a decree for the remaining Polish territory, while Hitler waited briefly for a possible Allied reaction to his early October "peace initiative." Frank pressed for complete independence from the army, and State Secretary Ernst von Weizsäcker urged that Poland not remain legally classified as occupied territory, for then it would be subject to provisions of international law, "to which we doubtless shall not submit."[45] On October 12 Hitler signed the decree creating a General Government under civilian administration headed by Frank, but the role of the army there was still left open.

Except for Wagner, however, the army was fast losing interest in Poland. On September 27 the stunned generals had learned of Hitler's intention to launch a November offensive in the west, when the predictable mud and fog would guarantee maximum ineffectiveness of Germany's air force and tanks.[46] The issue of the western offensive was now far more important to the generals than atrocities in Poland.[47] Moreover, officers like Rundstedt viewed assignment in the east as detrimental to their careers and displayed considerable lack of enthusiasm for establishing a permanent military administration.[48] And some of the generals worried about the impact of events in Poland on military discipline. Halder, for instance, noted on October 5: "Murder of Jews . . . Discipline! [*Judenmorde . . . Disziplin!*]."[49]

Perhaps sensing the army's disenchantment and predicting Brauchitsch's response, Hitler informed the army commander in chief that the military administration in the General Government would continue.[50] Under the impact of the rapid series of changes in Poland and the unexpected order for an autumn offensive in the west, Brauchitsch immediately expressed to Keitel his desire to give up the military administration in Poland.[51] In fact, the top military commanders were in disarray. On October 16 Groscurth noted that Halder was having a "complete nervous breakdown" and Brauchitsch was "helpless." In desperation and contempt he complained, "What circumstances! These are Prussian officers! A Chief of the General Staff must not collapse. All as 1914!"[52]

Wagner alone made one more attempt, arming Keitel with a memorandum of army demands regarding Poland: The responsibility of the military commander in Poland was not to be impaired by the granting of special powers to third parties. The appointment of officials to the civil administration was to take place solely through the army commander in chief upon nomination from the ministries and chief of the administration. Population resettlement programs of the Reichsführer-ss were to take place only in agreement with the army and not impair military interests. Finally, Frank was to come to Lodz and take up his administrative duties.[53] That evening Hitler held forth to the top Nazi leaders, a meeting Wagner missed, as he had just left Berlin to return to the army headquarters at Zossen.

Keitel never did raise Wagner's demands, since Hitler made it clear from the beginning of this meeting that the military role in Poland was over. There could not be two administrations alongside one another, and since Brauchitsch had requested that the army be relieved of these duties, it should be happy to be rid of them. Hitler then went on to sketch out Poland's future, where "devils' work" (*Teufelswerk*) was to be done. The Polish intelligentsia was to be prevented from reviving as a ruling class. The living standard was to be kept low, for the population was needed only as a source of "cheap labor." It was not Germany's task to restore order, but rather to let "the Polish chaos flourish" (*Poln. Wirtschaft höchster Blüte*). Both the new and the old Reich territory would be cleared of "Jews, Polacks and riff-raff" (*Juden, Polacken u. Gesindel*) through resettlement in Poland. A "harsh racial struggle" (*harten Volkstumskampf*) permitting no "legal restrictions" would be carried out, so that Poland would never again become a battlefield.[54] Nine days later the military administration in Poland was officially dissolved. As Groscurth succinctly noted, "In the General Government Minister Frank alone shall take over the administration and there 'exterminate!' [*ausrotten*]."[55] For the army, if not for other contenders, the struggle for power in Poland was over.

Although Hitler's shrill exhortations for a "harsh racial struggle" in Poland made clear the general direction Nazi policy was to follow, they were barren of specifics. This had a twofold effect quite typical of Hitler's method of ruling. On the one hand, these exhortations constituted a "green light" to the various Nazis descending on Poland that the restraints under which they had operated since the heady months of the *Machtergreifung* were now lifted. No one was going to be called to account for being too "ruthless" or "energetic." On the contrary, ambitious Nazis now had to prove themselves capable of living up to their rhetoric. The result was to unleash a chaotic terror in Poland whose virulence and emphasis varied with the local perpetrators, and whose vague goal was a violent "fundamental cleansing" of Germany's enemies. On the other hand, Hitler's exhortations were an incitement to Nazi leaders to produce proposals for policies that would turn his vague ideological pronouncements and emotional tirades into specific programs with well-defined goals. Those who authorized proposals most attuned to Hitler's wishes were awarded with enhanced powers to carry them out. Those who not only proved themselves capable of carrying out the drastic measures of "chaotic" terror but also displayed an organizational touch became the instruments of these more articulated policies. Those who did not accommodate themselves quickly enough were pushed aside. "Wild actions" gave way to centrally directed programs. Chaotic terror gradually became systematic terror. Such was the pattern of events in Poland in the fall of 1939.

The Shaping of Nazi Policy

Nazi plans for racial policy and Lebensraum in Poland took shape only during September, not before the invasion. When Heydrich met with his division heads on September 7, the "fourth partition" of Poland had already been decided, but not much else. Polish Jews, including those who had immigrated long ago and already attained German citizenship, were to be pushed out of Germany. The Polish leadership classes were to be "rendered harmless" (*unschädlich gemacht*) by being sent to concentration camps in Germany; the lowest classes left without education and "suppressed"; and the middling Poles put in provisional concentration camps in the border area and eventually deported to whatever remained of Poland.[56] One week later plans were being made. Heydrich discussed the Jewish question with his division heads and noted: "Proposals are being submitted to the Führer by the Reichsführer [Himmler], that only the Führer can decide, because they will be of considerable significance for foreign policy as well."[57] When Brauchitsch met with Hitler on September 20, he learned that "the idea of ghettos exists in general," but the details were not yet clarified. The following day Heydrich met with all his division heads, Einsatzgruppen leaders, and his expert on Jewish emigration, Adolf Eichmann, to convey the details of what had been decided. Concerning the Polish leadership, the policy remained unchanged: the top leaders were to be sent to camps in Germany; those in the middle echelon (now defined as teachers, clergy, nobles, legionnaires, and returning officers) were to be arrested and deported to rump Poland. The "primitive" Poles were to be migrant laborers for the German economy and then gradually resettled. The former German territories were to become German provinces.

This expansion of German Lebensraum could not, of course, be accomplished without a solution to the Jewish question as well. "The Jewish deportation into the non-German region, expulsion over the demarcation line is approved by the Führer," the protocol noted. Since this process would be spread over the next year, the Jews in the meantime would be concentrated in ghettos in cities, "in order to have a better possibility of control and later of deportation." Hence it was urgent that the Jews disappear from the countryside and be sent to the cities "as quickly as possible." This concentration action was to be carried out within three to four weeks! Only then could one achieve a "systematic dispatching" of the Jews to Poland in freight cars, along with 30,000 "Gypsies."[58]

Heydrich expanded upon these directions in an express letter or *Schnellbrief* sent to the Einsatzgruppen leaders on the same day of September 21, 1939. He reiterated the distinction between the strictly secret ultimate goal or *Endziel* (deportation/expulsion), which would take time, and the preliminary short-term measures (concentration in cities). The areas of Danzig–West Prussia, Poznan, and East Upper Silesia were to have priority. As for the rest of Poland, concentration was to take place along railway lines, except in the territory east of Cracow and north of the Slovak border. Conceding that the details of the operation could not be laid down in Berlin, Heydrich did, however, insist on uniform policy to a certain extent. Councils of elders were to be appointed in each Jewish community and held fully responsible for carrying out German orders. All measures were to be carried out in closest agreement with local German authorities. In particular, the interests of the army were to be kept in mind.[59]

The following day, when Heydrich had his "unsatisfactory" meeting with Brauchitsch, he informed the commander in chief of the "intended measures: to begin with, Jewish deportation from the countryside to the cities." Brauchitsch demanded that these movements be directed by military, not civilian, authorities—"no unauthorized actions by civilians. Otherwise it will come to clashes." Heydrich also revealed the significance of not including the area east of Cracow in the concentration measures. "A Jewish state under German administration by Cracow. Also all Gypsies and other undesirables in there."[60]

On September 30 Heydrich met with Halder, who once again pressed the army's concerns over the disruptions that would be caused by rapidly moving the Jews into the cities. Heydrich relented and wrote his Einsatzgruppen leaders again. He reiterated his directive of September 21 that all measures were to be taken in closest cooperation with the local military authority. The decision over the timing and the intensity of the concentration of Jews still remained in the hands of individual Einsatzgruppen leaders, Heydrich wrote, but was dependent upon not disturbing military interests.[61] The army commanders were informed that the Heydrich *Schnellbrief* of September 21 (of which they had received copies) referred only to "preparatory measures."[62] A disappointed Heydrich spoke to his division chiefs on October 3 of the "old army-SD problem."[63]

The last days of September saw several further developments concerning the Nazis' plan for Lebensraum and racial policy. The final negotiations with the Soviet Union resulted in an unexpected change in the demarcation line, whereby Germany now surrendered Lithuania to the Russian sphere of influence and got in return territory in east central Poland around the city of Lublin up to the Bug River. Moreover, it was agreed that the ethnic Germans in the Soviet sphere would be repatriated to Germany.[64]

When Hitler talked with one of his advisers on eastern Europe, Alfred Rosenberg, on September 29, he indicated that all Jews, including those from the Reich, would be settled in this newly acquired territory between the Vistula and the Bug Rivers. Along the new German boundary, ethnic Germans from all over the world would be resettled. Between the areas of German and Jewish settlement would be the Polish region. An *Ostwall* or eastern wall was to be created on the Vistula, separating the Jewish and Polish regions. Whether "after decades" (*nach Jahrzehnten*) the German settlement belt would be moved eastward, only time would tell.[65]

By the end of September the Nazis had developed a grandiose program of demographic engineering based on racial principles that would involve moving hundreds of thousands, indeed ultimately millions, of people like so many pieces on a checkerboard. It was not the result of any long-held blueprint. Rather it emerged from the unpredictable circumstances in the year of 1939, including Poland's refusal to accept vassal status in Germany's New Order, Stalin's decision to reach an agreement with Nazi Germany on the basis of a Polish partition, and the west's refusal to accept another fait accompli in eastern

Europe. Though improvised in September 1939, these policies were fully consonant with Hitler's underlying ideological assumptions: a need for Lebensraum in the east justified by a social Darwinist racism, a contempt for the Slavic populations of eastern Europe, and a determination to rid the expanding German Reich of Jews. They were also consonant with the emotional rage and hatred that arose in Hitler when the stubborn Poles, whom he had favored with a nonaggression pact in 1934 and a slice of Czech territory in 1938, rejected his offer for a continuing albeit junior partnership at the expense of Soviet territory to the east. Hitler had merely to annunciate the guiding ideological principles and express the depth of his emotional antipathy toward Poles and Jews; it could be left to his ambitious chieftains, especially in this case Himmler and Heydrich, to give them concrete shape.

This basic Nazi plan was also very much in tune with widely held views and hopes in German society concerning the construction of a German empire in the east based on racial and social Darwinist principles. The rapid emergence of the general outlines of the Nazi plan was not dependent upon the proposals of outside experts, although attempts to cope with the myriad details of local problem solving would be. There was no shortage of those who now eagerly sought to contribute to this historic opportunity for the triumph of German racial imperialism in the east. And the more the hopes and visions of these eager helpers foundered on stubborn reality, the greater their willingness to resort to ever more violent solutions. The broad support for German racial imperialism in the east was one foundation upon which the future consensus for the mass murder of the Jews would be built.[66]

The actual details of the massive deportation and resettlement programs had yet to be worked out. The institutions, techniques, and personnel had still to be put in place. In the meantime the terror could be intensified, liquidating potential Polish opposition, offering a proving ground for Nazi personnel, and reducing through murder and flight the ultimate number of Poles and Jews to be expelled.

The German Terror

In the first weeks of the Polish campaign, the Einsatzgruppen carried out more than 10,000 arrests in fulfillment of their assignment to "neutralize" potential anti-German elements of the population.[67] On September 3 they were ordered by Himmler to shoot all insurgents, defined loosely as anyone who endangered German life or property. The exact number of Einsatzgruppen executions in this period is not contained in their reports, but the number was clearly not insignificant. The Polish historian Szymon Datner has compiled statistics recording executions carried out by the Germans on Polish territory in this period: 12,137 in September and another 4,199 up to the dissolution of the military regime on October 25, 1939. However, his statistics do not distinguish Einsatzgruppen killings from others. As early as September 4, the quartermaster of General Blaskowitz's 8th Army deemed the turning over of "suspicious" persons to the Einsatzgruppen as "inexpedient" because only in the rarest cases was "sufficient evidence" subsequently adduced. Other army units were far less squeamish, however. The military police (*Feldgendarmerie*) turned over so many people to the Einsatzgruppen for execution that on September 15 Heydrich asked the OKW to give the military police instructions to carry out such shootings themselves.[68]

As the horror mounted through the month of September, not only the Einsatzgruppen but also the army and Waffen-SS units were involved in mass shootings. When the Germans captured Bydgoszcz, a major site of ethnic German deaths in the first days of the war,[69] mass shootings were subsequently carried out by "police, SD-Einsatzgruppen and troops." According to one report received by Major General Braemer, commander of the rear army area including Bydgoszcz, the total number of Polish civilian victims by September 8 was 200–300; according to another, 400. The following day, September 9, a clearing action in Bydgoszcz resulted in yet another 120 shootings, and 20 more Poles were shot in the main square on September 10 in retaliation for the wounding of a German soldier. When Roland Freisler, subsequently the notorious People's Court judge, arrived in Bydgoszcz to set up a special tribunal and inquired how many judgments had already been issued, Braemer noted, "I can only say that until now only the troops themselves have spoken, and many hundreds of civilians were shot for carrying weapons or for resistance."[70]

Other incidents soon followed in which Jewish victims became increasingly prominent. At Rozan a military police sergeant and a Waffen-SS artillery man drove 50 Jews "into a synagogue and shot them *without any reason*."[71] On September 11 Groscurth noted that SS-Standarte Deutschland "had shot Jews by the row without judicial proceedings."[72] On September 18 the music director of the SS-Leibstandarte shot 50 Jews in Blonie. This event was apparently common enough that the commander of the Army Group South, Rundstedt, had to answer, in response to an inquiry from the commander of the 10th Army, Reichenau, that at least from the army no order had been issued to shoot Jewish civilian prisoners.[73] On September 22 "near Pultusk 80 Jews were slaughtered like cattle by the troops."[74] On September 20 the 14th Army reported "mass shootings, especially of Jews" by the Woyrsch Einsatzgruppe.[75] When the commandant in Wloclawek learned of SS intentions to arrest all the male Jews, he protested that one could not simply arrest 10,000 people, for their internment would be impossible. An SS man, the adjutant of Standartenführer Nostitz of SS-Totenkopfstandarte Brandenburg, replied that they would arrest as many as the prisons held, and "in any case, they would be shot."[76]

In addition to the mass shootings, the German authorities deliberately added to the stream of refugees in Poland set in motion by the invasion. Once again, Jews were prominent both among those making their own decision to escape from German-occupied territory and among those expelled from their homes by German order. In northern Poland Einsatzgruppe V reported from Graudenz on September 7 that virtually all leading male Jews had fled, and "the exodus of the other Jews is being prepared." The Jewish community was even ordered to create a "migration fund" (*Auswanderungsfonds*), into which proceeds from the sale of Jewish businesses were deposited. Out of 350 Mlawa Jews, the Einsatzgruppe shoved 66 men and 3 women into the yet unoccupied Polish territory "in agreement with the local military commander."[77] Later in the month Einsatzgruppe V reported that it was blocking bridges to prevent the return of Poles and Jews who had fled. And on September 28 it boasted that "Jews in huge columns are being pushed over the demarcation line."[78]

The situation was similar in the south. From Czestochowa Einsatzgruppe commander Schäfer reported on preparations for the "intended expulsion of the Jews."[79] On September 12 the OKH quartermaster general ordered a border guard unit to "shove" Jews from East Upper Silesia over the San River. When the Soviet armies entered eastern Poland several days later, explicit orders were issued to prevent Polish and Jewish refugees from returning to western Poland, with weapons if necessary. To facilitate this task, the 14th Army asked Einsatzgruppe I units to clear the villages along the demarcation line of unreliable elements and, once again, to shove the Jews living there over the San River.[80] In late September General Brandt in East Upper Silesia proposed evacuating the "masses of Jews" in the region from Bedzin to Czestochowa as a preliminary to the later evacuation of all "ethnically foreign elements" and their replacement by ethnic Germans from the Soviet-occupied regions of Galicia and Volhynia—a notion that uncannily anticipated Himmler's own proposals.[81]

Once the demarcation line was moved from the San to the Bug, similar events occurred there in October. Army reports indicated that because of the high water many of the refugees drowned, and others were shot by the Russians. Conspicuous among the victims were the Jews of Cholm and Hrubieszow, many of whom were shot outright by German police units. Soviet complaints about and resistance to this flood of refugees grew, until in late October they threatened to block the return of ethnic Germans to the west in retaliation.[82]

Gradually the terror began to shift away from sporadic mass shootings of Jews and Poles to a more systematic "liquidation" of particular categories of people deemed especially dangerous to permanent pacification and, in the case of the incorporated territories, the wholesale deportation of further groups deemed obstacles to "Germanization." This transformation from chaotic to systematic terror began first in West Prussia in October 1939. Throughout the Polish borderlands the local Volksdeutsche had been mobilized into auxiliary units known as the Selbstschutz to protect their communities against Polish attack in the first days of the war. In many regions, especially in West Prussia, leaders of the Volksdeutsche community had been arrested and taken off shortly before the war, and in some places, such as Bydgoszcz, the ethnic German communities had suffered heavy losses.[83] Perhaps as many as 6,000 ethnic Germans were killed in the first days of the war.[84] When the German army quickly swept past most of the ethnic German communities, the bands shifted their attention from self-defense to revenge, settling scores with those who had not fled in time. In mid-September a unified Selbstschutz was officially founded on the basis of these ad hoc self-defense units, as ss officers arrived and summoned all ethnic Germans capable of bearing arms to report. Gottlob Berger on Himmler's staff was placed in charge, and district commanders in the Warthegau, Upper Silesia, and West Prussia were appointed. By far the most notorious of these commanders was Himmler's personal adjutant, ss-Oberführer Ludolph von Alvensleben of West Prussia. He presided over six inspectorates headed by ss officers from the Reich, but below that level local units remained under ethnic Germans who had proven themselves in the first weeks of the war.[85] By October 5 Alvensleben's West Prussian Selbstschutz comprised 17,667 men and had already executed 4,247 Poles.[86]

The Gauleiter of Danzig–West Prussia, Albert Forster, thus had at his disposal both Alvensleben's Selbstschutz and numerous Danzig police units (the Eimann Wachsturm or "storm guard" and Einsatzkommando 16 of Kriminalrat Jakob Lölgen) plus a special sD unit from Allenstein of Sturmbannführer Dr. Franz Oebsger-Röder at his disposal when he returned from the meetings with Hitler in early October that had resulted in the decree for incorporating the border territories into the Third Reich. Forster set the second phase of the terror in motion when he announced that West Prussia would become a "blossoming, pure German" (blühende, rein deutsche) province in a short time and that all Poles would have to be dislodged or driven off (verdrängt).[87] Whatever further incitement was needed was added in mid-October by Heydrich, who, fearing that the civil administration due to replace the departing military might somehow limit his freedom of action, ordered the "liquidation of Polish leadership" (*die Liquidierung des führenden Polentums*) by November 1.[88] The sense of urgency was felt even at the local level, as Oebsger-Röder noted: "The liquidation will be able to be carried out for only a short time. Then the German administration as well as other factors outside the NSDAP will make direct actions impossible." He then outlined the course of action in Bydgoszcz: "physical liquidation of all those Polish elements who a) in the past have been in any way prominent on the Polish side, or b) in the future could be carriers of Polish resistance," and "evacuation or resettlement" (*Aussiedlung bezw. Umsiedlung*) of all Poles from West Prussia, both natives and so-called Congress Poles, that is, those that had come there from the east since 1919.[89] By October 20, Oebsger-Röder wrote, the police and Selbstschutz together had carried out a wave of arrests against Polish teachers in the regions, and the first Congress Poles had been deported. The arrest of the remaining Polish intelligentsia, especially members of Polish nationalist organizations, was imminent. "It is planned to liquidate the radical Polish elements."[90] Kriminalrat Lölgen of Einsatzkommando 16, also operating in Bydgoszcz, noted: "The intended measures as well as all the actions of the state police up until now found the full approval of the Reichsführer-SS, to whom I was able to make a presentation in the Danziger Hof on the evening of October 20."[91]

The Bydgoszcz terror also encompassed the clergy, as only 17 of 75 Catholic priests were left in their positions. After the "extermination of the radical Polish priests" (*das Ausrotten der radikal-polnischen Pfarrer*), it was assumed that the survivors were either sufficiently shaken or weak-hearted and apolitical that no further difficulties from the church were expected.[92] By early November more than 1,000 Congress Poles had been deported from Bydgoszcz, and the trains going east were filled as increasing numbers fled in anticipation of Nazi measures.[93] Lölgen counted the action against the intelligentsia as good as concluded after another 250 were killed in the first week in November.[94] But Oebsger-Röder was not satisfied. "Even in the next months and years a considerable number of pure and conscious Poles will still have to be reckoned with." The Germans ought therefore to devise clever ruses to provoke, identify, and shoot them.[95]

The Nazi terror in Bydgoszcz may have been more intense than elsewhere in West Prussia, but the general outlines were the same everywhere. Polish intelligentsia, nationalists, Catholic priests, Jews, "Gypsies," and even Catholic Germans, ethnic Germans married to Poles, and anyone else denounced by at least two Volksdeutsche for whatever personal reasons were gathered in the camps that sprang up in West Prussia. Alvensleben toured the province, continually complaining to his Selbstschutz officers that too few Poles had been shot. This set the standard for his subordinates. The Landrat of Kreis (county) Berent near Danzig boasted that he had not yet liquidated 2,000 Poles but was close. One Selbstschutz commander, ss Standartenführer Wilhelm Richardt, told the men in the Karlhof (Karolewo) camp that he did not want to have to build big camps and feed Poles, and that it was an honor for Poles to fertilize German soil with their corpses.[96]

Only a few cases of lack of enthusiasm for or even opposition to the Selbstschutz killings are documented. One inspectorate chief, Standartenführer Norbert Scharf, was relieved for not having called the Poles "to account" (*zur Rechenschaft*) in the required manner. At the subsequent hearing, it was revealed that he had had a mere 300 people liquidated by his inspectorate by early October![97]

When Untersturmführer Wilhelm and his Selbstschutz entered the town of Pelplin on October 23, 1939, they encountered Gendarmerie Hauptwachtmeister Hahn, who on orders of Bürgermeister Seedig, had armed the SA (Sturmabteilungen or "brown shirts") and Hitler Youth as auxiliary police to block the Selbstschutz from carrying out its task. When Wilhelm announced that these measures had been ordered by the Reichsführer-ss, Hahn replied "in a blustery voice" that the Reichsführer-ss, whom he did not know, did not "interest him in the slightest" and furthermore his immediate superior was the Bürgermeister. The deputy mayor telephoned the Landrat and was told that nothing should be undertaken to interfere with the Selbstschutz, whereupon Seedig promptly fired his deputy mayor. Only when the Selbstschutz returned the next day, supported by the SD and threatening to use weapons against his bewildered and unwilling auxiliaries, did Hahn give way.[98]

The total number of victims of this orgy of murder and deportation in West Prussia cannot be ascertained with any precision. Even in the autumn of 1939, Oebsger-Röder lamented, "In any case despite all toughness in the end only a fraction of the Poles in West Prussia will be destroyed (approximately 20,000)."[99] In February Gauleiter Forster reported that 87,000 people had been evacuated from Danzig–West Prussia.[100]

Jews did not figure prominently among the victims in West Prussia because it was not an area of dense Jewish population to begin with and most Jews had fled from this most indefensible part of Polish territory before the Germans arrived. For instance, only 39 Jews remained in the area around Bydgoszcz in early October. A month later both city and countryside were reported free of Jews or *judenfrei*, as the Jews had been "removed" (*beseitigt*) through "expulsion [*Verschickung*] and other measures."[101] The latter meant, of course, murder. In villages throughout West Prussia where individual Jews or families had remained, it was proclaimed a "shameful situation" that local Selbstschutz leaders were expected to remedy without delay through direct action.[102]

The chaotic terror also made itself felt in the Warthegau in the fall of 1939. When the time came for more systematic action in December, Sturmbann-führer Albert Rapp noted that it was extremely difficult to make a reliable list of politically active Poles, since their numbers had been so "sharply reduced through flight, shooting, or arrest." Gauleiter Greiser's policy toward the Poles was referred to as the "Three-Ex System: Expulsion, Exploitation, Extermination" (*Drei-A System: Aussiedeln, Ausbeuten, Ausrotten*).[103]

The terror in Southeast Prussia took place somewhat later, for Gauleiter Koch had not been able to send his men in from East Prussia until October.[104] When Brigadeführer Dr. Dr. (*sic*) Otto Rasch arrived in Königsberg in November as the new inspector of the Security Police and Security Service (Sipo-SD), he found that large numbers of prisoners who had been arrested by the Einsatzgruppen were still scattered in former camps for Autobahn workers. Rasch suggested liquidating the activists, and Heydrich approved as long as the liquidations were "unobtrusive." Rasch himself checked which prisoners were to be killed, and the executions were carried out in forest areas. This apparently did not remain sufficiently inconspicuous, and in January 1940 Rasch set up a "temporary" camp in the former Polish army barrack of Soldau on the border of East Prussia and the newly incorporated Southeast Prussia. It served both as a site to complete the liquidation of Polish intelligentsia (which Rasch continued to direct personally) and as a transit center for deportations to the General Government scheduled for the early months of that year. As the supply of anti-German elements, "criminals," "asocials," and "shirkers" never ended, the "temporary" camp at Soldau became a permanent fixture where some 1,000 political prisoners and 1,558 mentally ill perished.[105] Among the Polish border regions annexed to the Third Reich, Upper Silesia was the site of the least extensive executions, with a total of 1,400–1,500 victims in September 1939.[106]

Flurbereinigung was not reserved solely for the incorporated territories. What began in West Prussia and the Warthegau in the fall of 1939 and passed through Southeast Prussia in the winter reached the General Government in the spring. Certainly at that point the General Government was no stranger to the frequent murder of Poles. As Hans Frank told a correspondent of the *Völkischer Beo-bachter* on February 6, 1940, if he had to hang a placard for every seven Poles shot, as was done in the Protectorate of Bohemia, "then the forests of Poland would not suffice to produce the paper for such placards."[107] Despite the bravado, however, Frank did attempt to bring the killing under tighter control at this time by insisting upon his prior approval for the carrying out of death sentences and an end to "mass executions."[108]

Frank hoped for the Germanization of his colonial domain in the long run, but meanwhile the deportation of Poles from the incorporated territories was swelling the ranks of the embittered intelligentsia and leadership cadres. When the offensive in France diverted the world's attention elsewhere, Frank seized the opportunity to act. On May 30, 1940, he informed a meeting of police officers of his intention to carry out a "pacification program" that would "make an end in quick tempo of the masses of individuals in our hands who stir up resistance or are otherwise politically suspicious." This "would cost the lives of some thousands of Poles." Confidentially, Frank said, it was an order from the Führer, who had told him: "What we have now identified as the leading class in Poland must be liquidated." This so-called AB-Aktion (*allgemeine Befriedung* or general pacification) was to be carried out exclusively by the Higher ss and Police Leader (HSSPF) in the General Government, Obergruppenführer Friedrich Wilhelm Krüger.[109]

The systematic liquidation in 1939–40 of Poles noted for their education, nationalism, or social status made it clear that the Nazis were capable of murdering by the thousands. By one estimate, the number of Poles executed by the Germans had reached 50,000 by the end of 1939.[110] In the Germans' view it was but one step to ensure the permanent rule of Germany in the conquered Polish territories. Complementary to this murdering of thousands was the "resettlement" of hundreds of thousands, eventually even millions. The expulsion of undesired elements—Poles, Jews, "Gypsies"—to the east and the recovery of valuable German stock to be settled in their place were to provide the real biological basis for the consolidation of German Lebensraum. Nazi Jewish policy was at least temporarily subsumed into these experiments in demographic engineering. When the problems of massive population resettlement proved insurmountable and a solution to the Jewish question had to be separated out and temporarily postponed, the Germans would be able to draw from this period of terror in Poland a lesson of immense importance. It was in many cases easier to murder than resettle.

3

The Search for
a Final Solution
through Expulsion,
1939–1941

Two aspects of Nazi Jewish policy in Poland in the period between 1939 and 1941 are particularly prominent: expulsion and ghettoization. The first is what the Germans sought to do in this period, and the second is what they actually did. Too often, however, these policies and this period have been seen through a perspective influenced, indeed distorted and overwhelmed, by the catastrophe that followed. The policy of Jewish expulsion—and its relationship to resettlement policies in general—was for many years not taken as seriously by historians as it had been by the Nazis themselves.[1] Conversely, the policy of ghettoization has all too often been seen as an integral, even conscious, preparatory step toward extermination, while to the Germans at the time it was a temporary improvisation, a "necessary evil" that followed from the failure of expulsion plans. These policies are the focus of the next two chapters. They will be studied not from hindsight but rather as the Germans conceived, implemented, and experienced them between 1939 and 1941. In short, an attempt will be made to see these policies in their own right, as the crux of Nazi Jewish policy in Poland before the Final Solution.

EICHMANN AND THE NISKO PLAN

Already in September 1939 many Polish Jews had fled into the eastern portions of Poland that fell into Soviet hands, and many others were deliberately pushed over the demarcation line by German police and army units.[2] The protocol of Heydrich's meeting with his Einsatzgruppen leaders on September 21 recorded Hitler's approval of the "deportation of Jews into the non-German area, expulsion over the demarcation line." Did this mean two sequential phases of one policy or two parallel policies?[3] Heydrich's and Hitler's references to a *Judenstaat* or *Reichs-Getto*, first east of Cracow and then around Lublin, make it clear that they never seriously assumed that the Jewish question was going to be solved solely by expulsion over the demarcation line. The existence of a Jewish reservation at the furthest extremity of the German empire, therefore, was approved and encouraged. One participant in Heydrich's September 21 meeting took that encouragement to heart. He was Adolf Eichmann.

Eichmann, an obscure official in Heydrich's SD working on the Jewish question, had risen to prominence as the organizer of Jewish emigration from Austria following the Anschluss.[4] His Zentralstelle für jüdische Auswanderung (Central Agency for Jewish Emigration) in Vienna had become the prototype for SS policies between the Kristallnacht and the outbreak of the war, and Eichmann had also been placed in charge of a similar office in Prague in recognition of his achievements. However, emigration opportunities were rapidly diminishing in 1939, and prospects for continuing emigration after the outbreak of war were even dimmer. Eichmann was a man whose career faced a dead end unless he could adapt to the new situation. Many of his tactics—internment of one family member in a concentration camp until the rest had completed all preparations for emigration, sending Jews illegally out of Austria across the "green frontier"—already constituted expulsion. Formal approval for the continuing expulsion of Jews into the Soviet sphere opened a wide vista for the revitalization of Eichmann's career. In a striking example of an ambitious Nazi seizing the initiative from below in response to vague signals emanating from above, Eichmann set out to prove himself the master deporter and expeller of Jews into the district of Lublin and beyond.

On October 6, 1939, Eichmann met in Berlin with Oberführer Heinrich Müller, the head of the Gestapo. According to Eichmann's version of the conversation, Müller ordered Eichmann to contact Gauleiter Wagner in Katowice concerning the deportation of 70,000–80,000 Jews from East Upper Silesia. "These Jews shall be sent in an easterly direction over the Vistula for the purpose of expulsion." Jews from nearby Mährisch Ostrau, a town in the eastern corner of the Protectorate, could be included, especially those who had fled over the border from Poland during the fighting. "This activity shall serve first of all to collect experiences, in order . . . to be able to carry out evacuations of much greater numbers."[5]

Before going to Katowice, however, Eichmann first visited Mährisch Ostrau, where on October 9 he assembled his Prague staff—Rolf Günther, Theo Dannecker, and Anton Brunner—and explained their coming task. By order of

Baltic Sea

Gdynia
Danzig
•Königsberg

DANZIG

EAST
PRUSSIA

SUWALKI

WEST
PRUSSIA

•Allenstein

•Grodno

•Bydgoszcz

Soldau
S. E.
PRUSSIA

•Białystok

•Poznan
WARTHEGAU

Chelmno•

Lodz•

•Treblinka

•Warsaw
WARSAW
DISTRICT

Sobibor

RADOM
DISTRICT

Radom•

Czestochowa•

Kielce•

Lublin•
LUBLIN
DISTRICT

GENERAL
GOVERNMENT

Sosnowiec-Bedzin

Nisko•

Belzec•

EAST
UPPER
SILESIA

Katowice•

Cracow•
Auschwitz

Tarnow•

CRACOW
DISTRICT

•Lwow

GALICIA
DISTRICT

Tarnopol•

Drohobycz•

Stanislawow•

•Czortkow

Horodenko•

Kolomyja•

	Prewar boundary of Poland
	General Government boundary
	District boundary
	Gau boundary
	Incorporated Territories
	General Government
	Soviet-occupied Poland
	Soviet-occupied Poland in 1940; District Galicia

of the General Government as of August 1941.

I. POLAND, 1940

Müller in Berlin, a Jewish transport from Mährisch Ostrau and another from Katowice were to be assembled to take an "advance party" to a region southeast of Lublin, where it would erect a village of barracks to serve as a "transit camp for all subsequent transports." In contrast to subsequent deportations, in which no attention need be paid to the age or sex of the deportees, this first group was to contain only male Jews capable of physical labor, especially engineers, carpenters, artisans of various kinds, and at least ten doctors. These first trainloads were also to serve a second purpose as "model transports" (*Mustertransporte*). The Jews themselves were to be involved in carrying out an orderly implementation of German directives. "That is necessary in the interest of preserving a certain 'voluntary character' and also to obtain an unobtrusive as possible departure of the transport."[6]

On October 9 Eichmann and Rolf Günther traveled to nearby Katowice, where they met with Major General Knobelsdorf and the chief of the military administration, Fitzner, and on the following day with Gauleiter Wagner. In Katowice, Eichmann's plans had suddenly grown. Now Mährisch Ostrau and Katowice were to provide two 1,000-man transports each, and after the four transports had been sent, a report would be submitted to Heydrich that would "probably" then be shown to the Führer. They would then wait "until the general deportation of Jews is ordered." This could confidently be expected, because "the Führer has ordered first of all the shifting of 300,000 Jews from the Old Reich and Austria." Wagner, Knobelsdorf, and Fitzner all promised their support.[7]

Eichmann's expanding plans were not confined to Katowice and Mährisch Ostrau, however. While he was in Katowice, his deputy in Vienna, Hans Günther, was preparing both German officials and representatives of the Jewish community for deportations. On October 10 he informed Jewish leaders that they were to prepare a list of 1,000–1,200 workingmen, especially carpenters, cabinetmakers, and mechanics, for deportation. Moreover, four of the Viennese Jewish leaders were to report to Eichmann in Mährisch Ostrau with clothing for a three- or four-week stay.[8] German officials received the "strictly confidential" information that the Führer had ordered the resettlement of 300,000 Reich Jews in Poland, in the course of which Vienna would be completely cleared of Jews in about three-quarters of a year.[9] A week later Gauleiter Josef Bürckel, grateful at the prospect of getting rid of his Jews, invested Eichmann with "full powers" to carry out the resettlement action, and two transports per week were being planned.[10]

Eichmann was not only steadily increasing the number of transports but, in doing so, also changing the nature of the project. Müller had authorized him to

carry out experimental deportations of Jews from the newly incorporated territory of East Upper Silesia, and allowed that Eichmann might add some Jews
from the bordering areas of the Protectorate, especially Polish Jews who had
recently fled there. Eichmann immediately put the Protectorate deportation on
an equal basis with those from East Upper Silesia, and then began organizing
for a steady stream of semiweekly trains from Vienna. The focus was clearly
shifting to the regions where Eichmann had organized Jewish emigration in the
prewar period and thus had his own trusted staff in place. And he was clearly
hoping—indeed assuming—that his experiment would succeed, and these initial
transports would become the basis for an ongoing deportation program.

Before this grandiose scheme could mature, however, Eichmann had to find a
location for his "transit camp." On October 12 he flew with the Sipo-SD inspector in the Protectorate, Oberführer Dr. Franz Walter Stahlecker, to Cracow and
Warsaw, and traveled by car to explore the area in question. On October 15
Eichmann reported his success. The deportation trains were to be sent to Nisko
on the San, on the western border of the Lublin district.[11]

By now Eichmann was quite bursting with confidence that his experiment
would mature into a full-fledged program. This can be seen in his reply to inquiries from Oberführer Arthur Nebe, chief of the Criminal Police (Kripo). On
the day Eichmann had left for Poland in search of his transit camp, Nebe had
called to ask when he could deport his Berlin "Gypsies." If he could not do
it soon, he might have to go to the expense of building a camp for them.
The idea of deporting "Gypsies" was not new, of course, as Heydrich himself had mentioned deporting 30,000 "Gypsies" from Germany in the meeting
of the Einsatzgruppen leaders on September 21. Upon his return Eichmann
answered that "continuous transports now depart regularly," for the present
from Vienna, Katowice, and Mährisch Ostrau. "The simplest method . . . is to
attach some train cars of Gypsies to each transport." Nebe's experts should
contact Eichmann's men, the Günther brothers (Hans in Vienna and Rolf in
Mährisch Ostrau and Katowice), to work out the details. The start of deportations in the Old Reich would come in three to four weeks, Eichmann confidently
concluded.[12]

The first transport from Mährisch Ostrau was loaded with 901 Jews on
October 17 and departed on the morning of the 18th. The first transports from
Vienna (912 Jews) and Katowice (875 Jews) departed soon after, on October
20.[13] Eichmann was already back in Nisko when the Mährisch Ostrau transport
pulled into the station at noon on October 19. Eichmann had taken great effort
to disguise the true nature of the expulsion. Deportees had had to sign a
document stating that they were voluntarily going to a "retraining camp."[14] In

Vienna, Eichmann cynically painted rosy pictures of the Jews creating for themselves a new existence in the territory between the San, Bug, and Vistula, where they would be free of the legal restrictions imposed upon them in the Third Reich.[15] But the reality proved quite different. The first transport was marched out of Nisko across the San River to a swampy meadow near the village of Zarzecze and put to work erecting barracks. The following morning the best workers were selected from the group, and the rest were marched away eastward and told never to return. The subsequent transports from Vienna and Katowice were treated similarly.[16]

But what Eichmann clearly hoped would blossom into a full-fledged ongoing deportation and expulsion program from all Reich territories was stopped in its infancy by Müller's intervention from Berlin. While Rolf Günther was completing posttransport business in Katowice on October 20, a telegram arrived via Mährisch Ostrau conveying Müller's order "that the resettlement and deportation of Poles and Jews in the territory of the future Polish state requires central coordination. Therefore permission from the offices here must on principle be in hand." Günther inquired if the second transports from Mährisch Ostrau and Katowice planned for the next week could depart, and was informed that on the basis of an order from the Reich Security Main Office (Reichssicherheitshauptamt or RSHA), "every evacuation of Jews had to be stopped," including those planned from Mährisch Ostrau and Katowice.[17]

Eichmann hurried off to Berlin to salvage what he could of his ambitious dreams, with limited success. On October 24 he telephoned to Mährisch Ostrau that indeed the deportation of Jews from the Protectorate was to cease until further notice. In particular, the women intended for the next transport could not be included. However, Eichmann did agree to Günther's suggestion that because preparations were already far advanced, at least the men could be deported "in order to preserve the prestige of the police here." This could be done by attaching a partial transport of 400 Jewish men from Mährisch Ostrau to the transport still scheduled to leave Katowice on October 27. However, Eichmann warned from Berlin, the complete details of every transport had to be reported to Müller at least two days in advance.[18] In addition to the transport of October 27, carrying 1,000 Jews from Katowice and 400 from the Protectorate, a second transport from Vienna with 672 Jews had departed on October 26.[19] A small transport of 323 Jews from Prague was assembled and dispatched from Mährisch Ostrau on November 1, but it was halted in Sosnowiec (Sosnowitz) after a telegram arrived from Eichmann warning that a bridge was down over the San.[20] An attempt to send yet another Vienna transport failed when the military claimed all transportation for itself on the day it was scheduled.[21] With that, the Nisko experiment came to an end, although the camp itself remained in existence until the following April. Then the camp was dissolved on the order of HSSPF Friedrich Wilhelm Krüger in the General Government, and the 501 remaining Jews returned to Austria and the Protectorate.[22]

Why did the Nisko experiment come to such an abrupt halt? Certainly the local Landrat protested the "invasion," and the military authorities in the area complained that they would have to protect the incoming Jews against the "justified displeasure" (*berechtigten Unmut*) of the local population or "tolerate and even encourage" pogroms.[23] But this protest came after the fact and could not have influenced an SS decision sent from Berlin even as the first transport was arriving in Nisko. Likewise, Hans Frank later objected to deportations, but in mid-October he was traveling from Berlin to Poznan (Posen) to Lodz and back to Berlin, awaiting the imminent dissolution of the military administration and unsuccessfully fighting to have Lodz included in his future General Government rather than in the Warthegau. That he was in any position to know about, much less waste political capital on protesting, Eichmann's scheme, is most unlikely.[24] Russian protest could scarcely have been decisive, since local German authorities continued to shove Jews over the demarcation line well into December, when Frank finally ordered Krüger to put a stop to such expulsions in order to avoid endangering good relations with the Soviet Union.[25] No doubt the military was placing great claim on rail transportation as it hurriedly shifted forces to the west for the offensive still scheduled for mid-November. But neither the military nor Göring, who was busy looting Poland, had forbidden *all* transports, as Eichmann himself found out upon inquiry.[26] Nor had Eichmann been operating totally without Müller's knowledge and was now being called to account. In that case Nebe would never have known about Eichmann's impending deportations, nor would Eichmann have openly invited him to add train cars of "Gypsies" to his "continuous" transports.[27]

Clearly the stop order came from Himmler personally. Himmler let Gauleiter Bürckel in Vienna know this in no uncertain terms when the latter accused Arthur Seyss-Inquart, at that time Frank's deputy in the General Government, of preventing the deportation of Viennese Jews that he so ardently desired. Himmler justified his decision on the basis of "technical difficulties."[28] Himmler had just gained jurisdiction over the resettlement of ethnic Germans, and for him the most decisive factor at the time was probably the arrival of the first Baltic Germans in Danzig on October 15.[29] The problem of finding space in West Prussia and the Warthegau for the incoming Volksdeutsche now took priority over deporting Jews from East Upper Silesia and especially from Austria and the Protectorate. For the next year, in fact, the deportation plans of the Nazis in eastern Europe would be inextricably connected to the resettlement of the ethnic Germans, for whom space had to be found in the incorporated territories. Eichmann's shift in emphasis to deporting Jews from Austria and the Protectorate simply did not provide lodging and livelihoods for incoming Volksdeutsche where Himmler needed it. Nor, as it turned out, did deporting Jews even from the Warthegau serve Himmler's new priority, for it did not open up the kinds of lodging and livelihoods best suited to the newcomers. While the Nazis never wanted openly to admit it and struggled against such a conclusion for months, it turned out that, at least temporarily, consolidating Lebensraum in the incorporated territories and solving the Jewish question were not complementary but competing goals. The result was that for the time being priority was given to the consolidation of Lebensraum through ethnic German resettlement, and a solution to the Jewish question was either postponed or sought in forms other than deportation eastward. Eichmann's Nisko experiment thus demonstrated not only the scope for local initiative within the Nazi system of government but also its limitations when it clashed with clear priorities set from above.

THE BALTIC GERMANS, THE FIRST SHORT-RANGE PLAN,
AND THE WARTHEGAU DEPORTATIONS

When Germany reached agreement with the Soviet Union on September 28, 1939, to repatriate ethnic Germans from the Soviet sphere, Heinrich Himmler succeeded in obtaining from Hitler the jurisdiction over "strengthening Germandom." This put Himmler in charge of both resettling the ethnic Germans and eliminating the "injurious" influence of alien populations in the areas to be "Germanized." In short, Himmler now controlled population movements both coming and going. It was a classic example of those who best anticipated Hitler's desires receiving their reward in new grants of power. Himmler was now in a position to overcome the obstacles to population transfers that Brauchitsch had placed in front of Heydrich on September 22. Himmler also moved to establish an economic base for his operations. Göring had already received the economic fruits of conquest, with jurisdiction over the seizure of all Polish and Jewish property in the incorporated territories. But Himmler used his new positions to insist on control over the distribution of agricultural land necessary for resettlement, which Göring conceded.[30]

On October 30, 1939, Himmler issued the overall guidelines for the activities of the RKFDV in the area of population expulsion. By February 1940, that is in four months, the following populations were to be transferred to the General Government: (1) from the incorporated territories, *all* Jews (estimated by the

RKFDV deputy Creutz at 550,000); (2) from Danzig–West Prussia, all "Congress Poles," that is, Poles who had moved to the former German areas after 1919; and (3) from the Warthegau, East Upper Silesia, and Southeast Prussia, a yet-to-be-determined number of especially anti-German Poles. The population transfers were to be arranged between the respective HSSPF, with Krüger of the General Government deciding which cities and districts received which transports. However, the Jews were to be transferred specifically to the territory between the Vistula and the Bug Rivers (to which the Jews of the General Government west of the Vistula were also to be sent the following year). Care of the deportees in the General Government was to be left to the local Polish administration. The Sipo-SD inspector of the General Government, Bruno Streckenbach, immediately reported to Frank that Himmler aimed to move no fewer than one million people in the next four months.[31]

While the HSSPF had to cope with the reality of moving even a fraction of the people targeted in Himmler's orders, two officials of the Rassenpolitisches Amt (RPA or Office of Racial Policy), Erhard Wetzel and Gerhard Hecht, articulated the racial theories underlying this vast scheme of population movement. They produced a document that might easily be dismissed as sheer fantasy, except that much of its thrust was subsequently incorporated into Himmler's own memorandum for Hitler on the treatment of foreign populations in the east.[32] Wetzel and Hecht noted that in the newly incorporated territories, only 7% of the population was German, 5% was Jewish, and the rest Polish. "Consequently, the necessity arises for a ruthless decimation of the Polish population and, as a matter of course, the expulsion of all Jews and persons of Polish-Jewish mixed blood." The German portion of the population had to be strengthened by the resettlement of the ethnic Germans, first from the Soviet Union but ultimately from southeastern Europe and even the western hemisphere, Palestine, and Australia. Only a small portion of Poles was suitable for "Germanization," which was defined as a "genuine ethnic transformation" (*echte Umvolkung*), the "intellectually and spiritually complete entry" (*geistig und seelisch mittragende Eintreten*) into the ethnicity of another people, something that could be achieved only after one or two generations, not from the mere adoption of German language and culture. This was possible only for a small number of racially suitable Poles. If they were politically "neutral" and willing to send their children to German educational institutions, they could remain. Racially suitable anti-German Poles were to be deported, but their "racially valuable" (*rassisch wertvolle*) children, if not more than 8–10 years old, would be sent to the wholesome environment of a German family or military orphanage. Polish intelligentsia and political activists, Congress Poles, the racially unsuitable lower class, people of mixed Polish-Jewish extraction, and even first-degree German *Mischlinge* (Germans with two Jewish grandparents) would be deported without exception. Ultimately perhaps 1 million Poles would remain and 5.6 million Poles, along with 530,000 Jews from the incorporated territories as well as the Jews of Germany, Austria, and the Protectorate, would be sent east. The problem of overpopulation in the Polish *Reststaat* or rump state did not bother Wetzel and Hecht at all. The racially degenerate population there was increasing too quickly in any case. "If only for the purpose of preventing the rapid increase of the population in these areas, the expulsion of Poles from Reich territory into this area is urgently necessary."

In the Polish *Reststaat* the Polish "national ideal" had to be combated ruthlessly by keeping education and culture to the most primitive level. Polish population growth would be kept down by restricting medical care to the bare minimum necessary to prevent the spread of epidemics to the Reich. Birth control would be encouraged and hygiene discouraged; homosexuality would be declared nonpunishable. While the Jewish population was also to be curtailed by such policies, Wetzel and Hecht felt that in other ways the Jews could be "treated more leniently" (*erleichtert behandelt*) than the Poles in order to maximize animosity between the two races. Better education would make the Jews "fit for emigration" and was less dangerous because "the Jews have no such real political force as the Poles, with their greater Poland ideology."

If the German authorities in Poland, who were to be on the receiving end of this flood of uprooted people, were not about to entertain Wetzel's and Hecht's notion (bizarre only in retrospect) of preferential treatment for Jews over the Poles, they certainly were attracted to the idea that the magnitude of their Jewish problem would be lessened by decreases in the Jewish population brought about by depressing the Jews' living conditions. Seyss-Inquart noted on returning from his inspection tour of the General Government in late November: "This territory [Lublin] with its extreme marshy nature can, in the view of the district governor Schmidt, serve as a Jewish reservation," which "could induce a severe decimation of the Jews [*eine starke Dezimierung der Juden*]."[33] Hans Frank, in a speech blustery even by his standards, informed a meeting of General Government officials in Radom on November 25, 1939, that one-half to three-quarters of the Jews, including also all those from the Third Reich, would be sent east of the Vistula. "Make short work of the Jews," he exhorted. "What a pleasure, finally for once to be able to tackle the Jewish race physically. The more that die, the better."[34]

In addition to Seyss-Inquart and Frank, the Propaganda Minister Joseph Goebbels also grasped and recorded in his diary the nature and intensity of the racial struggle to be carried out in Poland. On October 10 he noted: "The Führer's verdict on the Poles is devastating. More like animals than human beings, totally stupid and amorphous. . . . The Führer has no intention of assimilating the Poles. They are to be forced into their truncated state and left entirely to themselves." A week later Goebbels watched with Hitler a screening of recent film footage from Warsaw. "And then footage from the ghetto film. Never seen anything like it. Scenes so horrific and brutal in their explicitness that one's blood runs cold. One shudders at such crudeness. This Jewry must be destroyed [*Dieses Judentum muss vernichtet werden*]." A visit to Lodz on November 2 reinforced his conviction. "Drive through the ghetto. We get out and inspect everything thoroughly. It is indescribable. They are no longer human beings, they are animals. Thus our task is no longer humanitarian but surgical. One must cut here, and indeed quite radically. . . . This is already Asia. We will have much to do here to Germanize this region." In early December Goebbels reported to Hitler on a trip to Poland. "He listens to everything very carefully and totally shares my opinion on the Jewish and Polish question. We must exorcise the Jewish danger. . . . The Polish aristocracy deserves its demise."[35]

There were clearly many Nazis in Berlin and Poland who were intoxicated by Himmler's vision of vast population transfers to be completed in four months and who welcomed the loss of life, particularly Jewish life, that this would entail. For the ss officials who had the impossible task of making performance match Himmler's pronouncements, however, blustery speeches and bloodthirsty diary entries would not suffice. They had to develop the machinery and techniques to uproot and move thousands upon thousands of people. In the process of failing to meet Himmler's unrealistic deadline, they learned a great deal about what was and what was not possible. These were lessons that were not forgotten, and eventually the Nazi machinery would be able to transform even-more-fantastic visions of Hitler and Himmler into reality.

The practical work began in late September, even as the German-Russian agreement for the return of the ethnic Germans was being signed. The army was ordered to clear space in the city of Gdynia (Gotenhafen) and did so in a manner that "did not distinguish itself significantly" from the later eviction procedures of the ss. But within days Himmler was officially entrusted with all matters pertaining to resettlement, and he established an *Einwanderungszentrale* or immigration center in Gdynia to organize the entry of the Baltic Germans and the exit of Poles. As the first Baltic Germans arrived on October 15, the momentum picked up. Ultimately, some 40,000 people were forced out of Gdynia and deported to Radom and Kielce in the General Government. This constituted nearly one-half of the population of Gdynia, as well as almost one-half of those deported from Danzig–West Prussia by the end of January 1940.[36] It was soon apparent that Gdynia would not suffice, and Himmler ordered that Poznan be prepared to receive Baltic Germans as well. As these Baltic Germans poured into Poznan, internment camps were feverishly prepared to hold the uprooted Poles until they could be deported. Internment, first of the intelligentsia, began on November 4, 1939.[37]

Coordination could not be delayed any longer, and on November 8, 1939, a meeting of all the HSSPF on former Polish territory met in Cracow. Krüger, who chaired the meeting, insisted from the beginning that the "wild resettlement [*wilde Umsiedlung*] must be stopped immediately." With no fewer than one million Poles and Jews to be deported by the end of February, and with some 100,000 ethnic Germans from Volhynia and the Ukraine, 30,000 from the Lublin region, and 20,000 from other parts of the General Government in addition to the Baltic Germans to be resettled, the transfer of the population had to be undertaken "in a planned manner." According to Krüger's Sipo-SD commander, Bruno Streckenbach, ultimately all Jews and Poles in the Old Reich and incorporated territories would be deported, but only the Jews and Congress Poles of the incorporated territories were targeted for the end of February. The remaining Poles would be investigated, and the "undesirable" ones would be deported in 1941. The trains would begin running in mid-November (that is, when the redeployment of the German army was to be complete). One important exception was made. Because the retention of Lodz within the Warthegau had not been finalized, evacuations "even of Jews" were not to be undertaken from there for the moment. Thus because at that time Lodz might have remained a part of the General Government, making population transfers from there superfluous, what was to become the single largest concentration of Jews in the incorporated territories was not to be included in the impending deportations.[38]

HSSPF Koppe returned to Poznan to organize the population transfers. On November 11 a special staff for the placement of Baltic Germans was created under Reichsamtsleiter Dr. Derichsweiler, and a special staff for the evacuation of Poles and Jews was formed under Sturmbannführer Albert Rapp.[39] Rapp composed the initial draft of a circular to various officials announcing the deportation of 200,000 Poles and 100,000 Jews between mid-November and the end of February for the "necessary cleansing and security" of the Warthegau. All politically active Poles were to be included. While economic considerations were to be subordinated to security concerns, the deportations were to be "coupled" with the arrival of ethnic Germans. Indeed, Poles removed from their homes and businesses in favor of the arriving ethnic Germans were to form the "nucleus" though certainly not the full quota of the deportees. The War-thegau Jews—except those in Lodz—could be deported within hours and thus included when expedient to fill gaps and prevent delays.[40]

The official circular sent on November 12, 1939, contained significant changes from Rapp's initial draft. The goal of procuring housing and liveli-hoods for incoming ethnic Germans was placed on an equal footing with se-curity and cleansing. In addition to politically minded and nationalistic Poles, the "intellectual leadership, the entire intelligentsia" (*die geistig führende Schicht, die gesamte Intelligenz*) as well as the criminal element were to be removed. Despite the earlier prohibition, 30,000 Jews from Lodz were also to be included. And much more concern was expressed for economic factors. If not implicated, Polish manual workers and minor employees were to be exempted because they were "urgently needed" for labor. Mayors, Landräte, and economic leaders were to be consulted to prevent the deportation of economically indispensable Poles. The evacuation of every Pole was "to be prepared individually," and the "indiscriminate mass clearings" (*wahllose Massenräumungen*) of streets and neighborhoods was forbidden.[41]

Between November 16 and December 4 Rapp produced no less than twelve different sets of regulations covering every conceivable aspect of the deporta-tions; held two coordinating conferences on the scheduling of transportation and the handling of property, respectively; and finally made a personal in-spection tour to visit all Regierungspräsidenten, Oberbürgermeister, and Land-räten.[42] Only one set of regulations (of November 24) specifically referred to the deportation of Jews. In their case the Jewish councils were to be directly in-volved and held personally responsible for the assembly of the required number of Jews and for the orderly carrying out of the deportation.[43] This was to be no "wild resettlement" but one meticulously prepared in every detail.

In West Prussia Gauleiter Forster was on less amicable terms with Heinrich Himmler and less enthusiastic about cooperating with his resettlement scheme. Forster had been heard to remark about Himmler, "If I looked like him, I would not speak about race at all" (*Wenn ich so aussehen würde wie der, würde ich erst gar nicht von Rassen reden*).[44] Forster was openly critical of the way in which Himm-ler was handling the resettlement of ethnic Germans. To Goebbels he com-plained about "the hair-raising organizational abuses during the evacuation of the Baltic Germans. These cry out to high heaven."[45] Perhaps because of For-ster's lack of cooperation in resettling ethnic Germans, Himmler on October 28, 1939, ordered an end to the deportation of Poles from West Prussia.[46]

The ban was not permanent, however. On November 5, 1939, Ulrich Grei-felt, Himmler's deputy for the RKFDV, urged that full use be made of available transport to deport "Jews and Poles" in order "to create further lodging possibilities for the ethnic German repatriates from Latvia and Estonia."[47] In November HSSPF Richard Hildebrandt held a series of meetings in which he held out the prospect of deporting 400,000 people in the following year, but he announced that the target for December 1939 was a mere 10,000. These were to include as usual all Jews as well as families of executed Poles and those posing any security problem, radical and politically undesirable elements, and Polish peasants whose farms were suitable for ethnic German settlers. After the wild deportations of the preceding weeks, the thrust of Hildebrandt's message was in fact quite conservative. "Unauthorized expulsions have to stop," he noted. The economy was not to be disturbed. Those performing necessary economic functions had to be exempted. Moreover, there was little desire to take on more Baltic Germans. "In the Danzig district itself the Baltic Germans will no longer remain but rather be sent on."[48]

On November 28 Heydrich intervened from Berlin, drastically scaling down the immediate task facing the Germans in the incorporated territories. In wording similar to his famous *Schnellbrief* of September 21, Heydrich distinguished between a "short-range plan" (*Nahplan*) and a "long-range plan" (*Fernplan*), which permitted the Germans to return to the realm of the possible while still keeping faith with their ideology. According to the short-range plan, "enough Poles and Jews are to be deported that the incoming Baltic Germans can be housed. The short-range plan will be carried out *only in the Warthegau* [italics mine], because for the moment Baltic Germans are being brought only there." Since the expected number of Baltic Germans was 40,000, double that number, 80,000 Poles and Jews, had to be evacuated by December 16, 1939.[49]

If the other incorporated territories were temporarily reprieved, Koppe and Rapp still faced the formidable task of deporting 80,000 people in less than three weeks. In an extraordinary display of brutal efficiency, they surpassed their goal, deporting 87,833 people in 80 trainloads by December 17. Rapp summarized the operation in two lengthy reports.[50] Numerous obstacles had had to be overcome, he boasted. The coordination of so many agencies—the Landräte were in charge of the local operations, the office of the HSSPF provided central planning, the Sipo-SD provided local help in selecting the victims, the Reichsbahn provided transportation, and the police and Selbstschutz carried out the evacuations themselves—meant that a breakdown anywhere threatened the entire operation. Communications had been very poor, and finally courier service was instituted. The behavior of the Landräte was mixed. "Where it was a question of a young officer or SS leader, the entire operation was tackled with personal verve. The older Landräte typical of the German administrative bureaucrat assured at least an orderly operation in the selection of the persons and the organization of the evacuations. Only in the individual cases did Landräte lack from the beginning the necessary hardness for the evacuation."

The erection of internment camps had proved valuable for processing the deportees and reducing to a minimum the length of time the trains spent at the deportation stations. There had been considerable difficulty with the trains. Of the eleven that the operation was to use, only five came back, and in eight, not four, days; the rest were commandeered by the Wehrmacht or the authorities of the Polish railway system (Ostbahn) in Cracow. Almost insuperable difficulties stood in the way of finding substitute trains. Moreover, the train personnel of the Ostbahn, almost entirely Polish, were not interested in helping the operation run smoothly and in fact sometimes refused to work or sought to sabotage the operation. Officials in the General Government had also proven inadequate. Unsuitable arrival stations had been selected; local authorities there had not been informed, and the local preparations had been poor. "The taking over of transports was repeatedly refused, and in general little understanding was shown by the receiving officials."

The selection of the deportees had been a difficult process as well. To be evacuated were Jews, anti-German and politically active Poles, and Poles who were of the intelligentsia and leadership elite. The deportees thus had a racial, a political, and a social component, but the priority was to include Poles who posed an "immediate danger to Germandom" in the Warthegau. Constructing reliable lists of politically active Poles had been difficult because their numbers had been "sharply reduced through flight, shooting or arrest," and the census material on the intelligentsia and leadership elite was also inadequate. Thus, compiling lists of these two categories had required extensive preparation. Counting the Jews, including the 230,000 in Lodz who had not been hitherto included, the total number of potential deportees came to 680,000. With three trains daily, the 600,000 who still remained could be deported in six to seven months.

Strangely, nowhere in Rapp's reports did he record how many Jews were among the 87,000 "Poles and Jews" deported from the Warthegau in December 1939. On several later occasions SS officials referred only to the deportation of Poles in this episode.[51] Indeed, the primary thrust of what was to become known as the "first short-range plan" (1. *Nahplan*) had not been to solve the Jewish question but rather to remove dangerous Poles and find space for the Baltic Germans.

Nonetheless, the train that departed from Konin to Ostrowiec on December 1 carried 900 Jews.[52] Moreover, most of the ten trains from Lodz under the first short-range plan carried Jews. This was not mentioned, much less proclaimed as a success in any of the summary reports, for it was in fact evidence of a breakdown in the system, namely, the failure of the local authorities in Lodz to identify and seize dangerous Poles. When one of Rapp's men visited the city on November 30, 1939, he had been dismayed to find that absolutely no preparations had been made for the deportations. Stadtkommissar Schiffer seemed oblivious to the fact that he was responsible for coordinating the Lodz deportations. The orders containing the criteria for determining the list of deportees had just arrived, and no one could find more than a fraction of the earlier lists and files compiled by the Gestapo. The police president, ss-Brigadeführer Johannes Schäfer, suggested that one could always deport the "Jewish proletariat," for which no list would be needed.[53]

Lodz was assigned a quota of 15,000 "Poles and Jews," but "above all politically suspicious and intellectual Poles were to be evacuated." Owing to the loss of the Gestapo materials, a card file of only 5,000 names could be compiled. In turn, these hurriedly composed lists proved hopelessly incomplete, and only 2,600 of those listed could be taken into custody. "In order to reach the quota of 15,000, one had to fall back upon Jews" (*musste daher auf Juden zurückgegriffen werden*). The Jewish council was used as an intermediary to solicit volunteers among Jews interned in a camp in Radogocz, which netted 1,000.

Police president Schäfer and the Oberbürgermeister then decided that the "only practical method" was nighttime raids on entire apartment buildings in the Jewish quarter. On the night of December 14–15 a raiding party of 650 Schutzpolizei (Schupo) and 80 men of the NSKK (National Socialist Drivers Corps) seized 7,000 Jews between 8:20 P.M. and 4 A.M. Between 5,600 and 5,850 were deported in three trains the following evening. On December 16 a second raid caught 2,000 Jews, who along with the remaining Jews from the first raid were deported in three trains on December 17.

Rapp's representative Richter bitterly attacked the city administration in Lodz. The initial call for Jewish volunteers had been doomed to fail, because those responding to the call were made to stand in line for hours in the freezing cold. The first razzia or roundup, once in motion, was not stopped, even when twice as many Jews had been seized as planned. No holding camps were available, but to have released Jews already seized would have been an "intolerable loss of prestige" for the German authorities. Thus the trains had to be overfilled. Because the cattle cars were provided with neither straw nor provisions, Richter wrote in his report, "not all the deported persons, especially the infants, arrive at the destination alive." The city officials had made no lists and did not even know how many people had been deported from Lodz. They estimated 8,400, but Richter estimated 9,600–9,900.[54]

Few other reports from the first short-range plan mentioned Jews at all. In Kreis Konin the local Landrat wanted to deport 6,200 Jews and 5,000 Poles. In the first of two trains from Konin, on December 1, 900 of the 1,102 deportees were Jews.[55] The Landrat of Kreis Schroda noted that while Jews had constituted just less than 1% of the prewar population, as of December 12, 1939, none remained.[56] The police chief of Sieradsch had already arranged "on his own initiative" to deport 300–400 Jews in 16 train cars to Lublin in mid-November. Richter deemed the police chief to be "very competent."[57] In Kreis Weichsel a commando of Einsatzkommando 11 did not wait for such clever local initiative. On November 14, 1939, the mayor of Alexandrow had been ordered to force all the Jews in town to emigrate toward Warsaw within ten days.[58]

The first short-range plan concentrated on the expulsion of individual Poles who were placed on the deportation lists because of their particular political or social status or because they possessed lodgings and businesses needed for incoming Baltic Germans. Local Germans who had to "fall back" on indiscriminately seizing and deporting Jews were in effect admitting that they had not diligently carried out the identification and seizure of Polish activists and intelligentsia and thus were not eager to report the actual number of Jews deported. Likewise, Richter's critical remarks on the Lodz deportations, primarily of Jews, were omitted from Rapp's self-congratulatory reports.

But even if the thrust of the first short-range plan lay elsewhere, Berlin had in no way forgotten about the Jewish question. On December 19, in preparation for a meeting of RSHA division heads, Heydrich's SD Jewish desk (*Judenreferat*) submitted an "in-house" note on the "Final Solution of the German Jewish problem."[59] Heydrich's Jewish experts posed the question "whether a Jewish reservation shall be created in Poland." The protocol of this RSHA meeting does not survive. However, four results are known. First, on December 21 Müller forbade "until further notice a deportation of Jews from the Old Reich including Austria and the Protectorate to occupied Polish territory." Second, on the same day Heydrich announced that "the central preparation of security policy matters in carrying out evacuations in the east" was necessary. Therefore he was appointing Adolf Eichmann as his "special adviser" (*Sonderreferent*) in Amt IV (Müller's Gestapo) of the RSHA.[60] Thus the ban that had shut down the Nisko plan continued in force, but the originator of that plan had suffered no career setback. Third, an Einwandererzentralstelle (EWZ) or central agency for immigration was headquartered in Poznan, with branch offices in Gdynia and Lodz. The center of ethnic German resettlement had clearly shifted to the Warthegau.[61]

Fourth, the conference produced the first version of the "second short-range plan" (2. *Nahplan*), which was to entail "the complete seizure of all Jews without regard to age or gender in the German Ostgauen and their deportation into the General Government."[62] When Himmler had ordered the deportation of all Jews from the incorporated territories on October 30, 1939, the exact border between the expanded Third Reich and the General Government had not yet been determined. It was still unclear on which side of the boundary the two areas of greatest Jewish population—Lodz in the Warthegau and Sosnowiec-Bedzin in East Upper Silesia—would be placed, and hence whether such deportations would involve as few as 170,000 or as many as 550,000 Jews. By late December 1939 it was clear that both Lodz and Sosnowiec-Bedzin had been incorporated into the Third Reich.[63] Thus, according to the even higher estimate of the second short-range plan, 600,000 Jews were to be deported by the end of April by "combing through" the new territories from the north and west, at a deportation rate of 5,000 Jews per day, beginning sometime after January 15, 1940. To ensure that the territories were "totally cleared of Jews," in principle no deferments were to be granted for employer claims of economic indispensability.

On January 4, 1940, Eichmann held a meeting in Berlin attended by the Jewish experts of the Sipo-SD in the four Gaue of the incorporated territories as well as the General Government. In addition, representatives of the economic, transportation, and finance ministries and Göring's HTO attended. It was the first of many such interministerial conferences that Eichmann would organize in the coming years. "On the order of the Reichsführer-SS the evacuation of all Jews from the former Polish occupied territories is to be carried out as a priority," Eichmann announced.

Without explanation, Eichmann's quotas for the "immediate evacuation of Jews" (*sofortige Judenevakuierung*) totaled only 352,000–357,000 instead of the 600,000 targeted in the first draft of the second short-range plan: East Prussia, 30,000; East Upper Silesia, 120,000–125,000; and the Warthegau, 200,000. Danzig–West Prussia would evacuate 10,000 Poles and 2,000 Jews. "The Warthegau will moreover immediately evacuate 80,000 Poles, in order to create space for the ethnic Germans from Galicia and Volhynia. The Warthegau has by now already evacuated 87,000 Poles." A deadline could not yet be set, because arrangements in the General Government for reception were not yet complete. "A long-range plan would be worked out, which would be divided into a number of short-range plans." In any case, the evacuees would be deported to all four districts within the General Government (and not just to Lublin). The evacuations would not begin before January 25, and a final conference would be held beforehand with the participation of Heydrich.[64]

By the turn of the year, therefore, the Nazi attempt to find a Final Solution to the Jewish question through expulsions into Polish territory had made little practical progress. Since Hitler's statement to Rosenberg in late September that all Jews, including those in the Old Reich, would be sent to the region between the Vistula and the Bug, and Himmler's orders of October 30 to deport all Jews from the incorporated territories by the end of February, very little had been accomplished, other than the almost complete disappearance (through flight, "wild deportations," and murder) of the Jews from West Prussia and former German territory of the western Warthegau.[65] But some clarity had been achieved. The deportation of Jews from the Old Reich had been indefinitely postponed, and top priority was given to Jews in the incorporated territories. Centralized coordination of the deportations had been established under Heydrich's special adviser, Eichmann, who had tried to cut through the confusion, caused by mixing the deportation of Poles and Jews, which pervaded the German documents of these months. The Poles, he had said, were to be evacuated to make room for the ethnic Germans. All Jews were to be deported immediately and as a "matter of priority" because they were Jews. Eichmann assumed that both deportation programs could be carried out simultaneously. But in this he was to be thwarted once again.

THE CURBING OF NAZI DEPORTATION PLANS, JANUARY–FEBRUARY 1940

Nazi deportation policy became the center of an internal debate in January and February 1940 that resulted in a considerable cutback in ss plans for massive transfers of population, including a near total postponement of deportations aimed at making even the incorporated territories *judenfrei*. Effective criticism was launched from a number of vantage points: by people within the ss itself, by officials of the General Government, by economists of both the army and Göring's empire, and by some of the Gauleiters affected. Ultimately, an alliance between Frank and Göring forced concessions from Himmler, whose own concerns had also placed constraints upon the deportation program.

In the Warthegau the major targets of deportation had been Polish intelligentsia, political activists, and nationalists, not "Congress Poles," who had emigrated there since 1919. This was in accord with Himmler's October 30 order, in which Congress Poles had been targeted for deportation only in Danzig–West Prussia. Inevitably, the Polish elites targeted for deportation contained elements of the population that were well educated, spoke the German language, and knew German culture. There was a strong suspicion among the Nazis that many educated Poles were falsely trying to pass as ethnic Germans, and apparently much revenge taking among Volksdeutsche against those who had accommodated themselves to Polish rule. The result was that many people were deported who subsequently complained to officials of the General Government that they were really Volksdeutsche. For Himmler and his racial theorists, who were trying to maximize the ethnic German element in the incorporated territories and to save for Germandom those Polish elements capable of "Germanization," this was an intolerable hemorrhage of valuable racial material. Himmler thus forbade deportation of cases of contested Volksdeutsch status without his specific permission and ordered that henceforth denunciation by other ethnic Germans was not sufficient to settle the issue. Himmler further ordered that only Congress Poles and Jews were to be deported for the moment, not longtime residents, who required more careful screening.

This raised considerable difficulties for the deportation technicians, however. The collecting camps were already mostly full of politically implicated Poles, and the long-term residents were the ones with the best apartments most suitable for the Baltic Germans. On the other hand, the Congress Poles were simple workers indispensable for keeping the economy going and without property suitable for the incoming Baltic Germans.[66] In short, the Nazis had tied themselves in knots with conflicting demands concerning the deportations. Possible Volksdeutsche and Poles suitable for Germanization were not to be deported; yet places had to be found for the incoming ethnic Germans. The economy was not to be disrupted, but the Congress Poles—mostly laborers—were to be the first to go.

A second problem emerged over the methods of deportation. Rapp had, in typical ss style, expressed considerable sympathy and praise for the "overburdened" German officials who had surmounted great obstacles in accomplishing their task of evicting 87,000 people in 17 days, without once mentioning the catastrophic fate of the deportees. But other German officials, particularly those in the General Government who had had to cope with their arrival, did not mince words. At Eichmann's January 4 conference in Berlin, Hauptsturmführer Mohr of the General Government summarized the complaints of his colleagues. Trains had arrived carrying far more than the stipulated contingent of deportees, and local officials were totally unprepared to provide for such numbers. The deportees had been locked in cattle cars for as many as eight days, without even the opportunity to remove their human waste. Owing to the extreme cold, one train had arrived with over 100 cases of frostbite. Other reports complained that the deportees had arrived without having received food or drinking water for the entire trip, and many had been robbed of even the most basic necessities, such as bedding and utensils, to say nothing of sufficient money to make a new start. Eichmann promised to remedy all these difficulties. Each transport would be strictly limited to 1,000 deportees, each of whom would be provided with ten days' rations and 100 zloty. Timely notification to Cracow would be made of each departing train. In severe cold, the women and children would be protected "if possible" by sending them in passenger cars. "Disciplined" behavior by the guards would be ensured.[67]

In the Warthegau, Gauleiter Greiser shared his critical reaction with Goebbels, who noted that the Gauleiter was having "lots of problems with Himmler, who is behaving very autocratically, especially in regard to the evacuation question." Goebbels wasted no time in discussing the Reichsführer's difficulties with Hitler. "Himmler is shoving whole peoples around at the moment. Not always successfully."[68]

The economic mobilization experts of the military's Armaments Inspectorate in Poland also provided a barrage of criticism—although most certainly not from a moral or political point of view. When Rapp briefed one staff officer and one intelligence officer before the December deportations, he reported that they not only had "no objections at all" but expressed "their full understanding."[69] When local army officers intervened on behalf of Poles threatened with deportation, General Petzel made it clear that such behavior contradicted the prescribed attitude toward Poles and would "damage the prestige of the Wehrmacht."[70] But protest on economic grounds was vigorous. In the fall of 1939 the military had argued without success that Polish industrial capacity would best serve the German war economy if left in place. Frank and Göring had Hitler's backing for a piratical policy of removing everything from Poland beyond what was necessary to assure a "bare existence" for the inhabitants. In December the Economic and Armaments Office (Rüstungswirtschaftsamt) of the OKW tried again and appealed directly to Himmler to take the interests of the war economy into account. Himmler's resettlement schemes threatened economic paralysis in both the incorporated territories and the General Government by removing indispensable workers from the former and overfilling the latter.[71] Such appeals apparently had no effect, however, until the catastrophic winter deportations caused Hans Frank to join his otherwise hated military rivals in protest.

Frank's initial view of the resettlement potential of the General Government had been considerably more cautious than that of Himmler and the RPA theorists, Wetzel and Hecht. Frank estimated that ultimately the General Government could absorb no more than an additional 1–1.5 million people, because the land was relatively poor and already overpopulated. Thus the General Government might be able to absorb the Jews of the incorporated territories (600,000 in his estimation) and those of the Old Reich, Austria, Sudetenland, and Protectorate (bringing the total to 1 million). In addition, it could absorb the Polish intelligentsia and nationalists, as well as the Polish peasants whose land was needed for ethnic German resettlement. But any attempt to settle some 6 or 7 million Poles—as envisaged in the RPA memorandum—was possible only with "a revolutionary reorganization" (*einer umwälzenden Neuordnung*) of the east whereby superfluous Poles could be sent east, to Siberia for example. Additional space in the General Government could also be created, Frank noted, by resettling the millions of Jews, perhaps in Madagascar.[72]

The winter deportations sobered Frank and his associates considerably. At a meeting of leading officials in the General Government on January 19, 1940, Krüger noted that 80,000 Poles and Jews had been deported from the incorporated territories as quickly as possible as an emergency measure to make room for the incoming Baltic Germans, and at least another 30,000 Poles and Jews had been shoved into the General Government "illegally." This was a "modern tribal migration" (*moderne Völkerwanderung*), the implications of which Berlin had unfortunately failed to recognize. Moreover, scheduled for 1940 were the movement of the Volhynian Germans from the Soviet zone, the exchange of 14,000 Ukrainians and Belorussians from the General Government for 60,000 Poles on the Soviet side of the demarcation line, the movement of 30,000 ethnic Germans from beyond the Vistula, the internal uprooting of some 120,000 Poles for Wehrmacht training sites in the General Government, and finally the shipping of some 1 million Poles for work in the Reich. Frank noted that according to the "long-range plan," the deportation of 600,000 Jews into the General Government was to have begun on January 15. However, he had pointed out to all concerned the "absolute impossibility" of carrying out these deportations as in the past. The resettlement action had thus been postponed until March, which would allow for a considerable improvement in methods.[73]

If Frank and the Germans in the General Government opposed receiving a vast deportation of Jews at this time, German officials in the Warthegau were also concerned about finding housing and jobs for the renewed immigration of Baltic Germans, of whom 1,200 were scheduled to begin arriving daily from Stettin (Szczecin) to Poznan on January 7. Officials in Poznan calculated that it was "unconditionally necessary," in order to ensure "the seizure of good housing," that the first deportees be Polish intelligentsia who were also politically incriminated. Politically incriminated Poles without usable housing as well as "Gypsies" could be deported later, when the "housing action" had been concluded. The list of Poles to be evacuated for political reasons was thereupon divided into three categories, of good, average, and poor housing. Less than 10% of the proposed evacuees, however, were rated in the first category.[74]

As in Poznan, German officials in Lodz faced the renewed influx of Baltic Germans, due to arrive there beginning January 9, with trepidation. On January 11 Koppe pleaded with Heydrich for two trains daily to deport Poles and Jews in order to make room for the ethnic Germans. He was quickly informed that neither trains nor reception capacity in the General Government were available.[75] Once again, officials in Lodz fell back on solving their problems through measures against the Jews. While "the evacuation of Poles had to be undertaken individually," Jews could be cleared in mass from areas with "better Jewish apartments." While Poles could not be sent into the General Government, the wealthier Jews chased out of their good apartments could be sent into the area of the prospective ghetto. The evacuation of Jewish apartments and the transfer of the former owners to the future ghetto were therefore ordered to begin "immediately."[76] Within days, teams of SS men from the "evacuation staff" and Schupo began clearing Jewish apartments with the goal of 50 per day. In one frantic stretch, they surpassed themselves and cleared 399 apartments in three days. The method was declared a success and continued.[77]

As of January 14, 1940, Koppe was already aware that for the moment the General Government could receive no deportations, but he still thought that the "second short-range plan . . . basically encompassed only the deportation of the Jews." However, when the deportations were resumed, an exception was now to be made for those Poles who would be deported "in direct connection with the placement of Baltic and Volhynian Germans."

Six days later, however, Koppe informed officials of the Warthegau of a further change of plans and priorities. By agreement of the RSHA, General Government, and Reich Transportation Ministry, the Jewish evacuation of the second short-range plan was now to be preceded by an "intermediate plan" (Zwischenplan) whose sole purpose was to provide housing and jobs for incoming Baltic Germans. But in the process of providing jobs and housing, no one either of possible German origin or vital to the economy was to be deported.[78] Despite the "pervasive good will" of the Reichsbahn and Ostbahn, however, no trains could be allocated for the intermediate plan before February 10, and Lodz—now destined to be the center for receiving 100,000-130,000 Germans from Volhynia and Galicia[79]—could not be served before February 20.[80]

In addition to the arrival of the Volhynian Germans in January, several economic complications also arose in the same month—both attributable to the intervention of Hermann Göring. On the one hand, the official economic status of the General Government was revised. The conquered land was no longer merely to be pillaged but rather to be made productive. Frank's bargaining position concerning the economic impact of the resettlement program was thus enhanced.[81] On the other hand, 800,000 agricultural workers were to be brought into the Reich by mid-March 1940,[82] and the Warthegau was assigned a quota of 100,000. It made sense, therefore, to avoid "a double resettlement" in which "racially suitable" Poles were deported to the General Government only to be shipped back to the Reich as agricultural laborers.[83] As Rapp explained to a meeting convened in Poznan on January 11, 1940, to discuss the labor issue: "To the previous program of evacuation and placement of Baltic and Volhynian Germans, the deportation of the Polish agricultural workers demanded by the Reich has now been added."

The Trustee for Labor, Obersturmbannführer Kenzia, declared the Warthegau quota of 100,000 "impossible." By the end of 1939, 20,000 workers had already been sent to the Reich. As a result, Jews had had to be used for the harvest, but now there were no more Jews in the Poznan region. "First of all the Warthegau's needs for agricultural labor had to be ensured, the evacuations to the General Government therefore had to be stopped." Rapp informed Kenzia that in order to lodge 12,000–15,000 Volhynian Germans in the Warthegau, farms would have to be emptied. However, landless agricultural laborers, in contrast to landowners, would not be deported. Otherwise, for the moment only urban populations were being deported. Sturmbannführer Hans Ehlich of the RSHA conveyed Himmler's desire that for security reasons all Polish labor reserves of the incorporated territories be exhausted before the more hostile Polish workers of the General Government were imported. Moreover, these workers were to be both volunteers and racially acceptable. The conference concluded that a sufficient number of volunteers was guaranteed if the Poles were given a choice between deportation to the General Government and work in the Reich.[84]

The Germans made an attempt to sort out the various conflicts and priorities of Nazi resettlement policy at a top-level meeting on January 30 that was chaired by Heydrich and attended by the leading police officials from the east as well as by representatives of the RKFDV, RSHA, and Göring's HTO. Heydrich proclaimed that no fundamental objections had been raised against the deportations on the part of the General Government, only complaints against the way in which they had been carried out, in particular exceeding the announced numbers per train. With the creation of a *Referat* for Jews and Evacuation—IV D 4—within the RSHA under Adolf Eichmann, central direction would remedy this deficiency. It was now an urgent matter to deport 40,000 Jews and Poles to "make room" (*Platzschaffung*) for the rest of the Baltic Germans. This would be followed by "another improvised clearing" of 120,000 Poles to provide space for the Volhynian Germans. Since the Reichsführer had forbidden the deportation of anyone possibly of German origin, only Congress Poles were to be taken. While the Baltic Germans had been urban people (to be resettled in cities like Gdynia and Poznan), exclusively rural populations would have to be removed to provide space for the Volhynian Germans (which effectively eliminated Jews from consideration in this case).

After the deportation of 40,000 Poles and Jews for the Baltic Germans and of 120,000 Poles for the Volhynians, "the evacuation to the General Government of all Jews from the new eastern Gaue and 30,000 Gypsies from the Reich shall take place *as the last mass movement* [italics mine: *als letzte Massenbewegung*]." The Volhynian action would commence in March, and the deportation of Jews and "Gypsies" would in turn begin only after this was completed. Almost incidentally, Heydrich also announced that in mid-February 1,000 Jews from Stettin would be deported to the General Government because their apartments were urgently needed.

Concerning Polish agricultural workers for the Reich, Heydrich noted that between 800,000 and one million were needed in addition to the Polish prisoners of war. Heydrich also noted Himmler's concession that a "racial selection" (*rassische Auslese*) of Polish workers was impossible for the moment. However, after all these deportations, a racial selection of those suitable for resettlement in the Reich would follow. Heydrich intended to create Central Agencies for Emigration (Umwandererzentralstellen) in the incorporated territories to examine and classify the entire population according to personality, race, health, security risk, and labor ability.

Although the deportation of Jews from the incorporated territories had been postponed, apparently the two highest ranking representatives of the General Government, Frank's deputy Seyss-Inquart and his HSSPF Krüger, did not take kindly to their concerns being characterized as merely complaints against procedures, not basic objections. Krüger noted the tremendous difficulties caused by the Wehrmacht's uprooting of 100,000-120,000 Poles within the General Government for its own purposes, and Seyss-Inquart mentioned transportation difficulties and food shortages within the General Government that would require imports from the Reich. Heydrich brushed their concerns aside, noting that 100,000 Jews could be put in work camps to build the *Ostwall* and their families could be distributed among the Jews already living in the General Government.[85]

Eichmann's plan to deport all Jews from the incorporated territories had suffered not one but two setbacks in a single month. First, in mid-January the deportation of Jews called for in the second short-range plan had been postponed in favor of an intermediate plan to make room for incoming Baltic Germans. Then, at the end of the month, Heydrich had postponed the Jewish deportations once again, now to take place as the "last mass movement" after a further deportation of rural Poles to make room for the Volhynian Germans. Furthermore, the burden of selecting and deporting to the Reich vast numbers of Polish workers had been added to the tasks of the deportation technicians.

The situation became even more complicated when Göring met with Hans Frank and Heinrich Himmler, along with the Gauleiter of the incorporated territories and the state secretaries of the major ministries, at Göring's Karinhall estate on February 12, 1940. The first priority, Göring stated unequivocally, was to strengthen the war potential of the Reich. The task of the new Gaue was to maximize agricultural production—to be the granary of Germany. The economy in these eastern territories could only be maintained if sufficient manpower were at hand. Moreover, the Reich itself needed manpower from these areas. "All evacuation measures are to be directed in such a way that useful manpower does not disappear." But to Göring this did not mean a stop in Jewish deportation, both from Germany and the incorporated territories, as long as the trains were sent in an orderly manner and with prior notification.

The opinions of the Gauleiters were mixed. No deportations from his East Prussia had taken place so far, Koch said. Even Jewish labor was necessary for road construction, in addition to the Poles who worked in factories and on the land. If Polish prisoners of war were sent back to the Old Reich, East Prussia would need 115,000–120,000 additional Polish agricultural workers. Forster's Danzig–West Prussia contained 300,000 recently immigrated Poles, Jews, and asocials, of which 87,000 had been sent off. Only 1,800 Jews remained. He was ready to deport shirkers on public support and could thus estimate deporting another 20,000 in the coming year. Greiser had likewise deported 87,000 from the Warthegau. Wagner in Upper Silesia had carried out no deportations, but was ready to part with 100,000-120,000 Jews and 100,000 unreliable, recently immigrated Poles. Frank insisted that the continuation of previous deportation methods would make restoration of orderly administration in the General Government impossible. Allying himself openly with Göring, Frank declared that even Himmler's starkly reduced resettlement plan was conditional upon solving the food situation, and its tempo was dependent upon being reconciled with the "necessities of war."

Faced with the decided lack of support for major deportations on the part of Göring, Frank, and at least several of the eastern Gauleiters, Himmler moved to save what he could. Of the eight million Poles on German territory, certainly no more than 300,000 had been evacuated so far, he noted. He needed space for 70,000 Baltic and 130,000 Volhynian Germans, and the latter had to be settled on Polish farms in a strip along the border with the General Government. Given the difficulties of resettlement and the necessities of war, Himmler conceded the temporary postponement of bringing in a further 40,000 Lithuanian Germans, 80,000–100,000 Bukovinian Germans, and 100,000–130,000 Bessarabian Germans, as well as the ethnic Germans west of the Vistula. However, the 30,000 ethnic Germans east of the Vistula would have to be taken into the eastern Gaue because their present homeland was destined to become the "Jewish reservation" or *Judenreservat*. In any case, Himmler assured them, he and Frank "would agree upon the procedures of future evacuations."[86]

A consensus on just what had been decided at Karinhall seemed decidedly absent. Göring had opposed the further deportation of any Polish workers eastward and emphasized the absolute priority of agricultural production and strengthening Germany's war potential. On the other hand, he had not opposed the orderly deportation of Jews. Himmler had announced his intention to complete the Baltic and Volhynian operations, and explicitly noted that the latter required dispossessing Polish peasants whom Göring did not want disturbed. On the other hand, he made no mention at all of any imminent deportation of Jews. Himmler seemed to think that by scaling back the pace of ethnic German resettlement and indefinitely postponing Jewish deportation, he could sufficiently minimize disruption in both the incorporated territories and the General Government so as to continue with his cherished project, despite Frank's and Göring's objections. For Himmler at this time, the consolidation of Germany's new Lebensraum through Volksdeutsche resettlement clearly had priority over deporting Jews.

Frank related his own interpretation of what had transpired to officials of the General Government on several occasions in early March. "We shall still receive at least 400,000–600,000 Jews into the country. Only then can we gradually talk about what must happen to them. . . . First of all there is a plan to transfer all of them to the eastern part of the General Government on the border with Soviet Russia, and that we shall also carry through. . . . It is indescribable, what views have formed in the Reich that the region of the General Government east of the Vistula is increasingly considered as some kind of Jewish reservation." In any case, Göring had decided in Himmler's presence at Karinhall that "no resettlement actions may be undertaken in the General Government without the prior approval of each individual resettlement action by the Governor General." He, Frank, now had full power to stop evacuation trains. "In general, the great resettlement ideas have indeed been given up. The idea that one could gradually transport 7½ million Poles to the General Government has been fully abandoned. It is now only a question of the transfer of some 100,000-120,000 Poles, some 30,000 Gypsies, and a still to be determined number of Jews from the Reich, because the final goal shall be to make the German Reich free of Jews. That that shall not occur in a year and especially not under the circumstances of war, Berlin also recognizes."[87] Given the contrasting views of Himmler and Frank over what had been decided, the clash between them was fated to continue. The struggle over Nazi deportation and resettlement policy was not over.

THE INTERMEDIATE PLAN, THE STETTIN DEPORTATIONS, AND THE VOLHYNIAN ACTION, FEBRUARY–JULY 1940

One reason Himmler at Karinhall acted as if Göring's and Frank's opposition did not apply to his scaled-down deportation plans was that two such operations were getting underway even as the meeting was taking place. Already on January 20 the branch offices of the Gestapo in the Warthegau had received instructions for an intermediate or *Zwischen* plan to procure lodging and employment for the rest of the incoming Baltic Germans. The deportation program, utilizing 40 trains, had began two days earlier on February 10 and was scheduled to conclude on March 3, 1940. The destinations were in the districts of Cracow, Radom, and Warsaw, but not Lublin.[88] Every effort was made to ensure that the barrage of complaints over the first short-range plan would not be repeated. Each deportee was to have the proper allotment of food, clothing, and Polish currency, and each train—composed of passenger rather than box cars—was to carry only 1,000 people.[89]

Several problems emerged despite the careful planning. Even before the deportations began, the Reichsbahn tried to cut its commitment from 40 to 38 trains. And in mid-February the Reichsbahn confessed that it could not keep to the schedule and that the empty trains would not return on time.[90] Various local authorities begged to include undesired Poles whose presence was considered a burden but whose removal would in no way "make room" for Baltic Germans. These requests were systematically rejected.[91] As the program neared its end, even Rapp pleaded for its expansion. By adding five more trains, employment could be found for all the Baltic Germans. By overloading the last three trains by 10–15%, the camps could be emptied. Eichmann rejected both pleas.[92] Frank complained as well, noting that "despite his protests even now Polish peasants from Poznan and West Prussia were being resettled in the General Government. . . . The methods by which the Warthegau is governed are not very likeable," he concluded.[93]

The intermediate plan was completed on March 15, credited with a deportation total of 40,128 Poles.[94] The final statistics made no mention of Jews at all, but once again this does not reveal the full impact of the resettlement program on the Jewish population of the Warthegau. In Lodz, Jews continued to be removed from the center of the city to the future ghetto to provide housing for the Baltic Germans.[95] And 1,200 Jews were deported from Kreis Konin to Lodz on March 3.[96] Subsequently, on March 7, the Jewish council in Cracow noted the arrival of 421 Jews.[97] It is most likely that these 421 Jews were among the 999 deportees from Konin to the General Government attributed to the *Zwischenplan*.[98] The fate of the other Konin Jews sent to Lodz at this time is not known, but most of them were presumably also deported to the General Government. It is not likely to have been a mere coincidence that on March 7 Rapp asked Eichmann to what destinations in the General Government Jews could be sent.[99]

On a far smaller scale than the intermediate plan but much more spectacular for the attention it drew was the deportation from Stettin that Heydrich had announced at the end of January. In the early hours of February 12, the very day that Göring, Himmler, and Frank were meeting at Karinhall, some 1,100–1,200 German Jews were rounded up in Stettin and transported to the General Government.[100] Within days, foreign press reports gave graphic descriptions of how the Jews of Stettin, even the occupants of two homes for the elderly—some over 80 years old—were roused from their beds, forced to sign away all their property except one suitcase, a watch, and a wedding ring, and taken to the freight station by ss and sa men. According to a Swiss correspondent, preparations for similar deportations from other cities in northern Germany were being made. The State Secretary of the Foreign Office, Ernst von Weizsäcker, inquired whether there was any truth to the foreign press allegations that the Stettin deportation was the beginning of more-general measures.[101] Both Walter Schellenberg and Heinrich Müller of the RSHA claimed that the Stettin affair was an individual action to make room for returning Baltic Germans, not a prelude to wider measures.[102] The Foreign Office then requested that such deportations be carried out "in a noiseless and cautious way" so as not to excite attention abroad.[103] This request was immediately followed, however, by the deportation of 160 Jews from Schneidemühl in Pommern on March 12.

The Reich Chancellery and the German Foreign Office received copies of a report—mailed anonymously in Berlin and allegedly based upon the findings of a Polish-Jewish relief committee, the Quakers, and the Red Cross—providing a ghastly description of both deportations.[104] The deportees were forced to march on foot from Lublin in temperatures of $-22°$ centigrade in deep snow to villages without food or lodging. By the time the Schneidemühl deportees had arrived, 230 of the Stettin Jews had already died. The anonymous reports claimed that the district governor of Lublin, Zörner, had disclaimed any responsibility and that Göring had been informed. Upon inquiry by the Foreign Office, Eichmann claimed that the Schneidemühl Jews had been sent only as far as Poznan, and had then been brought back to the Reich, though not to Schneidemühl itself, where their apartments were needed by others.[105]

Helmuth Wohlthat of Göring's Office of the Four-Year Plan informed the Foreign Office that rumors continued to circulate among foreign diplomats, including the Americans, of imminent large-scale deportations. The Foreign Office noted that "because of the special attention that President Roosevelt gives to the development of the Jewish question," and in view of Germany's interest in U.S. neutrality, some unofficial statement was desirable that the deportation of the Jews from the Old Reich was not under consideration. Wohlthat was prepared to be the vehicle for such informal reassurances. This became unnecessary, however, when Göring himself intervened on March 23, 1940, notifying Himmler: "The Governor General has complained to me about the fact that even now deportations of Jews from the Reich are being carried out, although the reception possibilities do not yet exist. I hereby forbid such deportations without my permission and without proof of agreement on the side of the Governor General."[106] Göring's intervention, enforcing his position at the Karinhall conference, threatened to stop Himmler's deportations totally unless the latter now lived up to his own Karinhall promise to carry out deportations only in agreement with Frank. At first some of the Nazis, particularly Greiser in the Warthegau, were reluctant to face this unpleasant fact. Greiser's initial reaction, upon hearing of Göring's stop order, was to insist that it applied only to the Stettin affair and not to the Jews of Lodz, whom he was planning to deport. This, he insisted, had been agreed upon at Karinhall.[107] But once again Himmler gave priority to ethnic German resettlement over the deportation of Jews. He reached agreement with Frank on the second short-range plan for the immediate deportation of 120,000 Poles and 35,000 "Gypsies" to make room for the Volhynian Germans. Fully in accord with the sequence announced by Heydrich on January 30, the deportation of the Jews from the Warthegau would follow the Volhynian action and thus was not expected to begin until August. When the Jews did arrive, Frank still intended to send them over the Vistula.[108]

The "Volhynian action," or more precisely the expulsion of Poles to make room for ethnic Germans from Volhynia and Galicia, for which preparations had been underway for two months, was to be carried out in an even more organized manner than outlined in the intermediate plan. In early February members of Rapp's staff had visited the Landräte of the eastern areas of the Warthegau to prepare for the "simultaneous" evacuation of Poles and resettlement of the Volhynian Germans.[109] Many problems were noted, especially in relation to the novelty of dealing with rural rather than urban Poles. There were few medium-sized Polish farms and even fewer large estates. Farms suitable for German settlers could only be created by dispossessing on average three Polish farm families and consolidating these parcels for a single German family.[110] Preparations had to be disguised. German commissions had to stop openly investigating Polish villages, for the Poles would be warned of their imminent deportation and thereupon slaughter their livestock and destroy their crops. In any case, the exchange of possession should take place either before or after, not during, the spring harvest.[111]

Koppe ordered the compilation of a "farm file" (*Hofkartei*) in each county or Kreis, registering the best Polish farmsteads. The departure of settlers from Lodz was to be timed so that the Germans arrived early in the morning and could be installed in their new farms the same day. "Evacuations and installations must take place in rapid succession for tactical reasons." However, care was to be taken that the German settlers be kept out of sight at the moment of dispossession to be spared psychological stress.[112]

The Germans also had to devise methods of screening and selection to accommodate both Himmler's concern for people of possible German origin and Göring's demands for Polish agricultural workers. For this a system of three camps was devised. All dispossessed Poles would be brought to Camp I on the Wiesenstrasse in Lodz, which served as a "processing camp" (*Durchschleusungslager*) for racial and medical examinations. Those destined for deportation to the General Government would be sent to Camp II, a "transition camp" (*Übergangslager*) on Luisenstrasse. Those deemed suitable for work in the Reich would be sent to Camp III (Konstantynow). In both Camps I and II extreme care was to be exercised that no one of possible German origin was deported, which included anyone—regardless of political views—who had applied for membership on the German *Volksliste*; were members of the German Evangelical, German Catholic, or Polish Evangelical churches; or had relatives who were German citizens or were serving in the German military. Entire families could be sent to Camp III if they appeared racially suitable for Germanization. Otherwise only temporary or "seasonal" or "migrant" workers were sent to Camp III without families.[113]

Despite all these preparations, the first transports of the second short-range plan did not involve the seizure of farms and the processing of Poles through the three-camp system. In the first week of April, three trains carrying 2,663 Jews departed the camp at Glowno outside Poznan.[114] Thereafter the new procedures for deporting Poles to either the General Government or labor in the Reich were put to the test—initially without great success.

On April 20 Rapp wrote a blistering memorandum summarizing the magnitude of the failure. Few Poles—"frequently only 10%" of the evacuation quota—were actually being taken. Even in the Kreise merely neighboring on the evacuation sites, Polish farmers spent only a few hours on their farms feeding the livestock, which not only thwarted the evacuation program but also endangered the harvest. At the present rate, only 20,000 of the 120,000 Poles targeted for resettlement would be seized. The other 100,000 would be roving the villages and presenting an intolerable security risk. Rapp recommended suspending the operation until the "resettlement staffs" (*Ansiedlungsstäbe*) were removed from the villages, where their presence gave early warning and their work provided inadequate information for the Umwandererzentralstelle (UWZ) in any case; evacuation and resettlement could then be carried out suddenly across entire Kreise.[115]

Himmler was furious at the delay, for to him the key issue was not how many Poles were evacuated but how many ethnic Germans were settled and how quickly. Himmler wrote Greifelt, insisting that the placement of the Volhynian Germans had to be carried out "as unbureaucratically and thereby as quickly as possible," for conditions in their camps were "very bad." Moreover, the Volhynians had suffered the shock of leaving their homes, trekking through the harsh winter, living in squalid camps, and suffering illness and often even the loss of a child. His goal was to settle 100 families per day and be finished by the end of August. This placement was not final and could be adjusted the following spring.[116] At the same time, Albert Rapp was removed from his position in Poznan and replaced by Rolf-Heinz Höppner; Herman Krumey, head of the office of the UWZ in Lodz, was placed in charge of resettlement in the Warthegau.[117]

Indeed, Himmler had reasons for displeasure that transcended the slow pace of Volhynian resettlement. His grandiose design for a sweeping racial reorganization of eastern Europe had been steadily whittled away. In the fall of 1939 he had envisaged the deportation of about one million people (including *all* Jews) from the incorporated territories into the General Government by the end of February 1940, and eventually the removal of all so-called racially undesirable elements from these lands. By March 1940, however, Frank was boasting that the idea that one could gradually transport 7½ million Poles to the General Government had been "fully abandoned." Moreover, the Jewish deportations had been postponed repeatedly—most recently to August—and Göring had invested Frank with a virtual veto power over them. Even the resettlement of ethnic Germans had been scaled back and was now bogged down. But if Frank could go over Himmler's head to Göring, Himmler now sought to relegitimize his threatened dream by going over Göring's head to Hitler.

Since his pronouncements of the previous autumn, Hitler had played no visible role in shaping racial policy. In a typical example of the "institutional Darwinism" of the Third Reich, implementation had been left to a struggle between his subordinates while the Führer himself turned his attention to loftier matters of grand strategy, in particular preparations for the offensives into Scandinavia, the Low Countries, and France. But by spring Hitler seemed to have lost faith in his resettlement plan, at least insofar as it concerned the Jews in Lublin. According to the Foreign Office liaison to Führer headquarters, Walther Hewel, Hitler told Colin Ross on March 12, 1940, that

> the Jewish question really was a space question which was difficult to solve, particularly for him, since he had no space at his disposal. Neither would the establishment of a Jewish state around Lublin ever constitute a solution as even there the Jews lived too close together to be able to attain a somewhat satisfactory standard of living. . . . He, too, would welcome a positive solution to the Jewish question; if only he could indicate a solution; this, however, was not possible under present conditions when he had not even sufficient space for his own people.[118]

Word of this change of heart on Hitler's part must have reached Himmler very quickly, for already in early April HSSPF Krüger in the General Government rejected the expulsion of Jews from Warsaw to the Lublin district.[119] The brilliant success of German arms in the first two weeks of the French campaign, however, gave Himmler the opportunity in late May to seek Hitler's approval for his racial design, which stood in stark contrast to the pragmatic arguments of Göring and Frank and included an even more radical solution for the Jews than the now faltering Lublin reservation.

On May 9, 1940, Himmler reemphasized in an order the task of selecting from the populations of the incorporated territories and the General Government those people of alien nationality who on the basis of their "racial fitness" (*rassischen Eignung*) were suitable for "Germanization." This racial "*Auslese*" (a German term for special wine made from the choicest late-gathered grapes) was to be brought to the Reich and placed in a work environment separate from other foreign workers and conducive to the most rapid Germanization.[120] As for the other Poles, he remained committed to the notion that those who were not "racially amalgamable" (*rassisch verschmelzbar*) could remain in the eastern provinces only as long as their labor was needed. Thereafter they were "in the course of the next 5–10 years, without exception and mercy, to be deported into the General Government, the catchment basin [*Sammelbecken*] of Germany's racially unfit."[121]

Himmler then proceeded to draft his May 1940 memorandum "Some Thoughts on the Treatment of the Alien Populations in the East," which was reminiscent of the Wetzel-Hecht memorandum of November 1939.[122] The 15 million people of the General Government and the 8 million of the incorporated territories—"ethnic mush" (*Völkerbrei*) in Himmler's view—were to be splintered into as many ethnic groups as possible for "screening and sifting" (*Sichtung und Siebung*). "The basis of our considerations must be to fish out of this mush the racially valuable, in order to bring them to Germany for assimilation." (*Das Fundament in unseren Erwägungen sein muss, die rassisch Wertvollen aus diesem Brei herauszufischen, nach Deutschland zu tun, um sie dort zu assimilieren.*) The key to this sifting process was education. Schooling for the non-German populations was to be minimal—arithmetic calculations to 500, writing their names, lessons in obedience to Germany, honesty, and industriousness, but no reading. Racially valuable children would be permitted higher schooling, but only in Germany. Their parents would have to choose between parting with their children or coming to Germany themselves. Deprived of their racially valuable stock and dumped together in the General Government along with those from Germany "of the same racial and human type," the various ethnic groups would gradually disappear—the smallest like the Kaschubs within four or five years, then the Ukrainians, Goralians, and Lemkos, and finally the largest, the Poles, over a considerably longer period of time. This nondescript population of "denationalized" peoples would then serve as a reservoir for migrant labor to Germany.

Along with the denationalization (in fact, cultural genocide) of the various ethnic groups of eastern Europe, the Jews were also to disappear, but in a different way. "I hope completely to erase the concept of Jews through the possibility of a great emigration of all Jews to a colony in Africa or elsewhere." (*Den Begriff Juden hoffe ich, durch die Möglichkeit einer grossen Auswanderung sämtlicher Juden nach Afrika oder sonst in eine Kolonie völlig auslöschen zu sehen.*) Concerning this systematic eradication of the ethnic composition of eastern Europe, Himmler concluded: "However cruel and tragic each individual case may be, this method is still the mildest and best, if one rejects the Bolshevik method of physical extermination of a people out of inner conviction as un-German and impossible." (*So grausam und tragisch jeder einzelne Fall sein mag, so ist diese Methode, wenn man die bolschewistische Methode der physischen Ausrottung eines Volkes aus innerer Überzeugung als ungermanisch und unmöglich ablehnt, doch die mildeste und beste.*)

On May 25—that is, a week after the German army reached the English Channel and just as it was closing in on the best units of the French and British armies trapped at Dunkirk—Himmler discussed his memorandum with Hitler. Himmler's timing was impeccable, and he scored a great triumph. "The Führer read the six pages through and found them very good and correct [*sehr gut und richtig*]," Himmler noted. Moreover, "the Führer desires that I invite Governor General Frank back to Berlin, in order to show him the memorandum and to say to him that the Führer considers it correct." Himmler then asked if Hitler would authorize Lammers of the Reich Chancellery to distribute copies to the eastern Gauleiters. Also to be initiated was Göring's man in the incorporated territories, Winkler, among others, with the message that the Führer had "recognized and confirmed" (*anerkannt und bestätigt*) the memorandum as setting out authoritative guidelines. Hitler agreed.[123]

This episode is of singular importance in that it is the only firsthand account by a high-ranking participant—Himmler—of just how a Hitler decision was reached and a *Führerbefehl*, or Hitler order, was given in respect to Nazi racial policy during this period. The initiative came from Himmler. However, he did not present Hitler with a precise plan; it was rather a statement of intent, a set of policy objectives. The details of implementation would be left to Himmler. Hitler indicated both his enthusiastic agreement and the men with whom the information could be shared, but he himself gave no specific orders to the likes of Göring, Frank, and the eastern Gauleiters. He simply allowed it to be known what he wanted or approved. Presumably business was often conducted in such a way in the Third Reich.

Himmler's enthusiastic memorandum writing on this subject continued into June, when he countered the argument that Polish labor would always be necessary in the incorporated territories for economic reasons. He set out as his guiding principle: "One only possesses a land when even the last inhabitant of this territory belongs to his own people." Anything less only invited "blood mixing" (*blutliche Vermischung*). Thus the alien population had to be forced off the land into the cities for construction work. Then gradually seven-eighths of them would be deported to the east and one-eighth would be Germanized. Agricultural labor would be supplied by young German men and women eager to save money for their own farms. "I am convinced that in the east we can get by without native Polish labor in the long run, and that we cannot and must not leave Poles in the eastern provinces for economic reasons."[124]

Frank was still under the impression that the idea of deporting 7½ million Poles to the General Government had been "fully abandoned." He had agreed with Himmler to accept a few hundred thousand Poles and all the Jews, and even this prospect was daunting enough:

> We will in the future have to accept several hundred thousand Poles, and there is no doubt that we will have to do it in the coming years, if one wants to solve the Polish problem in the Reich. If we do not accept them directly and legally, then it will proceed in an illegal way. However, we must make this sacrifice to the German Reich. I have declared to the Führer and also to the Reichsführer-ss Himmler that we have no other interest other than to be ready to the furthest limit of our ability as the receptacle of all elements that stream into the General Government from outside, be they Poles, Jews, Gypsies, etc.

As for the Jews, not hundreds of thousands but millions would burden the General Government when the Reich's eastern provinces were cleared of them. This was a great dilemma for Frank, because these Jews were not rich. "In the General Government there are no rich Jews anymore, rather for the most part only a Jewish proletariat." He, like Himmler, could still not envisage a solution of physical extermination, however. "In the end one cannot simply starve them [the Jews] to death," his Sipo-sD commander Streckenbach confessed to a meeting of the ss and police, to whom Frank had just given orders for the liquidation of thousands of Polish intelligentsia.[125]

Frank did not meet with Himmler (as Hitler had suggested), but he did meet with Heydrich on June 12, 1940. Frank must have made a convincing case for his difficulties in the General Government, since it was agreed for the time being—"in view of the dire situation there"—not to go beyond the deportations already agreed upon, that is, the Volhynian action then in progress and the Jewish deportations to begin "presumably" in August.[126] But this was scant consolation to Frank, who was becoming increasingly desperate. In a letter to Lammers of the Reich Chancellery, he lamented the economic crisis in the General Government and added: "Just as impossible, in its catastrophic effects no longer bearable, is the continuation of resettlement." The General Government was far more densely populated than Germany. "It is quite impossible, in view of the totally wretched food situation in the General Government, that the resettlement actions can be continued beyond the amount of the last resettlement plan agreed upon with the RFSS." A "comprehensive discussion" of the "eastern problems" was thus "urgently necessary."[127] For the beleaguered Frank, therefore, a surprising order from Himmler suddenly stopping the impending evacuation of Jews into the General Government was a veritable deliverance.[128] Himmler had found his colony in Africa for the Jews—the island of Madagascar!

THE ARMY, FROM ABDICATION TO COMPLICITY

In October 1939 the German army had washed its hands of responsibility in Poland, and the military administration had been dissolved. Nonetheless, military personnel remained in the east not only to perform strictly military functions but also to continue administrative tasks for the as yet inadequately staffed civil administration. While the top army commanders knew perfectly well that a policy of systematic liquidation of Polish elites and mass deportation was to ensue, this information had not been shared with the officer corps at large or even with the generals who would be left behind in Poland. The latter in particular found themselves witnesses to mind-boggling atrocities, which they could only comprehend as the arbitrary and unauthorized actions of local ss units or the product of Himmler's sinister designs. To a few generals at least, such atrocities all too clearly revealed the sordid nature of certain elements within National Socialism but did not necessarily reflect state policy. To their credit they protested vociferously, though in the end ineffectively, for not only Hitler but also Brauchitsch and Halder were unreceptive to such objections from the east.

For a brief period, however, these graphic reports of the Polish horrors were not only permitted but also widely circulated among the generals on the western front. This was due to an unusual combination of circumstances. The generals had been dismayed in late September when Hitler announced his intentions for a fall offensive against France. The mud and fog of November threatened to neutralize the armor and air power upon which any chance of military success depended. For most of the generals, it was Hitler's mad determination to risk all under the least propitious conditions, not the criminal nature of the regime so clearly revealed in Poland, that fueled their discontent. In this atmosphere of discontent and even tentative intrigue and opposition, real resisters of conscience were able to collect and disseminate information on events in Poland among an officer corps briefly receptive to such evidence.

When the weather was so bad that it forced cancellation of the autumn offensive and saved Hitler from himself, the generals took hope that military victory was again possible. In these circumstances Brauchitsch, who himself had temporarily faced a "crisis of confidence," was able to silence the messengers of atrocities in Poland, and the protesting generals were abandoned to face the ruination of their military careers. For the vast majority of the officers, the spectacular victory in France then seemed to confirm the genius of the man they had considered mad six months earlier. It is this tragic descent of the army from an abdication of responsibility to the brink of active complicity that we must now trace.[129]

October was a month of growing consternation among the generals. Only the most ardent Nazi among them, Walter von Reichenau, was capable of openly confronting Hitler and urging a cancellation of the fall offensive.[130] Unwilling himself to confront Hitler, Halder at least tolerated tentative preparations for a coup to be undertaken by men such as Lt. General Heinrich von Stülpnagel, Colonel Hans Oster, and Major Helmuth Groscurth, *if* the offensive could not be postponed. Stülpnagel frequently visited the western front but could find only Wilhelm Ritter von Leeb among the three army group commanders (the others being Fedor von Bock and Gerd von Rundstedt) ready to act against the regime, though they all opposed the fall offensive. Before Brauchitsch and Halder also toured the west to collect testimony against the offensive, the latter confessed to Groscurth "with tears" in his eyes that for weeks he had gone to Hitler with a pistol in his pocket but could not bring himself to shoot the man. But he did indicate to Groscurth as late as November 2, 1939, that if Hitler did not cancel the offensive within three days, he would support the coup. At a climactic meeting on November 5, when Brauchitsch submitted to Hitler a memorandum opposing the fall offensive, Hitler exploded into one of his famous tirades. After 20 minutes an "ashen-faced" (*kreidebleich*) Brauchitsch emerged and told Halder of Hitler's threat to stamp out "the spirit of Zossen" (the OKH headquarters). Halder inferred that the plot was known, hurried back to headquarters to burn all evidence, and henceforth progressively distanced himself from all forms of opposition.[131]

What the military advice of the generals could not accomplish, the weather did—successive postponements of the western offensive into January 1940. When on January 10 an airplane carrying German military plans strayed off course and landed in Belgium, Hitler ordered a definite postponement until May while new plans were devised. During this prolonged "phony war" the disturbing reports from the east multiplied.

In West Prussia Lt. General Max Bock first sought to negotiate with the HSSPF Hildebrandt for an end to the extensive executions being carried out by Alvensleben's Selbschutz. Executions were to be carried out only for reasons of security and in an orderly manner by appropriate units. When this had no effect,

Bock complained directly to Forster that reports from his commanders uniformly warned of the "vast agitation and powerful emotional stress" (*ungeheuere Erregung und starke seelische Belastung*) on the troops. Moreover, continuation of such actions threatened the security of the area "because the Poles, aside from the necessarily harsh measures of confiscation and eviction, were driven into desperation by the closing of churches, the shootings of priests, through the destruction of Saints' images before their eyes, through the constant threat that all Poles must disappear as quickly as possible from this country and through the constant insecurity of their own lives, which would only intensify with the approaching winter and increasing distress." In an area where 10% of the population were Germans scattered on individual farms, German troop strength did not suffice to ensure security against understandable acts of desperation by Poles who had nothing more to lose.[132]

In the neighboring Warthegau, General Walter Petzel noted in a report that reached both the OKH and OKW that "reconstruction work" was endangered by ss units that displayed a tendency to form a "state within a state" and carried out their "special racial tasks" without regard for the effects upon the troops.

> In almost every large town public shootings took place through these units. The selection was totally nonuniform and often incomprehensible, the implementation frequently disgraceful. In many districts all Polish peasants were arrested and interned with their families. . . . In the cities evacuations were carried out in which entire apartment buildings were indiscriminately cleared. . . . In many cities actions were carried out against the Jews, which degenerated into the worst excesses. In Turek . . . a number of Jews were driven into a synagogue, forced to crawl through the bench seats while singing and constantly being beaten by ss men with whips. They were then forced to take down their pants, to be beaten on their naked behinds. One Jew, who out of fear had gone in his pants, was forced to smear excrement in the faces of the other Jews.[133]

Col. General Johannes Blaskowitz, the commander in chief in the east, was likewise impressed by the raging terror in the General Government. When Lt. Colonel Helmuth Stief from the Operations Division of the General Staff visited, Blaskowitz opened his heart for three-quarters of an hour and urged him to "make use of it" with the OKH. Stief himself was deeply shaken and wrote his wife: "The most prolific invention of atrocity propaganda is in poor comparison to what an organized murdering, robbing, and plundering band is doing there, with supposed tolerance from the highest quarters. . . . This extermination of entire families with women and children is only possible through subhumans who do not deserve the name German. *I am ashamed to be a German*" (italics mine).[134]

Blaskowitz sent off his own report on November 27, 1939. He noted that the Einsatzgruppen worked "almost exclusively as execution commandos" and that the police had "so far accomplished no visible task of keeping order but rather only spread terror among the population." This "blood lust" (*Blutrausch*) was an intolerable burden for the army, "because all this happens in the 'field grey' uniform." The present situation was making it impossible to utilize the country for the benefit of the troops and the war economy, for "with violence alone the security and peace of the land cannot be restored."[135] When this report reached Hitler, he dismissed it as evidence of the "childish attitude" (*kindliche Einstellung*) and "salvation-army methods" (*Heilsarmee-Methoden*) of the military leadership.[136]

Men like Groscurth gathered the information from Poland and sought to mobilize the officer corps into action. But "a decision to act is not taken. One is a soldier, bound by his oath, loyal to the Führer, etc., but above all one clings to his position and has an elegant wife," Groscurth noted in a particularly scornful reference to Brauchitsch, whose divorce and remarriage to an ardent Nazi woman had been made possible by a large cash gift from Hitler.[137] Groscurth sought to prevail upon Halder, once again in vain. The chief of staff now spurned all such importuning with a ready list of six reasons for following Hitler to the end: Such resistance in wartime was against tradition. There was no successor. The younger officers were not reliable. The internal mood was not ripe for opposition. It was intolerable that Germans remain the "slaves" (*Helotenvolk*) of England. And Ludendorf had carried out his 1918 offensive against the advice of others, without the judgment of history going against him.[138]

Unsuccessful in Berlin, Groscurth visited the western front from December 18 to 22 in an attempt to stir some response there with his Polish materials, including yet another Blaskowitz report delivered to Berlin in six copies on December 8.[139] Groscurth noted some success in arousing "great agitation."[140] Even the cautious Fedor von Bock wrote in his diary: "I hear of events from the 'colonization' of the east that frighten me." Furthermore, Bock discussed with other generals the need for a fuller clarification of the situation in Poland, though this was temporarily countered by assurance from Brauchitsch that Blaskowitz had subsequently settled his difficulties through discussions with Frank.[141]

On January 13, 1940, Groscurth tried to move Halder once more, but the latter was increasingly intoxicated by "the great possibilities for success" militarily and "railed at all those people, who thought of a putsch . . . most were only reactionaries and wanted to turn back the wheel of history."[142] Blaskowitz also saw Brauchitsch on January 17, but the commander in chief flatly refused to submit anything from Blaskowitz to Hitler. His meeting with Halder the following day was likewise futile.[143]

Unable to persuade Brauchitsch and Halder, the protestors were at least able to create the mood of a "crisis of confidence" vis-à-vis the commander in chief by virtue of his weak leadership and a broad antipathy toward the SS. Major General Kurt von Tippelskirch of the OKH noted in his diary: "In the case that a different attitude is not taken, the commander in chief has no guarantee that it will not explode."[144] To exercise some damage control Brauchitsch asked to meet with Himmler. Before the meeting both Himmler and Heydrich tried to secure a copy of the apparently now famous Blaskowitz report that Groscurth had circulated among the western commanders.[145] What transpired at the Himmler-Brauchitsch meeting of January 24 is not known, but Brauchitsch attempted to give a pacifying report to the western commanders: Himmler had said there was nothing to do about the past, but he would do everything in his power to prevent further occurrences in the future.[146] Brauchitsch also sent his own "neutral objective emissary," Major Kossman, to investigate matters on the spot but got no comfort when the latter returned with a "devastating report."[147] In late February Brauchitsch then turned—in Groscurth's words—to "negotiate again with Himmler over tea."[148]

Himmler was conciliatory. As Brauchitsch reported to Halder, Himmler admitted that "mistakes" had been made but said that it was his "intention to carry out his difficult tasks as discreetly as possible with little shedding of blood. He wants good relations with the army." To show his good will, Himmler offered the labor of 2½ million Jews to dig antitank ditches on the eastern border, a possibility Brauchitsch promised to look into.[149] The behavior of the army was not beyond reproach either, Himmler added. There were cases of slaughtering animals and socializing with Poles![150]

With alacrity Brauchitsch hurried to pass on the good tidings from Himmler in order to pacify his generals and to repress his critics. On February 7, 1940, he sent a letter concerning the "Army and the SS" to all his army and army group commanders. He asserted that "harsh measures against the Polish population" were inevitable for securing German Lebensraum and demanded that all criticism of Nazi racial policy, a policy "made necessary by the forthcoming battle of destiny of the German people," cease.[151]

In addition to meeting with Himmler twice and issuing this apologia for Nazi racial policies in Poland, Brauchitsch took one other measure to stifle his critics: he sacked Groscurth from his position in the OKW. Before his ignominious departure to a battalion command—"insolence and degradation," he noted—Groscurth received yet further discouraging news about Halder. The chief of staff had claimed "the situation in the east would later be forgotten—*it was after all not so bad*" (italics mine). Groscurth concluded, "It is pitiful and beyond understanding." Brauchitsch would believe nothing, and "in the decency of Halder I no longer believe in any form—from these people nothing more is to be expected."[152]

Despite the departure of Groscurth there was one more round to be fought in this unequal struggle for the conscience of the German army. Since his unsatisfactory meeting with Brauchitsch in mid-January, Blaskowitz had continued to accumulate material on events in Poland. When Brauchitsch visited the headquarters of the eastern command on February 20, Blaskowitz had his ammunition ready—26 pages of notes including a report from General Alexander Ulex, commander of the southern border region, and a list of 35 specifically dated incidents of flagrant atrocity.[153] The Ulex report noted that the violent actions of the police displayed an "incomprehensible lack of human and ethical sensitivity, so that one could almost speak of animalization" (*unbegreiflichen Mangel menschlichen und sittlichen Empfindens, so dass man geradezu von Vertierung sprechen kann*), and his headquarters knew of only a "tiny fraction" of the violence taking place. "The only way out of this disgraceful situation that stained the honor of the entire German people" was the total removal of all police units with their officers, Ulex concluded.

The Blaskowitz notes were worded more circumspectly to appeal to some remnant of utilitarian rationality, but given the context, the condemnatory thrust was quite clear. "It is a mistake to slaughter some 10,000 Jews and Poles, as is now happening, for in view of the size of the population neither the idea of the Polish state will be eliminated nor the Jews removed in that way. On the contrary, the manner of this slaughter causes the greatest harm, complicates our problems and makes the situation far more dangerous than it would have been with a considered and purposeful behavior." The counterproductive results were many. Enemy propaganda was given the most effective material imaginable. What the enemy radio reported so far was only a minute fraction of what was taking place, and one had to assume that the outcry abroad would grow "all the more as the abominations had actually happened." The public violence against the Jews caused the "deepest revulsion" and even aroused sympathy for the victims among the previously anti-Jewish Poles, thus threatening to unite Poles and Jews in common hatred against Germany. The prestige of the army, which was forced to stand by helplessly in the face of these atrocities, could never be restored in the eyes of the Polish population. But worst of all was the "moral depravity that will spread like a plague in the shortest time" among good Germans. At the moment "the attitude of the troops to the ss and police wavers between loathing and hate," but "when the highest officials of the ss and police demand violence and brutality and praise it publicly, then in the shortest time only the brutes rule. Surprisingly quickly the like-minded and the deviant personalities come together, as is the case in Poland, in order to give full vent to their animalistic and pathological instincts."

Finally, such behavior could only lead to Polish resistance. Especially disruptive were the deportations, in which people were torn from their houses and sent off "totally without means." That the widespread fear and panic caused by the resettlement turned to "measureless hatred through the numerous children starved to death on every transport and train cars full of frozen people" was only too obvious. "The view that one could intimidate and repress the Polish people with terror will surely be proven false. The capacity for suffering of these people is much too great for that. . . . The often expressed view that a small Polish resistance is quite desirable, because one then has the opportunity to decimate the Poles in grand style, is looked upon lightheartedly." But in fact the danger of resistance, to which the Poles were being driven irresponsibly, was real. It would jeopardize the military security and economic exploitation of the east and, thanks to the many weapons still hidden about the land, would cost much German blood.

Upon returning to Berlin, Brauchitsch was confronted with a letter from the 90-year-old World War I hero and oldest living field marshal August von Mackensen expressing concern over the "outrages" in Poland and urging that something be done to prevent "the prestige and honor" of the German army from being besmirched by the deeds of "hired subhumans and released criminals."[154]

At this point Brauchitsch did nothing short of enlisting the services of Himmler himself to put an end to the carping and criticism. Himmler had earlier sent an indirect feeler to Brauchitsch about the possibility of his clarifying the Polish situation to the western commanders, but Brauchitsch had declined. Brauchitsch now reversed himself and on February 20 invited Himmler to speak before all the army and army group commanders. Himmler initially refused, saying he had no desire to appear before a large group to "excuse himself." Brauchitsch's intermediary, Tippelskirch, assured him that it was not to "excuse but enlighten." Himmler was still reluctant and proposed speaking only to a small group of sympathetic men. In particular, he did not want Georg von Küchler (who had referred to an ss unit in Poland as a "blot" or *Schandfleck* on the army), Leeb, Blaskowitz, or Ulex present.[155] After some further delay, however, Himmler accepted the invitation, proposing an evening meeting with dinner because the atmosphere "would be more conducive to the possibility of a comradely discussion of these still difficult problems." Brauchitsch obliged, and the meeting was scheduled for March 13 at Rundstedt's headquarters in Koblenz.[156]

In Koblenz Himmler made it clear that ss actions in Poland were not unauthorized excesses by either subordinate commanders or himself. "No wild actions by lower officers—even less so by me," his handwritten notes insisted.[157] "In this group of the highest officers of the army I can quite openly say it: I do nothing that the Führer does not know," General Ulex remembered Himmler stating. General von Weichs recalled, "In conclusion, he [Himmler] emphasized that he always followed the orders of the Führer, but he was prepared in some things that perhaps appeared incomprehensible to take responsibility for the Führer before the people and the world, because the person of the Führer cannot be connected with these things." Apparently no one chose even to raise the question of events in Poland in the ensuing discussion, although Blaskowitz was there and at least one of his reports was well known to virtually all of the officers present.[158]

Brauchitsch's tactic was successful. Himmler's speech to the generals brought to an end the simmering discontent of many and the overt criticism of a courageous few concerning German policy in Poland. Increasingly the generals turned their attention to the impending attack on France, and the spectacular victory there had a mesmerizing effect on them, for many had experienced the formative stages of their military careers in the four horrendous years of stalemated trench war on the western front. In their eyes Hitler was confirmed as a man of genius and destiny, who to the great good fortune of Germany had triumphed over the hesitation of the generals. As Quartermaster General Wagner—a onetime critic—put it, "to the Führer alone is due the fame, because without his will it would never have come to such a course of action."[159]

The fates of the protestors varied. Blaskowitz continued to collect evidence on ss atrocities, which he tried to submit to Keitel in late April in two folders. The latter would not read them. Blaskowitz was removed from Poland in early May 1940. He was the only colonel general of the Polish campaign never to receive the field marshal's baton.[160] General Georg von Küchler, who had so angered Himmler in the fall of 1939, was far more supportive of Nazi racial policy when he returned to the east in the following summer. On July 22, 1940, he issued orders to the 18th Army forbidding any criticism of "the ethnic struggle being carried out in the General Government, for instance, the treatment of the Polish minorities, of the Jews, and of Church matters" because the "final ethnic solution" (*endgültigen völkischen Lösung*) to the centuries-old struggle on the eastern boarder required "unique, harsh measures."[161]

Between September 1939 and the summer of 1940 a fatal transformation had occurred in the position and attitude of the army, the one organization capable of removing Hitler from within, or at least setting limits on Nazi depravity abroad. Faced with the knowledge of the regime's intentions to carry out systematic murder and deportation in Poland, the top commanders had followed a policy of washing their hands. Brauchitsch had put it euphemistically, that he would shield the army from events that threatened to impair its discipline and spirit. The panic over the fall offensive in the west briefly moved some to consider a coup, but these plans collapsed as precipitously as the broken nerves of Brauchitsch and Halder in the face of a 20-minute Hitler tirade. Those few who were motivated more by revulsion over the atrocities in Poland and the criminal nature of the regime in general than by panic over the ill-considered fall offensive in the west tried unsuccessfully to keep the flames of discontent alive. As the prospects for a successful western offensive rose and Brauchitsch enlisted Himmler himself to legitimize Nazi policies in Poland, the critics were silenced. The victory in France only completed a process long underway. Abdication of responsibility by the army for the fate of the civilian populations that their military conquests brought under Nazi sway was complete.

The capacity to measure events by the traditional moral norms of the military caste, which, however antidemocratic and anti-Semitic, still involved notions of honor and chivalry and entailed certain obligations toward unarmed civilians, was still alive in 1939. So was the ability to articulate moral indignation. This ability to describe the policies of the regime in terms of dishonor and shame threatened to puncture the Nazis' world of moral inversion, in which they were able to hollow out and pervert traditional German values such as loyalty, obedience, and law and order and to enlist the bulk of the German population in either active support or passive acceptance of their murderous policies. By the summer of 1940, however, this capacity to measure events by the moral standards of a bygone world—to recall Germany to its senses—had been effectively smothered, and a major obstacle to the radicalization of Nazi racial policy had been removed.

Thus long before the Final Solution became the centerpiece of Nazi racial policy and the Jews its primary victims—but when the murderous nature of such racial policies was nonetheless already clear—criticism of these policies was no longer tolerated within the army. But the long descent of the army was not complete. In 1941, with the "war of destruction" against the Soviet Union and the Final Solution, the army would move from abdication of responsibility and passive complicity to outright participation in this crusade against the "Jewish-Bolshevik" enemy.

THE MADAGASCAR PLAN

The German victory in France provided an impetus for the radicalization of Nazi racial policy in a number of ways. Himmler's stance vis-à-vis Göring's and Frank's inhibitive arguments based on economic pragmatism was greatly strengthened, and the euphoria of victory provided the perfect moment for Himmler to elicit Hitler's reconfirmation of sweeping plans for the total removal not only of all Jews but also of all Poles from the expanded territory of the Third Reich, and for the reduction of the east European populations under German occupation to a denationalized helot status. Victory had likewise completed the transformation of the attitude of the army officer corps to one of adulation for Hitler's military genius and self-strangulation of any anti-Nazi criticism, particularly of Nazi racial policy. But the victory radicalized the situation in other ways as well. The occupation of territory in western Europe, with hundreds of thousands of additional Jews, ensured that the Nazis would no longer seek a solution to the Jewish question solely in terms of the Third Reich and the General Government. It was now a Europe-wide Jewish question that they would feel obligated to solve. This had always been implied in theory; now it was the case in practice as well. And finally, the expectation of an imminent peace settlement not only with France but also with Great Britain seemed to place at Germany's disposal both the colonial empire of the former and the merchant shipping of the latter. It was out of this conjuncture of factors that the Madagascar Plan was born, offering the prospect of a final solution to the Jewish question in Europe through the total removal of the continent's entire Jewish population. It was a heady and intoxicating vision to those who had experienced the bottlenecks of demographic engineering in eastern Europe over the past nine months and thus rekindled the flames of Nazi determination and fanaticism in this regard. However fantastical in retrospect, the Madagascar Plan was an important psychological step on the road to the Final Solution.

Among those advocating the removal of European Jewry from the continent, no potential resettlement area exercised such a faddish attraction in the years before World War II as the island of Madagascar, a French colony off the coast of Africa in the Indian Ocean. The idea was huckstered by the British anti-Semites Henry Hamilton Beamish and Arnold Leese, as well as by the mysterious Georg de Pottere (using the pseudonym Egon van Winghene).[162] The Polish, French, and British governments all toyed with the idea in the late 1930s, as did the Joint Distribution Committee, however briefly.[163] The Poles, with the concurrence of the French, even sent a three-man investigating team (the Lepecky commission) to study the feasibility of relocating Polish Jews there. After a 13-week investigation, Lepecky concluded that 5,000–7,000 families could be settled on Madagascar, although the more optimistic of the two Jewish members of the commission thought a mere 500 families was the maximum.[164]

If such a fantastic idea was seductive even to the French and the Poles, obviously it could not escape attention in Germany. From 1938 to the spring of 1940, various Nazi luminaries—Streicher, Göring, Rosenberg, Ribbentrop, and Frank—and even the fellow traveler Hjalmar Schacht mentioned the idea.[165] Just ten days before the Anschluss Eichmann had been instructed to collect material for a "foreign policy solution" to the Jewish question, along the lines being explored by Poland and France.[166] Presumably after the Anschluss Eichmann was too busy with coercing emigration in Vienna. There is no evidence that actual planning for a Jewish resettlement in Madagascar, as opposed to mere references to the possibility, took place among the Nazis until June 1940, when imminent French defeat seemed to place the territories of the French empire at Germany's disposal.

The initiative in this case came not from within the ss or the circle of Streicher's *Der Stürmer*, but rather from Franz Rademacher, the newly appointed head of the Jewish desk of the German Foreign Office (the so-called Referat D III or *Judenreferat*). Rademacher was an ambitious young jurist and diplomat, a self-made man of proletarian origins who had just returned from the German embassy in Montevideo.[167] Surveying the tasks of his new domain, Rademacher wanted to escape the humdrum paperwork involved in resolving specific cases of individual Jews with foreign policy implications. This had been the main task of the *Judenreferat* in the prewar period, but it seemed of little significance to Rademacher now that the war had broken out. He wanted to get down to fundamental questions. "In my opinion, therefore, the question in Jewish affairs is to be decided in accordance with German war aims," he wrote on June 3, 1940, in a memorandum to his superior, Undersecretary Martin Luther of Abteilung Deutschland, the most nazified division of the German Foreign Office. "One question must be clarified, whereto with the Jews?" Rademacher posed several possibilities: "a) all Jews out of Europe. b) separation between eastern and western Jews; the eastern Jews, which supply the regenerative and Talmudic recruits for the militant Jewish intelligentsia, stay, for example, in the district of Lublin as a pledge in German hands, so that the American Jews remain paralyzed in their fight against Germany. The western Jews on the other hand are removed from Europe, to Madagascar for example." Rademacher wanted to undertake a detailed feasibility study of these possibilities, so that the less nazified and more traditional Political Division of the Foreign Office did not preempt all planning for the peace treaty with France and, with its "inherently imperialistic way of thinking," ignore the racial question. Rademacher thus asked Luther to ascertain Ribbentrop's basic war aim in regards to the Jewish question.[168]

If the possible concentration of east European Jews around Lublin was an idea already tried and found wanting, the concept of shipping all European Jews to Madagascar appeared all the more a panacea to Germany's frustrated demographic engineers. The idea spread like wildfire. Two weeks after Rademacher broached it to Luther, both Ribbentrop and Hitler himself mentioned the plan to use Madagascar for a Jewish reservation to Foreign Minister Galeazzo Ciano and Mussolini in their talks in Munich on June 18 over the fate of the French empire.[169] Two days later, on June 20, Hitler repeated his intention to resettle the European Jews in Madagascar to the head of the German navy, Admiral Raeder.[170]

The well-informed Heydrich got wind of the Foreign Office brainstorm and moved quickly to protect his jurisdiction. On June 24, 1940, he wrote Ribbentrop to remind the foreign minister that in January 1939 Göring had placed him in charge of Jewish emigration from all Reich territory, a policy he had successfully pursued until the outbreak of the war. Now the "whole problem" (*Gesamtproblem*) of some three and a quarter million Jews in the German sphere could no longer be solved by emigration, and "thus a territorial final solution becomes necessary" (*Eine territoriale Endlösung wird daher notwendig*). Heydrich asked to be included in any forthcoming discussions on the subject that the foreign minister might be planning. Ribbentrop immediately conceded Heydrich's jurisdiction. Rademacher was informed that the foreign minister had "in principle agreed to the preparation of an expulsion of the Jews from Europe," which was to go forward "in closest agreement" with the agencies of the Reichsführer-SS.[171]

By early July the word on Madagascar had reached Hans Frank in the General Government. On July 10 his HSSPF Krüger reported on the new plan. Jewish deportations would no longer take place from Germany into the General Government, including "the expulsions that were to have begun in August." Now all Jews, including those already in the General Government, were to be sent to an African colony "that the French government must turn over to Germany for this purpose."[172] The situation of the Germans in the General Government was thus vastly transformed. Not only were they freed from the expected deluge of Jews from the Third Reich scheduled to begin in August, but they now expected to be relieved of the Polish Jews already in the General Government as well. The suddenly reprieved Frank could hardly contain his glee as on several occasions he boisterously expounded upon this astonishing turn of events—this "colossal relief" (*kolossale Entlastung*)—to the "amusement" (*Heiterkeit*) of his assembled court.[173]

The word on Madagascar naturally spread to all levels of the German administration in the General Government. As early as July 1 the SD man Gerhard Mende blurted out to Adam Czerniakow, chairman of the Jewish council in Warsaw, "that the war would be over in a month and that we would all leave for Madagascar."[174] In Warsaw plans to commence building two ghettos on the edge of the city, beginning in July, were brought to an immediate standstill. An "order from Cracow was issued to stop all work on ghetto construction in view of the fact that, according to the plan of the Führer, the Jews of Europe were to be sent to Madagascar at the end of the war and thus ghetto building was to all practical purposes illusory [*daher eine Gettobildung praktisch illusorisch sei*]."[175] The Kreishauptmann (county chief) of Krasnystaw reported in early September that many of the Jews in his district had German names that they now spelled according to Polish conventions, for example, Zygelszyper instead of Ziegelschipper. For ease of record keeping, he was ordering the use of German spelling. In his view this did not endanger any German interests, for "when they go to Madagascar after the war, they can get themselves Madagascar-style names there."[176]

If the German officials of the General Government were greatly relieved, the implications of the Madagascar Plan were less gratifying to those of the incorporated territories, especially Greiser in the Warthegau. In a meeting between Greiser and Frank at the end of July, the Gauleiter of the Warthegau noted that according to Himmler the Jews were now to be sent overseas. "That depends naturally upon the duration of the war." But in the Warthegau the deportation of the Jews had been expected for the summer of 1940, and a solution to the Jewish question there, where allegedly 250,000 Jews (in fact 160,000) were packed into the ghetto in Lodz, could not remain unresolved through the winter:

> Should the war last still longer, then one will have to find an interim solution. . . . It had been planned to transport them in a suitable manner to the General Government, and it had been intended to clarify the form of this transfer today. In the meantime the new decision had arrived, and he greatly valued the possibility of the transfer being cleared up, because for the

Warthegau . . . it would be an impossible situation [*ein unmöglicher Zustand*] to keep these Jews, packed together in the ghetto, over the winter. In any case, therefore, one had to find an interim solution that offered the possibility of deporting these Jews to some other territory.

But Frank, Krüger, and Streckenbach were not about to oblige Greiser. They were now preparing to deport their own Jews to Madagascar. As plans were being drawn up for this move, they advised Greiser to see that the Lodz Jews were considered first in line. As for the General Government, according to Himmler it still faced the influx of some 30,000 "Gypsies." Moreover, only 58,000 of the 120,000 Poles of the Volhynian action had arrived so far, and after that there were population exchanges involving 20,000–30,000 ethnic Germans from Lithuania and 41,000 Poles from Gdynia. To the final plea of Greiser's HSSPF, Wilhelm Koppe, "that the situation regarding the Jews in the Warthegau worsened day by day" and that the ghetto there "had actually only been erected on the condition that the deportation of the Jews would begin by mid-year at the latest," Frank was unmoved. The Warthegau might have priority when it came to Germanization; but his territory also had important tasks to fulfill for the Reich, and its food situation was desperate as well.[177]

Meanwhile in Berlin work on the Madagascar Plan proceeded feverishly in Rademacher's Judenreferat in the German Foreign Office and now also in Eichmann's office for Jews and evacuations in the RSHA.[178] Rademacher made contact with agencies of the SS and the Interior Ministry as well as with the party. By early July he submitted his first reports.[179] "The imminent victory gives Germany the possibility and, in my opinion, also the obligation to solve the Jewish question in Europe," he wrote. "The desirable solution is: All Jews out of Europe." (*Der bevorstehende Sieg gibt Deutschland die Möglichkeit und meines Erachtens auch die Pflicht die Judenfrage in Europa zu lösen. Die wünschenswerte Lösung ist: Alle Juden aus Europa.*) In the peace treaty France would be forced to cede the island of Madagascar to Germany as a mandate. Strategic points would be placed under a police governor of the SS. "The Madagascar solution means, as seen from the German point of view, the creation of a superghetto [*Grossgettos*]. Only the Security Police has the necessary experience in this area." The Jews would be held financially liable for the real estate given them on Madagascar, and all their European property would be transferred to a special bank for this purpose. On the island they would not be subjected to a colonial administration. This would be a "superfluous overlap of authorities" with the police governor; moreover, their treatment as a colonial people would cause an uproar among American Jews. Instead they would be given autonomy under the police governor, with their own mayors, police, postal administration, and so on. Rademacher thought such "generosity" (*Grossmut*) toward the Jews could be used as propaganda to Germany's benefit.

Rademacher continued his researches over the next several months. Consultations with the well-known demographer and president of the Bavarian State Office of Statistics, Dr. Burgdörfer, revealed that even if 4.9 million Jews from Europe and 1.6 million Jews from elsewhere in the world, excluding the United States and the Soviet Union, were resettled in Madagascar and the native population were left in place, it would still create a population density of only 16 per square kilometer. This was about average for the earth's surface and one-tenth of the population density of Germany. Burgdörfer and Rademacher, in total disregard of the realities, fecklessly concluded that this population density could preserve itself within the natural capacity of the island. Dr. Schumacher of the Freiburg Mining Academy assured Rademacher that, aside from graphite, there were no significant mineral deposits on Madagascar. In *Meyer's Lexicon* Rademacher read that the hot and humid coastal climate of Madagascar was "very unhealthy for Europeans," but that the highlands were cooler and more wholesome.[180]

But above all Rademacher became intrigued by the economic side of the Madagascar Plan and drew up, for submission to Helmuth Wohlthat of Göring's Four-Year Plan, a memorandum on the foundation of an intra-European bank for the utilization of Jewish property. The main idea was to replace Jewish economic influence in Europe with that of Germany in one blow, without disrupting the economy of any country. Jewish assets would be administered in trusteeship by the bank and gradually liquidated to pay for the entire cost of the resettlement operation. Property in Madagascar would likewise be administered by the bank in trusteeship and gradually transferred to the Jews. The bank would then continue to function as the economic intermediary between the Jewish reservation in Madagascar and the outside world, since no direct economic contact between the Jews and others would be permitted.[181] On August 15, 1940, Rademacher received word via Luther of a conversation between Hitler and the German ambassador to France, Otto Abetz, in which the Führer had stated his intention to evacuate all Jews from Europe after the war.[182] Rademacher thus had every reason to believe in the full seriousness of the plans he was concocting.

Eichmann and his Jewish experts in the RSHA were also busy. Already on June 25, one day after Heydrich's letter to Ribbentrop and a week after Hitler first mentioned Madagascar to Mussolini, a minor official of Eichmann's office, Jagusch, informed Dr. Paul Eppstein of the Reich Union of Jews in Germany that a plan existed for a total solution to the Jewish question through the removal of all Jews from the German sphere in Europe ("and insofar as possible also England") to a colonial territory.[183] On July 3 Eichmann and Dannecker met with Jewish leaders from Berlin, Prague, and Vienna (Josef Löwenherz, Jakob Edelstein, and Frantisek Weidmann in addition to Eppstein) and declared that after the war a total solution to the Jewish question would be pursued, for which individual emigration would not suffice. Eichmann assigned the Jewish leaders the task of compiling (within 24 hours!) a list of considerations that would have to be taken into account for such a solution involving four million Jews. But the Jewish leaders showed interest only in Palestine, which the two Nazis rejected as a possibility.[184]

Eichmann and Dannecker proceeded unperturbed by the lack of enthusiasm on the part of the Jewish leaders and by mid-August had completed their own draft of a plan—a neatly printed brochure, complete with table of contents and maps, entitled "Reichssicherheitshauptamt: Madagaskar Projekt." A copy was sent to Rademacher on August 15.[185] Eichmann and Dannecker noted that "with the addition of the masses of the east, a settlement of the Jewish question through emigration had become impossible. . . . To avoid the lasting contact of other peoples with Jews, an overseas solution of insular character must be preferred above all others." Thus the four million Jews in the German sphere— one million per year over four years—were to be sent to Madagascar.[186] The RSHA plan contained no nonsense about demonstrating Germany's generosity to the world by granting Jewish autonomy. Internally, the mandate would be a "police state." Jewish organizations would be created, but their sole function would be to enforce SS orders as quickly as possible. Above all the plan emphasized that the total direction of the project—from financing to transport to security—would be under Reinhard Heydrich, who had been named special deputy for Jewish emigration by Göring in January 1939. In addition to discussing the administrative apparatus for deportation from the various countries in the German sphere, the report proposed sending an advance party to Madagascar to ascertain, among other things, the possibility of erecting camps to increase reception capacity. A special deputy of Himmler's was to be named to take part in the peace negotiations insofar as the Madagascar Plan was involved.

Rademacher was not deterred by Eichmann's evident determination to monopolize all aspects of the Madagascar Plan and exclude the participation of other agencies. In a late-August summary of the development of the plan, Rademacher proposed an extensive division of labor: (1) the Foreign Office would be in charge of negotiations both for the peace treaty and for special treaties with other countries to regulate the Jewish question; (2) the SS would be in charge of collecting the Jews in Europe and administering the island ghetto; (3) the utilization of Jewish property through a special bank would be supervised by Wohlthat of the Four-Year Plan; (4) propaganda would be prepared internally by Dr. Eberhard Taubert of Antisemitische Aktion under Goebbels and externally by the Information Division of the Foreign Office; (5) Viktor Brack in the Führer's Chancellery would coordinate transportation. Rademacher requested Ribbentrop's approval to invite the various participating agencies to a conference at the Foreign Office to put together a preparatory commission.[187]

There is no record of Ribbentrop's response to Rademacher's last proposal. No Foreign Office conference was held; no preparatory commission was sent. Further work on the Madagascar Plan within the Foreign Office ceased. Moreover, Rademacher's counterpart in the RSHA, Adolf Eichmann, fared no better. As late as December 1940 he told Bernhard Lösener of the Interior Ministry that the Madagascar Plan was still sitting on Heydrich's desk, awaiting his signature.[188] The Madagascar Plan was born and died of military circumstances. The defeat of France and seemingly imminent victory over Great Britain promised both the colonial territory and the merchant fleet necessary for a massive overseas expulsion of the European Jews. Just as quickly, the failure to defeat Great Britain, fully apparent in September 1940, made realization of this plan impossible. The frenetic urgency behind its preparation in the summer months suddenly dissipated.

Like a spectacular meteor, the Madagascar Plan blazed across the sky of Nazi Jewish policy, only to burn out abruptly. It was no less real for its brief existence. There can be "no doubt that during this period both Rademacher and Eichmann tackled the plan in full earnest."[189] More important, it was also taken seriously by the Nazi leadership. To Frank's great relief and Greiser's disappointment, the impending deportations from the Warthegau to the General Government were canceled. Frank in turn temporarily ordered the end of ghetto construction as pointless. These men were not carrying out an elaborate sham; they were making real decisions based on the Madagascar Plan as a real part of Nazi Jewish policy in the summer of 1940.

It is also clear that had the Nazis carried out the plan as they intended, it would have been a murderous operation.[190] Whatever the illusions of the naive and dilettantish Rademacher, the Nazi demographic engineers in east Europe had already demonstrated that "decimation" of the uprooted was not only no deterrence but even an added attraction to their population policies. This was not yet the Final Solution—a compulsive and comprehensive program to murder every last Jew that the Nazis could lay their hands on—but it was nonetheless genocidal in its implications. As such, it was an important psychological step toward the Final Solution that emerged a year later. In the fall of 1939 the Nazis had assumed a rapid solution to the Jewish question through deportation to the region of Lublin, only to find the task more difficult and much more time-consuming than they had anticipated. The alacrity with which the Madagascar Plan was seized upon as a panacea for the Nazis' inability to solve the Jewish question is a measure of the frustration level that had been reached. Once again the alluring vision of a quick and total solution to the Jewish question cast its magic spell, only once again to disappoint. The desire, indeed the "obligation," to solve the Jewish question still weighed heavily upon them, and the greater the frustration the lower the threshold to systematic mass murder.

THE LAST SPASMS OF EXPULSION POLICY, FALL 1940–SPRING 1941

As prospects for the imminent realization of the Madagascar Plan declined with Germany's military fortunes in the Battle of Britain, Germany's Jewish policy based upon expulsion faced a dead end. The idea of a Polish reservation had proven impossible to realize immediately; no new vistas had opened up overseas. Yet old habits, thought patterns, and temptations died hard, and from the fall of 1940 through the spring of 1941 the expulsion policy spasmodically revived as local Gauleiters along the borders of the Third Reich—in both east and west—successfully prevailed upon Hitler to rid them of some of their unwanted Jews through piecemeal deportations into Vichy France and the General Government. Hitler's open encouragement inspired the demographic engineers to produce yet further plans for the massive population transfer of Poles in 1941, and also induced Frank's grudging acquiescence. Once again, however, practical obstacles proved too great, and the plan remained mostly unrealized. But the key obstacle to the massive transfer of Poles—preparations for Operation Barbarossa, the invasion of the Soviet Union—also fueled further planning for the expulsion of Jews. Expulsion remained the central theme or leitmotiv of Nazi demographic engineering well into the spring of 1941.

West

With the defeat of France, Alsace and Lorraine had been annexed to the Third Reich and joined to the Baden and Saarpfalz Gaue of Robert Wagner and Josef Bürckel, respectively. Beginning in July the Germans began deporting Jews, "Gypsies," "asocials," criminals, the mentally ill, and ardent French nationalists out of those newly annexed territories into France. That Himmler saw these population expulsions in the same light as the expulsions from the incorporated territories in the east can be seen in his speech to officers of the Waffen-ss in Metz: "Exactly the same thing took place in Poland at 40° below zero, where we had to ship out thousands and tens of thousands and hundreds of thousands, where we had to have the toughness—this you should hear but then immediately forget—to shoot thousands of leading Poles."[191] By mid-November the Germans had deported 47,187 people from Lorraine and by December 23,790 from Alsace (including 3,259 Jews). Another 71,537 who had fled Alsace (including 17,875 Jews) were barred from returning.[192]

In this massive upheaval of humanity, it is not surprising that someone perceived the possibility of including the German Jews of Baden and Saarpfalz, thus making these Gaue *judenfrei*. According to Eichmann, it was the Gauleiter of Baden, Wagner, who made the proposal to Himmler, and the latter, without even considering the possible complications, was "too impulsive" not to agree.[193] However impulsive the decision may have been, preparations for the deportations were secretly and carefully made well in advance, and involved close cooperation between the local authorities of the Gauleiter, the police, and the experts of Heydrich's RSHA. According to Lösener, on the basis of a Hitler order, Himmler authorized the deportations on September 30, that is, very soon after it must have become apparent that the war with Britain was not going to be won that fall. On the basis of a decree of the Ministry of the Interior in Baden dated October 15, local authorities were to be informed on October 21 of measures to be taken the following day.[194]

Early on October 22, teams of police equipped with lists descended upon the Jews in every village in Baden and Saarpfalz and with no more than two hours' notice brought them to collection points. The roundup proceeded according to very precise guidelines. The deportees were permitted 50 kilograms of baggage and 100 RM in cash; everything else was confiscated. The closing up of apartments was carefully regulated, even to the point of obtaining receipts for pets turned over to obliging neighbors. During the arrests the Jews were to be properly treated; excesses were to be avoided.[195] In Walldorf near Heidelberg, four Schupo and four men of the reserve police took part in the roundup of 19 Jews, indicating that the ratio of police to deportees was quite high.[196]

To Heydrich's satisfaction the roundups proceeded "without friction or incident" and were "scarcely noticed by the population." Nine trains—two from Saarpflaz and seven from Baden—departed with the 6,504 German Jews on October 22 and 23 for Vichy France. The trains had been arranged by Eichmann in conjunction with the Transportation Ministry, and he sat anxiously in his car at the demarcation-line crossing point in Chalon-sur-Saône "bathed in sweat" until the last train passed into Vichy territory. When the French discovered whom they had allowed over the border, they lodged the German Jews in camps at Gurs and Riversaltes in the Pyrenees and Les Milles near Aix-en-Provence—camps originally constructed for Republican refugees from Spain.[197]

But if the deportation had run smoothly, the ensuing diplomatic and political complications quickly made clear the limits of such an expulsion policy in the west. Vichy France, like Hans Frank's General Government, had no desire to become a "dumping ground" for the Jews of the Third Reich. On October 27 General Doyen, head of the French delegation to the armistice commission meeting in Wiesbaden, protested to the German delegation. Nine trains, with over 6,000 German citizens, registered as "expellee transports" (*Transporte Ausgewiesener*) had been accepted by French officials in the mistaken belief that they contained French citizens from Alsace-Lorraine. There were rumors that these transports of German Jews were destined for Portugal, but the French government wanted immediate information concerning "what final travel goal the Reich government planned for these expellees."[198]

The German armistice commission delegation, wanting to know how to respond, asked the Foreign Office for information and instructions. The Foreign Office, likewise uninformed, consulted the RSHA. First Eichmann's deputy Rolf Günther verbally and then Heydrich formally in a letter conceded that the reported deportation had indeed been carried out and without any warning to the French. It had been done by order of the Führer, they insisted. Ribbentrop thereupon ordered that the French demand be handled "dilatorily."[199]

As in the case of the Stettin/Schneidemühl deportations in the spring, the Foreign Office was also informed in gruesome detail by an anonymous letter, this time sent to Friedrich Gaus of the Legal Division, whose wife was one-quarter Jewish. He sent it to Undersecretary Luther, whose Judenreferat forwarded it to the Gestapo. In addition to alleging that the action had taken place under the initiative of Gauleiters Bürckel and Wagner, the writer claimed that plans for a similar deportation from Hessen had been temporarily postponed owing to the French protest. Among the victims transported were World War I veterans and the residents of old people's homes, including some who had to be carried to the trains on stretchers. Several people—eight in Mannheim alone and in Karlsruhe three—had committed suicide when faced with the deportation notice. Because suitable accommodation and provisions were lacking in the Pyrenees camps for the deportees—mostly elderly men and women—the French government was considering sending them to Madagascar as soon as the seaways were open. By this last comment, Luther scribbled, "Very interesting!"[200]

Another interested party emerged in the form of officials of the Interior Ministry. Ministerialrat Hans Globke requested a copy of the French protest note from Rademacher, noting that the Interior Ministry was the competent agency for the Jewish question inside Germany. When Rademacher protested that the deportations to France were primarily a foreign policy question and that the Interior Ministry had not even had the courtesy to inform the Foreign Office beforehand, Globke replied that the Interior Ministry would gladly have done so, but it had had no foreknowledge of the deportations either.[201]

Meanwhile the French persistently returned to the issue at Wiesbaden. The issue climaxed with a note of November 18, 1940: "The French government can in fact no longer provide asylum to these foreigners. It most urgently proposes that the Reich government immediately take the necessary measures so that they are transported back to Germany and the expenditures arising from their stay in France are repaid."[202] General Heinrich von Stülpnagel, head of the German delegation, complained bitterly that the current negotiations were extraordinarily overburdened and aggravated by this issue, on which he had been waiting nearly a month for instructions.[203] But Ribbentrop continued to insist that the matter be handled dilatorily. Stülpnagel was to be informed that the deportation had taken place by the order of the Führer and that the return of the deported Jews, as proposed by the French, was out of the question.[204]

If the French were powerless to force the Germans to take back the Jews deported from Baden and Saarpfalz until the Germans wanted to murder them in death camps in Poland nearly two years later, the Vichy regime was not so powerless that it could not prevent further large-scale deportations now that it was forewarned. On November 14, 1940, a train carrying 280 Luxembourg Jews reached Portugal under an ongoing agreement between that country and Germany that if further transportation to the Americas did not work out, the Jews would be returned. Such was the case this time, and the unfortunate Luxembourg Jews were sent back to Bayonne in German-occupied France on November 20. There the SD-Sonderkommando chief in Bordeaux, Herbert Hagen, Eichmann's erstwhile colleague at the Jewish desk of the SD and traveling companion to Palestine in 1937, took charge. On November 26 he sent the Luxembourg Jews in four train cars toward unoccupied France, only to have the French authorities at Orthez on the demarcation line refuse entry.

The French immediately lodged a complaint at Wiesbaden, and the military in Bordeaux complained that the continued presence of the Jews in that strategic zone was intolerable.[205] Thirty-eight of the Luxembourg Jews were then successfully infiltrated into unoccupied France on a regular passenger train on

December 21, and when the Germans refused to take them back, France protested repeatedly.[206] To Foreign Office requests for information, armistice delegation complaints, and army demands that the Luxembourg Jews be removed from Bayonne, the RSHA replied only in late February 1941 that the SD in Bordeaux was gradually deporting the Jews stranded in Bayonne and that most of them were already gone.[207] The Bordeaux military confirmed in May that all the Luxembourg Jews had been dispersed, some over the Spanish border and some into Vichy France.[208] The German armistice commission delegation wanted assurances not only that the episode of the Luxembourg Jews was over but also that the SS would refrain from deporting other Jews over the demarcation line. The RSHA promised that these had been "special individual measures: These actions are concluded."[209] But this assurance did not come until July 9, 1941, when the Einsatzgruppen were rushing into the Soviet Union, on the verge of carrying out a quite different policy from expulsion toward the Jews.

Poland

Though not without some conflict and misunderstanding, Himmler, Heydrich, Göring, and Frank had reached agreement on the resettlement schedule for 1940. Under the intermediate plan and the second short-range plan, the General Government was to accept uprooted and dispossessed Poles from the incorporated territories in order to make room for the repatriation and settlement of Baltic and Volhynian Germans. The deportations were to be completed by late July and then followed by the massive expulsion of all Jews from the incorporated territories. This agreement, reconfirmed between Heydrich and Frank on June 12, 1940, was subsequently changed in three ways. First, the pace of the Volhynian resettlement was much slower than expected, and this action was not in fact completed until January 1941. Second, the Madagascar Plan led to the cancellation of the total expulsion of the Jews of the incorporated territories, despite Greiser's attempts in both March and July to at least empty the Lodz ghetto. And third, with the cancellation of the mass expulsion of Jews, first Himmler and then Hitler prevailed upon Frank to accept a modest expansion of the second short-range plan to include four additional small resettlement programs over the last four months of 1940.

The expulsion of Poles from the Warthegau to make room for Volhynian Germans began on May 6, 1940, and ended more than eight months later on January 20, 1941. Over this span, 92 trains carried 89,293 Poles and 2,663 Jews (the latter in three transports from Poznan) from the UWZ in Lodz into the General Government.[210] As anticipated in Rapp's critical and pessimistic report of late April, catching the Poles designated for resettlement proved difficult. The branch office of the UWZ in Gostynin reported an average capture rate of 44% in late May, but noted that this average disguised a significant variation. On the first day of an action, the capture rate could reach 75%, but it would drop precipitously the next day to 25%. Many Poles were not sleeping at home at night, and a search of the nearest forest significantly improved numbers.[211] Two months later the capture rate remained around 40%. The Poles were frequently forewarned, indeed all too often by greedy Volksdeutsche who tried to use the impending deportations to extort the sale of livestock and equipment at bargain prices.[212]

HSSPF Koppe proposed that the SD set up an extensive network of agents to uncover the Poles' warning system, and the Order Police requested reinforcements.[213] The latter were indeed heavily engaged. For instance, between September 9 and December 13, units of Police Battalion 44 participated in 71 resettlement actions, often in overwhelming force. It was not unusual for 200–300 policemen to descend on an area to seize less than half that number of Polish families.[214] In three of these actions in Kreis Schroda, the battalion had capture rates of 81%, 59%, and 87%.[215]

Apparently Police Battalion 101 enjoyed less numerical superiority over its prey: "In actions night and day without pause, 100% of the battalion's strength was employed in all the districts of the Warthegau. On average some 350 Polish peasant families were evacuated daily. . . . During the peak of the evacuation period they [the men of the battalion] could not return to quarters for eight days and nights. The men had the opportunity to sleep only while traveling at night by truck. . . . In the biggest action, the battalion . . . evacuated about 900 families." In all, the battalion evacuated 36,972 people out of a targeted 58,628 —a capture rate of 63%.[216]

An intensified search for escapees also met with success. By early November the UWZ in Lodz reported to Eichmann that over 4,000 Poles had been captured who had earlier evaded resettlement and then been placed on wanted lists.[217] But Höppner held out no hope that Poles would not continue to be forewarned of German resettlement actions as long as every agency in the Warthegau had no choice but to hire Polish employees.[218]

The deporters encountered additional problems arising from the behavior of ethnic Germans already living in the eastern provinces at the time of their incorporation, many of whom saw the repatriates less as racial comrades than as unfairly favored competitors for Polish property. They not only attempted to extort property from Poles designated for deportation, thus giving them early warning, but also descended on the farms of the newly settled Volhynian Germans and helped themselves to items they claimed to have lent to the former Polish owners.[219]

Even more significant, the local ethnic Germans resented the priority given to the repatriates in receiving the pick of Polish farms and demanded an "improvement" (*Besserstellung*) of their own position by having Poles dispossessed and deported on their behalf as well. The resettlement authorities rejected this demand on several grounds: trains for additional deportations were not available, the placement of the repatriates was urgent, and Polish farmers would have no incentive to keep up their farms if that merely led to their property being given to covetous neighboring ethnic Germans. The resettlement authorities asked for patience, since it was the Führer's order that ultimately these regions be cleared of all Poles. In reality, local German officials winked at and even abetted the widespread practice of ethnic Germans taking over Polish farms. As one sd officer reported quite simply, "The Poles were made to understand they had to disappear."[220]

Another problem emerged from the policy, presumably insisted on by Frank, that old and sick Poles were not to be included in the deportations. Local German authorities in the Warthegau complained that such a practice was untenable in the long run because those left behind without family support were destined to become a "burden" on public welfare. While one German ss officer thought most sick and elderly Poles could be left with relatives and only "quite few" Poles would become a welfare burden, Höppner took the problem more seriously. He noted ominously, "Under the circumstances other measures must be taken against nontransportable people."[221] The problem must have remained on Höppner's mind, for the following spring he asked that all Poles suspected of having tuberculosis be registered and deported.[222]

Another problem the Germans faced was the constant temptation to increase the deportations. Even as the Volhynian resettlement action was just beginning, different German agencies attempted to expand the second short-range plan. In mid-May the military approached the uwz branch office in Konin for help in clearing the southern half of that Kreis to create a vast training ground and shooting range.[223] By late June the staggering dimensions of the project involving the resettlement of 80,000 people (including 8,000 Volksdeutsche and 4,000 Jews) were clear.[224] Both Höppner in Poznan and Eichmann's deputy in Berlin, Rolf Günther, noted that no deportations to the General Government could take place without the agreement of Göring, Frank, and the Reich Transportation Ministry. Höppner advised Krumey in Lodz to make it clear that without such prior agreement, the uwz camps would accept no transports sent to them. And Günther advised "local resettlement measures" (*örtliche Umsiedlungsmassnah-*

men) within the Warthegau in place of deportation to the General Government.[225] In late July the issue became moot when the military decided to postpone constructing the extensive training grounds in Konin until after the war.[226]

In the fall of 1939, when the Lublin district was first being considered as the future *Judenreservat*, Frank's HSSPF Krüger concluded that this would necessitate moving the ethnic Germans living there (estimated at 22,000) back to the Reich, and Frank had obtained Himmler's approval.[227] This project took on a life of its own and expanded even after the Lublin reservation was first canceled and then superseded by the Madagascar Plan. Just as Himmler was meeting with Hitler on May 25 to present his plan to resume the demographic restructuring of east Europe, his demographic engineers in Poznan learned of Himmler's intention to resettle ethnic Germans from the General Government in the Warthegau. However, in contrast to the procedure for repatriating Baltic and Volhynian Germans from outside the German sphere, by which Poles in the incorporated territories were dispossessed and simply dumped into the General Government, Himmler now proposed an orderly exchange of farms between Poles and ethnic Germans, with each family taking its own personal possessions, equipment, and livestock, beginning in August 1940.[228]

By late June the plan had expanded to encompass not just ethnic Germans from the Lublin district—the so-called Cholmer Germans—but *all* ethnic Germans in the General Government, estimated at 80,000.[229] Eichmann and Günther in Berlin seem to have not yet been informed, for on July 1, 1940, Günther wired Höppner that according to the Heydrich-Frank agreement of June 12, no deportations beyond the Volhynian action and the evacuation of Jews scheduled for August could take place. Höppner telephoned in reply that the RSHA had already sent a team from the Einwandererzentralstelle to Lublin, so Heydrich must have already taken the decision.[230] One week later Höppner was at Eichmann's Referat IV D 4 in Berlin, where the "halt to the evacuation of Jews into the General Government" was announced. Höppner was assured that once facts and figures had been collected on resettling the Cholmer Germans in the Warthegau, Frank's approval would be obtained.[231] Thus it can be suspected that Himmler and Heydrich had already secured Frank's acceptance in principle of the Cholmer Aktion as a reciprocal concession for canceling the evacuation of the Jews.

When the figures were gathered, the prospective number of ethnic Germans to be resettled dropped first to 34,000 and then 30,000 (from the earlier estimate of 80,000). The number of Poles was set at 50,000, so that some smaller Polish farms could be consolidated. Himmler's notion of an "exchange settlement" (*Tauschsiedlung*) was also modified. Poles and Germans would still trade farm for farm and take their personal possessions. However, because the Polish farmers of the Warthegau were often more prosperous than their German counterparts in the General Government, equipment and livestock would remain in place. The action was scheduled to begin in early September.[232]

The decision to resettle the ethnic Germans of the General Government in the summer of 1940 is significant because of the insight it provides into Himmler's outlook at the time. Unlike the Baltic, Volhynian, and Bessarabian Germans, the ethnic Germans of the General Government were not being rescued from territories conceded to the Soviet sphere by the Hitler-Stalin nonaggression pact and partition agreement. Residing within the German sphere, the Cholmer Germans were in no imminent danger. And after the cancellation of the Lublin plan, even the prospect of their having to live within a Jewish reservation, which had provided the initial impetus for their repatriation, was no longer a concern. In short, Himmler's desire to repatriate these ethnic Germans and settle them in the incorporated territories was not just a reactive rescue measure. This was not a program imposed simply by circumstance but rather one to be carried out for its own sake. The vision of Germanizing the new borderlands—both east and west—fired Himmler's imagination as a historic mission of great consequence. This was the construction of German Lebensraum as understood at the time. The scope of these resettlement and Germanization schemes would soon be dwarfed by the *Generalplan Ost*, and two years later the Germans would be attempting to reverse their resettlement work of 1940 by expelling Poles from the Lublin district and creating new German settlements in the very areas from which ethnic Germans had been so recently removed. With ethnic German resettlement as with the Madagascar Plan, hindsight is not the proper yardstick by which to measure Himmler's ideological horizon in the summer of 1940.

The first train of the Cholmer Aktion departed from Lodz to the Lublin district on September 2, 1940, and the last departed December 14. The total number of expelled Poles was 28,365 in 48 trains, considerably less than the 50,000 initially envisaged.[233] The slow pace of the Volhynian resettlement, the cancellation of the Jewish evacuations, and the reduced scale of the Cholmer Aktion apparently paved the way within the framework of the second short-range plan for three more expulsion programs from incorporated territories other than the Warthegau. In the Saybuscher Aktion 17,413 Poles were deported in 18 trains from East Upper Silesia between September 23 and December 14. In the Mlawa Aktion of November 10–20, 10,700 people were deported in 11 trains, at least one of which carried Jews, from the Zichenau district annexed to East Prussia. And finally, in the Litauer Aktion of December 5–17,

6,607 Poles and 3,259 Jews were deported from East Prussia via Soldau in 10 trains.[234]

In June 1940 Frank had been frantic over the desperate conditions in the General Government and the imminent massive deportation of Jews from the incorporated territories. By the fall of 1940, the expulsion of Jews into the General Government had been canceled and that of Poles had remained at a relatively modest level. Frank had reason to be pleased with himself, and at a rare meeting of the eastern Gauleiters in Hitler's apartment on October 2, 1940, he could not resist boasting to Hitler about his success in the General Government. He noted in particular that the Jews of Warsaw and other cities were now all sealed in ghettos. Baldur von Schirach, the attentive Gauleiter of Vienna sitting on the other side of Hitler, immediately burst in that he had 50,000 Jews that Frank must take. Koch of East Prussia noted that so far he had deported neither Jews nor Poles from the Zichenau region; "obviously" the General Government must take them now. Frank protested that this was impossible. Hitler as usual took no explicit decision and did not even mention the Jews specifically, but he did indicate his general line of thinking to the assembled Gauleiters. The population density of the General Government, he noted, was unimportant. It was only to be a "Polish reservation, a great Polish work camp" (*eine polnische Reservation, ein grosses polnisches Arbeitslager*). Polish leaders and intelligentsia were to be killed and the people kept at such a low standard of living that they would have to export migrant labor to the Reich to survive.[235]

To resist the growing pressure, Frank cited the army's opposition to further expulsions and informed both Himmler and Greiser on November 2 that before the end of the war any further shipments of Jews and Poles to the General Government were impossible. He had thus instructed his officials to halt and turn back any transports from neighboring areas.[236] Two days later, however, Frank met with Hitler, only to learn of his "urgent wish" that more Poles be taken into the General Government.[237] Hence presumably the addition of the Mlawa and Litauer Aktionen at this time. In December Hitler was even more insistent, declaring to Frank that "Polish resettlement in the General Government was in line with his policy and that measures necessary to carry out this resettlement had to be taken during the war, because after the war they would involve international difficulties."[238]

The renewed deportations were to include not only Poles but also Jews. Baldur von Schirach's pleas for Frank to take the Austrian Jews off his hands had fallen on fertile ground. On December 3, 1940, Lammers informed Schirach that "the Führer had decided after receipt of one of the reports made by you" that the 60,000 Jews still in Vienna would be "deported most rapidly, that is, still during the war, to the General Government because of the housing shortage prevalent in Vienna."[239] For Frank the handwriting was on the wall; the flood-gates of expulsion, so nearly closed just several months earlier, now threatened to open and swamp the General Government once again. The best he could do was bargain over the methods of deportation and for more economic support. As he conceded to his state secretary, Josef Bühler, he "still saw fit to put up some resistance in this matter, even if this resistance could not be maintained in the long run."[240]

With Hitler's encouragement, expulsion fever among the Germans was clearly on the rise. Eichmann's resettlement experts in the east were summoned to Berlin on December 17 for a meeting to plan the "third short-range plan" (3. *Nahplan*) for the resettlement of ethnic Germans from Bessarabia, Bukovina, Dobrudja, and Lithuania.[241] On January 8, 1941, Heydrich told Frank's HSSPF Krüger what had been decided at that meeting. To make room for the ethnic Germans, Heydrich intended to deport no less than 831,000 people in the coming year. In addition, the army wanted 200,000 people relocated to the General Government to create vast training areas. Thus over one million people were to be moved to the General Government within the framework of the third short-range plan, some 238,500 by May. This was to be accomplished with two trains, each of 1,000 deportees, per day. On top of this, 10,000 Jews from Vienna were also to be resettled in the General Government.[242]

By its own statistics—that is, not including the refugees who fled on their own and the "wild" deportations—the SS had deported a total of 286,161 people to the General Government between December 1939 and January 1941 (87,833 in the first short-range plan of December 1939, 40,128 in the intermediate plan of February/March 1940, and 120,321 in the second short-range plan—all from the Warthegau—and 37,879 in the three small actions from Upper East Silesia, Zichenau, and West Prussia that had just been concluded).[243] Thus Heydrich was actually planning to deport almost as many people into the General Government in the next four months as had been deported in the previous thirteen, and four times as many in the coming year as had been in the last. In short, the Nazis hoped in 1941 to dwarf the demographic upheavals they had already engineered.

Once again, however, the grandiose schemes of the Nazis reflected their ambitions more than their capacities. Unlike the previous year, the problem was no longer opposition from Frank. Hitler's wishes in this matter were all too clear, and Frank accepted the expulsions as "one of the great tasks that the Führer has set for the General Government." He therefore explicitly forbade any criticism of the expulsions "out of any rudiments of humanitarian convictions or considerations of expediency."[244] Nonetheless the transportation situation in the months before Barbarossa made realization of the expulsions on the planned scale unattainable.

Between late January and the end of March, 17,086 Poles and 2,140 Jews were deported through the UWZ in the Warthegau.[245] At least one trainload of Jews from a collection camp at Dirschau (Tczew) in West Prussia, near Danzig, was sent to Warsaw in early March.[246] On February 1 the Jewish community in Vienna was told of the plans to deport 10,000 Jews from there by May. In fact, five trains took approximately 5,000 Jews to small villages in southern Poland between February 15 and March 12.[247] As in the case of the deportation of German Jews from Stettin and Baden-Saarpfalz, the departure of the first train from Vienna brought forth another anonymous letter. It claimed that most of the Jews sent from Stettin and Vienna the previous year were already dead; that many, including 35 women, in the first transport had committed suicide; and that 8,000 "non-Aryan" Christians in Vienna were also marked for deportation. Rademacher in the Foreign Office complained to the Gestapo that "with every Jewish measure such a complaining letter arrived." Could not the sender be discovered, so that he could no longer send his "songs of lament" (*Klaglieder*) to the world?[248]

The German military in Poland, preparing for the invasion of the Soviet Union, was dismayed by the increased strain on the housing shortage and disruption within the army's security zone threatened by the vast deportations of the third short-range plan. Since Frank's state secretary Bühler declared that "he was powerless" to prevent them, the 17th Army in southern Poland appealed to the OKH to contact the RSHA directly. Perhaps heartened by finding allies among the military, Bühler also protested to the RSHA, citing a Göring letter of February 28, 1941, stating that necessities of war must have precedence over racial policies no matter how desirable the latter might be in their own right.[249]

But the end of the deportation was in sight. On February 21 Eichmann's deputy Günther informed the resettlement experts in the east of a "confidential" communication from the Transportation Ministry that the Reichsbahn "for obvious military reasons" was no longer able to provide the full number of evacuation trains agreed upon for the first part of the third short-range plan. In the near future even a limited allocation of trains for evacuation might no longer be possible. Despite this warning, two trains per day were promised by the Reichsbahn for early March.[250] But on March 15 Heinrich Müller issued the decisive stop order: "For reasons already known" no more evacuations from the incorporated territories and Vienna could be carried out until further notice. As to how long that might be, Müller could offer no information.[251]

A week later Krüger announced that the resettlement of Poles and Jews into the General Government had been stopped. Frank was able to relay the even more gratifying news "that the Führer had informed him in a discussion on March 17 that in the future resettlement in the General Government would be made dependent upon the possibilities of this territory." At the same time, moreover, Hitler had brought up a related topic and "promised that in recognition of its achievements the General Government would be the first territory made free of Jews" (zugesagt, dass das Generalgouvernement in Anerkennung seiner Leistungen als erstes Gebiet judenfrei gemacht werde). This would occur "within a reasonable space of time" (in absehbarer Zeit).[252]

Indeed, since the Madagascar Plan and the cancellation of the expulsion of Jews into the General Government in the summer of 1940, the resettlement programs of the Germans in the east had taken little account of the Jews. But the top Nazis had not ceased to ponder the issue, particularly following the decision to attack the Soviet Union. In February 1941 Hitler ruminated openly about the Jewish question in front of Martin Bormann, Keitel, Albert Speer, Robert Ley, and Hewel. The war would speed a solution, he noted, but it also brought forth many more difficulties. Originally he had only thought of breaking the power of the Jews in Germany, but now his goal had to be the exclusion of Jewish influence in the entire Axis sphere. In many countries, such as Poland and Slovakia, this could be done directly by the German authorities. In a country like France, however, it would be much more difficult, but all the more important. "If he only knew where one could put several million Jews, there were not so many after all." (Wenn er nur wüsste, wo man die paar Millionen Juden hintun könnte, so viel seien es ja gar nicht.) When he remarked that he would make France provide Madagascar, Bormann questioned how the Jews could be sent there during the war. Hitler replied that one would have to consider that problem. He would provide the entire German navy for that purpose, except that he would not subject it to the risk of torpedo attack. "He was thinking of many things in a different way, not exactly more friendly." (Er dächte über manches jetzt anders, nicht gerade freundlicher.)[253] What did Hitler mean?

"A Territory Yet to Be Determined"

Did Hitler and his closest associates, such as Heinrich Himmler, arrive at a fundamental decision for the systematic mass murder of all European Jews in the German sphere already in the early months, perhaps even in January, of

1941?[254] I would argue otherwise. The decision for Barbarossa did not alter the existing determination to create a Europe free of Jews, but expulsion and commensurate population decimation—not systematic extermination—remained the central vision. What did change, clearly, was the destination of the expelled Jews. Active consideration of Madagascar had ceased the previous fall, although occasional references to that island as a future destination continued to surface for months.[255] For those privy to the secret preparations for Barbarossa and the presumed rapid defeat of the Soviet Union, however, territory to the east now beckoned as a possible solution to the question once posed by Foreign Office Jewish expert Franz Rademacher: "Whereto with the Jews?"

In a circular of October 30, 1940, to all major police headquarters in Germany, Heydrich wrote about "plans for the settlement of the Jewish question in the German sphere of influence in Europe after the conclusion of peace." This would take the form of "evacuation overseas."[256] The vision of an overseas evacuation was still officially maintained by Eichmann more than a month later. On December 3, 1940, he explained to the Interior Ministry's racial expert Bernhard Lösener the relatively small role that the Jews played in the latest deportations to Poland. "The deportation of the Jews will be carried out according to several short-range plans and one long-range plan." The short-range plans concerned only the deportations of Jews that were necessary to make room for repatriated Germans. For example, he noted, 3,000 Jews were being included in the deportations from East Prussia into the General Government to make room for Germans from Lithuania, and another 1,700 would follow. But such deportations were to be as limited as possible, because within a "reasonable space of time" (*absehbarer Zeit*) the long-range plan—which provided "that the Jews would be deported from the entire European sphere dominated by Germany to Madagascar within the framework of a four- or five-year plan after the end of the war"—would make them "superfluous."[257]

The following day, December 4, Eichmann submitted to Himmler a very brief summary of the current status of "the Jewish question." Through emigration, 501,711 Jews had already departed from the Altreich, Austria, and the Protectorate. Following the imposition of Nazi control in those areas, Jewish deaths had exceeded births by 57,036. In total, 315,642 Jews remained. In contrast, with regard to all of Europe and "the final solution of the Jewish question," no similar progress to date could be reported. Eichmann wrote cryptically: "Through resettlement of Jews from the European economic sphere of the German people to a territory yet to be determined. [*Durch Umsiedlung der Juden aus dem europäischen Wirtschaftsraum des deutschen Volkes in ein noch zu bestimmendes Territorium.*] In regard to this project, some 5.8 million Jews must be taken into consideration."[258] Clearly, the Jews targeted for resettlement now also included those of Germany's new allies in southeastern Europe, thus increasing the total from 4 million in the Madagascar Plan of August 1940 to 5.8 million. And now Madagascar was no longer mentioned. In its place, for the first time the destination of Jewish expulsion was designated vaguely as "a territory yet to be determined."

It can be inferred from Himmler's address to the Gauleiters on December 10, 1940, that this "territory yet to be determined" was not Poland. In his notes for the speech, Himmler wrote that the General Government, ruled "ruthlessly" by Germany, was to be a "reservoir of labor" for Germany. He then added: "Jewish emigration and thus yet more space for Poles." (*Judenauswanderung und damit noch mehr Platz für Polen.*)[259] This was on the eve of the finalization of two important policies of which Himmler was presumably already aware: the third short-range plan for sending more than a million Poles from the incorporated territories into the General Government, and the decision to invade the Soviet Union by the following spring. The latter, though it obviously could not be mentioned much less talked about openly, was to provide the "territory yet to be determined" for Jewish expulsion. This in turn would break the demographic logjam in the General Government and create space for the realization of the former. At the turn of the year the Nazi demographic engineers thus had not one but two plans to prepare, one relatively openly (expelling Poles into the General Government) and one secretly (expelling Jews into conquered Soviet territory).

Outside the inner circle, of course, references to plans for expelling Jews into the Soviet Union could not be made openly without compromising the secrecy surrounding the preparations for Barbarossa. Thus the continued use of code language about "a territory yet to be determined." The most detailed reference to this planning is contained in a document written by Eichmann's close associate Theodore Dannecker on January 21, 1941.

In conformity with the will of the Führer, at the end of the war there should be brought about a final solution of the Jewish question within the European territories ruled or controlled by Germany.

The Chief of the Security Police and the Security Service [Heydrich] has already received orders from the Führer, through the Reichsführer-ss [Himmler] as well as the Reichsmarschall [Göring], to submit a project for a final solution. On the basis of the present extensive experience of the offices of the Chief of Security Police and the Security Service in handling Jewish issues, and thanks to the preparatory work carried out for so long, the project in all its essentials has been completed. It is now with the Führer and the Reichsmarschall. It is certain that its execution will involve a tremendous amount of work whose success can only be guaranteed through the most painstaking preparations. This will extend to the work preceding the wholesale deportation of Jews as well as to the planning to the last detail of a settlement action *in the territory yet to be determined* [italics mine].[260]

Such references continued to be made by personnel of the RSHA in the following month. In a letter to Undersecretary Martin Luther of the Foreign Office on February 5, Heydrich himself referred to a "later total solution to the Jewish question" (*späteren Gesamtlösung des Judenproblems*) to be achieved through "sending them off to the country that will be chosen later" (*nach dem zukünftigen Bestimmungslande abzutransportieren*).[261] On February 14, 1941, Bruno Streckenbach also wrote Luther from the RSHA, confirming that a "total evacuation from Europe" was planned "after the conclusion of peace."[262]

That Heydrich had indeed prepared and submitted a plan to Göring is confirmed in a meeting of the two on March 26, 1941. Point 10 of Heydrich's memorandum recording the meeting stated: "Concerning the solution to the Jewish question, I reported briefly to the Reichsmarschall and submitted my draft to him, which he approved with one amendment concerning the jurisdiction of Rosenberg and ordered to be resubmitted."[263] The reference to Rosenberg's jurisdiction—he was soon to be designated the future minister of the occupied Soviet territories—indicates once again that the proverbial territory yet to be determined in regard to the "evacuation" of European Jews was the Soviet Union.[264]

Awareness of Heydrich's plan and especially its timing do not seem to have been widespread, and Hitler's own statements at this time, even in confidential circles, were sufficiently unclear as to be open to conflicting interpretations contingent upon the predisposition and wishful thinking of his listeners. After meetings with Hitler and Frank on March 18, 1941, Goebbels confided to his diary: "Vienna will soon be entirely Jew-free. And now it is Berlin's turn. I am already discussing the question with the Führer and Dr. Frank."[265]

Goebbels wasted no time in pressing the matter. Two days later, on March 20, his deputy Leopold Gutterer met with Eichmann and a representative from Albert Speer. Gutterer told his colleagues of Goebbels's recent "conversation at the lunch table of the Führer." Goebbels had drawn Hitler's attention to the fact that 60,000–70,000 Jews still resided in Berlin. "One gathered from the conversation that it was no longer tolerable that this very day the capital city of the national socialist empire lodged such a large number of Jews. . . . In this conversation *the Führer admittedly did not personally decide* that Berlin had to be made free of Jews immediately, but *Dr. Goebbels was convinced* that an appropriate proposal for evacuation would certainly win the Führer's approval" (italics mine). Eichmann noted that Heydrich, "who is entrusted by the Führer with the final evacuation of the Jews" (*der vom Führer mit der endgültigen Juden-evakuierung beauftragt sei*), had made a proposal to Hitler eight to ten weeks earlier that could not yet be carried out only because the General Government was not in a position at the moment to take a single Jew or Pole "from the Altreich." There was, however, a "written order of the Führer" for the evacuation of 60,000 Jews from Vienna whom the General Government had to accept. But only 45,000 Jews from Vienna were on hand at the moment, so possibly one could remove 15,000 Jews from Berlin. One could not, however, consider working Jews needed for production. Speer's deputy backed Goebbels's position, noting that the Jews used 20,000 apartments in Berlin at a time when the city had a shortage of 160,000–180,000. At the end of the discussion, Eichmann was asked to prepare for Goebbels a proposal for the evacuation of the Jews from Berlin.[266]

Goebbels's interpretation of Hitler's remarks as a signal soliciting immediate evacuation proposals was incorrect, and his hopes for an early evacuation of Berlin were dashed. On March 22 he noted that "the Jews, it turns out, cannot be evacuated from Berlin because 30,000 of them are working in armaments factories."[267] Goebbels sought consolation. "Because the evacuation of Jews from Berlin unfortunately cannot at the moment proceed to the desired degree, Dr. Goebbels has given instructions to prepare a badge for the Jews."[268] On his orders, the Propaganda Ministry pressed the issue, only to learn that a marking proposal from Heydrich was still tied up in negotiations with Göring.[269] Goebbels's marking proposal, like his deportation initiative, remained for the moment without result.

Hans Frank, who had attended the same Hitler luncheon as Goebbels on March 18, came away with a very different impression of Hitler's expectations and intentions. A week later he related his own version to his followers in the General Government. Over the next "several decades" (*einigen Jahrzehnten*) or "15–20 years" the General Government was to be completely Germanized. For the moment the resettlement of Poles and Jews there was to be stopped. Moreover, Hitler had promised that in the future the General Government would be the first territory made *judenfrei*. This would occur "within a reasonable space of time" (*in absehbarer Zeit*).[270] Frank clearly understood this to be a long-term, not a short-term project. In the following month he approved the establishment of a self-sufficient ghetto economy in Warsaw, based on the assumption that the ghetto would still be there in five years. Coincidentally, when Eichmann had used the same expression about "a reasonable space of time" with Lösener the previous December, he too had referred to making Europe *judenfrei* "after the end of the war within the framework of a four- or five-year plan."[271]

If Heydrich was busy drafting and submitting plans in the early months of 1941, what did Himmler think about this? There is an indication that at least in one regard he was somewhat troubled. In early 1941 Himmler approached Viktor Brack of the Führer Chancellery and expressed concern that "through the mixing of blood in the Polish Jews with that of the Jews of western Europe a much greater danger for Germany was arising than even before the war." Such a concern made sense in Himmler's bizarre thinking only if a massive concentration of eastern and western Jewry was actually being envisaged in some area of resettlement. A man privy to an alleged Führer decision to murder all the Jews of Europe in the near future would scarcely have worried about the political and biological implications of offspring who would not reach adulthood for twenty years! Himmler asked Brack, who had been working with the "many scientists and doctors" assembled by Bouhler for the euthanasia program, to investigate the possibility of mass sterilization through X-rays. Brack submitted a preliminary report on March 28, 1941, which the Reichsführer acknowledged positively on May 12.[272] Thereafter, however, Himmler showed no further interest. This could be one hint, given the dearth of other evidence, that at this time Himmler and Hitler, at least in private, began discussing the possibility of solutions even more radical than expulsion and sterilization.

Between the fall of 1939 and the spring of 1941 the Nazis envisaged for their newly won Lebensraum a convulsive population policy based on racial principles. In the minds of Hitler, Himmler, and others, the western portions of Poland were to be annexed to the Third Reich and totally Germanized through the resettlement of ethnic Germans from the Soviet sphere and the expulsion of "harmful" and "undesirable" elements of the population, meaning most Poles and all Jews. Central Poland was to be a vast reservoir of cheap Polish labor— deprived of its present and potential leadership through extensive executions, denationalized by a systematic repression of Polish culture, raided for what the Nazis considered its most valuable biological elements by a process of selection and "Germanization" (*Eindeutschung*) or "re-Germanization" (*Wiedereindeutschung*), and forced to work on German terms by means of a deliberately depressed standard of living. The Jews fit into this scheme only partially. Like the Poles, they had to be removed from German territory, but what then? Unlike Poles, Jews could not be recruited for labor in the Third Reich; Jews could not be subject to selection for Germanization. Jews ultimately had to be separated even from the Polish population and insofar as possible simply "disappear," although so far Himmler rejected the "Bolshevik method of physical extermination of a people out of inner conviction as un-German and impossible." Thus the idea of expelling the Jews first to a special reservation at the easternmost edge of the German sphere (Lublin), then to a "super-ghetto" on the island of Madagascar, finally into the Soviet Union captured the imagination of the Nazis.

If the ultimate inspiration and authority for Nazi racial policy was Hitler, this did not preclude an important role for his subordinates. Hitler proclaimed and legitimized goals and, when he chose, refereed disputes. The initiative for particular actions and the drawing up of plans were usually in the hands of Hitler's close followers—his vassals. It was Heinrich Himmler who, in the euphoria of victory over Poland in mid-September 1939 and again over France in late May 1940, obtained Hitler's approval for the most sweeping plans for the demographic reorganization of eastern Europe along racial lines. It was the Gauleiters, Wagner and perhaps Bürckel in the west, Schirach in Vienna, and Koch in the east, who prevailed upon Hitler to permit the resumption of piecemeal deportations in the fall of 1940. Hitler's open encouragement quickly induced Himmler and Heydrich to plan once again for mass expulsions of Poles and Jews in 1941.

Despite Hitler's support for radical racial policy and his undisguised obsession with the Jewish question, however, the polycratic Nazi system left considerable maneuvering room for his vassals to criticize, modify, or even within limits oppose policies sanctioned by the Führer in the name of other recognized needs and priorities. Hitler's approval allowed policies to be tried but did not make them immune from political reality. Thus Himmler's plans for extensive demographic engineering through massive expulsions proved easier to imagine than to carry out. Nazis like Göring were concerned to maximize rational economic exploitation for the war effort, and Nazis like Frank resisted the limitless dumping of Poles and Jews into the General Government. The need to provide those ethnic Germans repatriated from further east with housing, farms, and businesses required a pragmatic selection of propertied Poles for deportation. As Eichmann told his officials in the Warthegau in June 1940, it made no sense to deport landless agricultural laborers because that made no farms available for incoming ethnic Germans.[273] The same could be said for the Jews, who were already deprived of their property and crowded into miserable ghettos in the Warthegau. Therefore, although the Jews were at the bottom of the Nazis' racial hierarchy, they were relatively ignored in the expulsions that the Nazis actually carried out in this period. Many Jews fled before the Nazi advance in the fall of 1939, and many were either killed or deported in the chaotic terror that followed. Many others fled subsequently, often after they had lost their homes, land, and businesses. About 10,000 Jews were included in the deportations of the first short-range plan of December 1939, 1,000 Jews were deported from Stettin in February 1940, and more than 3,800 from Konin and Poznan that spring. And nearly 24,000 Jews were deported in late 1940 and early 1941 from the incorporated territories, Baden-Saarpflaz, and Vienna. It was clear that this in no way constituted a solution to the Jewish question, however, for this was a pittance in comparison to the hundreds of thousands of Poles, Frenchmen, and ethnic Germans being moved about by the Nazis at this time. Eichmann's attempts to get full-scale Jewish deportations underway in October 1939, January 1940, and again in the summer of 1940 all came to naught. Other priorities and considerations always intervened. The Nazis' self-imposed Jewish problem was proving itself intractable to solution through expulsion.

But the relatively small numbers of Jews deported so far did not mean an open repudiation of the Nazis' avowed ideology. The concept of Lebensraum, as articulated and practiced between late 1939 and early 1941, implied a long-term process of consolidation. On several occasions Hitler remarked that his eastern Gauleiters had ten years to tell him that Germanization of their provinces was complete, and he would ask no questions about their methods.[274] Likewise Hitler told Rosenberg in September 1939 that only time would tell if Germanization would "after decades" expand beyond the incorporated territories. Himmler's concept that a land belonged to the German people only when every last tiller of the soil was German also implied years, even generations, of consolidation. The removal of ethnic Germans from the General Government to the Warthegau, especially the Cholmer Aktion in the last half of 1940, shows that Himmler's resettlement schemes of 1939–40 were undertaken in their own right, not just as improvised rescue operations, and that he was not yet thinking beyond racial consolidation in the incorporated territories.

In such a time frame the Nazis could keep faith with their anti-Semitic principles by planning to eventually expel the Jews to Lublin, Madagascar, or the Soviet Union while temporarily conceding priority to the need to rescue and resettle endangered ethnic Germans, though not without rising frustration among the zealots. The Jewish question was just as important, though temporarily not as urgent, as the resettlement of ethnic Germans.

The decision to invade the Soviet Union, however, would put the concepts of Lebensraum and racial policy in a different light. Driven on by his own fervent anti-Bolshevism, his vision of Soviet territory as the fated land of German

Expulsions	Dates	Total No.	Jews
"Wild deportations" over the San and Bug	Sept. 1939	20,000	20,000
"Wild deportations" from West Prussia	Sept. 1939–Jan. 1940	87,000	?
Nisko	Oct. 1939	5,035	5,035
1. *Nahplan*	Dec. 1939	87,833	10,000
Stettin (Szczecin)	Feb. 12, 1940	1,100	1,100
Zwischenplan	Feb. 10–Mar. 15, 1940	40,128	1,200
2. *Nahplan*			
Volhynian Aktion	May 1940–Jan. 1941	91,956	2,663
Cholmer Aktion	Sept.–Dec. 1940	28,365	none
Saybuscher Aktion	Sept.–Dec. 1940	17,413	none
Mlawa Aktion	Oct. 10–20, 1940	10,700	1,000
Litauer Aktion	Dec. 5–17, 1940	9,766	3,259
Alsace	July–Dec. 1940	23,790	3,255
Lorraine	July–Dec. 1940	47,187	?
Baden-Saarpfalz	Oct. 22–23, 1940	6,504	6,504
Luxembourg	Nov. 1940–April 1941	280	280
3. *Nahplan*			
Warthegau	Jan.–Mar. 1941	19,226	2,140
Vienna	Feb. 15–Mar. 12, 1941	5,000	5,000
Danzig–West Prussia	Mar. 1941	2,000	2,000
Totals		503,000	At least 63,000 (approx. 12.5%)

expansion, his increasing sense of himself as a man of destiny who must accomplish everything in his own lifetime, his frustration with the military stalemate in the west, and the pervasive and ceaseless activism that possessed his own psyche as well as the Nazi movement, Hitler opted for Barbarossa. This had an intensely radicalizing effect. The ideology of Lebensraum put into practice between 1939 and 1941 was a policy of gradual racial consolidation, a policy quite radical in its methods but less so in its foreign policy implications. The invasion of the Soviet Union transformed Lebensraum from the practice of gradual racial consolidation into one of limitless expansion.

The Nazi view of the Jewish question could not help but be radicalized as well, on both practical and ideological grounds. Limitless expansion into the Soviet Union meant ever more Jews. A problem that had proved intractable even in the Old Reich, incorporated territories, and General Government threatened to reach immense proportions with the addition of Belorussia, the Ukraine, the Baltic, and beyond. The whole sequence of thwarted expulsion plans between 1939 and 1941 had both accustomed the Nazis to thinking in terms of an imminent final solution to the Jewish question and frustrated them as, like a mirage, this vision of a *judenfrei* German empire continually receded before their advance. The time was ripe to break the vicious circle, to ensure that further gains in territory did not mean an increasing burden of Jews. Murder was in the air as the Germans prepared for a *Vernichtungskrieg* or "war of destruction" against the Soviet Union, and in these circumstances the Soviet Jews could hardly be spared the fate awaiting so many others.

This tendency was intensified by the fundamental position of the Jewish-Bolshevik identity in Nazi ideology. When the Nazis invaded Poland in September 1939, the fate of the Polish Jews could wait but the fate of the Polish intelligentsia could not. Even before Hitler's and Himmler's vision of vast demographic upheaval emerged in the euphoria of victory, the Einsatzgruppen had been targeted to carry out the immediate genocidal elimination of all potential carriers of the Polish national ideal. As the Nazis prepared to confront communism in 1941, neither the Soviet commissars nor Soviet Jews could wait; both would have to be eliminated by the onrushing Einsatzgruppen, for ultimately they were perceived as one—the political and biological manifestations of the same Jewish-Bolshevik menace. Insofar as the Nazi solution to the Jewish question was concerned, the era of expulsion ended when military preparations for Barbarossa brought the last evacuation transports in Poland to a halt in mid-March 1941. The era of mass murder was about to begin.

4

The Polish Ghettos

GHETTOIZATION

The starting point of Nazi Jewish policy in eastern Europe had been Heydrich's September 21 conference with the Einsatzgruppen leaders. On that occasion Heydrich had stipulated the immediate (within three to four weeks) concentration of Jews "in ghettos" in cities in order to facilitate "a better possibility of control and later deportation."[1] Heydrich's following *Schnellbrief* stipulated precisely the setting up of councils of "Jewish Elders"—composed of 24 males in each community—to be "fully responsible in the literal sense of the word" for the execution of German orders. By the late 1930s the Germans had learned the virtues (from their point of view) and techniques of operating through Jewish leaders at once recognized by the Jewish community and imposed and manipulated by the Germans. This was not a lesson that had to be relearned in Poland, since Heydrich ensured that it would be a cornerstone of Nazi Jewish policy there from the beginning. Aside from this, however, Heydrich was vague about the nature and organization of Jewish life in the cities. He noted that the "concentrations of Jews in the cities for general reasons of security will probably bring about orders forbidding Jews from entering certain quarters of the cities altogether, and that—in view of economic necessity—they cannot for instance leave the ghetto, they cannot go out after designated hours, etc." But these were suggestions, not explicit orders. "Obviously the tasks at hand cannot be laid down in detail from here," he conceded in a statement that would hold true not only for ghettoization but for many other future measures of Nazi Jewish policy.[2]

The concentration of Jews in the cities was not accomplished within Heydrich's three-to-four-week time frame. Brauchitsch's opposition had led Heydrich on September 30 to inform his Einsatzgruppen leaders that the timing of concentration was dependent upon not disturbing military interests.[3] In terms of Nazi intentions at that time, even more serious was the nearly complete frustration of the subsequent deportation of Jews to Lublin or Madagascar.

GENERAL GOVERNMENT (1939–1942)

Governor General: Hans Frank
HSSPF: Friedrich Wilhelm Krüger
Bds Bruno Streckenbach (Oct. 1939–Mar. 1940)
     Eberhard Schöngarth (Mar. 1940–July 1943)

Main Offices
Interior: Eberhard Westerkamp (Oct. 1940–Jan. 1942)
Food and Agriculture: Hellmut Körner (Oct. 1939–July 1941)
                      Karl Naumann (July 1941–)
Labor: Max Frauendorfer (Nov. 1939–Sept. 1940)
Economy: Walter Emmerich (June 1940–)
Population and Welfare: Friedrich Arlt (Oct. 1939–Sept. 1940)
                       Lothar Weirauch (Sept. 1940–)

District Offices:
CRACOW
District Governor: Otto Wächter (Nov. 1939–Jan. 1942)
SSPF: Julian Scherner

LUBLIN
District Governor: Friedrich Schmidt (Oct. 1939–Jan. 1940)
                   Ernst Zörner (Feb. 1940–Apr. 1943)
SSPF: Odilo Globocnik (Nov. 1939–Sept. 1943)

WARSAW
District Governor: Ludwig Fischer (Oct. 1939–)
SSPF: Paul Moder (–Aug. 1941)
      Arpad Wigand (Aug. 1941–June 1942)

RADOM
District Governor: Karl Lasch (Oct. 1939–Aug. 1941)
                   Ernst Kundt (Aug. 1941–)
SSPF: Friedrich Katzmann (Nov. 1939–July 1941)
      Carl Albrecht Oberg (July 1941–Mar. 1942)

GALICIA
District Governor: Karl Lasch (Aug. 1941–Jan. 1942)
                   Otto Wächter (Jan. 1942–)
SSPF: Friedrich Katzmann (July 1941–)

Jewish urban ghettos, intended as temporary way stations on the road to complete deportation, now became a factor with which local German authorities unexpectedly had to cope on a long-term basis. Little guidance came from Berlin, which continued to dream of deportation plans and was reluctant to confess that its schemes were not viable and that the Jews had become "stuck." Local authorities in the General Government and the incorporated territories were thus left to fend for themselves. In this light, ghettoization policy as practiced in Poland in 1940 and 1941 would be the direct result, not of Heydrich's Schnellbrief of September 21 ordering the concentration of Jews in cities, but rather of the Germans' failure to carry out the subsequent deportations envisaged therein.

If an idea of ghettoization was present from the beginning, just how and when the idea was to be given concrete form varied greatly. The need to deal with the problems caused by uprooting and concentrating the Jews; the desire to plunder Jewish property and exploit Jewish labor; the need to find housing for the influx of German officials, businessmen, military personnel, and Volksdeutsche into the same cities in which the Jews had been concentrated; and the parameters set by ideology were everywhere approximately the same.[4] Nevertheless, a policy that took all these considerations into account, especially given the lack of clear guidelines from above, was never a matter of unanimity among the local German authorities.

At the core of the dispute over ghetto policy was a split between "attritionists" and "productionists." The former saw the decline, indeed even the "dying out," of the Jewish population as the desired goal. For them the ghettos were vast concentration camps facilitating the total extraction of Jewish wealth through the leverage of deliberate starvation. In contrast, the "productionists" viewed their task, at least until that future point when the Jews were finally taken away, as the minimization of the burden of the ghettoized Jews on the Reich through the maximization of their economic potential. For them the ghettos were potential economic units whose labor could be rationally organized to make them self-sufficient or, even better, able to contribute to the German war economy. In this policy dispute the "productionists" gradually prevailed over the "attritionists" until Berlin intervened in favor not just of attrition but of immediate and systematic mass murder. But that comes later. The previous chapter dealt with what the Nazis wanted to do to solve the Jewish question between the invasion of Poland and Barbarossa. This chapter examines what they actually did in the conquered Polish territories.

Lodz

Ghettoization came first to the Warthegau, but even there only with great reluctance, after the deportation of the Jews of Lodz—a much more popular policy with the local German authorities—proved impossible. As early as September 20, 1939, the chief of staff of Blaskowitz's 8th Army, Hans Felber, anticipated Heydrich and assumed that the Lodz Jews—whom he deemed "a dreadful rabble. Filthy and crafty" (*Ein entsetzliches Pack. Dreckig und verschlagen*)—would be deported.[5] A month later Frank wanted to deport 50,000 Jews from the city, but this was considered unfeasible by the army.[6] After the military administration in Poland was dismantled and actual planning for the deportation was underway in November 1939, Frank's HSSPF Krüger decided that until the final allocation of Lodz to either the Warthegau or the General Government, no evacuations—"even of Jews"—would be undertaken from there.[7]

Faced with this delay in the deportation of the Lodz Jews, Greiser decided to ghettoize. "They [the Jews] have hoarded colossally," he claimed. They would remain in the ghettos "until what they have amassed is given back in exchange for food and then they will be expelled over the border." (*Sie haben ungeheuer gehamstert. . . . bis das von ihnen Zusammengeraffte im Austauschverfahren gegen Lebensmittel zurückgegeben ist und dann werden sie über die Grenze abgeschoben.*)[8]

On December 10 Greiser's Regierungspräsident for the district of Kalisch and Lodz, Friedrich Uebelhoer, conceded that the "immediate evacuation" of the Lodz Jews (whose number he grossly overestimated at 320,000) was not possible. He ordered that the Jewish question in Lodz be solved "temporarily" through the concentration of all Jews in a "closed ghetto." Since existing proposals for a ghetto were inadequate, Uebelhoer formed a special working staff of representatives from his office, the party, the Order and Security Police, the local Totenkopf ss unit, the Chamber of Industry and Trade, the Finance Office, and the housing, construction, health, and food offices of the city administration, and charged it with drawing up a plan for a ghetto in the northern part of the city, where most of the Jews lived.[9]

According to Uebelhoer, many questions had to be decided: the boundaries of the ghetto, the resettlement of Poles and Germans living there, the shifting of traffic patterns, the plans and materials for sealing and guarding the ghetto, the measures to combat epidemics, preparations for sewage removal and disposal of corpses, and the procurement of provisions for feeding and heating. Only when all these preparations had been made and sufficient manpower was on hand would Uebelhoer order the "sudden" creation of the ghetto. At a set hour the guards would take up positions along the predetermined boundary, and construction of the barriers would begin. Immediately thereafter the Jews living outside the ghetto boundary would be dealt with by the Order and Security police. Those capable of work would be placed in labor barracks, and those not capable of work would be shoved into the ghetto. Provisioning would take place through the food office of the city administration, but only in return for the valuables that Uebelhoer assumed the Jews were hoarding. Internal governance of the ghetto would be in the hands of the head of the Jewish council, who would establish departments for food, health, finance, housing, registration, and security. The last of these duties was to be performed by a Jewish police or *Ordnungsdienst*.[10] Planning along these lines continued through January 1940. Creation of the ghetto was finally decreed on February 8, and it was sealed as of April 30.[11]

The creation of the Lodz ghetto had a major impact. Not only was it the first major ghetto in the German empire, but it became the model to be studied before the creation of other ghettos. Although the Lodz plan was often modified to suit the tastes of local German authorities, the basic features of its parallel German and Jewish bureaucracies (and police) reappeared again and again. The Lodz ghetto was even destined to become "a 'tourist attraction' that never failed to excite the most lively interest of visitors from the Old Reich" (*eine "Sehenswürdigkeit," die dann immer wieder das lebhafte Interesse der Besucher aus dem Altreich hervorrief*).[12] Ghettoization of the remaining Jewish communities in the Warthegau followed in the spring and early summer of 1940.[13]

The number of Jews trapped inside the sealed ghetto turned out to be far lower than Uebelhoer's original estimate. The Statistical Office of Lodz retroactively estimated 219,860 Jews in the city as of January 1, 1940. By the beginning of May, when the ghetto was sealed, it estimated only 162,000.[14] This represented a net decline of over 57,000 Jews. Where these Jews went is not clear from the German records. Upon the announcement of the ghetto, many Jews scattered to the countryside within the Warthegau. In March, for instance, a *Judenrazzia* in the town of Hinterberg in the northern Warthegau uncovered many Jews from Lodz and other cities who were staying with friends and relatives and had not registered with the police.[15] Some may have been smuggled into the deportations of the "intermediate plan" of February and March. Since voluntary departure for the General Government, prodded by the confiscation of homes and businesses, was possible until the ghetto was sealed, most of the Jews who left Lodz probably took this course. Certainly the authorities of the General Government in the area bordering Lodz complained about "illegal Jewish evacuations and unauthorized border crossings." Flooded by "this illegal Jewish immigration," the Kreishauptmann across the border constructed ghettos in Lowicz and Glowno to control the influx.[16] The Polish historian

Czeslaw Madajczyk estimates that the Jewish population of the Warthegau dropped from 385,000 to 263,000 between September 1939 and February 1940 and to 247,000 by September 1940. Yehuda Bauer has documented a drop in the Jewish population of all the incorporated territories from 692,000 to 460,000 over this period.[17] Clearly much movement was taking place that was not recorded in the tidy statistics of the Umwandererzentralen in Poznan and Lodz or in Eichmann's office in Berlin.

The sharp decline in the Jewish population of Lodz in these months was of little consolation to Gauleiter Greiser or Uebelhoer. The latter had been adamant from the start that the ghetto would not be permanent. He had declared in December 1939: "The creation of the ghetto is of course only a transition measure. I shall determine at what time and with what means the ghetto and thereby also the city of Lodz will be cleansed of Jews. The final goal in any case must be that we burn out this plague-boil." (*Die Einstellung des Gettos ist selbstverständlich nur eine Übergangsmassnahme. Zu welchen Zeitpunkten und mit welchen Mitteln das Getto und damit die Stadt Lodsch von Juden gesäubert wird, behalte ich mir vor. Endziel muss jedenfalls sein, dass wir diese Pestbeule restlos ausbrennen.*)[18] In fact, however, Greiser and Uebelhoer were not free to eliminate the ghetto when they chose. Greiser's attempt to have the deportation of Lodz Jews exempted from Göring's order of March 23, 1940—which stopped any Jewish emigration to the General Government until the resettlement of the Volhynian Germans was complete—failed totally.[19] And in late July Greiser was almost frantic when the Madagascar Plan once again postponed the elimination of the Lodz ghetto until a satisfactory conclusion of the war with England, but his protests were once again in vain.[20]

While awaiting the imminent deportation of the Lodz Jews, the German authorities only gradually faced up to the unwelcome reality that the ghetto was not going to disappear quickly. Until the ghetto was sealed on April 30, 1940, the Germans had undertaken no provisioning of the Jewish population, although they were aware that the food supplies within the ghetto would not last long.[21] Indeed, the whole point of the ghetto was to force the Jews to disgorge their "hoarded wealth" in exchange for food.

The Germans also displayed little interest in exploiting the Jewish labor force, for it was thought that the full employment of Jewish skilled workers would require more raw materials than were available and would impede the development of the textile industry for which Lodz was famous. In early April when the head of the Jewish council, Chaim Rumkowski, proposed to the Lodz mayor, Dr. Karl Marder, that he be empowered to organize ghetto labor and production in order to purchase food for the poor Jews in the ghetto, Marder granted him the right to impose forced labor. Rumkowski was also asked to submit lists of the work skills and machines available in the ghetto. But the Germans did not expect that Jewish labor would contribute more than 15% of the ghetto's food costs.[22]

The emphasis continued to remain on extraction rather than production at a conference of Lodz city officials held on May 27, 1940. Marder admitted that money would soon have to be found to finance food purchases for the ghetto. The city authorities calculated that they could secure the necessary funds from four sources: (1) the extraction of all currency from the ghetto, (2) the sale of goods produced by skilled Jewish labor, especially textile workers, within the ghetto, (3) the providing of unskilled Jewish labor for construction work in the city, and (4) "in the future" the sale of goods held in the storehouses of the Litzmannstädter Warenhandelsgesellschaft (LWHG or Lodz Commodity Trading Company, a subsidiary of the Lodz branch of the Haupttreuhandstelle Ost, HTO, or Main Trusteeship Office East) which had been formed in December 1939 as a receiving company for textiles and other goods confiscated from Jewish businesses). The conference participants felt that at best Jewish skilled labor could earn 15,000 RM daily, a small amount of the total needed. Calculating that roughly 5 million RM were still in the ghetto, and that 100,000 RM would be needed per day in June, increasing to 200,000 RM per day in July, the Germans could forecast that an economic crisis requiring financing from the LWHG would occur by the end of July.[23] This looming crisis did not alarm them, however, because they expected the Jews to be deported in August. Thus the business arrangement finalized in early June, whereby the LWHG supplied raw materials to the ghetto and took over the finished textile products for sale, with 70% of the proceeds deposited in an account for purchasing food for the ghetto, was still just a stopgap measure, not a major change in ghetto policy.[24]

By July differences among the German authorities over financing and feeding the ghetto began to emerge. The head of the section within the Food Supply and Economic Office of the city government who had been made responsible for managing ghetto affairs was a 38-year-old businessman from Bremen named Hans Biebow. A party member since 1937, he had made his fortune in the coffee import business before taking up his administrative duties in Lodz in May 1940.[25] In July he was still insisting that food purchases for the ghetto could only be made from surplus stocks, thus in no way endangering the provisioning of the city. But he was aware of the potential crisis looming. In his monthly report he noted that Rumkowski, who was fulfilling his tasks "quickly and reliably," was trying to secure the employment of as many Jews as possible. According to Rumkowski, the money for purchasing food was drying up and poverty was increasing rapidly. "To what extent one can believe him," Biebow wrote, "the month of August will prove."[26]

But if Biebow awaited events, one of his staff, Alexander Palfinger, was already articulating suspicions of Rumkowski's attempt to increase Jewish employment. In Palfinger's view the Jews still possessed large amounts of precious metals and other valuables. "Given the mentality of the Jews," it was quite certain that they would surrender such highly valued reserves only in a time of the "most extreme exigency" (*allergrösster Not*). Only when the Jews were convinced that labor could not supply their needs would they part with these valuables, he concluded.[27]

In early September Biebow moved closer to Rumkowski's view. The impoverishment of the Jews had increased considerably in August. Fully 70% of the population had no means to buy food and were dependent upon the community. By the end of August, however, food deliveries to the ghetto had stopped because the community itself had no more money to purchase the supplies of food already available in the German stockpile.[28]

Another source of anxiety for Biebow was Gauleiter Greiser's attempt to take for himself the income of the working Jews now that he had been unable to deport the ghetto inhabitants to the General Government in August as previously planned. Immediately upon returning from his meeting with Frank at the end of July where he had unsuccessfully sought an "interim solution" for the Lodz Jews while awaiting realization of the Madagascar Plan, the Gauleiter ordered that all wages above 10 pfennigs per hour for Jewish laborers working for private firms were to be transferred to his own "reconstruction account of the NSDAP." The Lodz mayor, Dr. Marder, protested vigorously. The Jews of Lodz were already working on projects important to the war economy, and Marder was of the opinion that in view of the overall shortage of labor the question of mobilizing Jewish manpower was becoming paramount. Yet the new order of the Gauleiter would have the effect of depriving the Jews of any incentive to work. It was the mayor's aim to ensure that the Jews were provided for out of their own efforts and not through public means. It might seem to make no difference ultimately whether Jews were provided for by wages for their own labor or by subsidies from the HTO, but only the former provided the incentive for them to strive for self-financing. After some negotiations, and faced with increasing emphasis on the imminent prospect of needing HTO funds to subsidize the ghetto, the Gau authorities finally agreed to permit 35% of Jewish wages to be retained by the workers, while Greiser's special account received the remaining 65%.[29]

By early October the situation was obvious to Biebow. The cessation of food deliveries for some days in September had produced no outpouring of hoarded valuables from the ghetto. He had to ask Regierungspräsident Uebelhoer to provide funds for further food deliveries.[30] Although every effort had to be made "to facilitate the self-maintenance of the Jews through finding them work" (*durch Arbeitsbeschaffung die Selbsterhaltung der Juden zu förden*), this would be impossible without "continuous and initially high subsidies" because the "large-scale employment of Jewish labor" required considerable lead time to procure contracts and erect factories. Weeks would pass before the anticipated income would secure the provisioning needs of the Jews. In the meantime stockpiling for the winter could not be put off any longer, and the 4 to 5 million RM needed for this were simply not available from the Jews. Subsidies were therefore needed "as quickly as possible."[31]

Biebow did not get all the financing he wanted. He had been led to believe that the LWHG, funded by looted Jewish property, would provide a subsidy when it was needed. Instead, the LWHG offered a six-month loan of only 3 million RM at 4½% interest, which Rumkowski and the Jewish council signed for and were obligated to repay. When Biebow doubted the Jews' ability to repay the loan and suggested that the interest payment be treated as a "pro forma" matter, he encountered great astonishment. After all, he was told, it was a matter of "public money."[32] Nevertheless, the loan represented a turning point in German policy. The ghetto was no longer a temporary device for extracting Jewish wealth before deportation. It was now a more permanent institution in whose economic productivity the Germans had a vested interest.

The fateful change of perspective was finally articulated and officially approved at a meeting on October 18, 1940, where "it was established at the outset that the ghetto in Lodz must continue to exist and everything must be done to make the ghetto self-sustaining." (*Es wurde eingangs festgestellt, dass das Getto in Litzmannstadt weiter bestehen müsse und alle Kräfte in Bewegung gesestzt werden müssten, um das Getto aus sich heraus selbst zu erhalten.*) Biebow's office, now renamed the Getto Verwaltung or ghetto administration, was made directly subordinate to the mayor and placed in charge of coordinating the mobilization of Jewish labor throughout the entire district. Its task was to obtain from its labor contracts the "greatest possible surplus" which would be used to maintain the ghetto.[33]

Not everyone was reconciled to this basic change in German ghetto policy, however. To Alexander Palfinger, Biebow's sullen deputy, the very idea of a self-sustaining ghetto bordered on heresy. For Palfinger, "especially in the Jewish question the National Socialist idea . . . permits no compromise" (*speziell in der Judenfrage die nationalsozialistische Idee . . . keine Kompromise erlaubt*). To seek a solution to the problem purely through a "salesmanlike negotiating ability" (*kaufmännischen Verhandlungsfähigkeit*) was to forgo a real solution to the ghetto problem. Palfinger's desires ran along different lines. "The rapid dying out of the Jews is for us a matter of total indifference, if not to say desirable, as long as the concomitant effects leave the public interest of the German people untouched; inasmuch, however, as these people in accordance with the instructions of the Reichsführer-SS are to be made to serve the state interest, the most primitive conditions for this must be created." (*Völlig gleichgültig, um nicht zu sagen wünschenswert, ist uns das rasche Absterben der Juden insolange als die Begleitererscheinungen das öffentliche Interesse des deutschen Volkes unberührt lassen; sofern jedoch weisungsgemäss (Reichsführer SS) dieses Volk staatlichen Interessen dienstbar zu machen ist, müssen die primitivsten Voraussetzungen hierzu geschaffen werden.*)[34]

However, the pragmatic views of the mayor of Lodz, Dr. Karl Marder, and his handpicked ghetto manager, Hans Biebow, stood in sharp contrast to Palfinger's desire for murderous attrition. Ghetto policy would now develop in a very different direction. As Marder later explained, as long as the ghetto was a "transition measure" not intended to last the year, the major task of the ghetto administration had been the "drawing off of the wealth of the ghetto inhabitants in order to supply their necessities of life." Now the character of the ghetto had to be "fundamentally altered." It was no longer to be "nothing more than a kind of holding or concentration camp" but rather an "essential element of the total economy . . . a one-of-its-kind large-scale enterprise [*ein Grossbetrieb sui generis*]."[35]

Having conducted the first large-scale experiment in ghettoization because the Jews had not been deported in 1939, the Germans in Lodz now prepared to conduct the first large-scale experiment in creating a ghetto economy because the Jews had likewise not been deported in 1940. Neither development was planned or desired in its own right but was a response to the need to do something about the Lodz Jews short of having them die out on the spot.

The odious Palfinger was still the exception, not the rule. Bilked of a "rapid dying out of the Jews" and frustrated by the appointment over his head of the Johnny-come-lately businessman Biebow and, even worse, Biebow's assistant Friedrich Wilhelm Ribbe, while he considered himself to be the real architect of the ghetto administration, Palfinger left for Warsaw to see if he could get his way there.[36] His parting gesture, an obvious ploy to draw attention to what he considered the intolerable coddling of Jews in Lodz, was an attempt to order 144,000 eggs per week for the ghetto, first from Poznan and then from Berlin. The embarrassed Biebow and Ribbe were left to explain that the request had been made without their knowledge.[37]

Warsaw

While the ghettoization of the Lodz Jews proceeded from a single initiative of Greiser's and was carried out under Uebelhoer's supervision in one continuous action, ghettoization in Warsaw proceeded in fits and starts. The ghetto was not sealed until November 1940, and a reorganization of the ghetto administration for the purpose of economic self-sustenance did not occur until May 1941. Warsaw was, in short, more than a half-year behind the pace set in Lodz. Even more clearly than in Lodz, the course of events in Warsaw illustrates the lack of central and long-term planning and the resulting improvised nature of German ghettoization policy.

On November 4, 1939, Standartenführer Dr. Rudolph Batz ordered the Warsaw Jewish council, in the name of the military commandant, General Neumann-Neurode, to concentrate the Jews into certain blocks of the city within three days. But the following day a delegation from the Jewish council approached the general, who knew nothing of the order and told them to wait for written confirmation. Two weeks later the leader of the council, Adam Czerniakow, recorded with relief that the ghetto had been postponed for several months.[38] Instead of a ghetto, the army ordered the formation of a "quarantine area" (*Seuchengebiet*) in the predominantly Jewish section of the city. It was off-limits to Germans, but Poles and Volksdeutsche could live there, and Jews could still live and work elsewhere.[39] Ironically, just as the ss initiative to set ghettoization in motion failed, Dr. Ludwig Fischer, governor of the Warsaw district, was securing Frank's approval for "a special ghetto" in the former Polish capital.[40]

In the next months rumors of both deportation and ghettoization circulated among the Warsaw Jews.[41] Concrete preparations for the latter resumed after the turn of the year when Fischer appointed Waldemar Schön to head a newly formed Resettlement Division within his district government. Schön was a 36-year-old government and party official who had joined the NSDAP and SA in 1930.[42] The first idea he worked up was for a Jewish ghetto on the east bank of the Vistula across the river from Warsaw. This short-lived plan was rejected at a meeting on March 8, 1940, when it encountered stiff opposition from city officials. Such a ghetto would disrupt the economy, since 80% of the city's craftsmen were Jews. Moreover, it would not be possible to feed the Jews in such a closed ghetto, they protested.[43]

As in Lodz, the Warsaw planners then grasped at the idea of solving their Jewish question through deportation and cast their eyes on the Lublin district as a "catch basin" (*Sammelbecken*) for all the Jews of the General Government. However, in April HSSPF Krüger disabused them of the notion that deportation to Lublin was a viable solution.[44] In the meantime two top health officials—SA-

Oberführer Dr. Jost Walbaum of the General Government and Dr. Kaminski of the Warsaw district—successfully pressed for the erection of walls around the quarantine area.[45] The walls were to be built and paid for by the Jews. "A ghetto in spite of everything," Czerniakow concluded.[46]

But the Germans were not satisfied, and ghetto planning continued with the goal of completing resettlement within its boundaries before winter. This time Schön came up with the idea of two suburban ghettos—Kolo and Wola to the west and Grochow to the east—that would disrupt neither the economy nor city traffic.[47] This effort received impetus from a major economic conference in the General Government on June 6–7, 1940. In order to ensure reliable registration and rational use of Jewish forced labor, the conference concluded that "it was necessary that the nomadicized Jews be settled in cities" (*wäre es notwendig, dass die nomadisierenden Juden in Städten sesshaft würden*). Thus in all cities measures were to be taken to erect work camps, concentration camps, and ghettos "so that the Jews cannot move about freely."[48] This was as close as it ever came to a uniform policy for ghettoization in the General Government. However, this decision was almost immediately nullified the next month, when Cracow ordered a halt to all ghetto building, which was now considered to be "for all practical purposes illusory" in view of the impending deportation of Europe's Jews to Madagascar.[49]

In the end it was not Schön and the Resettlement Division but doctors whose intervention proved decisive in tipping the scales in favor of a sealed ghetto. In Warsaw the newly arrived Dr. Lambrecht, head of Fischer's Health Division, looked at the epidemic statistics and concluded "with absolute certainty" that spotted fever or typhus would spread throughout the district that winter. He concluded that ghettoization was urgent for the protection of the increasing troop concentrations in the area. Fischer's Division for Internal Administration backed the Health Division and lamented that "until now clearly no unified treatment of the Jewish problem has been established in Cracow."[50] On September 6 SA-Oberführer Dr. Walbaum personally gave Frank a statistical overview of the epidemic problem and pressed for an immediate ghettoization in Warsaw. On September 12 Frank approved a sealed ghetto there, "above all because it is established that the danger from the 500,000 Jews is so great that the possibility of the roving about of these Jews must be prevented."[51]

Because the Germans felt that it was urgent to complete the ghettoization before winter and Schön's suburban dual ghetto plan would have required four to five months to realize, they agreed to form the ghetto in the quarantine area, where most of the Jews already lived and some walls had already been constructed. The concentration of Jews in this area had been steadily increasing, for all incoming Jews as well as all Jews giving up apartments elsewhere in the city had since August been allowed to take up residence only in the quarantine area.[52] Schön's Resettlement Division was entrusted with the task of implementation. At the same time, other towns in the district were also to construct ghettos.[53]

In Lodz the Germans had justified ghettoization quite simply as a means of extracting—in exchange for food—the last wealth of the Jews before deportation. In Warsaw deportation was not imminent, and the Germans elaborated a more complex series of justifications. The urgent recommendation of German medical personnel to seal off the Jews as a necessary measure to prevent the spread of epidemics had been the actual occasion for the decision in late summer 1940, and it was cited by both Schön and the district governor, Fischer, as a major factor. They also noted as motives the desirability of removing Jewish political, moral, and cultural influence on life in Poland, and ending Jewish black-marketeering and price speculation.[54] After the fact, two further benefits of ghettoization were claimed. One was aesthetic: the "Jewish imprint" (*jüdische Gepräge*) had disappeared from Warsaw, which now "displayed clean streets."[55] The other was practical: ghettoization had allowed all the above to be achieved with a relatively small claim on German supervisory personnel.[56]

Whatever the particular reasons of the moment, ghettoization was fully consonant with the basic assumptions and long-term goals of Nazi Jewish policy, which aimed at a total removal of the Jews from the German sphere. In Lodz ghettoization had been intended as a transition, a temporary, ad hoc measure in preparation for deportation, but deportation was subsequently canceled. In Warsaw ghettoization was to a degree a conscious substitute for a no-longer-imminent deportation. As a later German commissioner of the ghetto, Heinz Auerswald, wrote, "Decisive for it [ghettoization] was first of all the desire to segregate the Jews from the Aryan environment for general political and ideological reasons." (*Massgebend dafür war in erster Linie der Wunsch, die Juden aus allgemeinen politischen und weltanschaulichen Gründen von der arischen Umwelt abzusondern.*)[57] But the Germans in Warsaw were no more willing than those in Lodz to admit that this was a permanent solution. There was a basic activist drive among some of the Nazis to give witness to the fact that they were not stuck, that the Jewish problem was not beyond solution, and that ghettoization was still a way station to a final solution. As Waldemar Schön concluded: "We want to show the world that in the framework of our colonial work, we are able to cope with the Jewish problem even when it emerges as a problem of masses. The parasite of all peoples is in spite of everything being made useful to the human community in a new-found way. The development of the Jewish district in Warsaw represents in practice a preliminary step to the exploitation of Jewish labor in Madagascar planned by the Führer."[58]

Two major problems faced the Germans in setting up the Warsaw ghetto: to learn the techniques of ghetto management and to decide on final boundaries. The first was done by consciously drawing on the experience of others. In early September the head of the Lodz Jewish council, Chaim Rumkowski, was brought to Warsaw, and in mid-September a number of officials traveled from Warsaw to Lodz.[59] The head of Kreis Lowicz, Heinrich Werner Schwender, also reported on the ghetto he had set up in May 1940 in response to the influx of Jews from the Warthegau that spring. Above all he emphasized the benefits of working through the Jewish council and its police or *Ordnungsdienst*. In Lowicz the latter were equipped with riding whips, and the Germans had succeeded in controlling the Jewish element and imposing forced labor with practically no supervisory personnel.[60]

As the Germans gathered their information, they were besieged with requests to keep various buildings and areas outside the ghetto walls. The German authorities tried to fulfill as many of these requests as possible, and the result was a steady reduction in the size of the ghetto.[61] Between early October and mid-November, 113,000 Poles and 138,000 Jews were moved in a massive population exchange. But the exchange was by no means equal, as 30% of the population was crowded into 2.4% of the city's territory.[62] By the Germans' own statistics, the ghetto had a population density eight times the city average.[63] This situation was made even more catastrophic in early 1941, when between January and March the Germans moved all the Jews in the district of Warsaw west of the Vistula into the ghetto to make room for the evacuation of Poles expected from the incorporated territories as part of the third short-range plan. With this influx of an additional 66,000 Jews, the total population of the Warsaw ghetto reached its maximum of 445,000, of which 130,000 were refugees from outside the city.[64] In Warsaw the Nazis had created a ghetto nearly three times the population of the one in Lodz, and together the two ghettos contained nearly one-third of all Polish Jews under Nazi control.

The creation of a sealed ghetto, cutting the Jews off from employment and business on the outside, required a restructuring of their economic position. Schön established a Transferstelle or transfer station, which began to function in December 1940, to act as the economic intermediary between the incarcerated Jews and the outside world. The job of the Transferstelle was to provide food and raw materials to the ghetto and to negotiate contracts with the outside on its behalf. The food and supplies were to be paid for by the goods that the ghetto produced, and the Transferstelle was the sole judge in assessing the value of the Jewish goods delivered to it. The Transferstelle was thus in the position either to stimulate and encourage the economic activity of the ghetto, making it a contributor to the German war economy, or to strangle its economic activity and starve its inhabitants.

That Schön's inclinations tended toward the latter can be seen by two factors. The first was his appointment of none other than Alexander Palfinger, the disgruntled former official of the Lodz ghetto administration, to the head of the Transferstelle. Palfinger had never hidden his attitude toward the Jews. As the ghetto historian Emanuel Ringelblum noted, "The director of the Transferstelle makes it a practice not to talk to Jews. There are dignitaries like that, who won't see a Jew to talk with as a matter of principle. They order the windows of the Transferstelle kept open because of the stench the Jews make."[65] The second indication of Schön's attitude was his own description of the Transferstelle's purposes and tasks. On the one hand, it was to contribute to the war effort by extracting foreign exchange from the ghetto and by fulfilling outside contracts, especially for the military. On the other hand, it was to preside over both the extraction of necessities of life "hidden" in the ghetto and the "effective and continuous exploitation of the labor and economic potential of the Jews for maintaining the Jewish district until the complete liquidation of Jewish property at the time of the evacuation to Madagascar." The Transferstelle had to tread a thin line between maximized exploitation and extraction on the one hand and what Schön termed "premature impoverishment" (vorzeitiges Verarmen) on the other.[66] Given the prevailing attitude, it is not surprising that Schön and Palfinger erred considerably on the side of "premature impoverishment."

Schön systematically ignored the catastrophic economic consequences of ghettoization. In contrast to the district's situation report to Cracow, which emphasized the massive economic disruption, Schön described the economy as "essentially undisturbed."[67] When the head of the Division for Food and Agriculture, Karl Naumann, suggested in early December 1940 that the ghetto not be supplied with food that month to force the Jews to use up their smuggled food and hidden cash, Dr. Lambrecht of the Health Division warned against causing an outbreak of epidemic through "artificial famine" (künstliche Hungersnot). Schön sided with Lambrecht, and Naumann promised the supplies.[68] Two days later, however, Naumann's office refused to honor a letter from Schön's division and forbade the importing of food into the ghetto after all.[69] Schön apparently did nothing to alter the situation, for most of the promised supplies were in fact not forthcoming, as Czerniakow noted in increasingly desperate letters.[70]

By mid-January reports had reached Cracow that food supplies to the ghetto had been stopped completely.[71] Schön was unmoved by Czerniakow's pleas. His division had no interest in the complaints of the Jewish council, he said, with one exception. "The delivery of soap . . . must be carried out, lest the Jewish council can rightfully maintain that German offices are increasing its difficulties in carrying out hygienic directions." Schön's expressed concern for the soap supply, however, did not stop the city's public health officer, Dr. Wilhelm Hagen, from accusing the Transferstelle of obstructing his efforts to combat epidemics.[72] Schön, Palfinger, and Naumann, it would seem, were more than ready to preside over the "dying out" of the Warsaw Jews.

In Cracow, however, Frank was going through one of his mercurial changes of mood. At the beginning of the year he had reluctantly supported Hitler's wishes concerning the deportations of the third short-range plan. When they were indefinitely postponed in mid-March, Frank quickly relaxed into a more pragmatic stance. It was not "practicable" to carry out "vast ethnic experiments" (*grosse volkspolitische Experimente*) at the moment, he said, and quoted Göring approvingly: "It is more important that we win the war than implement racial policy." (*Es ist wichtiger, dass wir den Krieg gewinnen, als Rassenpolitik durchsetzen.*) One had to be happy over every Pole or Jew working in a factory, whether he "suits us or not," Frank insisted.[73]

It was a propitious time for Dr. Walter Emmerich, the head of the Economic Division of the General Government, to present Frank with a 53-page memorandum written by his adviser, Dr. Rudolf Gater, the head of an economic "think tank" called the Reichskuratorium der Wirtschaftlichkeit (Reich Board for Economic Efficiency). This memorandum analyzed the economic viability of the Warsaw ghetto and concluded that organizational changes had to take place immediately.[74] The crux of the problem for Emmerich and Gater was that once the ghetto had been sealed and the population cut off from its normal economic activity, it consumed more than it produced. This created a negative balance or deficit in the economy of the ghetto, whose duration was estimated at five years. Once the existing wealth of the ghettoized Jews had been liquidated, the Germans would have to face one of four choices: (1) subsidize the ghetto, (2) accept the consequences of inadequate provisioning, (3) harness the Jews to productive labor, or (4) loosen the seal around the ghetto to allow the resumption of direct economic ties with the surrounding population. Public health officials would oppose the last possibility, and the undesirability of the first required no comment. Thus one could view the ghetto either "as a means . . . to liquidate the Jews" (*als ein Mittel . . . das jüdische Volkstum zu liquidieren*) or as a source of labor that had to be sufficiently fed to be capable of productive work. The bulk of the report sought to analyze the conditions necessary to achieve the third option, a self-sufficient, working ghetto. It concluded that to provide minimal provisions for the ghetto inhabitants without a subsidy, 60,000 Jews would have to be employed producing "exports" for the outside world.

Schön and Palfinger's existing policies were totally inadequate to this task. Schön claimed that the ghetto inhabitants possessed wealth worth six months' food supply and that pressure "through a ban on food deliveries" (*durch Sperrung der Nahrungsmittellieferungen*) was necessary to extract this wealth before one could worry about organizing production. Gater insisted that nothing approaching this kind of wealth existed in the ghetto. If production were not organized within three months, one would have to reckon with "a considerable loss of life" (*einer erheblichen Stockung des Lebens*) within the ghetto. Gater also criticized the plan for the Transferstelle, working through the Jewish council, to totally control a highly centralized ghetto economy on the Lodz model. The council lacked sufficient authority and organization for such a task, and the Transferstelle could not possibly control every aspect of an economy of nearly 500,000 people.

Frank ordered Emmerich to obtain the views of the Warsaw district governor, Dr. Ludwig Fischer, before he would call a meeting on the subject. Two days later Fischer claimed that the ghetto was working out very well. Allegedly, 40,000 Warsaw Jews were already employed (15,000 within the ghetto and 25,000 in camps), and the epidemic situation had improved by 50%. According to Fischer, "If developments continued as at present, one did not need to reckon with special difficulties in the ghetto, all the less because provisioning had been guaranteed."[75] What followed was a dramatic debate between the Cracow-centered "productionists" and the Warsaw "attritionists."

The confrontation began at an initial meeting on April 3, 1941, attended by the leading officials from both Warsaw and Cracow. Governor Fischer presented a rosy picture of the situation. The Jews had "considerable means" at their disposal; sufficient food supplies were at hand in the ghetto, "so that in the next months there is no danger at all of famine." Trade and production in the ghetto were going forward. Jewish craftsmen were extensively employed. Emmerich, however, brushed this fantasy aside:

In all economic reflections regarding the ghetto, one must free oneself from the notion that it is still going well in the ghetto and that supplies are still available there. The ghetto is not a business that can be liquidated within a year, but rather was created for the long haul and therefore economic planning for the long haul must also ensue. . . . The starting point for all economic measures has to be the idea of maintaining the capacity of the Jews to live. [*Ausgangspunkt für alle Massnahmen auf wirtschaftlichem Gebiet gegenüber dem Ghetto sei der Gedanke gewesen, die Lebensfähigkeit der Juden zu erhalten.*] The question is whether one can succeed in solving this problem in a productive manner, that is, to create so much work for the ghetto and to withdraw so much output from the ghetto, that a balance is produced.

In a scarcely veiled reference to Palfinger and Schön, Emmerich noted that in setting up the Transferstelle, the "question of personality" had played a great role. Dr. Gater, Emmerich's adviser, then provided a detailed and pessimistic analysis of how the necessary economic balance for the ghetto was to be achieved. Emmerich concluded that the participation of large German companies and the provision of credit would be required to set the ghetto economy in motion, and 65,000–70,000 Jews would have to be employed in productive labor. Only then could the creation of the ghetto be considered a success.

Schön, for whom the meeting must have been quite uncomfortable, dismissed Gater's presentation as "too theoretical." Nonetheless, neither he nor Fischer dared to contest the general consensus of the meeting that a way had to be found to put the ghetto on a productive footing. This consensus was supported by Frank, who concluded, "The responsibility that the government took on with the creation of a Jewish district of 500,000 human beings [*Menschen*] is very great, and a failure would always be blamed on the authorities of the General Government."[76]

Four days after this meeting, Palfinger composed a blistering "exposé" of the Emmerich report. The report had been drawn up by "impractical and unrealistic theoreticians" whose facts were wrong. Employment prospects in the ghetto were so good, Palfinger claimed, that soon the ghetto administration would be able "to stock a reserve fund." Moreover, these theoreticians failed to realize that economic considerations had to be subordinated to "purely political" ones. For example, they were so politically uninformed that they calculated the needs of the ghettoized Jews as if they were Aryans. Palfinger provided a different measure. "A work animal from whom a human being demands output was never the subject of profound contemplation concerning its needs. On the contrary . . . the one who maintains the animal regulates its food supply according to its productivity." The authors of the report ignored the fact that for political reasons the highest authorities desired "a radical course" on the Jewish question and that the living standard of the ghetto inhabitants was to be depressed to the level of an "internment camp" regardless of the total output of the Jewish masses.[77]

Palfinger's exposé was in vain. On April 9, 1941, Cracow officials submitted to Frank a draft for reorganizing the administration of the Warsaw ghetto. It specifically stated that the district governor of Warsaw was to act "within the framework of guidelines provided by the central authorities of the General Government."[78] They argued, "Such an instruction is necessary because the district chief of Warsaw wants to decide this question alone, without reaching the necessary agreement with superior authorities." Direct administrative responsibility for the ghetto was to be taken from the Resettlement Division and placed under a newly created commissioner for the Jewish district who would supervise the activities of both the Transferstelle and the chairman of the Jewish council. The latter was now to be considered the equivalent of a "mayor" of the ghetto.[79] Frank was emphatic that the Germans in the Warsaw district would abide by the guidelines of the central authorities, and instructed his Undersecretary Kundt to inform Fischer accordingly.[80]

A final meeting—again with the district governor of Warsaw attending—was held on April 19, 1941. Fischer's objections to the decree were explicitly overruled by Frank, who insisted that "this entire question of the Warsaw ghetto must be considered as a concern for the General Government and not just as one for the district." Fischer thus had to keep in touch with the central authorities and give them the opportunity to become involved before any measures could be taken. The head of the Emissionsbank, Dr. Fritz Paersch, voiced concern that, like Lodz, the Warsaw ghetto could not be maintained without a government subsidy. Fischer disagreed, noting that unlike Lodz, the Warsaw ghetto had not been stripped clean of all equipment and means of production. In any case, if they had not created a closed ghetto and had continued to let the Jews run around, the danger would have been much worse. On this issue Frank emphatically agreed with Fischer:

> One would have to choose the lesser evil here. That one cannot dissolve the ghetto and leave the Jews in freedom, over that there is still full agreement. Moreover the Führer had told him that the General Government shall be the first area fully freed of Jews. It was not therefore a question of a permanent burden but rather of a typical war phenomenon, perhaps even a Reich defense measure. Even if this measure should incur expenses, it would still be for him a reassuring feeling to have half a million Jews under control.

It was agreed, however, that the situation in Warsaw was unique and not to be copied elsewhere in the General Government.[81]

The conference of April 1941 brought about a change of both policy and personnel. A Viennese banker with a "half-Jewish" wife, Max Bischof,[82] was hired to head the Transferstelle with the specific task of achieving economic self-sufficiency for the ghetto. He was promised a government subsidy if it proved necessary. He also received the assurance that, once he had worked into the job, he could have Palfinger recalled.[83] Schön was moved to another position in the Warsaw district. Heinz Auerswald was appointed commissioner of the Jewish district. Auerswald was a lawyer whose Nazi party membership was seemingly nominal, for at least on one occasion he could not remember when he had joined.[84] Auerswald and Bischof faced an awesome task. As Auerswald confided to Bischof, he had been unpleasantly surprised to learn that despite past assurances of high employment in the ghetto, almost no one was working. Furthermore, the Transferstelle had in fact procured only about 5–10% of the ghetto's basic needs for food and supplies. Under these circumstances it was necessary to tolerate gaps in the ghetto cordon.[85]

Czerniakow's diary for the month of May records a truly astonishing turnabout in German behavior. On May 5 Dr. Gater and another economic adviser from Cracow, Meder, visited the ghetto and suggested that the merchants there establish direct contact with merchants outside. The next day Palfinger suspiciously asked what Gater and Meder were doing in the ghetto, but he solicitously informed Czerniakow that he would "do everything to improve the food supply." On May 8 Schön's assistant, Otto Mohns, told Czerniakow that the ghetto would receive a budget of 24 million zloty, that all requisitions of Jewish property in the ghetto were henceforth forbidden and to be reported immediately, that Jewish militia would be allowed to replace ruthless guards in Jewish work camps outside the ghetto, and that the government was increasing the Jewish council's share of rental income from 4% to 10%. On May 12 Czerniakow met with Auerswald, who "announced that his attitude toward the council was objective and matter-of-fact, without animosity." And on May 21 Czerniakow was even received by the district governor, Dr. Fischer. "At the very beginning he contended that starving the Jews was not his objective. There is a possibility that the food rations would be increased and that there will be work or orders for the workers." In addition to these assurances Fischer had a request as well. "He pointed out that the corpses lying in the street create a very bad impression. . . . The corpses, he said, must be cleared away quickly." Returning to the topic of food, "he added that it is possible that we may receive additional food contingents for the police and Community staff." That afternoon Czerniakow met with Auerswald and Bischof. "In between the lines I sensed a certain displeasure with Transfer." In early June Czerniakow noted the difference made by Palfinger's successor: "What a climate in Transfer with Bischof."[86]

In May 1941, therefore, a fundamental change—parallel to that in Lodz the previous fall—occurred in German policy toward the Warsaw ghetto. The attritionists were out and the productionists had prevailed. The ghetto was not to be starved to death but made into a productive entity. Theoretically, the government was even prepared, if necessary, to partially subsidize the cost of keeping the ghetto alive, though self-sufficiency was certainly the goal. The timing was as ironic as it was tragic. Just as German officials in Poland were preparing to deal with the Warsaw Jews in a more utilitarian and less murderous manner, Germans in Berlin were preparing to unleash a war of destruction against the Soviet Union, with fateful consequences for Soviet Jewry. But while mass murder was not going to be the product of local initiative from German authorities in Poland, where the trend was running in just the opposite direction, these same local authorities were not going to resist the new impulses emanating from Berlin. There were all too many Nazis in Poland ready to preside over the "dying out" of the Jews as soon as that was in fashion once again.

Cracow, Radom, and Lublin

Ghettoization in the other three districts of the General Government— Cracow, Radom, and Lublin[87]—followed a different pattern. Beginning in the capital city of Cracow in 1940, German authorities decided to reduce the Jewish population by expelling Jews to other parts of the General Government. This set in motion waves of expulsions as authorities in the district capitals of Radom and Lublin followed suit in the spring of 1941. Faced with a vast influx of German military personnel in preparation for Barbarossa, German urban administrators sought to alleviate the housing shortage by expelling Jews into the smaller surrounding towns. There local German authorities struggled to cope, shifting their Jews to particular towns in the district, where in turn the unwelcome Jews were often crowded into particular residential quarters. This incessant uprooting and shifting of Polish Jews temporarily tapered off after the spring of 1941, when the reduced Jewish populations of Cracow, Lublin, and Radom were officially ghettoized, only to be set in motion again in the spring of 1942, when the Jews of Poland were shipped from their new residences to the death camps of Operation Reinhard. Their places were taken temporarily by trainloads of Jews from Germany, Austria, and Czechoslovakia, until the latter were also sent on the last, fatal train ride. Thus most Jews of southern Poland were uprooted, impoverished refugees, moved about as helpless pawns in a vast demographic chess game, and this frenetic shifting only came to an end when they and the Central European Jews who followed them had all been murdered.[88]

The initial impetus for this series of internal population transfers occurred in Cracow on April 12, 1940, during a discussion of the housing shortage in that city. It was "absolutely intolerable" to Frank that "thousands and more thousands of Jews slink around and take up apartments" in the city that the Führer had honored by making it the capital of the General Government. He thus intended to make Cracow "the most Jew-free city" in the General Government through "a vast evacuation operation" that would remove 50,000 Jews and leave only 5,000 or at most 10,000 indispensable skilled workers. Once this was accomplished, one could build clean German residences and "breathe German air."[89]

The Jews of Cracow were given until August 15, 1940, to leave the city voluntarily. If they did so, they would be allowed to take their belongings and choose where they wished to settle. The local German authorities throughout the General Government were specifically warned to place no obstacles in the way of such voluntary resettlement, so that the Jews who left Cracow would not become a "rural plague" (*Landplage*) on the outskirts of the capital. Ultimately, only Jews who were important to the city's economic life would be allowed to remain. Jews who did not leave Cracow by August 15 would be subject to forced deportation without the right to take property.[90]

Frank justified the expulsion to the district heads on the grounds that the Jewish population of Cracow had increased 50% since the conquest of Poland and was the primary cause of the housing shortage. According to the statistics of the Jewish community itself, the Jewish population of Cracow was 65,488 at the end of November 1939. Despite the arrival of 4,400 Jews during the first short-range plan and 421 Jews during the intermediate plan, as well as more than 4,000 others by April 1940, a commensurate departure of Jews had left the total population at 66,110—a gain of less than 1%.[91] Statistical reality was not, of course, the driving force behind Frank's plan, which met with Hitler's approval when the two men met on July 8.[92]

As of July 21 only 3,689 Jews had left Cracow, and Major Ragger of the Office of Population and Welfare (Bevölkerungswesen und Fürsorge) ordered the Jewish council to prepare three lists, each of 1,000 unmarried male Jews capable of work, to be expelled in succession on August 16, 17, and 18.[93] Different sections of the city were then to be cleared, until the Jewish population was reduced to 10,000 economically useful Jews living in the Kazimir district.[94] In early August Frank altered the quota slightly, calling for the expulsion of 45,000 Jews and permitting 15,000 to remain. Moreover, Frank emphatically emphasized "that the entire action had to bear the stamp of humanity" (*dass die ganze Aktion den Stempel der Menschlichkeit tragen muss*).[95]

By August 19, 1940, Ragger could report that 22,000 Jews had left the city voluntarily, but the expulsion of 3,000 unmarried Jews capable of labor had been a total failure. Of the 3,000 listed by the Jewish council, only 70 had reported. The regiment of Order Police in Cracow, aided by Polish police, had thereupon been ordered to arrest 5,000 Jews by list, but they netted only 500 unfortunates, who were sent to forced labor breaking stones.[96]

A furious Standartenführer Dethoff on Krüger's staff contacted Ragger and demanded the arrest of the current Jewish council and the creation of a new one. If it did not function either, then both were to be "put against the wall" (an die Wand gestellt). Ragger asked his superior, Dr. Siebert of the Department of Internal Administration, to be relieved of his responsibilities for the resettlement of Jews from Cracow. Siebert told him to do nothing regarding Dethoff's orders about the Jewish council. The commander of the Order Police, Lt. Colonel Köber, also summoned Ragger and announced he would no longer accept Ragger's requests for police. All such orders would have to come through Dethoff on the staff of the HSSPF.[97]

While the Germans engaged in recriminations and threats, the Jewish council courageously pointed out that the obvious reason for the total failure of the roundup lay in the contradictory nature of German orders. Virtually all those Jews who were on the list for expulsion quite naturally exercised the option to leave Cracow voluntarily with their property before August 15. The council advocated continuing the hitherto successful process of voluntary departure.[98] Indeed, by the end of August a total of 26,000 Jews had left Cracow; the number reached 35,000 by the end of September.[99]

Local German authorities, already burdened with the flight and deportation of Jews and Poles from the incorporated territories, faced the prospect of a new influx of Jewish refugees from Cracow with alarm. The Kreishauptmann of Krakau-Land, the countryside county surrounding the city, complained that because the Jews had been given the choice of where to resettle, his region had been swamped, overcrowding had ensued, rents had been driven up, and epidemic threatened.[100] The Kreishauptmann of Jaslo, in a rather transparent attempt to give weight to his arguments, reported that many Poles were

disturbed by the handling of the Jewish problem. The Poles cannot understand at all why Cracow shall be made pure of Jews when these elements could be better controlled and would be less conspicuous in the larger city than is the case in small towns and in the countryside. The prospect of a later general settlement of the Jewish problem can be no consolation to the population here, which must take upon itself the present invasion of Cracow Jews. The Poles even ask why the local German officials are burdened with still more difficulties in the already unavoidable intercourse with Jews and they do not truly believe in a later total evacuation of the Jews, because otherwise the Cracow operation would not have been necessary.[101]

In Tarnow the Germans complained that the influx of 4,000 Jews from Cracow had considerably aggravated the shortage of housing and upset popular feeling.[102] The Kreishauptmann of Opatow reported that he was carrying out "a systematic dejudaizing" of that city's market area, and that a ghetto would be built if possible. However, that required a reduction of the Jewish population to 2,500, and it was now highly questionable whether an emigration of Jews to neighboring areas was possible.[103] Other Kreise also reported the attempt to create ghettos or at least to concentrate the Jews in certain quarters or towns.[104]

In Cracow the Germans were not pleased with the course of events either, though for the opposite reason that the reduction of the Jewish population was not proceeding quickly enough. In early October direction of the resettlement was taken out of Ragger's hands and assigned to the Stadthauptmann of Cracow, Dr. Schmid. Final screening of Jews important to the economy was to be completed quickly, followed by police actions to expel all others.[105] In fact, economic screening was complex and time-consuming. Six weeks later not only had no further expulsions taken place, but according to reports many Jews were already slipping back into the city from the surrounding region. By one account the Jewish population of Cracow was back to 50,000, by another to 60,000. A furious Governor Wächter berated Schmid and placed leadership of the resettlement action in the hands of Obersturmbannführer Pavlu under his direct supervision.[106]

This time brutal action was quickly forthcoming. On November 29 and December 3 and 9, a series of police razzias were carried out by Police Battalion 311, the Polish municipal police, and the German Kripo to demonstrate to the Jews "the seriousness of the situation." The German Security Police estimated that some 20,000 Jews left Cracow in the month of December.[107] Since the local authorities were once again faced with a simultaneous influx from Cracow and the incorporated territories, there arose cries of despair that they were saturated with refugees beyond their capacity to absorb any more.[108] But the authorities in Cracow still wanted to reach their quota of a maximum of 15,000 Jews, and they set about preparing a limited number of new identity papers and residence permits for those who would be allowed to remain. By the end of February 1941, 27,000 expulsion orders had been issued, and preparation for a ghetto in the Podgorze quarter had been made.[109] Throughout February transports of Jews set out from Cracow to other parts of the General Government.[110] Then on February 27 the old identity papers were declared invalid for further residence in the city, and on March 3 the order for ghettoization was issued.[111]

The escalation of German policy in Cracow was in no small way a product of the frustration produced by the contradictions and impracticality inherent in that policy—a pattern similar to the dynamic of escalating resettlement schemes as well. Attributing the housing shortage to an influx of Jews (an allegation not supported statistically), Frank ordered all but the economically useful Jews to leave the city. Spurred by the threat of later deportation and the immediate inducement of being allowed the opportunity to take their property with them, the Jews were to depart voluntarily. The remaining 15,000 Jews were to be concentrated in the Kazimir district, but nothing was said about ghettoization. The whole operation was to "bear the stamp of humanity."

In reality, even the threat of deportation without property was not sufficient to induce 45,000 Jews to depart voluntarily, especially since their arrival elsewhere was invariably met with hostility and resistance. And the prolonged process of identifying those Jews whose economic usefulness would earn them exemption from deportation delayed the police razzias until late in the year. In the end, of course, the expulsions did not "bear the stamp of humanity." And instead of being concentrated in Kazimir, the remaining Jews were ghettoized in Podgorze.

In the course of following the Cracow model of shrinking the Jewish urban populations through expulsion to the rural towns and villages and then ghettoizing the remnant, the German authorities in Radom and Lublin faced a further pressure in the spring of 1941. The massive German military buildup in the General Government before Barbarossa made demands for housing even more acute. Not only did the military therefore resist the arrival of Polish refugees from the incorporated territories under the third short-range plan, but they also added their voice in support of expelling Jews from urban areas and squeezing the remnant into overcrowded ghettos.[112]

In the Radom district, the Germans in the capital city had already begun deporting Jews to neighboring towns in December 1940—following Cracow's lead and long before any pressure from the military related to Barbarossa.[113] "This resettlement of the Jews proved necessary," a Radom official noted, "because a sealed lodging of the Jewish population in a specific Jewish district—for this only the old city is in question—will only be possible for some 10,000 Jews."[114] Ghettoization in other cities of the Radom district followed as a result of a meeting held on March 29 by the district governor, Karl Lasch: Kielce on March 31, and Czestochowa, Skarzysko-Kamienna, Opatow, and Ostrowiec in April.[115]

The March/April timing suggests the Barbarossa connection in the Radom district, but this should not be overemphasized. The move toward ghettoization both began earlier and continued later. In Kielce, for instance, the Stadthauptmann indicated as early as January 23, 1941, that he wanted to erect a ghetto in his city "as soon as the weather situation permitted." But the intended ghetto had room for only 15,000 of the 20,000 Jews in Kielce. He thus proposed a population exchange with the Kreishauptmann of Kreis Kielce, sending 5,000 Jews to the town of Checiny and taking 2,500 Poles into the city of Kielce. The Kreishauptmann agreed, but Governor Lasch declared that the question of ghettos had to be examined more carefully.[116]

In May 1941 approval for building a ghetto in Checiny was finally granted, although once again ghettoization "was stopped in view of the danger of epidemic existing at the time."[117] This was a rare, if not unique, occasion in the General Government in which the obvious relationship between ghettoization and epidemic led to realistic, preventive behavior rather than counterproductive, self-fulfilling prophecy. On July 3, 1941, long after the military had moved on, the Kreishauptmann of Kielce finally gave the order to "immediately" construct the ghetto in Checiny and carry out the resettlement agreed upon the previous January. This was done by early August.[118]

In the Lublin district the military pressure can be clearly documented.[119] In early March the 17th Army commander urgently requested a halt to the entry of further refugees "because the available housing is fully needed for newly arriving troops." A week later Frank's state secretary, Bühler, noted that "urgent military considerations have necessitated the immediate evacuation of 10,000 Jews from the city of Lublin into the district."[120] And on March 25 Governor Zörner explained the domino effect that was taking place. Ten thousand Jews were being moved out of the city, and Poles were being moved into the evacuated Jewish quarter. In turn, "the freed-up Polish quarter was being placed at the disposal of the Wehrmacht."[121]

In Lublin the beginning of evacuations from the city was announced to officials on March 9, 1941. On the following day, 1,100 Jews were dispersed to four small towns, and another 1,200 were deported on March 12.[122] On March 24 the creation of the ghetto was declared. Jews who did not want to live in the ghetto were free to leave the city with their possessions and to settle in other communities in the district. Since the ghetto would only accommodate 20,000, some 15,000 additional Jews were to leave the city. If not enough Jews left of their own accord, forced deportations were to ensue, with only 25 kilos of luggage permitted. This was to exercise "a certain pressure" to reach the quota voluntarily. In fact, the goal was not met, and the ghetto of Lublin continued to hold close to 40,000 Jews.[123]

As elsewhere, the expulsion and flight of the Jews from the district capital to the smaller towns led to vociferous complaints.[124] But unlike in Radom, this did not set off a chain reaction of ghettoization in other towns of the Lublin district, which remained relatively unghettoized. As one official commented in February 1942, on the eve of the mass destruction, "In the district of Lublin, with one exception, regular and sealed ghettos do not exist. There are many Jewish quarters and special Jewish communities, but these are not specially isolated."[125] Indeed, as Bogdan Musial has noted, ghettoization in the Lublin district led to the uprooting and dispersal rather than the concentration of the Jewish population.[126]

The ghettoization of the Polish Jews took place roughly in three waves: Lodz along with the Warthegau and the bordering western portions of the Warsaw district in the spring of 1940; Warsaw and the rest of its district in the fall of 1940; and the districts of Cracow and Radom and the city (but not the district) of Lublin in the spring of 1941. Lodz and Warsaw served as concentration points for Jews of the surrounding regions; Cracow, Radom, and Lublin expelled Jews to the surrounding areas. In Lodz the Germans rationalized ghettoization as the most effective means of depriving the Jews of the last remnants of their property before deportation. In Warsaw a number of reasons were given, but concern about epidemics provided the actual impetus for the oft-postponed decision. In Cracow, Radom, and Lublin the shortage of housing—intensified by though not originating in the increasing military presence in the spring of 1941—was invoked above all other reasons. Thus the ghettoization of the Polish Jews occurred at different times, in different ways, and for different reasons. Moreover, the degree to which the ghettos were sealed or closed varied greatly.[127] In short, there was no common or unified ghettoization policy.

Nevertheless, underlying the diversity was a common assumption that produced a common result: Aryans did not live together with Jews. As attempts to remove the Jews and send them elsewhere failed, the ghettos became great "warehouses" to store an unwanted population in isolation from the rest of society. By late spring of 1941 an apparent and precarious stabilization set in. The ghettoization was mostly complete, the endless shuffling of people from one place to another declined, and the pragmatists concerned with maximizing the economic potential of the ghettos had prevailed, at least in the short run, over the more radical Nazis favoring a policy of attrition through deliberate starvation. The stabilization was only apparent and temporary, however, for the invasion of the Soviet Union would ultimately have an immensely radicalizing effect on Nazi Jewish policy, from which no Jews in the German empire—and those in Poland in particular—would be spared.

If the Germans were of two minds on the purposes of ghettoization, there was complete consensus on the need to exploit both the property and the labor of Polish Jewry while excluding them from normal economic life. The differences of opinion were merely over who would control and benefit from the spoils of this exploitation. The result was an avalanche of anti-Jewish decrees and measures, as well as considerable internecine warfare, as various Nazi authorities tried to stake their claims in Jewish affairs. If there were both winners and losers among the German factions, the Jews could only lose in this sordid competition.

In this rush to stake a claim in Jewish affairs, many of the major anti-Jewish measures were anticipated by local authorities. For instance, Uebelhoer in Lodz had ordered the marking of Jews on November 14, 1939, only to have to alter his decree to conform to Greiser's general decree on marking for all of the Warthegau.[128] Likewise, the district governor of Warsaw, Fischer, had issued his own marking decree before Frank's edict for the General Government on November 23, 1939.[129] The army frequently helped itself to uncompensated Jewish labor, and the Security Police in Warsaw had worked out arrangements with the Jewish council there for the regular supply of workers, before the Frank edict of October 26, 1939, imposed a general obligation for forced labor on all male Jews between 12 and 60 years old.[130] The Warsaw district anticipated by a month the General Government edict of January 24, 1940, on registering Jewish property. The army had anticipated General Government legislation on blocking Jewish accounts.[131] And Heydrich had ordered the formation of Jewish councils in his Schnellbrief of September 21, which Frank then repeated in his decree of November 28, 1939.[132]

When the central authorities did not follow the lead of local initiators, the latter often tried to shame the former into doing so. Jews were forbidden to use the railways in the General Government on January 26, 1940, except in cases of special permission. The Warsaw district granted such permission only in the case of the death of a relative or when Jewish officials were summoned to visit German authorities. Aside from representatives of the American Joint Distribution Committee being allowed to visit Cracow by express train, only third-class travel was permitted. The Germans in Warsaw expressed their dismay upon discovering that officials in Cracow permitted the representatives of Jewish welfare organizations not only to travel by express train but to travel second class and in sleeping cars. Such measures were "out of place, because one could not expect a German to travel in the same section of an express train or sleeping car with Jews."[133]

Property

Among the vast array of anti-Jewish measures, obviously the control of Jewish property and Jewish labor generated the most intense interest among the Germans. Germany's predatory policy toward all property in Poland inevitably overlapped with measures aimed specifically at Jewish property. Göring had made a claim on all Polish (and hence Polish Jewish) property in October 1939, with the establishment of the HTO but was soon forced to make compromises. Himmler secured control of landed property in the incorporated territories for the resettlement of ethnic Germans, and Frank succeeded in establishing his own trusteeship office for the General Government.[134] In the early period Göring and Frank engaged in a policy of easy plunder, "skimming off the cream" in Raul Hilberg's words.[135] That a total expropriation of Jewish property was assumed from the beginning, however, can be seen from the earliest decrees of the military occupation. On September 6, 1939, the transfer, sale, leasing, donation, or encumbrance of any property that was even partially of Jewish ownership was forbidden. In mid-September the guiding principle was annunciated: "The future goal of the treatment of Jews in economic life must be their total exclusion and the transfer of their businesses to Aryan hands."[136]

It was much easier to decree the freezing of Jewish property, however, than to actually take possession of it. During the wild expulsions of 1939 no doubt much property, both Jewish and Polish, fell into the hands of both the Reich Germans, who descended upon Poland as if they were on a gold rush,[137] and the ethnic Germans, who claimed the right to ample compensation for twenty years of suffering under Polish rule. The deportations of the first short-range plan from the Warthegau in December 1939, however, required the German authorities to develop techniques for seizing property in a more systematic manner. Albert Rapp, the coordinator of these deportations, chaired a meeting of all interested parties to work out the procedures. The HTO was to provide trustees for businesses, town officials were to secure the apartments of the deportees, and banks were to freeze their accounts. Before departure, each deported Pole or Jew was to fill out a form listing all his property. To prevent loss of property, inventories were to be quickly compiled, and plundering was to be punished with the death penalty.[138]

The decision to concentrate Jews in a ghetto in Lodz offered a new challenge and opportunity to develop techniques of expropriation. A major motivation behind the decision for ghettoization in Lodz had in fact been the desire to force the Jews, before deportation, to turn over what was supposed to be their hoards of hidden wealth in return for food. But the Germans were determined to secure as much as they could even before ghettoization was finalized. Once the boundaries were designated, various agencies were assigned the task of ensuring that nothing of value remained within. The Litzmannstädter Warenhandelsgesellschaft (the HTO subsidiary for receiving Jewish property) was assigned the task of taking all finished and unfinished products, as well as raw materials and equipment, from the ghetto site and also of ascertaining what individual businesses were worth moving. The Lodz Union of Industrialists (Verband Lodscher Industrieller) was to check on the presence of any industry. Various officials of the city administration were responsible for the confiscation of food supplies, household goods, and retail trade. The SS was in charge of valuables such as gold and silver. The HTO would continue closing Jewish businesses, with the help of inventory lists compiled by agents of the Chamber of Industry and Trade (Industrie- und Handelskammer). All seized goods were to be sent to collection points for assessment and sale, with proceeds going to the accounts of the HTO.[139] To maximize the take from areas outside the ghetto boundaries, the edict decreeing ghettoization on February 8, 1940, stipulated that no one moving in could take more of his possessions than he could carry without special means of transportation.[140] The despoilment of the Lodz Jews, therefore, was to be a joint operation of the city administration, police, Göring's HTO, and various organizations of the business community.

The lure of Jewish property was sufficiently strong, however, that the German authorities found themselves in a constant struggle to ward off unauthorized confiscation. As men in SS uniforms were often involved, Uebelhoer induced the Lodz police president, Johannes Schäfer, to take a strong stand against any unauthorized interventions in the economy by SS personnel.[141] A strict division of labor and spoils was to be adhered to. The SS and police were to be in charge of the confiscation of valuables and precious metals, the RKFDV of farm land, and the HTO of factories and businesses. In addition, the HTO delegated the seizure of urban real estate, housing, and furnishings to the mayors of the cities and to the Landräte in the rural towns and villages, while raw materials were to be seized by a special staff under Major General Buehrmann.[142] Since apartment furnishings and moveable property were especially vulnerable, the Oberbürgermeister was moved to issue special warnings in regard to their unauthorized confiscation.[143]

Ironically, the greatest challenge to controlling illegal confiscation in Lodz came from the Criminal Police (Kripo). The Kripo successfully petitioned for its own headquarters within the ghetto on the grounds that all Jews were "more or less criminally inclined," and that it needed quarters on the spot to do its job effectively.[144] In the eyes of the Food Supply and Economic Office of the city government, in charge of supplying the ghetto with provisions in exchange for

Jewish valuables, the Kripo was engaged less in fighting smuggling and other illegal activities than in conducting a systematic looting of the ghetto which constituted nothing less than "sabotage." The Food Supply and Economic Office had already reached agreement with the Gestapo and other agencies that all Jewish valuables were to be exchanged for food. The Kripo's actions not only threatened the orderly supply of food to the ghetto but also threatened to spread epidemic, since the Kripo furtively avoided the prescribed disinfection of all goods leaving the ghetto.[145] The protest was partially effective, and an agreement was worked out between the Kripo and the Food Supply and Economic Office, soon to be renamed the ghetto administration. By its terms, the Kripo was the sole authority in charge of carrying out confiscations within the ghetto, but all confiscated goods had to be turned over to the ghetto administration. Kripo officials inside the ghetto were to get extra uniforms (because their work was so unclean) and extra pay in recognition of the additional income they brought to the ghetto administration. Moreover, Kripo officials were to be allowed first chance to purchase the goods they had confiscated at the price assessed by the ghetto administration for the purpose of liquidating Jewish property.[146]

The Kripo in Lodz was not the only agency that felt it did not receive a fair share of the spoils in return for the role it played in confiscating Jewish property. In the General Government, where registration and confiscation of Jewish property had been ordered on January 24, 1940, with Frank's Trusteeship Office in charge, the Kreishauptmann of Krasnystaw voiced a similar complaint. In his Kreis 1,125 Jewish houses had been confiscated, a task that the Trusteeship Office could never have accomplished without the help of local officials. "It is nothing more than just and equitable that we, that is, the Kreis officials, above all dispose of the houses and the income derived from that. Unfortunately, the trusteeship branch office objects in this regard, but ignores the fact that it would not have this income if we had not confiscated the houses."[147]

In general, however, disputes over Jewish property in the General Government were less strident than in the incorporated territories. Since the Jews were poorer, much less was at stake. On the other hand, the significance of Jewish labor was relatively greater in the General Government.[148] Thus the control of this labor was vigorously contested.

Labor

On October 26, 1939, Frank's government issued an edict imposing forced labor on all Jews of the General Government and authorizing implementation through the HSSPF, Friedrich Krüger.[149] Until then the local German authorities had rounded up Jews for forced labor on an ad hoc basis. The disruption and fear caused by such roundups induced the head of the Warsaw Jewish council, Adam Czerniakow, to negotiate an agreement with the Security Police, whereby the Jewish council would supply and pay for a labor battalion on a regular basis.[150] Other councils followed Czerniakow's example, and labor roundups diminished, though they never ceased entirely.[151]

Krüger was quite aware that local roundups constituted a relatively irrational use of Jewish labor potential. The Polish Jews had various crafts, he noted, and "it would be a pity if this manpower were not profitably employed." But this question could not be solved immediately; rather, it required the systematic registration of all male Jews by profession. This was to be carried out by the Jewish councils under the supervision of the local mayors. In the meantime the Jews could continue to be employed in labor columns on urgent projects as determined by the district governors.[152] The Jewish councils received their instructions to construct card files of Jewish workers in late January, and then revised instructions in mid-February. The task was to be completed in early March 1940.[153]

Meanwhile, Krüger's superiors, Frank in Cracow as well as Heydrich and Himmler in Berlin, were enthusiastic about the prospect of a vast labor force. To a correspondent from the *Völkischer Beobachter*, Frank boasted that his Jews "work very honestly, yes, they even volunteer for it. . . . The model of the eastern Jew is unknown to us; here the Jew works."[154] On January 30, 1940, Heydrich mentioned the possibility of putting several hundred thousand Jews in forced labor camps to work on fortifications and other construction projects in the east. Several days later Himmler dangled before Brauchitsch the prospect of 2½ million Jews digging antitank ditches on the eastern border, an offer the latter promised to examine.[155]

Once the card files were complete, several questions remained open. Who was to assign or allocate Jewish labor? And were the Jews to be concentrated in large-scale projects as envisaged by Himmler? As usual, the Germans in Poland did not resolve these questions in a uniform manner. In the Warsaw district the SD, which had been in charge of Jewish labor, surrendered its jurisdiction in April 1940 to Fischer's Labor Division, which set up its own regulations and insisted that all requests for labor be processed through its offices. The SD was moved to make this concession because the administration of Jewish labor was too much for its overburdened personnel.[156] In Lublin, on the other hand, the district SSPF, Odilo Globocnik, despised Frank's district civil authorities and jealously guarded his prerogatives. Thus it was the police that issued regulations in May 1940 governing the use of Jewish labor, and it was to Globocnik's Lublin headquarters or to Sipo branch offices that application had to be made for Jewish labor.[157]

The control of Jewish labor was then caught up in a wider debate over supervision of the entire Jewish community, and more specifically the Jewish councils. At a lengthy meeting on May 30, 1940, the General Government's Sipo inspector, Brigadeführer Bruno Streckenbach, complained that police control of the Jews had been infringed upon because all sorts of agencies were making requests of the Jewish councils, including "planless" demands for labor. A basic decision was needed concerning who should supervise the Jewish councils. In Streckenbach's opinion the Security Police should be the sole supervisor because of its past experience with the Jews. All those desiring something of the Jews should go through his agency. In the area of forced labor in particular, unified management was desirable, and this would be the way to achieve it. The greed for Jewish wealth was sufficiently widespread that Streckenbach felt it necessary to disclaim any need on the part of the Security Police to enrich itself.

Dr. Ernst Zörner, the district governor of Lublin, opposed Streckenbach and leveled an indirect criticism against Globocnik. In Lublin the Jews stood around in the city streets and were not effectively mobilized for labor. It was thus necessary that the civil administration be given authority in this area. Only local officials were sufficiently acquainted with local conditions to efficiently utilize the Jewish councils for the employment of Jewish labor. The SD simply did not have sufficient personnel for this task.

Fischer backed Zörner, noting that in Warsaw the SD had been so overburdened that it had already transferred the supervision of Jewish labor to the civil administration. Frank did not contest SS jurisdiction vis-à-vis the Jewish councils for maintaining order and conceded that he had named the HSSPF as the central authority for Jewish forced labor. However, he was now of the opinion that requests for and allocation of Jewish labor should be handled through the local civil authorities, "obviously" in close cooperation with the Sipo-SD. A comprehensive settlement of this question had to be found, and he expected proposals from his district governors within two weeks.[158]

The first step in resolving the issue was taken at a two-day economic conference of General Government officials on June 6 and 7, 1940.[159] Dr. Max Frauendorfer, head of the Labor Division of the General Government, announced a compromise. In principle, administration of Jewish labor was a police matter. In practice, however, allocation of such labor would now take place through the Labor Division in agreement with the police, although registration of Jewish labor would continue to remain in police hands. He intended to employ Jews in the normal labor market for pay. "One could not forget that the Jews, so long as they were there, had to be provided for in some way."[160]

Frauendorfer would also be in charge of organizing forced labor, but its rational use would be possible only when "the nomadicized Jews" became stationary in the cities and could be registered. Certainly not all Jews could be placed in camps, given the inherent difficulties of administration, security, supply, and financing; hence the need to employ Jews in the free economy. But in agreement with the military commander in Poland, Jews would be employed on the "so-called green frontier" between the Bug and the San Rivers. This would be an experiment. Only the future would show how far one could go in this direction. The conference concluded that the Jews were to be put to work, and both ghettos and work camps were to be erected to prevent the Jews from moving about freely.

A week later HSSPF Krüger decided to concede even greater jurisdiction over Jewish labor to the Labor Division. In a personal letter to Frauendorfer, Krüger announced that he was sending over the card indexes of Jewish laborers compiled by the police. Further registration would henceforth be the task of the Labor Division, as would be the selecting of Jews for forced labor and the regulating of their working conditions. The police would restrict itself to enforcement.[161]

On July 5, 1940, Frauendorfer sent a circular letter to all the labor offices of the General Government outlining a uniform policy for Jewish labor. The utilization of Jewish labor was "urgently necessary," he wrote, because many Polish workers had been sent to Germany, and "moreover, in contrast to the Jews in the Reich, good skilled workers and craftsmen are found among the Jews obligated to compulsory labor." The allocation of Jewish labor was to take place only through the local labor offices of the district Labor Divisions. In all suitable cases an attempt should be made to employ Jews in the free labor market, since this would best utilize their skills for the common good and also secure a living for them and their families. So far there had been no regular pay for Jewish labor, since this had been left to the Jewish councils. However, the resources of the councils were exhausted. Now, to maintain the strength of the workers and the livelihood of their families, and to avoid sickness and epidemic, this basic principle had to be set aside, and regular pay had to be provided at a rate of 80% of what a Pole would earn for the same job. Only Jews who were not employed in the free economy would be summoned to forced labor. In general, forced labor would only be used for big projects for which large numbers of workers would be kept in camps under guard.[162]

This policy occasioned opposition on two counts. First, those who had become accustomed to having free labor were dismayed at the prospect of now being required to pay for it. There were a few exceptions, such as the military's Rittmeister Hans Schu in Warsaw, who had informed Czerniakow that he did not want "slaves" and was already paying for his workers.[163] In contrast, in the Kreis of Pulawy the military response was to employ higher paid Poles exclusively rather than to pay Jews anything.[164] The Kreishauptmann of Jaslo complained that road construction firms did not want to hire Jews, even at 80% of the Polish wage, because among other things they were already too poorly fed to be worth paying for such physical labor.[165] In Miechow the authorities complained that they kept the towns clean with unpaid Jewish labor. The communities had no money for this, but the Jewish councils obviously did, since they were caring for the poor Jews. Thus the local German authorities requested permission to use unpaid Jewish labor for street cleaning.[166] And the Kreishauptmann of Czestochowa also complained bitterly about the alleged inability of the Jewish councils to pay for Jewish forced labor. "Naturally if one takes the expressions of the Jewish council as the measure of the capacity of the Jews, then in fact all of the recent work carried out by Jewish forced laborers would have to have been paid, because according to the Jews they already stood on the brink of financial collapse half a year ago. I assume that even this regulation can be lost locally and have acted accordingly." (*Ich nehme an, dass auch diese Vorschrift örtlich verliert werden kann und habe danach gehandelt.*)[167] Frauendorfer continued to insist, however, that the 80% wage rate be adhered to, because "otherwise maintaining the strength of the working Jews would not be guaranteed."[168]

More serious, however, was the conflict that broke out between Globocnik and the labor offices in the district of Lublin.[169] Frauendorfer had ordered that employment in the free economy be given priority, and had stipulated that only the labor offices had the right to assign labor; but Globocnik had no intention of allowing such stipulations to stand in the way of filling his labor camps for the construction of fortifications between the San and the Bug. The idea for a massive use of Jewish forced labor to construct fortifications—an *Ostwall*—along the demarcation line had first been broached to the military by Himmler in early February, and Brauchitsch had promised to look into the possibility. By June the military had approved a more limited plan for fortifications—antitank ditches or *Panzergraben*—between the San and Bug to be constructed with Jewish labor supplied by the authorities of the General Government. Even though this construction was rendered militarily obsolete by virtue of the quick German victory in France, work went forward anyway.[170]

Globocnik envisaged a Jewish labor force of 30,000 unskilled workers and 1,000 craftsmen to be at work in SS camps along the demarcation line by August. He urgently requested these workers from the officials in Lublin and Cracow. In particular, the first camp at Belzec needed 3,000 workers immediately.[171] Globocnik did not simply wait upon others, however. On the night of July 22–23, SS men seized 300 Jews in a razzia in Lublin without notifying the Labor Division. Protesting labor officials were curtly informed that a change in labor policy was expected shortly, and that in the meantime the SS would procure Jews in Lublin through razzias as needed.[172] The chief of the district's Labor Division, Oberregierungsrat Jache, met with Globocnik's representatives the following day. A tenuous compromise was worked out. The labor offices would officially process the razzia victims and transfer them to the SS on the basis of a retroactive application from Globocnik. In return, the SS would refrain from "further special measures" for procuring labor for the border fortifications until it had secured authorization from Frank and Krüger.[173]

On August 6, 1940, another major conference, chaired by Frauendorfer, was held in Cracow to discuss labor allocation. His deputy, Dr. Gschliesser, explained the necessity of shifting the use of Jewish forced labor from miscellaneous services for local authorities to large-scale employment for politically significant projects. The largest of these projects was the fortifications in the district of Lublin, and so some equalization of labor supply among the various districts had to be worked out. HSSPF Krüger's representative announced that camps for 15,000 workers were almost ready, and capacity would be quickly raised to 30,000. Not to be excluded entirely, representatives for water control projects and road construction recorded their need for 7,000 and 12,000 Jews, respectively. Jache of the Lublin Labor Division noted some friction in recent relations with the SS, but requested that the latter provide him with help for mustering and guarding Jewish labor. After some debate with Unterfsturmführer Dr. Hofbauer, Globocnik's representative, it was agreed that the SS would make a special effort to round up the Jews capable of work in the district of Lublin, but "with the agreement and participation of the competent labor offices." The district Labor Division heads of Warsaw and Radom promised to send Jewish workers to Lublin as well. Cracow claimed to currently need all its available Jewish labor for road and dam construction but did not foreclose the possibility of sending labor to Lublin later.[174]

Jache was in a difficult position. He needed Globocnik's help to mobilize the required number of workers but wanted this help on his own terms, whereby the labor offices and not the SS ultimately decided who went to the camps. Globocnik seemed willing to play by the rules, declaring himself ready to carry out razzias as the Labor Division reported the numbers needed, leaving registration and allocation to the latter and promising to respect the certificates of exemption issued by the labor offices to Jews already placed in other jobs.[175]

The great roundups were carried out in the district of Lublin on the night of August 13–14, seizing 7,296 Jews.[176] However, the Labor Division was immediately swamped with complaints that the ss was either excluding local labor offices entirely or permitting them only to register workers while reserving allocation to itself and shipping off to ss camps almost all of those seized, including many with labor office certificates of prior employment. Local ss men ignored labor officials' protests, citing "secret orders" from Globocnik.[177]

Zörner's deputy, Hans Damrau, wrote a scathing letter to Frank in Cracow denouncing Globocnik's duplicity. Not only were many important projects involving Jewish labor disrupted and jeopardized by the independent measures of the ss, but also Globocnik's secret orders violated Frank's own instructions concerning jurisdiction over Jewish labor. This put the labor officials in an "undignified position" that was "intolerable." The "prestige" of German administrative authorities was threatened, for such contradictory policies could not remain hidden from the Poles. Since more roundups were imminent, he urgently requested that Globocnik be given clear instructions to prevent a repetition.[178]

Jache also asked Globocnik to postpone any further razzias until the labor officials had completed a new registration. The card files they had received from the ss had proven to be most unreliable, and in order to avoid further disruption to the economy, it was important to provide those Jews in productive employment with up-to-date identity cards that exempted them from the roundups. Globocnik promised to wait only four days, until August 20, and then, ignoring a Labor Division last-minute appeal for a further postponement, resumed his roundups. This produced new complaints of high-handed ss behavior in complete disregard of local economic interests and labor office certificates.[179] The Labor Division retaliated by assigning most of the incoming trains of Jewish laborers from Radom and Warsaw to water control and road construction, on the grounds that Globocnik had taken the Jews of Lublin exclusively for his own camps. Moreover, the district governor, Zörner, a longtime foe of Globocnik's, ordered the labor offices to cease all registration of Jewish labor seized in ss roundups.[180] The Labor Division was not in a position to manage without the ss, however. It had no transit camps and guards to handle the trainloads of Jewish workers now beginning to pour in from Radom and Warsaw. Once again an agreement had to be reached with Globocnik over sharing the allocation of the incoming forced laborers in return for the use of ss guards and camps in Lublin.[181]

Twice more in the fall of 1940 Globocnik's ss carried out razzias without informing the Lublin district Labor Division.[182] Finally, at the end of November, another agreement was reached, whereby the police were to report any need for Jewish labor to the Labor Division. Only if it could not supply the requested number of laborers could the police undertake razzias, with the number and place agreed upon in advance with the Labor Division. No Jews with valid work papers were to be included.[183]

By then, however, the issue was practically moot. Already in September the influx of labor from the other districts had eased the pressure for roundups in Lublin. From Warsaw alone, 15 transports brought Jews—some volunteers but increasingly forced laborers—to the camps. Warsaw Jews were distributed between 13 camps for water control, 6 for road construction, and 5 for border fortifications. Extensive reports were collected detailing the terrible conditions under which the Jewish workers from Warsaw labored. This would not, however, deter Warsaw authorities from their own work camp experiments the following spring.[184]

By October Globocnik was sending Jewish workers from his own camps to those for water control and road construction. This turned out to be not an act of cooperation on his part, but merely an attempt to transfer to others the care of Jews exhausted beyond the capacity for further work. Echoing the reaction of many others, an inspector for the water control project noted, "The Jews who . . . have been delivered from the Jewish camp at Belzec unfortunately had to be released, because they had been driven to the utmost by those in charge there (ss) and were totally incapable of work."[185] When the ss camp at Belzec was dissolved, the Jewish workers from Warsaw and Radom were to be returned to their districts, and those from Lublin transferred to road construction.

However, a Lublin official complained to Cracow that once again Globocnik was totally uncooperative. Over 400 Jews were unaccounted for. "Because in such large numbers they could not really all have been shot," the official suspected that the ss had accepted money for their release.[186] But such complaints became irrelevant in late December and early January when, with the onset of winter, the last of the water control camps in Lublin were temporarily closed as well.[187]

In 1940 some 21,000 Jewish forced laborers, including 5,253 from the Warsaw district and 7,223 from the Radom district, worked in labor camps for border fortifications (8,000), road construction (3,000), and water control projects (10,000). Of no military value and of limited economic utility, this program of forced labor was ruinous for the Jewish workers involved and financially draining for the Jewish councils, which were often left with the "double burden" of both paying the workers and maintaining their families.[188]

In the spring of 1941 the focus of German attention shifted from construction of fortifications to preparations for Barbarossa, and conflict with the ss over the allocation of Jewish labor diminished. Camps for water control projects became the new Jewish labor priority. Fifteen camps were opened in the Warsaw district in April 1941 for this purpose. Eventually 6,100 Warsaw Jews were sent to these camps, and a further 1,500 and 2,000 to camps in the Cracow and Lublin districts, respectively.[189] Very quickly news reached Warsaw about the terrible conditions and inhuman treatment in the camps, reports that were soon confirmed by the return of "physically and psychically broken" survivors. Despite the conditions of mass starvation in the ghetto, it was soon impossible to find volunteers, and German authorities forced the Jewish council and police to fill the recruitment quotas through impressment.[190]

As a result of mushrooming complaints, in early May a delegation including a captain Meissner of the Schupo and a member of the Jewish Self-Aid Society, Dr. Gamsej Wielikowski, visited a number of the camps to report on conditions. Wielikowski reported terrible food shortages in all camps, compounded by poor sanitation and medical care, and in many cases mistreatment by the guards. In some camps the workers had received no pay at all. Indeed, one camp employer shamelessly announced that, after wage deductions for food, shelter, salaries for the guards, and medical care, his workers owed him 2,000 zloty![191] Meissner, while admitting that no one had received the prescribed food rations and that brutality and corruption were common among the guards, nonetheless blamed the sickness and death rates on the unusually wet and cold weather on the one hand and the "inferior human material" (*das minderwertige Menschenmaterial*) recruited by the Jewish council on the other. Complaining bitterly that the workers were sick and starved even before they set off for the work camps, Meissner concluded, "One has the impression, from the nature of the human material recruited for labor by the Jewish council, that the Jewish residential district perceives the work camps as an institution for disposing of its inferior elements."[192] Apparently it did not occur to the captain that after half a year of systematic starvation, the ghetto was not brimming with hordes of strong, healthy workers being held back out of sheer spite.

The Jewish council summarized the complaints from the camps and noted that if the Germans wanted the Jewish council to be able to fulfill the tasks assigned to it, it had to possess "a minimal popularity" within the population. The present situation was discrediting the Jewish council without supplying satisfactory workers. Changing the conditions in the camps would accomplish the latter far more effectively than "the most intensive action of the Jewish police."[193]

The man in charge of the water control projects in the Warsaw district, Goebel, tried to dismiss the Jewish complaints "because it is certainly known to all involved that the Jews do not like to work and try everything to sabotage their use for labor." He then added that the various grievances, whose existence he had just denied, had in any case been remedied.[194] However, Auerswald, commissioner of the ghetto, and the district expert for Jewish labor, Kurt Hoffmann, visited several camps to see for themselves, and they concluded that the work conditions were inadequate to maintain the Jews' ability to work, and the piecework system of pay was so faulty that even normal productivity would provide the workers no profit. Auerswald had already agreed, in response to complaints about the brutality and corruption of the camp guards, to dismiss them and replace them with Jewish police.[195] At a meeting on May 22, two days after his visits to the camps, Auerswald ordered further reforms. Before leaving for the camps, workers were to be fed for a week, naturally out of the ghetto's overall food allocation. Those no longer able to work would be returned from the camps as quickly as possible. Medical supplies to the camps would be increased. The pay system would be reexamined.[196]

Auerswald then decided to dissolve all the old camps and test his reforms in three new camps untainted by the previous mistakes. Several people warned against pursuing the camp experiment any further. Meissner noted that the old camps had each cost four and a half times as much to build as the value of the labor performed there.[197] And Dr. Wielikowski noted that the kind of work being expected had so exhausted Polish workers in the prewar period that they had to be rotated every three weeks. To make Jews, malnourished and debilitated for the past 20 months, perform such labor under conditions of inadequate food supply if not downright hunger, could only have catastrophic consequences. In the camps 239 Jews had already died since spring.[198]

But Auerswald would not be deterred from his experiment. When Jewish workers fled from the first new camp at Drewnica (which was guarded by Jewish police and not surrounded by barbed wire) and others were reluctant to volunteer, he threatened Czerniakow. The latter noted in his diary, "The Jews, according the Auerswald, should show good will by volunteering for labor. Otherwise the ghetto would be surrounded by barbed wire. . . . The ring will be tightened more and more and the whole population will slowly die out."[199] But Auerswald's threats could not change the stark fact that his "model camp" at

Drewnica was a failure. Almost immediately the vast majority of the workers there were incapacitated by swelling feet, and an outbreak of spotted fever made it impossible to send replacement workers. In the end, productivity was not improved over the miserable level of the old camps.[200]

Warsaw's experience with water control camps was not unique. Hoffmann noted that by late August the use of Jewish labor in camps throughout the General Government was in steady decline. "The inclination to use Jewish labor in camps is, after many bitter experiences, no longer great. The cost stands in no profitable relationship to the labor output." A month later Hoffmann noted that the decline in work camps had continued, and all the water control camps in Lublin had also been dissolved.[201] By the end of summer, only 2,359 Warsaw Jews were employed in camps outside the ghetto, and by October this had dropped to 600.[202]

Among the civil authorities at least, the work camp was an idea whose time had passed. When the suggestion to revive the camps was broached at a Warsaw conference in March 1942, it aroused no enthusiasm. On the basis of past experience, Hoffmann said, he wanted "no camps of emaciated men, no impossible work demands that even German workers could not surmount" (*keine Lager von ausgemergelten Menschen, keine unmöglichen Arbeitsansprüche, die selbst deutsche Arbeiter nicht bewältigen können*).[203] But the civil authorities were not going to have anything to say about Jewish labor much longer. Dr. Max Frauendorfer ominously informed his district officers in June 1942: "It must be expected that in the future the police themselves will undertake the utilization of Jewish labor to a certain extent, especially for the armaments industry."[204] A second era of ss labor camps was at hand, and the ss now had a different kind of camp in mind for those Jews whom they were not going to put to work.

PRODUCTION OR STARVATION,
THE GHETTO MANAGERS' DILEMMA

The proponents of creating ghetto economies designed to achieve self-sufficiency had triumphed in Lodz and Warsaw, but their triumphs were qualified by several serious factors. First, novel economies had to be created out of virtually nothing; productive capacity and market relations had to be established where none existed. Second, an impoverished, uprooted, and isolated population had to be kept alive and put to work despite the ravages of starvation and disease. The German authorities did succeed in fostering the creation of ghetto economies in both Lodz and Warsaw, albeit along strikingly different lines. But in neither ghetto did they cope adequately with the devastating attrition of hunger and epidemic. The constraints under which the ghetto managers operated were too great to overcome.

The ghetto was a temporary phenomenon—existing longer than had been expected initially but nonetheless destined for liquidation at some point in the future—and thus ranking low in any claim on priorities. More important, the inhabitants of the ghettos were at the bottom of the Nazi racial hierarchy, according to which even the surrounding Polish population—though itself kept, by Hitler's explicit order, to a bare subsistence standard of living—axiomatically had a greater right to scarce wartime food supplies than the Jews. Thus the ghetto managers were free to improvise ghetto economies only as long as they worked with marginal resources not previously claimed by others. What they could not do was achieve a reallocation of resources, especially food, to benefit Jews at the expense of anyone else.

Against such factors the ghetto managers could not fully prevail. A precarious "stabilization" was achieved, and the decimation of the Jewish population through hunger and disease was only partially stemmed.[205] Nonetheless the Polish ghettos in this period should not be seen as some covert scheme cynically perpetrated by local German authorities to carry out gradual extermination, although Jews within the ghettos understandably drew such conclusions.[206] The local Germans in fact had every inducement to maximize ghetto productivity and drew the obvious conclusion that starving Jews did not make the most productive workers. The starvation rations were maintained in spite of, not because of, their efforts.

Lodz

At a meeting on October 18, 1940, the Lodz authorities had finally admitted to themselves that the ghetto was going to continue to exist and had to be made self-sufficient. In the following weeks a series of further meetings were held to hammer out policies to this end. The first of these, under the chairmanship of Uebelhoer's deputy in Lodz, Dr. Moser, on October 24, dealt with feeding the ghetto. The ill-disposed and not-yet-departed Alexander Palfinger took the protocol. According to Moser, the "differences of opinion" between various agencies dealing with the ghetto were "no longer a matter for discussion." While the ghetto was a "most unwelcome institution" (*eine höchst unwillkommene Errichtung*), it nevertheless was a "necessary evil" (*notwendiges Übel*) and had to be fed. That it was not a normal consumer of food required no comment. It would be provided the kind and amount of food that the ghetto administration and Reich food supply authorities agreed was necessary, but provisioning the civil population could not be "impaired or disadvantaged even in the slightest for the benefit of the Jews" (*auch nur geringfügigst zugunsten der Juden beeinträchtigt, bezw. benachteiligt*). Moreover, the Jews were to be supplied only with goods of the lowest quality, and the prices for goods delivered from the ghetto were to be fixed at a level suitable to this "more or less dubious merchandise."[207] Such policies, at least as interpreted and recorded by Palfinger, hardly constituted an auspicious beginning for the establishment of ghetto self-sufficiency.

A conference on November 9, 1940, under Uebelhoer's chairmanship, struck a rather different note. Uebelhoer immediately backed the complaint of the Lodz mayor, Dr. Marder, against a Finance Office proposal to collect back taxes from the account established to purchase ghetto provisions. He promised to seek clarification of the issue in Berlin. Biebow then outlined his plans for the ghetto economy. Contracts in hand from the military fully claimed the ghetto's skilled labor, and no further contracts could be signed at the moment. To enhance the ghetto's productive capacity, Biebow suggested that the HTO turn over all its unused or nonfunctioning machinery, especially such items as sewing machines and carpenter's benches. Restoration and maintenance of the machinery would be the ghetto's responsibility. Jewish labor was to be used solely for government projects requiring a large supply of labor. All requests were to be directed solely to the ghetto administration. Jewish labor was not to be put at the disposal of private firms. The military was to be prevailed upon not to contract private firms to do jobs that could be done by the "interned Jewish labor who were a public charge on the Reich."

Concerning the food supply, Biebow proposed a saving and rationing of food through the establishment of large common kitchens. Food supply should approximate "prison fare," with working Jews getting more than nonworking Jews. Uebelhoer agreed to this, as long as the supplementary rations for hard labor were provided at the workplace to prevent them from being shared with family members. Dr. Marder was asked to prepare a plan for food supply based upon a study of prison fare and medical opinion concerning the "nutritional minimum." To ensure that no cost for maintaining the ghetto fell to the Reich, further savings were to be achieved through a ban on the use of electricity and heating in the ghetto after eight o'clock in the evening.[208]

Biebow's concept of a highly centralized ghetto economy, with all contracts and allocation of labor decided solely through the ghetto administration, reflected the dictatorial predisposition and earlier proposals of the Jewish council chairman, Chaim Rumkowski, for centralized management from within the ghetto as well. In April 1940 Rumkowski had proposed to Marder that in order to purchase food for the ghetto and support the poor Jews, he alone be empowered to organize ghetto labor and production and to distribute the provisions earned in this manner.[209] Rumkowski had been authorized at that time to impose forced labor on all Jews in the ghetto.[210] But the German emphasis had been on extraction of Jewish wealth, not production, until the fall. Only then did the Germans come to share Rumkowski's wider concept of sustaining ghetto life through production.

In the following months Biebow went beyond collecting unused machinery in the Warthegau from the HTO. Through the Finance Ministry in Berlin, he also arranged for the delivery of machinery confiscated from German Jews. By March 1943 Biebow boasted of a machine inventory of 18,000 items.[211] He also toured Germany looking for contracts.[212] Biebow was constantly adding new workshops and factories and introducing new industries. The initial emphasis had been on textiles. By the spring of 1941, however, the Lodz ghetto was producing cabinets, furniture, shoes, and gloves, and performing tannery, furrier, upholstery, and locksmith work.[213]

Employment statistics reflected the economic transformation. In October 1940, 5,000 textile workers were employed in the ghetto. By December this figure had risen to 15,000.[214] Hopes for putting Jews to work outside the ghetto were not realized, for only 2,148 were employed outside between December 1940 and April 1941.[215] But employment within the ghetto rose steadily in the spring of 1941. By summer Marder claimed that 40,000 Jews were at work in the ghetto. A year later this figure was 53,000. And in the spring of 1943, it was 80,000, which is to say almost the entire ghetto population at that time.[216] Income earned by Jewish labor was estimated at 3.3 million RM for 1941, rising to 19 million for 1942. Moreover, initial reservations about the "dubious" quality of Jewish goods proved unfounded. A mistrustful Wehrmacht had originally given contracts only for tailoring, but once convinced of the "quality work" of the ghetto workers, was soon ordering military supplies of all kinds. All this was achieved, Biebow boasted, with a German administration of only 180 employers and 160 workers.[217]

Despite the burgeoning growth of the ghetto economy—in Isaiah Trunk's words, "the most industrialized ghetto in all of Eastern Europe"[218]—Biebow faced two difficulties. The first was the ghetto's balance of payments, which was always made precarious by the artificially depressed prices for goods produced by Jewish labor, the falsifications of German bookkeeping, and the constant attempts of various German authorities to lay their hands on the wealth being produced by Jewish labor.[219] One outrageous example of the last was the attempt by the city government in January 1941 to impose a lump sum tax of 275,000 RM per month on the Jewish community to compensate for a drop in the city's real estate and business tax revenues. The HTO paid taxes only on the actual rental income from its confiscated Jewish property, but thousands of Jewish apartments and businesses stood empty and thus produced no tax revenue. It seemed only logical to the city government that the Jews should make up the revenue shortfall brought about by their resettlement in the ghetto. This piece of chicanery was blocked by Uebelhoer, but the city government never ceased to complain about alleged costs, both direct and indirect, of the ghetto for which it was not being compensated.[220]

The precarious balance was maintained because, in addition to the ghetto's earned income, the ghetto administration also received the proceeds from the confiscation and liquidation of Jewish valuables. By its nature, this additional income was steadily decreasing. Thus Biebow never felt free from the threat that the ghetto would not be able to pay its way. The only way out, in his mind, was to constantly increase the productivity of the workers.[221] This was achieved by extending the workweek from 54 to 60 and finally to 72 hours and imposing draconian factory discipline.[222]

This intensification of exploitation immediately confronted Biebow with a second problem, however. The workers from whom he was demanding greater productivity were being steadily weakened, indeed slowly starved to death, by an utterly inadequate food supply. In October 1940 it had been suggested that the ghettoized Jews be provided with "prison fare." After various consultations this was officially approved the following month, with the limiting proviso "that the Jews receive this food only to the extent that in no case will the provisioning situation in Litzmannstadt be negatively affected."[223]

As the winter deepened, the food situation became increasingly more desperate. No food had been stockpiled for winter. In January Biebow reported:

The plight in the ghetto is so great that the Jewish Elder felt compelled to hand over to his communal kitchens the potato scraps that had been delivered for horse fodder, in order at least to be able to prepare lunch for the productively active workers in the workshops. . . . In practice the ghetto lives from hand to mouth, and each further shortfall in a food delivery earmarked for the Jews results in inescapable famine. . . . In calculating the needs of the population in Litzmannstadt and in the resulting allocation and delivery for the German and Polish population, apparently the ghetto is never included. It would be advisable that the attitude of the market control authorities fundamentally change, for the fact remains that the head as well as the other competent authorities of the ghetto administration must occupy themselves day after day with the question of feeding the ghetto, because either the deliveries are not as large as promised or allocated provisions are suddenly withdrawn for allegedly more urgent needs. Inevitably the necessity arises to drop other equally important tasks of the ghetto administration, which is especially disadvantageous to the mobilization of Jewish labor.[224]

The chroniclers of the Lodz ghetto noted the growing desperation as well: "With the current increase in the death rate, a minimum of three days' wait to bury the dead, sometimes even ten days, has become an everyday occurrence." The death counts in January and February were 1,218 and 1,069, almost reaching the July 1940 maximum of 1,366.[225]

In addition to the desperate need for food, Biebow noted that the shortage of coal was so great that meals could not be cooked even if potatoes were available, and workers were not coming to the unheated factories because they simply could not withstand the cold, the intensity of which Biebow had verified through personal inspection.[226] In mid-January a meeting took place between Uebelhoer's deputy, Dr. Moser, the provincial food authorities, and the ghetto administration on the question of supplying the ghetto. It was readily admitted that provisioning for the ghetto had reached neither the approved prison fare level nor the amounts promised by the food authorities. Biebow complained, moreover, that wholesalers refused to deliver even those goods not in scarce supply. He was assured that the wholesalers would be instructed to honor his requests. Moreover, it was decided that henceforth 10% of the city's coal allotment would be delivered to the ghetto, for otherwise the factories could not function.[227]

Biebow noted a slight improvement in the situation in the second half of January, but the hope that prison-level rations would be attained by February proved unfounded. In fact, deliveries of the main staple—potatoes—barely reached one-quarter of that level. "Catastrophe" and "famine" threatened, and it was obvious that productivity must suffer in such circumstances. Even the horses, so essential for transporting goods, were starving; yet all efforts to procure fodder had been in vain.[228]

The auditor examining the ghetto administration books calculated that the Jews were being fed on 23 pfennigs per day, though prison fare was at least double that. The auditor also commented on the lack of "proper understanding" concerning the ghetto. Requests for food and raw materials as well were met with the standard reply that nothing was available for the Jews. "It is thereby completely overlooked that these requests serve much less the interest of the Jews than the appropriate exploitation of Jewish manpower for the good of the Reich." (*Dabei werde vollständig übersehen, dass diese Anforderungen viel*

wen
Arb
(
rea
was
hor
of t
on
the
fan
bee
out
app
to
ing
lei
the
en

po
Au
wo
wl
in

the Jewish ghetto workers, who were far more productive th
counterparts, at least receive the same rations. Their provis
able," worse even than in any Jewish work camp or pri
bürgermeister, Werner Ventzki, promised to try but
Gauleiter [Greiser] has repeatedly refused to imp
Jews on principle, in view of the fact that su
involved not inconsiderable difficulties."[235]
time and the ideologically grounded axi
be expected to sacrifice or suffer in or
even the soundest arguments we
constraint the ghetto manager
It must be remembered
Jews was based exclusi
work, this was demo
in just the opposi
then they cou
over the a

deportations that began in January 1942), the ghetto was receiving too much food, Biebow replied with vehemence. In 1940 provisioning had been set at prison standards, he wrote, but this had not been met for more than a year. Moreover, what was delivered was of inferior quality. "No one can make the assertion that the ghetto inhabitants can remain fit for employment in the long run on the rations allocated to them. . . . The rapidly climbing death statistics provide the clearest proof of the food supply situation. . . . Anyone familiar with the situation in the ghetto knows that the workers literally collapse at their workplaces because of debilitation."[233] The city's public health officer fully supported Biebow's position. What was allocated to the Jews on paper was not in fact delivered, and thus provisioning was well below prison standards, leading to "downright famine." In such a situation "one could no longer demand of a Jew that he work." Furthermore, since epidemics prevailed among the hungry, the doctor warned of increased danger in that regard as well.[234]

A year later the situation had worsened, and Biebow once again asked that

...an their Polish
...ions were "intoler-
...son camp. The Ober-
...eld out little hope. "The
...rove the provisioning of the
...pplying the German population
...Given the inherent scarcities of war-
...om that on principle no one else could
...der to improve the food supply of the Jews,
...re doomed to failure. This was the ultimate
...could not surmount.

...that if after mid-1941 the argument for feeding the
...ely on the rationale that without food they could not
...nstrably not the case earlier. Initially, the argument had run
...e direction, namely, that if one did not find work for the Jews,
...d not be fed. In that argument the productionists had prevailed
...ritionists, albeit only partially.

Warsaw

In Warsaw those Germans advocating a reorganization of the ghetto economy had prevailed in May 1941, but this proved too late to stem the skyrocket-
ing death rate within the ghetto produced by half-a-year's starvation. The death
rate had risen above 1,000 in the month of February, over 2,000 in April, and
nearly doubled to 3,800 in May. A report of the military's Oberfeldkommandant
in Warsaw of May 20, 1941, described the situation vividly: "The situation in
the Jewish quarter is catastrophic. The corpses of those who have died of
starvation lie in the streets. The death rate, 80% from malnutrition, has tripled
since February. The only thing that is issued to the Jews is 1½ pounds of bread
per week. No one has yet been able to deliver potatoes, for which the Jewish
council made a prepayment of several millions. . . . The ghetto is becoming a
cultural scandal, a source of infection and a breeding place of the worst subhumanity."[236] "A quantum leap in deaths for May of this year showed that the
food shortage had already grown into a famine," Auerswald concluded. "The
provisioning of food thus constituted our most urgent task." Auerswald did
provide some extra supplies to the Jewish Self-Aid Society (JSS) to increase the
daily meals it provided from 30,000 in May to 120,000 in August. "Owing to the
general impoverishment of the Jews prevailing since the outbreak of the war,"
however, even these supplementary rations did not stem the rising death rates

until they peaked at 5,550 in July and 5,560 in August. Thereafter a modest decline and stabilization set in.[237]

During this period of soaring death rates, a number of Germans held out to the starving Jews the prospect of a general improvement in the food supply. In late May Fischer told Czerniakow of such a "possibility," and in early July Auerswald even said the Jews might be allocated "Polish rations" by August. By late July, however, Auerswald conceded that "the rations for the Jews will not be increased next month." And on August 19 Czerniakow was finally told that the prospects for a food increase were dim. "Auerswald declares that Cracow is also inclined not to starve out the ghetto Jews. However, the rations cannot be increased at this point because the newly captured territories absorb a lot of food."[238]

In October Max Bischof complained that the "unconditionally necessary" provisions for workers in the economy were lacking. He was vehemently supported by Auerswald. All aspects of Auerswald's policy toward the Jews—tighter sealing of the ghetto, ending Jewish black-marketeering and smuggling, preventing the spread of epidemics, as well as exploiting Jewish labor—depended upon "securing a necessary nutritional minimum for the working Jewish population." The present rations, less than one-third the level provided in the Lodz ghetto, were "absolutely insufficient." Governor Fischer, a onetime attritionist, continued to argue that the war was a conflict "with Jewry in its totality" and that the Germans would be justified in striking "destructively" against "these spawning grounds of Jewry, from which all world Jewry is constantly renewed." In the meantime, however, if the Jews were to work, they had to receive "sufficient rations."[239]

Frank, like Greiser in the Warthegau, refused on principle to approve any increase, noting that "even for the Polish population hardly anything more can be provided."[240] This was at least partially circumvented on the local level, however. Although the bread ration was not increased, Bischof arranged for the delivery of some other supplies, especially potatoes.[241] Czerniakow noted pessimistically: "The food rations were to be increased. The mountain gave birth to a mouse. . . . The bread ration is to remain as before; not a chance of increasing it." However, he did note that minuscule amounts of potatoes, sugar, and marmalade, and one egg per month per person, were promised.[242]

Bischof's efforts focused mainly not on a general increase in rations for the entire ghetto population but rather on supplemental rations provided by German employers to their Jewish workers. In the winter he was able to get this supplement at least for those involved in war production. The resulting increase in workers' productivity was so "extraordinary" that Bischof thought other private firms could be induced to follow suit. However, he noted, only 8% of the winter potato supply that he had procured for the ghetto had actually been delivered.[243]

From the beginning Auerswald and Bischof were fully aware that official food supplies to the ghetto were totally inadequate to sustain life. "The amount of legally delivered food is utterly insufficient to effectively counter the famine situation existing in the Jewish district," Auerswald stated bluntly in a report that the Cracow authorities deemed inappropriate for publication.[244] This had two results. On the one hand, the malnutrition meant ravaging epidemics, for Auerswald knew perfectly well that the "food and health situations are closely connected."[245] On the other hand, in their desperation to ward off starvation, the Jews smuggled extensively, which threatened to spread the hunger-induced epidemics beyond the ghetto walls. Unable to break the vicious circle simply by feeding the Jews enough to restore their health, Auerswald became increasingly perplexed about how to deal with the interrelated problems of smuggling and epidemic.

At first Auerswald announced a rather simple policy to Czerniakow. "He [Auerswald] indicated that so far as smuggling is concerned the authorities are looking the other way but that he will take the sternest measures against people leaving the ghetto. The reason—the epidemic."[246] But spotted fever spread beyond the ghetto anyway, and Auerswald blamed this on the Jewish smugglers. His relatively lenient attitude gave way to a harsher tone and more stringent measures. "Only the most drastic steps against vagabonding Jews (death penalty!) and above all the creation of borders that assure an actual demarcation and control can help here."[247] This required a significant shrinking of the ghetto through moving the walls inward to the middle of the streets, so openings could not be made through the back walls of border houses.[248]

Initially the German authorities decided on an even more drastic shortening of the wall to facilitate more-effective guarding by cutting off the smaller southern sector of the ghetto entirely. The city public health officer, Dr. Wilhelm Hagen, vigorously opposed the idea, appealing over Auerswald's head to Mayor Ludwig Leist "that it is insanity [ein Wahnsinn] to carry out such a measure at the present time." Given the increase in spotted fever, any such massive movement of peoples would be a "catastrophe."[249] The idea of eliminating the southern sector was in fact eventually given up, but even so some 60,000 Jews in the ghetto were uprooted once again in the extensive boundary changes.[250]

Auerswald's other antismuggling proposal—the death penalty for leaving the ghetto—was decreed by Frank on October 15, the very day he refused Bischof's request for additional food supplies for the Warsaw ghetto.[251] The logical connection between these two decisions did not escape the attention of a hundred government, military, and ss doctors from all over the General Government who were meeting at that time at Bad Krynica under the chairmanship of SA-Oberführer Dr. Jost Walbaum, Frank's chief of public health.[252] Professor Kudicke, who had been appointed special deputy for combating spotted fever, raised the important question "with great caution." Speaking "purely academically without making any value judgment" (*rein akademisch ohne irgendein Werturteil*), Kudicke noted that one could not successfully combat the spread of epidemic without removing its cause. He had noted in earlier reports that the considerable scarcity of food led to a situation in which

> without doubt the Jewish population simply broke out of the ghettos in which there was nothing to eat. . . . If one wants to prevent that in the future, then one must use the best means for this, namely, provide more sufficient provisioning of the Jewish population. This is beyond my power—I may be quite open—this is beyond the power of all of us. For me the matter is clear, and I also know that the difficulties are so great that the shortage may possibly never be removed in this regard.

Therefore, Kudicke concluded, the attempt to combat the spread of epidemic might quite simply fail.

On this discouraging note Dr. Walbaum apparently felt the need to intervene.

> You are completely right. Naturally it would be the best and simplest to give the people sufficient provisioning possibilities, but that cannot be done. That is connected to the food situation and the war situation in general. Thus shooting will be employed when one comes across a Jew outside the ghetto without special permission. One must, I can say it quite openly in this circle, be clear about it. There are only two ways. We sentence the Jews in the ghetto to death by hunger or we shoot them. [*Man muss sich, ich kann es in diesem Kreise offen aussprechen, darüber klar sein, es gibt nur 2 Wege, wir verurteilen die Juden im Ghetto zum Hungertode oder wir erschiessen sie.*] Even if the end result is the same, the latter is more intimidating. We cannot do otherwise, even if we want to. We have one and only one responsibility, that the German people are not infected and endangered by these parasites. For that any means must be right.

The protocol indicates that Walbaum's remarks were greeted with "Applause, clapping" (*Beifall, Klatschen*).

Dr. Lambrecht, the chief public health officer of the Warsaw district, supported Walbaum. It was utopian to think one could seal the ghetto so that not a single infected Jew could leave. Thus one must naturally approve of shooting Jews outside the ghetto without permission. He himself had recommended that "the provisioning of the Jews in the ghetto be improved, because the greater the pressure in the ghetto, all the greater the pressure on the borders. Unfortunately the necessary food supply could not be approved, because nothing was there. But it is always better in any case, that the Jews starve in the ghetto than that they sit scattered about the city and die there. . . . One must be logical, and it is thus appropriate to proceed against the Jews much more severely than before." Lambrecht's remarks, like Walbaum's, were greeted with "applause, clapping." The appetite for thinking clearly and logically about starving Jews had grown quite strong in the medical profession, which, having urged ghettoization to prevent the spread of epidemics, was now eager (like the attritionists) for the "rapid dying out" of the Jews for the same reason.[253]

The death penalty for leaving the ghetto, so enthusiastically supported by the doctors, was announced to the ghetto on November 6. The first executions were carried out two weeks later. Four days after the first executions, an extraordinary conversation occurred in which Czerniakow talked with Auerswald for $2\frac{1}{2}$ hours about the latter's "historical role and responsibility" and the "rationality of official measures."[254] Perhaps because there was a significant decline in the incidence of disease,[255] perhaps because of Czerniakow's effort, Auerswald's attitude on the smuggling question softened. Instead of shooting all those caught leaving the ghetto, he acceded to Czerniakow's request to work for the release of many of them. When finally successful, he told Czerniakow that "had he known how complicated the whole business was, he would not have undertaken it." Czerniakow replied that he should "listen to the voices of his conscience above all."[256]

If Auerswald did not solve the food problem and struggled with the problem of smuggling, he and Bischof were more successful—though only gradually—in creating the basis for a ghetto economy in Warsaw. Massive unemployment within the ghetto was a major obstacle. Early in 1941, before the change of ghetto managers in May, the German authorities had intended to deal with the employment question by creating labor camps on a very large scale. There were plans for sending 25,000 Jews back to the Lublin district and for employing another 25,000 in water control projects in the Warsaw district itself. With such an outflow of labor, a "noticeable easing" within the ghetto had been expected.[257] As already noted, however, the work camp did not prove to be the answer either for the ghetto's unemployment problem or for the effective exploitation of Jewish labor.

In addition to the ill-fated work camps, the German ghetto managers attempted to deal with the employment problem along four lines. The first was to set up workshops in the ghetto. Auerswald claimed this to be a great success, but in fact his statistics indicated only the most modest improvement. By September employment in the workshops had reached only 3,055 out of a total of 36,198 registered employed. This stood in stark contrast to the 69,862 unemployed, down from 76,102 in June.[258] It stood in even starker contrast to the 53,000 employed at this time in Lodz, although that ghetto had only one-third the population.

The second approach was to carry out yet another registration of Jewish workers, with the promise of better rations for those who complied and the threat of fines against those who did not. But registration went very slowly. As Hoffmann noted, "The fear of the Jewish population to appear before the labor office is based on the fact the until now such measures were taken only for the purpose of camp labor." This mistrust would only be overcome by finding work for those registering.[259]

The third approach was to stabilize and revive economic life within the ghetto by freeing it from past threats and restrictions. Confiscation and other counterproductive interventions were halted. Various controls on the possession of currency were lifted, and an amnesty was decreed for hidden wealth in order to encourage its use in the economy. The Jewish council was allowed various banking and credit privileges to facilitate economic changes, and the previous fees for economic transactions were sharply lowered. Various departments of the Jewish council that had hitherto handled economic functions were dissolved and replaced by "corporations" that would henceforth operate on a business rather than bureaucratic basis.[260]

And finally, a concerted attempt was made to attract German employers to the ghetto. Articles about Jewish skilled workers were placed in various German newspapers; newsletters were sent to various economic organizations in Germany; the dispensers of public contracts, particularly involving armaments, were approached.[261] In Warsaw, in contrast to Lodz, the Wehrmacht was initially a reluctant employer.[262] More successful was the attempt to attract private firms. A major inducement was the fact that the ghetto administration had gotten out of the business of trying to run workshops. "Since in the long run the Transferstelle could not assume the economic risk for these shops, German firms have been introduced to direct the shops and obtain orders for them."[263] Thus in contrast to the highly centralized and controlled economy in Lodz, the ghetto authorities in Warsaw began to foster a kind of "ghetto-free enterprise"—one that offered possibilities to both German as well as Jewish capitalists. For instance, Bischof denounced Czerniakow's imposition of forced welfare contributions on wealthier Jews on the grounds that it was "ruining the capital market."[264]

Inevitably, the more open economy of the Warsaw ghetto meant that Bischof's Transferstelle did not and could not have the same kind of control as exercised by Biebow in Lodz. While the Transferstelle was expected at least to supervise economic exchange between the ghetto and the outside world, in fact a whole underground economy grew up. Contracts were arranged and raw materials and finished products were delivered without the knowledge or approval of the Transferstelle.[265] Bischof was certainly aware of some of what was going on, because he complained that "Aryan firms avoid the formal requirement of the Transferstelle's approval procedures," and that the inadequate sealing of the ghetto "was misused to an extraordinarily great extent for illegal trade with the Jewish district."[266] However, Auerswald and Bischof were even less inclined to take decisive measures against this kind of illicit economic activity than they were against smuggling. They were more concerned with the serious problems that still threatened the precarious ghetto economy in the winter of 1941–42: the around-the-clock power failures and cutoffs that made even a shift to night work impossible, the frequent shortages of raw materials, and the constant transportation stoppages that bedeviled the economy.[267]

Despite all these measures, Bischof had little to show for his efforts in the first half-year. Taking stock in mid-October 1941, a discouraged Bischof confessed that economically the ghetto was a "field of ruins."[268] However, in early 1942 a significant change in the ghetto economy began to occur. The driving force behind this economic change was the altered attitude among many Germans toward the potential of Jewish labor which paralleled a change in the German attitude toward Soviet prisoners of war and other captive populations. After the desperate winter of 1941 on the eastern front, early victory was no longer taken for granted. Germany had to gird for the long haul. The hoards of Soviet prisoners, or more precisely the minority that had survived the terrible decimation of the first nine months of the Soviet-German war (over two million had perished by April 1942!), were now a scarce commodity. Likewise, demands for Polish labor increased.[269] At a conference in late March 1942, Hoffmann informed Auerswald and other district authorities of the new situation. All the Russians working in the civilian sector and half of those working for the army were being sent back from Poland to Germany. Hundreds of thousands of Poles were also being sent to the Reich. The ghetto was now a reservoir of labor that was needed for tasks important to the war economy.[270]

In the months of April and May, demands for Jewish labor rose dramatically.

New firms opened operations in the ghetto and others expanded their operations there. In May the death rate dropped below 4,000 for the first time in a year.[271] Production figures skyrocketed. That portion of the economy registered in Transferstelle statistics had produced exports worth 3,736,300 zloty in January 1942. This increased regularly each month, so that in June this figure reached 14,458,200 zloty and in the first three weeks in July 15,058,558 zloty.[272]

The reversal was clearly apparent on June 18, 1942, when Fischer's deputy Hummel announced to leading officials of the General Government:

> Contrary to earlier expert studies, we have been so successful in activating the ghetto economically that state subsidies have not yet been necessary. In the ghetto approximately 25,000 Jews worked in enterprises important to the war economy, while 3,000 Jews were employed in external work. . . . The monthly exchange between the ghetto and the Aryan sector at the moment amounted to 6 million; in addition to that was an unregistered exchange of perhaps some 2 to 3 million. For better or worse, the inhabitants of the ghetto lived off this exchange. He [Hummel] hoped that in the foreseeable future the city of Warsaw would be relieved of the burden of the nonworking Jews.[273]

Despite all the disadvantages under which it labored, the ghetto economy in Warsaw had clearly turned the corner.

Yet the ghetto was living on borrowed time, for it was precisely in the spring of 1942 that the great onslaught against the Polish ghettos began. In the case of Warsaw this onslaught was not the product of local initiative, either as the last recourse of frustrated ghetto authorities because the ghetto had stubbornly survived their attempts to starve it, or as the way out of an economic impasse in which the ghetto population could not be viably supported. In Warsaw the turn to mass murder would destroy an economic experiment that was in fact beginning to bear fruit.

From the beginning of the war the concentration of the Jews had been seen as a temporary measure to facilitate their control and imminent expulsion. Even when more-formal ghettoization ensued—in different places at different times in different ways for different reasons—the ghetto was still not regarded as a permanent fixture, just one that was going to last longer than the Germans had initially expected. Imminent expulsion had become expulsion in the indeterminate future, and ghettoization was merely an intermediate measure.

Once in existence, ghettos invariably gave rise to a German bureaucracy of ghetto managers. Among themselves they were fully agreed on one aspect of their task. The Jewish councils were an invaluable instrument through which they exercised their control. They were vital, indeed indispensable, in relieving the Germans of much of the burden of managing the ghetto. As Schön's assistant Mohns noted: "It is in the interest of the onerous administration of the Jewish district that in any case the authority of the Jewish council is maintained and strengthened."[274] Moreover, the Jewish councils served as lightening rods, attracting to themselves much of the hostility and frustration of the interned Jews. "When deficiencies occur," wrote Auerswald, "the Jews direct the resentment against the Jewish administration, and not against the German supervisors."[275]

If the ghetto managers were agreed upon the expediency of working through the Jewish councils, there was less clarity and consensus on the issue of ghetto maintenance. On this point Isaiah Trunk has expressed a different view, arguing that there was a clearly understood goal in Nazi ghettoization policy, even if that policy was imperfectly implemented:

> It was the set task of the German occupation authorities . . . to see to it that the Jews decreased in numbers by the impositions of economic measures that were designed to achieve pauperization, epidemics, and an increased death rate. Try as they did, they could not achieve these aims completely. Their intentions were to some degree frustrated . . . because of the neutralizing influence of . . . a subjective factor in the attitude of some of the German ghetto overlords toward the Jews—the last vestiges of humaneness in some of them, or varying degrees of corruption or moral depravity in others.[276]

Without any doubt, there were many German authorities who advocated and welcomed the attrition of the Jewish population through the exploitation and ghettoization measures of 1939–41. But it is misleading to state that attrition was the "set task" of the German authorities which, despite the Germans' best efforts, was partially mitigated by either corruption or the last vestiges of humaneness.

On the contrary, aside from preparing the Jews for eventual expulsion, which included concentrating them and excluding them from the regular economy, there simply was no "set task." Without clear direction from above about what to do with the Jews while their expulsion was repeatedly postponed, local authorities were forced to improvise. For some, indeed, the ghetto was to be merely a vast urban internment camp in which a "natural diminution" of the Jewish population was the expected and desired result. But this turned out to be a minority view. The prevailing view that emerged among the local Germans, who were left more or less to themselves by Berlin, was to "store" the Jews in ghetto "warehouses" in such a way as to minimize the burden upon the German authorities.

That the Jews were viewed as an undesirable burden is not in question. German occupation policy and anti-Jewish measures had indeed created a "self-fulfilling prophecy" in which the appearance and behavior of Polish Jewry confirmed the Nazi anti-Semitic stereotype. Ruthless expropriation and exploitation of labor combined with a totally inadequate food supply, terrible overcrowding in poor housing, and utterly inadequate sanitation and medical care turned Polish Jewry into a starving, disease-ridden, impoverished community desperately struggling for survival through "illegal" smuggling, bribery, and black-market activities.[277] In the eyes of the occupying Germans, they posed an ever increasing threat to public health, economic order, and aesthetic standards. As is evident in their documents, at least some of the ghetto managers understood that this "vicious circle" had been set in motion by German policy, with whose adverse effects they were left to cope. It was not their intention or expectation to change the fundamentals of German occupation policy, however. Rather, their goal was to mitigate temporarily the burden by creating a self-sufficient ghetto economy that would sustain the Jewish population until it could be expelled.

They behaved in this way, for the most part, neither out of a desire to maximize the opportunity for corrupt self-enrichment nor from the last vestiges of humaneness—though there was much of the former and a little of the latter—but because this was how they conceived of their duty to the Third Reich. This was how they helped Germany cope with the Jewish question until the central authorities took the problem off their hands. They did not see this duty as a preliminary to the death camps. Men who conceive of themselves as part of a covert scheme to decimate the Jewish population do not openly appeal for improved rations, or boast to their superiors of their success in combating epidemics, lowering death rates, or harnessing the ghetto population to self-sustaining labor.[278]

If the behavior of the German ghetto managers did not indicate the existence of a premeditated plan for the extermination of the Jews, of which ghettoization was to be the initial or preliminary stage, it also did not reveal the existence of any political mechanism of automatic and inevitable radicalization through local initiative from below. The trend in ghetto management was not toward radicalization but rather toward increasing economic rationality and utilitarianism. As Yisrael Gutman has written, "It soon became evident to the Germans that they could not have it both ways: starve the Jews and annihilate the ghetto and at the same time take advantage of Jewish manpower."[279] Even before the failure of the

German Blitzkrieg against the Soviet Union and the growing awareness of the need to mobilize economically for a long war, the ghetto managers had opted for the latter. The changing perspectives on the war only reinforced a process already underway.

But the ghetto managers always saw their task as a holding action, not the ultimate solution to the Jewish question. As Auerswald noted, "The best solution would apparently still be the removal of the Jews to some other place."[280] They always knew that one day the ghettos would disappear, and they never dreamed of resisting or opposing when that day came. Indeed, many yearned for the day when they would be free of their unwelcome and frustrating burden. Thus once Berlin had resolved how to settle the Jewish question, their new duty was to facilitate the liquidation of the very ghettos they had previously sought to maintain.

5

Germany and Europe

German-occupied Poland, as the demographic center of the Jewish population under Nazi control and the site of the regime's first attempts to engineer the racial transformation of conquered Lebensraum, was the key "laboratory" for Nazi experimentation in racial persecution from September 1939 to June 1941. Given both the size of the population subjected to persecution and the radical extent of the measures employed, events in Poland have tended to eclipse the measures of Nazi racial persecution within Germany's pre-1939 borders during this period. While certainly the persecution of German Jews was less radical than that of Polish Jews at this time, nonetheless the isolation, impoverishment, exploitation, and humiliation of German Jews accelerated drastically. In addition, the Roma and Sinti, referred to as *Zigeuner* or "Gypsies," experienced persecution that had chilling parallels to that of the Jews. And most crucially, with the killing of the German handicapped, especially by carbon monoxide in the gas chambers of the "euthanasia" centers, the Nazi regime discovered how it could harness the scientific, medical, and organizational capacities of modern society to implement its racial projects through systematic mass murder.

The Persecution of German Jewry

Following the November 1938 pogrom, the Nazi regime pursued what Wolf Gruner has called a "double strategy" of coerced emigration on the one hand and the "segregation of those remaining within a controlled community" on the other.[1] With the outbreak of war in September 1939, the already limited possibilities for coerced emigration were drastically diminished even further, and the alternative of collective expulsion was repeatedly postponed. This left German authorities to concentrate on intensifying the persecution of the "controlled community" of German Jews. Several measures that had been briefly considered but then vetoed in the wake of Kristallnacht—marking and ghettoization—

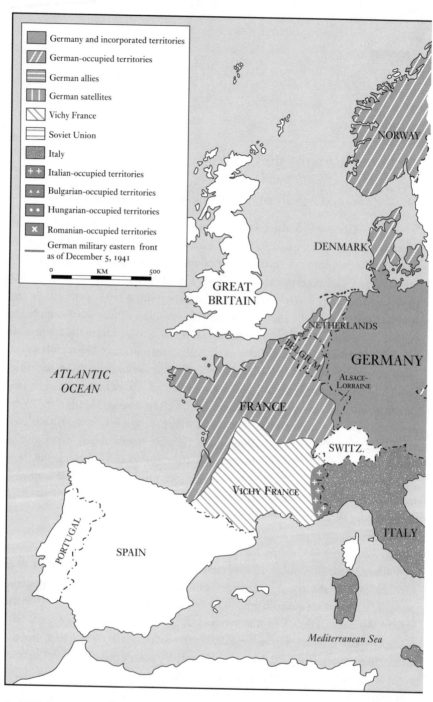

Germany and incorporated territories

German-occupied territories

German allies

German satellites

Vichy France

Soviet Union

Italy

Italian-occupied territories

Bulgarian-occupied territories

Hungarian-occupied territories

Romanian-occupied territories

German military eastern front
as of December 5, 1941

0   KM   500

NORWAY

DENMARK

GREAT
BRITAIN

NETHERLANDS

BELGIUM

GERMANY

ALSACE-
LORRAINE

ATLANTIC
OCEAN

FRANCE

SWITZ.

VICHY FRANCE

ITALY

PORTUGAL

SPAIN

Mediterranean Sea

2. EUROPE, DECEMBER 1941

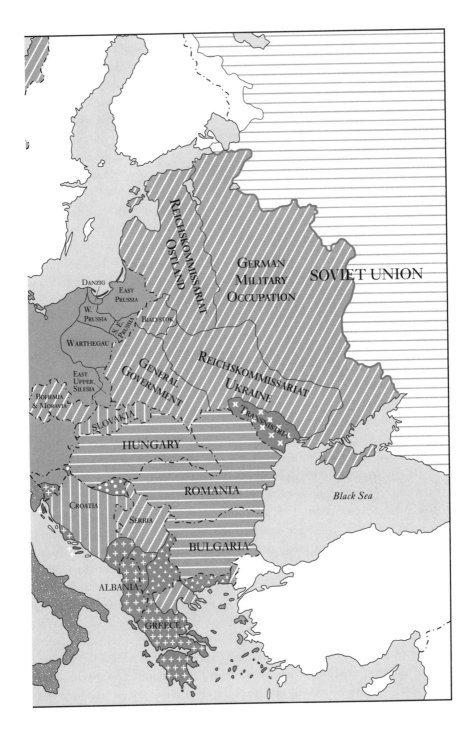

DANZIG
EAST PRUSSIA
W. PRUSSIA
S. E. PRUSSIA
BIALYSTOK
WARTHEGAU
EAST UPPER SILESIA
BOHEMIA & MORAVIA
SLOVAKIA

REICHSKOMMISSARIAT OSTLAND

GENERAL GOVERNMENT

GERMAN MILITARY OCCUPATION

SOVIET UNION

REICHSKOMMISSARIAT UKRAINE

TRANSNISTRIA

HUNGARY

CROATIA
SERBIA

ROMANIA

Black Sea

BULGARIA

ALBANIA

GREECE

had been imposed in Poland but remained off-limits within Germany. But the persecutors still had plenty of scope to devise an endless cascade of new anti-Jewish measures. These increased the suffering of the German Jews in roughly five ways, through (1) intensifying their isolation and concentration, (2) accelerating their impoverishment, (3) eroding yet further their legal rights and status and subjecting them to intensifying terror, (4) deepening their humiliation and degradation, and (5) expanding the exploitation of their labor. Measures in the first four categories paved the way for the ultimate collective expulsion and annihilation of German Jewry. Ironically, measures in the last category had unexpected countervailing consequences, at least temporarily.

Measures for the isolation of German Jews had, of course, begun long before the outbreak of the war and had taken many forms, from forbidding mixed marriage or sexual relations with non-Jews to banning Jews from swimming pools and beaches, park and gardens, theaters and cinemas, public libraries and museums, and hotels, restaurants, and cafés.[2] The persecution of German Jews had made their continued life in small towns and villages both economically impossible and socially unbearable. The result was intensified concentration in the form of urbanization, as they fled to the anonymity of larger cities.[3] In addition, in the months following the outbreak of war, Jews were forced to leave the western border regions.[4] In Marian Kaplan's words, many Jews "were turned into refugees within Germany."[5]

A second form of concentration, a kind of substitute ghettoization, then occurred as German Jews were increasingly forced into so-called Jew houses (*Judenhäuser*). Although the construction of ghettos had been rejected in the post-Kristallnacht planning period, proposals had been made to exempt Jews from the rent protection laws, thus permitting German landlords to demand their immediate eviction. This proposal was rejected by Hitler, however, in order to avoid the disruptive consequences of massive and sudden homelessness.[6] Instead, as far as possible Jews were to be concentrated in individual houses. The legal basis for this was provided by a law of April 30, 1939, modifying the rental rights of Jews. A Jew could be evicted by a landlord if the landlord obtained certification from the municipal authorities that other housing was available. And municipal authorities could compel Jewish homeowners to take in Jewish renters.[7] This created a situation in which municipal authorities, in conjunction with local party leaders and police (and in Berlin, Albert Speer's office as well), gradually concentrated the Jewish population in clusters of specifically Jewish houses. By mid-1941 the process had gone a step further. In May 1941 the ss in Vienna ordered that all Jews in that city could reside in only three districts, thus coming very close to creating de facto ghettos.[8] Elsewhere, many municipal authorities began creating Jewish "residence camps" (*Wohnlager*) in old barracks or other rundown, disused buildings. At least 38 such residence camps were eventually established.[9] The largest of these was in the barracks of an old fort in Müngersdorf outside Cologne, into which 2,000 Jews were crammed, 20 to a room.[10]

Several kinds of isolation measures immediately followed the outbreak of the war. First, German Jews were subjected to both a curfew and restricted shopping hours, so there would be far less time and occasion to mix with the non-Jewish population. Second, they were cut off from information and communication. In September 1939 Jews had their radio sets confiscated. Then in 1940 their private telephones were taken, and in the following year they were banned from using public telephones. In that same year they were forbidden access to rental libraries, and in 1942 even to buy newspapers and magazines.[11]

In the last months of 1938 and first months of 1939, the German Jews had been subjected to a massive and systematic expropriation of their property, as "voluntary aryanization" had been replaced by "compulsory aryanization."[12] By the outbreak of war, the German Jews had been stripped of the bulk of their property, but that did not stop the German bureaucracy from inventing yet further measures to intensify the process of impoverishment. Some of these measures confiscated what little property Jews still had through what Uwe Adam termed "legalized raiding."[13] For instance, on November 15, 1939, the notorious "expiation tax" was increased from 20% to 25%. And in December 1940 the wages of Jewish workers were subjected to a 15% "social equalization tax" on the grounds that Jews did not contribute to Nazi charitable and relief organizations.[14] In the following years Jews were ordered to surrender a variety of specific items, such as furs, electrical appliances, typewriters, calculators, duplicating machines, bicycles, cameras, and binoculars. In the city of Dresden they were even ordered to surrender safety razors, new combs, and hair scissors.[15]

Other measures prohibited German Jews from receiving supplies that other Germans still received. Most devastating in this regard were the numerous restrictions on rationing. Propaganda Minister Joseph Goebbels set the tone when on November 17, 1939, he demanded that Jews not be allowed ration cards for the purchase of chocolate products, an idea that the Reich Food Ministry immediately embraced.[16] The Nazis soon went from the symbolic to the serious. In December 1939 the first of many cuts in food rations for Jews was ordered, a process that would ultimately leave the entire community hungry and malnourished. And this was quickly followed by prohibitions against Jews receiving ration cards for shoes, clothes, and textile fabrics.[17] Jews were even barred from purchasing many nonrationed food items, both by specific prohibition and by limiting shopping hours to ensure that permitted items would be sold out before Jews had access.[18] Also, German Jews were prohibited from receiving the many supplementary wage payments received by German workers, such as holiday pay, family and children's allowances, and birth, marriage, and death benefits.[19]

German Jews were also increasingly deprived of legal protection and subjected to the unfettered terror of the police state. In October 1939, shortly after the outbreak of the war, Himmler ordered the immediate arrest and incarceration in a concentration camp of any Jew who failed to comply immediately with any instruction or who demonstrated antistate behavior in any other way. And the following spring he ordered that all Jews in concentration camps were not to be released for the duration of the war.[20] German Jews were, therefore, particularly at the mercy of local police authorities and the zeal with which they exercised the virtually unlimited power over Jewish life that Himmler had granted them. Aware of their vulnerability, German Jews were exacting in their obedience to the law. Nevertheless, as Eric Johnson has shown, the percentage of the Gestapo cases involving Jews in the town of Krefeld rose from 20% in the prewar period to 35% during the war, even though Jews represented an almost infinitesimal portion of the German population at large. Caught between Gestapo zeal and popular denunciation, German Jews were many times more likely to have a case started against them, and were many more times likely to receive much harsher sentences than "ordinary" Germans.[21]

While Himmler issued decrees that in practice allowed for the disappearance of Jews into the concentration camp system on the slightest pretext and left them defenseless before the whim of local police authorities, the state secretary of the Interior Ministry Wilhelm Stuckart became fixated on the idea of stripping German Jews of their German citizenship.[22] Jews in the Sudentenland, the Protectorate, and the incorporated territories had not, of course, been granted German citizenship when these regions became part of the Third Reich. When Himmler set forth his procedures for the "re-Germanization" of selected inhabitants in the incorporated territories, and proposed categorizing those who were clearly ineligible as "dependents" (*Schutzangehöriger*) of the German Reich, Stuckart was perturbed by both the legal disorder that had arisen and the anomaly that non-Jewish populations in the incorporated territories would have a lower status than German Jews. He therefore proposed that German Jews also be reduced to the status of "dependents." Wilhelm Kritzinger, ministerial director of the Reich Chancellery, could not understand the purpose of creating a special legal position for German Jews "in view of the fact that in the not-so-distant future the Jews will have disappeared from Germany."[23] And his boss,

Hans Lammers, obtained Hitler's decision in December 1940 emphatically rejecting any decree that would mention Jews as "dependents" of the Reich.

Undeterred, Stuckart sponsored various meetings and presided over various legislative drafts that now aimed at making German Jews immediately stateless. When the final draft was submitted to Hitler on May 27, 1941, he once again rejected it because, as Lammers reported to Bormann, "he is of the opinion that after the war there will be no Jews in Germany anyway and thus it is not necessary to enact a regulation that is hard to administer, ties up manpower, and still does not bring about a basic solution."[24] Hitler thought that a regulation simply depriving German Jews residing abroad of their citizenship (and property) would be sufficient, and this was precisely the formula eventually enacted in November 1941.

Notwithstanding Stuckart's failure to deprive the German Jews of their citizenship, they were subjected to a continuing barrage of prohibitions that served no purpose other than to gratuitously humiliate and degrade them. As of October 20, 1939, Jewish authors could not be cited in German Ph.D. dissertations unless it was absolutely indispensable for academic reasons, and then only if the Jewish sources were clearly marked as such. In the same month Jews were forbidden to serve as volunteer firefighters.[25] The year 1942 was a particularly fertile one for the creative bureaucrats of persecution. Perhaps precisely because their victims were fast disappearing into death camps in the east and their years of accumulated expertise in Jewish affairs would soon be professionally irrelevant, they hastened to construct legislative monuments to their own zeal. In Leipzig signs were to be posted in all bakeries and confectioneries that cakes would not be sold to Jews and Poles. In Dresden, where Jews had been forced to surrender their safety razors and combs, they were also forbidden to buy cut flowers. Jews were not to own pets or have their hair cut by non-Jewish barbers. They were not to buy national costumes or use previous professional titles and professional designations when dealing with German officials.[26]

All of these measures furthering the isolation, concentration, expropriation, impoverishment, intimidation, incarceration, and humiliation of German Jews created a climate and situation conducive to their subsequent deportation and destruction. In the exploitation of Jewish labor, however, the persecutors inadvertently created complications that would briefly slow the process of deportation and destruction. Before the outbreak of war, the forced labor of German Jews was in practice limited. Unemployed Jews fit for work were required to register with their local labor offices, which were to assign them to menial, hard-labor jobs segregated from non-Jewish workers.[27] By the summer of 1939, some 20,000 Jews were working at such assigned jobs.[28]

A conference on February 28, 1939, sponsored by the Interior Ministry and chaired by Bernhard Lösener, explored the labor obligation of Jews in case of war. The participants, representing the Security Police, Order Police, Wehrmacht, and Theodor Eicke's concentration camp system, were unanimous that all male Jews, 18–55 years old, would be obligated to hard forced labor (such as road construction). Since this work was considered an alternative to the compulsory military service performed by male Germans, it was to be less attractive and thus take place "in a military form" in "special camps."[29] Further planning along these lines did not in fact take place before the outbreak of the war. In the first months thereafter, only the Nazi authorities in Vienna seriously explored the possibility of building large labor camps for the internment of Austrian Jews and discovered that the cost of such an enterprise would be very high.[30]

With Hitler's approval of plans to deport all Reich Jews to the Lublin reservation, long-term plans for the mobilization and exploitation of Jewish labor seemed irrelevant. Indeed, many of the projects employing Jewish forced labor were set aside as nonpriority items, and demand for Jewish labor sank. Many of those Jews already caught up in forced labor were sent instead to help bring in the fall harvest, before being replaced by large numbers of Polish prisoners of war who arrived in Germany in late October. Jews at forced labor were then assigned such menial tasks as snow removal. As both Germany's labor shortage and the presence of Jews in Germany were still thought of as short-term situations, there was as yet no thought of incorporating Jews into the war economy in any significant way.[31]

The context for thinking about Jewish labor changed significantly in the spring of 1940. Deportation of Reich Jews to the east was postponed once again, and the idea of the Lublin reservation was given up. Emigration from the Third Reich was still pursued in theory but increasingly restricted, first by limited avenues of exit and second by the prohibition against male Jews of military age leaving. At the same time, the labor shortage in German industry became ever more critical. At this point all Jews (males 15 to 55 years old and females 15 to 50) were ordered to register for labor, not just those who were unemployed and on welfare. Moreover, in May and June 1940 Jews were assigned jobs in industry, including the armaments sector, for the first time, though still as unskilled rather than skilled workers.[32]

The appetite of German industry for Jewish labor was whetted. Here was a pool of workers from whom maximum work could be extracted for minimum pay, but for whom, unlike foreign workers, barracks did not have to be constructed and translators did not have to be provided. Increasingly, Jews were shifted from unskilled to skilled jobs, and by October 1940 the number of Jews in forced labor reached 40,000.[33] Beginning in Vienna, and subsequently in the rest of the Reich, increasingly draconian measures were taken to replenish the exhausted reservoir of Jewish labor. The age limits of 55 for men and 50 for women were ignored. Jewish communal authorities were forced to reduce the numbers of their own employees, and the newly unemployed Jewish community officials, as well as participants in training camps for emigration run by the Jewish communities, were incorporated into the forced labor pool. Jews who had been certified unfit for work were subjected to new examinations. And the systematic recruitment of women intensified.[34]

How thoroughly the forced labor of German Jews had been integrated into the war economy was graphically demonstrated in the fall of 1940. In October, Fritz Todt, the man in charge of Germany's highway construction, bypassed the usual labor authorities and directly approached the RSHA concerning the desperate need for manpower. The RSHA in turn demanded that the Reichsvereinigung der Juden (Reich Union of Jews) provide 10,000 Jewish men for road construction within five days. Given the near total mobilization of Jewish labor that had already been achieved, this demand proved impossible to meet. The RSHA gave exceptional permission for the Gauleiter of the Warthegau, Arthur Greiser, to provide Polish Jews for work on the Frankfurt an der Oder–to–Poznan stretch of Autobahn under construction, even though this meant housing Polish Jews in labor camps within pre-1938 German boundaries. A similar exception was made for the use of Polish Jews on road construction in Silesia.[35]

As the labor shortage intensified, the Reich Labor Ministry also approached Greiser with a plan for procuring a further 73,000 Polish Jews from the Warthegau for labor in Germany.[36] The state secretary of the Labor Ministry, Dr. Friedrich Syrup, argued that "because the present employment situation makes necessary the utilization of all available manpower reserves, the employment of these Jews cannot be dispensed with."[37] At this point, however, pragmatic considerations concerning the war economy's labor needs collided with the ideological priorities of the Nazi regime for a *judenfrei* Reich. Just one week after Syrup informed local labor offices that the 73,000 Jewish workers from the Warthegau would be made available, Goebbels pressed Eichmann to help him rid Berlin of its Jews as quickly as possible.[38] Much to his astonishment Goebbels discovered that "the Jews, it turns out, cannot be evacuated from Berlin because 30,000 of them are working in armaments factories. Who would have ever thought that possible."[39]

The degree to which years of effort to create a *judenfrei* Reich were being overturned by Germany's labor needs became clear, and the RSHA now intervened:

For years it has been the aspiration of the Reich Security Main Office [RSHA] to cleanse Reich territory of Jews. The difficulties that this task has encountered are known. It will not do that on the one hand Jews are with extraordinary effort shipped out while on the other hand let back in. Until now only one exception has been made, namely, for the construction of the strategically important stretch of highway between Frankfurt an der Oder and Poznan. . . . A further shifting of Jewish workers from the eastern territories, especially into Old Reich territory, is indefensible.[40]

In addition to the RSHA, Hitler also intervened. On April 7, 1941, Syrup had to rescind his previous communication because "the Führer has now decided that Jews from the General Government and the Warthegau are not to be employed on Reich territory."[41] Thus a limit to employing Jewish forced labor, regardless of economic exigency, had been set.

The shaping of Nazi policies concerning the use of Jewish labor is instructive in several ways. First, this was an area of both extreme polycracy and consensus. The number of authorities involved—from the Reich Labor Ministry, ss, Office of the Four-Year Plan, Interior Ministry, Party Chancellery, and Wehrmacht at the top to the local labor offices, communal authorities, party organizations, and industries at the bottom—was nearly endless.[42] Yet despite the inevitable friction and jurisdictional quibbling, there was virtual consensus on pursuing seemingly paradoxical policies. The Nazi regime attempted to maximize the exploitation of German Jewish labor while it simultaneously reduced the productivity of these same workers through minimal wages, increasingly inadequate food and housing, and other debilitating forms of persecution.[43] As in so many other realms of Nazi policy, the circle was to be squared through fear and coercion.

Second, when the fundamental ideological priority of making Germany *judenfrei* was challenged by the economic priority of importing additional Jewish labor to alleviate the labor shortage, ideological priority prevailed. This was one of the rare occasions when Hitler felt moved to intervene. And the outcome foreshadowed the ultimate fate of German Jewish labor, when even their position as skilled workers in the armaments industry would only delay but not prevent their deportation and death.

The Persecution of the "Gypsies"
Alongside the Jews in Europe, the people known as "Gypsies" had for centuries been a dispersed minority subjected to a pervasive negative stereotype. They were characterized as rootless itinerants and alleged to be habitually parasitical, criminal, unclean, lazy, promiscuous, and unreliable. Again as in the case

of the Jews, the trend toward emancipation and democratization in Europe had neither eliminated widespread prejudice against "Gypsies" nor granted them full equality before the law. Not surprisingly, therefore, the Nazi regime posed a special danger to the "Gypsies"—first to the Sinti of Germany and then to the Roma throughout Europe as well. However, the route the "Gypsies" traveled to Auschwitz was an even more twisted road than that of the Jews.[44]

The "Gypsies" held no prominent position in Hitler's hate-filled Weltanschauung, and the Nazi regime never committed itself outright to a comprehensive program, analogous to the Final Solution of the Jewish question, aimed at systematically killing every last "Gypsy" within the German grasp. Numerically insignificant[45] and socially marginalized within German society, the "Gypsies" were viewed as a "nuisance" and a "plague" but not a dire menace locked in a life-or-death struggle with Germans. Nonetheless, a clear majority of German and Austrian "Gypsies" were eventually killed by the Nazi regime, as were many thousands of others throughout the German empire.[46] The fact that the Nazi regime could carry out such a genocidal assault[47] against a people who were of no particular concern to its leader demonstrates how dangerous can be the combination of pervasive popular prejudice, institutionalized racism, and a bureaucratic police state that develops the habit of solving problems through repression and mass murder.

In the prewar years the "Gypsies" in Germany were affected by the Nazi regime in a number of ways. Some Nazi measures did not target the "Gypsies" explicitly but nonetheless affected them disproportionately because they were stereotypically associated with behaviors deemed "asocial," such as begging, vagrancy, and avoiding steady work. Especially victimized in these cases were itinerant "Gypsies," as well as so-called white Gypsies or Germans who exhibited a "Gypsylike" lifestyle. The racist thinking legitimized under the Nazi regime identified individual characteristics and behaviors with the allegedly inherited and immutable qualities of "races." Thus the "Gypsies," stereotypically considered criminal, were also disproportionately vulnerable to the law against dangerous career criminals (November 1933) and the decree for preventive crime fighting (December 1937). In a fateful chain, "Gypsies" were stereotypically identified with what the Nazis deemed asocial behavior, this asocial behavior was criminalized, and potential criminals were deprived of due process and subjected to indefinite "preventive custody."[48] Consequently, in 1938 and 1939, over 2,000 German and Austrian "Gypsies" were placed in concentration camps.[49]

The "Gypsies" were likewise disproportionately subjected to compulsory sterilization under the law for the prevention of genetically diseased offspring

(July 1933). They had merely to be declared "feebleminded" to be legally sterilized. For cases when the victims were obviously too bright for such a pretext, two public health officials, Fred Dubitscher and Robert Ritter, developed the concepts of "moral" and "disguised mental retardation," by which indifference and nonconformity to societal norms on the one hand, and cleverness and cunning on the other were declared to be the very symptoms that confirmed hereditary mental retardation justifying sterilization.[50]

In addition to general measures that disproportionately affected "Gypsies," there were measures aimed explicitly at them. For instance, many municipal authorities complained that the itinerant "Gypsies" were both a burden and a blemish upon their communities. In 1935 the municipal authorities in Cologne created a camp to concentrate and control them. Following this precedent, a camp was created in the Berlin suburb of Marzahn to remove itinerant "Gypsies" from sight during the summer Olympics of 1936. Many other cities followed this example, and the camps became permanent.[51]

The Nuremberg Laws proclaimed in September 1935 did not mention the "Gypsies," but ensuing commentaries and implementation decrees did. Along with Jews, "Gypsies" were declared persons of "alien blood" ineligible to be Reichsbürger or to marry persons of German blood.[52] It was thus necessary to be able to determine who was legally a "Gypsy." Since the "Gypsies" were Christian, the method used to define Jews by the religious affiliation of their grandparents provided no solution. The Interior Ministry therefore created a research office (first within its department of public health but later relocated in the Criminal Police) under a specialist in the "biology of criminality," Dr. Robert Ritter, to provide criteria for judging who was a "Gypsy." Ritter and his team set out to research and exhaustively record the genealogy, in particular the exact proportion of "Gypsy" blood, of all "Gypsylike" people in Germany. His subjects were then classified as "pure Gypsy" (*reinrassiger Zigeuner*); "Gypsy hybrid" (*Zigeunermischling*) of two kinds, either mostly German or mostly "Gypsy"; and "non-Gypsy" (*Nichtzigeuner*).[53]

So far Ritter's model followed the Interior Ministry model for defining Jews. But Ritter then added a bizarre ideological twist. He claimed that "pure Gypsies," a bare 10% of those classified, were an inherently itinerant but relatively harmless group who could be left to their natural ways if kept separate from the rest of the population. But the numerically predominate *Zigeunermischlinge* were the product of generations of mixing with the most asocial and inferior elements of the German population, and this unwholesome mixture was biologically destined to criminality and parasitism and constituted a danger to society requiring a solution.[54]

Himmler embraced Ritter's findings, declaring that the "Gypsy problem" was a "matter of race" and that it would be "necessary to distinguish between pure and part-Gypsies in the final solution of the Gypsy question."[55] It was not unusual in Nazi Germany for categories of behavior and belief to be routinely commingled with racial categories, as in the case of partisans, Bolshevism, and Jews, or criminality, immorality, and "Gypsies." Such sloppy thinking posed no problem for the perpetrators, because this commingling was always mutually supportive of more radicalized persecution. But the Ritter-Himmler notion that "pure Gypsies" were less criminal and less dangerous than *Zigeunermischlinge* did pose a problem. Were the Nazis to invent measures favoring the "pure Gypsies" over the *Zigeunermischlinge* of both lesser and greater degrees of German blood? Or were they to succumb to the temptation simply to apply the model of Jewish legislation, in which decreasing degrees of Jewish blood corresponded with lesser severity of persecution? Would Ritter's pseudoscience and Himmler's racial fantasy prevail, or would sheer bureaucratic habit and momentum?

With the outbreak of war, the initial reaction of the Nazi regime was to include both Reich Jews and "Gypsies" in the general plans for *Flurbereinigung* or "basic cleansing" through expulsion into the General Government. On September 21, 1939, Heydrich announced to his division heads and the Einsatzgruppen leaders the "systematic dispatching" of Jews as well as 30,000 "Gypsies" into the non-German region of conquered Poland.[56] The following day he confirmed to Brauchitsch the intention to concentrate all Jews east of Cracow, along with "all Gypsies and other undesirables" (*alle Zigeuner und sonstige Unliebsame*).[57] When Eichmann began the first trial deportations of the Nisko operation, he was immediately approached by the head of the Kripo, Arthur Nebe (under whom police jurisdiction of the "Gypsies" had been placed), about quickly deporting the "Gypsies" of Berlin to avoid the cost of building a camp for them. Eichmann thought the simplest solution would be to attach "Gypsy" cars to each Jewish transport. This could begin almost immediately in Vienna and within three to four weeks for transports leaving the Old Reich.[58]

On October 17, 1939, one day after Eichmann had communicated his proposal to Nebe, Hitler met with Keitel and emphasized that Reich territory was to be cleared of "Jews, Polacks, and riffraff" (*Juden, Polacken, u. Gesindel*).[59] Hitler did not specifically mention "Gypsies," but clearly they were included under the notion of "riffraff." On the same day Heydrich notified Kripo stations throughout Germany of Himmler's order that "Gypsies" and "Gypsies of mixed blood" were not to leave their current residence or whereabouts. Those "Gypsies" who were "subsequently apprehended" were "to be kept in special assembly camps until their final deportation."[60] To help decide who exactly was to be apprehended, incarcerated, and deported, the "Gypsies" and *Zigeuner-mischlinge*, once deprived of their freedom of movement, were to be counted. During this process key information was to be collected. Had they held regular work in the past five years? Had they economically sustained themselves and their families? Did they have a permanent residence? Did they have Aryan spouses?[61] Just how this information would have been used, and by what criteria "Gypsies" would have been exempted from deportation is unclear, for the plan to deport "Gypsies" as well as Jews in fall 1939 was subsequently canceled.

Deportation as a solution to the "Gypsy question" was opposed by both Dr. Ritter and Dr. Leonardo Conti of the Interior Ministry. They advocated sterilization because a mere geographical shifting of "Gypsies" did nothing to stop their propagation.[62] Nonetheless, the plan to deport all Jews from the incorporated territories and all "Gypsies" from the Reich was revived by Heydrich on January 30, 1940. However, this was only to take place "as the last mass movement" following a series of deportations that would make space for repatriated ethnic Germans in the Warthegau.[63] But just as the SS jumped the queue and deported Jews from Stettin and Schneidemühl in February 1940 in order to secure housing for incoming Baltic Germans, it likewise carried out a hasty, ahead-of-schedule partial deportation of "Gypsies" in May 1940.

The pretext for the May 1940 deportation apparently came from the German military, which on January 31, 1940, asked Himmler to forbid the presence of "Gypsies" in the western border regions "as soon as possible" because they allegedly constituted an espionage danger.[64] Himmler did not in fact act "as soon as possible." Only on April 27, 1940, did he issue the order to deport a specific quota of "Gypsies" and "Gypsies of mixed blood" from western Germany to the General Government: 1,000 from Hamburg and Bremen; 1,000 from Düsseldorf, Cologne, and Hanover; and 500 from Frankfurt and Stuttgart. And the roundups themselves did not begin until May 16, just as the western offensive was making the military rationale irrelevant.

The procedure of these roundups and deportations was an eerie foreshadowing of the subsequent Jewish deportations from Germany of 1941 and 1942. The immediate fate of the deportees, however, was similar to that of Poles expelled from the incorporated territories and dumped into the General Government. The transport from Stuttgart was unloaded in Jedrzejow in the district of Radom, and the deportees were dispersed among surrounding villages and left to fend for themselves. The deportees from Cologne were similarly unloaded in Platorowo in the district of Warsaw and dispersed. The Hamburg transport was sent to the Lublin district, where the deportees were immediately put to work in Globocnik's Belzec labor camp and later dispersed. Though never subjected to systematic extermination, the vast bulk of these deported "Gypsies" (80% in the case of the Hamburg transport) perished in Poland.[65]

As late as July 31, 1940, the HSSPF in the General Government, Krüger, still expected to receive 30,000 "Gypsies" from the Old Reich.[66] And in July 1940 the Kripo authorities in Salzberg were told of an imminent "Gypsy" deportation scheduled for late August.[67] But, as in the case of the often postponed deportation of Jews, the deportation of the "Gypsies" was put off indefinitely.[68] Like the earlier concentration of the Polish Jews in preparation for expulsion, Himmler's order of October 17, 1939, had similarly deprived the "Gypsies" of freedom of movement in preparation for deportation. Now they too were stuck; particularly in Austria and the Protectorate, virtually all of the "Gypsies" were incarcerated in camps.[69] Only on Alsatian territory annexed to the Third Reich did local German authorities have some success in expelling "Gypsies" as part of a broader "cleansing" campaign aimed at a long list of "undesirables."[70]

The intended deportation was to have included both "Gypsies" and *Zigeunermischlinge*. The Ritter-Himmler notion of focusing discriminatory measures on the *Zigeunermischlinge* and giving preferential treatment to the "pure Gypsies" seems to have faded away in the first two years of the war, even on the part of the SS. Not surprisingly, others involved in persecution of the "Gypsies" even more readily applied anti-Jewish models. For instance, in 1937 "full-blooded Gypsies" as well as persons of marked "Gypsy" appearance had been excluded from military service. Then in February 1941, the OKW ordered the expulsion "for racial reasons" of both "Gypsies" and *Zigeunermischlinge* from active service. In practice "Gypsy hybrids of predominately German blood" were permitted to remain in the service, and mainly "Gypsy hybrids of predominately Gypsy blood" were expelled. Interestingly, the presence of "Gypsies" in the military seems to have been the occasion for Hitler's only two recorded comments on them.[71]

"Gypsies," like Jews, were increasingly subjected to forced labor, but unlike Jews they did not graduate into skilled factory jobs. In 1942 "Gypsies" were subjected to the same labor and social equalization laws (15% surtax on wages) that had been promulgated for Jews.[72] Only the Interior Ministry seemed interested in rejecting the trend toward the simple application of anti-Jewish measures to "Gypsies" and instead devised special measures in line with Ritter's theories. The Nuremberg legislation and commentaries prohibited marriages between Germans on the one hand and Jews or Jewish *Mischlinge* of the first degree on the other. But it did not forbid marriage between Jewish *Mischlinge* or between Germans and *Mischlinge* of the second degree. Breaking with the Nuremberg model, the Interior Ministry on June 20, 1941, instructed local authorities to subject marriages involving *Zigeunermischlinge* to special scrutiny and prohibited the marriage of Germans to *Zigeunermischlinge* with even one-quarter or less "Gypsy" blood.[73] The Ritter notion had been temporarily eclipsed in 1941, but it had not disappeared entirely.

In the period between 1939 and 1941, therefore, the persecution of the "Gypsies" ran more parallel to that of the Jews than it did either before or after. Before the war much of the persecution of "Gypsies" resulted from the disproportionate impact of more general measures against "asocials," and only gradually was the "Gypsy problem" defined in clear racial terms. Between 1939 and 1941, however, Jews and "Gypsies" were to be deported together as part of the same vast program of "ethnic cleansing" and demographic engineering. Both deportation programs, with notable exceptions, were unrealized. The discriminatory measures of concentration and deprivation of freedom of movement, forced labor exploitation, isolation, and humiliation were often identical. Only with the invasion of the Soviet Union and the emergence of the Final Solution did the treatment and fate of Jews and "Gypsies" begin to diverge again.

Killing the Handicapped

Anti-Semitism had been a pervasive European tradition for many centuries. Racial imperialism, justifying the conquest and domination (and not infrequently the decimation if not elimination) of allegedly inferior and backward peoples, had characterized Europe's expansion for half a millennium. But it was not until the 19th century that both movements received the pseudoscientific gloss of modern social Darwinist and racist rationalization. The latest, scientifically legitimized, tributary to flow into the river of Nazi ideology was the eugenics movement.[74]

Underlying the eugenics movement was a belief that human inequality was based on heredity and hence the conviction that limiting the procreation of inferior people and maximizing that of superior ones would improve mankind. Early in the 20th century, for instance, eugenics advocates in the United States successfully pushed for laws in many states authorizing the sterilization of individuals deemed to be the carriers of hereditary defects such as mental retardation. Thus behavior that today would be viewed as the product of a combination of environment and heredity was seen solely in terms of heredity; and individual behaviors were conflated with group behaviors, which were likewise explained solely in terms of heredity. In particular, subjective judgments about the value of individual qualities such as intelligence, diligence, and sobriety were increasingly equated with either race or class, and entire races and classes were ranked as hereditarily superior and inferior. In the United States, poor people, nonwhite peoples, and recent emigrants were the focal point of this prejudicial thinking and considered the carriers of inferior traits threatening to cause society-wide degeneration.

The eugenics movement was international, but in Germany it took on a particular cast. First, it was entrenched in the universities and enjoyed widespread respectability. Second, it was strongly nationalistic and *völkisch*, hence both supportive of the notion of Germanic, Nordic, or Aryan superiority and susceptible to anti-Semitism. Third, a German lawyer, Karl Binding, and a German eugenicist, Alfred Hoche, went beyond the typical advocacy of sterilization and openly argued for laws permitting the state to kill those judged "unworthy of life." In doing so, they deliberately confused arguments for euthanasia, that is, permitting the ending of life on an individual and voluntary basis, with the state-authorized killing of people deemed "degenerate" and "unworthy."[75] While the very rise of National Socialism discredited the most openly racist and anti-Semitic tendencies in the American eugenics movement,[76] in Germany those whom Henry Friedlander calls "the practitioners of race hygiene—anthropologists, geneticists, psychiatrists, and physicians"—embraced with enthusiasm the new Nazi regime, its anti-Semitism, and its crusade against "racial degeneration."[77] In its assault on those considered a threat to the hereditary health of the German people, the Nazi regime would have prestigious allies in the German medical and academic communities.

In comparison to the "twisted road" that led to the mass killing of Jews and "Gypsies," the path to the killing of the handicapped was extraordinarily straight. As early as 1935 Hitler had revealed his intention in the case of war to implement "euthanasia."[78] As the war became imminent, concrete preparations were already underway. In May 1939 Hitler instructed his accompanying physician, Dr. Karl Brandt, to set up an advisory committee to prepare for the killing of mentally ill children. This committee adopted the cover name Reich Committee for the Scientific Registering of Serious Hereditary and Congenital Illnesses. At some undetermined point Brandt brought to Hitler a petition from the parents of a severely deformed child—Gerhard Herbert Kretschmar (the so-called Knauer child), born February 20, 1939—asking that the child be put to death. Hitler authorized Brandt to investigate, and if the facts of the case were confirmed, to authorize euthanasia. Brandt visited the family near Leipzig, and the child was killed on July 25, 1939. Brandt and Philipp Bouhler of the Party Chancellery were then authorized to perform "euthanasia" in similar cases.[79]

Hitler, Brandt, and Bouhler had no intention of waiting for similar petitions, however. Rather, the regime was going to seek out its victims. On August 18, 1939, the Interior Ministry circulated a decree in which physicians and midwives were ordered to report all cases of "deformed" newborns.[80] Specific medical conditions were listed, with the focus on visible physical deformity rather than mental illness.

The program for adult "euthanasia" also took shape in the last weeks before the outbreak of the war. Initially Hitler placed Dr. Conti, the state secretary for health in the Interior Ministry, in charge of organizing this program, but Conti was soon shoved aside by Brandt and Bouhler, who thus were in charge of both the adult and the infant killing programs.[81] According to Werner Heyde, the future head of the medical division of the "euthanasia" program, he was invited to a meeting in July 1939, which was also attended by Brandt, Bouhler, Conti, and another Interior Ministry official, Herbert Linden. At this meeting Heyde learned of the imminent "euthanasia" of the adult mentally ill and the need to recruit physicians to serve as experts. In subsequent meetings, which stretched into the fall, it became clear to him that Brandt and Bouhler were in charge.[82] At some point Hitler himself met with Hans Lammers of the Reich Chancellery, Conti, and Bormann. According to Lammers, Hitler endorsed ending "the worthless lives of seriously ill mental patients." Indicating the depth of his disgust and loathing for these unfortunates, Hitler invoked the example of those who "perpetually dirtied themselves" and "put their own excrement in their mouths as if it were food." In contrast to the "Gypsies," the handicapped, like the Jews, were an object of Hitler's deep emotional hatred, and he was fully involved in the decisions taken to kill them.[83]

While preparations for a systematic, countrywide program of "euthanasia" continued into the fall of 1939 after the outbreak of war, victory in Poland opened the way for a series of local killing actions against the handicapped on Germany's eastern borders. These killing actions victimized not only Polish patients in institutions in the incorporated territories of Danzig–West Prussia and the Warthegau but also German patients from the Altreich territories of Pomerania and East Prussia. The killing began in West Prussia in the last ten days of September and involved the same units—the Eimann commando, Einsatzkommando 16, and the Selbstschutz—that were so notorious in killing Polish intelligentsia and nationalists, among others.

In short, the Polish handicapped were an additional group of undesired Poles that fell victim to the mass killing that engulfed West Prussia in the fall of 1939. Hitler, Himmler, Lammers, Bormann, and other top Nazi leaders (including Bouhler, Brandt, and Conti) arrived in Danzig on September 19 and met with the Gauleiter, Albert Forster. Presumably Forster's chief health officer, Prof. Dr. and Oberführer Grossmann, met with Conti.[84] Three days later, on September 22, the Eimann commando began killing Polish patients in the mental hospital at Conradstein (Kocborowo) south of Danzig. By early December, some 1,800 patients from Conradstein had been shot by Eimann's men and other helpers in the forest of Szpegawski, where an overall total of some 7,000 victims were buried.[85] As Conradstein was partially cleared, patients from other institutions—Schwetz (Sniecie), Mewe (Gniew), Silberhammer (Srebrzysk), and Riesenburg (Prabuty)—were transferred there as well. The last of these was in fact on Altreich territory in East Prussia. Nonetheless, of its 700 German patients transferred to Conradstein, some 300 were shot upon arrival.[86]

A second major killing site of the handicapped was the Piasnitzer forest northwest of Gdynia, where ultimately some 10,000 people were killed and buried. As in Conradstein to the south, the killing of patients from the mental hospital in Neustadt (Wejherowo) by members of Einsatzkommando 16 began in the later part of September and ended in early December.[87] At a third site, the so-called death valley near Konitz (Chojnice), patients from the nearby mental hospital were among the total of some 2,000 victims of the local Selbstschutz.[88]

The reduction of patients in some of these institutions and total evacuation in others caused a scramble among the German occupiers for the available buildings. Parts of Conradstein remained in service as a mental hospital, but by the end of October 1939 some evacuated buildings as well as new barracks were being used as a transit camp for incoming ethnic Germans—first from Latvia but later from Lithuania and Bessarabia. The facility at Schwetz was used as an old people's home for Baltic Germans. The children's home at Mewe was taken over by the Wehrmacht. The facility in Riesenburg was first used as a transit camp for Poles sent to Germany as workers or to be "Germanized" and was subsequently taken over by the army to be used again as a hospital. The Selbstschutz in Konitz used part of the hospital there as a prison. Military police were lodged in Neustadt.[89] In short, the buildings that became available were soon put to other uses, but no single need for space—such as housing for incoming Baltic Germans—dominated the grab for spoils or motivated the killing process.

The killing of institutionalized mental patients in West Prussia spread next to Pomerania. After a visit to Poland, Gauleiter Franz Schwede-Coburg saw the opportunity to rid himself of the Gau's mental patients. He quickly secured Himmler's support and approval by promising to turn over several of the vacated institutions to the Waffen-SS. With the help of his HSSPF, Emil Mazuw, and beginning in late October, 1,400 patients from five hospitals, in Stralsund, Ueckermunde, Treptow, Lauenburg, and Meseritz-Obrawalde, were loaded on trains and shipped to Neustadt in West Prussia. Here they were unloaded, taken to the Piasnitzer forest in trucks, and shot by members of Eimann's commando. The two totally evacuated institutions—Stralsund and Lauenburg—became Waffen-SS barracks; the other three continued to serve as mental hospitals.[90]

While the gunmen of West Prussia were helping to kill selected patients from Pomerania, medical personnel from the mental institutions in Pomerania came to the Warthegau to help select future victims. Dr. Johannes Banse, having selected some of his patients in Ückermunde for death, brought his expertise to the mental hospital in Treskau (Owinska) north of Poznan. In early November a commando of ss men from Einsatzgruppe VI of Erich Naumann appeared and gradually cleared the hospital. Victims of all but the last evacuation on November 25 were taken to the nearby forest and shot. Some surviving 100 patients of German nationality were then moved to the hospital at Tiegenhof (Oziekanka), and the property was taken over for use as a Waffen-ss barracks.[91]

The connection between the killing of mental patients in West Prussia, Pomerania, and the Warthegau, and the coordinating role of Himmler and the central "euthanasia" authorities in Berlin becomes even clearer in light of the continued killings in the Warthegau in December 1939 and January 1940. By October Dr. Albert Widmann, the chief chemist of the Criminal Technical Institute (KTI) of Nebe's Criminal Police (Kripo) within the RSHA, had become an adviser to the euthanasia planners on the method of killing. Widmann advocated the use of bottled carbon monoxide, and by late November gas chambers were being constructed at the first two sites selected to be killing centers, Grafeneck and Brandenburg.[92] The decision to construct gas chambers using carbon monoxide was not taken without testing, as Volker Riess has now shown. In October 1939 the ss chemist Dr. August Becker, who would subsequently be lent by Himmler to the euthanasia program and who described himself as a "gassing expert," arrived in Poznan. In Fort VII, which Naumann had taken over for use as a concentration camp, Becker had a provisional gas chamber constructed. Here he tested both carbon monoxide and an agent that was handled in the same way as Zyklon B.[93] Apparently the carbon monoxide gassing proved most satisfactory, and the last transport of patients from Treskau on November 25 was gassed in Fort VII.

The evacuation of the next Warthegau mental hospital in Tiegenhof began on December 7. Here too Dr. Banse had visited and categorized the patients. By the time the evacuations were broken off shortly before Christmas, 595 patients had been taken to Fort VII and gassed. One of these gassings, on December 13, was observed by the visiting Heinrich Himmler. After the turn of the year, the evacuations were quickly completed, and 442 patients were taken away between January 8 and 12, 1940. By now the patients were being gassed not in the improvised gas chamber in Fort VII but in a sealed truck into which bottled carbon monoxide was introduced.[94]

This first gas van was operated by a commando under Herbert Lange, formerly the chief of staff of Naumann's Einsatzgruppe VI. Presumably because of the logistical difficulties and lack of secrecy in bringing victims to Fort VII and then transporting the corpses to some forest for burial in mass graves, the killers had improvised the idea of the gas van. This enabled them to bring the gas chamber and bottled carbon monoxide to the victims and then conveniently drive into a nearby forest for body disposal.

On January 15 Lange's commando made its first visit to the Warthegau mental hospital at Kosten (Koscian), where once again the peripatetic Dr. Banse had already categorized the patients. Over the next week, 534 local patients were killed. Most of the facilities were taken over by the Wehrmacht, with the exception of several buildings that were used to house yet another wave of transports carrying some 1,000 patients from Pomerania to Kosten. The beds of murdered Polish patients were quickly filled by German patients expelled from Pomerania.[95]

Lange's work was not done. Disguised with a painted sign proclaiming "Kaiser's Kaffeegeschäft" (Kaiser's Coffee Company), Lange's gas van apparently worked so well that it continued its journeys around the Warthegau in the spring of 1940. At the request of HSSPF Wilhelm Rediess in East Prussia, Lange's commando was then "rented" to the transit camp at Soldau. There, between May 21 and June 8, 1,559 German mental patients from East Prussia and 250–300 Polish patients from the annexed territories of southeast Prussia were gassed. Rediess was transferred to Norway, and he left without paying the bill of 10 RM per head for Lange's killing services.[96]

Although these early killing actions in the eastern borderlands were not as systematic and uniform as the subsequent "euthanasia" program directed by Aktion T4 in Berlin, they were nonetheless not "wild" actions carried out solely on local initiative. The killing of Polish mental patients began in West Prussia immediately after Hitler and Himmler, as well as Brandt, Bouhler, and Conti, visited Danzig on September 19. This killing was one facet of a much wider program instigated by the Nazi leadership that aimed at eliminating many categories of undesired Poles. Local Nazi leaders in neighboring Pomerania and also Himmler perceived the advantage of employing the same killers to reduce the number of German mental patients. Having gained experience in selecting which German patients were to be sentenced to death, medical personnel from the Pomeranian institutions then visited the mental institutions in the Warthegau, and large numbers of patients—mostly Polish—were in turn killed, first by shooting and then by poison gas. The former was carried out by local SS, the latter by a Kripo chemist dispatched from Berlin. Finally, after gassing had been carried out in the mobile van of the Lange commando in the Warthegau, it traveled to East Prussia to gas both German and Polish patients there. In short, both Polish and German mental patients were killed in a succession of actions that affected West Prussia, Pomerania, the Warthegau, and East Prussia. And in each successive action, killers who had just gained experience lent their expertise to the next action. The 7,700 victims[97] of these eastern borderlands killings were but the first installment of the genocidal assault on the German handicapped that, after careful planning, was now getting underway.

In the first two years of the war, the systematic, countrywide "euthanasia" program that emerged had four distinguishable but overlapping procedures with four distinct sets of victims: infants, adults, institutionalized Jews, and concentration camp prisoners. As outlined above, planning for infant euthanasia had been placed in the hands of Hitler's physician, Brandt, and the head of the Führer Chancellery, Bouhler, who added to their team Linden of the health department of the Interior Ministry and one of Bouhler's deputies, Viktor Brack. Once Linden's office had circulated the decree of August 18, 1939, requiring health officials to report "deformed newborns," the other pieces of the program were put into place. A panel of three doctors was set up to review the forms and pass sentence of life or death on those infants selected for consideration by nonmedical personnel under Brack. Special wards were established in selected hospitals, eventually at least 22 throughout the country, where doctors were recruited to kill the infants sent to them. This was usually done by an overdose of common medication, large supplies of which were made available by the ever helpful chemist of the KTI, Dr. Widmann. Local health authorities were given the task of persuading parents to send their children to the killing wards through the deceptive promise of special medical treatment. If necessary, financial assistance was promised. Still-recalcitrant parents could be threatened with loss of custody. Over time the age limit moved from infants and children under three to older children and even in some cases teenagers. At the same time, fatal diagnoses expanded to include learning disabilities and behavior problems. By the end of the war, some 5,000 children had been murdered by this program.[98]

The program for adult euthanasia was much larger and more centralized. The same team of Brandt, Bouhler, Linden, and Brack were in charge, but the program was too big to be managed directly by Brack's staff within the Führer Chancellery. Thus a central headquarters was established at 4 Tiergartenstrasse, from which the program received its designation T4. Following the infant euthanasia method, the Interior Ministry circulated a decree on September 21, 1939, requiring all hospitals, nursing and old-age homes, sanatoriums, and so on, to fill out questionnaires on all patients who had been institutionalized for more than five years or committed as criminally insane, were of non-Aryan race, or had one of a long list of specific conditions (including "feeblemindedness") and were unable to work. While a panel of three doctors had been sufficient to judge the children's forms, T4 had to recruit a large pool of some 40 doctors to process this second set of forms. Teams of T4 physicians also descended upon institutions that did not return forms (or were suspected of falsifying them) and compiled their own lists of patients who were deemed to fall under these criteria.[99]

The killing method for adults differed from that for children. Based on Widmann's advice and the carbon monoxide experiments of his associate Dr. Becker, in Poznan, six special "euthanasia" killing centers were created. In the first center, Brandenburg near Berlin, some twenty functionaries and program advisers (including Widmann and Becker of the KTI and a Stuttgart policeman, Christian Wirth, as well as a large party of key doctors) put on a demonstration gassing in January 1940. The German adult handicapped were thus the first group of victims to be systematically gassed by the Nazi regime. In addition to the six killing centers, T4 created a transport company, Gekrat, that collected the doomed patients from their respective institutions by bus. They were taken first to "transit institutions" for a temporary stay and then to the killing centers. Following their deaths by carbon monoxide, families of the victims received falsified death notices. By August 1941 over 70,000 people had perished in the gas chambers of Brandenburg, Grafeneck, Hartheim, Sonnenstein, Hadamar, and Bernburg.[100]

Initially, Jewish mentally and physically handicapped patients were judged in the same way as others. If the panel of doctors reviewing the forms submitted to T4 concluded that Jewish patients met the criteria for euthanasia, they were placed on the list of patients to be taken from the institution in question and transported to one of the killing centers. Such a situation of non–racial discrimination was not tolerated for long, however. On April 15, 1940, Herbert Linden asked local health authorities to submit the names of all Jewish patients in their jurisdictions. Beginning in June 1940 these Jewish patients were transferred as entire groups to various assembly centers, from which they were dispatched to the "euthanasia" gas chambers on Reich territory. As camouflage, Gekrat replied to inquiries that the transports of Jewish patients had been sent to an asylum in Chelm (alternatively spelled Cholm) in the Lublin district of the General Government. Death notices were even mailed back from Chelm to add to the deception. Thus Jewish patients were killed in the same way as other T4 victims, but they were selected on a different basis. Degree of disability, case history, and prognosis were irrelevant. Simply being both a Jew and a patient was a death sentence. There was one significant exception, however, the patients of the all-Jewish hospital and nursing home in Bendorf-Sayn. Apparently it had not been subjected to T4 registration, and its patients were deported along with the Jews of Koblenz in 1942. They were killed in Poland as part of the Final Solution rather than in Germany as part of the T4 program.[101]

In the spring of 1941, T4 cooperation with the SS was extended into the concentration camps in what became known as Operation 14f13. Himmler wanted to use the T4 killing centers to exterminate some of his prisoners. As Henry Friedlander has plausibly argued, the Führer's Chancellery and T4 officials apparently insisted on the use of T4 physicians and forms to preserve their formal control over the "euthanasia" process. Thus teams of T4 doctors were dispatched on periodic visits to the concentration camps, much as they had visited to fill out the forms in recalcitrant hospitals. They did not conduct medical examinations but confined themselves to completing the forms on the basis of information supplied by SS camp doctors. The main factors determining the doctors' judgment were race, health, criminal record, camp behavior, and ability to work. For Jewish prisoners, needless to say, race alone was often sufficient for a death sentence. The killing took place at Hartheim, Sonnenstein, and Bernburg.[102]

By the summer of 1941, both knowledge of and unease about the "euthanasia" program had become increasingly widespread. Especially conspicuous were the transport and killing of the adult handicapped. Already in 1940 Himmler had closed down two of the notorious killing centers, Grafeneck and Brandenburg, because of public unrest, only to replace them with Bernburg and Hadamar.[103] However, the regime's various measures of deception and subterfuge were ineffective, in large part because the killing took place on German soil. Moreover, unlike the Jews and "Gypsies," the victims were not an isolated racial minority toward whose fate the majority had long been indifferent at best. The growing public unease emboldened a handful of courageous churchmen, especially Bishop Clemens August Graf von Galen of Münster in his sermon of August 3, 1941, to go public in their protest. Shortly thereafter, on August 24, Hitler ordered a halt to the adult "euthanasia" program in its current form. The large-scale culling of hospitals and mass transport to the killing centers came to an end.[104] Other forms of the "euthanasia" program, however, not only continued but even intensified. Children's "euthanasia" was expanded to older age groups. Operation 14f13, which was just getting underway in 1941, continued to grow. Its total number of victims approached 20,000 by the end of the war. And a much more decentralized and unobtrusive "wild" euthanasia of adults in hospitals (similar to the methods used for children) replaced the conspicuous program just suspended. Indeed, according to Friedlander, "more victims of euthanasia perished after the stop order was issued than before."[105]

Even while the number of "euthanasia" victims continued to increase, the diminished duties of the killing centers suddenly made a large staff of professional killers experienced in gas chamber operations available for other assignments. Many of them would reappear in Poland in 1942 to play a central role in the genocide of the Jews. Gerald Reitlinger, in his early history of the Final Solution, was one of the first historians to note the direct connection between both the personnel and gas chamber technology of the "euthanasia" program and the later Final Solution. As he did in the case of Jewish victims of the Final Solution, however, he vastly understated the number of "euthanasia" victims, putting the total number at 50,000-60,000.[106] Raul Hilberg scarcely mentioned "euthanasia" in the 1961 edition of *The Destruction of the European Jews*, but he devoted a number of pages of the expanded and revised 1985 edition to the connection between the "euthanasia" program and the subsequent killing of Jews. He concluded, " 'Euthanasia' was a conceptual as well as technological and administrative prefiguration of the 'Final Solution' in the death camps."[107] The pathbreaking work of Ernst Klee inaugurated a period of intense study of the Nazi murder of the handicapped. This has led to the realization, articulated perhaps most eloquently by Michael Burleigh and Wolfgang Wippermann[108] and by Henry Friedlander, that the connection between Nazi "euthanasia" and the Final Solution goes well beyond personnel, technology, and procedure. The killing of the handicapped and the Jews were two essential elements of the Nazis' wider vision of creating a racial utopia. The former was to cleanse the German race of its "degenerate" or "defective" elements. The latter was to destroy its ultimate enemy. They were two campaigns in the same crusade.

THE NAZI SPHERE OF INFLUENCE

Between September 1939 and April 1941, Nazi Germany won control over most of Europe. A sphere of influence extended in (as Hilberg phrased it) a "semi-circular arc" from Norway south to the Pyrenees and then east to the Aegean and Black Seas. Here the Nazi regime faced a very different situation than it did within the Third Reich and German-occupied Poland, in terms of both the freedom to impose its own Jewish policies and the demographic weight of its potential victims.

German relations with the other countries within its sphere of influence varied tremendously. Some territories (Luxembourg, Alsace-Lorraine, and northern Slovenia) were annexed outright. Some territories (the Netherlands and Norway) that had been conquered and occupied were dominated by party and ss functionaries, while others (Belgium, northern France, northern Greece, and Serbia) were under military administration. In some conquered territories semiautonomous puppet governments ultimately dependent on and serving at Germany's pleasure (Vichy in southern France, as well as newly created Slovakia and Croatia) were permitted. Among the conquered countries, only Denmark retained its own government operating by its former constitution.

In addition to the conquered countries, a number of countries signed on as Germany's military allies. Italy had been an ally even before the outbreak of war, but Germany's military success brought Hungary, Romania, and Bulgaria into the fold as well. All but Romania were "revisionist" powers aggrieved by the territorial settlements at the end of World War I, and all harbored territorial ambitions that could not be realized without German military success.

Ultimately these regions were within Germany's empire but not within its projected Lebensraum. The Nazi regime did not aim to drastically transform the racial composition of these countries, aside of course from the eventual removal of their Jews. Rather, Germany wanted to incorporate the economic— and in the case of its allies also the military—potential of these regions into its war effort, and to do so with the least drain on its own resources. Thus Germany had to concern itself with practical limits and pursue avenues of influence rather than command. Germany would have to work with and through the various governing bodies in these territories and gain their assent and cooperation in implementing Jewish policy in a manner quite different from its rule in the eastern European areas designated as Germany's Lebensraum. In addition to the ss and the military, the German Foreign Office would have a significant role to play.[109]

The Jewish populations in the semicircular arc were a different kind of target as well. Not only did an array of legal barriers and political intermediaries stand between the Jews and the Nazi regime, but the Jews were also much more widely and thinly dispersed. The Warsaw ghetto contained more Jews than all of France; the Lodz ghetto more Jews than all of the Netherlands. More Jews lived in the city of Cracow than in all of Italy, and virtually any medium-sized town in Poland had a larger Jewish population than all of Scandinavia. All of southeast Europe—Hungary, Romania, Bulgaria, Yugoslavia, and Greece—had fewer Jews than the original four districts of the General Government. While Germany was experimenting with policies of expulsion, expropriation, ghettoization, and forced labor in Poland from 1939 to 1941, Jewish policies within its sphere of influence in these same years were necessarily much more muted.

Emigration

The Nazi regime was clearly committed to making its entire sphere of influence *judenfrei* in the long run. The Madagascar Plan envisaged the expulsion of 4 million Jews from an expanding German empire that included the newly conquered territories in the west. In December 1940, when Germany was putting its Balkan alliance system in place, Eichmann prepared figures for Himmler that projected the expulsion of 5.8 million Jews from Germany's "European economic sphere." The Jews of southeastern Europe were now to be included as well.[110] Just two weeks earlier Hitler had assured the Hungarian Prime Minister Pal Teleki that he considered "the solution to the Jewish question for Europe as one of the greatest tasks of the peace."[111]

But whatever the long-term goal, the short-term priority of the Nazi regime was to make the Third Reich the first territory in Europe to be free of Jews. This meant that Germany temporarily used its influence not to facilitate but rather to hinder the emigration of Jews from elsewhere in Europe and monopolize the scant emigration possibilities for its own Jews. One thread that ran through Germany's diplomatic activities in the 1939–41 period, therefore, was the effort to arrange for the continuing emigration of German Jews while simultaneously blocking the exit of other Jews.

Within weeks of the outbreak of war in Poland in September 1939, the Foreign Office passed on to Heydrich's Security Police an inquiry of the International Committee of the Red Cross (ICRC) concerning the continuation of Jewish emigration. On Heydrich's behalf, Kurt Lischka, head of the Central Agency for Jewish Emigration in Berlin, replied that, as before, Jewish emigration was desired. However, the Reichsvereinigung der Juden in Germany would not be allowed to contact the ICRC so that the latter's important tasks would not be "debased" by involvement in Jewish emigration. The ICRC agreed not to concern itself.[112] Meanwhile Lischka in the Security Police, Göring's representative Helmuth Wohltat, and the Foreign Office representatives Emil Schumburg and Ernst Eisenlohr of Referat Deutschland reached an agreement that not only would Jewish emigration continue during the war but it would be furthered by every available means, as long as German interests were not hurt. In this regard, the Foreign Office urged denying emigration approval to Jewish professionals and intellectuals, who would be useful to the enemy's economy and propaganda.[113]

As the spreading war naturally restricted the already diminishing emigration possibilities open to German Jews, the German Foreign Office actively sought to keep open the few remaining routes. In September 1939 Britain was still willing to honor permission that had been granted to 1,450 German Jews to enter Palestine, if they could pick up their permits in Triest. The Foreign Office, with the approval of Gestapo chief Heinrich Müller, negotiated Italy's agreement to this arrangement by promising to take back any Jews who were refused entry to Palestine after entering Italy.[114] As Italy prepared to enter the war in May 1940, however, it refused to grant further transit visas to German Jews in order to avoid having them stranded in Triest when war broke out.[115]

With the Italian route closed, the Foreign Office, the SS, and the Reich Agency for Emigration (Reichsstelle für Auswanderungswesen) cooperated on maximizing the tenuous route through the Soviet Union and Manchukuo to Shanghai by simplifying the paperwork. Previously each applicant had to procure the necessary permits from the internal authorities and then a "certificate of nonobjection" (*Unbedenklichkeitsbescheinigung*) from the Foreign Office before seeking visas from the embassies of the Soviet Union, Manchukuo, and Japan. As of the summer of 1940, the emigration authorities filled out the paperwork of applicants approved by the RSHA. After screening the applicants to eliminate the undesired emigration of certain professions, Referat D III in the Foreign Office sent lists to the appropriate embassies with the request to grant transit visas.[116] Several thousand Jews used the Siberian route to the Far East until it too was closed by the German invasion of the Soviet Union in June 1941.

To maximize the limited possibilities for the emigration of Jews from Germany, Austria, and the Protectorate, the Nazi regime sought whenever possible to block Jewish emigration from elsewhere. In this regard an ominous phrase was used. In order not to disadvantage Jewish emigration from the Third Reich and "in view of the doubtless imminent final solution to the Jewish question" (*in Anbetracht der zweifellos kommenden Endlösung der Judenfrage*), Weintz on Himmler's staff informed the Foreign Office in September 1940 that further Jewish emigration would not be permitted even from the General Government.[117]

Blocking Jewish emigration from territories directly under German control was one thing. To block Jewish emigration from other countries in Europe was another, often involving conflicting priorities. In February 1940 the Lithuanian government requested permission for Polish Jewish refugees there to transit through Germany to Italy. The request was backed by the Italians, who did not want their shipping companies to lose out to Soviet ships on an alternative route through Odessa to Palestine. And the German consulate in Kaunas (Kovno) urged favorable consideration in view of the fact that Lithuania had accepted 1,500 Jews expelled from Suwalki. The Foreign Office too was favorably disposed, but the SS was adamantly opposed. The route through Odessa was open to Lithuania, and if Italian shipping companies had unused capacity, they should be more aggressive in soliciting business with German Jews.[118]

The Hungarian government also requested permission for Jews to transit through Germany to Lisbon in September 1940. Eichmann urged that the request be rejected because the all-too-perceptible lack of "emigration possibilities" for German Jews would only be further impaired by competition with Hungarian Jews. As Hungary was granting transit visas to German Jews, however, the Legal Division in the Foreign Office successfully asserted that both politeness and reciprocity necessitated permitting the transit of Hungarian Jews.[119] In another exceptional case, Eichmann and his adviser in Slovakia, Dieter Wisliceny, agreed to a onetime transit of Slovakian Jews across Germany to Lisbon, but only on the conditions that the transport be sealed, the Jews be beyond military age, and unclaimed shipping space be available.[120]

Faced with increasing requests for exceptions, the RSHA adamantly reaffirmed existing policy on May 20, 1941, in a circular dispatched from Eichmann's office over the signature of Walter Schellenberg:

> According to the communication of the Reich Marshal of the Greater German Reich [Göring] Jewish emigration is to be intensively carried out even during the war. . . . Because insufficient emigration opportunities are available at the moment, mainly via Spain and Portugal, for Jews from Reich territory, emigration from France and Belgium would mean a renewed impairment of these opportunities. In consideration of this fact and in view of the doubtless imminent final solution of the Jewish question, emigration of Jews from France and Belgium is thus to be prevented.[121]

Jewish emigration from the Third Reich continued to be permitted, in fact, until October 18, 1941.

Western Europe
Even while hindering Jewish emigration from countries within its European sphere, the Nazi regime attempted to influence the local treatment of these trapped Jews, with both the short-term goal of destroying their political and economic position and the long-term goal of preparing for their total "evacuation." In Western Europe, the German occupation authorities in France took the lead.

France had been partitioned into different areas. Alsace-Lorraine was annexed to the Third Reich, and the northern departments of Nord and Pas de Calais were administered by the military commander for Belgium and Northern France, headquartered in Brussels. The rest of France was divided into occupied and unoccupied zones. The former was directly administered by the German military commander in France (Militärbefehlshaber [MBH] in Frankreich), headquartered in Paris. The puppet government of Marshal Petain had its capital at Vichy in the unoccupied zone in the south. With less than 1,000 German officers and officials in the occupied zone and none in the unoccupied zone, the German military administration by necessity had to work through the French bureaucracy and police that remained in place throughout France.[122] With the exception of Dr. Werner Best—Heydrich's recent deputy in the RSHA—as head of internal affairs, the military administration of General Otto von Stülpnagel was staffed by a homogeneous group of traditional, nationalistic conservative military men whose temperament and outlook occasionally clashed but also frequently overlapped with Nazi ideology.[123]

As was typical of German occupation regimes, a plethora of other German agencies also struggled to gain influence and power in France. Two in particular played a key role in Nazi Jewish policy. The Foreign Office was represented by the embassy of Otto Abetz, which was headquartered in Paris rather than Vichy and had a loosely defined jurisdiction over all political questions in both zones. Abetz was not a traditional career diplomat but instead an early member of Bureau Ribbentrop—a Nazi party foreign policy advisory group—who had long consorted with French rightists. His deputy was a former businessman with experience in France, Rudolph Schleier, and his adviser on Jewish affairs and liaison to the Security Police was the ambitious, rabidly anti-Semitic Sturmbannführer Carltheo Zeitschel. Both Schleier and Zeitschel were longtime Nazis.[124]

The military had been successful in initially curtailing the role of the SS in the western campaign and subsequent occupation, excluding in particular the formation of Einsatzgruppen. The SS was thus represented by a lightly staffed Security Police headquarters under Befehlshaber der Sicherheitspolizei (BdS) Helmut Knochen. However, among his men were three close associates of Adolf Eichmann with considerable experience in "Jewish affairs": Kurt Lischka, former head of the Central Agency for Jewish Emigration in Berlin; Herbert Hagen, Eichmann's former supervisor at the Jewish desk of the SD; and most notorious, the 27-year-old Theo Dannecker, who served as Knochen's *Judenreferent*.[125]

In France it was Best and Abetz, not Knochen, who took the initiative. In early August, Abetz had an audience with Hitler during which the latter affirmed his intention to evacuate all Jews from Europe once the war was over.[126] Upon his arrival in Paris, Abetz met with Werner Best. Together they prepared a series of proposals for anti-Jewish measures in the occupied zone (prohibition of Jews returning over the demarcation line into occupied France, registration of Jews in the occupied zone, marking Jewish businesses, and placing abandoned Jewish businesses under trusteeship), which could be implemented by the French authorities and also serve as the foundation for the subsequent removal of Jews from unoccupied France as well. These proposals were dispatched as "very urgent."[127]

Best submitted a somewhat different summary to his own staff members in the military administration, including a request to examine the possibility of removing all Jews from the occupied zone. Their reaction was mixed. They noted the priority of preserving order and security, and the expediency of leaving administrative measures to the French bureaucracy. Above all, they feared that broaching the racial question might awaken annexation fears among the French. Expulsion of all Jews from the occupied zone was deemed impractical. But they shared the view that Jews represented a dangerous anti-German element and that selective measures excluding Jews from exercising economic and cultural influence were desirable.[128] In any case, the military was made aware of Hitler's general approval for action on the Jewish question as early as August 26, 1940.[129]

Official approval of Abetz's specific proposals through the Foreign Office went more slowly, since the Foreign Office asked the opinions of Göring's Office of the Four-Year Plan and Heydrich. Hoppe, Wohltat's deputy for the Four-Year Plan, felt the proposals were "not expedient."[130] Foreign Office Undersecretary Martin Luther questioned whether the psychological preparation of the French was at hand and thought it advisable that the proposed measures be carried out by the Vichy regime so that it "bore the responsibility in case of failure."[131] It required two inquiries to arouse the attention of Heydrich, who had no objection to the proposals but considered it "indispensable" that the Security Police, with its experience in Jewish matters, take over supervision of enforcement through the French police.[132]

On September 27 and October 16, 1940, the military administration in Paris issued two decrees authorizing anti-Jewish measures. The first defined a Jew as someone who adhered to the Jewish religion or had more than two Jewish grandparents. As proposed by Abetz and Best earlier, it prohibited Jews from returning across the demarcation line into the occupied zone and provided for the registration of all Jews and the marking of all Jewish businesses in the occupied zone.[133] The second degree, urged by Brauchitsch, required registration of Jewish property as a preparation for confiscation and aryanization.[134]

The first anti-Jewish decrees of the military administration in France are noteworthy in several respects. First, the initiative came neither from Berlin nor from the local ss and police. While the initiators, Best and Abetz, both had a strong ideological commitment to National Socialism, their proposals found ready acceptance in the conservative nationalist Stülpnagel circle, even if it did not consider Jewish matters to be of particularly high priority.

Second, these decrees paralleled anti-Jewish legislation issued independently in Vichy. On July 22, 1940, the Vichy regime permitted the denaturalization of "undesirables" who had attained citizenship after 1927, and on August 27 it lifted the prohibition against anti-Semitic publications. The *Statut des juifs*, issued on October 3, defined Jews on the basis of race and excluded them from various professions. And the following day French prefects were authorized to intern foreign Jews in camps. All this was done without pressure from the Germans, who were still trying to find their own path.

What emerged from these independent German and French initiatives was a cycle of mutual intensification. Best, having heard of the imminent *Statut des juifs*, felt a sense of urgency to issue the German decree first: "It was consciously judged necessary to have it antedate the French law in order that the regulation of the Jewish question appeared to emanate from the German authorities."[135] With the second German decree concerning the registration and aryanization of Jewish property, Vichy in turn felt pushed toward a "preemptive strategy." Alarmed that the Germans might take Jewish property for themselves and wanting to assert its sovereignty in the occupied zone, Vichy quickly agreed to cooperate in order to ensure the appointment of French trustees.[136]

Third, the legislation of both the military administration and Vichy provided a model for others.[137] On October 28, 1940, the military administration for Belgium and Northern France also issued two edicts. One—like the two military decrees in Paris—defined Jews, prohibited their return, and ordered the registration of Jews as well as the marking and registration of Jewish businesses. The second, like Vichy's *Statut des juifs*, excluded Jews from public offices and other important positions.[138]

The next German initiative in France stemmed from Theo Dannecker. Assured that Hitler was still pressing for the total evacuation of European Jewry "after the war" and that Heydrich had been entrusted with planning "the final solution project" (*Endlösungsprojekt*), Dannecker was energized. On January 21, 1941, he recommended the creation of a center for Jewish affairs in France to harness French officialdom to the "tremendous amount of work" and "most painstaking preparations" that had to be done "preceding the wholesale deportation of the Jews" to a "territory which has yet to be determined." In Paris, the military administration and Abetz gave their approval.[139] In Berlin, Heydrich and Streckenbach confirmed to Undersecretary Luther in the Foreign Office that planning was underway for a "later total solution" through "deportation to a territory to be determined in the future."[140]

Vichy was thereupon persuaded to create a Commissariat-General for Jewish Affairs (CGQJ) headed by a Xavier Vallat, a man who combined anti-Semitism with a strong dose of French nationalist anti-German sentiment.[141] Best urged that Vallat be informed of the German goal of a "total dejudaizing" (*vollständigen Entjudung*) of Europe. He also urged the military to press the newly appointed general commissar to intern some 3,000–5,000 especially dangerous Jews, including those holding French citizenship, and to make timely preparations for the later "emigration" of all French Jews.[142] The Germans found Vallat willing to expand Vichy anti-Jewish measures but not willing to take part in the more "disagreeable" policies of "expulsions and internment," which he claimed were not in his jurisdiction.[143] Despite Vallat's partial recalcitrance, Abetz correctly perceived that through the CGQJ the Germans would gain the leverage for extending anti-Jewish measures from occupied to unoccupied France.[144]

The Germans did not come away empty-handed. In May 1941, 3,733 foreign Jews (but not French Jews) were arrested by the French police and interned in the Pithiviers and Beaune-la-Rolande camps in the occupied zone.[145] More important, anxious to assert Vichy sovereignty throughout France, Vallat proposed legislation in the summer of 1941 extending both the registration of Jews and aryanization of Jewish property to the unoccupied zone—what Michael Marrus and Robert Paxton term the "gravest step yet" in Germany's success in enlisting French help to accomplish what it could not do on its own.[146]

Dannecker initiated the creation of yet another institution that would prove useful to Germany's eventual deportation of French Jewry when, in August 1941, he began pressing for the creation of a French *Judenrat* or Jewish council to replace all existing Jewish organizations. By threatening to go ahead on his own in the occupied zone, Dannecker leveraged Vallat into persuading Vichy to decree a General Union of French Jews (Union Générale des Israélites de France) in both zones and dissolve all other Jewish organizations on November 29, 1941.[147]

In short, German dependency on French manpower and institutions in France had been overcome by a combination of Vichy's own indigenous anti-Semitism as an integral part of its National Revolution as well as by German manipulation of Vichy's phobic determination to symbolize French sovereignty in the occupied zone. The Jews of France had been defined, registered, expelled from various professions, expropriated, and subjected to the jurisdiction of a Jewish council. In all this, the initiatives had come from either Vichy or Abetz, Best, and Dannecker, but the German military had proved quite accommodating as long as its priority—the maximum exploitation of France with minimum German manpower—was not threatened.

The German occupation regime in the Netherlands differed from that in France in important ways.[148] First, the Dutch government had fled into exile. The civil service left behind remained intact, under the direction of its collective Secretaries-General, but there was no equivalent to the puppet Vichy regime at the top. Second, German power resided in a Reichskommissariat dominated by Austrian Nazis, while the military played a subordinate role and the Foreign Office had a mere "representative" or *Vertreter*, Otto Bene, at the Hague with no mandate equivalent to that of Abetz in France. The Reichskommissar was Dr. Arthur Seyss-Inquart, a key figure in the Anschluss and subsequently Frank's deputy in the General Government. Two Austrian cronies held key positions: Generalkommissar Dr. Hans Fischböck (who had been active in despoiling Austrian Jewry and in advising Göring and Schacht during negotiations with George Rublee of the International Refugee Committee in 1938–39) for finance and economics, and Generalkommissar Dr. Friedrich Wimmer for administration and justice. Third, the ss would achieve an exceptionally strong position. Seyss-Inquart's chief potential rival was his own Generalkommissar for security, yet another Austrian, Hanns Rauter, who was also HSSPF reporting directly to Himmler. Despite the rivalry between Seyss-Inquart and Rauter for control of Jewish policy, both were doctrinaire National Socialists and anti-Semites. In France, Abetz, Best, and Dannecker had to deal with a strong military authority which, though not opposed to persecution of the Jews, did not share their sense of priorities. In the Netherlands there was no such difference among the German occupiers.

Although the German occupation regime in the tiny Netherlands had more civilian personnel and police than the MBH had for all of France,[149] it still needed to operate through the Dutch administration. Thus Dutch sensibilities were taken into account, and initially the Germans proceeded quite cautiously against the 140,000 Jews in the Netherlands. For instance, purging the civil service of Jews took place in stages. On August 28, 1940, Wimmer issued instructions that in the future no one of Jewish ancestry (even one grandparent) was to be appointed to public office. On October 18 Dutch civil servants were confronted with forms to fill out—one set for Aryans and another for non-Aryans. On November 4 Wimmer instructed the Dutch Secretaries-General to dismiss Jewish civil servants. The Secretaries-General, after "prolonged discussion" and "grave crises of conscience," agreed to implement a "temporary suspension" rather than "dismissal" of their Dutch Jewish colleagues.[150] This pattern, in which the Dutch administrators stayed at their posts and promulgated decrees on German instruction after achieving minor mitigation, was to be repeated. The harnessing of a compliant, dutiful, and impeccably efficient Dutch officialdom to implement Nazi racial policy was to be one of the keys to the record fatality rate of Dutch Jews in comparison to other west European countries.[151]

A decree for registering Jewish businesses, accompanied by an even more thorough definition of who was a Jew, was issued on October 22, 1940. The registration of all Jews and even *Mischlinge* was in turn ordered on January 10, 1941. Nowhere was the expertise of the Dutch bureaucracy felt more acutely than in the comprehensiveness of its registration procedures and the difficulty in forging its identity cards.[152] Unlike in France, however, the subsequent despoiling of Jewish property was primarily to the benefit of a flood of German businessmen and especially the Dresdner Bank rather than the Dutch.[153]

The incremental but methodical legislative approach to the persecution of Dutch Jewry in the Netherlands was temporarily interrupted by a series of unusual events in February 1941. The German Stadtkommissar for Amsterdam, Heinrich Böhmcker, toyed with the idea of setting up a ghetto in January 1941 and encouraged Dutch Nazis to harass and abuse Jews in the city.[154] Marauding Dutch Nazis encountered resistance in the Jewish quarter of Amsterdam on February 11, and after the ensuing scuffle, one Dutch Nazi died of his injuries. Böhmcker summoned Jewish leaders and ordered the founding of a Jewish council in Amsterdam, which was immediately charged with maintaining order and procuring the surrender of all weapons in Jewish hands. After a German police patrol encountered resistance from the Jewish owners of a previously vandalized ice cream parlor on February 19, the Germans reacted violently. The ice cream parlor owner was shot, and a police razzia descended upon the Jewish quarter, seized some 425 young Jewish men as "hostages," and sent 389 of them to Mauthausen, where (along with several hundred more Jews seized in a raid in June) they subsequently perished. When a strike or "riot" of Dutch workers followed on February 25–26, the Germans threatened the newly formed Jewish council with even more massive retaliation of deportation and shooting. The Jewish council implored the strikers, whose efforts were being broken by German repression in any case, to stop.[155]

After the February events and the founding of the Amsterdam Jewish council, the Germans in the Netherlands accelerated preparations for the total "evacuation" of the Dutch Jews, while at the same time the SS was trying to assert a larger role in shaping Jewish policy. This paralleled similar actions by Dannecker in France and, as there, traced back to Reinhard Heydrich. In April 1941 Heydrich ordered the creation of a Central Office for Jewish Emigration in the Netherlands, "which would serve as an example for the solution to the Jewish question in all European countries." The Central Office for Jewish Emigration in Prague was cited as the model for funding, and Eichmann's associate Erich

Rajakowitsch was transferred from that city to employ similar methods in the Netherlands. Moreover, two Jewish functionaries of the Prague office were brought to Amsterdam to consult with the two heads of the Dutch council, Abraham Asscher and David Cohen, and a representative from the council was sent to Lisbon to procure credit from the American Joint Distribution Committee to help finance emigration.[156]

Rauter preferred calculated methods under the control of the ss to the uncontrolled violence instigated by Böhmcker. He thus indicated to Seyss-Inquart on April 18, 1941, that the work of the new Central Office was—on Heydrich's orders—to be carried out under the supervision of the Security Police commanded by Dr. Wilhelm Harster. A modest tug-of-war between Seyss-Inquart and Rauter followed. At a meeting on May 19, 1941, Seyss-Inquart's Generalkommissar for finance, Fischböck, and not Rajakowitsch, was put in control of funding.[157] In August, Harster attempted to boost Rajakowitsch's position, establishing a special department for Jewish affairs (Sonderreferat J) under the latter. The Sonderreferat J was to be in charge of all Jewish affairs and was to be the sole body empowered to issue orders to the Jewish council. Seyss-Inquart managed to assert a continuing role in Jewish policy, especially for Böhmcker, but one upshot of increasing cooperation between the ss and Seyss-Inquart's bureaucrats was an agreement to extend the authority of the Amsterdam Jewish council to all Dutch Jews.[158]

A further ominous development in the Netherlands was the increasing integration of the Dutch police into the machinery of persecution. After the events of February 1941, the Germans installed Sybren Tulp, a pro-German admirer of Hitler and a member of the NSB (Dutch National Socialist Party) since 1939, as chief constable of the Amsterdam police. A retired lieutenant colonel in the Royal Dutch East Indian Army, Tulp had considerable experience in the police enforcement of racial discrimination. He established two new units within the Amsterdam police: the Amsterdam Police Battalion, composed of 300 demobilized soldiers stationed in barracks, and a bureau for Jewish affairs. It was Tulp's Amsterdam police, not the Germans, who in June 1941 arrested the 300 German Jews who composed the second group of "hostages" sent from the Netherlands to Mauthausen as a retaliation measure. And it was Tulp's police who enforced the German measures expelling Jews from public life in the fall of 1941. Here again most arrested offenders were turned over to the Germans and perished in Mauthausen.[159]

Ultimately, the rivalry between Seyss-Inquart and Rauter over the control of Jewish policy did not slow the persecution. In the Netherlands as in France, the definition and registration of the Jews, as well as their expulsion from the economy and the expropriation of their property, had been accomplished with the cooperation of the native civil service. Moreover, a Jewish council that conveyed German orders had been established, and the Dutch police had been transformed into an instrument of German enforcement.

Belgium had neither a Vichy-style government with its own anti-Semitic agenda nor a highly Nazified occupation regime whose leaders intrigued for control over Jewish policy. Yet in the end the result was much the same for the 52,000 Jews (90% of them foreigners) residing there. The military administration copied the anti-Jewish legislation of France with two decrees issued on October 22, 1940. Jews in Belgium were thereby defined, registered, excluded from public office and various professions, and barred from returning from abroad. But the aryanization process followed more closely the model employed in the Netherlands, in part, perhaps, because the Belgians displayed a certain "aversion" at least to acquiring Jewish real estate. In contrast to the German authorities in the Netherlands, who incited the February 1941 attacks on Jews in Amsterdam, the chief of the military administration, Eggert Reeder, moved against a noisy group of Belgian anti-Semites who attempted an attack on the Jewish district in Antwerp on Easter Monday in 1941. Reeder wanted no interference or challenge to his control of Jewish policy from either an ss independent of his supervision or Belgian collaborators. Perhaps because he himself held ss rank, he was relatively successful in this regard. On August 29, 1941, Jews were forbidden to move from Brussels, Antwerp, Liège, and Charleroi, so that these four cities would be the "collection points" of Belgian Jewry. And at the same time as the establishment of the General Union of French Jews in France, the Belgian Jews were provided with the Association of Jews in Belgium (Association des Juifs en Belgique) on November 25, 1941, although in contrast to France the Belgian association was directly subordinate to Reeder's military administration, without the Security Police as intermediary.[160]

Despite the slower pace and seeming laxity of anti-Jewish measures in Belgium in comparison to France and the Netherlands, in all three countries the preparations needed for a total evacuation of the Jews out of Europe "after the war" were mostly in place in late 1941. When German Jewish policy changed to evacuation "to the east" during the war, the groundwork had already been laid.

Southeastern Europe

In the political context of the late 1930s, the Jews of eastern Europe were at quadruple jeopardy. As beneficiaries and supporters of liberal and revolutionary political movements promising equal rights, they were both excluded by and the natural targets of authoritarian, antiliberal, and anticommunist political movements coming to power in almost every country in eastern Europe as one "Wilsonian democracy" after another collapsed. As symbols of capitalism and modernization in a time of world depression and painful economic transition, they were the natural scapegoats for economic distress and greed. As a dispersed, "international" minority, they were both shunned and targeted by political movements engaged in nation building on the basis of integral, ethnic nationalism. And finally—in addition to such factors facilitating indigenous anti-Semitism—there was a major external factor. In a geographic zone that was caught between the declining influence of the west, the threat of the Soviet Union, and the rising power of Nazi Germany, the Jews were easy pawns in the geopolitical calculations of east European leaders currying Hitler's favor.

Other factors in addition to Jewish vulnerability were of course at work. Within many countries in eastern Europe, anti-Semitism was more cultural than racial. A not insignificant distinction was made between unassimilated, alien, and foreign Jews and highly assimilated native Jews. In contrast to National Socialist racial doctrine, it was often the easily identifiable alien Jew who was the political symbol for various grievances and was conceived of as the real threat. Moreover, the desire to preserve some symbolic independence from the Nazi regime often made this double-standard and less-than-total compliance concerning the native Jews a point of pride with east European states allied to Germany. When German military fortunes began to falter and some of the east European countries began to see their remaining Jewish populations as political credit with the west, this small countervailing sentiment proved significant in the survival of pockets of east European Jewry.

German leverage in this situation could be exercised in several ways. Internally, the traditional authoritarian regimes in eastern Europe were challenged by New Right or fascist-style political movements for whom anti-Semitism was often a priority issue. Often the Old Right would adopt anti-Semitic measures to preempt the issue and take the wind out of the sails of their opponents, both to gain domestic support and to influence Nazi Germany's inclination to support or abandon these fascist challengers. Even more important, the east European countries were obsessed with the post–World War I boundary settlements, and an increasingly powerful Germany had no qualms about exploiting its position as a territorial arbiter to reward its friends and punish its enemies. This was, in the end, the most important leverage the Nazi regime had to set its east European allies on the path to mass murder, but it was also leverage that would become less effective as German military fortunes flagged.

Not all east European countries sought to accommodate Hitler. Czechoslovakia was destroyed even before the outbreak of war, and when Poland and

Yugoslavia in succession spurned Hitler's offers of alliance, they were conquered and dismembered. Two remnant puppet states—Slovakia and Croatia—were created in 1939 and 1941, respectively. Romania, Hungary, and Bulgaria on the other hand sought accommodation with Nazi Germany in the period from 1938 through 1940. It is in these countries that the combined effects and shifting balance of the factors of anti-Semitism, territorial greed, and Nazi power can be seen.

Slovakia was the first puppet state created by Germany when it completed the occupation and dismemberment of post-Munich Czecho-Slovakia in March 1939. The Slovak state was to be a showcase of the benefits of cooperation with the Third Reich, and Germany thus placed some value on preserving the appearance of Slovak independence. One of the first measures of the new Slovak regime was the anti-Jewish legislation of April 18, 1939, curtailing the role of Jews in the professions and economy but providing—by Nazi racial standards—a rather unsatisfactory definition of who was a Jew, as pre-1918 converts to Christianity were exempt.[161] In 1940 the struggle for power within Slovakia between the hard-core fascist Hlinka Guard of Prime Minister Vojtech Tuka and Sano Mach, the clerical fascists of the president, Father Tiso, and the authoritarian nationalists (favoring a regime both more secular and autonomous from Germany) of Ferdinand Durcansky, began to tip in favor of Durcansky, who served as both interior and foreign minister.[162] In May 1940 Mach, deemed by Undersecretary Ernst Woermann in the German Foreign Office as "one of our best friends in Slovakia," was ousted from key positions and replaced by Durcansky supporters—including one "whose wife is said to be of Jewish origin."[163]

With victory in the west, the Germans were less concerned to preserve the appearance of Slovak independence and more concerned to impose a compliant regime to their liking. A diplomatic troubleshooter, Manfred von Killinger, was dispatched to Bratislava (Pressburg) in June. He recommended that Durcansky—"ensnared" by "plutocratic Jewish circles"—"absolutely must disappear from the Government." The clever Durcansky, he warned, was trying to avoid this fate by playing the Germanophile and, in his capacity as minister of the interior, ordering stores in Bratislava to put up "Jews not wanted" signs. Killinger urged that Mach and Tuka be made interior and foreign ministers, respectively, and that Germany appoint "a commissioner with the Slovak Government who keeps an eye on all happenings."[164]

On German demand, Durcansky was dismissed, and Tiso, Tuka, and Mach were summoned to a meeting with Hitler at the Berghof on July 28, 1940. Hitler warned that there were "forces at work (Jews, Freemasons, and similar elements) that wished to prevent harmony" between Germany and Slovakia, adding that "Germany demanded that Slovakia should adhere loyally and unequiv-ocally to the German cause in her domestic politics."[165] Killinger was appointed the new ambassador to Slovakia and instructed to install a system of "German advisers," including one for the "Jewish question."[166] This was none other than Dieter Wisliceny, a close associate of Adolf Eichmann's. As Heydrich explained to Undersecretary Luther in the Foreign Office, Wisliceny was to be subordi-nated to the adviser for police affairs, Dr. Hahn, since all Jewish questions were being handled in the RSHA.[167]

Killinger's predecessor as ambassador had complained that in Slovakia "the Jewish question has in no sense been brought nearer a solution."[168] In the days following Wisliceny's arrival on September 1, 1940, however, the legislative assault on Slovakia's 89,000 Jews quickly picked up pace. On September 3 the government was given the power to issue Jewish legislation by decree without further parliamentary approval. On September 16 the Central Office for the Economy was created to oversee aryanization of Jewish property, registration of which had just been made mandatory. And on September 26 a Judenzentrale was established and all other Jewish organizations were dissolved.[169] Slovakian subservience to German Jewish policy had been firmly established.

Hungary was in several ways a kindred spirit with Germany in the interwar period. It suffered far more territorial amputation as a result of the Treaty of Trianon than Germany did from Versailles and hence was implacably "revision-ist." Hungary was also the scene of a "white terror" counterrevolution against Bela Kun which had strong anti-Semitic overtones. And the anti-Semitic dema-gogue Gyula Gombos had served as prime minister from 1932 until his death in 1936. Hungary was no stranger to the currents of anti-Semitism, which its own pro-Nazi radical right vigorously advocated. Yet Hungary also had all the pre-tensions of a former great power and no desire to be reduced to the status of a second-rate satellite of Nazi Germany or drawn into another military defeat. Hence Hungary attempted a perilous balancing act that postponed but ulti-mately did not prevent either the defeat of Hungary or the destruction of Hungarian Jewry.

On March 5, 1938, in a bid to coopt elements of the radical right opposition and build a broader political base, Prime Minister Kalman Daranyi announced that he would come to grips with the inordinate influence of the Jews in Hun-gary. The Anschluss in mid-March, which brought the Third Reich to a com-mon border with Hungary, added a foreign policy motivation. The First Jewish Law, with broad support in Parliament and from the churches, was signed by Daranyi's successor, Bela Imredy, and came into effect on May 29, 1938. It provided a religious definition (1919 was the cutoff date for conversions) of Jews and (exempting combat veterans, widows, and orphans) sought to reduce Jewish participation in the professions, economy, and culture to 20%.[170]

As early as November 1937 Hitler had dangled the prospect of territorial recovery before visiting Hungarians and had tried to enlist the Hungarians for war on Czechoslovakia during Horthy's and Imredy's respective visits in August and September 1938. The Hungarians equivocated and remained relatively passive during the Czech crisis. Nonetheless, following the Munich Agreement, Hungary was allotted a slice of southern Slovakia by Germany in the First Vienna Award of November 3, 1938. Imredy, having proclaimed the Jewish question settled after the First Law, thereupon proposed further anti-Jewish legislation and appointed a pro-German foreign minister, Istvan Csaky.[171]

When Csaky met with Hitler on January 16, 1939, he broached the Jewish question. Hitler—just two weeks before delivering his famous Reichstag prophecy—was emphatic: "He was sure of only one thing, the Jews would have to disappear from Germany to the last man." Moreover, "for him the Jewish problem did not exist for Germany alone; Germany would support every nation which takes up this fight."[172] Two months later, upon the final dissolution of Czecho-Slovakia, Hungary received its second territorial award in the form of the Carpatho-Ukraine. At the same time, Hungary joined the Anti-Comintern Pact and left the League of Nations.[173]

When Imredy's successor, Pal Teleki, informed Ribbentrop about the agreement within the Hungarian parliament on the new anti-Jewish legislation, the two men expressed "hearty agreement" that Germany and Hungary had a common future.[174] The Second Jewish Law was approved in May 1939. It employed the language of race in its definition of a Jew but contained so many exemptions that in practice the definition remained religious. It banned Jews from government service and established a 6% quota or *numerus clausus* for many professions and access to higher education.[175]

As it did during the Czech crisis in 1938, Hungary still clung to its neutrality in September 1939 and declined to permit the transit of German and Slovak troops for the campaign against Poland. But German victories and growing influence over Romania, another holder of territories coveted by Hungary, proved too great a temptation. In the Second Vienna Award of August 30, 1940, Hitler ordered the return of the northern half of Transylvania from Romania to Hungary. Teleki promptly announced his intention to adopt further anti-Jewish legislation, which was to be "clear, radical, and simple, without the complications and loopholes for evasion of its predecessors."[176] And the Hungarian ambassador in Berlin warned of German impatience: "I find the evolution of the Jewish question of such far-reaching importance that it may have a decisive impact on German-Hungarian relations, nay . . . I must state in full knowledge of my responsibility that it will in fact become decisive." Meeting with Hitler in Vienna on November 20, 1940, Teleki not only signed the Tripartite Pact but also affirmed that after the war the Jews should be removed from Europe.[177]

In short, between November 1938 and November 1940, Hungary had gained three pieces of territory, swelling its Jewish population from 450,000 to 725,000. But in the process it had introduced two pieces of anti-Jewish legislation and promised a third. And more important, it had committed itself to both the ultimate expulsion of its Jews and Hitler's future wars.

In contrast to Hungary, Romania was one of the great territorial beneficiaries of the post–World War I settlement. This fact shaped the fate of Romania and its Jews in two ways. First, Romania was a natural ally of the western powers trying to preserve the treaty settlement and a natural target of the revisionist powers. Second, in addition to the Jews of the Old Kingdom, Romania contained three other distinct Jewish communities: the Magyarized Jews of Transylvania, the Habsburg-Germanized Jews of Bukovina, and the eastern Jews of Bessarabia. If all three were viewed as foreign, the Bessarabian Jews were considered especially alien and unassimilable.

Romanian vulnerability to German leverage was twofold. Externally, as German power increased and western power declined, Romania's isolated position became diplomatically and militarily hopeless. Internally, Romania was afflicted with not just one but two radical right, anti-Semitic movements (the Iron Guard of Corneliu Codreanu and the Christian-National Party of Alexander Cuza and Octavian Goga), for which Nazi Germany was a source of both inspiration and financial and political support. Romania's only bargaining chip was the Ploesti oil vital to Germany's war machine. In the end, this was enough to save Romania from the fate of the other east European benefactors of the treaty settlement—Czechoslovakia, Poland, and Yugoslavia—but not from that of becoming a German satellite.

When the two radical right movements combined received 25% of the vote in 1937, King Carol named Octavian Goga prime minister. Goga's government launched a wave of anti-Semitic measures, which stripped 200,000 Jews of citizenship.[178] King Carol ousted the Goga government the following year, and in the ensuing upheaval Codreanu and many leaders of the Iron Guard were murdered. In anger Germany withdrew its ambassador from Bucharest and gave asylum to the new Iron Guard leader, Horia Simia. Upon his return in February 1939, the German ambassador Fabricius made it clear that Romanian-German relations would improve when Romania took the proper stance on the Jewish question. Romania instead played the economic card, reaching an agreement in March 1939 that gave Germany full access to Romanian oil and placed Romania fully in the German economic orbit.[179]

The Nazi-Soviet Non-Aggression Pact of August 1939, whose secret protocols consigned Bukovina and Bessarabia to the Soviet sphere and the Ploesti oil fields to the German sphere, followed by Germany's victory in the west in May/June 1940 rendered Romania helpless. When the Soviet regime delivered an ultimatum for the cession of Bukovina and Bessarabia in late June 1940, the Germans recommended full compliance. Bulgaria, which had lost territory to Romania in the Balkan wars of 1912–13, and Hungary then pressed similar claims over southern Dobrudja and Transylvania, respectively.

The desperate Romanians did everything in their power to belatedly win German favor, such as inviting a German military mission and leaving the League of Nations. As with the Slovak government in the summer of 1940, Romania was visited by the Foreign Office troubleshooter Manfred von Killinger in June, and the prime minister (Gigurtu) was summoned to meet with Ribbentrop and Hitler in late July. On both occasions, the Jewish question was discussed.[180] Not surprisingly, the Romanian government quickly issued a large volume of anti-Jewish measures. One law was modeled after the Nuremberg decrees, providing a racial definition of Jews and banning intermarriage. Other measures banned Jews from the military, civil service, and various careers that involved contact with the public (including even sports teams).[181]

Romanian efforts to save itself from further territorial amputation were in vain. The Bulgarian claim was conceded, and in the Second Vienna Award of August 30, 1940, northern Transylvania was transferred to Hungary. With the loss of Bukovina, Bessarabia, and northern Transylvania, Romania's Jewish population dropped from 728,000 to 302,000.[182] The disastrous loss of territory spelled the end of Carol's royal dictatorship. The Germans backed Carol's abdication and the formation of a coalition government of two protégés: Marshall Ion Antonescu, who had been rescued from arrest under Carol by German intervention, and the Iron Guard. German troops entered the country to "protect" the oil fields, and the new government issued another barrage of anti-Jewish laws that provided for the expropriation of Jewish real estate, the gradual dismissal of Jews from commerce and industry (i.e., "romanization" of the economy), limits on Jewish doctors and lawyers, and work service in place of military service.[183]

Antonescu's dependence upon Germany only increased in January 1941, when the Iron Guard revolted in an attempt to seize total power. Some 120 Jews were killed in the Iron Guard violence.[184] Hitler opted for Antonescu, permitting him to crush the revolt. However, Horia Simia and the Iron Guard leadership were granted asylum in Germany once again, being held in reserve as an alternative should the Antonescu government prove insufficiently subservient to German wishes.[185]

Bulgaria was another southeast European country nursing irredentist ambitions, although its territorial grievances traced not so much to the post–World War I settlement as to Bulgaria's defeat in the Second Balkan War. Bulgarian Jews constituted less than 1% of the population and were not particularly distinct, while the Turk and Greek minorities were much more numerous and loomed much larger in the popular consciousness. Bulgaria's radical right movement, the Ratnitsi, was indeed anti-Semitic but primarily obsessed with the recovery of Macedonia.

Bulgaria's recovery of a sliver of territory from Romania in the summer of 1940 irresistibly whetted its appetite for more, and Bulgaria moved toward closer ties with Nazi Germany as the necessary precondition. King Boris conceded the inevitability of anti-Jewish legislation under these circumstances and preferred that Bulgaria institute its own rather than await a German dictate. Ratnitsi influence had already penetrated the government when Petur Gabrovski was made minister of the interior in October 1939, and he in turn placed Aleksandr Belev in charge of Jewish affairs. But only in the summer of 1940 did they get the green light to proceed, and Belev visited Germany to study its anti-Jewish legislation. The resulting Law for the Defense of the Nation registered the Jewish population and curtailed its political and economic activities, but exempted veterans, spouses in mixed marriage, and converts. Read in the Bulgarian parliament in November and passed in December 1940, it occasioned considerable criticism from prestigious Bulgarian politicians. Nonetheless, it was signed by King Boris on January 15, 1941. As the historian Frederick Chary has concluded, "There was really no Jewish problem even in the Nazi sense in Bulgaria, but the German alliance created a need for one."[186] Of all the southeast European countries that became entangled in the anti-Semitic consequences of the German alliance system, none did so with less indigenous impetus and greater cynicism than Bulgaria.

By the end of 1940, when Germany turned to concrete preparations for the invasion of the Soviet Union and securing its Balkan flank, it had already established both diplomatic and economic domination over most of southeast Europe. Through the power to redistribute territory as well as the clever exploitation of internal political rivalries, Nazi Germany had established an alliance for its war against the Jews as well.

6

Preparing for the "War of Destruction"

Perhaps no area of Holocaust studies has been more intensively researched and debated over the past several decades than the nature and timing of the decisions that led to the emergence of the Final Solution.[1] Although many issues are still contested, there is widespread agreement among scholars in several areas.

First, most historians agree that there is no "big bang" theory for the origins of the Final Solution, predicated on a single decision made at a single moment. It is generally accepted that the decision-making process was prolonged and incremental. The debate is rather about the nuances of weighting and emphasis. Which in a series of decisions and events should be considered more important, more pivotal, than others?

Second, there has been a shift toward emphasizing continuity over discontinuity.[2] The policies of Jewish expulsion pursued between September 1939 and March 1941 implied a massive decimation of the Jewish population. If completely implemented, they would have been seen as fulfilling Hitler's January 1939 prophecy that the next war would mean the end of Jewry in Europe. Between the spring and summer of 1941, plans for the *Vernichtungskrieg* entailed the death of millions of people in the Soviet Union. In such an environment of mass death, clearly Soviet Jewry was in grave peril. Indeed, in the light of past Nazi actions in Poland, Nazi plans for the war of destruction *implied* nothing less than the *genocide* of Soviet Jewry. When large numbers of people had been shot, Jews had always been shot in disproportionate numbers. When massive expulsions had been planned, it was never intended that any Jews would be left behind. And when food had been scarce, Jews had always been the first to starve. Now mass executions, mass expulsions, and mass starvation were being planned for the Soviet Union on a scale that would dwarf what had happened in Poland.

Within the framework of a war of destruction, through some unspecified combination of execution, starvation, and expulsion to inhospitable territories, Soviet Jewry, along with millions of other Slavs, would eventually be destroyed. In the months following the June 1941 invasion of the Soviet Union, this vague vision of *implied genocide* in the future, unspecific about timetable and means, gradually evolved into what the Nazis called "the Final Solution to the Jewish question," a program of systematic and total mass murder of every Jewish man, woman, and child within the German sphere of power. Even though the escalating stages of population decimation, genocide, and Final Solution can be articulated, the lines between these stages as reflected in actual Nazi documents and practice cannot be so sharply drawn.

Third, most scholars accept that a simple, linear, top-down model of decision-order-implementation does not capture the amorphous and unstructured nature of the Nazi decision-making process. Rather, Nazi policy evolved through an unsystematic dialectical interaction of mutual radicalization between central and local authorities involving numerous variations of exhortation, legitimization, and support, as well as decisions and orders from above; and intuition, initiative, and experimentation, as well as obedience from below. The relative weighting of center and periphery, Hitler's precise role, and the timing and context of key turning points in this complex process are still contested issues.

Fourth, there is consensus that just as the decision-making process cannot be properly studied by focusing solely on Hitler and the central authorities, likewise the initiation and implementation of evolving Nazi policy cannot be studied by focusing solely on the ss. However crucial the roles of Himmler, Heydrich, and the Higher ss and Police Leaders (HSSPF), as well as the Einsatzgruppen and other police formations under their command, the picture is incomplete without the military, the civil administration, the ministerial bureaucracy, the economic planners, and local collaborators and police auxiliaries. The historian faces an especially daunting task in trying to formulate viable generalizations about the respective roles of the different institutions and organizations in the face of almost infinite local variation.

Finally, most—though certainly not all—scholars in the field have gravitated toward the position first articulated by Christian Streit and Alfred Streim over 20 years ago that there was no decision or order for the murder of all Soviet Jews before the invasion.[3] Preparations for Operation Barbarossa set in motion a fateful chain of events, and the murderous "war of destruction" quickly opened the door for the systematic mass murder of first Soviet and then European Jewry.

In a meeting with his highest-ranking military commanders on July 31, 1940, Hitler noted that the destruction of the Soviet Union would remove England's last hope.[4] The army chief of staff Franz Halder noted ominously, "The master of Europe and the Balkans is then Germany. Decision: In the course of this conflict Russia must be finished off. Spring 1941."[5] After postponing the invasion of England in September and briefly toying with a Mediterranean strategy against the British empire, Hitler again discussed the invasion of the Soviet Union with his generals on December 5. Two weeks later he officially ordered that all preparations for Operation Barbarossa—the invasion of the Soviet Union—were to be complete by mid-May 1941.[6] On January 9, 1941, Hitler justified the decision for Barbarossa in pragmatic terms. The "smashing" (*Zerschlagung*) of the Soviet Union would cause the English to give up, enable Japan to attack the United States in the Pacific, engage the Soviet army while it was still weak in leadership and armaments, and relieve Germany's economic dilemma by opening up Russia's immense riches while simultaneously allowing a reduction in the German army to the benefit of the air force and navy. Germany would then have the capacity to wage war against continents without fear of defeat.[7]

Hitler's initial remarks to the military leadership about the invasion of the Soviet Union were thus cast in terms of traditional Great Power hegemony—a way of thinking that was not unfamiliar to officers who had passed their formative years in the Kaiserreich of Wilhelm II. Within several months, however, discussion of Barbarossa took on the additional dimension of an ideological and racial war of destruction.

In late February 1941 General Georg Thomas, head of the War Economy and Armaments Office (Wehrwirtschafts- und Rüstungsamt) submitted plans for the economic utilization of the conquered territories. Göring relayed Hitler's response on February 26. The Führer was in full agreement on the economic issues; Thomas was in fact appointed Göring's coordinator for a unified economic policy on conquered Soviet territory. Göring also passed on Hitler's view that in order to pacify and secure these territories for maximum exploitation, one would have to destroy communism, and that required "taking care of the Bolshevik leadership as soon as possible" (*zunächst schnell die bolschewistischen Führer zu erledigen*).[8]

Alfred Jodl, chief of staff of the OKW, met with Hitler on March 3 to discuss the military's initial draft plan for the occupation of the Soviet Union. Hitler emphatically set out the principles upon which the plan had to be revised.

> This imminent campaign is more than just a battle of weapons; it also entails a conflict between two worldviews. . . . The Jewish-Bolshevik intelligentsia, the "suppressor" of these peoples until now, must be removed. . . . Moreover, we must avoid under all circumstances that in place of a Bolshevik now a nationalist Russia is allowed to emerge, which as history proves will in the end again be hostile to Germany. It is our task to construct as quickly as possible with a minimum of German military power socialist state forms that are dependent upon us. These tasks are so difficult that one can not burden the army with them.

Accordingly, Jodl issued the following instructions for the new draft. The operational zone of the military was to be kept very shallow. Behind this zone, no military administration was to be erected. Instead, Reich commissars would be installed, and the bulk of the police would operate there. The question whether SS units would have to operate alongside the Secret Military Police (Geheime Feldpolizei) in the combat zone as well remained to be examined with Himmler. "The necessity of immediately rendering harmless all Bolshevik leaders and commissars argued for that. Military courts had to be excluded from all these questions. They were only to concern themselves with legal matters among the troops."[9] Two days later Halder was briefed by Quartermaster General Wagner on the new draft being prepared in accordance with Hitler's guidelines and Jodl's instructions. Halder noted approvingly that the army must "not be burdened with administrative tasks. Special missions of the Reichsführer-SS."[10]

The new draft was completed on March 13 and signed by Keitel. The issue of SS units operating even within the shallow operation zone of the army had been decided in favor of the SS. "In the army operation zone, in order to prepare the political administration, the Reichsführer-SS receives by order of the Führer special tasks that result from the final battle to be settled between two opposing political systems (*die sich aus dem endgültig auszutragenden Kampf zweier entgegengesetzter politischer Systeme ergeben*). Within the scope of these tasks the Reichsführer-SS operates independently and under his own responsibility." Details of army-SS cooperation were to be settled in continuing negotiations, but it was already determined that the army would provide logistical support for SS units operating in the combat zone.[11]

Negotiations with the SS began the same day, and as before the invasion of Poland, they were conducted between Quartermaster General Wagner and Heydrich.[12] Even while the negotiations were in progress, Hitler left Halder and

Wagner in no doubt about one major task of the SS units: "The intelligentsia put in by Stalin must be exterminated. The controlling machinery of the Russian empire must be smashed. In Great Russia force must be used in its most brutal form. The ideological ties holding together the Russian people are not yet strong enough, and the nation would break up once the functionaries are eliminated."[13]

Despite the army's experience with SS units in Poland—in Blaskowitz's words, they had worked "almost exclusively as execution squads"—Wagner and Heydrich arrived at a draft agreement on March 26. The draft reaffirmed that the "special commandos of the Security Police" (later to be called Einsatzgruppen, their subunits and Einsatzkommandos or Sonderkommandos) would operate on their own responsibility. They were to receive logistical support from the army but their operational instructions—concerning "executive measures against the civilian population"—were to come from Heydrich. Close cooperation with the army was to be ensured through the contact between an Einsatzkommando liaison officer and the intelligence officer (I c) on the staff of each army. The military would be kept informed of all instructions from Hedyrich to the Einsatzgruppen. Brauchitsch signed the agreement one month later.[14]

By one account, Wagner emerged from one negotiating session "with halting steps and flushed cheeks" (*mit verhaltenen Schritten und geröteten Wangen*).[15] With this agreement the military knowingly opened the way for the SS to carry out mass executions on Soviet territory. Given Hitler's remarks directly to Jodl and Halder and as relayed by Göring to Thomas, the military leadership could have been in absolutely no doubt about the intended systematic murder of communists. Moreover, they knew that Hitler equated the Jews with Bolshevism. Indeed, on March 3 he referred explicitly to the removal of "the Jewish-Bolshevik intelligentsia." Indeed, many in the military shared his belief in this equation. Army propaganda, for instance, spoke of "commissars and party functionaries, mostly filthy Jews" (*Kommissare und Parteifunktionäre, meist dreckige Juden*).[16] In short, as the fate of the Jewish-Bolshevik intelligentsia and communist functionaries was to be summary execution, it is very difficult to believe that the German military leadership was not fully aware several months before the invasion of the Soviet Union that mass killings of both communists and Jews would occur.

Indications of military attitudes and expectations about the invasion of the Soviet Union, however, lie not solely in the agreement with the SS over the Einsatzgruppen but also in other preparations being made in the spring of 1941. For unlike in Poland, this time the military was not merely going to stand aside while the SS carried out its murderous work. It would have an active role to play. Keitel's March 13 order, besides conceding freedom of action to the SS in the combat zone, also pointed to two other areas affecting the military. First, "The behavior of the troops toward the population and the tasks of the military courts will be separately regulated and ordered." Second, special uniform guidelines for the economic administration of the occupied territories would be forthcoming from General Thomas as Göring's deputy.[17] Finally, there was a matter of omission. Although Hitler and his generals were agreed on a strategy of vast encirclements calculated to capture large numbers of prisoners of war, Keitel's order made no mention of preparations for handling Soviet POWs. It was in these areas that the military's readiness for participation in Hitler's "war of destruction" in Russia was truly revealed.

On March 30, 1941, Hitler addressed a gathering of some 200 military officers for two and a half hours. The signals Hitler had given to Jodl, Wagner, and Halder about the nature of the Russian campaign were now made clear to a much wider circle. Halder took extensive notes on the fateful speech:

> *Clash of two ideologies.* Crushing denunciation of Bolshevism, identified with asocial criminality. Communism is an enormous danger for our future. A communist is no comrade before or after the battle. This is a war of destruction. If we do not grasp this, we shall still beat the enemy, but 30 years later we shall again have to fight the communist foe. We do not wage war to preserve the enemy. . . .
>
> *War Against Russia.* Extermination of the Bolshevist Commissars and the communist intelligentsia. The new states must be socialist, but without a new intellectual class of their own. A primitive socialist intelligentsia is all that is needed. We must fight against the poison of disintegration. This is no job for the military courts. The individual troop commanders must know the issues at stake. They must be leaders in this fight. The troops must fight back with the methods with which they are attacked. Commissars and GPU [Soviet political police] men are criminals and must be dealt with as such. This need not mean that the troops shall get out of hand. Rather, the commander must give orders that express the common feelings of his men.
>
> This will be very different from the war in the west. In the east, harshness today means lenience in the future. Commanders must make the sacrifice of overcoming their personal scruples. ObdH Order.
>
> *Noon:* All invited to lunch.[18]

The murder of Soviet "commissars" and the limiting of military court jurisdiction that Hitler asked of his generals in this speech were dealt with in the following months in a way that demonstrated how willing the generals were to "overcome their scruples." On May 6, 1941, two drafts were submitted by Lt. General Eugen Müller of the OKH to the OKW. The first dealt with the jurisdiction of military courts on occupied Soviet territory (*Kriegsgerichtsbarkeiterlass im Gebiet Barbarossa* or simply *Barbarossa-Erlass*) and the second—designated as procedures for carrying out orders issued on March 31—was destined to become known as the *Kommissarbefehl*.[19]

Work on limiting the jurisdiction of military courts had in fact already begun in early March,[20] but a completed draft, delayed possibly by preparations for the unexpected invasion of Yugoslavia, written by Dr. Rudolf Lehmann, chief of the OKW legal division, was not submitted to Jodl and Major General Walter Warlimont of the OKW until April 28. "Guerrillas" (*Freischärler*) and other civilians were to be dealt with by the troops through "all means at their disposal including annihilation of the attackers," not through military courts. There was no obligation to prosecute troops for criminal actions against civilians except when necessary to preserve discipline. "In judging such deeds it had to be taken into consideration that the collapse of 1918, the later suffering of the German people, and the struggle against National Socialism with the countless blood sacrifices of the movement were clearly traced back to the influence of Bolshevism, and no German had forgotten this."[21]

The Lehmann draft was discussed by Halder and Müller of the OKH. Halder noted: "Order to troops along lines of last Führer address to the generals. Troops must do their share in the ideological struggle of the eastern campaign."[22] A draft by Müller containing several additions was then returned to the OKW on May 6. A justificatory preamble on measures needed to pacify the conquered territory had been added:

In this connection it must be established that beyond the usual military resistance this time the troops will encounter, as an especially dangerous element from the civilian population disruptive of all order, the carriers of the Jewish-Bolshevik worldview. There is no doubt that wherever he can, he will use his weapon of disintegration deviously and from behind against the German military engaged in battle or pacifying the land. The troops therefore have the right and obligation to secure themselves fully and effectively against these disintegrative powers.

In the body of the text, the Müller draft provided for collective reprisal against villages from which attacks had issued when it could not be expected that individual perpetrators could be found quickly. Finally, the draft explicitly prohibited prosecution of German soldiers for punishable offenses against civilians that were committed "out of bitterness over the atrocities or disintegrative work of the carriers of the Jewish-Bolshevik system."[23]

Lehmann reworked the draft once again. He added the explicit statement that military courts had no jurisdiction whatsoever over civilians. "Otherwise the danger exists that the troops will shove off onto the courts matters that are uncomfortable to them, and in this way . . . the opposite will occur from what should be achieved." To make the matter "somewhat more palatable" (*etwas schmackhafter*), however, Lehmann reworked the preamble and omitted the references to "the carriers of the Jewish-Bolshevik worldview" and "Jewish-Bolshevik system," emphasizing instead the rationale of military security.[24] This draft was signed by Keitel on May 13.[25]

The other draft submitted by Müller to the OKH on May 6 concerned the army's role in the treatment of so-called commissars in the light of Hitler's repeated demand for the elimination of the "Jewish-Bolshevik intelligentsia" and party functionaries. In the army operation zone, commissars constituted "a heightened danger for the security of the troops and the pacification of the conquered territory. . . . They must therefore be removed." Those captured by the troops were to be taken to an officer who, satisfied with the identification, was to order and carry out the shooting immediately. Commissars attached to the Red Army "are not recognized as soldiers. The provisions valid for prisoners of war are not applicable." This also applied to commissars in the administration and party whom the troops encountered. On the other hand, technical experts in economic enterprises were to be seized only if they resisted the German military. In the rear areas, commissars other than those attached to the army were to be turned over to the Einsatzgruppen.[26]

Warlimont recommended to Jodl a greater distinction between military and civilian commissars. Military commissars were to be treated as in the OKH draft, that is, not recognized as POWs and disposed of at the latest in the transit camps. Civilian commissars who opposed German troops were to be treated according to the Barbarossa-*Erlass*, while those not guilty of anti-German actions would be investigated later to decide whether they should be turned over to the Einsatzgruppen. Jodl's response was to suggest justifying the entire policy as a reprisal action.[27]

The final version of the *Kommissarbefehl* was signed by Keitel on June 6. Again, a justificatory preamble was added:

In the struggle against Bolshevism, we must not assume that the enemy's conduct will be based on principles of humanity or international law. In particular, hate-inspired, cruel, and inhuman treatment of prisoners of war can be expected on the part of all grades of political commissars, who are the real leaders of resistance.

The attention of all units must be drawn to the following:

1. To show consideration of these elements during this struggle or to act in accordance with international rules of war is wrong and endangers both our own security and the rapid pacification of conquered territory.

2. Political commissars have initiated barbaric, Asiatic methods of warfare. Consequently they have to be dealt with immediately and with maximum severity. As a matter of principle they will be shot at once whether captured during operations or otherwise showing resistance.

Therefore any commissars in the combat zone even suspected of resistance were to be dealt with according to the Barbarossa-*Erlass*. Military commissars found among prisoners were to be treated not as POWs but separated out immediately and shot.[28] Commissars apprehended in the rear areas were to be turned over to the Einsatzgruppen.

The response of the officer corps to this complex of orders ran along three tracks. First, a few protests can be documented. General Field Marshal Fedor von Bock objected that any German soldier was now free to shoot Russian civilians at will, and asked Brauchitsch to restore military court jurisdiction over crimes against Russian civilians.[29] Oberstleutnant Hennig von Treschkow argued that if international law was to be broken, it should be left to the Russians to do it first.[30] Ulrich von Hassell decried Brauchitsch and Keitel's supineness in allowing Hitler to shift the "odium" for murder from the SS to the army.[31]

A second tack—taken by Brauchitsch—was to parry criticism by issuing several supplementary decrees that could be used by officers who were so inclined to mitigate some of the effects of the *Kommissarbefehl* and Barbarossa-*Erlass*, an indication that Brauchitsch received a more widespread critical response from his officers than can be documented. On May 24 he issued the so-called *Disziplin-Erlass*, which permitted officers some leeway. It noted that the Barbarossa-*Erlass* applied to severe cases, and that officers could impose lesser penalties (such as imprisonment on reduced rations, chaining, forced labor) according to circumstances. It also enjoined officers to maintain discipline and avoid willful outrages. Soldiers could not do as they pleased vis-à-vis the civilian population but were bound by the orders of their officers.[32] Then in connection with the *Kommissar-befehl*, Brauchitsch issued another mitigating order on June 8. Civilian commissars were to be shot only if their anti-German behavior was "especially recognizable" (*besondere erkennbare Handlung oder Haltung*). And the shooting of military commissars in the rear areas outside the combat zone was to take place only on the order of an officer.[33]

A third response, however, did much to neutralize the mitigating effects of Brauchitsch's supplementary orders. Various meetings were held among large groups of officers to explain the Barbarossa orders. Surviving documentation of these discussions provides no support for those who have claimed that there was a widespread "conspiracy of silence" or tacit consensus among the officers to sabotage these orders. At several of these meetings the ss's responsibility for carrying out its own "political" tasks and the noninvolvement of the army was stressed,[34] but at other meetings the need for army understanding of and support for "political" tasks was emphasized more explicitly. Standartenführer Nockemann informed a meeting of intelligence officers (I c's) on June 6 that the final removal of Bolshevism was necessary in order to secure the occupied territories, and thus according to the existing orders one had to proceed with "extreme hardness and harshness."[35] Müller's legal adviser, Dr. Erich Lattmann, held meetings on May 16 and 24 in which he made it clear that in the case of civilians there would be no military court jurisdiction, no sentencing, only battle with weapons. Every guerrilla was to be shot; if an attacker could not be apprehended, collective measures were necessary. "No setting on fire, but 30 men to be shot."[36] During another discussion on May 26 it was advised that before the army turned captured commissars over to the SD, intelligence officers should interrogate them, since "many of the non-Jewish commissars are no doubt only fellow travelers and not convinced of the communist ideas" (*viele der nichtjüdischen Kommissare sind zweifellos nur Mitläufer und nicht von der kommunistischen Idee überzeugt*).[37] On June 10 and 11 Müller himself briefed army officers in Allenstein and Warsaw. "Legal sensibilities" (*Rechtsempfinden*) had to give way to the necessities of war, Müller insisted. "A return to the ancient usage of war. . . . One of the two adversaries must remain dead on the ground. Exponents of the enemy attitude must not be conserved but finished off."[38] And on June 18 Oberkriegsgerichtsrat Dr. Weber told the officers of the 11th Army: "Every officer must know that . . . political commissars are to be taken aside and finished off. Every battalion commander must know that he can order collective forcible measures."[39]

Finally, guidelines for troop behavior were distributed at the divisional level on June 4, with instructions that they were to be made known to the troops at the beginning of the invasion. The opening section stated: "Bolshevism is the deadly enemy of the national socialist German people. This disintegrative worldview and its carriers must be combated by Germany. This struggle demands ruthless and energetic measures against bolshevist agitators, guerrillas, saboteurs, Jews, and complete elimination of any active or passive resistance."[40] Among the various orders issued by the military, this was the only explicit mention of Jews. Significantly, they were equated with those categories of people—guerrillas, saboteurs, agitators, resisters—whom not just the Einsatzgruppen but even the military were to shoot on sight.

Between the invasion of Poland and the invasion of the Soviet Union, therefore, the German military had evolved from passive if complaining bystanders to accomplices and participants in building Hitler's New Order. How had such a descent come to pass?[41] On the one hand, the military was responding to a political situation. Having frequently warned Hitler against the consequences of his gambles and having been proved wrong time and again, the military jumped on the Hitler bandwagon in the wake of the fantastic triumph over France. They no longer had faith in their own judgment against the Führer's intuition, sense of destiny, and incredible luck. Moreover, they wanted to protect their own institution against the rising influence of the ss. Expecting a short war, they were prepared to take on some of the "devil's work" themselves as the necessary price of preserving their position, stature, and influence in the New Order.

But more than loss of nerve and political expediency on the part of the military was at work. Two experiences from their formative years in World War I haunted and obsessed the senior German officers. First was the blockade that had slowly strangled Germany's capacity to wage war and allowed a nation of despised shopkeepers to outlast the military prowess of the Kaiserreich. Second was the traumatic collapse at the end, when virtually all they had cherished was swept away by defeat and revolution—a collapse blamed on a "stab in the back" from Marxist and internationalist-pacifist (and therefore naturally Jewish) influences that had subverted the home front.

Thus in many ways the outlook of Germany's military elite vis-à-vis the Soviet Union overlapped axioms of National Socialism. The Nazi leadership and the German military elite shared the geopolitical, social Darwinist postulate that Germany must seize Lebensraum in the east to make itself blockade-proof and secure its position as a world power. They shared a low regard for Slavs, who were fitting objects of Germany's colonial exploitation and domination. They were both obsessed with anticommunism. The conquest of the Soviet Union and the extirpation of Bolshevism would revenge the stab in the back of 1918 and remove forever a subversive, disintegrative threat that was their political nightmare. The malignancy of communism justified in their minds all kinds of drastic preventive measures, no matter how divergent from international law and the traditional norms of the professional soldier. And last but not least, like the Nazis (and like conservatives throughout Europe), the officer corps accepted the equation of Bolshevism with the Jews.

For Hitler, Bolshevism was merely the most recent and nefarious manifestation of the eternal Jewish threat. His anti-Bolshevism was a derivative of his racist anti-Semitism. For the old elites, the anti-Bolshevik crusade was primary, but it also energized their anti-Semitism. In the looming war of destruction against the Soviet Union, considerations of military expediency, anticommunism, and anti-Semitism would all play a role. Military conquest, systematic repression and terror, and deliberate starvation would consume many victims, but Soviet Jewry was certain to be disproportionately affected. This escalating murder of Soviet Jewry would in turn open the way to the Final Solution.

PREPARATIONS OF THE SS

In Poland considerable friction had arisen between the Einsatzgruppen and the military because of the lack of prior agreement and coordination, which contributed to a more limited ss role in the invasion and occupation of the Scandinavian and west European countries in 1940. Himmler and Heydrich strenuously sought to avoid a repetition of such conflict and any limitation on the scope of their role during Barbarossa. In negotiations between the military and the ss, they obtained Brauchitsch's agreement that special units of the Security Police and SD, the Einsatzgruppen, would operate in close cooperation with the army, from which they would receive logistical support, and that they would carry out "executive measures against the civilian population" as ordered by Heydrich.[42] Although the Einsatzgruppen were to be the vanguard of the ss presence on occupied Soviet territory, numerous other units under Himmler's command were also being mobilized for the looming "war of destruction." ss manpower preparations for Barbarossa involved Order Police battalions and Waffen-ss units as well as Himmler's own command staff or Kommandostab and specially selected HSSPF.

Apparently Heydrich began negotiations with Brauchitsch concerning the deployment of the Einsatzgruppen alongside the advancing troops very early in 1941. In February he confided to an ss man named Künsberg, whose team of specialized pillagers of documents and valuables on behalf of the German Foreign Office Heydrich was eager to get attached to the ss, that such conversations were underway.[43] Although an agreement was not signed by Brauchitsch until April 28, Heydrich, his chief of personnel Bruno Streckenbach,[44] and the Gestapo, Kripo, and SD main offices in the RSHA were already selecting leading officers in March, with final approval reserved for Himmler. The selection of lower-echelon officers, according to Streckenbach, was more haphazard. Streckenbach negotiated with the Sipo, Kripo, and SD over their respective quotas and then requested lists from the various branch offices around Germany of men who were both suitable for front duty and not indispensable in their current jobs. Streckenbach conceded that it was "not always" the worst men who were offered up by the branch offices.[45] Presumably many eager and ambitious SS men lobbied their chiefs for the opportunity to prove themselves and advance their careers, especially as a number of Gestapo and SD branch offices were being downsized and their existing leadership positions downgraded.[46]

In late April, Heydrich told Streckenbach to increase yet further the number of men assigned to the Einsatzgruppen, at which point all pretense of individual selection gave way to the assignment of entire units en bloc. On May 21, 1941, the entire class of cadets from the Security Police officer training school in Berlin-Charlottenburg was designated for Einsatzgruppen duty.[47] So too was a class of Criminal Police preparing for promotion exams.[48] All four companies of Reserve Police Battalion 9, stationed in Berlin, were likewise assigned. And the many reservists of the Waffen-SS already assigned were supplemented by an entire Waffen-SS battalion in July.[49] An array of support staff ranging from communications specialists and translators to drivers, mechanics, and secretaries was also designated for Einsatzgruppen duty. Finally, some additional manpower would be added from the native population as the Einsatzgruppen moved into Soviet territory. A sense of the relative contribution from each of these sources can be seen in the breakdown of the 990 men of Einsatzgruppe (EG) A in October 1941: 89 Security Police, 41 Criminal Police, 35 Security Service, 133 Order Police, 340 Waffen-SS, 172 drivers, 87 auxiliary police, 51 translators, and 42 clerks, secretaries, and communications specialists.[50] The other Einsatzgruppen were somewhat smaller, and the total manpower approached 3,000.[51]

Three Einsatzgruppen were originally envisaged for the north, central, and southern fronts, respectively. Eventually a fourth was added for the Romanian front. Each of these in turn was divided into two Sonderkommandos (SK) and two Einsatzkommandos (EK). The former were to operate in the "rear operation areas" (rückwärtige Armeegebiete) close behind the front, while the latter operated in the "rear army areas" (rückwärtige Heeresgebiete) somewhat further back. In addition, an advanced commando or Vorkommando for Moscow was attached to Einsatzgruppe B on the central front.

As in Poland, Heydrich did not hesitate to draw from his stable of highly educated Nazis. Of the four Einsatzgruppen commanders, three held a total of four doctorates: Dr. Dr. Otto Rasch of EG C, Dr. Franz Walter Stahlecker of EG A, and Dr. Otto Ohlendorf of EG D. Of the seventeen SK, EK, and Vorkommando chiefs, a further seven held the doctorate: Dr. Martin Sandberger (SK 1a), Dr. Erich Ehrlinger (SK 1b), Dr. Walter Blume (SK 7a), Dr. Erhard Kroeger (EK 6), Dr. Otto Bradfisch (EK 8), Dr. Alfred Filbert (EK 9), and Prof. Dr. Franz Six (Vorkommando Moscow). Some were taken from the upper ranks of the RSHA in Berlin: Nebe, Ohlendorf, Six, Sandberger, Filbert, Blume, and Erwin Schulz (EK 5). Rasch and Stahlecker commanded the Security Police headquarters in Königsberg and Prague. Many others were branch office Security Police and Gestapo chiefs: Rudolf Batz (EK 2) from Hanover, Günther Hermann (SK 4b) from Brünn, Heinz Seetzen (SK 10a) from Hamburg, and Gustav Nosske (EK 12) from Aachen.

Whatever their immediate previous postings, most of these officers had risen through Heydrich's SD. They virtually all shared the same ideological outlook concerning Jews, Bolsheviks, and Slavs and Germany's imperial future in the east as well as attitudes and dispositions of "energetic ruthlessness," initiative, and activism that were the common characteristics of the SS intellectual elite.[52] If the top officers were handpicked, there is no indication that ideological reliability was ever seen as a necessary distinguishing criterion among the candidates under consideration.[53]

Those assigned to the Einsatzgruppen before the invasion slowly assembled at the border police training school in Pretzsch and the neighboring towns of Düben and Bad Schmiedeberg in Saxony in the months of May and June. They were often visited and inspected by Streckenbach, who was in charge of assembling and equipping them.[54] Heydrich and Müller reportedly appeared on one or more occasions. More important, many of the officers either remained in Berlin or returned there for frequent meetings with key division heads of the RSHA—Hans Nockemann, Arthur Nebe, Heinrich Müller, Walter Schellenberg, and Otto Ohlendorf—and other experts for detailed discussions of the forthcoming mission.[55] In addition, a meeting of all the Einsatzgruppen officers took place in Berlin with Heydrich on June 17, 1941, and Heydrich addressed the closing ceremony in Pretzsch before the units moved out.[56] And the manpower of at least Einsatzgruppe D gathered together for several days in Düben to create some sense of unit identity before departing for the front.[57]

If it is clear that the officers and men of the Einsatzgruppen were prepared for their mission, precisely what orders they received before the invasion has been a subject of considerable dispute. According to the testimony both of Ohlendorf at the International Military Tribunal and of an additional five indicted EG officers (Blobel, Sandberger, Blume, Nosske, and deputy commander of SK 7b Waldemar Klingelhöfer) at the Einsatzgruppen trial before the American Military Tribunal in Nuremberg in 1948, the Einsatzgruppen officers were given an order for the killing of all Soviet Jews by Streckenbach (and in some versions Heydrich) just days before the invasion. This version was disputed only by the terminally ill commander of EG C, Otto Rasch, and the commander of EK 5, Erwin Schulz, who claimed to have received such an order only in mid-August 1941.[58] The Ohlendorf account was generally accepted even after Streckenbach, hitherto presumed dead, returned from captivity in the Soviet Union and denied transmitting such an order.[59] In the ensuing judicial investigation of Streckenbach, only one of the five surviving codefendants of the now executed Ohlendorf, Klingelhöfer, continued to accuse him of transmitting the comprehensive killing order. Two others, Sandberger and Blume, exonerated Streckenbach but maintained they had received such a preinvasion order from Heydrich. Nosske now sided with Schulz, who remained consistent in his account of a mid-August order. Of the eight additional EK and SK commanders subsequently found and interrogated, four (Batz, Jäger, Filbert, and Zapp) supported the existence of a preinvasion comprehensive killing order, though none supported Ohlendorf's original version that it had been disseminated by Streckenbach; two (Bradfisch and Prast, Seetzen's deputy for SK 10a) claimed to have received such an order later; and two (Ehrlinger and Kroeger) denied ever having received such an order.[60]

Out of the welter of conflicting and changing testimony, and from his own preparation of the judicial case against SK 4a, Alfred Streim concluded that Ohlendorf had organized a conspiracy among the original defendants (which only Rasch and Schulz would not join) to provide false testimony as part of a legal defense strategy of binding orders, and that the hapless Streckenbach had been chosen as the alleged disseminator because he was presumed dead.[61] In the last decade most historians have accepted the Streim thesis and do not rely on the early testimonies of the captured Einsatzgruppen officers.[62] More credence is given to the surviving SS documentation, scant in comparison to the military documentation elucidating the development of the *Kommissarbefehl* and *Gerichtsbarkeitserlass*, and to the general mood and outlook on the eve of the Nazis' "war of destruction" against the Soviet Union.

Shortly before the invasion, a list of instructions for the officers of the EG and EK, with particular emphasis on close cooperation with the military, was reproduced in 75 copies. The text was emphatic: "Relations with the military are determined by the OKH order of March 26, 1941, which is to be observed exactly. The most loyal cooperation with the military is to be preserved on the basis of this order."[63]

On June 29, 1941, Heydrich wrote to his Einsatzgruppen commanders in order to "remind" them of verbal explanations he had made to them in Berlin on June 17. No obstacle was to be placed in the way of the "self-cleansing efforts" (*Selbstreinigungsbestrebungen*) of anticommunist and anti-Jewish circles. On the contrary, such "self-defense circles" were to be incited, intensified, and if necessary pointed in the right direction, but "without leaving a trace" (*spurenlos*), so that later they would be unable to invoke any German order or political assurance. Because such measures were possible only in the earliest period of military occupation, the EG and EK, in closest cooperation with the military, had to send at least advance commandos as quickly as possible into the newly conquered territories.[64]

On July 2 Heydrich wrote to the HSSPF on the eastern front, noting that, unlike Kurt Daluege of the Order Police, he had been unable to meet with them in Berlin in order to provide them with the "basic instructions" (*grundsätzlichen Weisungen*) for the jurisdiction of the Security Police and SD. Thus he was now sending them "in compressed form" (*in gedrängter Form*) his "most important instructions" to the Einsatzgruppen with the request that they adopt them as their own. The "short-term goal" (*Nahziel*) of political and security pacification was the prerequisite for the "long-term goal" (*Endziel*) of economic pacification, and all necessary measures were to be carried out with "ruthless severity" (*rücksichtsloser Schärfe*). To avoid any possible confusion concerning the role of the EG in the overall campaign, Heydrich once again referred explicitly to the OKH order of March 26, 1941 (signed by Brauchitsch on April 28).

The EG were to undertake all arrests and executions necessary for political pacification. Explicitly included among those to be executed were all functionaries of the Comintern and all communist career politicians; the higher, middle, and lower echelon functionaries of the Party and its various committees; *Jews in party and state positions* (italics mine); and other radical elements (saboteurs, propagandists, snipers, assassins, agitators, etc.), insofar as they were not necessary for political or economic expertise. In particular, economic experts were not to be so totally liquidated that no suitably trained people survived. And once again Heydrich noted that anticommunist and anti-Jewish "self-cleansing efforts" were to be encouraged without leaving any trace of German involvement or obligation.[65]

In addition to this fragmentary documentation concerning the tasks of the Einsatzgruppen, Heydrich had addressed the Einsatzgruppen commanders in Berlin and the entire manpower at the closing ceremony in Pretzsch. According to Erwin Schulz,[66] over the years the most consistent (and in my opinion most reliable) witness among the EG officers, Heydrich spoke in general terms but in a way that revealed the expectations to which his officers would be held. They faced a conflict of unprecedented harshness in a life-and-death struggle between two worldviews. They had to secure the rear areas against partisans. The Jews constituted a special danger and, as had been learned in Poland, had to be dealt with "more severely" (*schärfer*).[67]

Such verbal incitement, along with the explicit orders to shoot all Communist Party functionaries and all Jews in state and party positions, as well as to undertake all other executions deemed necessary for pacification, could have left the EG officers with little doubt about what was expected of them. With the sole limitations of not straining relations with the military and not liquidating every last economic specialist, their performance would be measured by their execution counts. In such circumstances, all Communist Party members, all Jews in leadership positions, and all male Jews of military age were obvious targets and especially endangered, but anyone deemed a potential enemy was vulnerable. And if the Wehrmacht proved to be a willing partner in the "war of destruction," the EG commanders were free to escalate the killings.

The Einsatzgruppen were clearly intended as the vanguard of the SS presence on Soviet territory, and their key role has undoubtedly been magnified in historical perspective because of the surviving daily Einsatzgruppen reports that would record their subsequent actions in detail. But their prominence must not obscure the fact that numerically they were only one—and indeed the smallest—contingent among the SS forces Himmler planned to deploy for his "special tasks." Far more numerous but far less prominent in the surviving documentation were the additional 21 battalions of Order Police (not including Reserve Police Battalion 9, whose men were divided among the Einsatzgruppen, and Police Battalion 69, whose men were dispersed to guard various Organisation Todt units) assigned to take up positions on occupied Soviet territory. This constituted a manpower pool of some 11,000 men compared to the 3,000 of the Einsatzgruppen.[68]

In 1936 Heinrich Himmler had gained centralized control of the uniformed Order Police, added "and Chief of German Police" to his title of Reichsführer-SS, and delegated power to two men. Parallel to Heydrich's political police or Gestapo, the criminal investigative police or Kripo, and the intelligence service or SD) (consolidated into the Reichssicherheitshauptamt or RSHA in 1939) was the Main Office of the Order Police (Ordnungspolizei) under Kurt Daluege. Daluege's domain included the urban police or Schutzpolizei (Schupo), the rural police (Gendarmerie), and small town or community police (Gemeindepolizei). In addition to these forces dispersed at the precinct level, however, he aspired to large, paramilitary units of barracks police. By 1938 he had 8,930 men organized into police companies called Polizei-Hundertschaften of 108 men each as well as 3,389 men in company-size police training units. Of the 20,000 Order Police who took part in the invasion of Austria in March 1938, many were in these units. Police units were also involved in the occupation of the Sudetenland in October 1938 and Czech lands in March 1939. To swell the potential numbers of the Order Police, Daluege created a Police Reserve of 91,500 men that could be called to full-time duty in time of mobilization. The military made available for the Police Reserve German men born between 1901 and 1909, whom they deemed too old to be suitable for conscription into the army in any case.[69]

The outbreak of war affected the Order Police in a number of ways. The police companies were merged into police battalions of approximately 500 men each, 17 of which were attached to the German armies that invaded Poland. Increased to 21 battalions by the end of 1939, they became involved not only with traditional police work but also in the executions, ethnic cleansing, and ghetto guard duty inherent in the Nazi regime's occupation.[70]

While the war offered Daluege and the Order Police new fields of action, its demands also posed a threat to his manpower. Many of his best units were formed into a police division of 16,000 men that was put at the disposal of the army. Another 8,000 career policemen were transferred to the military police or Feldgendarmerie.[71] In compensation, the Order Police was allowed to recruit volunteers: 9,000 from those born between 1918 and 1920, 17,000 from those born between 1909 and 1912—together constituting the so-called 26,000-man action—and 6,000 ethnic Germans from the newly occupied territories in the east. The number of young men who volunteered for a draft-exempt career in the police far exceeded the allotted quota. Himmler directly siphoned into the SS those volunteers deemed most desirable, despite the complaints of many who felt deceived. Even so, the Order Police could be quite selective (including a criterion of political reliability) in accepting some 13,100 men (half the number promised) out of an initial pool of 160,000 applications.[72]

Over the first 12 months of the war, the number of police battalions swelled to 101.[73] As older reserve policemen were called up to fill in posts at the precinct level, many additional career policemen were thereby released for duty in police battalions (PB). The rank and file and junior officers of some 20 additional battalions were made up primarily of older reservists, although the cadres of noncommissioned officers and commanders of these "pure reserve battalions" were still career policemen.[74] And finally, the recent volunteers were formed into 30 battalions (numbered 251–56 for the classes of 1918–20 and 301–25 for the classes of 1909–12). If the battalions of older reservists were made up of middle-aged men who were conscripted primarily because they held jobs not essential to the war economy and who received scant training, the new 200- and 300-level battalions, in contrast, were made up of carefully selected young men who came from the generation with the highest Nazi Party membership in German society and who were self-selected for a police career in a Nazi police state. They also received extensive training.[75] Twelve of the 21 battalions (not including PB 9 and 69) that were assigned to occupied Soviet territory in the summer of 1941 were 300-level.[76] Some of these units had spent many months in Poland or the Protectorate, acclimatizing to the police work of racial imperialism, before crossing the border.[77] However, the police battalions assigned to Barbarossa also included some of the "pure reserve battalions" composed of rather randomly selected middle-aged conscripts who would be sent into action with little preparation.[78]

Following Himmler's centralization of the police in 1936, Daluege's Order Police were increasingly transformed in two ways. The first was militarization, a trend seen most clearly in the formation of battalions and then police regiments, initially committed to occupation duty but before the end of 1941 assigned even to frontline service.[79] The second was the amalgamation of the Order Police, both in personnel and ideological indoctrination, with the ss. Generally the police are the least likely institution to resist the creation of a police state, and even before 1936 the German police quickly and eagerly adapted itself to its enhanced position within the Nazi dictatorship. A seductive combination of career interest, institutional prominence, and ideological affinity led many police officials to seek party membership. By February 1942 Daluege could report that 76% of the officers corps of the Order Police were party members and 30% were members of the ss. For reserve officers, also specially selected as suitable for officer training, party membership stood at 67%, though ss membership dropped sharply to 7%.[80] For a "pure reserve battalion" like RPB 101, 25% of the middle-aged rank-and-file reservists held party membership. This stood in sharp contrast to the career noncommissioned officers, of whom 63% held party membership and 22% were in the ss.[81] The rank and file of the 300-level battalions, younger in age and recruited more selectively, were more frequently party members than their middle-aged reservist counterparts.[82]

Clearly Himmler sought to indoctrinate all the new recruits, both young and old, who were added to the rapidly expanding Order Police in the early years of the war. The training guidelines of January 23, 1940, insisted that battalion members be educated "for toughness" (*zur Härte*) in order to fulfill their wartime duties. Basic training was to emphasize an introduction to police work, physical fitness, use of weapons, and "strengthening of character and worldview."[83] Himmler required a further three months of intense military and ideology instruction for the reserve police battalions after their basic training, to be completed by June 30, 1941.[84]

For Himmler, all police were to be formed into "soldierly warriors," and the "plumbline" of all such training was the National Socialist worldview. Every day, or at least every other day, the men were to be informed about current events and their proper understanding in ideological perspective. Every week officers were to hold thirty- to forty-five minute sessions on some theme through which the educational goals of National Socialism could be expressed. And monthly sessions were to be held on the most important themes of the time.[85]

Numerous materials were circulated among the police to provide the basis for these ideological training sessions.[86] Pre-Barbarossa issues contained articles by such Nazi luminaries as Alfred Rosenberg; Dr. Leonardo Conti, discussing "biological victory"; and Prof. Dr. Walter Gross, discussing racial selection and population policy. On June 10, 1941, an entire issue of one of the circulars was devoted to "Jews and criminality." Other topics included "the blood community of the German Volk" and "the greater German Reich."[87]

While these specific materials—especially in comparison with the verbal and visual monuments to Nazism of Goebbels and Speer—might strike the contemporary reader as an ineffective mixture of Nazi platitudes and tedious verbiage with little capacity to inspire, they were part of a wider institutional socialization. Himmler and Daluege placed great emphasis on cultivating the professional culture of a soldierly police force imbued with a cluster of particular values: tough and decisive ruthlessness, a firm belief in German racial superiority, an unquestioning acceptance of Germany's right to empire in eastern Europe and the commensurate obligation to assert itself there as the master race, and an aversion to Jews and Bolsheviks as both contemptible and dangerous. This professional culture established norms of behavior and values, in many cases an intensified or radicalized version of attitudes already widespread in German society, which even "ordinary Germans" drafted or recently recruited into the police would feel compelled to measure up to. Indoctrination, institutional socialization to a professional culture, and peer pressure for conformity were mutually reinforcing.[88]

The explicit orders given to the Order Police battalions on the eve of the invasion varied widely. In Police Battalion 309, previously stationed in Radom in the General Government, Major Weiss not only issued the *Kommissarbefehl* and Barbarossa decree but also went much further. He explained to his officers that this would be a war against Jews and Bolshevism, and he wanted it understood that his battalion would proceed ruthlessly against Jews. In his view, the meaning of the Führer's order was that the Jews, regardless of age, were to be destroyed.[89]

In the case of Police Battalion 322, Major General Dr. Retzlaff addressed the men before their departure from Vienna on June 6. Every man was to do his best for the Führer, the Volk, and the fatherland, he exhorted, and "every man of the battalion should be conscious that he had to behave toward the Slavic people as a member of the master race and show that he was a German." Before crossing the border on July 2, the men were instructed to shoot not just political commissars but any civilian with a weapon. "They were to proceed vigorously with toughness, determination, and ruthlessness." (*Es ist hart, entschlossen und rücksichtslos durchzugreifen.*)[90]

In Reserve Police Battalion 65, a Bremen salesman and reservist wrote his wife on June 24: "The major says that every suspect must be immediately shot." But he was not particularly impressed. "Well, I'm in suspense," he continued sarcastically. Not hiding his antipathy toward his officers, he suggested that they might shoot as they had in the comfort of the officers' casino in Oslo, where they had previously been stationed. "The gentlemen fancy themselves as very important and martial," while he in contrast "face[d] the future calmly."[91]

In contrast to the Einsatzgruppen, the police battalions differed in composition and command, were not uniformly briefed, and were issued varying instructions on the eve of the invasion. Some, like Police Battalion 309, were ready to inaugurate a "war of destruction" and launch a genocidal attack on Soviet Jews almost immediately. Others would come to these tasks more gradually.

If the Einsatzgruppen of Reinhard Heydrich and the Order Police of Kurt Daluege were initially the two main sources of SS manpower that crossed onto Soviet territory, Himmler kept some additional forces under his direct control. On April 7, 1941, he formed a special staff (Einsatzstab) that was officially designated as the Kommandostab Reichsführer-SS (command staff of the Reichsführer-SS) on May 6. Also in early May he pulled together disparate SS units in Poland and the Netherlands into the First and Second SS Brigades and a SS Cavalry Brigade. These three units were placed directly under the Kommandostab Reichsführer-SS, that is, under Himmler's personal command. With the addition of several other smaller units, this force of Waffen-SS troops numbered some 25,000 men. The First SS Brigade and the SS Cavalry Brigade in particular, over 11,000 men, would become deeply involved in anti-Jewish actions on Soviet territory by late July 1941.[92]

To coordinate future joint activities by these three branches of SS and police forces on Soviet territories, Himmler named three HSSPF for the north, center, and south fronts, and a fourth was projected for the Caucasus (Hans-

Adolf Prützmann, Erich von dem Bach-Zelewski, Friedrich Jeckeln, and Gerret Korsemann, respectively). The office of HSSPF had been approved in 1937 for the purpose of mobilizing and directing all SS and police forces in each defense district (Wehrkreis) in Germany. Thirteen men were appointed to these positions in 1938. Additional HSSPF were created for Vienna in 1938; southern Austria, the Protectorate, the Warthegau, Danzig–West Prussia, and the General Government in 1939; and Norway and the Netherlands in 1940.[93] On May 21, 1941, Himmler confirmed an agreement with the military, analogous to the agreement concerning the Einsatzgruppen, that the HSSPF on Soviet territory would receive logistical support from the rear army area commanders but their operational instructions and "special tasks" from Himmler directly. For these tasks they would jointly employ the Security Police, Order Police, and Waffen-SS in those areas.[94]

Himmler conceived of the HSSPF as his personal representatives and hand-picked men whose qualities promised no scruples about transcending bureaucratic jurisdictions and asserting SS interests and Himmler's own agenda. The tabula rasa of occupied Soviet territory promised especially wide scope for energetic HSSPF to exploit the full potential of their peculiar and somewhat ill-defined positions as well as to enhance Himmler's influence and control. The HSSPF would also play a crucial role in maintaining Himmler's authority over his powerful subordinates Heydrich and Daluege, in asserting SS interests against his Nazi rivals on Soviet territory, and in the deploying of all of his forces for the looming "war of destruction."[95]

ECONOMIC AND DEMOGRAPHIC PREPARATIONS
FOR "OPERATION BARBAROSSA"
By Christopher R. Browning and Jürgen Matthäus

In addition to plans regarding the smashing of the Red Army and the policing of the occupied territory, German preparations for the "war of destruction" revealed expectations for the future of the region as part of the Reich's sphere of influence. On the level of official ideology and propaganda, these expectations gravitated around the concept of Lebensraum as outlined—though only sketchily—by Hitler since the 1920s. In concrete political terms, the importance of Lebensraum meant focusing even more on the resettlement issue, which, since the occupation of Poland and the agreement with the Soviet Union over the transfer of ethnic Germans into the Reich, had been one of Himmler's key tasks in his capacity as Reich Commissioner for the Strengthening of Germandom (Reichskommissar für die Festigung deutschen Volkstums,

RKFDV).[96] At the same time, huge benefits for the German war economy were anticipated from the exploitation of the occupied Soviet Union. Imports of agricultural products would ensure the food supply in Germany and thus prevent the kinds of shortages and the resulting discontent that occurred in World War I. Accordingly, German preinvasion plans addressed the interrelated problems of resettlement and economic utilization.

From the beginning, economic planning for Barbarossa implied demographic decimation—a readiness not just to accept but to impose a staggering loss of life on the civilian population of the conquered Soviet territories. In February 1941 General Georg Thomas's memorandum on the prospect of immediate economic gain from the invasion of the Soviet Union met with Hitler's approval.[97] On May 2, 1941, the state secretaries of various ministries met with Thomas. They agreed on making it a priority to supply the army with food from within Russia and to ship other essential agricultural products like oils and grain to Germany. "In doing so," the summary protocol laconically stated, "umpteen million people will doubtless starve to death, if we extract everything necessary for us from the country." (*Hierbei werden zweifellos zig Millionen Menschen verhungern, wenn von uns das für uns Notwendige aus dem Lande herausgeholt wird.*) With regard to the remaining infrastructure, industrial production was to take place only in sectors of special demand (transportation, iron, textiles). Beyond that, care was be taken to secure "the vast areas between the main transit roads" by allocating "special troops" to "select areas of special importance that have to be protected."[98]

The protocol of the meeting exemplifies German planning for the occupation of the Soviet Union. It camouflages a deliberate decision on the life or death of vast parts of the local population as a logical, almost inevitable development and quickly moves on to matters of practical implementation. This seemingly sterile, task-oriented rationale resulted from a way of thinking that, because of its total detachment from any concern for human life—with the exception of those privileged to be regarded as members of the German Volk— was racist to the core.

Despite what appears to be a general preinvasion agreement in theory on the aim of exploitation, however, the matter would in practice become contentious. Economic resources could be extracted in two ways: by as far as possible making everything, from production factors to final products, available for the short-term German war effort; or alternatively by leaving the existing infrastructure in place and exploiting the local workforce with a view toward producing beyond immediate German demands. The main protagonists in the ensuing economic debate were Hermann Göring and his office of the Four-Year Plan; General Thomas and the War Economy and Armaments Office; Heinrich Himmler in his capacities as Reichsführer-SS, police chief, and RKFDV; and Alfred Rosenberg, the designated Reich minister for the occupied eastern territories (Reichsminister für die besetzten Ostgebiete).

Since late March it had been evident to top Nazi leaders that Rosenberg, chief ideologue of the Nazi Party and officially involved in a number of activities from foreign policy to the looting of assets, would soon receive a huge boost in power.[99] When Heydrich submitted his draft for a "solution of the Jewish question" to Göring on March 26, 1941, the Reichsmarschall requested—alongside a warning to the troops about the danger from GPU members, political commissars, Jews, and others, "so that they would know whom in practice to put up against the wall"—the addition of references to Rosenberg's future competencies.[100] Two days later, Himmler had an appointment to speak at the opening of the Institute for Research into the Jewish Question (Institut für die Erforschung der Judenfrage) in Frankfurt; he changed his mind, however, and left the lectern to Rosenberg.[101] The expert on eastern Europe declared that the problem would be solved "for Germany . . . when the last Jew has left the area of Greater Germany" and "for Europe . . . when the last Jew has left the European continent."[102] In early April he had a meeting with Hitler, who assured him, as Rosenberg confided to his journal, of his great expectations—"Rosenberg, now your great hour has come!"—and asked him about "the current Jewish element in the Soviet Union and other matters."[103] Rosenberg also noted in his journal: "What I do not want to write down today, but what I will nonetheless never forget."[104]

In April and May, when the "Barbarossa orders" were under consideration, Rosenberg wrote a number of memoranda for Hitler that outlined his vision for the occupied Soviet Union. In his first memorandum he stressed the need for the total destruction of the "Jewish-Bolshevist state apparatus" (jüdisch-bolschewistische Staatsverwaltung) and for the resettlement of unwanted ethnic groups.[105] The same topic occupied his private thoughts at this time. "The East," the Reval-born politician speculated in his diary, "is something fundamentally different from the West with its cities, industry, discipline. One can only imagine the desolation in the most drastic terms." (Der Osten ist etwas grundsätzlich anderes als der Westen mit seinen Städten, Industrie, Disziplin. Man wird sich die Verödung nicht schlimm genug vorzustellen haben.)[106] In regard to the "Jewish question," Rosenberg anticipated that a "temporary solution" (zeitweilige Übergangslösung) would have to be found that included forced labor and ghettoization.[107] For the Ukraine he expected a "decisive solution" through removing Jews from offices, forming work columns, and creating ghettos like that in Lodz "as far as the Jews have not been driven out by the Ukrainians themselves." "Ostland," an artificial geopolitical construct that comprised the Baltic States and parts of Belorussia, was to be transformed "by Germanization of racially suitable elements, by being colonized with Germanic peoples and by resettlement of racially unwanted elements" (*durch Eindeutschung rassisch möglicher Elemente, durch Kolonisierung germanischer Völker und durch Aussiedlung nicht erwünschter Elemente*).[108] As a result of his more long term perspective, Rosenberg favored a less radical approach regarding the treatment of these "enemies" in the course of Operation Barbarossa than what was planned by the Wehrmacht.[109]

While the meeting on economic policy of May 2, 1941, was highly relevant for Rosenberg's task, it is unlikely that he attended, since he was briefed that day by the army on the plans for the attack and the separation of tasks between Wehrmacht and ss as outlined in the Heydrich-Wagner agreement.[110] However, his ideas were very much along the lines of those who envisaged the starving to death of millions of people. Phrased in his nebulous jargon, this rationale entered into the structure Rosenberg outlined for his ministerial and regional apparatus. In a memorandum with general instructions for the Reich commissioners (Reichkommissare) in Ukraine, "Ostland," and other areas that were to be occupied, Rosenberg described the coming war as a "fight for the food supply and raw materials for the German Reich as well as for Europe as a whole, a fight ideological in nature in which the last Jewish-Marxist enemy has to be defeated." (*Kampf um die Ernährung und Rohstoffversorgung sowohl für das Deutsche Reich als auch für den ganzen europäischen Raum, ein Kampf weltanschaulicher Natur, in dem der letzte jüdisch-marxistische Gegner niedergerungen werden muss.*)[111]

In the weeks before the beginning of Operation Barbarossa, economic experts drew up further plans presenting a similar scenario of mass starvation and massive exploitation. Of special importance were guidelines on economic policy finalized by the Wirtschaftsorganisation Ost, Gruppe Landwirtschaft on May 23, 1941.[112] Claiming "approval from the highest authorities" (*Billigung der höchsten Stellen*),[113] the (unknown) authors of the twenty-page set of guidelines proposed to radically alter the structure of the Russian economy by establishing a "primacy of food supply" (*Primat der Ernährung*)[114] for the benefit of German troops, the German population, and the rest of German-dominated Europe. The key to success was the subdivision of the Soviet Union into two geo-economic entities according to agricultural productivity: the "deficit zone" (alternatively, "forest zone" or "hunger area") (*Zuschusszone, Waldbauzone,*

Hungergebiet) in the north, especially the industrial centers of Moscow and Leningrad; and the "surplus zone" or "black-soil zone" (*Überschusszone, Schwarz-erdezone*) in the south, including the Caucasus.[115]

The surplus generated by cutting the economic connections between the two zones was to be, literally, swallowed up by the occupying army (two-thirds or more of its provisions were to be extracted from occupied Soviet territory, one-third or less were to be supplied by France). As already envisaged in the meeting on May 2, the German economy was also to benefit directly from imports of fats and grain from the "surplus area."[116] While the population in the south, as the producers of an agricultural surplus, could hope for a subsistence minimum (*lebenswürdige Zustände*),[117] those living in the "hunger area" had little if any chance of surviving. "Many tens of millions of people will become redundant in this area and will die or have to emigrate to Siberia. Attempts to prevent the local population from starving to death by importing surpluses from the black-soil zone will only be at the expense of provisioning Europe. They endanger Germany's capacity to hold out in war, they endanger Germany's resistance to blockade. Absolute clarity must prevail in this regard." The economic experts rationalized, moreover, that even if the German administration were to want to move food from the south, such attempts would be doomed to fail owing to the lack of transport facilities.[118]

These guidelines, together with the summary of the May 2 meeting—the grimmest expression of German intent toward the civilian population in the Soviet Union—envisaged that millions would disappear, either by death from starvation or through the "evacuation" of "useless eaters."[119] The guidelines were not, however, a blueprint for the measures that were actually taken after the beginning of Operation Barbarossa.[120] If they had been, the people in the Baltic States and parts of Belorussia might have fared better than they did. According to the planners, although these areas were part of the "deficit zone," special German interests had to be taken into account. Because of their high degree of agricultural cultivation, Lithuania, Estonia, and Latvia were to be treated "exactly like the newly incorporated districts" of former Poland. For Belorussia, the prime producer of meat in relative proximity to the German market, it was seen as desirable—"also for political reasons: conflict between Belorussians, Lithuanians and Russians" (*Grossrussen*)—to proceed "with care" (*pfleglich zu behandeln*); only the future would show "how far this is possible."[121] Jews were not explicitly mentioned in the guidelines. The prime target groups of the German policy of withholding vital food supplies were the people living around Moscow and Leningrad as well as "Russians" (*Grossrussen*), who were collectively regarded as political enemies. With the exception of parts of Russia and the environs of Leningrad, where the 900-day siege indeed created mass death by starvation, the Germans managed to occupy only those areas of the Soviet Union that the guidelines had earmarked either as "surplus zone" or as exceptional parts of the "hunger zone" where special interests demanded a less destructive policy.

However imprecise, the thrust of Germany's preinvasion economic planning had ominous implications not only for Soviet civilians but also for the many prisoners of war that predictably would result from the Wehrmacht's encirclement strategy.[122] It would embitter the population, which would only aggravate Germany's attempts to pacify the conquered country and trigger escalating terror and repression on a massive scale.[123] And it implied catastrophic consequences for Soviet Jewry, who, as elsewhere under German control, would always have the last claim on scare food supplies.

All agencies involved in preinvasion planning agreed that a "solution to the eastern questions"[124] entailed a vast range of measures directed against different groups of the population. For Hans Frank, the prospect of Barbarossa aroused expectations for the expulsion and decimation of European Jewry in general and the Jews in his area of influence in particular. On the eve of the invasion, June 19, Hitler, Goebbels, and Frank discussed the Jews of the General Government. Goebbels noted: "Dr. Frank talks about the General Government. There they are already looking forward to being able to expel the Jews. Jewry in Poland is gradually going to wrack and ruin. A just punishment for its instigation among the peoples of the world and its plotting of the war. The Führer, of course, prophesied this for the Jews." (*Das Judentum in Polen verkommt allmählich. Eine gerechte Strafe für die Verhetzung der Völker und die Anzettelung des Krieges. Der Führer hat das ja auch den Juden prophezeit.*)[125] However, Frank did not seem to have heard in this conversation anything beyond Hitler's assurances of the previous March, for he did not relate it to his followers in the General Government for more than a month. Once again the General Government was to be freed of its Jews "in a reasonable space of time" (*in absehbarer Zeit*). The General Government was envisaged as a kind of "transit camp" (*Durchgangslager*), implying ultimate expulsion eastward.[126] At the same time, Frank wrote Lammers in the Reich Chancellery, requesting annexation of the Pripet marshes to the General Government. Here he hoped to resettle the Jews from the General Government, so they could do useful work for the Reich.[127]

Not all top Nazi officials perceived the Jewish question as the most pressing item on the political agenda. In a speech on June 20, 1941, before an audience described in his manuscript as "the closest participants in the eastern problem," Rosenberg explained that even he, the ideologue, followed specific political goals, most notably "to organically cut out state entities [*Staatsgebilde*] from the gigantic territory of the Soviet Union and to prop these up against Moscow in order to free the German Reich for centuries to come from the Eastern nightmare [*östlichen Alpdruck*]." He outlined two enormous challenges: "1. To secure the German food supply and war economy; this is the big task of the Reichsmarschall [Göring], and 2. To liberate Germany for eternity from the political pressure of the east; this is the political aim in this fight." On the central planning level, feeding the German people (*deutsche Volksernährung*) was the priority. As before, Rosenberg presented ideology-driven decisions on the fate of the local population in terms of economic necessity: "We indeed do not see any responsibility to also feed the Russian people from within these areas of agricultural surplus. We know that this is a harsh necessity that remains untouched by sentiment. Doubtless, very extensive evacuations will be necessary, and for sure Russiandom has very harsh years ahead of itself." For Rosenberg, Belorussia had the potential of becoming a "very well suited catchment area" for "many unsocial elements" not only from the Baltic States but also from the General Government and the annexed parts of Poland, especially the "Wartheland"—an indication that the idea of removing Jews and other "unwanted" groups to the east had gained further ground.[128]

In addition to the practical measures taken to prepare for the war of destruction against the Soviet Union, in particular the formation and training of the Einsatzgruppen, Himmler—like so many others[129]—reveled in the coming possibilities for demographic engineering that would dwarf the experiments of the previous 18 months. On June 12–15 he met with top SS leaders (including Heydrich and the three future HSSPF for the Russian front: Bach-Zelewski, Prützmann, and Jeckeln) at his renovated Saxon castle in Wewelsburg. According to Bach-Zelewski, Himmler said: "It is a question of existence, thus it will be a racial struggle of pitiless severity, in the course of which 20 to 30 million Slavs and Jews will perish through military actions and crisis of food supply." (*Es gehe um eine Existenzfrage, daher werde es zu einem Volkstumskampf von unerbittlicher Härte kommen, in dessen Verlaufe durch die Kriegshandlungen und die Ernährungsschwierigkeiten 20 bis 30 Millionen Slawen und Juden umkommen würden.*)[130]

On June 24, just after the invasion, Himmler met with one of his demographic planners, Professor Konrad Meyer. Himmler gave him the task—along with "guidelines and advice"—of sketching out a *Generalplan Ost* for future settlement. A quick three weeks later, Meyer submitted his initial draft to Himmler, but apparently the war had gone so well that a plan based on the June 24 "guidelines and advice" was now out of date. Himmler considered the plan already "superseded" (*überholt*) and sent Meyer back to work on it.[131]

Himmler never lost sight of the Russian campaign as a vast racial and ideological conflict that involved more than Jews. On July 13 he exhorted some of his Waffen-ss troops in Stettin (Szczecin) to carry out the "struggle of races" against the Asiatic horde—"the same subhumanity, the same inferior races" that had threatened Europe since the Huns, Magyars, and Tatars, but who now appeared under the banner of Bolshevism. And on July 20 he was in Lublin, where he gave his support to Globocnik's plans for re-Germanizing a region from which Himmler had evacuated the ethnic Germans just one year earlier in the Cholmer Aktion.[132]

Himmler's planning for vast population decimation and expulsion on the one hand and German settlement on the other continued relentlessly. One version of the *Generalplan Ost* was circulated to the Ostministerium in the spring of 1942. The comments made on the plan by Erhard Wetzel pointed out an important change since Meyer had received his guidelines from Himmler in June 1941. The current plan envisaged the expulsion of 31 million Slavs into Siberia (very close to Bach-Zelewski's Wewelsburg figure), with 14 million permitted to remain. According to Wetzel, however, the figures did not add up. "Only if one proceeds on the basis that the approximately 5–6 million Jews who live in this region were already removed before the evacuation, can one reach the figure of 45 million in the alien population. The comments of the plan indicate, however, that the Jews are included in this 45 million." It was perfectly clear to Wetzel, however, that with the Final Solution, the Jews were already being "liquidated" (*liquidiert*), and therefore the resettlement of the Jews referred to in the plan was "superfluous" (*erübrigt sich*). It was also clear that the Germans could not "liquidate" either the Poles or the Russians as they could the Jews.[133] Indeed, the next version of *Generalplan Ost*, offered by Meyer in May 1942, renounced even the notion of deporting the non-Jewish population.[134] In short, sometime after Himmler gave Meyer the "guidelines and advice" for the *Generalplan Ost* on June 24, 1941, a fundamental change had taken place.[135] A solution to the Jewish question was no longer part of the wider framework of a vast decimation and expulsion of Slavs but had gained an autonomy and priority it had not enjoyed earlier. But this fateful development took place after the invasion and not during the preinvasion planning.

In considering the German preparations for Barbarossa, it would be misleading to concentrate solely on the plans of higher officials. For instance, material expectations were not restricted to high-level plans for the exploitation of the occupied Soviet Union for the benefit of the national economy. Corruption, profiteering, and favoritism connected with Nazi anti-Jewish policy had reached endemic proportions already before 1941, most notably in regard to the "aryanization" of Jewish businesses. Since the Anschluss of Austria in spring 1938, the combination of territorial expansion and anti-Jewish measures had proved to be of direct benefit, financially and otherwise, to individuals and groups willing to take advantage of the massive redistribution of property from Jews to "Aryans."[136] The total war against the Soviet Union promised a free-for-all limited only by the availability of assets and the application of restrictions on looting by German agencies themselves. It was not just Hitler's cronies deployed in high-ranking positions in the east but also ordinary Germans— soldiers, bureaucrats, administrators—who expected to profit. Their prospects ranged from "organizing," that is, stealing food and items of daily use and sending home all kinds of goods and valuables, to acquiring farmland in connection with plans "for settlement in the east" (*für die Sesshaftmachung im Ostraum*) and—as in the case of Wehrmacht field marshals von Leeb and von Rundstedt— being granted significant cash gifts by Hitler.[137]

The common though unofficial acceptance of the slogan "*enrichissez-vous*" or "enrich yourselves" was not an aberration from the idealized image of the German public servant in the east but an important part of it. The authors of the economic guidelines of May 23, 1941, pointed out that the successful exploitation of the occupied east depended on the "maximum initiative and eagerness to serve" (*grösste Initiative und Einsatzfreudigkeit*) of staff. Shortage in numbers had to be compensated for with personal energy and the ability to make up one's mind quickly; wrong decisions were better than none. "The men have to understand," the guidelines explained, "that they have only themselves to rely on [*allein auf sich gestellt*] and that in the vast spaces they cannot wait for orders to arrive from above in writing or via telephone. They have to work by themselves and with utmost vigor on the basis of these guidelines. They also should not demand anything from above as these demands, at least in the first months, cannot be satisfied anyway."[138]

In the run-up to the attack, the Nazi leadership made sure that the need for personal initiative in the absence of clear-cut orders could be met. Himmler appointed his HSSPF in the east—Bach-Zelewski, Jeckeln, Prützmann, and Korsemann (projected for the Caucasus)—from among those of his generals who were ambitious, ruthless, and intelligent enough to anticipate what their superiors wanted.[139] All had some experience in administering the "Jewish question" in the Reich, most notably Bach-Zelewski in his capacity as Security Police chief in East Prussia and HSSPF in Silesia.[140] In appointing representatives who had proven their reliability, Himmler followed a bureaucratic style that had increasingly influenced German policy making since 1933. Characterized by improvisation and rival competencies, this style suited Hitler's preference for delaying or altogether avoiding pressing decisions.[141] In mid-October 1941, at a crucial stage in the war and in the development of the Final Solution, Hitler confided to his entourage that he had adopted the habit of holding back outgoing correspondence for three or four days. He admitted that there would always be problems that he himself had to settle; however, he would rather leave it to others. "Where would I be," Hitler stated, "if I would not find people to whom I can entrust work which I myself cannot direct, tough people of whom I know they take the steps I would take myself. The best man is for me the one who bothers me least by taking upon himself 95 out of 100 decisions." (*Wohin käme ich, wenn ich nicht Leute meines Vertrauens fände zur Erledigung der Arbeiten, die ich nicht selbst leiten kann, harte Leute, von denen ich weiss, sie greifen so durch, wie ich das tun würde. Der beste Mann ist für mich der, welcher mich am wenigsten bemüht, indem er 95 von 100 Entscheidungen auf sich nimmt.*)[142] The weeks after June 22, 1941, were to show that the willingness to act independently on the basis of general principles and vague guidelines and thus to relieve the overburdened Führer of the need for a decision extended well beyond the circle of his closest associates.

7

Operation Barbarossa and the Onset of the Holocaust, June–December 1941

Jürgen Matthäus

On June 22, 1941, the first day of Operation Barbarossa, German army units swept across the border into the Soviet Union. Within a few months the Wehrmacht had conquered a vast strip of land that extended from the Baltic Sea in the north via Belorussia to the southeastern Ukraine. Unlike previous campaigns, this Blitzkrieg did not proceed according to plan. Despite defeats in many battles and an immense loss of men and material, the Red Army was able to stop the German advance, forcing the Wehrmacht into a winter campaign for which it was not prepared. What followed might appear in hindsight as a protracted German retreat that ended in unconditional surrender. In late 1941, however, the extended front line in the east not only demonstrated the Reich's unbroken military power; it meant suffering and death for millions of people in the occupied parts of the Soviet Union.[1]

From the beginning, Germany adopted a policy of terror that, though foreshadowed in earlier plans for this war of destruction, gathered momentum over time. Already by the end of 1941, the death toll among noncombatants was devastating. Between 500,000 and 800,000 Jews, including women and children, had been murdered—on average 2,700 to 4,200 per day—and entire regions were reported "free of Jews." While many Jewish communities, especially in rural areas, were targeted later, the murder of Soviet POWs reached its climax in this early period. In the fall of 1941, Red Army soldiers were dying in German camps at a rate of 6,000 per day; by the spring of 1942, more than 2 million of the 3.5 million Soviet soldiers captured by the Wehrmacht had perished. By the time of their final withdrawal in 1943/44, the Germans had devastated most of the occupied territory, burned thousands of villages, and depopulated vast areas. Reliable estimates on total Soviet losses are difficult to arrive at; a figure of at least 20 million people seems likely.[2]

In looking for answers to the questions how, when, and why the Nazi persecution of the Jews evolved into the Final Solution, the importance of the war against the Soviet Union can hardly be overestimated. Ever since Operation Barbarossa became an object of research, it has been stressed that the murder of the Jews in the Soviet Union marks a watershed in history, a quantum leap toward the Holocaust.[3] Still, despite new research based on sources from east European archives, historians continue to struggle with key questions: What turned men from a variety of groups—Wehrmacht, SS, German police and civil agencies, allied troops, local collaborators—into perpetrators, and how did they interact in the course of this "realization of the unthinkable"?[4] How important were orders, guidelines, and instructions issued by Berlin central agencies compared with factors at the local and regional level? What were the driving forces of this process and what were their origins? In addressing these questions, historians have to confront the inappropriateness of monocausal and linear explanations as well as the impossibility of comprehensive understanding. In looking for reasons how, when, and why the "Final Solution" came about, this chapter focuses on developments that were especially relevant for Germany's crossing the threshold from instances of physical abuse and murder to systematic extermination.

GERMAN PERCEPTIONS AND EXPECTATIONS
REGARDING "THE EAST"

Ideological bias influenced more than just the strategic grand designs and military orders drawn up by the top leadership in preparation for the war against the Soviet Union. When Wehrmacht soldiers, SS men, and other Germans crossed the border toward the east, they brought with them more or less fixed images of the region and the people they would encounter. Combining collective stereotypes established in the 19th century with Nazi propaganda slogans and political interests that found expression in the "Barbarossa orders," these predominantly negative images determined how reality was perceived. Both "endless vastness" and "living space," "the east" implied a threat to the present as well as a promise for the future. In its origin and function "the east" was also closely associated with other ideological concepts—most notably "the Jew" and "Bolshevism." Hitler's ideas regarding "living space" or Lebensraum in the east, hardly original and with strong utopian elements, were well known through his own writings and speeches and those of his closest

Baltic Sea

RUSSIA

Leningrad

Tallinn

ARMY
GROUP
NORTH

Moscow

Riga

REICHS-

Liepaja

Memel

KOMMISSARIAT

Smolensk

ARMY GROUP CENTER

Kaunas

Tilsit

Vilnius

Mogilev

Köenigsberg

OSTLAND Minsk

EAST
PRUSSIA

BIALYSTOK
(Admin. by
E. PRUSSIA)

Slutsk

Gomel

Kursk

GERMANY

Warsaw

Brest-Litovsk

REICHSKOMMISSARIAT

Kharkov

GENERAL
GOVERNMENT

Rovno

Zhitomir

Kiev

UKRAINE

ARMY GROUP SOUTH

Cracow

Lwow

DISTRICT
GALICIA

Dnepropetrovsk

Rostov

Kamenets-
Podolsky

TRANSNISTRIA

Iasi

Odessa

Black Sea

—————— Front as of Dec. 5, 1941
—————— Reichskommissariat boundary
- - - - - - German Army Group dividers
////// Military occupation zones

3. OCCUPIED SOVIET TERRITORY, DECEMBER 1941

followers.[5] It is much more difficult to gauge the mind-set of Germans outside the narrow, Berlin-based circle of Nazi leaders. Despite their fragmentation along social, organizational, and other lines, the representatives of the occupying power—military officers, soldiers, administrators, policemen—shared perceptions and expectations that formed the background to German policy in the Soviet Union.[6]

Images of "the east" had influenced German policy making since World War I, when the German army first occupied parts of the Russian empire. This element of continuity is most obvious when looking at the attitudes toward Russia of commanding Wehrmacht officers, the majority of whom had served during the Great War. Afterward, military conflict between the two countries was perceived as being deeply rooted in history, a struggle in which Germanic peoples fought Slavs for "the defense of European culture against the Muscovite-Asiatic deluge." The occupation of eastern Poland, parts of the Baltic area, Belorussia, and Ukraine during World War I had also confronted German soldiers with the peoples of eastern Europe. Members of the officer corps in particular regarded the local population not only as different but as degraded and unable to appreciate western values. On the sliding scale of backwardness, the lowest place was reserved for the eastern Jews. Urban ghettos appeared to German soldiers as remnants of medieval times, their occupants filthy and repulsive.[7]

During World War I, the German army had been unable to secure the captured areas. The threat by *franc-tireurs* (irregulars) in the west seemed small compared to the danger posed by "bandits" and later communist infiltrators in the east.[8] For many officers more than twenty years later, the lessons of the Great War loomed large. In mid-June 1941 the Army High Command's (Oberkommando des Heeres, OKH) legal expert Lt. General Müller told officers of Panzer Group 3 that the expected severity of the coming war called for equally severe punitive measures against civilian saboteurs. To prove his point, he reminded his audience of the brief Russian occupation of Gumbinnen in Eastern Prussia in 1914 when all inhabitants of villages along the route from Tilsit to Insterburg were threatened with execution if the railway line was damaged. It did not matter that the threat was not executed. "In cases of doubt regarding the perpetrator," the general advised for the future, "suspicion frequently will have to suffice." (*In Zweifelsfragen über Täterschaft wird häufig der Verdacht genügen müssen.*)[9]

Another crucial element of ideological continuity after 1918—the identification of Jews with Bolshevism—linked old anti-Semitic stereotypes with the new fear of a communist world revolution. Right-wing ideologues and Nazi propagandists like Alfred Rosenberg and Joseph Goebbels tried to paint communism as an aberration from European history, an Asiatic phenomenon alien to all accepted moral categories of the West.[10] Affinity to these notions explains to some extent why, compared with the loyalty displayed toward the Nazi state well into its final hours, German military officers had few problems disregarding their oath to protect the democratic system of the Weimar Republic. Hitler's movement offered promises to all strata of the nationalist elite but had special appeal for the military, since it called for more than a revision of Versailles and offered a chance for rapid remilitarization. Early indications of the army's eagerness to support the Nazi regime include acquiescence to the murder of political opponents, among them former chancellor and army general Kurt von Schleicher during the so-called Röhm Putsch in late June/early July 1934; and the military's attitude toward Jews. Not waiting until the Nuremberg laws, the army was quick to enact its own anti-Jewish measures, which excluded Jews from military service and prohibited officers from being married to "non-Aryans."[11]

Staff officers of bourgeois upbringing might have resented "Stürmer"-style slogans and the actions of Nazi thugs, but they had no sympathy for either Jews or communists. In late 1935, in a leaflet drafted by the Reichskriegsministerium, Soviet party functionaries were referred to as "mostly dirty Jews" (*meist dreckige Juden*).[12] Four years later, the Allgemeine Wehrmachtsamt of the Wehrmacht High Command (OKW), subsequently heavily involved in the planning of Operation Barbarossa, published a training brochure titled "The Jew in German History" that spelled out what remained to be done regarding the "Jewish question." All traces of "Jewish influence" were to be eradicated, especially in economic and cultural life; in addition, the "fight against world Jewry, which tries to incite all peoples of the world against Germany," had to be continued.[13] Firmly enshrined in anti-Jewish policy and supplemented by a barrage of propaganda, the phantom of "Jewish Bolshevism" had by June 1941 assumed a life of its own that drastically diminished the military's ability to perceive reality. The involvement in the murder of Jews and other civilians during Operation Barbarossa of staff officers who were later to support the military opposition against Hitler indicates their acceptance of basic Nazi notions.[14] In view of the willing self-integration of leading Wehrmacht officers into the upper echelons of the Third Reich and their support for Hitler's course toward war, Nazi ideology with its focus on an internal and external enemy provided not a straitjacket but a fitting new uniform for traditional sets of belief.

If the German army's commanding officers harbored a deep-seated animosity toward communist Russia combined with an ingrained as well as politically motivated anti-Semitism, this cannot be said with the same certainty of the Wehrmacht's rank and file. For young recruits of 1941, World War I, though an important part of family history, school education, and national memory, seemed remote. Most of them knew "the east" only from books, school lessons, and propaganda. The German attack on Poland in September 1939 had been orchestrated by a campaign of lies about what the Poles had done to a former (and future) area of German settlement. So far, little research has been done on the role of ideological indoctrination in the behavior of Wehrmacht soldiers or, for that matter, any other group deployed in the east; the prevailing though largely unsubstantiated assumption has been that efforts in this direction were largely futile.[15]

It has to be taken into account, however, that beginning with the Polish campaign, Nazi propaganda had its strongest ally in German occupation policy itself. As the measures adopted rapidly worsened conditions in the east, despised elements of the local population appeared increasingly subhuman, and this in turn helped to erode remaining moral scruples among German soldiers who had to deal with them. Nowhere was this vicious circle of dehumanization more obvious than in the case of Polish Jews, who came to be presented and perceived as the personification of the Nazi caricature of the "eternal Jew." Atrocities committed by both ss and Wehrmacht in the Polish campaign were at least partly the result of this imagery and the "master race" or *Herrenvolk* mentality systematically fostered since 1933.[16]

After the conclusion of the Molotov-Ribbentrop pact on August 23, 1939, anti-Bolshevism had to be toned down in public.[17] At the same time, the death toll during the Polish and other campaigns had started to erode the relative homogeneity of the prewar officer corps, a development greatly accelerated after the beginning of Operation Barbarossa with its heavy losses, especially among lower-ranking troop officers.[18] Even if, as is often claimed, the success of deliberate attempts at selling Nazi notions to the soldiers was limited before June 1941, the ideologically highly charged atmosphere and the conditions at the eastern front had a massive impact on how the members of the Wehrmacht perceived and legitimized what they did. At least until Stalingrad, German soldiers mentally endured the hardships of the campaign against a determined enemy not only out of sheer obedience or compliance with group pressure but also because of certain convictions, including the projection of their own destructive impulses onto the enemy.[19]

In this respect, the political leadership's sense of reality turned out to be correct. In his speech before army leaders on March 30, 1941, in which he called for the "destruction of Bolshevist commissars and the communist intelligentsia" (*Vernichtung der bolschewistischen Kommissare und der kommunistischen Intel-*

ligenz), Hitler advised his officers to give orders "in harmony with the sentiment of the troops" (*im Einklang mit dem Empfinden der Truppe*).[20] In mid-September 1941, in one of his nightly musings about the recent past, Hitler conceded that at the time of the attack he had expected expressions of procommunist sentiments within the Wehrmacht. "Those who took part in it," he assumed, "have now surely learned their lesson, but before no one knew how it really looked over there."[21]

The Nazi concept of ideological war implied replacing traditional rules of discipline and subordination with a more flexible system that allowed German functionaries on all levels to act promptly and aggressively. In early May 1941 Colonel General Hoepner, commander of Panzer Group 4, which was to be deployed with Army Group North, legitimized the coming war as a "defense of European culture against a Muscovite-Asiatic deluge" (*Verteidigung europäischer Kultur gegen moskowitisch-asiatische Überschwemmung*) and a "warding off of Jewish Bolshevism" (*Abwehr des jüdischen Bolschewismus*)[22] Days later, General Müller stated, in regard to the treatment of commissars and the local population, that this campaign would be different from previous ones; the Wehrmacht had to expect resistance from the "carriers of Jewish-Bolshevist ideology," and it was called upon to shoot "locals who participate in the fighting as partisans or intend to do so . . . during battle or while trying to escape." Any crimes committed by members of the Wehrmacht as a result of "exasperation about atrocities or the decomposition efforts by the carriers of the Jewish-Bolshevist system" were not to be persecuted as long as they did not threaten discipline.[23] This was the tenor of the Erlass über die Ausübung der Gerichtsbarkeit und über besondere Massnahmen der Truppe (Decree on the exercise of military court jurisdiction and special measures of the troops) signed by Keitel on May 13, 1941, and sent down by Brauchitsch to the level of army commanders on May 24.[24]

The line drawn between "legitimate" and "unacceptable" activities of the local population remained elusive, allowing a wide range of interpretation. In a meeting of intelligence (I c) officers, General Müller's leading legal expert explained that in deciding whether a crime committed by a German soldier threatened the discipline of the troops, his motivation for the crime should be the key factor.[25] The OKW's Abteilung Wehrmachtspropaganda (Division of Military Propaganda) had issued guidelines for the conduct of the campaign in Russia which called for "ruthless and energetic measures against Bolshevist instigators, partisans, saboteurs, Jews, and total eradication of any active or passive resistance."[26] In their final version, the guidelines stressed the "subhuman nature" (*Untermenschentum*) of the future enemy.[27] OKW chief Keitel signed the "commissar order" on June 6, 1941;[28] shortly thereafter, his department for POWs laid down plans for the treatment of captured Red Army soldiers (commissars and Jews were not mentioned) that followed the guidelines regarding the treatment of the population at large.[29]

It is widely accepted that "the troops of ideological warfare"—the members of the Einsatzgruppen—were motivated by firm ideological convictions. Compared with the three million soldiers who flooded across the border, Heydrich's Einsatz- and Sonderkommandos seem almost insignificant in size. The majority of Einsatzgruppen personnel came from outside the Security Police and the SD. Units of the Order Police and Waffen-SS fulfilled similar functions either within or outside the Einsatzgruppen framework. The question raised by Christopher Browning in his pathbreaking case study of Reserve Police Battalion 101 as to how "ordinary" these men were needs to be extended to all direct perpetrators.[30] The absence of comparative research makes it difficult to come up with more than general conjectures. It seems evident, however, that the issue is very much linked to the institutional history of the SS and police in the Third Reich.

Since the mid-1930s ideological training had been part of the curriculum of German policemen. After 1936 when Himmler was appointed chief of the German police, in addition to his position as Reichsführer-SS, he felt the need to integrate more firmly the component parts of his empire. On the organizational level, these efforts proved largely futile owing to the intense rivalry between the different agencies within his apparatus. The office of HSSPF, designed to link SS and police functions, in fact increased the degree of decentralization by creating "little Himmlers" bound into the existing structure by their personal allegiance to the Reichsführer rather than by bureaucratic ties.[31] On the ideological level, however, the self-image of a Staatsschutzkorps (state defense corps)—a diversified security agency that would defend the Reich against inner enemies just as the Wehrmacht provided protection against external foes—began to take root among the officers of the SS and police even before the war.[32] Regarding the Jewish question, the term "education for murder" coined by Konrad Kwiet aptly describes the long-term effects of this process.[33] As Ian Kershaw has pointed out, propaganda "was above all effective where it was building upon, not countering, already existing values and mentalities."[34] Like Wehrmacht soldiers and the German population at large, members of the SS and police were subjected daily to anti-Semitic messages. Gripping images like in the 1940 movie *Jud Süss* (The Jew Süss) reinforced what was taught in police and SS schools.

Indoctrination was not an end in itself, but closely linked to political practice. Beginning with the enactment of the first anti-Jewish measures and the upsurge of street violence against Jews after January 1933, the police formed an integral part of the machinery that generated the "Final Solution." Even if policemen harbored no anti-Semitic feelings beyond what was considered "normal" in prewar Germany, the activities of Nazi thugs, opportunistic profiteers, and eager bureaucrats deeply affected individuals of all ranks as well as the police as an institution. Prejudices, indoctrination, and the ever increasing practice of persecution made ss and policemen perceive the Jewish question not in abstract terms but as a pressing problem that—for the benefit of the regime, the security apparatus, and their own careers as well—needed to be addressed. The focus on transmitting applicable as opposed to abstract knowledge meant that many of the teachers and students at ss and police schools were members of the Einsatzgruppen and that, in turn, officers involved in "fieldwork," like Adolf Eichmann, lectured at these schools.[35]

Ideological factors operated on many levels. In compiling reports on what happened on Soviet territory before Operation Barbarossa, German agencies could rely to some extent on the help of local informers. In the Baltic States or western Ukraine, annexed to the Soviet Union after 1939, the anti-Semitic bias of nationalists dovetailed with the prejudices of German officials. Lithuanian activists who had fled their country as a consequence of the Soviet takeover formed an especially important group. Via the Stapostelle Tilsit, the Reich Security Main Office (RSHA) Amt IV (Gestapo) in Berlin received regular reports from across the border with Lithuania that were sometimes read by Heydrich and Himmler. In late May 1941 the Tilsit Stapo office under Hans-Joachim Böhme noted changes in the composition of communist functionaries in Lithuania in favor of Russians and Jews. "The Jews in Soviet Lithuania," Böhme concluded, "are primarily active as spies for the Soviet Union."[36]

Prewar orders by the German military leadership regarding the future treatment of captured Red Army soldiers and political commissars leave no doubt about the importance of ideological factors preceding Operation Barbarossa. These orders were more radical than Heydrich's prewar instructions to the Einsatzgruppen, which called for the destruction of specific, though vaguely defined, groups of the population. However, Heydrich had reason to believe that Security and Order Police officers were less influenced by the wording of directives than by their own interpretation of what needed to be done in the east. Before the attack on Poland, Heydrich had charged the Einsatzgruppen with fighting all inimical elements behind the front line (*Bekämpfung aller reichs- und deutschfeindlichen Elemente in Feindesland rückwärts der fechtenden Truppe*), similar to the task of the Security Police in the Reich. This formula provided unit commanders with sufficient legitimization for acts of terror directed against the Polish population.[37] Based on this experience, in 1940 Heydrich issued more stringent guidelines for the deployment of Security Police and SD in Norway. While "enemies of the Reich" were to be neutralized, the "necessity for an absolutely correct conduct" had to be taken into account. All measures had to be implemented "with the greatest sensitivity toward tact," since this was not "a campaign on enemy territory."[38] For the Balkan campaign in spring 1941, no such caveat seemed necessary; in fact, Heydrich came up with a much wider definition of enemy groups that included communists and Jews.[39] In planning for Operation Barbarossa, it must have been clear to the leader of the Security Police and the SD that the likelihood of his officers in the field committing acts of violence against the civilian population increased with the vagueness of the guidelines issued to them.

EARLY ANTI-JEWISH MEASURES AND THE MID-JULY TURNING POINT

Despite the design of the campaign as a war of destruction against the Red Army, potential enemies of German rule, and millions of unwanted civilians, some remaining barriers still had to be overcome on the way to the Final Solution. In June 1941 a solution to the Jewish question was still envisioned by the German leadership in terms of forced resettlement that, though inherently destructive, did not amount to the systematic mass murder of all Jewish men, women, and children. Precedents set in the early weeks of the Barbarossa campaign would prove crucial in the turn to systematic and total mass murder.

The area first affected by the German war machine's deliberate targeting of civilians was the German-Lithuanian border strip. In the early morning hours of June 22, a battalion of the 176th Infantry Regiment launched its attack on the town of Garsden (Gargždai) but faced heavy resistance from Soviet border troops. Surprised by the Germans and armed only with handguns, these units defended parts of the town until, in the afternoon, they were almost completely wiped out by the overwhelming force of the enemy. Infantry Regiment 176 suffered more than 100 casualties on this first day of the war—among them 7 dead officers. In advancing further east, it left securing the town to German border police (Grenzpolizei) from the city of Memel. The Memel unit, with the assistance of local Lithuanians, separated 600 to 700 Jews from the rest of the civilian population. The border police were not sure how to proceed, and telegraph messages were exchanged between Memel, the Stapostelle Tilsit, and the RSHA.[40]

The next morning, while Berlin remained undecided about what to do, the leader of the Stapostelle Tilsit, Hans-Joachim Böhme, the officer who had transmitted reports from Lithuanian informers to Berlin before the war, ordered the border police to select 200 male Jews from among the detainees. They were then marched, together with one woman, across the border to a field where they were guarded by members of the German customs service. It is not clear what instructions were issued to the Stapostelle Tilsit before the attack. During his trial in the late 1950s, Böhme claimed to have received three orders from the RSHA: one regarding the closing of the border, a second outlining the tasks of the Einsatzgruppen—to which his unit did not belong—and the third regarding executions in the border area. Since the Tilsit Stapostelle and SD did not have enough men for the execution of the 201 Garsden Jews, the police commander in Memel supplied upon request a Schutzpolizei (Schupo) platoon of one officer and 25 men. On June 23 the platoon rehearsed the execution in the police barracks before driving the next day to Garsden, where Böhme and the Tilsit SD leader Werner Hersmann were waiting for them. While waiting for their execution, the Jews—among them old men, the wife of a Soviet commissar, and at least one 12-year-old child—had to hand over their possessions and dig their grave. Security Police and SD men of the Stapoleitstelle Tilsit abused the victims, especially an old rabbi with a beard and caftan; one person was shot for not digging fast enough.

In the early afternoon of June 24, the remaining 200 Jews were executed in a court-martial-like procedure that included the reading of the death sentence "for crimes against the Wehrmacht on order of the Führer" and the Schutzpolizei officer, with sword drawn, giving the order to fire. Victims and perpetrators were no strangers to each other. Many of the Jews living in Garsden at the time of the German attack had escaped from Memel after its incorporation into the Reich in early 1939. Decades later, some of the defendants and witnesses in the West German court case remembered the names of the victims. According to the verdict, the soap manufacturer Feinstein from Memel called out to his former friend and neighbor, a police sergeant who stood in the firing squad: "Gustav, shoot well!" After the execution, the Memel Schutzpolizei men discussed what they had done. In reassuring each other, comments were made like "Good heavens, damn it, one generation has to go through this so that our children will have a better life." (*Menschenskinder, verflucht noch mal, eine Generation muss dies halt durchstehen, damit es unsere Kinder besser haben.*)[41]

On June 24 Böhme and Hersmann met with Brigadeführer Franz Walter Stahlecker, the chief of Einsatzgruppe A. During the postwar judicial proceedings, the defendants claimed that Stahlecker had ordered Böhme to shoot all

Jews in the border area including women and children.[42] However, wartime evidence suggests that this was not the case. In a report sent to Berlin about a week after the first mass execution, Böhme wrote only that Stahlecker gave his "general approval to the cleansing actions" (*grundsätzlich sein Einverständnis zu den Säuberungsaktionen erklärte*) close to the border.[43]

From Garsden, Böhme's unit, now referred to as Einsatzkommando Tilsit, moved on. After joining the Wehrmacht in shooting 214 persons including one woman in the town of Krottingen and 111 "persons" in Polangen for allegedly attacking German soldiers, Böhme's men met with Himmler and Heydrich in Augustowo on June 30. Again, the wording of Böhme's report on what was discussed is crucial for understanding the situation at the beginning of Operation Barbarossa: "The Reichsführer-ss [Himmler] and the Gruppenführer [Heydrich] who by coincidence were present there [in Augustowo] received information from me *on the measures initiated by the Stapostelle Tilsit* [italics mine] and sanctioned them completely." (*Der Reichsführer-ss und der Gruppenführer, die dort zufällig anwesend waren, liessen sich über die von der Staatspolizeistelle Tilsit eingeleiteten Massnahmen unterrichten und billigten diese in vollem Umfange.*) Böhme also mentioned consultations with state officials—the Regierungspräsident in Gumbinnen, the East Prussian Oberpräsident and Gauleiter Erich Koch, who was soon to become Reichskommissar for the Ukraine—about incorporating parts of the occupied border regions into Eastern Prussia. Böhme's unit continued its killing spree in Lithuania, claiming by July 18, 1941, a total of 3,302 victims.[44]

South of the Lithuanian sector of the front, equally destructive precedents were being set. Few of the early killings show as obvious a link to Jew-hatred as the mass murder of Jews in Bialystok on June 27, 1941, in which men of Police Battalion 309 and other units subordinated to the Wehrmacht's 221st Security Division killed at least 2,000 Jews. More than 500 persons including women and children were driven into a synagogue and burned alive; those trying to escape were shot. Wehrmacht units blew up adjacent buildings to make sure that the fire did not spread across the city. The scarcity of wartime documentation on this massacre is to some extent compensated for by investigative material compiled by a West German court after the war.

After an order had been given to search for Red Army soldiers and Jews, a few determined officers initiated the murder and dragged others along. The West German court identified some of the perpetrators within the ranks of Police Battalion 309 as "fanatic Nazis," such as "Pipo" Schneider, a platoon leader in the 3rd company; and Captain Behrens, commander of the 1st company. Schneider showed little respect for military obedience, openly dismissing his company commander as a "cowardly weakling," and made no secret of his conviction that the Führer would "no longer feed these dirty Jordan slouchers" (*diese dreckigen Jordanlatscher nicht mehr am Fressen halten*). Together with Behrens, Schneider transformed his ideas into action. Jewish men whose outward appearance corresponded to anti-Semitic stereotypes became their first victims: beards were set on fire, some Jews were forced to dance or to cry "I am Jesus Christ," and Orthodox Jews were shot in the streets. A police officer who expressed discomfort at such acts was rebuked with the words "You don't seem to have received the right ideological training yet." (*Du bist wohl ideologisch noch nicht richtig geschult.*) Higher-ranking officers—among them the battalion commander and the commanding general of the 221st Security Division—stood by. The general did not begin to take notice that men under his command were running amok until the executions had reached a park next to his headquarters, and he later tried to cover up the massacre as a reprisal.[45]

The mass murders in Garsden and Bialystok in late June reflect most of the features of what Raul Hilberg has called the "first killing sweep."[46] The perpetrators used their image of the "enemy" and the pretexts of "retaliation" and "pacification" to legitimize the selection and execution of undesirable persons, primarily Jews, without waiting for specific orders from above. If the murder of Jews on occupied Soviet territory did not result from a preconceived master plan,[47] the sequence, speed, and scope of the killings must have been connected to regional factors and the dynamics of ad hoc decision making. In the process, traditional elements of hierarchy lost their importance. Men from different agencies—the Security Police, the Wehrmacht, the Order Police—interacted. The authority to inflict suffering and death on civilians became detached from military rank and status, with lower- and middle-ranking officers taking the initiative while their superiors provided support, encouragement, or ex post facto legitimization. In this way the limits of what was regarded as acceptable in dealing with selected groups within the civilian population were expanded.

This approach did not become standard procedure overnight. At the time of the killings in Garsden, the 10th Regiment of the 1st ss Brigade, which as part of the Kommandostab was deployed further south, understood its task of "cleansing the border regions" in a much narrower way than Einsatzkommando Tilsit. Instead of killing civilians, it seems to have merely guarded bridges.[48] Through the month of July, however, additional units available to Himmler—his Kommandostab and battalions of Order Police—increasingly became involved on a massive scale in mass murder, thus marking the end of the first stage of destruction.

As they did in the meeting with Böhme in Augustowo, Himmler and his leading officers fomented the local killing process, often in more subtle ways than by directly ordering what was to be done. Frequent visits by Himmler, the HSSPF, Heydrich, or Daluege ensured that word about the "success" of radical measures got around quickly and that officers who were reluctant or tardy adapted to the new possibilities.[49]

How the presence of high-ranking officials influenced the course of events in the field can be seen from the visits by Himmler, Daluege, and Bach-Zelewski to Bialystok in early July 1941. Hours before Himmler arrived in the city, Police Battalion 322 had looted the Jewish quarter, taking out 20 truckloads of food and other supplies, but it did not massacre Jews like Police Battalion 309 just days earlier. In fact, the three persons shot by Police Battalion 322 were Poles.[50] After his arrival the Reichsführer-SS addressed Bach-Zelewski; the commander of the Rear Army Area Center, von Schenckendorff;[51] the commander of Police Regiment Center (to which Police Battalion 322 belonged), Max Montua; and the officers of Police Battalions 322 and 316 as well as of the SD. According to postwar testimonies by participants, Himmler talked about the organization of the police in the east and inquired about the measures taken that day in the Jewish quarter. One witness claimed to have heard from others at the time that Himmler had complained about the small number of Jews arrested and had called for a more active course in that direction.[52] One day later, on July 9, Order Police chief Daluege came to visit Police Regiment Center in Bialystok and delivered a speech on the fight against the "world enemy of Bolshevism." Between July 8 and July 11, perhaps even starting on the evening of Himmler's visit, at least 1,000 Jews—all men of military age—were driven to the outskirts of the city, where they were shot by members of Police Battalions 322 and 316 under the direction of the Security Police and the SD.[53] This sequence of events in Bialystok seems to imply a causal connection, but at the very least encouragement from above had the effect of speeding things up. However, in light of the earlier massacre in Bialystok in late June and other mass killings in localities that high-ranking officers from Berlin had not visited, it seems evident that the presence of the Reichsführer-SS and his lieutenants was not required to trigger the murder of Jews.[54]

On July 11, 1941, possibly in reaction to the earlier killings by Order Police units in Bialystok,[55] the commander of Police Regiment Center, Montua, transmitted an order by HSSPF Bach-Zelewski according to which all Jews age 17 to 45 convicted of plunder were to be shot ("alle als Plünderer überführten Juden im Alter von 17–45 Jahren sofort standrechtlich zu erschiessen"). To prevent "places of pilgrimage" (*Wallfahrtsorte*), the executions had to be carried out in a clandestine way and reported daily; no photographs or onlookers were allowed.

The following piece of advice Bach must have received, directly or indirectly, from Himmler, whose concern for the well-being of his officers was notorious: "Battalion commanders and company chiefs have to make special accommodations for the spiritual care of the men participating in such actions. The impressions of the day have to be blurred by having social gatherings. In addition, the men have to be continuously lectured about the necessity of measures caused by the political situation." (*Die seelische Betreuung der bei dieser Aktion beteiligten Männer haben sich die Batls.-Kdre. und Kompanie-Chefs besonders angelegen sein zu lassen. Die Eindrücke des Tages sind durch Abhaltung von Kameradschafts-abenden zu verwischen. Ferner sind die Männer laufend über die Notwendigkeit der durch die politische Lage bedingten Massnahmen zu belehren.*)[56]

By visiting their men behind the front line, Himmler and some of his closest associates both provided and gathered important information on how to synchronize the "pacification" efforts. But while backing what had been done already and appealing to the men's sense of initiative in a rapidly escalating situation, they did not call directly for the killing of unarmed civilians irrespective of age or gender. The absence of specific orders from Berlin to kill all the Jews east of the border is reflected in the fact that the incoming reports described the first victims of physical annihilation as local Jewish men of military age, especially Jewish intelligentsia in leadership positions in the community.[57] However, from the beginning the delineation of the target group was not clear-cut. The massacre in Bialystok on June 27 shows the perpetrators' lack of inhibitions about killing even those Jews who were the least suspicious and the most vulnerable. And among the 201 persons shot in Garsden on June 24 there were a boy, one woman, and several Jews from Memel who but for the Nuremberg laws were German.

To some extent, the sequence of German anti-Jewish measures adopted in the occupied Soviet Union followed the model first established in Poland. In contrast to the Polish campaign and its aftermath, however, during Operation Barbarossa arrests, confiscation of property, exclusion from certain professions, introduction of badges or other markings, and separation from the gentile population were from the beginning directly linked with numerous acts of mass murder perpetrated by different agencies. Recent research has confirmed that in many cases units of the Wehrmacht delivered the first blows.[58] More-systematic steps were later taken by the Security Police and the SD as well as, in the Reichskommissariate, by representatives of the civil administration. What might appear from a post-Holocaust perspective as a centrally planned and uniformly applied pattern of stigmatization, dispossession, concentration, and annihilation was in the first months of Operation Barbarossa an incoherent, locally and regionally varied sequence of measures characterized on the part of German officials by increasing violence and its acceptance as normality in "the east."

The destructive energies released by the German attack on the Soviet Union were primarily directed against the enemy army. In any military campaign troops can perpetrate atrocities, but Operation Barbarossa was an exceptional war for which the German leadership had deliberately defined new parameters of conduct. Criminal orders from above and violent impulses from below created a climate of unmitigated violence. This can be seen from the available evidence on the killing of captured Red Army soldiers by frontline troops and the conditions in camps for Soviet POWs and civilians.[59] In late June in the city of Minsk the local military commander established a camp that housed at times up to 100,000 Soviet POWs and 40,000 civilians, predominantly men of military age. Conditions in the camp were terrible; even Germans voiced their disgust.[60] In the following weeks, units of the Security Police and SD in conjunction with the army's Secret Military Police (Geheime Feldpolizei) screened both prisoner groups, taking out an estimated 10,000 for execution. Many of the men selected were Jews; however, a significant number of Jews were also among the approximately 20,000 persons released from the Minsk camp in mid-July.[61]

As in preinvasion memoranda and plans, German officials in the field hid ideological bias behind practical rationalizations, mostly by presenting anti-Jewish measures as part of a wider policy of "pacifying" the occupied area. This is true of the events in Bialystok and of a number of other killings. In late June/early July, units of the Waffen-SS Division "Wiking" were, according to a report by a staff officer of the 295th Infantry Division, randomly shooting large numbers "of Russian soldiers and also civilians whom they regard as suspicious," among them most likely 600 Jews in Zborov in Ukraine.[62] Following a request from the 6th Army, SK 4a of Einsatzgruppe C killed 17 non-Jewish civilians, 117 "communist agents of the NKVD," and 183 "Jewish communists" in Sokal. According to Hoepner, commander of Panzer Group 4, "individual communist elements, especially Jews," were responsible for the "rather rare instances of sabotage."[63] In Drobomil, EK 6 arrested approximately 100 persons, mostly Jews, under the pretext of retaliation for NKVD murders and shot them. Reports on events in Kaunas (Kovno), Lwow (Lemberg), and Tarnopol (Ternopol) linked the execution of Jews to earlier killings of prisoners by Soviet authorities, thus artificially creating a causal connection that ignored the Jews among the NKVD victims and helped to gloss over the anti-Jewish feeling of German units.[64] Sometime before mid-July, 4,000–6,000 male Jews in the western Belorussian city of Brest were arrested and shot by men of Police Battalion 307 and the 162nd Infantry Division as part of a "cleansing action."[65] In

Lithuania, German security agencies continued setting precedents that were later to become a standard part of the overall process. In early July 1941 SS Colonel Karl Jäger of EK 3 reported that 7,800 Jews had been killed so far in Kaunas "partly by pogrom, partly by mass executions." To systematically "cleanse" the countryside of Jews, a small mobile unit was set up; in Kaunas, a ghetto was to be created within the next four weeks.[66]

All along the front line, German military and police agencies executed Jews in reprisal for alleged attacks on troops or for being plunderers, members of the intelligentsia, saboteurs, or communists. Beginning in mid-July, Jewish communities were confined to "Jewish quarters" in segregated parts of towns and cities.[67] Central though hardly coherent guidelines regarding ghettoization were issued weeks later.[68] How great an area could be "secured" and "pacified" depended to a large extent on the working relationship between leading Wehrmacht and Einsatzgruppen officers.[69] In the Latvian city of Liepaja, where shots were occasionally fired at Wehrmacht soldiers, the navy commander in late July requested and received the help of police forces for solving the Jewish problem.[70] Einsatzgruppe B leader Arthur Nebe reported that the "excellent" (*ausgezeichnet*) cooperation with the Army Group Center "has proven to be successful especially in the liquidation actions in Bialystok and Minsk and has not failed to affect other commandos." (*Diese Methode hat sich besonders bei den Liquidierungs-Aktionen in Bialystok und Minsk gut bewährt und ihre Wirkung auf die übrigen Kommandos nicht verfehlt.*)[71] Dieter Pohl has estimated that in Eastern Galicia SS and police units killed more than 7,000 Jews by the end of July 1941, before the area was incorporated into the General Government.[72] At the same time, Einsatzgruppe B reported 11,084 murder victims, predominantly Jews.[73] For all the Einsatzgruppen, the total at the end of July was 63,000 persons, about 90% Jews.[74] The perpetrators no longer thought of total annihilation as a utopian idea. In early July a member of Reserve Police Battalion 105 wrote home to Bremen that "the Jews are free game. . . . One can only give the Jews some well-intentioned advice: Bring no more children into the world. They no longer have a future." (*Die Juden sind Freiwild. . . . Man kann den Juden nur noch einen gut gemeinten Rat geben: Keine Kinder mehr in die Welt zu setzen. Sie haben keine Zukunft mehr.*)[75]

The killings in the first five weeks of Operation Barbarossa were of crucial importance for the later sequence of events. What had previously been regarded as logistically difficult, morally questionable, and politically dangerous became a new point of reference for German occupation policy. Starting in Garsden and Bialystok, the last taboo—the killing of women and children—eroded. On July 3 the I c officer of the 295th Infantry Division reported from Zloczow that "Jews and Russians including women and children" were murdered in the streets by Ukrainians.[76] From Lithuania, Jäger's EK 3 was reporting small but increasing numbers of women among the victims of executions.[77] In late July significant numbers of women seem to have been among the victims of pogroms in Lwow and Grodek Jagiellonski.[78] Police Regiment Center ordered its subordinate police battalions to provide execution statistics specifying the number of Russian soldiers, Jews, and women shot.[79] Around the turn of July/August 1941, other units—the 1st SS Brigade subordinated to HSSPF Jeckeln, Einsatzgruppe B (EK 9) and C (SK 4a)—started to shoot women and children in larger numbers.[80] In early August the previously quoted member of Reserve Police Battalion 105 from Bremen wrote: "Last night 150 Jews from this village were shot, men, women, and children, all killed. The Jews are being totally eradicated."[81]

By that time, a standardized method of mass murder had been adopted. The Jews were first rounded up, then brought, in groups of varying size depending on circumstances, to a more or less remote execution site, where the first arrivals were forced to dig a pit. The Jews had to undress and line up in front of the mass grave; they were then either shot into the pit or were murdered after being forced to lie on top of those already killed.[82] What the perpetrators presented as an "orderly" execution procedure was, literally, a bloodbath. In the vicinity of cities, what could be called "execution tourism"—all kinds of Germans on or off duty looking on and taking pictures—abounded despite orders to the contrary.[83] Unlike the execution in Garsden, in later killings the reading of a verdict, however fabricated, was dispensed with. No officer gave a command to fire; instead, the executioners shot randomly, often with submachine guns. Coups de grâce were rarely delivered, and those who were shot but not immediately killed were left to die from their wounds or from suffocation after the pit was covered with soil. "Order" was restored for the murderers at the end of the day when they reentered the world of seemingly normal values or when they attended, as advised by Himmler, their "social gatherings."[84]

As in the planning stages of Operation Barbarossa, economic considerations were but one factor that guided German policy toward the Jews. While the army and later the civil administration stressed the need for qualified Jewish laborers, early experiences pointed to their dispensability. For the Wirtschaftsstab Ost, the case of the oil refinery in Drohobycz (Drogobych) initially seemed to prove that Jewish experts were needed only for a short transition period. Since things worked well without any Jews (ganz judenfrei), it recommended that they should be confined to ghettos.[85] Ghettoization had the additional advantages of providing economic opportunities for Germans and reliable locals and of excluding Jews from the food market. According to Göring's economic experts, skilled Jewish laborers were to remain employed in the war industry only if they were crucial for maintaining the required level of production and could not be replaced.[86] In late July, Berlin economic planners abandoned the grand designs for economic policy developed before the war in favor of practical measures for the immediate benefit of the war effort. For the Jews, that meant concentration in ghettos and forced labor in work columns.[87] Nevertheless, there was uncertainty about which Jews should be killed and which should be regarded as temporarily indispensable. As the Wirtschaftsstab Ost phrased it in its first report: "Unresolved is the question of the Jews who at this time remain deadly enemies, but who are at least temporarily needed economically owing to their large number." (*Ungelöst Frage der Juden, die diesmal Todfeinde bleiben und doch wirtschaftilich wegen grosser Zahl mindestens vorläufig notwendig.*)[88] Those responsible for the enactment of anti-Jewish measures noted that their victims tried to make sense of the confusing and contradictory German measures, often by assuming "that we will leave them alone if they eagerly do their work."[89]

In this rapidly changing situation, contact between the command centers and the units in the field were of mutual benefit. When on June 29, 1941, Heydrich reminded the Einsatzgruppen chiefs of the need for "self-cleansing measures" by the local population, he also insisted that leaders of advance units had to have "the necessary political sensitivity" (*das erforderliche politische Fingerspitzengefühl*) and requested regular reports.[90] On July 1 Heydrich demanded "a maximum of mobility in the organization of tactical operations" (*grösste Beweglichkeit in der taktischen Einsatzgestaltung*) by pointing to his unsatisfactory experience in Grodno, where during a visit four days after the occupation of the city, he and Himmler had not found one representative of the Security Police and the SD.[91] The following day he notified "in condensed form" the HSSPFs—who had been dispatched to the east after having met with Daluege, but not with Heydrich—about the "most important instructions" issued to the Einsatzgruppen: to further the final aim of "economic pacification" (*wirtschaftliche Befriedung*), stern political measures were to be adopted. The list of persons to be executed comprised functionaries of the Communist Party, people's commissars, "Jews in party and state positions," and "other radical elements (saboteurs, propagandists, snipers, assassins, instigators etc.)."[92] We can tell from the reasoning for mass killings offered in the reports from the Einsatzgruppen, Wehrmacht, and police units that Heydrich's categories in fact described the prime target groups. It is not clear, however, whether incoming reports from the field were tailored to meet the instructions from Berlin or whether Heydrich tried to adapt his somewhat belated notification to the actions of his subordinates behind the German front line.

Heydrich's obsession with monitoring the activities of his units behind the advancing front line stemmed largely from the fear of going too far too quickly, a fear he shared with Himmler. At this stage, instead of providing explicit orders for the rapid expansion of the killing process, the ss and police leadership in Berlin seems to have followed a course that can be described as controlled escalation. The delegation of power in the absence of unambiguous guidelines from above greatly increased the danger of subordinate officers getting out of control; thus, reliable information about what went on in the field was crucial. The incoming reports from the Einsatzgruppen were edited at the RSHA and, in the form of the so-called *Ereignismeldungen*, distributed to other government agencies in order to inform them about as well as adapt them to the course of events in the east. Himmler's infamous speech of October 1943 in which he talked to a large audience of Nazi officials about the implementation of the Final Solution was not his first attempt at spreading responsibility for the murder of the European Jews.[93]

Officers at the periphery could expect that their reports would be received by an influential circle of high-ranking officials. For the purpose of presenting it to Hitler, the RSHA gathered "illustrative material" (*Anschauungsmaterial*) on the "work of the Einsatzgruppen in the east."[94] On July 4 Heydrich reiterated his supreme interest in functioning communications between periphery and center while announcing that local Security Police and SD offices in the border region were authorized to perform "cleansing actions" in occupied territory after consultation with the Einsatzgruppen. Heydrich might have had the case of Böhme's Einsatzkommando Tilsit in mind when he threatened to withdraw this authorization if these additional units intended "further actions" (*ein weiteres Vorgehen*) beyond those agreed upon with the Einsatzgruppen "for the purpose of operational coordination" (*zwecks einheitlicher Ausrichtung der zu ergreifenden Massnahmen*).[95] As late as mid-August the Reichsführer-ss sent out reminders for regular reports to his most trusted officers deployed in the east.[96]

In the minds of Himmler and Heydrich, the potential dangers of excessive zeal were manifold. First, despite the cordial relations in the field and the agreement between Wagner and Heydrich, the army could still be antagonized to such a degree that the conflicts of the Polish campaign might reemerge. Second, the thin, but for internal as well as external reasons essential, veil of secrecy could tear, exposing the true nature of German measures in the east. Richard Breitman has recently shown that this fear was indeed well founded, since the British had broken the German Order Police code for radio messages and intercepted execution reports and other incriminating material.[97] Third, Himmler was committed to caring for the psychological needs of his men, and he feared that the persistent use of extreme violence posed a threat to the coherence, loyalty, and postwar effectiveness of the troops. Fourth and most important, given the Nazi leadership's obsession with preventing a situation similar to 1918, the quiet on the home front was not to be endangered. Economic considerations that already in the planning stages of the war enabled the branding of entire groups of the local population as redundant and dispensable were not an end in themselves but resulted to a significant degree from the Nazi leaders' determination to avoid putting an undue burden on the German Volk. Concern about potential unrest led to the official stop of the "euthanasia" killings (Aktion T4) in August 1941. "The Führer," Heydrich explained to his subordinates in early September, "has repeatedly stressed that all enemies of the Reich use—like during the [First] World War—every opportunity to sow disunity among the German people. It is thus urgently necessary to abstain from all measures that can affect the uniform mood of the people." Heydrich ordered that "my approval is sought before taking any especially drastic measures" but left a loophole in cases of "imminent danger."[98]

As before, Hitler himself displayed trust in the rapid adaptation of his men and the population at large. While he initially expected that some Wehrmacht soldiers still harbored sympathy for communism,[99] he was nevertheless sure that the situation across the border would have the desired effect of removing remaining inhibitions. His orders regarding the treatment of Soviet POWs and the civilian population contributed decisively toward this development. In addition, the German propaganda machine expanded on existing stereotypes by stressing that "millions of German soldiers are witnesses today of the barbarity and wretchedness of the Bolshevist state." (*Heute sind Millionen deutscher Soldaten Zeugen der Barbarei und der Verkommenheit des bolschewistischen Staates.*) What they saw there went, according to the official line, far beyond anything known so far about "the Jewish slave state." (*Ihre furchtbaren Einblicke in die Verhältnisse dieses jüdischen Sklavenstaates stellen das in den Jahren bisher dem deutschen Volk bekannt Gewordene noch weit in den Schatten.*)[100]

Recent evaluations of letters and photographs by Wehrmacht soldiers point to a certain discrepancy between propaganda slogans and the more complex "eastern experiences" of many Germans. Jews did not figure prominently as objects of photographic imagery or as topics in the correspondence between German soldiers and their families back in the Reich.[101] Much more dominant in this phase of the war were the primitive conditions, filth and the lack of hygiene, which over time retreated into the background thanks to what Omer Bartov calls the "barbarization of warfare" that especially affected frontline soldiers.[102] In the comparatively few instances when the Jewish question was referred to, Jews were depicted primarily in terms of official propaganda and familiar stereotypes. Accordingly, early dispatches from the east presented Jews as snipers or instigators of atrocities committed against German soldiers. One of the most graphic examples is a letter written from Tarnopol in early July 1941. The writer, after referring to mutilated bodies left by the retreating Soviets in the city's courthouse, minced no words about what happened next:

> Revenge was quick to follow. Yesterday we and the SS were merciful, for every Jew we found was shot immediately. Today things have changed, for we again found 60 fellow soldiers mutilated. Now the Jews must carry the dead out of the basement, lay them out nicely, and then they are shown the atrocities. After they have seen the victims, they are killed with clubs and spades.
>
> So far, we have sent about 1,000 Jews into the hereafter, but that is far too few for what they have done. The Ukrainians have said that the Jews had all the leadership positions and, together with the Soviets, had a regular public festival while executing the Germans and Ukrainians. I ask you, dear parents, to make this known, also father, in the local branch [of the NSDAP]. If there should be doubts, we will bring photos with us. Then there will be no doubts.
>
> Many greetings, your son Franzl.[103]

In hindsight, the available documentation for the early weeks of the campaign indeed corroborates Hitler's view that his men would function well and that the unity of the home front was not in imminent danger. At the same time, in his pronouncements before his closest advisers Hitler expressed less interest in the Jewish question than in other, broader problems. This can be seen from the course of a meeting on July 16, 1941, at which Göring, Rosenberg, Lammers, Bormann, and Keitel were to receive Hitler's view on key issues of policy making. Before addressing the specifics of the issues at hand, Hitler made some general remarks: German propaganda would again have to stress that the Wehrmacht stepped in to restore order and that the Reich was taking over a mandate. However, "all necessary measures"—including shootings, forced resettlement—were to be accelerated, since "we will never leave these areas again." To achieve "a final settlement" (*endgültige Regelung*) of German control over the area, it was essential "to cut the gigantic cake into manageable pieces so that we can, first, dominate it, second, administer it, and third, exploit it." Using Stalin's call for partisan warfare as a pretext, Hitler stressed the "possibility of *eradicating* whatever *puts itself against us*." (*Möglichkeit*, auszurotten, *was* sich gegen uns stellt.)[104]

Taking up Hitler's demand to transform the occupied territory into a "Garden of Eden" and his decision to hand over the area west of the river Düna to civil administration, Rosenberg tried to stress the importance of treating the local population differently—for Ukrainians he even envisaged a limited degree of independence.[105] Göring objected: all thoughts would have to focus for the time being on securing the food supply. The matter was left undecided, and it might have been in that context that Hitler mentioned—as recorded by Rosenberg in his diary—that "all decrees are but theory. If they do not meet the demands, they will have to be changed."[106] Hitler and his cronies moved on to the issue of sharing some of the territorial spoils with Germany's allies, followed by lengthy discussions on the relative merits of the various contenders for the positions of Reichskommissare. Here again, everything depended on quick, energetic action. When Rosenberg objected to the idea of having Erich Koch, Gauleiter of East Prussia, administer the Ukraine for fear that he might act too independently, he was told by Göring that he "could not *always lead* his regional representatives *around by the nose*, rather they would have to work quite independently." (*Rosenberg könne die eingesetzten Leute ja nun nicht* ständig gängeln, *sondern diese Leute müssten doch sehr selbständig arbeiten.*)[107]

When Rosenberg brought up the "question of securing the administration," Hitler stated that he had repeatedly called for better weapons for the police in the east and added, "Naturally, the vast area must be pacified as quickly as possible; this will happen best by *shooting anyone who even looks sideways at us.*" (*Der Riesenraum müsse natürlich so rasch wie möglich befriedet werden; dies geschehe am besten dadurch*, dass man Jeden, der nur schief schaue, totschiesse.)[108] Field Marshal Keitel stressed that, since one could not guard "every barn and every railway station," the local population needed to know "that anybody would be shot who did not behave properly and that they would be held responsible." Although Himmler did not attend this meeting, his interests were taken into account by the other participants and in the order for the establishment of the civil administration drafted by Lammers, the chief of the Reich chancellery.

Rosenberg's final remarks in his diary reflect the atmosphere during the meeting:

At 8 we were nearly finished. I had received a gigantic task, very likely the biggest the Reich could assign, the task to make Europe independent from overseas countries and to make this safe for centuries to come. I did, however, not receive complete authority, since Göring as plenipotentiary for the Four-Year Plan had the right, for a *short* while even precedence, to interfere in the economy, which if done without clear coordination could possibly endanger the political aims. In addition Koch in Kiev, the most important city, who will lean more toward Göring than me. I have to watch carefully that my directives are followed. . . . When we parted Göring shook hands with me and expressed his hope for a good collaboration.[109]

The meeting on July 16 can be interpreted as the clearest expression of what Browning has termed the first turning point in the decision-making process that led up to the Holocaust.[110] Linking inclusion and exclusion—the two basic aims that had characterized German resettlement policy since fall 1939—the participants and especially Hitler presented "positive" visions for the German Volk at large that were to transform the rugged east into a "Garden of Eden" while at the same time calling for negative, in fact highly destructive, measures against any sign of noncompliance among the local population. In this context, the correlation between the east and the Jewish question in its broader meaning played an important, yet undefined role. At the time, the Nazi leadership might have shared the doubts expressed at the periphery that mass shootings of Soviet Jews were, as a report by the Kommandostab on the killings in the Baltics put it, the way in which "the Jewish problem can be fundamentally solved" (*das jüdische Problem einer grundsätzlichen Lösung zugeführt werden kann*).[111] Similarly, in early July following the pogroms in Kaunas the commander of Army Group North, von Leeb, had voiced his agreement with Franz von Roques, commander of the Rear Army Area North, that "in this manner the Jewish question will probably not be solved. The most secure means would be the sterilization of all male Jews."[112] Nevertheless, Hitler and the top leadership refrained from addressing the issue and left it to their men in the field to decide how to proceed.

Although the meeting of July 16 did not result in any specific directives in regard to the Jewish question in the east, it was crucial for defining the parameters of subsequent policy. One day later, Hitler signed a set of orders that formally established the civil administration in the occupied east.[113] These orders guaranteed that Himmler's jurisdiction over security matters and Göring's over the war economy remained intact, thus creating the precarious imbalance of agencies within which Rosenberg and his ministry had to operate.[114] At the same time, following the appointment of the first representatives of the civil administration, the persecution of the Jews in the occupied parts of the Soviet Union took on a new, more systematic form.[115] Rosenberg's men found conditions that to a large degree had already been determined by events during the preceding weeks. However, not all of these events, including those leading up to the large-scale murder of the Jewish population, had been brought about solely by Germans.

Since the early stages of the war against the Soviet Union, non-Germans—in a kind of tacit division of labor—participated in anti-Jewish violence to a significant extent. The scope of their involvement ranged from assistance in identifying, persecuting, and ghettoizing Jews to the carrying out of pogroms, "cleansing measures," or other acts of physical violence. The perpetrators were resident gentiles, collaborators brought in from other areas, and soldiers or policemen of countries allied with or controlled by the Reich.[116] Heydrich's order to the Einsatzgruppen to foster "self-cleansing measures" by the local population against communists and Jews indicates that these crimes would not have been committed without Operation Barbarossa.[117] Thus, German policy is key to the understanding of non-German involvement. It is also evident that some gentiles, despite the risks involved, provided vital support for Jews who tried to escape from Nazi persecution.[118] Yet the question remains concerning the extent to which non-German assistance was important for shaping anti-Jewish policy at this stage in the process and later on.

Lithuania—home to the largest concentration of Jews in the Baltic and the site of early instances of mass murder—poses this question with particular urgency. Here, unlike in other parts of the occupied Soviet Union, with the exception of Latvia and western Ukraine, locals were from the beginning of German rule until its end deeply involved in the murder of the Jews. At the outbreak of the war and in some cases before the arrival of German troops, pogroms swept the country. In the city of Kaunas, according to reports by EK 3, some 3,800 Jews lost their lives in these outbursts.[119] Neighboring Latvia, which had been completely occupied by the Wehrmacht by July 10, was the site of similar scenes, though on a smaller scale. In Riga, the capital, an auxiliary police unit under nationalist Viktors Arajs in agreement with Einsatzgruppe A killed several hundred communists, Jews, and other "undesirable" persons by mid-July.[120] In western Ukraine (Volhynia and Eastern Galicia annexed by the Soviet Union in September 1939) approximately 24,000 Jews were murdered by Ukrainians; by the end of July, pogroms supported by the Germans had claimed the lives of at least 5,000 Jews in the Eastern Galician capital Lwow alone.[121] Some of the most notorious killing units of the Holocaust operated far beyond the borders of their home countries. Auxiliary police units from Latvia and Lithuania helped to carry out the mass murder of Jews deep in Belorussia, while Ukrainians (and other ethnic groups) trained in Trawniki near Lublin served as guards for German death and concentration camps.[122] Clearly, this astonishing degree of involvement in murder was not merely the result of German instigation; there were other, indigenous factors at work.

German preinvasion memoranda indicate that stereotypes about "the east" and its inhabitants allowed a certain degree of differentiation in regard to the relative qualities of different despised ethnic groups. For the dual purpose of exploitation and domination, Russians were seen, together with the Jews, as least desirable, while Ukrainians and the peoples of the Baltic States fared comparatively better. Hitler applied a similar hierarchy but, because of his political grand design regarding "the east," was unwilling to grant preferential treatment to Ukrainians, Latvians, and others regarded as racially inferior. At the same time, German policy exploited ethnic rivalries and residual local anti-Semitism, as well as national ambitions, to facilitate gaining control of the occupied territory. Using these factors helped implement the vision Hitler expressed during the meeting on July 16, 1941, of cutting up "the gigantic cake" for easier German consumption.[123]

The absence of any sincere desire on the part of politicians in Berlin to foster non-German self-determination did not deter nationalist groups from the Baltic States and Ukraine from seeking the assistance of the Reich against Moscow. Following the annexation of their countries by the Soviet Union in 1939/40, scores of political refugees left Lithuania, Latvia, Estonia, and western Ukraine, sometimes using the opportunities created by the resettlement of ethnic Germans agreed upon by Berlin and the Kremlin.[124] Members of the respective security services had special reasons to escape before the Soviet NKVD took control. Pranas Lukys, who had worked for the Lithuanian secret police (Saugumas) and after the war was Böhme's codefendant in the West German "Einsatzkommando Tilsit" trial, was one of them. The available evidence, sketchy as it is, given the absence of thorough research on the activities of Baltic émigrés in Nazi Germany, suggests that Lukys's career was not an exception. Having crossed the border together with some fifty other secret policemen, he was interned in a camp near Tilsit. Preinvasion reports by the Stapostelle Tilsit prove that the Germans were aware of the potential usefulness of these Lithuanians for the pending war against the Soviet Union. The Tilsit office sent Lukys and some other Saugumas men to an assignment with the Security Police near Lublin in the General Government, where they stayed until their transfer to Memel in spring 1941. From there, one night before the beginning of Operation Barbarossa, they were sent across the border to Lithuania to prepare subversive activities against the Red Army.[125]

In preparation for the attack, the Reich provided nationalists and anti-

Bolshevists not only with a safe haven but also with opportunities to organize and direct propaganda efforts and to plan for the future following the Soviet withdrawal. One of the most well-known Lithuanian expatriates in Berlin, Kazys Skirpa, formed the Lithuanian Activists Front (LAF), which tried to transcend the longtime division separating the two bourgeois camps, the right-wing sympathizers of former president Antanas Smetona and the profascist "Iron Wolf" movement.[126] Skirpa and his men exploited anti-Jewish feeling and claimed that Jews formed the backbone of the Bolshevist system and thus had caused the loss of Lithuania's national independence. In a leaflet drafted in March 1941, the LAF gave instructions to its sympathizers across the border for the anticipated "hour of Lithuania's liberation":

> Local uprising must be started in the enslaved cities, towns, and villages of Lithuania or, to put it more exactly, all power must be seized the moment the war begins. Local Communists and other traitors of Lithuania must be arrested at once, so that they may not escape just punishment for their crimes (The traitor will be pardoned only provided he proves beyond doubt that he has killed one Jew at least). . . . Already today inform the Jews that their fate has been decided upon. So that those who can had better get out of Lithuania now, to avoid unnecessary victims.[127]

In the weeks before the beginning of Operation Barbarossa, the LAF intensified its propaganda efforts with German help by infiltrating anti-Soviet agitators, distributing propaganda leaflets, or broadcasting radio messages across the border. Because of its limited number of members, especially from among the prewar Lithuanian establishment, the LAF was more a symbol of anticommunism than a key political player. Even before the Wehrmacht had occupied the country, Lithuanian units of the Red Army, most notably its 297th Territorial Corps in the city of Kaunas, staged a mutiny that hastened the Soviet retreat. Following the Red Army's withdrawal, provisional military commanders and other Lithuanian agencies, including a provisional government in Kaunas, emerged to stake a claim for future self-rule if not independence.[128] Insurgents of the LAF and other anti-Bolshevists played an important role in the instigation of pogroms.

Compared with the reluctance of Germans to address their own crimes, the great number of German testimonies and photographs depicting pogrom scenes in the east is surprising. Most notorious are images and statements by bystanders on the killings that took place in Kaunas between June 23 and 28, 1941. "I became witness," a colonel stated in the late 1950s regarding the clubbing to death of male "civilians" by a young Lithuanian, "to probably the most frightful event that I had seen during the course of two world wars." A corporal from a bakers' company described a similar scene in Kaunas: "Why these Jews were being beaten to death I did not find out. At that time I had not formulated my own thoughts about the persecution of the Jews because I had not yet heard anything about it. The bystanders were almost exclusively German soldiers, who were watching the cruel incident out of curiosity."[129]

Public scenes like these, in an area controlled by the Reich and with Germans as onlookers, were unprecedented. In Lithuania and elsewhere, Wehrmacht officers watched with a mixture of approval and apprehension. On July 1, 1941, the war diary of the 1st Mountain Division in Lwow noted that during a meeting of unit commanders shots could be heard from the direction of the GPU prison as part of a "full-scale pogrom against Jews and Russians" (*regelrechten Juden- und Russenpogrom*) instigated by Ukrainians.[130] In Drohobycz, the local military commander observed "terror and lynch justice against the Jews"; the overall number of victims remained undetermined.[131] Even the most high-ranking military officers declared themselves unable to interfere. Field Marshal von Leeb, the commander of Army Group North, wrote in his diary about the killings in Kaunas that "the only thing to do is to keep clear of them." (*Es bleibt nur übrig, dass man sich fernhält.*)[132]

Some representatives of the occupying power openly applauded such outbreaks of mass violence. From Lwow, where pogroms had been raging for days, the secret military police reported on July 7 that "the fanatic mood was transmitted to our Ukrainian translators," who had been recruited from nationalistic circles. According to the report, these Ukrainians "were of the opinion that every Jew should be clubbed to death immediately." (*Ferner waren sie der Meinung, dass jeder Jude sofort erschlagen werden müsse.*)[133] In a number of places, Germans did not just look on favorably but actively participated in locally instigated atrocities against Jews, Russians, and communists, thus contributing to the radicalization of German measures.[134] In the long run, however, "spontaneous" violence by locals had to be channeled into organized crime. Since Heydrich's order of June 29 provided little assistance for solving practical problems, Security Police officers in the field looked for guidance to the Wehrmacht, which had already started to make systematic use of non-German collaborators.

From Kaunas, Erich Ehrlinger of EK 1b reported to the RSHA on July 1, 1941, that the local anti-Soviet "partisans" had been disarmed a couple of days earlier on order of the German military commander. To ensure their future availability, Ehrlinger continued, the Wehrmacht Feldkommandant had created an auxiliary police unit consisting of five companies from among the ranks of reliable collaborators. Ehrlinger presented this measure as at least partly motivated by social considerations: the auxiliary policemen had no jobs, were "without any means, partly without housing." The entire economic situation, including food supply for the local population, remained unclear. Of the two companies subordinated to EK 1b, one was guarding "the Jewish concentration camp created in Kaunas—Fort VII [one of the old fortifications of the city]—and carries out the executions." Several army units had adopted different policies in Lithuania. For Ehrlinger, the most pressing task was to solve the "Lithuanian question according to uniform guidelines." ("Im Interesse der deutschen Ostraumpolitik ist es aber unbedingt notwendig, dass die litauische Frage nach einheitlichen Richtlinien gelöst wird.")[135]

The speedy integration of local pogroms into the emerging pattern of German policy makes it extremely difficult to identify their specific driving forces. As can be seen from events in Kaunas and Lwow, considerations for German interests determined local actions at least indirectly. Once units of the Wehrmacht or the Security Police had started adopting a more long-term strategy, German preponderance became much more visible. As most of the available contemporary documentation originated from the Einsatzgruppen, it is not surprising that other agencies—German as well as non-German—appear less important.[136] Nevertheless, the reports from Security Police units provide essential information on the local setting and the mix of factors. Obviously, the perpetrators of early mass killings did not restrict their activities to Jews; and even where Jews were targeted exclusively, anti-Semitism seems not to have been the sole motive. On the same day that the "partisans" of Kaunas were disarmed, the Lithuanian provisional military commander issued an appeal to the population to beware of "raging Russians and Jewish communists."[137] In nearby Vilnius, Lithuanian aggression focused on Poles, the largest ethnic group in the city.[138]

In the interest of preventing an uncontrolled mushrooming of violence by non-Germans, Heydrich stepped in. On July 1, following an inquiry from the 17th Army under General Stülpnagel, he elaborated on his order issued two days earlier regarding what he termed "the nonprevention of self-cleansing measures by anticommunist and anti-Jewish circles." Heydrich called it "self-evident that the cleansing actions have to be directed primarily against Bolshevists and Jews." Poles, on the other hand, were to be exempted for the time being, "since they will be of special importance as initiators [*Initiativelement*] for pogroms as well as for gathering information."[139]

Despite his eagerness to make use of pogroms as expressions of local hatred against "Judeobolshevists," Heydrich was aware of their inherent dangers. Pogroms were dangerous weapons in the hands of nationalists who, according to

German reports, had previously used slogans like "Germans, Jews, and Russians out."[140] More important, given the complex mix of nationalistic, opportunistic, and anti-Semitic motives at work, pogroms contained a degree of unpredictability that ran counter to any systematic anti-Jewish policy as adopted in Germany and other parts of occupied Europe. The basic ingredients recommended by the RSHA—instigating pogroms and making use of local collaborators without officially sanctioning their auxiliary function—did not strike officials in the field as a recipe for an efficient occupation policy. "Spontaneous cleansing actions," a report by Einsatzgruppe A pointed out, "were insufficient to stabilize the rear army area, especially as the eagerness of the local population was quickly waning."[141] The further the Germans advanced, the less gentiles were inclined to stage pogroms. In Belorussia this tactic failed to work from the beginning.[142] Given the shortage of German manpower, the envisaged "stabilization" required the transformation of pogrom participants into regular policemen.

At that time, however, it was still unclear where the line should be drawn between enlisting local populations in the service of German security and blocking their national ambitions. In late June the 9th Army had notified Wehrmacht commanders in Lithuania that on order of the Führer agencies of the provisional government should be ignored. The only task for local Lithuanian agencies was to restore "quiet and order"; armed Lithuanian units were to be dissolved except where they carried out "purely police tasks." ("Nur Ausübung von reinen Polizeiaufgaben ist zu gestatten.")[143] On June 28, 1941, Colonel Bobelis, the Lithuanian provisional military commander in Kaunas, issued a call for volunteers from the former Lithuanian army to replace the so-called partisans. Days later as reported by Ehrlinger, a "Battalion for the Defense of National Labor" had been formed which, growing significantly in size over the following weeks, was subordinated to Karl Jäger's Einsatzkommando 3. As part of a unit referred to in German sources after its leader as "Rollkommando Hamann," these men contributed massively toward the staggering figure of 133,346 mostly Jewish murder victims reported by Jäger in mid-December 1941.[144]

While regional and local agencies were looking for a practical solution to the pressing question of how to police the occupied territory with a minimum of German manpower, the Berlin center played a characteristically ambiguous role. In the top-level meeting on July 16, 1941, Hitler had emphatically demanded that non-Germans should never be allowed to bear arms. ("Nie darf erlaubt werden, dass ein Anderer Waffen trägt, als der Deutsche! . . . Nur der Deutsche darf Waffen tragen, nicht der Slawe, nicht der Tscheche, nicht der Kossak oder der Ukrainer!")[145] The Führer's subordinates decided differently.

On July 25 Himmler noted that the tasks of the police in the east could not be fulfilled by men of the police and ss alone and ordered the organization of "additional protective units from the ethnic groups suitable to us in the conquered area as soon as possible."[146] Himmler's order marked the official creation of the Schutzmannschaften, which over time became, in addition to the German security divisions, ss units, and Order Police battalions, a crucial element in the "pacification" of the occupied territory.[147] In late 1941, 26 battalions with local policemen had been created, and 33,000 Schutzmänner were serving German interests; within a year this figure had multiplied to about 300,000 local policemen, who were deployed in a variety of functions.[148]

Containing the activism of locals and integrating them into German occupation structures sometimes created a larger problem than eliciting their initial support. The commander of the Rear Army Area North ordered in early August that, since the "pacification" of occupied Latvia had been largely achieved, there was no longer any reason "to tolerate unauthorized and uncontrolled arrests and far-reaching executive measures" by Latvian auxiliaries; henceforth, these measures had to be sanctioned by German authorities.[149] As the highest nonmilitary authority in the region, the HSSPF was in charge of supervising a rapidly growing auxiliary police force and integrating it into the emerging administrative structure.[150] After the civil administration had taken over, Rosenberg's representatives became involved in supporting these efforts. In a report written in mid-August, the Gebietskommissar (county commissar) in Mitau (Jelgava) defined it as one of his main tasks to establish discipline among local policemen, who, as a result of their involvement in the liquidation of the Jewish population, had lost all moral restraints. He took it as a sign of success that his order "to bring the surviving 21 Jews from Mitau alive to Illuxt" had been carried out despite the considerable distance between the two cities.[151]

Not just ideological affinities with the new rulers but material expectations provided from early on a major incentive for locals to join the ranks of auxiliary police units.[152] Since organized plunder and robbery formed an integral element of German occupation policy in general and anti-Jewish measures in particular, it is hardly surprising that parts of the local population wanted to improve their poor living conditions by trying to get a share of the loot. This factor was especially relevant for the recruitment of Soviet POWs into auxiliary police units and in areas like Belorussia, where gentiles had initially shown little enthusiasm to support the German effort to get rid of the Jews. Unable to fully control the activities of their own auxiliaries, Einsatzgruppe B vilified the so-called Order Service (Ordnungsdienst) created in Belorussia by the Wehrmacht and the Security Police as "organized bands of robbers."[153] Problems in asserting control over local collaborators in parts of Belorussia and Ukraine explain to some extent why Schutzmannschaft battalions were brought in from the Baltics to bolster up the German "pacification" effort whenever large-scale actions were required.[154] Once the civil administration had been firmly established in the western part of the occupied Soviet Union, however, Schutzmänner became the foot soldiers of German rule on a day-to-day basis. In conjunction with the Order Police, they contributed massively to the murder of Jews in the "second killing wave," which started in spring 1942, and to antipartisan warfare.[155]

Anti-Bolshevist partisans and auxiliary policemen were not the only locals who assisted the occupiers in their efforts to control and "pacify" the area. From the Baltic States via Belorussia to Ukraine, gentiles employed in official functions in city, town, and village administrations did their best to ensure that rules and regulations imposed by the Germans were adhered to. They became auxiliaries to the emerging administrative hierarchy, usually situated at its bottom, sometimes—as in the case of the Lithuanian, Latvian, and Estonian Security Police[156]—performing functions parallel to those of German offices. Accordingly, the degree of German involvement ranged from direct intervention to general supervision. Without the active support of mayors, city councils, housing offices, and a plethora of local administrators, the identification, expropriation, and ghettoization of the Jewish population especially in rural areas would have exceeded the limited logistic capabilities of German occupation agencies.[157]

In some cases, these local offices did more than provide preparatory help for the murder of the Jews. On June 30, 1941, less than a week after the occupation of the Lithuanian town of Alytus, the local police chief offered the German military commander to murder all the Jews in the district with the assistance of his auxiliary policemen. At this time, the Stadtkommandant did not take up the offer;[158] by September 19, however, more than 2,200 Jews in Alytus and surroundings had been murdered by a mobile commando of EK 3.[159] In August the women and children who had survived the first killings by Böhme's Einsatzkommando in the area east of the German-Soviet border fell victim to executions carried out by Lithuanian police units, partly without direct German participation.[160]

In conjunction with the Wehrmacht, military forces of allied or associated countries fought the Red Army on Soviet territory. As with local collaborators, the behavior of these non-German troops toward the Jews was influenced by a variety of factors.[161] While Hungarian soldiers seemed to have largely abstained from following the German example,[162] Romanian units on the southern sector of the front committed large-scale killings. Romanian politics had been heavily anti-Semitic since the late 1930s, reaching a first peak in the summer of 1940, when the surrender of Bessarabia and northern Bukovina to the Soviet Union was accompanied by outbreaks of violence against Jews.[163] In anticipation of Operation Barbarossa, commanders of the Romanian gendarmerie issued orders that called on regional officers "to cleanse the land" of Jews, to concentrate urban Jews in ghettos, and to bring about "the extermination on site of all Jews found in rural areas." The same language prevailed in other early pronouncements by Romanian officials, who expanded the target groups for "the act of ethnic cleansing" to include Ukrainians.[164] On June 19 the Romanian dictator Ion Antonescu ordered that "the names of all Jewish and communist agents or sympathizers are to be listed (by county)" and that their freedom of movement was to be restricted to enable the military "to execute further orders."[165]

After June 22, 1941, it seems as if Romanian military and police units wasted little time implementing their prewar plans, first targeting the area of Bessarabia and northern Bukovina, the territory occupied by the Soviet Union in 1940. Yet German involvement and other factors played an important role in propelling these killings. Einsatzgruppe D, lead by Otto Ohlendorf and attached to the German 11th Army adjacent to Romanian troops (3rd and 4th Armies), first observed, then tried to control and direct, the activities of their ally. Many of the executions were carried out as so-called reprisals, with a ratio of 50 Jewish victims for every Romanian or German soldier killed.[166] According to an estimate by Raul Hilberg, more than 10,000 Jews were murdered in July 1941 in Bukovina and Bessarabia by Romanian and German units.[167]

Like the pogroms in Lithuania, some of these early killings pointed toward the subsequent escalation to mass murder. On June 27 the German military commander ordered the evacuation of the civilian population of Sculeni, a recently occupied village in Bessarabia (Moldova). Officers from the Romanian 6th Mountain Regiment selected the Jews from among the evacuees, robbed them of their belongings, and forced them to dig mass graves. The Romanian soldiers then shot at least 311 Jews into the pit. About a month later, when the case came under investigation by Romanian army authorities, the officers involved claimed to have acted "pursuant to orders from our superiors." A postwar exhumation revealed corpses of men, old persons, women, and 33 children including 7 under the age of a year. One child seemed to have been burned alive.[168]

Romanian officers competed with their German colleagues in setting new parameters on how to deal with the Jews. Beginning on June 28, 1941, soldiers, gendarmes, and civilians staged a pogrom in Iasi, a city in northeastern Romania and a stronghold of the nationalist Right, that claimed the lives of thousands of local Jews. More than 4,000 survivors were put on trains marked with inscriptions like "Communist Jews" or "Killers of German and Romanian soldiers," and at least half of them died.[169] Again, German officials tried to mold disorganized mass violence into a controlled pattern. Preventing further "executions carried out by the Romanians in an unprofessional and sadistic manner" (*die von den Rumänen durchgeführten unsachgemässen und sadistischen Exekutionen*) was one of the tasks of Einsatzgruppe D until the formal Romanian takeover of Bukovina, Bessarabia, and Transnistria following the Tighina agreement of August 30, 1941.[170] In order to entice the Romanians into "a more planned procedure in this direction," Ohlendorf's men showed the way. Targeting first "newcomers" who had arrived in Czernowitz (Cernauti) following the Soviet annexation in summer 1940, Einsatzgruppe D quickly expanded the group of Jewish victims from men to women—200 were shot in Kishinev on August 1, 1941—and, shortly thereafter, children.[171]

Clearly, the Germans did not need Lithuanians, Latvians, Ukrainians, or Romanians to tell them that the Jews in the occupied area of the Soviet Union were to be treated as enemies. Whatever crimes non-Germans committed, it was the Germans who, by establishing a pattern of systematic persecution, posed a much deadlier threat to Jewish existence. At the same time, events like the pogrom in Kaunas or the murder of Jewish women and children in Sculeni presented important lessons for German observers and participants on all levels. Such atrocities contributed to the shaping of anti-Jewish policy by providing additional stimuli. But overall, Himmler's order of July 25, 1941, establishing auxiliary police units from within the local population—units that were to become indispensable tools for the implementation of the Final Solution—had in the long run a greater impact on the overall course of events than the pogroms or other uncoordinated killings committed by non-Germans.

TOWARD THE FINAL SOLUTION, AUGUST–DECEMBER 1941

By the beginning of August 1941, all factors were in place for passing the threshold to the murder of all Jews in the occupied Soviet Union. The German army had occupied the Baltic States and Belorussia, and in Ukraine had reached the Kiev-Kirovograd line; the encirclement battles of Uman and Smolensk/Roslawl were to add almost another half a million Soviet POWs to those already starving in German camps.[172] In mid-July, Heydrich had issued guidelines for the screening of camps for Soviet POWs that called for the identification of "all Jews."[173] At the end of the month, Göring had authorized Heydrich to prepare a "total solution of the Jewish question in the German sphere of influence in Europe." Starting in Lithuania, Alfred Rosenberg's civil administration took over from the Wehrmacht, while the areas of Bialystock and Galicia came under the control of East Prussia and the General Government, respectively. All across the occupied territory, regulations had been or were about to be issued that, following an unsystematic and locally varied pattern, set the Jews apart from the rest of the population. For those units of the Wehrmacht, ss, and police that were involved in "pacification," the mass murder of Jews and other noncombatants had become a matter of daily routine. The recruitment of local collaborators increased the German ability to bring death to the most remote villages. On occasion, the killings had been expanded to engulf women and children. German officials in the field envisaged an alignment or coordination of these developments toward a common goal, a *Gleichschaltung* of sorts that would transform extreme destructiveness into administrative normalcy, selective mass murder into genocide. This was to happen in the remaining months of 1941.

Beginning in late July, as a result of the failure to win a quick victory over the Red Army, German obsession with security increased. The Reich was, as Hitler put it, forced "to rule areas extending over 300 to 500 kilometers with a handful of people."[174] The army leadership compensated for that lack of manpower by an even more massive use of force.[175] In the eyes of the commanding officers, increased terror called for greater control of the troops involved. In consequence, the army addressed two issues in particular. The first was the danger of an erosion of discipline following the involvement of troops in violent acts against the civilian population. Given the eagerness of the military leadership to annihilate actual as well as imagined enemies, this danger could only be mitigated by cosmetic measures. For this purpose, soldiers and non-German auxiliaries were prohibited from participating in mass executions outside their line of duty.[176]

The other issue related to the necessity of legitimizing increased terror directed against civilians in areas well behind the front line. One way of doing this was to put greater stress on the predetermined segregation of the local population into "desirable" and "undesirable" groups. As the I c officer of the 221st Security Division put it, the key to "total political and economic pacification" was the "skillful utilization of interethnic rivalry while at the same time eradicating Jewry" (*souveräne Beherrschung dieses Volkstumskampfes unter gleichzeitiger Ausmerzung des Judentums*).[177] Across the occupied Soviet Union, the military followed this strategy with varying intensity. In the south, army commanders ordered that reprisals for anti-German activities should be directed against Jews and Russians, not Ukrainians; further north, Belorussians, Lithuanians, and Latvians were to be "protected" from the activities of Jews, Russians, and Poles.[178] Over time, the growing German fixation on eradicating "partisans" and potential sympathizers—Jews, former Red Army soldiers, "suspicious elements," and "wanderers"—blurred the borderline separating desirables from undesirables until all locals were seen as presenting a security threat.[179]

Three days after the July 16, 1941, meeting with Hitler on future German policy in the occupied eastern territories, Heinrich Himmler (who had not attended the meeting) started reassigning two brigades from his own Kommandostab—the SS Cavalry Brigade (consisting of the 1st and the 2nd SS Cavalry Regiments) to the HSSPF for Russia Center, Bach-Zelewski, and the 1st SS Brigade to the HSSPF for Russia South, Jeckeln. It was the task of this force of more than 10,000 Waffen-SS men, in conjunction with several Order Police battalions subordinated to the HSSPF, to "pacify" what was regarded as the main trouble spot in the occupied territory. While the SS Cavalry Brigade was sent into the Pripet marshes, a vast, almost impenetrable area that covered parts of Belorussia and the northern Ukraine, the 1st SS Brigade was deployed at its southern edge.[180] Much better equipped for swift, large-scale operations than the Einsatzgruppen, these units played an important role in the transition from a policy of selective mass murder to the wholesale destruction of Jewish life in the occupied parts of the Soviet Union.

The Kommandostab Reichsführer-SS had been formed in May 1941 from units of the Waffen-SS. Stationed in occupied Poland, its men had been subjected since early 1941 to the usual dose of ideological indoctrination reinforced by daily life in the east. The Waffen-SS officers could see the image of "The Eternal Jew" not only in local cinemas but also in the nearby ghettos of Cracow, Lublin, Tarnow, or Zamosc.[181] In the weeks before their deployment in the Pripet, the officers of the Kommandostab down to the company level were issued with guidelines that explained at great length how the military situation was to be assessed, orders given, and the "pacification of the rear army area and the territory of the political administration" achieved. By then, despite the efforts of the Waffen-SS to bolster their self-esteem vis-à-vis the Wehrmacht, there could be little doubt that theirs was not a military task in the traditional sense: "To gain ground is irrelevant. The aim of the fight remains solely the complete destruction of the encircled enemy."[182]

On July 21, 1941, Himmler had visited the commander for the Rear Army Area South, Karl von Roques, in Lwow.[183] While it is not clear what they discussed that day, the Jewish question was at least on von Roques's agenda.[184] Further north, Max von Schenckendorff, commander of the Rear Army Area Center, expected to receive support from the 1st and 2nd Cavalry Regiments for "cleansing" the Pripet marshes, where partisans had been reported.[185] The two

HSSPF in the area, Jeckeln in Russia South and Bach-Zelewski in Russia Center, provided the link between the military commanders and Himmler's units. Except for rather general instructions, these units had so far received few indications as to what their specific task would be. When Himmler visited the 2nd Cavalry Regiment on July 21, he spoke only in general terms about an "onerous task" (*schwere Aufgabe*).[186] From July 20 to 23 officers from the I c division of the Kommandostab (ss Captains May and Schneider) visited their counterparts at Army Group Center (Major von Gersdorff, Captain Henrici) for the first time. The officers of Army Group Center were already informed about the planned deployment of the ss Cavalry Brigade in Schenckendorff's rear army area and expressed their gratitude for the willingness of their brothers-in-arms to help them out.[187]

On July 27 the chief of the Kommandostab, ss Brigadier General Kurt Knoblauch transmitted Himmler's orders for the deployment of the ss Cavalry Brigade to HSSPF Bach-Zelewski and to the commander of the 1st ss Cavalry Regiment, Hermann Fegelein.[188] That same day, Fegelein passed the orders on to his subordinates. For the purpose of the "pacification" of the rear army area close to the main road (*Rollbahn*), "soldiers of the Red Army in civilian clothes and plunderers as well as armed civilians or civilians performing sabotage are to be shot according to martial law on order of an officer." The Reichsführer, Fegelein continued, had issued special instructions regarding the villagers in the Pripet. Criminal elements were to be eradicated, and Jews had to be treated "for the most part as plunderers." ("Juden sind zum grossen Teil als Plünderer zu behandeln.") In contrast to Bach-Zelewski's order to Police Regiment Center issued in early July, the target group was no longer specified according to age. Exceptions could be made for highly qualified persons like bakers and doctors; women and children were to be driven out of the destroyed villages together with the livestock.[189] One day later, elaborating on the tasks of his cavalry units in the swamps, Himmler reiterated that if the locals were "from the national point of view inimical, racially and individually inferior," they were to be shot and their villages burned down.[190] Until August 1 the 1st ss Cavalry Regiment, mostly its mounted troops, or Reitende Abteilung, killed 788 persons; five days later, the unit's death toll had approximated 3,000 "Jews and partisans" (*Juden und Freischärler*).[191]

The operation exemplified how the Wehrmacht, Waffen-ss, and police were working hand in hand. Military commanders from the Rear Army Areas Center and South applauded the actions of Himmler's men and awarded decorations.[192] In an order that prohibited the participation of individual soldiers in pogroms outside the line of duty, the commander of Rear Army Area South announced a directive from the OKH according to which any straying Red Army soldier captured after August 8 would be shot.[193] At the same time, the 1st SS Brigade under HSSPF Jeckeln submitted its first report regarding the "cleansing action" in northwestern Ukraine: some 800 male and female Jews aged 16 to 60 had been shot "for supporting Bolshevism and Bolshevist partisans."[194] On July 31, after visiting Hinrich Lohse, the newly appointed Reichskommissar Ostland, and HSSPF Prützmann in Kaunas, Himmler flew on to Baranovichi, where he seems to have met Bach-Zelewski.[195] One day later, the SS Cavalry Brigade passed on to its units the following communication: "Explicit order by RF-SS. All Jews must be shot. Drive the female Jews into the swamps." (*Ausdrücklicher Befehl des RF-SS. Sämtliche Juden müssen erschossen werden. Judenweiber in die Sümpfe treiben.*)[196]

Unit commanders adopted different approaches toward the implementation of what Himmler presented as an unequivocal order. On the afternoon of the same day, the commander of the Reitende Abteilung of SS Cavalry Regiment 1, Gustav Lombard, saw reason to assure his men that Himmler's order "re shooting of Jews" (*betr. Judenerschiessung*) was not meant as a reprimand. So far, Jews had been found only in the area of SS Cavalry Regiment 2, with the exception of the village of Bereska-Kartuska, where the Wehrmacht's 221st Security Division was in desperate need of laborers for road construction. Nevertheless, Lombard advised for the future: "Not one male Jew is to remain alive, not one family in the villages." (*Es bleibt kein männlicher Jude leben, keine Restfamilie in den Ortschaften.*)[197] In his attempt to interpret Himmler's order, Lombard drew on his experience with earlier directives from Bach-Zelewski, Fegelein, and Himmler. Subsequently, his unit reported the "de-Jewification" (*Entjudung*) of several towns and villages; in most places, all Jews including women and children were killed.[198] Franz Magill, commander of the 2nd SS Cavalry Regiment's Reitende Abteilung, took Himmler's order more literally. In a report dated August 12, the SS-Sturmbannführer explained that only "Jewish plunderers" had been shot, since skilled Jewish laborers were in demand for the Wehrmacht. He continued: "Driving women and children into the swamps did not have the success it was supposed to have as the swamps were not deep enough for sinking under to occur. After a depth of one meter a person for the most part hit firm ground, so that sinking was not possible."[199]

Although Himmler's "explicit order" (*ausdrücklicher Befehl*) did not precisely spell out that Jewish women and children were to be killed, some commanders interpreted it this way. Before mid-August the SS Cavalry Brigade claimed to have "shot in combat 200 Russians and additionally some 10,000 Jews and plunderers" (*im Kampfe 200 Russen und ausserdem an Juden und Plün-*

derern rund 10,000 Mann erschossen).[200] In the city of Pinsk, 5,000 to 8,000 men aged 18 to 55 were rounded up by Magill's Reitende Abteilung in cooperation with police reinforcements from the General Government (designated as Einsatzgruppe z.b.V.) and shot; shortly thereafter, another 2,000 Pinsk Jews including women, children, and older men were murdered.[201] Those commanders who did not receive Himmler's "explicit order" nevertheless knew what to do. For August 3 the 1st SS Brigade reported "Jewish actions" (*Judenaktionen*) involving some 500 executions; for the following days, after it had been subordinated to Field Marshal von Reichenau's 6th Army in agreement with the HSSPF South, the brigade reported "cleansing actions" (*Säuberungsaktionen*) that killed more than 1,500 Jews, among them at least 275 women.[202]

As in Lithuania, the murderers had adopted a more efficient killing practice of shooting with automatic weapons.[203] The fact that the target groups were described as "plunderers," "partisans," or "Bolshevists" while certain kinds of workers were exempted helped the perpetrators to envisage the killings as economically and militarily rational. In addition, the unit commanders of the Kommandostab presented their activities as part of a move to convince the local population that the Reich would maintain a continuous presence and that any fear for the return of the Red Army was unfounded. "A neutralization of the Jews," the chief of staff of the Kommandostab advised, "will also in this respect achieve miracles." (*Eine Unschädlichmachung der Juden wirkt aber auch in dieser Beziehung Wunder.*)[204] On August 13 the first massive German descent upon the Pripet came to a preliminary end with 13,788 "plunderers," predominantly Jews, shot, and 714 prisoners captured. No fight had taken place. The entire SS Cavalry Brigade with its roughly 4,000 men had lost 2 dead (who had driven over a mine) and 15 wounded.[205]

The activities of Himmler's Kommandostab units in early August undoubtedly mark an important step in the history of the Holocaust.[206] A vast area had been "cleansed" in several sweeps, and some rural communities had been completely wiped out. At the same time, however, the innovative aspects of the Kommandostab action should not be overrated. As Dieter Pohl rightly points out, "killings of [Jewish] women and children started already at the end of July in the Soviet Union."[207] On the other hand, the murder of *all Jews* in a given area was not initiated on a massive scale before fall, with the notable exception of Lithuania, and in some areas of the occupied Soviet Union did not begin before spring 1942. Two of the component parts of the Kommandostab—the SS Cavalry Brigade and the 1st SS Brigade—operated independently of each other, especially after the subordination of the 1st SS Brigade to the Wehrmacht's 6th Army in early August intensified the ever present communication problem.[208]

Even in the Pripet, a significant number of Jews, including men, remained alive—more than 20,000 in Pinsk—to be targeted a year later in another killing sweep.[209] The same ambiguity applies to the involvement of the Reichsführer-SS. In addition to Himmler's exhortations, it was the fervor and adaptability of his lieutenants that mark the importance of the Pripet sweep for the future course of events in the occupied Soviet Union.

In the attempt to clarify Himmler's role in the escalation of the killing process, historians have greatly stressed the importance of his visit to Belorussia in mid-August.[210] On Thursday, August 14, the Reichsführer, accompanied by a large entourage, spent a couple of hours in Baranovichi, where he met with HSSPF Bach-Zelewski; the commander of the 1st SS Cavalry Regiment, Fegelein; and the commander of the Rear Army Area Center, von Schenckendorff. There can be no doubt that the Pripet sweep figured prominently in their discussion. In the afternoon Himmler left by car for Minsk; for the morning of the next day, his appointment book noted "presence at an execution of partisans and Jews in the vicinity of Minsk."[211]

This was the closest Himmler came to directly observing the murder of the Jews in the occupied Soviet Union. After the war, as a witness before the International Military Tribunal in Nuremberg, Bach-Zelewski described how Himmler became nervous when watching the execution performed by men from Nebe's Einsatzgruppe B and afterward gave a speech that legitimized the killings as a necessary means of defense for which he would bear responsibility. According to other postwar statements by members of Einsatzgruppe B, the Reichsführer on this occasion issued an order for the liquidation of all Jews in the east (*Gesamtliquidierung der Juden im Osten*) and mentioned a directive from Hitler.[212]

In the afternoon Himmler visited a hospital with mental patients in Novinki near Minsk. There, he seems to have talked with Bach-Zelewski and Nebe about the possibility of killing methods other than shooting. Nebe's criminal technicians at the RSHA had already gathered practical experience during the murder of asylum inmates in the Reich and Poland.[213] In early September, more than 500 mental patients were gassed in Mogilev; on September 18 a similar "test gassing" by carbon monoxide took place in Novinki.[214]

August 15, 1941, marks a caesura in the history of the Holocaust for reasons other than Himmler's visit to Belorussia, however. For on that day and the following, EK 3 in Lithuania for the first time reported the incorporation of children in mass executions. In doing so, Jäger made no reference to any directive from above.[215] The claim that Himmler issued an all-encompassing killing order in front of the murder scene near Minsk is primarily based on self-serving postwar statements by his officers and on the mistaken assumption that Berlin agencies had to be the centers of decision making in regard to the carrying out of mass murder in the east.[216] As can be seen from the Pripet sweep, Himmler, like Heydrich, faced problems in adjusting his directives to events in the field. This was less the result of insufficient communication networks between center and periphery than an inevitable consequence of the Nazi system's proneness for lower-level initiative and ad hoc decision making. With the delegation of power to his commanding officers, it was not Himmler but the HSSPF, the leaders of the Einsatzgruppen, Kommandostab units, and police battalions who, in conjunction with the military and representatives of the emerging civil administration, decided matters of practical policy. Anti-Jewish measures adopted in the following months show how the pattern of interaction between local and central authorities solidified until the end of 1941.[217]

In the highly competitive Nazi bureaucracy, the newcomers of the Ostministerium had to mark their turf. This applied especially to Rosenberg himself, who was facing open hostility from Himmler and, despite their cordial farewell after the meeting with Hitler on July 16, a hardly warmer attitude from Göring. In regard to the Jewish question, Rosenberg provided the Reichskommissare with guidelines that, in addition to ghettoization, forced labor, and other discriminatory measures, called for "partial preliminary measures" (*vorbereitende Teilmassnahmen*) in anticipation of a Europe-wide solution after the war. At the same time his office stressed that the experiences gained in dealing with the Jews in the east could point in the direction of a "solution of the overall problem" (*für die Lösung des Gesamt-Problems richtungweisend*).[218]

While Erich Koch, Reichskommisar in the Ukraine, did not care much about paper plans, the more bureaucratic-minded Lohse, Reichskommisar Ostland, was looking for clues on how to proceed. In late July, he received Himmler twice,[219] then on August 1 he met with Rosenberg and others to discuss the economic and political situation in the Ostland. In talking about the Jewish question, which he deemed "an important problem," Lohse presented information that must have come from the Security Police or Himmler himself. So far, according to Lohse, about 10,000 Jews had been liquidated by the Lithuanians. The remaining Jewish population, including women, was to be relocated to work camps. Himmler would decide the fate of the 3,000 imprisoned "Bolshevists"; executions were performed every night. "According to the decision of the Führer," Lohse stated, "the Germanization of Reichskommissariat Ostland shall be the final aim; the Jews should be removed totally from this area." (*Nach der Entscheidung des Führers soll die Eindeutschung des Reichskommissariats Ostland das Endziel sein; die Juden sollten restlos aus diesem Gebiet entfernt werden.*)[220]

Toward that aim, "pacification of the population" (*Befriedung der Bevölkerung*) was paramount. The Gebietskommissar in Schaulen (Siauliai) in Lithuania—an area larger than Lohse's home Gau of Schleswig-Holstein—had only four policemen at his disposition, even though 50% of the population was Jewish.[221]

By perceiving the Jewish question as part of a wider set of problems—Germanization and pacification—the chief civilian administrator in the Ostland followed the reasoning of his colleagues from the SS, police, and Wehrmacht. Yet Lohse showed little inclination to accept their leading role. On August 2, 1941, he presented "preliminary guidelines for the treatment of the Jews" to the HSSPF Ostland, Hans-Adolf Prützmann, as a means of ensuring "a uniform implementation of even preliminary measures." The draft combined anti-Jewish measures enacted in Germany since 1935 and especially in occupied Poland since fall 1939 regarding definition, registration, marking, expropriation, forced labor and concentration, with even more rigid regulations specifically devised for the occupied Soviet Union. The countryside was to be "cleansed" of Jews; they were to be concentrated in urban ghettos. Lohse's guidelines envisaged that the ghettos would be hermetically sealed and that food supplies would not exceed a level necessary for keeping the inhabitants alive. In implementing the guidelines, the General- and Gebietskommissare were to take local, especially economic, conditions into account. In the entire five-page document there is no mention of the Security Police and the SD, in reference to either their previous actions or their future role.[222]

By the time these guidelines were drafted in Lohse's offices, Stahlecker's men had already gathered extensive experience with "preliminary measures" and were not willing to be pushed aside by the civil administration. Anti-Jewish regulations had been in place since the occupation of Lithuania, ghettoization had been initiated weeks ago, and executions were being carried out on a regular basis with the help of collaborators.[223] In dealing with the Jewish question, the Security Police and SD had followed their own economic considerations, which in fact was one of the reasons why Stahlecker had been pushing since late July for the creation of concentration camps in the Reichskommissariat.[224]

In response to Lohse's draft, Stahlecker wrote a memorandum that, with the aim of rebuking the civil administration's claim to sole responsibility for handling the Jewish question in the Ostland, summed up what his men had done so far and why. Stahlecker criticized Lohse's draft for being too much tied to the measures applied in the General Government while neglecting the prospect of a "radical treatment of the Jewish question possible for the first time in the east" (*die im Ostraum erstmalig mögliche radikale Behandlung der Judenfrage*). With the exception of artisans, Jews were not an important labor factor. Instead, they presented a security threat that had to be neutralized in the interest of the "absolutely necessary, quick pacification of the east" (*unbedingt notwendige, schnelle Befriedung des Ostraumes*). In addition to a total "cleansing of the Ostland of Jews," Stahlecker defined the prevention of Jewish procreation as a top priority of future policy. The Jews were to be resettled to "Jewish reserve areas" (*Judenreservatsräume*) where, men and women separated, they would be available for forced labor "unless in the meantime the total cleansing of Europe of all Jews has become ripe for decision" (*[f]alls nicht unterdes die Gesamtreinigung des europäischen Raumes von allen Juden spruchreif geworden ist*). Stahlecker concluded by calling for a meeting to discuss the issue, "particularly as the draft to a great extent touches on general orders from a higher authority to the Security Police which cannot be discussed in writing" (*zumal da der Entwurf grundsätzliche, schriftlich nicht zu erörternde Befehle von höherer Stelle an die Sicherheitspolizei erheblich berührt*).[225]

Stahlecker's reference to "general orders from a higher authority" could be interpreted as a hint toward a declaration of intent by the top Nazi leadership, perhaps even by Hitler, according to which, already in early August 1941, the fate of the Jews in the Ostland if not beyond was sealed. In light of contemporaneous events, as well as Stahlecker's aim in drafting his letter, however, such an assumption seems debatable. If such an authoritative statement from Hitler had been issued, Stahlecker, instead of presenting a lengthy rebuttal of Lohse's draft and alluding almost as an aside to a "higher authority," could have referred to it directly and thus ended any further debate. The same applies to an order from Himmler, although in this case the civil administration would have had greater possibilities to interfere. At the same time, similar references to this directive should have surfaced in other areas. Instead, as can be seen from the Pripet sweep of late July/early August, Himmler issued unclear instructions that achieved their desired aim only because of his commanding officers' zeal. In an earlier letter to Jäger relating to Lohse's guidelines, Einsatzgruppe A chief of staff Karl Tschierschky had used the term "directive" (*Weisung*) instead of "order." Other available documentation, most notably the extensive reports by Stahlecker and Jäger, does not mention any superior order that would have explained the sequence or ferocity of anti-Jewish measures.[226]

Later events indicate that in his response to Lohse the ambitious Stahlecker was trying to present something he hoped to receive from Berlin in the future as an order he already had in hand. For that purpose, he could use what he regarded as undue interference by the civil administration to pressure his superiors for support in enlarging his authority and role.[227] In calling for the economic exploitation of Jews as forced laborers until a Europe-wide final solution had been decided upon, Stahlecker expressed a view shared by his colleague Otto Rasch, the leader of Einsatzgruppe C operating in Ukraine.[228] For the time being, the success of such indirect pressuring of the Berlin center was limited. On August 24, 1941, Gestapo chief Müller informed Einsatzgruppen A and B that some of the newly appointed Gebietskommissare had requested a "halt in the execution of communists and Jews" (*Einstellung der Kommunisten- und Juden-Aktionen*). While Heydrich ordered that these requests be declined and reports sent to Berlin, thus providing protection to his jealous subordinates, he did not address the question of who was to authorize the executions.[229] In the absence of a clear-cut directive that could be used for the purpose of aggrandizement vis-à-vis Lohse, the best way for Stahlecker to ensure that the civil administration would give in was to convince Heydrich that his (Stahlecker's) vision of a "radical treatment of the Jewish question possible for the first time in the east" extended beyond the Ostland. Stahlecker's attempt, as we will see, was to have a deeper impact later in 1941.

In reaction to Stahlecker's intervention, Lohse inserted a clause into his guidelines stating that "further measures, especially by the Security Police" were not to be interfered with by the civil administration and that his aim was to ensure that "minimal measures" were adopted.[230] These modified guidelines, sent out on August 18, 1941, to the General-, Stadt-, and Gebietskommissare in the Ostland with the caveat not to have them published but rather orally transmitted to the Jewish councils, reassured Stahlecker. "Whereas full support for the agencies of the Reichskommissar especially regarding the Jewish question is, as far as we're concerned, self-evident," he wrote to his officers in late August, "currently we nevertheless have to concentrate on the final solution of the Jewish question through very different measures than the ones envisaged by the Reichskommissar." (*Wenn auch jede Unterstützung der Dienststellen des Reichskommissars gerade in der Judenfrage für uns selbstverständlich ist, müssen wir doch unser Hauptaugenmerk z.Zt. auf die endgültige Lösung der Judenfrage mit ganz anderen als den vom Reichskommissar vorgesehenen Mitteln richten.*)[231]

With these remarks Stahlecker alluded to the ongoing killings in the ghettos and the countryside. Since mid-August, as documented by Jäger, now Kommandeur der Sicherheitspolizei und des SD (KdS) in Lithuania, entire communities including women and children had been systematically wiped out.[232] At the same time, the target group had been expanded beyond Soviet Jews. On August 2 Jäger reported the execution of a Jewish couple with U.S. citizenship in Fort VII in Kaunas, months before Jews of all nationalities were formally subjected to the same treatment as their eastern brethren.[233] On September 1 Jäger recorded—in addition to the murder of almost 5,000 Jews and 109 inmates of a mental asylum in Mariampole—the killing of a German citizen married to a Jew.[234]

In Belorussia, which was partly integrated into the Ostland as Generalkommissariat Weissruthenien under Wilhelm Kube on September 1, 1941, the triad of Wehrmacht, SS, and police agencies were about to establish a similar pattern.[235] The security divisions and police battalions under Wehrmacht commander Walter Braemer and the commander of the Rear Army Area Center von Schenckendorff, the units of Einsatzgruppe B, and HSSPF Bach-Zelewski's men became active first in the area east of the former Polish-Soviet border. In a second sweep through the Pripet marshes, the SS Cavalry Brigade killed 14,178 "plunderers," 1,001 "partisans," and 699 Red Army soldiers; only 830 prisoners were taken.[236] During a joint training course on partisan warfare organized by von Schenckendorff in late September, Wehrmacht and SS officers—among them Bach-Zelewski, Nebe, and Fegelein—agreed on the inseparable link between Jews and partisans, which strengthened the need for interagency cooperation. Fegelein noted Schenckendorff's priorities in dealing with the Jewish question. Units staying in a locality for a longer period of time had to create ghettos or other confined quarters for the Jews "in case they cannot be exterminated at once." Theory and practice merged when the participants of the training course conducted a search in a village near Mogilev. In addition to "some Jews," they shot persons not living in the village.[237]

The efforts of Wehrmacht commanders in the field were greatly supported by the army leadership's determination to intensify pacification. In mid-September, Field Marshal Keitel (OKW) demanded "relentless and energetic measures especially also against the Jews, the main bearers of Bolshevism" (*ein rücksichtsloses und energisches Durchgreifen vor allem auch gegen die Juden, die Hauptträger des Bolschewismus*).[238] In his "guidelines for the fighting of partisans" issued in late October, Field Marshal von Brauchitsch (OKH) called for energetic "ruthless and merciless" action.[239] While Keitel's order left little doubt about how to address the Jewish question, Brauchitsch did not mention Jews specifically. For General Gustav Freiherr von Bechtolsheim, the commander of the 707th Infantry Division deployed in the Generalkommissariat Weissruthenien, the matter had already been settled, since he understood the phrase "enemy of the Reich" to cover "communists," stray Red Army soldiers, Poles, and "Gypsies." Similar to Wehrmacht commander Braemer, Bechtolsheim presented Jews as "the sole supporters that the partisans can find" and demanded their remorseless destruction.[240]

The murder of more than 2,200 men, women, and children in Mogilev on October 2 and 3, 1941, by SS and policemen under the command of HSSPF Bach-

Zelewski marked the turning point toward genocide in Belorussia. Units of Einsatzgruppe B had since late August begun killing women and children; in early October HSSPF Bach-Zelewski pushed for the "de-Jewification" of entire areas, to the extent that by the end of the year Jews were virtually extinct on prewar Soviet territory.[241] While the Security Police and the SD, most notably EK 8, moved from city to city and targeted Jewish communities (for example, in Vitebsk and Borisov in October, and in Gomel (Homyel'), Bobruysk, and Kritschev in November/December), Order Police battalions and Wehrmacht security divisions swept through the countryside, killing Jews, as Christian Gerlach writes, "almost incidentally" in their search for "politically suspicious civilians (Bolshevists, Jews and Gypsies)."[242] Further west, army and police units "cleansed" the area under civil administration. According to Bechtolsheim, Jews had to "vanish from the flat land and the Gypsies too have to be exterminated."[243] By the end of the year, the total death toll in Belorussia amounted to 190,000 Jews, while close to 320,000 were still alive; in the area under civil administration, approximately 60,000 Jews had been murdered—30,000 by detachments of Einsatzgruppe A—while 145,000 survivors remained alive for the time being.[244]

The deployment of forces across geographical and administrative boundaries indicates the task-oriented, flexible approach adopted by regional and local German officials. Following requests from leading military commanders—von Bock, Braemer, von Schenckendorff—to support the efforts of Bechtolsheim's 707th Infantry Division in the area under civil administration, SS and police units were sent to Belorussia from the north. In early October 1941 the Kaunas-based Reserve Police Battalion 11 in conjunction with two Lithuanian Schutzmannschaft battalions performed a series of killings in the area around Minsk. Major Lechthaler, the battalion commander, had since August built up the auxiliary police force in Lithuania as part of the Order Police apparatus established under the civil administration.[245] Following its arrival in Minsk, the battalion joined forces with Bechtolsheim's security regiments for the purpose of pacifying the area. According to reports by Bechtolsheim, in the second week of October approximately 630 "suspicious elements without ID cards, communists, and Jews" were shot by Reserve Police Battalion 11 and its Lithuanian auxiliaries under the command of the army's Secret Military Police (Abwehraussenstelle Minsk of the Geheime Feldpolizei) in the area Uzlany-Rudensk, and at least 1,300 persons by Lechthaler's men without the support of Wehrmacht units in Kliniki and Smilovichi.[246] Following other actions against Jews, communists, and "partisans"—54 Jews in Pleschtschenitzy, 1,000 in Kojdanov, and 1,775 in the Minsk civilian prisoner camp—Reserve Police Battalion 11 murdered 5,900 Jews in Slutsk and Kleck in the last half of October. At around the same time, Karl Jäger sent from Lithuania to Belorussia a detachment of his EK 3, which killed 620 male Jews, 1,285 Jewish women, and 1,126 children. In roughly three weeks, Lechthaler's and Jäger's men had massacred at least 14,400 men, women, and children.[247]

The basic problem faced by German authorities in Belorussia was not how to initiate but how to coordinate pacification in order to achieve better results while avoiding negative consequences. Concern with efficiency—not moral scruples—explained why Gebietskommissar Carl complained in late October about the action by Police Battalion 11 that killed several thousand Jews in Slutsk.[248] This concern grew in relation to the scope of the task that German officials had set themselves. In a letter to Lohse, Braemer stated that "despite the harsh measures" taken by Bechtolsheim, "a significant easing of the situation has not occurred yet."[249] With units of Einsatzgruppe B and the army following the advancing troops into Russia proper, the task of "pacifying the Ostland" had to a large degree be left to the police forces of the civil administration—the Security Police and SD units that, as BdS and KdS offices, had become stationary, the parallel structure of the Order Police apparatus (Befehlshaber and Kommandeur der Ordnungspoliziei, BdO and KdO, respectively) and its local auxiliaries —and the overarching office of the HSSPF. It was this attempt at coordination that prompted Bechtolsheim to order in late November that "the carrying-out of *large-scale* Jewish actions is not the task of the units of the [707th Infantry] Division," but instead would have to be performed by or on behalf of the civil authorities. "Where smaller or larger groups of Jews are encountered on the flat land," Bechtolsheim added, "we can dispose of them either on our own or concentrate them into designated ghettos in larger places where they will be handed over to the civil administration or the SD."[250]

A slightly different pattern of destruction emerged in Ukraine, where more rural Jewish communities existed than further north. East of the river Dnieper, most of the Jews had managed to get away before the arrival of the Germans.[251] When, beginning in September, Reichskommissar Koch's men took up their positions as civil administrators, they, like their colleagues in the Ostland, found in place procedures jointly established by the Wehrmacht, SS, and police. Army Group South was fighting its way east, killing Jews, "partisans," and captured Red Army soldiers along the advance routes. In the region that remained for the time being under military administration, the mass killings reached a new height in September.[252] Einsatzgruppe C acted in an intermediate function by attaching some of its units to the advancing armies (SK 4a to the 6th Army under von Reichenau, and SK 4b to the 17th Army under Hermann Hoth) and supporting the police work of HSSPF Russia South, Friedrich Jeckeln, with his Order Police and Waffen-SS units in the rear army areas. Further south, since August units of Einsatzgruppe D in conjunction with the 11th Army had been successful in asserting greater independence from the Romanian military.[253]

Bernd Boll and Hans Safrian, in retracing the advance of the 6th Army to Stalingrad, have shown the close cooperation between Wehrmacht and Security Police from the first days of the campaign. On August 9 in Zhitomir, a commando of Einsatzgruppe C and army units transformed the public hanging of two Jews into a festive spectacle that was followed by the execution of more than 400 Jewish men.[254] As in the other occupied areas, Order Police units attached to the HSSPF or the Wehrmacht participated heavily in the killings.[255] The division of labor between the 6th Army and Einsatzgruppe C found its clearest expression in the murder of Jewish children in Belaja Cerkov in late August. Their parents had been murdered earlier in a joint operation by the local military commander and SK 4a. For days the children, some only months old, were left without any food, until a staff officer raised the question what to do with them. The Wehrmacht Feldkommandant was convinced that "this scum had to be exterminated." The issue was brought to the attention of the commander of the 6th Army, Field Marshal von Reichenau, who decided that the "action had to be executed in an appropriate manner." The children were killed by Paul Blobel's SK 4a.[256]

Like his counterparts further north, HSSPF Jeckeln played a key role in coordinating and expanding the murder of the Jews. In Ukraine, Jewish women and children had already been killed by individual units since late July. For several weeks the number of killings remained relatively steady, but the threshold to genocide was crossed at the end of August. At that time, Jeckeln offered Wehrmacht commanders to relieve the crisis in Kamenets Podolsky, the destination of mass deportations by Romanian and Hungarian authorities, before the formal transfer of the city to the civil administration on September 1. As a result, about 23,600 Jews (mostly expellees from Hungary and including women and children) were murdered in that city between August 27 and 30 by Jeckeln's Stabskompanie (staff company), a detachment of Einsatzgruppe C, and Police Battalion 320.[257] The victims of the Kamenets Podolsky massacre constituted more than half the number of Jews killed up to that date in Ukraine by SS and police units. In late September, Jeckeln's, Blobel's, and Reichenau's men reached the peak of their genocidal cooperation with the murder of more than 33,000 Jews—men, women, and children—in the ravine of Babi Yar near Kiev.

For the month of August the units under the HSSPF South reported a total death toll of 44,125; by mid-October this figure had surpassed 100,000 men, women, and children.[258]

In large cities Einsatzgruppe C and the Wehrmacht would kill some Jews on arrival, register the remaining persons, and coordinate the modus and date for their murder with the HSSPF, the Security Police, or the Order Police. Guidance from higher authorities was not required. In Zhitomir, Blobel held a conference with the local military commander on September 10 to discuss what to do with the more than 3,300 Jews in the city. "The resulting decision," Einsatzgruppe C reported, "was the final and radical liquidation of the Jews of Zhitomir." On the morning of September 19, the Ukrainian militia helped to round up 3,145 Jews, who were brought in 12 trucks (some supplied by the military, others by the city administration) to the killing site, where they were shot.[259] Other urban communities in the area under military administration were targeted at about the same time. In Berdichev, where some 20,000 Jews had been forced into a ghetto in late August, more than 16,000 persons were killed by Police Regiment South, Reserve Police Battalion 45, and Jeckeln's Stabskompanie in the first half of September.[260] In late September the 17th Army under Heinrich von Stülpnagel approached SK 4a to exterminate the Jews in Kremenchug. In Vinnitsa, an estimated 10,000 persons fell victim to a combined action of EK 6 and Police Battalions 45 and 314; in Kirovograd, SK 4b and Police Battalion 304 murdered 4,200 Jews; in Dnepropetrovsk, the death toll was estimated at 15,000. The killing spree continued further east. At least 20,000 Jews were killed in Kharkov between December 1941 and January 1942 as part of a terror campaign that no longer differentiated between specific target groups but engulfed the entire civilian population.[261]

Along the southernmost sector of the front line, the turning point from mass murder to genocide was reached with the liquidation of the Jewish community in Nikolayev in mid-September 1941. Members of Ohlendorf's Einsatzgruppe D, assisted by the 11th Army, rounded up the Jews under the pretext of "resettlement" and shot approximately 5,000 men, women, and children. There seem to have been no survivors. A similar Aktion was staged in Cherson, bringing the death toll reported by Einsatzgruppe D for September up to 22,467 "Jews and communists."[262] When Himmler visited Ohlendorf's men in Nikolayev in early October en route from Kiev, he reassured them that the liquidation of Jews and political opponents was necessary to crush Bolshevism and to win territory for German settlement.[263] Such incentives added to the momentum of the killing process. In October the communities of Melitopol, Berdyansk, Mariupol, and Taganrog were targeted. Later that month, Romanian troops captured Odessa, the city with the largest Jewish population in the Soviet Union. After bomb explosions that killed high-ranking Romanian and some German officers, approximately 19,000 Jews were rounded up and shot in the city's harbor area by Romanians on October 23, 1941, and at least 500 men, women, and children fell victim to SK 11b of Einsatzgruppe D. Shortly thereafter, 16,000 more Jews were murdered outside Odessa.[264] With the occupation of the Crimea in October/November, the killing spree spread further to the southeast.[265] At the end of 1941, Ohlendorf's Einsatzgruppe reported that it had murdered approximately 55,000 Jews.[266]

In the minds of the killers, the problems of mass murder, even of orphaned children, had been reduced to logistics. At the end of September, the 454th Security Division reported that "in some places providing for Jewish children and infants who lost their parents presented some difficulties; but also in that respect a remedy has been found in the meantime by the SD." (*An einigen Orten bereitete die Versorgung elternlos gewordener jüdischer Kinder und Säuglinge teilweise Schwierigkeiten; auch insoweit ist jedoch inzwischen durch den S.D. Abhilfe geschaffen worden.*)[267] Again, leading Wehrmacht officers helped to rationalize the systematic slaughter of unarmed men, women, and children as part of ordinary warfare in the east. On October 10 the commander of the 6th Army, Field Marshal von Reichenau, issued his notorious order regarding the "behavior of the troops in the east" (*Verhalten der Truppe im Ostraum*) which called for the "elimination of the Asiatic influence in the European sphere of culture" (*Ausrottung des asiatischen Einflusses im europäischen Kulturkreis*) and "harsh but just punishment of Jewish subhumanity" (*Notwendigkeit der harten, aber gerechten Sühne am jüdischen Untermenschentum*).[268] Reichenau was commended by Hitler for his zeal, leading other army commanders to follow his example.[269]

In rural Ukraine, the Wehrmacht seems to have been less involved in the killings than it was in the Ostland. Here, the "cleansing of the flat land" was left to a larger extent to the civil administration with its units of Security, Order, and auxiliary police. In the cities of Koch's new fiefdom, especially in central and southern Ukraine and the area east of Kiev, there were few Jews left. As in Belorussia, the systematic killing sweep had progressed from the east to the west. In the administrative centers, Rosenberg's men wasted no time in getting involved. On October 1, the day of the official inauguration of the Reichskommissariat, 2,500 Jews were murdered in Ostrog in western Ukraine. The next communities targeted were Koch's capital Rovno, where in early November 17,000 Jews were killed, followed by massacres in Kostopol and Proskurov.[270] But in contrast to the area under military administration, most of the Jews in the Reichskommissariat Ukraine—according to an estimate by Dieter Pohl, approximately 300,000—were still alive at the end of 1941. They became the targets of a second huge killing wave that was jointly set in motion by German occupation agencies in spring 1942.[271]

Beginning in late 1941, those Ukrainian Jews left alive in the area under civil administration were forced into ghettos. However, ghettoization in western Ukraine was less systematic than further north, leaving many Jews, especially in isolated communities, in their old places of residence until the arrival of the murder squads.[272] Concentration in confined and easily controllable spaces was more important where the Germans wanted to exploit Jews for forced labor. At this stage in the war, few projects required as much Jewish forced labor as road construction projects. The most ambitious such project was the extension of the so-called transit road IV (Durchgangsstrasse IV), planned since autumn 1941. Conceived as the main supply line for the troops in the southern sector of the eastern front, the road was to extend more than 1,200 kilometers, from the General Government through Ukraine to Stalino in the Donets region.[273] Although construction work started on a massive scale only in 1942, preparatory work on the central and regional level had already begun in fall 1941.[274] Implemented under the control of the ss in conjunction with other agencies, the project marked the intermediate stage between pre-Barbarossa concepts of Jewish forced labor and "destruction through work" (*Vernichtung durch Arbeit*), which was to claim the lives of hundreds of thousands of camp prisoners in the second half of the war.[275]

THE FINAL SOLUTION IN THE EAST

Chronological and regional differences reflected in the reports by Einsatzgruppen, Wehrmacht, and police units support the idea that central planning and top-level decision making were one factor among many that contributed to the radicalization of anti-Jewish policy during the first six months of Operation Barbarossa. Officers in the field were the ones who decided whether a community was temporarily bypassed, decapitated by killing members of the "intelligentsia," or entirely wiped out. Their superiors sanctioned such lower-level initiative in a variety of ways. The Wehrmacht top brass preferred ex post facto orders that, based on the Barbarossa directives drafted before the invasion, made anti-Jewish measures seem to be an integral element of securing the occupied territory. Himmler and the ss and police leadership, not relying solely on feeble communication lines and incoming reports, joined their men in the east for brief stints to sanction and encourage energetic actions and shielded them from occasional criticism by rival agencies, most notably the civil administration. Rosenberg's Ostministerium tried to adjust to the situation it found when taking up office and at the end of the year favored coordinated measures that integrated rather than antagonized the police apparatus.

What drove the killing process in the initial stage of the war against the Soviet Union? Economic factors clearly played a role. Already in its planning stage, Operation Barbarossa had been designed as a war to ensure German supremacy in Europe and thus by its very nature implied a massive redistribution of wealth at the expense of the material and physical well-being of the population in the occupied territory. Once the campaign had started, actual German policy became increasingly less influenced by preinvasion plans than by the disparate dynamics of unfolding events that, though brought about by German agencies, often threatened to slip from their control. Already in late July the economic experts of the military found themselves pressured to abandon long-range plans for the solution of pressing short-term problems—to feed the troops in the east and to fill gaps in supplies for the home front.[276] While this focusing on practical key issues hardly offered the civilian population better prospects for sustenance than the initial plans,[277] it helped to shift the balance of political power from the center to the periphery, where regional and local authorities were expected to make decisions based on the prevailing conditions.[278]

With the further expansion of the front line to the east, more areas with little or no industry came under German control. Since fewer workers were needed for economic purposes, the remaining population appeared as "useless eaters."[279] At the same time, fewer Jews were falling into German hands, so that their perception as a burden on the German food statistics became less relevant in practice, especially since they received about half the rations allotted to non-Jews.[280] Even where Jews were regarded as "an extraordinary burden, especially in terms of food policy," as for example in the city of Brest Litovsk, this did not necessarily result in their being killed immediately. In Brest, in fact, even as the Jews' rations were officially cut and actual deliveries were reduced to almost nothing, Jewish labor, paradoxically, was increasingly valued more highly and exploited more thoroughly.[281] In other areas, German officials found the food supply abundant enough to provide Jews with sufficient rations; however, neither the supply situation nor the demand for Jewish artisans prevented the "final execution of the Jewish question."[282]

As in its first phase, the murder of the Jews took place in the context of sweeping "pacification" that left tens of thousands of civilians either dead or without housing and means of subsistence. Captured Red Army soldiers faced an even grimmer fate than other groups. According to estimates, in September the monthly death rate among Soviet POWs in the Rear Army Area Center was between 5,000 and 9,000 victims.[283] The number of Soviet POWs murdered by deliberate malnutrition or "selections" in this region increased drastically to 30,000 in October and 80,000 in November—staggering figures that surpassed the number of executions reported by the Einsatzgruppen.[284] Across the occupied territory, "Gypsies" and hospital patients were targeted for execution in varying intensity.[285] No reliable figures are available for civilian losses from starvation or disease caused by the German policy of exploitation and insufficient supplies.

For the creation of ghettos, the economic rationale was important but not paramount. The systematic extraction of economic value from Jews by forced labor and the smooth execution of mass murder both required confined spaces. For this dual purpose, it made sense to establish ghettos. Yet it remained an open question whether Jewish labor represented an asset valuable enough to be preserved. Different agencies favored different approaches in different areas. In the Baltic and in western Belorussia, the Security Police preferred to make use of the unprecedented possibilities created by the war for swiftly proceeding with the most drastic measures, while civil and military administrators were more inclined to exploit Jewish workers in the interest of long-term occupation policy. Nevertheless, men like Stahlecker used economic arguments to advance their plans for "reserve areas" and concentration camps. If Jews were regarded as useful workers, this did not preclude their murder. In mid-September Einsatzgruppe C warned that the main task of destroying the communist apparatus should not be subordinated to "the practically easier task of the exclusion of the Jews," who especially in western Ukraine formed the core of the workforce. In contrast to what the German administration had done for a long time in the General Government, "the solution of the Jewish problem" should be brought about "by extensive labor utilization of the Jews." According to the Einsatzgruppe, this "will result in a gradual liquidation of the Jews, a development which corresponds to the economic conditions of the country."[286] Two months later, Max Thomas, Rasch's successor as chief of Einsatzgruppe C, called for the "complete extermination of the Jews" in western Ukraine "to remove thereby the most fertile soil from Bolshevism." Jews, Thomas claimed, were "without any doubt less valuable as laborers compared with the damage they do as 'germ carriers' of communism."[287]

Even in its economic aspects, Operation Barbarossa was primarily an ideologically driven military campaign. While many Germans experienced war in the east as a rush to get rich, on the macroeconomic level the material benefits of mass murder were outweighed by the depletion of an increasingly scarce commodity: workers.[288] Already in 1941, ghetto administrators performed "selections" of those seen as fit for work and those deemed unfit—a phenomenon usually associated with the death camps established later in Poland—in a number of ghettos, such as Kaunas and Berdichev. But the categorization was not consistent or uniform, and some workers and their families remained alive for the time being while other men and women just as "fit" or "unfit" were killed.[289] As with anti-Jewish measures in general, ghettoization and the use of forced labor implied an interpretation of material usefulness that entailed the temporary preservation of laborers, their being worked to death, or their immediate murder. The capricious and arbitrary element inherent in German economic policy toward the Jews is hardly surprising given the fact that, as reflected in earlier plans for Operation Barbarossa, the extraction of economic value from the east was regarded as a means to the central aim of preserving quiet on the German home front.

With the beginning of the mass murder of children in mid-August, genocide of the Jews in the territory of the occupied Soviet Union had become a reality. No further escalation in the process was conceivable. It implied the physical elimination of all Jews, irrespective of gender, age, occupation, or behavior, and lead directly to the destruction of entire communities and the "de-Jewification" of vast areas. The question was no longer why the Jews should be killed, but why they should *not* be killed. In the eyes of German officials, especially outside the civil administration, the economic usefulness of Jews as forced laborers was far outweighed by their being perceived as a threat to security, even in the absence of an organized and efficient partisan movement; as "useless eaters" who contributed to the depletion of scarce food resources; as remnants of an "impossible condition" that could no longer be tolerated; or as "scum" that had to be exterminated. The importance of these factors in determining practical politics varied according to time and place. While each agency involved favored its own rationale, "pacification" served as the strongest overarching legitimization for mass murder.

In no respect is the available German documentation, with its tendency toward "clean" bureaucratic language and the hiding of individual sentiments behind standardized phraseology, more unreliable than in regard to motivation. Given the resources at their disposal, historians find it difficult to answer the question how, on the individual and the group level, the adaptation to mass murder was possible. In his book on the "ordinary men" of Reserve Police Battalion 101, the first study that seriously confronts the issue of motivation and its relevance for the carrying out of mass shootings, Christopher Browning stresses the importance of situational factors, especially group pressure to conform and the threat of isolation in case of dereliction.[290] On the other hand, the group of perpetrators was stratified enough to allow a separation of tasks—from drawing up plans to organizing transport to guarding the perimeters—that enabled reluctant individuals to at least occasionally abstain from directly participating in murder while still being involved in an Aktion. As in the process of persecution as a whole, division of labor was key to the deadly success of the Final Solution. A few committed, full-time killers (*Dauerschützen*) and a sufficient supply of short-term executioners were enough to get the job done and even allowed a small minority to abstain, either temporarily or consistently, without facing serious repercussions.[291] In this sense, the frequent claim by perpetrators after the war that they had only been guarding while others were shooting realistically describes the social interaction in the group and the mental defense mechanism resulting from the possibility of temporarily retreating from the crime scene and dissociating oneself from the devoted murderers.

In his monumental study on German occupation policy in Belorussia, Christian Gerlach presents a most disturbing account of the mind-set of a seemingly committed lower-ranking perpetrator, based on letters from police secretary Walter Mattner from Vienna to his wife written on the occasion of the mass murder in Mogilev in early October 1941. On his direct involvement in the shooting, Mattner wrote:

> When the first truckload [of victims] arrived my hand was slightly trembling when shooting, but one gets used to this. When the tenth load arrived I was already aiming more calmly and shot securely at the many women, children, and infants. Considering that I too have two infants at home, with whom these hordes would do the same, if not ten times worse. The death we gave to them was a nice, quick death compared with the hellish torture of thousands upon thousands in the dungeons of the GPU. Infants were flying in a wide circle through the air and we shot them down still in flight, before they fell into the pit and into the water. Let's get rid of this scum that tossed all of Europe into the war and is still agitating in America. . . . I am actually already looking forward, and many say here that after our return home, then it will be the turn of our own Jews. Well, I'm not allowed to tell you enough.[292]

Neither the gradual radicalization of anti-Jewish measures after 1933 and their dehumanizing effects on both Jews and non-Jews, nor the massive push toward physical elimination beginning with Operation Barbarossa, can fully explain the apparently smooth incorporation of child victims into the murder process. Much stronger means of legitimization were required than for killing adults, whose mere presence could be construed as a threat. In some cases, as in Belaja Cerkov, the murder of children was perceived as the consequence of the preceding murder of adults, as something required to bring the job to an end. The sterile logic of this argument stands in marked contrast to the way the killings were performed. This was not industrial murder in a confined space in which a poison gas did the killing; this was anything but a "nice, quick death." Mattner's testimony is clearly an exception insofar as he wants to convince himself—and his wife—that in murdering Jewish children he is protecting his own children and thus fulfilling his parental obligations. However, it provides a glimpse at the ease with which German perpetrators rationalized their participation in the most abysmal crimes and were transformed in the process. Not only did they get used to killing, they also learned how to live with it, and even impatiently waited for the killing process to engulf Jews from the Reich.

In addition, men in the field at times expressed with greater clarity where developments were heading than did top officials in Berlin. In a lengthy order issued in mid-November 1941 on the fight against partisans, Himmler stressed the need for complete annihilation and recommended "increased attention" to women and children in partisan-infested areas, but did not once mention Jews.[293] He thus fell short of the example set by Keitel in mid-September and Reichenau in October. In passing Reichenau's order on to its units, the Kommandostab leadership praised its usefulness in giving the men "a uniform, thorough inner orientation concerning the general questions of our struggle for life in the east." Not only would such an orientation make the troops look more self-confident in the eyes of the locals; it was also desperately needed because soldiers, "if only in individual cases caused by observing the misery in these areas," still acted insecurely and even handed out bread or other food to the local population.[294]

The men who brought death to civilians in the occupied Soviet Union were reacting not only to one another but also to their environment. Time (the stage reached in the persecution of the Jews and other "undesirables") and space (the conditions in the east and the occupiers' perception of them) intersected in summer 1941 to facilitate the crossing of the threshold to genocide. While the actual killings required deliberate decisions on the part of the direct and indirect perpetrators, they themselves could perceive their role as mere agents of destiny. It is no surprise that in one of his letters Mattner invokes Hitler's well-known "prophecy" of January 1939 that presented the "annihilation of the Jewish race in Europe" as an abstract consequence of fate without actors.[295] In late December 1941 the training journal of the Order Police expressed the eastern dimension of the necessity for a solution to the Jewish question in unusually frank, yet clinically sterile terms:

The word of the Führer [in his speech of January 1939] that a new war, instigated by Jewry, will not bring about the destruction of anti-Semitic Germany but rather the end of Jewry, is now being carried out. The gigantic spaces of the east, which Germany and Europe have now at their disposition for colonization, also facilitate the definitive solution of the Jewish problem in the near future. This means not only removing the race of parasites from power, but its elimination [*Ausscheidung*] from the family of European peoples. What seemed impossible only two years ago, now step-by-step is becoming a reality: the end of the war will see a Europe free of Jews [*am Ende des Krieges steht das judenfreie Europa*].[296]

For the Germans deployed in the east, basic social norms and rules did not apply. The combination of extreme forms of public violence and the attempt to re-create German Gemütlichkeit in the private sphere meant that even Germans who did not directly participate in mass murder found the idea of normality assuming a specific meaning.[297] Behind the façade of selfless devotion to the Fatherland, corruption and moral depravation were rampant. The city of Minsk can serve as an example. Rumors about alcoholic and sexual excesses (*Saufexcesse, Weibergeschichten*) spread back to the Reich and were officially investigated.[298] After the war, former members of the KdS described the office as a "pigsty" (*Sauhaufen*).[299] Trostinez, a camp complex where at least 40,000 people were murdered, was remembered by secretaries and other German women as a place where they would go for horseback riding or to pick up a fur coat from Jewish victims.[300] A KdS officer distributed thousands of bottles of vodka for consumption during and after mass killings—not exactly what Himmler had in mind when he called for the "spiritual care" of men performing executions.[301] The physical retreat from the occupied territories toward the end of the war enabled the perpetrators to psychologically dissociate themselves from their crimes and facilitated their more or less smooth integration, shielded by the myth of their own victimization, into postwar German society.[302]

While genocide by any other name was under way at the periphery, the possibilities of the east for solving the Jewish question were slowly being recognized in Berlin. Heydrich's planners in the RSHA were facing increasing pressure to address the practical sides of the problem in a European context. Goebbels and other Gauleiter tried to use their direct access to Hitler to speed up the deportation of German Jews;[303] at the same time, lower-ranking officials developed their own plans.[304] Again, Hitler preferred the role of observer to that of decision maker. In early October 1941 Heydrich showed signs of frustration over the discrepancy between prevailing expectations and the limited nature of what could be done. In a speech given to members of the occupation apparatus on October 2 in Prague, where he had just taken over the office of acting Reichsprotektor in addition to his position as chief of the Security Police and the SD, he stressed that the events of the previous years were interrelated and a prerequisite for the ultimate Germanization of the Reich's sphere of influence. Toward that aim, even those of good racial origin but bad character (*gutrassig Schlechtgesinnten*) would have to be put up against the wall; one could but imagine what Heydrich had in mind for those whom he regarded as racially inferior. The implementation of this vision, however, was a "question that the Führer will have to decide." But it was already possible "to gather the plans and the raw material." "We have to test the material," he concluded, "we have to take advantage of the available opportunities."[305]

Two days after his Prague speech, Heydrich met with representatives of the Ostministerium to discuss a lengthy agenda, including the "settlement of the Jewish question" (*Regelung der Judenfrage*). Heydrich stressed that a coordinated effort would be useful, especially to prevent economic considerations from jeopardizing his "plan of a total resettlement of the Jews from the territory occupied by us" (*Plan einer totalen Aussiedlung der Juden aus den von uns besetzten Gebieten*). He saw no need to quarrel with the civil administration, "since the implementation of the treatment of the Jews lies anyway in every respect in the hands of the Security Police" (*da die Durchführung der Behandlung der Juden in jeder Beziehung sowieso in den Händen der Sicherheitspolizei liegt*).[306] For his part, Rosenberg was clearly aware of this fact and favored cooperation in view of the approaching "great ideological struggle" (*grosse weltanschauliche Kampf*); at the same time, he gave Heydrich's superior Himmler to understand that some of his officers were performing "very violent actions" without the Reichsführer necessarily knowing everything that was going on. (*Manche SS-Führer sollen sehr gewaltsame Aktionen durchgeführt haben, ohne dass der Reichsführer-SS über alles im Bilde gewesen.*)[307]

Getting the Ostministerium out of the way was one thing, preparing the actual "total resettlement" another. His new position as acting Reichsprotektor enabled Heydrich to adopt a more proactive role. On October 10 he chaired a meeting in Prague with Eichmann and other resettlement specialists regarding a "solution of Jewish questions." The records of this meeting provide important insight into how the eastern periphery was perceived by the center. According to the protocol, the purpose of the meeting was to discuss ways in which the problem could be solved "for the time being" in the Protectorate and the Reich. Following their concentration in "temporary collection camps," the Jews in the Protectorate were to be deported to Lodz; in view of the resistance of the Lodz authorities, however, 50,000 of the "most burdensome" Jews were to be shipped to Minsk and Riga. The leaders of Einsatzgruppe B and C, Nebe and Rasch, would make space for some of these Jews and others from the Reich "in the camps for communist prisoners" in the area of military operations (*Operationsgebiet*); according to Eichmann, preparations for this had already begun. In addition, an unspecified number of "Gypsies"—as it turned out, 5,000 Sinti and Roma from Austria[308]—were to be deported, as the protocol put it, "to Stahlecker in Riga, whose camp is equipped according to the model of [concentration camp] Sachsenhausen." The protocol continued,

> Since the Führer wishes that by the end of the year the Jews be removed as far as possible from the German sphere, pending questions have to be solved immediately. The transport question too must not present any problems.

> (*Die zu evakuierenden Zigeuner könnten nach Riga zu Stahlecker gebracht werden, dessen Lager nach dem Muster von Sachsenhausen eingerichtet ist. Da der Führer wünscht, dass noch Ende d.J. möglichst die Juden aus dem deutschen Raum herausgebracht sind, müssen die schwebenden Fragen umgehend gelöst werden. Auch die Transportfrage darf dabei keine Schwierigkeit bedeuten*).[309]

In a press announcement Heydrich summed up the result of the meeting by stating that it was the "final aim" of the Reich "not only to exclude Jewry from having any influence on the peoples of Europe, but if possible to resettle them outside Europe." As Madagascar was by that time but a distant memory, Heydrich must have been referring to the east. "I have decided," he declared, "to go through these stages also in the Protectorate consistently and as quickly as possible." (*Ich habe mich entschlossen, diese Etappen auch im Protektorat folgerichtig und möglichst schnell zu gehen.*) The first deportations from the Protectorate were to take place the same week.[310] Obviously, Heydrich did not regard the practical implementation of Hitler's "wish" as a matter requiring any further Führer decision, even though deportation was expected to have drastic consequences for the people affected.[311] In taking the initiative, Heydrich adapted to Hitler's image of the "best man" who bothered him least[312] as well as to the example set by some of his officers like Nebe, Rasch, and Stahlecker.

While Heydrich and the other participants at the meeting had clear ideas where the deportations should start, they were vague on the destination. According to Christian Gerlach, no "camps for communist prisoners" existed at that time behind the front line with the exception of a forced labor camp in Mogilev, where more than 2,200 Jewish men, women, and children had recently been massacred on October 2 and 3.[313] The discussions in Prague indicate that

Stahlecker's attempt to prepare the stage for the "total cleansing of Europe of all Jews" by raising Berlin's awareness of the possibilities in the Ostland was starting to have an effect.[314] Provided with an expression of interest from his superior, Stahlecker could, as a first step, intensify his push for a concentration camp in the Riga area, an effort he had started back in late July. In early October the office of the BdS in the Ostland revived the project.[315] Characteristically, in pressing his case vis-à-vis the civil administration, the BdS Ostland and leader of Einsatzgruppe A did not refer to a directive from Heydrich but hinted at a "wish of the Führer" according to which Jews from the Protectorate and the Reich had to be accommodated.[316]

In Riga, Generalkommissar Drechsler, Lohse's chief administrator for Latvia, was not thrilled. The same day Stahlecker confronted him with the prospect of having more undesirable Jews added to his area of influence, Drechsler received a report from his subordinate in Liepaja informing him about the ongoing problems in getting rid of the Jews that were already there. After the men had been killed, the Gebietskommissar wrote, it was the turn of the remaining women and children. The actions taken by the police had not gone unnoticed: "Especially the shooting of women and small children, some of them screaming when led to the execution site, has created common outrage."[317] Higher up in the administration, however, the issue was addressed in a clean, bureaucratic manner. On October 11 Rosenberg's aide Otto Bräutigam attended a large meeting with Lohse and Wehrmacht commander Braemer.[318] Two days later Bräutigam noted for Rosenberg that the SD regarded the "liquidation of commissars and Jews" as a matter of course.[319] In Himmler's appointment book, there is a (as usual, cryptic) reference to a conversation with Heydrich on October 14 that included the topic of "executions."[320] One day later, Stahlecker submitted his first cumulative report on the activities of his Einsatzgruppe. It contained staggering death figures: a total of 125,000 Jews had been killed so far, more than 80,000 in Lithuania.[321] That same day, the first wave of deportations started. By November 5, some 25,000 victims had been transported to Lodz.[322]

While the Security Police in Riga were trying to speed up the construction of the planned camp for Jews so that it would be ready to receive the first deportees in early November,[323] Himmler visited Mogilev and Smolensk to consult with Bach-Zelewski and leading Wehrmacht officers.[324] Regulations were issued by police authorities for another wave of deportations from the Reich and the Protectorate to the area around Riga and Minsk to begin on November 1.[325] Most Jews in the east had been murdered in mass executions—a killing procedure that had proven its effectiveness despite Himmler's concern with psychological side effects for the perpetrators and repeated complaints from within the Nazi hierarchy.[326] However, other options were under consideration.

Experiments with gassings had already been conducted near Minsk and Mogilev in September.[327] Now, in late October, the experts from the "euthanasia" killings were offering to import their expertise to the east. In a draft letter to Lohse, Erhard Wetzel, the "race expert" in Rosenberg's ministry, reported the willingness of Viktor Brack, one of the organizers of the so-called Aktion T4 in Hitler's Chancellery, to assist in the production of gassing facilities. Eichmann had already agreed to this proposal and explained that in Riga and Minsk camps were to be created for Jewish deportees. The Ostministerium, Wetzel wrote, had no objections "if those Jews who are not fit for work will be disposed of with Brack's device." This would also ensure greater secrecy than mass executions, which, as seen in Liepaja, continued to create unwanted public attention. The remaining Jews, kept separate by gender over the winter, were to be transported "further east" the following spring.[328]

Despite an obscure and largely undocumented deployment of T4 personnel in the area of Minsk in early 1942, Brack's specific proposal for Riga was never implemented in this form. Beginning in November/December, carbon monoxide was used for the gassing of Jews in the occupied Soviet Union. The gas came not from bottles, as in the "euthanasia" killing centers on Reich territory, but from the exhaust pipes of trucks specifically designed for that purpose by Nebe's criminal technicians at the RSHA.[329]

In November administrators in the Ostland were still calling for "general directives" on anti-Jewish policy.[330] The need for clarification was increased by pressure from the Security Police to prepare for the arrival of the first deportees scheduled for mid-November and to speed up the ongoing killings of local Jews.[331] On November 9 Friedrich Trampedach, in charge of the political division in the RKO, sent an urgent request to the Ostministerium and Lohse (who was in Berlin at the time) to have the transports prevented and directed "further east."[332] Four days later, Georg Leibbrandt, head of the political division in Rosenberg's ministry, informed Trampedach that deportations to camps in Riga and Minsk were indeed "preliminary measures"; since the Jews were to be sent on, the Ostministerium had no objections. For further clarification, Trampedach should get in touch with the HSSPF.[333]

With the former HSSPF North, Prützmann, about to be replaced, it fell to his successor Jeckeln to solve the open questions. Where were the Jews to be sent, if only temporarily? In the Ostland, none of the camps mentioned in the communications from Berlin were ready.[334] Putting the Jews up in the existing ghettos seemed to present a solution, provided space could be created. What happened in Kaunas in late October with the murder of almost 10,000 Jews could indeed be perceived as "creating space"; in Minsk similar executions took place in early November that claimed the life of 12,000 Jews.[335] However, it is not altogether certain that the Aktion in Kaunas at least was directly caused by the deportations of Jews from the Reich. In fact the reverse might have been the case; not for the first time, the measures taken in Lithuania provided exemplary lessons for the entire area, in this case how to make room for deportees. In his postwar testimony, Jeckeln offered a different rationale by claiming to have received an order from Himmler in Berlin on November 10 or 11, 1941— around the time of the mass murder in Minsk and two weeks after the Aktion in Kaunas—according to which "all Jews in the Ostland down to the last man must be exterminated" (*alle sich im Ostland befindenden Juden bis zum letzten Mann vernichtet werden müssen*).[336]

Such a Himmler order, if it had actually been issued, would have settled the other unresolved question concerning what to do with the deportees once they had reached their destination. But confusion prevailed: On November 11 the first transport arrived in Minsk; the Jews from the Reich were immediately forced into the ghetto.[337] Two weeks later in Kaunas, the Security Police took the 5,000 German and Austrian deportees directly to Fort IX and shot them.[338] In Riga on November 30 all of the 1,000 Jews who had just arrived from Berlin and 3,000 local Jews already in the ghetto were executed. It was only after another large-scale murder action on December 8, with an estimated death toll of more than 25,000, that deportees were admitted into the ghetto.[339] In view of the different treatment of these early transports, Hans Safrian's argument "that in fall 1941 no general orders were issued which called for the immediate and indiscriminate murder of all Jews deported from Central Europe" is convincing.[340]

This assumption finds further support in what took place in the aftermath of the first killings of deportees. In the early afternoon of November 30, Himmler had a telephone conversation with Heydrich from Hitler's headquarters, in which he said there was to be "no liquidation" of the Berlin Jews deported to Riga. By that time, the more than 1,000 Jews who had arrived in Riga from Berlin were already dead. Himmler now warned Jeckeln against "arbitrariness and violation" of "guidelines given either by me or by the RSHA on my behalf" and summoned the HSSPF for a talk.[341] No such reaction, however, from Heydrich or Himmler is recorded for the murder of the almost 5,000 deportees who had been killed on arrival in Kaunas, including some 1,000 Berlin Jews. If Himmler had issued a previous directive for the killing of all Jews transported east, his subordinates in Minsk would have violated it by admitting all deportees to the ghetto and thus were liable to a similar reprimand—although for a dif-

ferent reason—to the one Jeckeln received. The fact that, in his macabre statistics of mass murder addressed to his superiors, EK 3 commander Jäger made no
reference to any instruction coming from Berlin or elsewhere regarding the
treatment of Jews deported from the Reich confirms the absence of an overall
directive for immediate killing.

In view of the communications received regarding deportations and given
the absence of clear guidelines from above, civilian authorities had until that
time indeed assumed that they would have a say in the treatment of Jewish
questions. After the murder of Reich Jews deported to the east, high-ranking
officials in the Interior Ministry conceded that they had lost control over the
course of events.[342] On November 15, in response to an inquiry from the Ostministerium that noted a complaint from the RSHA about the prohibition of
executions by his office, Lohse had specifically asked whether this inquiry was
meant to imply "that all Jews in the Ostland are to be liquidated."[343] That
same day, Himmler met with Rosenberg to discuss whether the Jewish question
was to be treated as a "police matter"—that is, an issue to be solved by the
Reichsführer-SS and Chief of German Police—or "as part of overall politics" as
envisaged by Rosenberg.[344] On the central level, the issue remained contentious.
In early 1942 Heydrich again claimed sole authority and urged the civil administration to replace their own guidelines regarding the treatment of Jews with a
version drafted by Eichmann. Days after the Wannsee Conference, held on
January 20, the matter was discussed in Berlin; only in autumn 1942 did Himmler grudgingly agree to a compromise that postponed indefinitely a clear delineation of tasks.[345]

In late autumn 1941 the military was also ready to get involved in the discussion over the new dimensions of the Jewish question. On November 20
Braemer, as Wehrmacht commander for Ostland, sent Lohse a letter that expressed the army's concern over the political and military implications of the
deportations: the presence of German Jews in the Generalkommissariat Weissruthenien added to the partisan movement; more important, shipping Jews to
the east seemed "in view of the tense transport situation, for the time being not
at all possible."[346] Raising the transport question touched the most sensitive
spot of the entire deportation project. Heydrich had previously mentioned that
Hitler had agreed to the deportations provided the means of transport would
not interfere with the needs of the military.[347] The complaint by the Wehrmacht
was successful. Except for one more transport that left Vienna on November 28,
no further deportations were to arrive in Minsk until spring 1942.[348]

The bottleneck created by the transport situation seems also to have been the
key factor in the termination of an attempt for an alternative solution to the dual

question of where to take the deportees and what to do with them. Götz Aly was the first historian to point to the possibility that, in fall 1941, a major killing site was planned for Jewish deportees in the occupied parts of the Soviet Union, most likely in Mogilev, the city in the rear area of Army Group Center where a forced labor camp had been established in late September or early October. Although there is no clear documentation on this project, the assumption that it existed is supported by several pieces of evidence, most notably a large order of Zyklon—a prussic acid used for disinfection as well as later in Auschwitz-Birkenau, in its "B" version, for gassing—to be shipped to Mogilev and Riga; and plans for installing crematorium ovens in Mogilev were developed in mid-November by the ss. No gassings with Zyklon B seem to have taken place in either Mogilev or Riga. By the time the first crematorium oven was delivered to Mogilev on December 30, the project had already been dropped in favor of alternative solutions. In 1942 the other ovens ordered were rerouted to Auschwitz.[349]

For other parts of the Ostland, in late November the deportation issue was settled. While more and more areas were reported as "free of Jews,"[350] deportations from the west had to be accepted.[351] Lohse was informed by his ministry that Heydrich had decided to select a different site for the camp planned near Riga;[352] in arriving at this decision, the Reichskommissar's opinion had not been requested. Subsequently, Lohse declined to get involved in the decision of how the Jews deported from Germany were to be treated.[353] In mid-December, Bräutigam responded to Lohse's enquiry of November 15, saying that he assumed that "in the meantime matters in regard to the Jewish question will have been clarified by oral discussions." In principle, economic aspects were to be disregarded; remaining questions were to be discussed directly with the HSSPF.[354]

Things were also straightened out within the ss. On December 4 Jeckeln, reprimanded days before for the murder of the Berlin Jews deported to Riga, met with Himmler and reported the killing of most of the Riga Jews.[355] Himmler cared more than ever about the morale of his men involved in the ongoing executions. In an order dated December 12, the Reichsführer advised unit commanders to hold "comradely get-togethers" (kameradschaftliches Beisammensein) at the end of days in which "enemies of the German people" had been subjected to "the just death sentence." These evenings were not designed for heavy drinking, but for leading the men through music and lectures "into the beautiful regions of German spiritual and cultural life."[356] Reality in the east, however, was very different from the ideas of the Reichsführer.

In the first six months of the war against the Soviet Union, the "material" was "tested" and "opportunities" were "used," as envisaged by Heydrich in his

Prague speech of October 2,[357] though not according to a preconceived, consistent, or centralized plan. Politics, it seems, has rarely been as regional if not local as in these months when a uniform pattern of mass murder had not yet emerged. Middle-level officials with overarching functions—most notably Himmler's HSSPF and Einsatzgruppen chiefs,[358] but also the rear army commanders of the Wehrmacht and the men of the civil administration—in cooperation with each other, filled the void created by the absence of a centralized decision-making process. In summing up their achievements for 1941, Einsatzgruppen officers stressed that "a radical solution of the Jewish problem" by killing all Jews had been, if only as a "vague notion," their aim from the beginning of the campaign.[359] By advancing in their reports all kinds of rationalizations, the Führer's men in the field confirmed that a mix of factors rather than one order from above had led to mass murder becoming a standard procedure of occupation policy. By the end of the year, the Berlin centers were fully aware of the lessons learned in the east for solving the Jewish question in other parts of Europe.

8

From War of Destruction to the Final Solution

The First Peak of Victory Euphoria and the Fate of Soviet Jewry
In the first month of the Barbarossa campaign, the Germans experienced stunning and exhilarating success. On July 8 Goebbels confided to his diary, "No one doubts anymore that we shall be victorious in Russia."[1] The following day he flew to meet Hitler, who pronounced the military situation "surprisingly positive." Two-thirds of the Soviet army and five-sixths of its tanks and airplanes had already been destroyed, Hitler claimed. "Of Bolshevism nothing more may be allowed to remain. The Führer intends to have cities like Moscow and Petersburg rubbed out." (*Der Führer hat die Absicht, Städte wie Moskau und Petersburg ausradieren zu lassen.*)[2] And one day later, July 10, the self-congratulatory Hitler proclaimed himself the Robert Koch of politics who had discovered in Jewry the bacillus of social decomposition.[3]

The mood of expectant victory intensified on July 16, 1941, when Hitler spoke at length to top Nazi leaders, including Göring, Bormann, Lammers, Rosenberg, and Keitel, but not in this case Himmler, and made what he termed "fundamental observations" (*grundsätzliche Feststellungen*). He proclaimed that Germany would never leave the eastern territories now occupied. Out of these territories he intended to create a "Garden of Eden." "All necessary measures—shootings, resettlements, etc." *(alle notwendigen Massnahmen—Erschiessen, Aussiedeln, usw.*) would be undertaken to accomplish this. It was thus fortunate that the Russians had given the order for partisan warfare, for "it gives us the opportunity to exterminate anyone who is hostile to us. . . . Naturally, the vast area must be pacified as quickly as possible; this will happen best by shooting anyone who even looks sideways at us."[4] (*er gibt uns die Möglichkeit, auszurotten was sich gegen uns stellt. . . . Der Riesenraum müsse natürlich so rasch wie möglich befriedet werden; dies geschah am besten dadurch, dass man jeden, der nur schief schaue, totschiesse.*) As usual, Hitler was not giving explicit orders, but the tenor of his speech was unmistakable. What role could Jews have in a German Garden of Eden? What could be expected of his subordinates when Hitler urged the shooting and extermination of all hostile elements? The euphoria of victory had elicited from Hitler both a utopian vision of a future Garden of Eden as well as the shrillest exhortations for intensified bloodletting. His subordinates were eager not to disappoint.

Most important for the fate of Soviet Jews was the reaction of Heinrich Himmler, who immediately acted to multiply many times over the limited manpower of the Einsatzgruppen committed to behind-the-lines pacification and mass killings. On July 19 he reassigned the ss Cavalry Brigade from his own Kommandostab to Erich von dem Bach-Zelewski, the HSSPF Center, for an impending sweep of the Pripet marches, and on July 22 he reassigned the 1st ss Brigade to the HSSPF South, Friedrich Jeckeln. The ss Cavalry contained nearly 4,000 men and the 1st Brigade over 7,200.[5] Himmler also reassigned at least 11 police battalions to the HSSPFs. This reinforcement added at least another 5,500 men.[6] And on July 25, 1941, he ordered the HSSPFs to form auxiliary police units from the Ukrainian, Belorussian, and Baltic populations, because "the task of the police in the occupied eastern territories can not be accomplished with the manpower of the police and ss now deployed or yet to be deployed."[7] By the end of the year there would be 26 police battalions on Soviet territory, and the number of native auxiliary police (Schutzmänner) under police command would reach 33,000.[8] In just a few days in late July, therefore, Himmler had set in motion the rapid buildup of precisely those units that would subsequently constitute the core of the killing squads of the Final Solution on Soviet territory.

Himmler also continued to visit his men in the field. Already on June 30, while visiting Augustowo, he and Heydrich had approved the killing of Jews by the Stapostelle Tilsit, and extensive killings of Jews in Bialystok had immediately followed the appearance there of Himmler and Daluege on July 8–9.[9] After giving his orders for the manpower build-up, Himmler traveled to the east once again. On July 31 he came to Riga and Baranovichi, meeting with HSSPFs Prützmann and Bach-Zelewski.[10] On that same day he issued an "explicit order" (*ausdrücklicher Befehl*) to a regiment of the recently dispatched ss Cavalry Brigade about to commence its sweep of the Pripet marshes: "All Jews must be shot. Drive the female Jews into the swamp."[11]

Several days after his July 31 meeting with Himmler, HSSPF Prützmann sent to the commander of Einsatzgruppe A, Franz Walter Stahlecker, a copy of the guidelines for the treatment of Jews that Hinrich Lohse, Reichskommissar for the Ostland, had just drafted, without consulting the SS. Prützmann offered Stahlecker the use of a plane to fly to Kaunas for a meeting with Lohse, which he considered imperative because the Security Police had "instructions" (*Weisungen*) that "in part contradict the draft" (*die z. Tl. dem Entwurf widersprechen*). Stahlecker did not fly to Kaunas but instead sent his commander there, Karl Jäger of Einsatzkommando 3, a three-page position paper that the latter was to transmit to Lohse orally.[12]

Stahlecker's position paper indicated that much more than a mere jurisdictional issue was at stake.[13] He complained that "the new possibilities in the east for a cleaning up of the Jewish question had not been taken into consideration" (*die im Ostraum gegebenen neuen Möglichkeiten zur Bereinigung der Judenfrage sind im Entwurf nicht berücksichtigt worden*). Lohse had failed "to keep in mind the radical treatment of the Jewish question now possible for the first time" (*die im Ostraum erstmalig mögliche radikale Behandlung der Judenfrage ins Auge zu fassen*). Rather than long-term ghettoization as in Poland, the situation required "an almost 100% immediate cleansing of the entire Ostland of Jews" (*eine fast 100% sofortige Säuberung des gesamten Ostlandes von Juden*). In a handwritten note at the end of the paper, Stahlecker added that the Lohse draft "to a great extent touches on general orders from higher authority to the Security Police which cannot be discussed in writing" (*grundsätzliche, schriftlich nicht zu erörternde Befehle von höherer Stelle an die Sicherheitspolizei erheblich berührt*).

What were the "instructions" or "orders" to the Security Police that Prützmann and Stahlecker referred to just days after Himmler's visit to Riga but that neither would put in writing? One indication might be found in the carefully collected statistics of Karl Jäger. Beginning on August 15, 1941, the number of victims claimed daily by EK 3 jumped sharply and henceforth included large numbers of women and children.[14]

In addition, various postwar testimonies, in which precise dating is always uncertain, take on added significance when they are correlated with Himmler's now established itinerary. On July 21, 1941, Himmler was in Lwow (Lemberg) in the Ukraine.[15] After the war the commander of Reserve Police Battalion 45, Major Franz, vividly remembered a conversation with his superior, Colonel Besser of Police Regiment South. In Franz's account, Besser told him that Himmler had ordered that the Jews in Russia were to be destroyed and that Police Battalion 45 was to participate in carrying out this policy. Several days later Reserve Police Battalion 45 began killing Jewish women and children in an action in Shepetovka. The diary of one of the policeman reliably placed the battalion in that town between July 24 and August 1, 1941.[16]

On August 12 Himmler met with HSSPF Jeckeln following the former's complaint about inadequate reporting from the 1st ss Brigade. The commander of EK 5, Erwin Schulz, testified in 1953 that he had been summoned to Zhitomir by his superior, Dr. Dr. Otto Rasch of EG C on either August 10 or 12. Rasch let his officers know that he had been reproached for not treating the Jews sharply enough. Rasch then informed his commanders that, on the basis of a binding order from Himmler, Jecklen had ordered that all nonworking Jews, women and children included, be shot.[17] Jeckeln himself then conducted the largest single massacre of the war to date at Kamenets Podolsky, and for the month of August reported that units under his command had "shot a total of 44,125 persons, mostly Jews."[18] As with Jäger's killing statistics in Lithuania, Jecklen's jumped dramatically in the weeks following Himmler's intervention.

On August 14–16 Himmler was back in Belorussia, and on August 15 he was "present at an execution of partisans and Jews in the area of Minsk." No immediate large-scale massacres on the scale of those of Jäger and Jeckeln followed, but Bach-Zelewski immediately requested a visit from the Warthegau expert in the gas-van killing of the mentally handicapped (the future commandant of Chelmno, Herbert Lange).[19] This visit did not in fact take place, but others involved in the design and mass production of gas vans subsequently testified that the impetus for the visit had been Einsatzgruppe B's complaints about the psychological burden of shooting women and children.[20] Thus the issue of shooting women and children presumably came up during Himmler's mid-August visit.[21] By the end of August, on the occasion of a visit to Minsk by Himmler's Order Police chief Daluege, Police Battalion 322 began to shoot Jewish women in significantly larger numbers than before.[22]

If there is a strong correlation between Himmler's documented actions (both the manpower build-up and trips to the east) and the intensified killing of Soviet Jews (and especially the inclusion now of women and children), there is also ample evidence that Berlin explicitly insisted upon being kept informed of what was happening. Heydrich, of course, received from the Einsatzgruppen commanders a regular flow of information that he fashioned into the notorious daily reports.[23] Heydrich's Gestapo chief, Heinrich Müller, made explicit at least one purpose of these reports. "The Führer is to receive reports from here regularly about the work of the Einsatzgruppen in the east." (*Dem Führer soll von hier aus lfd. Berichte über die Arbeit der Einsatzgruppen im Osten vorgelegt werden.*)[24] The ss Cavalry Brigade made detailed reports of its killing sweep in the Pripet marshes.[25] When the 1st ss Brigade in Ukraine did not make similar regular reports, it was rebuked by Himmler.[26] Jeckeln made frequent radio reports on the August killing actions of his police battalions in the Ukraine.[27] Clearly there was no gap between what was happening in the field and what was either known or desired by the top leadership of the Nazi regime.

While no single document conveys the exact date and manner of a decision for the Final Solution on Soviet territory, the period of mid-July to mid-August was fateful for Soviet Jewry. One scenario consistent with the existing evidence is that in mid-July Hitler, convinced that the military campaign was nearly over and victory at hand, gave the signal to carry out accelerated pacification and racial "cleansing" of Germany's new "Garden of Eden." His subordinates understood what such signals and exhortations meant, and Himmler in particular responded with alacrity. He massively increased the manpower of the killing forces behind the lines. Moreover, he traveled through much of the eastern territory, personally contacting his HSSPFs Bach-Zelewski, Jeckeln, and Prütz-mann. In the Pripet marshes he ordered his SS cavalry regiment to chase the Jewish women into the swamp. In Minsk he witnessed an execution and reportedly exhorted the men to carry out this difficult but historic task. For others not graced with a personal visit from Himmler, his orders and exhortations filtered eastward from the HSSPF to the Einsatzgruppen and police battalions. The major exception in this regard seems to have been Ohlendorf, who was initiated by Heydrich during a visit to Berlin in mid-August.[28]

In short, there was not a single, comprehensive killing order issued on a single date and disseminated by a single uniform method. The commanders of various killing units learned of their new tasks at different times and in different ways, and the Einsatzgruppen commanders were not the first to know. But despite the irregular manner in which the new policy was disseminated, by mid-August the results were virtually everywhere the same. German killing units— Order Police battalions and other SS units of the HSSPF as well as the Einsatz-gruppen—knew that they were expected to commence implementing the Final Solution on Soviet territory, and at least in some areas, particularly in Lithuania, commensurate killing operations were already underway.

The pivotal change in how the killers themselves conceived of what they were doing can be seen in the documents at several levels. The *Ereignismeldung* or event report of July 23, 1941, includes a lament by the commander of Einsatzgruppe B, Arthur Nebe, that even though his men were killing hundreds of Jews each day, given the vast number of Jews a solution to the Jewish question was not possible until after the war and then only through deportation.[29] Less than two months later, Nebe's counterpart for Einsatzgruppe C, Otto Rasch, reported in a very different vein. Then it was no longer a solution to the Jewish question that seemed impossible through shooting, but rather the economic reconstruction of the Ukraine "if the Jewish labor force is entirely discarded." He thus argued pragmatically for the temporary use of Jewish labor because it would still "result in a gradual liquidation of the Jews" but without damaging the economy.[30] These two reports, less than two months apart, are based on entirely different premises. The first still assumes mass deportation sometime in the future; the latter assumes a default position of comprehensive and immediate mass murder, from which any exemption has to be justified on the basis that it would lead to "gradual liquidation" in the end.

The same change is reflected in the letters of a reserve policeman from Bremen in Reserve Police Battalion 105, previously quoted in chapter 7. Noting the treatment to which Jews were being subjected, he wrote on July 7 that "the Jews are free game. . . . One can only give the Jews some well-intentioned advice: Bring no more children into the world. They no longer have a future." (*Die Juden sind Freiwild. . . . Man kann den Juden nur noch einen gut gemeinten Rat geben: Keine Kinder mehr in die Welt zu setzen. Sie haben keine Zukunft mehr.*) When he wrote exactly one month later, it was no longer a question of the dismal future for the Jews. "Here all the Jews are being shot. Everywhere such actions are underway. Last night 150 Jews from the village were shot, men, women, and children, all killed. The Jews are being totally eradicated." (*Hier werden sämtliche Juden erschossen. Überall sind solche Aktionen in Gange. Gestern nacht sind aus diesem Ort 150 Juden erschossen, Männer, Frauen und Kinder, alles umgelegt. Die Juden werden gänzlich ausgerottet.*)[31] Such was the difference between implied genocide in the future and the immediate reality of the Final Solution.

The Second Peak of Victory Euphoria and the Fate of European Jewry

As the Einsatzgruppen and other German units on Soviet territory shifted toward the comprehensive mass murder of Soviet Jewry in the weeks between mid-July and mid-August, the fate of European Jewry also hung in the balance. It is my conclusion that victory euphoria in mid-July marked not only the conclusion of the decision-making process leading to the mass murder of Soviet Jewry but also the point at which Hitler inaugurated the decision-making process that led to the extension of the Final Solution to European Jewry. What did the prospect that soon all Europe would be at his feet mean to Hitler?

Hitler seems to have put the European Jewish question on the agenda with renewed urgency, and the bacillus metaphor dominated his language. On July 22 he spoke to the visiting Croatian Marshal Kvaternik about his intentions concerning the Jews of Europe. Owing to a missing page in the protocol, the historian enters Hitler's monologue in midstream:

... for if even just one state for whatever reasons tolerates one Jewish family in it, then this will become the bacillus source for a new decomposition. If there were no more Jews in Europe, then the unity of the European states would no longer be destroyed. Where one will send the Jews, to Siberia or Madagascar, is all the same. He [Hitler] would approach each state with this demand.

(. . . *denn wenn auch nur ein Staat aus irgendwelchen Gründen eine jüdische Familie bei sich dulde, so würde diese der Bazillusherd für eine neue Zersetzung werden. Wohin man die Juden schicke, nach Sibirien oder Madagaskar, sei gleichgültig. Er werde an jeden Staat mit dieser Forderung herantreten.)*[32]

If Hitler was informing even a visiting field marshal from Croatia of his intention to approach every state in Europe and demand the total evacuation of the Jews, what was he saying to Himmler and Heydrich? That they received signals from Hitler to turn their attention now to the wider question of European Jewry—and this against the background of the signal to commence systematic mass murder on Soviet territory—seems clear.

Within Eichmann's Gestapo bureau for Jewish affairs, new manpower was added in this month of July. Sturmbannführer Friedrich Suhr was made Referent for the "Final Solution of the Jewish question," *especially for foreign countries.*[33] On July 31 Heydrich visited Göring and obtained his signature on a deceptively simple document of a mere three sentences—a document that presumably originated from Heydrich himself. Extending the powers entrusted to Heydrich on January 24, 1939, to organize a solution to the Jewish question through emigration or evacuation, this document authorized him (1) to make "all necessary preparations" (*alle erforderlichen Vorbereitungen*) for a "total solution of the Jewish question" (*Gesamtlösung der Judenfrage*) in the European territories under German influence; (2) to coordinate the participation of those organizations whose jurisdictions were affected; and (3) to submit a "comprehensive draft" (*Gesamtentwurf*) of this plan for a "Final Solution to the Jewish Question" (*Endlösung der Judenfrage*).[34] The authorization does not explicitly mention mass murder, of course. The question, then, is did Heydrich at this point still understand the Final Solution as the mass expulsion of European Jewry into inhospitable regions of a conquered Soviet Union (and accompanying decimation) in order to make the German empire free of Jews, or was "the Final Solution" a term now freighted with a new and even more fateful meaning?

Both immediate context and subsequent events indicate that the authorization of July 31 was understood as Heydrich's "charter" to draw up a "feasibility study" for the mass murder of European Jewry, procured from Göring in response to Hitler's incitement of mid-July. The new authorization was received by Heydrich, who already had a previous authorization, dated January 24, 1939, and signed by Göring, for coordinating Jewish emigration. When Jewish emigration gave way to successive plans for massive "resettlement," Heydrich had felt no need for a new authorization and cited the older one when relentlessly asserting jurisdiction over the Madagascar Plan in 1940 and other resettlement activities.[35] Moreover, he had just spent the previous months organizing the Einsatzgruppen, which exactly at this time were moving into a full-scale extermination campaign against Soviet Jewry. The historical context would thus suggest that Heydrich needed the July 1941 authorization, not to continue the emigration and expulsion activities over which he had long established unchallenged jurisdiction, but rather because he now faced a new and awesome task that would dwarf even the systematic murder program emerging on Soviet territory.[36]

It had taken five months for the murder of Soviet Jewry to emerge from early conceptions of a "war of destruction" to the first steps of full-scale implementation, and the Final Solution would be a far more complex program. Thus Hitler's instigation and the Göring authorization were only the first moves in a process that would stretch out over months. There was, after all, no precedent for the destruction plan that Himmler and Heydrich were to prepare. The task they faced posed daunting problems for which the solutions were not self-evident. Hence a seeming ambivalence continued to surround Jewish policy in the late summer and autumn of 1941. One possible conception of how the Final Solution might be implemented—through massive deportation to factories of death equipped with facilities to kill on an assembly-line basis through poison gas—emerged by October. But other options remained open as well, and the physical and political preparations even to begin implementing the Final Solution in this way were only in place in the spring of 1942.

Only at the end of this journey of innovation did the Final Solution take on an air of obviousness and inevitability that could not have been apparent to the perpetrators at the time. These pathfinders to the Final Solution, these inventors of a bureaucratically organized assembly-line mass murder, groped their way along a trail filled with contingencies and uncertainties. These uncertainties, however, must not disguise the fact that the perpetrators sensed what was expected of them and what they were looking for. The extermination camp was not an accident. It did not result from some mysterious process of spontaneous generation. It was a horrific monument to the perpetrators' problem-solving abilities, but they needed lead time to invent and construct it.

Tracing this path to the Final Solution is made difficult not only by the uncertainties of the perpetrators but also by the problem of evidence. Hitler operated in a very nonbureaucratic manner, verbally indicating his "wishes" and priorities.[37] No paper trail leads to the *Führerhauptquartier*. At the next echelon, the files of Himmler and Heydrich regarding the Final Solution were destroyed. The historian is left with copies of a few key papers—such as the Göring authorization, the Einsatzgruppen reports, and the Wannsee protocol—that Himmler and Heydrich sent to others, but not with the vital internal working papers at the coordinating center.

However, Hitler's words and Himmler's and Heydrich's actions at the center set in motion waves of political signals that radiated outward. Like expanding concentric circles, they encompassed more and more people who, reading these signals, became aware that something new was expected of them. Some documentation and witnesses did survive the war; they allow the historian to establish fixed points and thus to plot (or at least make informed speculations about) the course of these expanding concentric circles. When the historian discovers at what point certain perpetrators first knew that they were part of a program to murder the Jews of Europe, to be carried out in an unprecedented manner, he or she can then extrapolate backward in time and upward and inward through the hierarchy to calculate with some probability what had taken place at the center of the Nazi regime.

Another difficulty in assessing the evidence is the polycratic nature of the Nazi regime. Various Nazis received differing amounts of information and attained differing degrees of awareness. They also had differing interpretations and conceptions of how the Jewish question was to be solved and what Hitler expected of them. Thus they traveled by different paths and different timetables to the Final Solution. At any given point, therefore, what Frank, Rosenberg, or Goebbels understood about the state of Nazi Jewish policy could be quite different from what Himmler and Heydrich understood. It is this confusing and incomplete evidence that we must now survey to re-create Nazi Germany's path from the War of Destruction to the Final Solution.

The spectacular military successes in the Soviet Union and Hitler's mid-July exhortations created a new atmosphere and set off a series of reactions within Nazi Germany over the months of August, September, and October. These reactions took on different forms. Notable Nazi leaders as well as obscure lower- and middle-echelon officials pressed for immediate deportations. Those threatened with being on the receiving end of deportations objected. Others began to anticipate future events and either openly advocated or actually commenced the mass killing of Jews. And finally, within the ss and Führer Chancellery, a still relatively small group of men set about inventing the extermination camp as the technological and organizational solution to the task Hitler had posed to Himmler and Heydrich in July. These four reactions would sometimes run separately, sometimes intermingle, over the next three months.

Only at the end of October did the various strands of Jewish policy again come together, creating the initial outline of the course Nazi Germany was embarking upon. Until then the Nazi leadership envisaged solving their self-imposed Jewish question through expulsion, accompanied by no small amount of outright killing and attrition, in order to create a German empire free of Jews. Thereafter, the vision was clearer. No Jews were to escape the German grasp, and no Jews were in the end to be left alive. If before August 1941 the Jewish question was to be solved "one way or another," after October it was to be solved in one way—through the death of all Jews.

The exhilaration and euphoria of victory affected not only Hitler. The Nazi hopes placed in various emigration and expulsion plans over the years had been dashed. By late 1940 a solution to the Jewish question in Europe had, except for piecemeal emigration, been postponed until after the war. To a whole variety of Nazis, therefore, seeming victory over the Soviet Union offered both the time and the place to fulfill the commitment that had fueled Nazi Jewish policy. A veritable consensus and competition to resume deportations—the logical consequence of the expulsion policies of 1939–40—permeated the Nazi power structure in the late summer and fall of 1941. As a result, even while continuing his verbal exhortations, Hitler had to curb rather than encourage the deportation zeal of his followers.

Heydrich and Goebbels took the lead. In August 1941 both of them impatiently pressured Hitler for intensified Jewish measures, and especially for deportations from Germany. On August 15 Goebbels's state secretary, Leopold Gutterer, chaired a meeting attended mostly by party faithful but also by the Interior Ministry expert for racial questions, Bernhard Lösener, to discuss the issue of obligating the Jews to wear special markings. Gutterer justified this renewed attempt to have a hand in Jewish policy on the grounds that the marking of Jews was a matter vital to the morale of the German war effort. Blaming the Jews for every problem from the lack of housing to the shortage of strawberries, Gutterer noted that only 19,000 of the 70,000 Berlin Jews were working. The rest should be "carted off to Russia . . . *best of all actually would be to kill them* [italics mine]" (*nach Russland abkarren . . . am besten wäre es, diese überhaupt totzuschlagen*). Less rhetorically, Gutterer proposed numerous measures of intensified restriction and persecution, the precondition for the enforcement of which was the marking of Jews.

Eichmann then informed the gathering that a marking proposal had already been made to Göring, who had replied that it required the Führer's decision, and the RSHA had thus prepared a proposal that Bormann would present to Hitler. As for evacuating the Jews, Eichmann added, Heydrich had also already made this proposal to Hitler. The Führer had "rejected evacuations *during the war* [italics mine]" (*Evakuierungen während des Krieges abgelehnt*). However, he had allowed Heydrich to prepare a proposal for a "partial evacuation of the larger cities."[38]

Goebbels did not wait for Bormann to act on Heydrich's marking proposal. He met with Hitler on August 19. An unsigned Propaganda Ministry memorandum for Goebbels, dated August 17, was presumably written to prepare him for this meeting. The memo invoked the alleged disgust and embitterment of German soldiers returning from the east when they encountered Jews in Germany running around freely, buying up scarce goods, and occupying scarce apartments:

> It is clear that when the soldiers return from the war, they must find no more Jews. But it is equally clear that in the meantime harsh immediate measures must be enacted so that morale will not be poisoned by such grievances. Efforts in this direction founder upon such bureaucratic impediments as formalistic, juridical thinking, competency struggles, and dawdling. This last factor is further promoted by the line of thought that the Jews will soon disappear, and it is thus not worth shifting the machinery for drafting laws into high gear.

All the ministries and agencies concerned were agreed that marking was the prerequisite for all the intensified measures that were being planned.[39]

At the Goebbels-Hitler meeting on August 19, the Jewish question was discussed at length.

> The Führer is convinced his prophecy in the Reichstag, that should Jewry succeed once again in provoking a world war, this would end in their annihilation, is being confirmed. It is coming true in these weeks and months with a certainty that appears almost sinister. In the east the Jews are paying the price, in Germany they have already paid in part and will have to pay still more in the future.

> (*Der Führer ist der Überzeugung, dass seine damalige Prophezeiung im Reichstag, dass, wenn es dem Judentum gelänge, noch einmal einen Weltkrieg zu provozieren, er mit der Vernichtung der Juden enden würde, sich bestätigt. Sie bewahrheitet sich in diesen Wochen und Monaten mit einer fast unheimlich anmutenden Sicherheit.*

Im Osten müssen die Juden die Zeche bezahlen; in Deutschland haben sie sie zum Teil schon bezahlt und werden sie in Zukunft noch mehr bezahlen müssen.)

Apparently Goebbels, like Heydrich earlier, took the opportunity to press for immediate deportations, but without success, for he noted that "it is not yet possible to make Berlin a city entirely free of Jews." But Goebbels was consoled by the fact "the Führer has promised me . . . that *immediately after the end of the campaign* [italics mine] in the east, I can deport the Jews of Berlin" (*hat der Führer mir zugesagt, dass ich die Juden aus Berlin unmittelbar nach der Beendigung des Ostfeldzugs in den Osten abschieben kann*).

As for their subsequent fate in the east, Hitler hinted ominously, "Then they will be worked over in the harsh climate there." Even more threatening, he noted: "As for the Jewish question, today in any case one could say that a man like Antonescu, for example, proceeds much more radically in this matter than we have done until now. But I will not rest or be idle until we too have gone all the way with the Jews" (*bis auch wir dem Judentum gegenüber die letzten Konzequenzen gezogen haben*).[40]

On the more limited issue of marking, however, Goebbels was not disappointed. On August 20 and 21 the word was quickly telephoned around Berlin that he had obtained Hitler's approval for a marking decree.[41] Goebbels had stolen the march on Heydrich and the RSHA, which in turn had been ignoring the Reich Interior Ministry.[42] The last now moved belatedly to reassert its official but tenuous jurisdiction in the matter. State Secretary Stuckart presided over the meeting of August 29 held to draft the marking legislation. In the end, however, it was the RSHA that came away with the spoils. An RSHA draft formed the basis of discussion and was for the most part agreed upon. Moreover, the marking decree, dated September 1 and published on September 5, was issued in the form of a police ordinance because an ordinance was procedurally much quicker than a law. In addition, the tricky question of exempting foreign Jews of certain countries but not others could be handled by internal orders from Himmler in agreement with the Foreign Office, rather than in the public text of a law.[43]

The events of August are instructive in a number of ways. First, they illuminate the prevailing atmosphere. A Propaganda Ministry official like Gutterer could openly advocate, before a meeting of mostly party officials in Berlin, that the killing of German Jews was the optimal if as yet unattainable solution. Goebbels could confide in his diary Hitler's prophesy that in the future the Jews of Germany would pay the price currently being paid by Jews in the east. Murder was in the air. Second, Hitler was directly involved in the decision-making process and controlled the pace of events. Although proposals were initiated by others, decisions concerning both marking and deportations could be taken only by him.[44]

Third, with the likes of both Heydrich and Goebbels—soon to be joined by others—pressing for deportations, Hitler at this point exercised restraint despite his inflammatory rhetoric and ominous threats about the looming fate awaiting German Jews. It must be kept in mind, however, that in the context of August 1941, postponing deportations until after the war only meant a very short delay. Fourth, Hitler's decision to postpone the deportation of German Jews until after the war while simultaneously pushing for a rapid pacification in Russia indicates that the onslaught against Soviet Jewry as part of the "war of destruction" on the one hand and the Final Solution of the Jewish question in Europe on the other were as yet two separate programs or at least two distinct phases resulting from different decisions and involving different timetables. They did not merge into a single enterprise until later.

Finally, it should be noted that Hitler's prophesy and the murder of the Jews, already being realized on Soviet territory and anticipated for German Jews following victory, were not tied to a "world war" defined by American involvement. For Hitler the fulfillment of his prophecy need not wait upon American entry into the war.[45] Also, on August 20, the day after Goebbels visited the Führer headquarters, Himmler not only dined with Hitler but had lunch and a long walk with Göring.[46] Presumably the mood and expectations that Hitler shared with Goebbels were being expressed to the rest of the top Nazi leadership as well.

Proposals for deportation and murder were not confined to the top Nazi leaders in Berlin. In Poznan a group of ss officers deliberated about the Jewish problem in the Warthegau. On July 16, 1941, Sturmbannführer Rolf Heinz Höppner wrote to "dear comrade Eichmann," summarizing their discussions. After weighing the possibility of concentrating all Warthegau Jews in a huge labor camp, thus requiring fewer guards and lessening the chance of epidemic then threatening the ghettos, they considered two further proposals:

> There exists this winter the danger that all the Jews can no longer be fed. It should be seriously considered if it would not be the most humane solution to dispose of the Jews, insofar as they are not capable of work, through a quick-acting agent. In any case it would be more pleasant than to let them starve.
>
> In addition the proposal was made to sterilize all the female Jews in this camp from whom children could still be expected, so that with this generation the Jewish problem is in fact completely solved.

Asking for Eichmann's opinion, Höppner concluded, "These things sound somewhat fantastic but are in my opinion definitely feasible."[47]

There is no record of Eichmann's reply to Höppner, but clearly the two remained in close contact. On September 3 Höppner submitted to his two superiors in the RSHA, Ehlich and Eichmann, a proposal for a major restructuring and expansion of the UWZ to handle large-scale deportations in the postwar period involving not just Jews but other racially undesirable elements as well. The memo, he noted, had been drawn up "on the basis of the *recent* consultation" (italics mine) (*auf Grund der letzten Rücksprache*) with Eichmann in Berlin. This "recent consultation" would have taken place at virtually the same time that Eichmann altered the wording of one of his stock formulations. Where in past correspondence with the Foreign Office he had referred to the "imminent Final Solution" (*kommende Endlösung*), on August 28, 1941, he added the phrase "now in preparation" (*die kommende und in Vorbereitung befindliche Endlösung*).[48]

Basically Höppner wanted the UWZ transformed into a subsection of the RSHA within the Gestapo, in charge of both the areas from which people would be deported and the "reception territories" (*Aufnahmegebieten*). His concrete proposals concerning the latter had to remain "patchwork" (*Stückwerk*) for the moment

because I do not know the intentions of the Führer and the Reichsführer-SS, as well as the Chief of the Security Police and SD, concerning the shaping of this territory. I could well imagine that *large areas of the present Soviet Russia* are being prepared to receive the undesired ethnic elements of the greater German settlement area. . . . To go into further details about the organization of this reception area would be fantasy, because first of all the basic decisions must be made. It is essential in this regard, by the way, that total clarity prevail about what finally shall happen to those undesirable ethnic elements deported from the greater German resettlement area. Is it the goal to ensure them a certain level of life in the long run, or shall they be totally eradicated.

(*da ich die Absichten des Führers und des Reichsführers SS, sowie des Chefs der Sicherheitspolizei und des SD über die Ausgestaltung dieser Gebiete nicht kenne. Ich könnte mir vorstellen, dass man zur Aufnahme der im grossdeutschen Siedlungsraum unerwünschten Volksteile grosse Räume im jetzigen Sowjet-Russland bereitstellt. . . . Auf weitere Einzelheiten der Organisation dieser Aufnahmegebiete einzugehen, wäre Phantasterei, da zunächst die grundlegenden Entscheidungen ergehen müssten. Wesentlich ist dabei im übrigen, dass von Anfang an völlige Klarheit darüber herrscht, was nun mit diesen ausgesiedelten, für die grossdeutschen Siedlungsräume unerwünschten Volksteilen endgültig geschehen soll, ob das Ziel darin besteht, ihnen ein gewisses Leben für dauernd zu sichern, oder ob sie völlig ausgemerzt werden sollen.)*[49]

In late August / early September, it would appear that both in Poznan and in the RSHA in Berlin, planning and preparation for a new phase in Jewish policy were underway, and "total eradication" was being openly discussed. Moreover, great impatience and frustration was growing over the lack of "total clarity" because "basic decisions" had still not been taken.

At the other end of Europe, Sturmbannführer Carltheo Zeitschel, attached to the German embassy in Paris, was also growing impatient. He advised Ambassador Abetz on August 22, 1941, that "the progressive conquest and occupation of extensive eastern territory could now bring about a final satisfactory solution in no time to the Jewish problem in Europe." Unlike Madagascar, which would require waiting until after the war and overcoming great transportation difficulties, in the new territories one could begin concentrating the Jews somewhere even during the war. "It could not be such a big problem on this occasion if the Jews from all the other countries of Europe would be added and also those Jews now packed in ghettos in Warsaw, Litzmannstadt, Lublin, etc., were also deported there." Zeitschel immodestly urged Abetz to carry the idea to Ribbentrop, who in turn should urge it upon Himmler, Rosenberg, and Göring.[50]

In mid-August the occupation authorities in Serbia, faced with a growing insurgency, urged the deportation of Serbian Jews down the Danube to Romania or to the General Government.[51] Ignored, this request was vehemently repeated three times, on September 8, 10, and 12, now with the backing of Ribbentrop's roving ambassador, Edmund Veesenmayer.[52] The Foreign Office ruled out deportation to Romania, but Undersecretary Martin Luther asked his Jewish expert, Franz Rademacher, to discuss with the RSHA the possibility of deportation to Russia or the General Government. Rademacher telephoned Eichmann and jotted down the latter's cryptic response that "residence in Russia and GG impossible. Not even the Jews from Germany can be lodged there. Eichmann proposes shooting."[53] The Serbian Jews were not going to be given precedence over German Jews for deportation, and at the moment requests to deport German Jews had been blocked by Hitler. That Eichmann felt free to casually recommend shooting is evidence of the same mood and expectation seen in Höppner's memos and Gutterer's comments.

However, on September 14, the day after Eichmann told Rademacher that not even the German Jews could be lodged in the east, the deputy director of the political division of the Ostministerium, Otto Bräutigam, arrived at the Führer-hauptquartier with a proposal from his boss, Alfred Rosenberg. In retaliation for Stalin's deportation of the Volga Germans to Siberia, Rosenberg proposed the deportation of all Jews from central Europe to the east. Shunted aside by others at the Führer headquarters, Bräutigam finally found Oberst Schmundt of Hitler's staff, who much to his surprise immediately asked for Bräutigam's memorandum because "it was a very important and urgent matter, in which the Führer was very interested." When Bräutigam inquired the next day about the fate of the Rosenberg proposal, he was told that Hitler would first confer with Ribbentrop on it.[54]

Before Ribbentrop met with Hitler, however, he had thrust upon him yet other deportation proposals. As we have seen, on August 22 Carltheo Zeitschel in Paris had urged his superior, Otto Abetz, to propose using the newly conquered eastern territories for a solution to the Jewish question. At the same time, faced with growing opposition to the German occupation in France following the invasion of the Soviet Union, the military commander, General von Stülpnagel, had the French police carry out a wave of arrests between August 20 and 23. In the end, 4,323 men—all Jews—were interned in a camp at Drancy outside Paris. The German military wanted to deter further resistance but did not want to alienate the French administration or arouse resentment in the general population. Their priority was still maximum exploitation of France with minimum German manpower, a balancing act they hoped to maintain by making the Jews bear the brunt of German reprisal measures.[55]

This provided the impetus for Zeitschel to take the initiative once again with Abetz, who was preparing for his scheduled meetings with Ribbentrop, Himmler, and Hitler at the Führer headquarters on September 16. The internment camps were filled with Jews, Zeitschel noted to Abetz before his departure. The ambassador should ask Himmler to deport them to the east as soon as possible. This would free up the only camps available, so that more Jews could be interned.[56]

Pressure for deportation also came from various Gauleiter in Germany. On the night of September 15, Hamburg was bombed. The Hamburg Gauleiter Karl Kaufmann urged Hitler to permit the evacuation of Jews from the damaged city so that their lodgings could be redistributed to those made homeless.[57] The Gauleiter of Cologne also sent a delegation, including the head of the Stapoleitstelle Emanuel Schäfer and the party Kreisleiter Schaller, to Berlin to urge the evacuation of his Jews.[58]

Himmler and Heydrich were not inactive while this pressure for deportation was building up from various directions. On September 1, 1941, the two men met together. On the following day, Himmler met with his HSSPF in the General Government, Friedrich Wilhelm Krüger, and discussed the "Jewish Question–Resettlement from the Reich." (*Judenfrage-Aussiedlung aus dem Reich*)[59] Two days later Himmler met with his HSSPF from the Warthegau, Wilhelm Koppe, and probably discussed the deportation of 60,000 Reich Jews to Lodz.[60] If in both these meetings Himmler was seeking reception areas in order to persuade Hitler of the feasibility of beginning deportations from the Reich, he was apparently more successful in the second meeting than the first. On September 14 Eichmann informed the Foreign Office that Russia and the General Government could not receive Jews even from the Reich and thus certainly not from Serbia. If Krüger had persuaded Himmler of the impossibility of deporting Jews to the General Government, presumably because of the anticipated reaction of Frank, apparently Koppe offered more hope concerning the Warthegau, as subsequent events in mid-September revealed.

On the afternoon of September 16 Abetz met with Himmler and then Hitler. The latter expansively sketched to Abetz his vision of leveling to the ground the recently besieged Leningrad and turning Russian territory to the Urals into Germany's "India." Himmler also met with Greifelt and Meyer of the RKFDV to discuss a series of issues, including compensation to the Baltic Germans, the *Judenfrage*, "settlement in the east" (*Siedlung Ost*), and brickworks. The following day Ribbentrop met with Hitler in the afternoon and Himmler in the evening.[61]

Out of this cluster of meetings, Hitler seems to have reached the basic decision to proceed with the deportation of Reich Jews that just weeks earlier he had deferred until after the war. Neither Ribbentrop nor Rosenberg seems to have been informed, though they had each played a small role in the decision-making process. Gauleiter Kaufmann would later write: "The Führer immediately accepted my suggestion and issued the appropriate orders for the deportation of the Jews."[62] But it is not clear when Kaufmann actually learned that the Hamburg Jews would be deported. It is clear, however, that Himmler learned of Hitler's change of heart immediately and proceeded without delay to inaugurate the new policy.

On September 18, 1941, Himmler wrote Arthur Greiser in the Warthegau: "The Führer wishes that the Old Reich and Protectorate be emptied and freed of Jews from west to east as quickly as possible." (*Der Führer wünscht, dass möglichst bald das Altreich und das Protektorat vom Westen nach Osten von Juden geleert und befreit werden.*) Thus Himmler intended, "as a first step" (*als erste Stufe*), to deport the Jews of the Old Reich and Protectorate into the incorporated territories, "in order to deport them yet further to the east next spring" (*um sie im nächsten Frühjahr noch weiter nach dem Osten abzuschieben*). He therefore was going to lodge for the winter some 60,000 Jews in the Lodz ghetto. Himmler understood that this involved "difficulties and burdens" for Greiser, but requested his full support for the "Jewish migration" that would be arranged between Heydrich and the Warthegau HSSPF Wilhelm Koppe.[63] Himmler apparently tried to use the Hamburg bombing as a means of breaking down Frank's resistance to receiving any Jewish transports from the Third Reich, but without success. In early October Frank specifically vetoed a plan to evacuate two trainloads of Hamburg Jews to Hrubieszow in the Lublin district.[64]

What brought about this decisive turning point? Unless the likes of Rosenberg, Ribbentrop, and Kaufmann are to be credited with greater influence on Hitler than Heydrich and Goebbels, whose similar proposals a month earlier were unsuccessful, it is best to see the proposals and interventions of Rosenberg via Bräutigam, Zeitschel via Abetz and Ribbentrop, and Gauleiter Kaufmann more as the occasion than the basic cause of Hitler's change of heart.[65] A look at the correlation between Hitler's reversal and Germany's changing fortunes of war on the eastern front points to a second peak of German victory euphoria as a crucial factor in the timing of this decision.

Following the heady days of mid-July, the German war effort encountered increasing frustrations. While advance on the central front halted and the German military sought to consolidate its gains, refit its units, and prepare a final push on the now not-so-distant Moscow, Hitler attempted to persuade his generals to divert armored forces north and south for offensives against Leningrad and Kiev. Hitler made it clear that he gave priority to the capture of economic targets over Moscow, which he dubbed a "mere geographic concept." The generals resisted stubbornly and dragged their feet until Hitler unequivocally imposed his will on August 18. In the end Hitler successfully insisted that there would be no resumption of an offensive against Moscow until all his goals in the north and south had been achieved.[66] It was during this period of strategic stalemate with his generals that Hitler also resisted the pressures of Goebbels and Heydrich to begin immediate deportations from the Third Reich. But Goebbels also reported from his meeting with Hitler on August 19 that after several very difficult weeks, Hitler had expressed renewed hope. He would not only surround and starve out Leningrad and Kiev, but the refitted tank forces would reach Moscow before winter. "Then for all practical purposes at least the military striking power of Bolshevism is disposed of."[67]

The offensive in the north resumed first, and Leningrad was successfully cut off in early September. The Ukrainian campaign that Hitler imposed on his reluctant generals quickly followed. On September 12 Ewald von Kleist's tanks broke through the Soviet lines behind Kiev. On the same day German forces cracked the defensive perimeter around Leningrad. In the words of Alan Clark, this day could be "reckoned the low point in the fortunes of the Red Army for the whole war."[68] By September 16 Kleist had joined up with Heinz Guderian at Lokhvitsa to complete the vast Kiev encirclement. By September 26 Kiev had fallen and 665,000 Soviet prisoners had been taken.[69]

The resumption of successful offensives on the Leningrad and Ukrainian fronts, therefore, was the military context of Hitler's mid-September indication to Himmler that deportations from the Third Reich could begin. As the Soviet position in Kiev became increasingly desperate, Hitler met with Himmler, Heydrich, Goebbels, and what the latter termed a "great parade of notables" in lengthy meetings on September 23 and 24. Speaking with Heydrich, Goebbels expressed his desire to deport the Jews of Berlin as soon as possible. Heydrich replied that "this could occur as soon as we arrive at a clarification of the military situation in the east. In the end they should be transported into camps that have been erected by the Bolsheviks. These camps were erected by the Jews, so what could be more fitting than that they now also be populated by Jews." (*Das wird der Fall sein können, sobald wir im Osten zu einer Bereinigung der militärischen Fragen gekommen sind. Sie sollen am Ende [in die von den] Bolschewisten angelegten Lager [. . .] transportiert werden. Diese Lager sind von den Juden errichtet worden; was läge also näher, als dass sie nun auch von den Juden bevölkert werden.*) Speaking with Hitler, the propaganda minister learned, "The Führer is of the opinion that the Jews are to be removed from Germany step-by-step. The first cities that have to be cleared of Jews are Berlin, Vienna, and Prague. Berlin is first in line, and I hope it will be possible even in the course of this year to deport a significant portion of Berlin Jews to the east."

Goebbels's hope for deporting the bulk of Berlin's Jews by the end of the year stemmed from Hitler's extraordinarily optimistic views on the military situation, the clarification of which Heydrich had said was the one remaining obstacle to commencing deportation. Hitler thought the Kiev encirclement would be cleaned up in a few days, and then Germany would advance quickly on other fronts. "The spell is broken. In the next three to four weeks we must once again expect great victories." (*Der Bann ist gebrochen. Wir haben in den nächsten drei bis vier Wochen wiederum grosse neue Siege zu erwarten.*) Hitler believed that serious fighting would last until October 15, after which date Bolshevism would be routed. After relishing the destruction and starvation that awaited Leningrad, Hitler prescribed the same fate for Moscow. German preparations were sufficiently advanced that he once again contemplated the encirclement of Moscow by the fateful date of October 15.[70] Between mid-August and mid-September,

Hitler's expectations of quick victory had increased enormously. Was it mere coincidence that his reversal of policy concerning deportations took place at this time?

The need for "a clarification of the military situation in the east" posed by Heydrich to Goebbels was not long in coming. Having had his way with his generals, Hitler on September 6 had permitted Army Group Center to prepare for a decisive campaign to destroy the opposing Soviet forces.[71] On September 30, just four days after the fall of Kiev, Guderian's army began the offensive, and on October 2 the rest of the forces of Operation Typhoon struck along the central front.

The initial reports on the progress of Operation Typhoon indicated a tremendous success. Goebbels, who persuaded Hitler to return to Berlin on October 4 to give a speech at the Sportspalast, recorded his Führer's mood:

He looks at his best and is in an exuberantly optimistic frame of mind. He literally exudes optimism. . . . The offensive has been surprisingly successful so far. . . . The Führer is convinced that if the weather remains halfway favorable, the Soviet army will be essentially demolished in fourteen days.

(*Er ist von besten Aussehen, befindet sich in einer übersprudelnd optimistischen Laune. Er strahlt förmlich Optimismus aus. . . . Die Offensive ist bisher zu überraschenden Erfolgen gekommen. . . . Der Führer ist der Überzeugung, dass wenn das Wetter halbwegs günstig bleibt, die sowjetische Wehrmacht in vierzehn Tagen im wesentlichen zertrümmert sein wird.)*[72]

On October 6, one day before the double encirclement of Vyazma and Bryansk was complete, Hitler again spoke of deportations: "All Jews have to be removed from the Protectorate, not only to the General Government but straight on to the east." But Hitler voiced another reservation. "Only the great shortage of transport prevents this being done at once. Together with the Jews of the Protectorate all the Jews of Vienna and Berlin must disappear."[73] But expectations remained high. By October 7 the Germans had completed the double encirclement at Vyazma and Bryansk that ultimately led to the capture of another 673,000 Soviet troops. On that day Goebbels again noted: "It goes well on the front. The Führer continues to be extraordinarily optimistic." (*Der Führer ist weiterhin ausserordentlich optimistisch.*)[74] Despite the transportation difficulties and the need for military clarification noted by Hitler and Heydrich, preparations for the deportations were in any case already underway. As one official in Prague noted subsequently, the first transport from Prague on October 16 "required quite lengthy preparation beforehand, from at least mid-September."[75]

By the time of an October 10 conference in Prague, chaired by Heydrich,[76] no further reservations were recorded. In addition to Lodz, Heydrich mentioned Riga and Minsk as destinations for 50,000 deported Jews. Similar to his earlier statement to Goebbels, Heydrich declared that "Nebe and Rasch [given his earlier reference to Riga, presumably he means Stahlecker here, not Rasch] could take in Jews in the camps for communist prisoners in the theater of operations" (*könnten in das Lager für kommunistische Häftlinge im Operationsgebiet Juden mithineinnehmen*). Deportations were to begin around October 15, and 5,000 Jews from Prague would be deported in the first month. "Because the Führer wishes that by the end of this year as many Jews as possible be removed from the German sphere," Heydrich concluded, "all pending questions must be solved immediately. Even the transportation question must not present any problems." (*Da der Führer wünscht, dass noch Ende d. J. möglichst die Juden aus dem deutschen Raum herausgebracht sind, müssen die schwebenden Fragen umgehend gelöst werden. Auch die Transportfrage darf dabei keine Schwierigkeiten bedeuten.*)[77] The first deportation train, in fact, left Vienna on October 15, the same day that resistance died in the Vyazma pocket and panic spread through Moscow. This was also precisely the date Hitler had twice given to Goebbels on September 23 as when he expected the military verdict to be settled and serious fighting on the eastern front to be at an end. By the time the Bryansk pocket was liquidated on October 18, three more Jewish transports had departed from Prague, Luxemburg, and Berlin.[78]

The fundamental change in German policy at the center was not yet known on the periphery, where frustrated officials continued to press for deportation. The zealous Carltheo Zeitschel of the German embassy in Paris contacted Eichmann's local representative, Theo Dannecker, on October 8. Zeitschel reported that Ambassador Abetz had taken the Zeitschel proposal to Himmler and received the promise that the Jews in the concentration camps of the occupied territories could be deported to the east as soon as transportation was available. Zeitschel urged Dannecker not to let Himmler's "agreement in principle" be wasted. Every other week he should forward to Berlin the urgent request to deport the Jews of France as soon as possible.[79] Apparently Zeitschel had also worked on the military authorities in France. On October 14, 1941, Frank asked the Ostministerium leader about the possibility of deporting the Jews of the General Government to the east. Rosenberg noted that the military administration in Paris had brought up a similar idea. Unfortunately, for the moment he saw no possibility for carrying out such deportation plans, but he promised to facilitate them in the future.[80]

By early October one question concerning the deportation of the Jews had been settled. Hitler had, after initial hesitation, embraced the idea of deporting as many Jews as possible from within Germany's prewar borders by the end of the year. The other areas of the wider German empire aspiring to be included—the General Government, France, Serbia—were not yet, however, to be relieved of their Jews.

The limited deportation program approved by Hitler posed two major problems. The first was the question of reception areas. An overall plan for a total solution to the Jewish question, which Heydrich had been authorized to draw up on July 31, was not ready to be implemented. Where were the Jews deported from Germany to go? Himmler's answer was to buy time until the following spring by lodging them over the winter partly in Lodz but mostly in Minsk and Riga, much to the consternation of the local German authorities on the receiving end. The second problem concerned those unable to rid themselves of their unwanted Jews. Faced with what seemed to be an intractable situation, they began on their own initiative to anticipate a murderous solution. It is to these local manifestations of consternation and anticipation that we must now turn.

CONSTERNATION AND ANTICIPATION

Lodz, Riga, and Minsk

If the deportation of the Jews was fervently hoped for by many Nazis, local German officials fated to be on the receiving end had a different perspective. Already in the early summer of 1941, Hans Biebow of the Lodz ghetto administration had found his attempts to stabilize the ghetto economy threatened by the prospect of having all the other Jews of the Warthegau interned in Lodz as well. Biebow warned of the catastrophic consequences if this were done without both enlarging the ghetto and ensuring adequate food supplies. Nonetheless, in mid-July the Warthegau Gauleiter, Greiser, ordered Lodz to accept 2,900 Jews from the Leslau district. The German authorities in Lodz dragged their feet and delayed this transfer until late September.[81] By then, however, they were faced with a far greater threat in the form of Himmler's letter to Greiser of September 18 announcing that 60,000 German Jews would be lodged in Lodz over the winter. The numbers were quickly scaled down to 20,000 Jews and 5,000 "Gypsies," but the Lodz officials were still flabbergasted at the prospect. Biebow assiduously assembled counterarguments for his immediate superiors, Oberbürgermeister Ventzki and Regierungspräsident Uebelhoer. They promptly sent Biebow's counterarguments, over their own signatures, to Himmler.

These counterarguments noted the past history of the Lodz ghetto. Initially

the Jews lived solely off their hoarded goods, but such means of support eventually came to an end. Therefore, through great effort a "work ghetto" had been
created, "in which the Jews today earn 80% of their subsistence through their
own labor." Some 95% of ghetto production went to fulfill military contracts.
"If the Lodz ghetto were a pure decimation ghetto, then one could contemplate a
greater concentration of Jews" (*Wäre das Ghetto Litzmannstadt ein reines Dezimierungsghetto, dann könnte man an eine noch grössere Zusammenpferchung der
Juden denken*); however, it was a "finely tuned and thereby extremely sensitive
component of the defense economy" (*ein fein verästeltes und dadurch äusserst
empfindliches Wehrwirtschaftsgebiet*). Thus the addition of 20,000 Jews and above
all 5,000 "Gypsies" would have catastrophic consequences. Factories would
have to be closed to house the newcomers; military contracts would not be fulfilled; the ghetto would again have to be fed at the expense of the Reich; German
workers would no longer be freed for military duty by virtue of the ghetto's
contribution to military production; epidemics would break out and cross the
wire into the surrounding German population. For all these reasons the planned
importation of 20,000 Jews and 5,000 "Gypsies" was "intolerable."[82]

Himmler replied to Uebelhoer that while Ventzki (in fact Biebow) had written an "excellent" report, he did not appear to be an "old National Socialist." In
any case, their arguments were rejected from the start, because "endangerment
of work for the war economy" was "the most beloved counterargument in
Germany today . . . when one wants to refuse something." It was "obviously not
pleasant" to receive new Jews, but Himmler nonetheless asked Uebelhoer to
understand that this was necessary "in accordance with the will of the Führer
that the Jews should be driven out step-by-step from west to east" (*gemäss dem
Willen des Führers, dass die Juden von Westen nach Osten hin Stufe für Stufe
ausgetrieben werden sollen*).[83]

Before receiving this letter, however, Uebelhoer had gone to the Interior
Ministry in Berlin, investigated the situation, and written again to Himmler to
tell him that he (Himmler) had been deceived by Eichmann and Dr. Robert
Schefe of the Lodz Gestapo. Eichmann's claim to have consulted with Uebelhoer beforehand was false. His claim that the economic supervisor of the ghetto
had agreed to the plan was false, for that man—Biebow—was in fact the author
of the "excellent" report signed by Ventzki. Eichmann's claim that the ghetto
was subdivided into a work ghetto and a residence ghetto, so that adding people
to the latter would not affect the former, was false. Finally, the claim of Dr.
Schefe that the ghetto population had declined from 185,000 to 120,000 and
thus could easily hold another 25,000 was false. The population had dropped
from 160,000 to 145,000, but the ghetto had also been diminished in size.

Uebelhoer concluded by describing the methods of Eichmann and the Lodz Gestapo as "ugly Gypsylike horse-trading manners" (*von den Zigeunern übel-genommene* [sic] *Rosstäuschermanieren*) and suggesting that the Jews be sent to Warsaw instead.[84] Uebelhoer also induced General Thomas, head of the War Economy and Armaments Office, to make common cause with him.[85]

Himmler was not pleased and told Uebelhoer to read his letter again. "You have adopted quite the wrong tone and obviously forgotten that you were writing to a superior." (*Sie haben sich im Ton völlig vergriffen und offenkundig vergessen, dass Sie an einen Vorgesetzten geschrieben haben.*) He gave instructions that any further communications from Uebelhoer were to be sent back until this matter had been cleared up.[86] Heydrich took up the correspondence that Himmler now refused to pursue and harshly condemned Uebelhoer for his "oppositional attitude," his "totally unrestrained and hostile manner," his "deficient sense of belonging to the ss," and his pettiness in attacking subordinate ss officers who were only following orders. Unless he received from Uebelhoer an immediate explanation concerning his ability to continue working with Dr. Schefe in the future, Heydrich would draw the "appropriate conclusions."[87] Subsequently, Greiser covered for Uebelhoer and assured Heydrich that the Regierungspräsident had carried out his orders. Himmler suggested that "the good Uebelhoer" should take a vacation to sooth his nerves; if he came back recovered, Himmler would consider the matter closed. In the meantime he trusted that Uebelhoer had learned the lesson that the interests of the Reich were higher than the local church tower (*dass der Bau des Reiches höher ist als der Kirchturm von Litzmannstadt*).[88] Thus the deportations to Lodz were not deterred, but Uebelhoer's career survived intact.

Less spectacular but equally ineffective was the reaction of the German officials in Riga to the unexpected and unwanted deluge of Reich Jews. On October 11, 1941, Einsatzgruppe A commander Stahlecker informed the Generalkommissar of Latvia, Dr. Otto-Heinrich Drechsler, that he needed materials for a big concentration camp to be built to lodge Jews from the Reich who were being sent to Riga in accordance with the Führer's wish. Ten days later Sturmbannführer Rudolf Lange of EK 2 elaborated; it was a question of 25,000 Jews in a camp outside Riga.[89] Three days after that, on October 24, Reichskommissar for the Ostland, Hinrich Lohse, and Drechsler met with Lange to discuss the issue. Lange was insistent "that he was merely acting according to the order of Obergruppenführer Heydrich." He had been instructed to inform the authorities of the Reichskommissariat Ostland, which he had done. Drechsler complained that he had not been informed for the purpose of discussing the issue but merely notified after the fact. Because of the "salient political significance" of these measures, Lohse added, he intended to go to Berlin the next morning to clarify the matter. To a pointed question, Lange assured Lohse that "essential work" on the camp had not yet begun, so that irrespective of construction on the camp other decisions could be made.[90]

While Lohse was in Berlin to discuss the Jewish transports to the Ostland, the civil administration there was informed that the transports would begin arriving in Minsk on November 11 and in Riga on November 19. Thereafter, until December 17 transports of 1,000 Reich Jews would arrive every other day. Five of the Riga-bound transports would be sent to the ghetto in Kaunas. In Riga itself, a camp was under construction at Salaspils. Since it would not be completed in time, the first transport would be lodged in the former troop barracks at Jungfernhof.[91] Lohse's assistant, Friedrich Trampedach, telegraphed to the Ostministerium and to Lohse at the Hotel Adlon in Berlin an urgent request to stop the transports because the *Judenlager* ought to be located much further east.[92] In Berlin the Ostministerium Jewish expert, Erhard Wetzel, had just had very interesting discussions (which will be analyzed below) about the eventual fate of the Jewish transports to the Ostland. Dr. Leibbrandt of the political division of the Ostministerium could thus assure the Germans in Riga that the Jews were indeed going to be sent "further east. Camps in Riga and Minsk only temporary measures, therefore no objections on our part" (*weiter nach Osten. Lager in Riga und Minsk nur vorläufige Massnahmen, daher hier keine Bedenken*).[93]

When the military commander in the Ostland, General Braemer, learned of the intended deportation of 25,000 Reich Jews to Minsk, he too objected. Already the Jews of Belorussia—pro-Bolshevik and anti-German—were the "driving force" behind the resistance. The addition of German Jews, who according to Braemer were far superior intellectually to the Belorussians, would endanger security even more. Considering also the problems of food and transportation shortages, the military commander urgently requested that the Jewish transports be stopped. One week later Lohse tried to put an end to such protests, issuing instructions that "no objections were to be raised anymore to any kind of transport from the Reich."[94] Despite Lohse's attempt to override Braemer's objections, they were in this rare case of military exigency not without effect. Only 7 rather than the planned 25 Jewish transports were in fact sent to Minsk.[95]

Himmler and Heydrich were reluctant to compromise on the issue of Jewish deportations to Lodz, Riga, Kaunas, and Minsk. The transports could not be stopped entirely by local objection, although in the face of strong opposition in Lodz and Minsk the numbers of projected deportees were scaled back. Himmler and Heydrich were not unsympathetic about the problems posed to local authorities by virtue of this influx of Jews. They were more than willing to help local authorities mitigate overcrowding, not by halting the transports but rather by reducing the Jewish population through other means. And the consternation felt by local German authorities at the prospect of receiving more Jews made them only more ready to participate in mass murder when that time came.

Serbia

While some fated to receive new shipments of Jews from the Reich protested in vain, others viewing the seemingly intractable situation of the Jews within the Nazi empire drew their own conclusions, thus anticipating the Final Solution. In Serbia situational and ideological factors combined with deadly effect. On the one hand, the request to deport the Jews of Serbia had been vetoed in Berlin, leaving the Jews trapped in a country convulsed by a growing, communist-led insurgency. On the other hand, the German military forces occupying Serbia shared the views of the German military as it prepared for a war of destruction in the Soviet Union—above all, the stereotypical equation of Jews with communism. As a result, the first systematic massacre of European Jews outside Soviet territory was perpetrated by the German military in Serbia in October 1941.[96]

Following Yugoslavia's rejection of an alliance with Germany at the end of March 1941, Yugoslavia along with Greece had been overrun in the following month. The country was divided up among Germany's southeast European allies, although the Serbian heartland remained a German occupation zone under a military administration of unparalleled complexity and confusion. A Luftwaffe general—first Ludwig von Schröder, then Heinrich Danckelmann—served as military commander in Serbia (Militärbefehlshaber in Serbien), responsible to the Wehrmacht commander in Greece, Field Marshal Wilhelm List. The Serbian military commander had two staffs: a command staff, which exercised direct control over the regional defense battalions in Serbia and a more distant control over General Paul Bader's 65th Corps; and an administrative staff under State Councillor and Gruppenführer Harald Turner,[97] which supervised the activities of a Serbian provisional government, the German commandants in the four districts into which Serbia had been divided, the Sipo-SD Einsatzgruppe of Wilhelm Fuchs, and the 64th Reserve Police Battalion. In addition, Göring's Four-Year Plan was represented by a plenipotentiary for the economy, Hans Neuhausen, and the Foreign Office was represented by yet another plenipotentiary for all matters touching on foreign policy, Felix Benzler.

Even before the uprising in Serbia was triggered by the German invasion of the Soviet Union, German occupation authorities had already imposed the usual array of anti-Jewish measures: registration, exclusion from many occupations and social activities, expropriation of property, marking, and forced labor. Almost as an afterthought, all these measures had been applied to Serbian "Gypsies" as well. The German authorities in Belgrade anticipated the uprising, but initially assumed that police measures would be sufficient to counter resistance. Among the earliest police measures instituted were reprisal shootings of arrested communists. In addition, the Jewish community had to provide 40 hostages weekly, and Jews were explicitly among the 111 people executed in German reprisals by July 22.[98]

As the uprising and commensurate reprisals intensified, in late July Schröder's administrative staff disseminated guidelines for "deterrent and expiatory measures" (*Vorbeugungs- und Sühnemassnahmen*), which imposed many restrictions. Special care was to be taken to investigate the facts of any incident, for "measures unjustly enacted damage German prestige." Reprisal shooting was to occur only for actions committed after hostages had been arrested and sufficient warning had been given. And a close connection between the hostages and the perpetrators had to exist. However, the guidelines also permitted measures against the population of a location if they made themselves "coresponsible" (*mitverantwortlich*) by facilitating sabotage committed by others, by passively resisting German investigation, or by providing a supportive environment for anti-German activity. Thus in addition to arrested communists and Jewish hostages, who were hitherto used as reprisal victims, Serbians on the spot deemed coresponsible were now vulnerable.[99] This new reprisal policy was first put into effect on July 27, when Serbian police were forced at gunpoint to shoot 81 harvest workers rounded up in the fields near the site of an ambushed German car.[100]

Since German police measures were proving inadequate in stemming the growth of the partisan movement, the occupation authorities sought a more effective counterinsurgency policy. Field Marshal List urged a more active combat role for the troops of Bader's 65th Corps, but Bader's three divisions were undermanned, overage, poorly equipped, immobile, and still in training. Such units were unable to cope with the partisans.[101] The OKW refused reinforcements and instead emphatically urged an intensification of the reprisal policy begun on local initiative.[102] This proved not just inadequate but counterproductive.[103] Numerous German documents make it clear that Schröder's initial injunction to avoid injustices was a dead letter and that German reprisal policy was driving the population to the side of the insurgents. Saying that "in the Balkans life counts for nothing," an OKW German report conceded, "Even with the most unrestricted reprisal measures—up until the end of August a total of approximately 1,000 communists and Jews had been shot or publicly hanged and the houses of the guilty burned down—it was not possible to restrain the continual growth of the armed revolt."[104] In contrast to greater military involvement or increasingly draconian reprisals, a number of local German officials preferred expanded police measures, with particular emphasis on a strengthened and better-armed Serbian police. However, the ill-equipped Serbian police became increasingly demoralized and unreliable as partisan success grew.[105]

By late August drastic measures were required, but the Germans in Belgrade and List in Greece continued to advocate contrasting solutions based on starkly different interpretations of the partisan movement. The Belgrade Germans felt that the communists were the main force behind the insurgency, that the Serbian nationalists (including the Chetniks) had hitherto remained aloof and deliberately avoided confrontation with the Germans, and that the population at large still rejected communism even if it did not cooperate with the German troops against the partisans. The Belgrade Germans did not want to drive the communists and nationalists into a united front; rather, they wanted to work with the latter against the former. Thus in late August, Danckelmann (with the support of Turner, Benzler, Neuhausen, and Bader) asked the former Serbian minister of defense Milan Nedic, a popular figure with an anticommunist, pro-German record, to become president of a new Serbian government. It was hoped that he would have the popularity and prestige to win broad support and mobilize anticommunist sentiment.[106]

List reluctantly agreed to give the Nedic government a chance, but he flatly rejected the local diagnosis of the insurgency, insisting that it was not only a communist but also a Serbian national movement.[107] In two messages to Belgrade on September 4 and 5, List made clear his preference for intensified military action and repression in contrast to greater reliance on Serbian collaborators. He advocated "ruthless" measures against the insurgents and their families, such as "hanging, burning down of villages involved, seizure of more hostages, deportation of relatives, etc. into concentration camps" and also a more general "increased pressure on the population in areas where the insurgents are tolerated."[108]

List's behavior toward Serbia in September 1941 was typical of neither the rest of his career nor his character. He was neither a Nazi nor a traditional Prussian officer but a highly cultured and deeply religious man trained at a military academy in Munich before World War I.[109] No less prestigious a witness than Archbishop Angelo Roncalli, later Pope John XXIII, testified to List's strict efforts to protect Greek civilians from mistreatment by German soldiers and his efforts on behalf of food deliveries to Greece to avoid famine.[110] He was, moreover, no careerist willing to do anything to keep his position, nor a timid man afraid to stand up to Hitler. When ordered by Hitler to carry out an attack in the Caucasus in 1942 that he deemed suicidal for his troops, List refused and his military career came to an abrupt end.[111]

List's behavior in Serbia in September 1941 reflected the military frustrations of a professional soldier with little political sense. A strict disciplinarian with a paternalistic concern for the welfare of his troops, List found the insurgency and its "insidious" methods an outrageous affront to his sense of order and decency. The insurgents and the unruly Serbian people from whom they sprang had to be punished. And because List had a stereotypical image of "hotblooded" Serbs made cruel by centuries of Turkish domination, he felt they could only be disciplined with measures commensurate with their own violent nature.[112]

List, and indeed almost every German officer in the Balkans, was tormented by another concern—the damage to the prestige and image of the German army caused by its inability to cope with partisan tactics. The partisan success was more than just an embarrassment to their professional pride. If not checked, the increasing display of German military impotence could snowball into military disaster. In early September, when List fired off his exhortations for greater terror, this was no longer a fanciful prospect. Some Chetnik units were now entering the battle against the Germans, swept up in the wave of partisan success, and in the first days of September 175 Germans were captured in two separate incidents.[113] Thus List was reacting to two major setbacks of unprecedented proportions in the guerrilla war which clearly demonstrated that the thinly stretched German troops in Serbia were not only impotent to suppress sabotage and ambush but now threatened with piecemeal defeat.

As the German position continued to deteriorate, even the proponents of the Nedic experiment (and Nedic himself) concluded that the uprising could only be crushed with German forces.[114] List then moved to end what he considered the "intolerable chain of command" in Serbia in which a "vain" and "superficial" Luftwaffe general, who had been seduced by the political calculations of Turner and Benzler, outranked the army troop commander.[115] His request for the appointment of General Franz Böhme, a former Austrian officer who would presumably have few inhibitions about repression in Serbia, as "plenipotentiary commanding general" as well as his request for a frontline division were both granted.[116]

When Böhme arrived in Belgrade on September 18, he found fervent converts to List's call for "increased pressure on the population." A major punitive expedition by the 342nd division arriving from France was already being planned for the Sava Bend region around Sabac, a particularly dense area of partisan activity. The premise of the expedition was that the entire population had joined the insurgency, and that a horrifying example had to be made that would immediately become known throughout Serbia.[117] Orders were issued by Böhme that all men in the area between 14 and 70 years of age were to be placed in a concentration camp and the female population was to be driven off into the mountains. All inhabitants who participated in resistance or in whose houses weapons were found or who attempted to flee were to be shot and their houses burned down.[118] In a message to the troops, Böhme exhorted: "Your mission lies in a country in which German blood flowed in 1914 through the treachery of the Serbs, men and women. You are the avengers of these dead. An intimidating example must be created for the whole of Serbia which must hit the whole population most severely."[119]

On September 23, units of Lt. General Dr. Hinghofer's 342nd division entered Sabac. The male population was rounded up, held for two days without food, force marched to Jarak 23 kilometers away, and then marched back again four days later when the site proved unsuitable for a concentration camp.[120] Meanwhile, as German troops fanned out from Sabac, particular towns were earmarked for total destruction, and all suspected communists were shot.[121] Then the fury began to subside. On October 2 Hinghofer ordered that the female population was not to be driven off into the mountains but left in the villages to take care of the livestock and harvest. Two days later he ordered that shootings and burning of houses and villages be halted. By then over 20,000 men had been interned and 1,126 executed.[122]

The 125th regiment, sent from Greece, carried out a similar punitive expedition to Valjevo south of Sabac, but elsewhere the partisans remained on the offensive. Another German unit was overrun and captured at the end of September. Even more shocking to the Germans was the ambush of a communications unit near Topola on October 2: the German troops who surrendered were executed by machine-gun fire at close range.[123] Böhme's staff concluded that "no trace can be found of a deterrent effect from the clearing actions carried out so far," and they determined upon an even harsher policy.[124]

On September 16 Keitel had issued a general directive to implement Hitler's demand for the "harshest measures" against communist insurgency in occupied territories. Because human life in these countries often meant nothing and a deterrent effect could only be achieved through unusual harshness, Keitel asserted, he ordered that 50–100 communists be executed in retaliation for the death of each German soldier.[125] In the wake of the Topola ambush, Böhme's quartermaster, Captain Hans Faulmüller, drafted a proposal, also initialed by the chief of staff Colonel Max Pemsel, that "for every murdered German soldier, 100 Serbian prisoners are immediately to be shot." For the 21 men lost at Topola, Turner was "requested to select 2,100 prisoners in the concentration camps Sabac and Belgrade (predominantly Jews and communists)."[126]

On October 5, the day after his order for 2,100 reprisal executions, Böhme received a further counterinsurgency directive from List. List was responding to Böhme's request to deport to Germany all the interned Serbs at Sabac, for he opposed either holding them indefinitely or releasing them. List vetoed deportation and ordered that while all those caught in active resistance were to be shot immediately, men merely encountered in the area of operations were to be investigated. Those proven to be partisans were to be executed, those suspected were to be held as hostages subject to reprisal execution, and those not suspected of anti-German activities were to be released.[127] While in theory Keitel's and List's directives were not incompatible, in practice they would prove to be so. Future events would show that if prisoners had to be investigated and only the suspicious held as hostages, the reprisal ratio would be unobtainable; if the ratio was to be met, screening of prisoners would have to be dispensed with.

Böhme's staff proceeded to develop a general reprisal policy. Drafted by Faulmüller, initialed by Pemsel, and signed by Böhme, it was issued to all units on October 10, 1941. "In Serbia it is necessary because of the 'Balkan mentality' and the great expansion of the . . . insurgency movements, to carry out the orders of the OKW in the sharpest form. . . . In every command area in Serbia all communists, all those suspected as such, *all Jews* [italics mine], and a certain number of nationalist and democratically inclined inhabitants are to be seized as hostages." Of these hostages, 100 were to be shot for each German killed and 50 for each wounded.[128]

This reprisal policy of Böhme, Pemsel, and Faulmüller was not simply a minimal compliance with the Keitel guidelines. Not only did they adopt the maximum suggested ratio of 100:1 instead of the minimum of 50:1, but they also explicitly included "all Jews," a group which Keitel had never mentioned. Why did they do this? The German military in Serbia had long accepted the identification or at least the natural combination of communist and Jew. From the beginning of the uprising, reprisals had been carried out against "communists and Jews." Böhme, Pemsel, and Faulmüller were not breaking new ground.

While many officers may simply have accepted the communist-Jewish identification as an unquestioned and self-evident tenet of Nazi ideology, a narrowly professional and nonideological mode of thinking among other officers led to the same results. It was obvious to every German officer that the Jews in occupied countries would assuredly be among Germany's enemies. As List stated at his trial, "I can well understand from the view of the Jews that they worked against the Germans and that they combined with the communists. I say I can well understand that on the basis of events which had occurred."[129] Professional soldiers stood ready to defend their country against its enemies; they did not stand in judgment of or make their loyalty conditional upon the policies of their government, which created those enemies. As long as the anti-Jewish measures in Serbia were perceived and construed as measures against Germany's enemies, it did not require nazified zealots (though surely such were not lacking), merely conscientious and politically obtuse professional soldiers to carry them out.

The inclusion of all male Jews as hostages for reprisal shooting did not strike the Germans in Serbia as extraordinary or unusual. On the contrary, it was a course of action that must have seemed almost natural and obvious. The male Jews of the Banat and Belgrade had been interned in Belgrade since late summer, and a large group of Jewish refugees from central Europe, who had been stranded in Yugoslavia when their travel arrangements to Palestine had collapsed, had been interned in Sabac since June 1941.[130] Efforts by Turner and Benzler to deport the interned Jews to Romania or elsewhere had been vetoed by the Foreign Office and ss, and thus they remained in camps. List had likewise vetoed the deportation of the vast number of male prisoners rounded up in the Sava Bend and ordered the screening of prisoners and the holding of suspects as hostages instead. Thus the German military in Serbia found itself presiding over more and more camps whose inmate population could not be deported and could be decreased only by release, which they did not favor, or by hostage shooting.

Since the Serbian Jews constituted a group from whose ranks reprisal victims had already been selected for the past four months and whose blanket identification by the Germans with the elusive communist enemy obviated the bothersome and unreliable screening process now prescribed for Serbian prisoners, it is almost inconceivable that the military authorities would have given the Jews a special protected status among the internees and not included them in the hostage pool. And since the Jews were already interned while the communists for the most part defied capture, it had to be clear to Böhme and his staff upon whom the brunt of the reprisal shootings would fall.

Indeed, the 2,100 reprisal shootings for the Topola ambush were carried out exclusively against Jews and "Gypsies" in Belgrade and Sabac. In a fateful chain of associated stereotypes, Jews had been equated with communists and "Gypsies" with Jews. On October 9 and 11 a firing squad from the communications unit that had suffered the casualties of the Topola ambush shot 449 Jews. Its commander, Lieutenant Walter Liepe, noted that the men returned from the first execution "satisfied," but "unfortunately" his unit could not continue after the second day because of an assignment in the field. Other communications troops continued the executions in Belgrade thereafter.[131] In Sabac parts of the 750th regiment under Major Faninger and the 64th Reserve Police Battalion guarded the town and camp. The records of neither unit have survived, but one witness, a Serb forced to dig graves and bury the corpses, lived to testify to the mass executions of the Sabac Jews and "Gypsies" carried out by German soldiers at Zasavica on October 12 and 13, 1941.[132] In the case of Sabac, this had the grotesque consequence that central European refugees, mostly Austrian, were shot by troops of predominantly Austrian origin in retaliation for casualties inflicted by Serbian partisans on the German army!

Among the Germans in Belgrade, Harald Turner alone showed signs of ambivalence about using the interned Jews for the purpose of filling reprisal quotas. On October 17 he wrote in a personal letter:

> In the last eight days I had 2,000 Jews and 200 Gypsies shot in accordance with the ratio 1:100 for bestially murdered German soldiers, and a further 2,200, likewise almost all Jews, will be shot in the next eight days. This is not a pretty business. At any rate, it has to be, if only to make clear what it means even to attack a German soldier, and, for the rest, the Jewish question solves itself most quickly in this way. Actually it is incorrect, if one is to be precise about it, that for murdered Germans—on whose account the ratio 1:100 should really be borne by Serbs—100 Jews are shot instead; but the Jews we had in camps—after all, they too are Serb nationals, and besides, they have to disappear.[133]

But Turner's preferred solution for the necessary disappearance of the Jews had been deportation to Romania or elsewhere, and suddenly he saw the opportunity to press for this solution once more when Foreign Office Jewish expert Franz Rademacher and one of Eichmann's deputies, Friedrich Suhr, arrived in Belgrade on October 18.

The visit of Rademacher and Suhr had been set in motion much earlier. From mid-August through mid-September Benzler, incited by Turner and seconded by Ribbentrop's roving ambassador, Edmund Veesenmayer, had repeatedly urged the deportation of the Serbian Jews. Benzler had justified this request to make Serbia *judenfrei* on the grounds that the Jews made common cause with the communist uprising and no pacification could take place until they were removed.[134] Benzler's fourth appeal for deportation had been the occasion of Rademacher's inquiry to Eichmann about the feasibility of moving the Serbian Jews to Poland or Russia. Eichmann had rejected deportation and proposed "shooting."[135] Undersecretary Martin Luther thereupon informed Benzler that deportation was impossible; by "tough and uncompromising" methods, it had to be possible to keep the Jews from spreading unrest.[136]

The persistent Benzler did not quit. He went over the head of the Wilhelm-strasse bureaucracy and on September 28 wrote Ribbentrop "personally." He chided Ribbentrop for not providing the help he had been promised and invoked the support of the military for the immediate deportation of at least the 8,000 male Jews in Serbia.[137] Luther, who received a copy of this letter, was very irritated. He drafted his own memorandum for Ribbentrop. "If the military commander is agreed with Benzler to the effect that these 8,000 Jews prevent pacification action in the Serbian Old Kingdom in the first place, then in my opinion the military commander must take care of the immediate elimination of these 8,000 Jews. In other areas other military commanders have dealt with considerably greater numbers of Jews without even mentioning it." Luther requested Ribbentrop's authorization to discuss the question with Heydrich, due to return shortly from Prague. "I am convinced that in agreement with him we can come very quickly to a clear solution of this question."[138]

Luther's request of October 2 was initialed by Weizsäcker but went no further, for at the same time Weizsäcker received instructions from the foreign minister. Stung by Benzler's reproach of insufficient support, Ribbentrop now wanted to contact Himmler to clarify the question "whether he could not take over the 8,000 Jews, in order to move them to east Poland or anywhere else."[139] Luther had his authorization to contact Heydrich, which he used to achieve his aims, not Ribbentrop's.

Luther's meeting with Heydrich must have taken place when Heydrich briefly returned from Prague to Berlin on October 4, for on that same day he informed Benzler of his agreement with Heydrich to send representatives to Belgrade—Rademacher and Suhr.[140] "Purpose of the trip," Rademacher wrote, "was to check on the spot whether the problem of the 8,000 Jewish agitators, whose deportation had been urged by the embassy, could not be settled on the spot."[141] Rademacher and Suhr arrived in Belgrade on October 18, and Rademacher met with Turner the following morning. The latter informed him that the problem of the 8,000 male Jews was already three-quarters solved. Through an unexplained mix-up, it turned out that there had only been about 4,000 male Jews, "of which moreover only 3,500 can be shot" because 500 were needed by the police to maintain the ghetto they were planning to build. Of these 3,500 male Jews, 2,000 had already been shot in reprisal for attacks on German soldiers.

Just as Luther had hoped, the military was eliminating the Jews without even mentioning it. The problem of the remaining 1,500 Jews would have solved itself if Turner had simply turned them over to the army firing squads. Böhme's ratios already required over 4,000 additional reprisal shootings. To the army the problem now was not that there were too many Jews but that there were too few! But one obstacle stood in the way of the quick dispatch of the remaining 1,500 male Jews earmarked for reprisal execution, and this was Turner. He once again saw the chance to press for the deportation of the male Jews and expressed to Rademacher his bitterest disappointment that Benzler's earlier requests had been ignored. Rademacher explained the difficulties of sending the Jews to Romania, Poland, or Russia. "Staatsrat Turner could not close his mind to these reasons. However he urged as before the deportation of the Jews from Serbia."

Unable as yet to overcome Turner's insistence on deportation, Rademacher went on to visit Einsatzgruppe commander Wilhelm Fuchs and his entourage of Jewish experts. They reiterated that the problem of the male Jews could be settled within a week by having them shot as hostages. Already the number of incarcerated Jews did not suffice. On the following morning, October 20, Rademacher, Suhr, Fuchs, and Turner met together. Rademacher and Suhr explained the impossibility of deportation; Fuchs pressed to have the Jews shot within the framework of Böhme's reprisal policy. Faced with this united front, Turner made no objection. Rademacher could thus report: "The male Jews will be shot by the end of the week, so the problem broached in the embassy's report is settled."

As the fate of the remaining male Jews in Serbia was being sealed in Belgrade, events to the south of the capital, in the towns of Kraljevo and Kragujevac, were building to a crisis that would force the Germans to reconsider their reprisal policy. The 717th division of Major General Hoffmann was responsible for this region, and the reprisal order of October 10 was to him a veritable hunting license. When units of his division suffered casualties in an attack on Kraljevo on October 15 and 16, they went on a house-to-house search through the city, and by the evening of the 17th had shot 1,736 men and 19 "communist" women.[142]

The Kraljevo massacre was shortly followed by an even larger one in Kragujevac, when a German punitive expedition returning to the town suffered casualties and Hoffmann ordered immediate retaliation. The number of communist suspects, prison inmates, Jews, and even men rounded up from the surrounding villages considered "communist infested" left the Germans far short of their quota of 2,300. The German commander, Major König, an ardent critic of "soft" measures, had his troops seize 3,200 inhabitants from the city itself, including the students of the local high school, and they fired away on October 21 until the quota had been met.[143]

List and Böhme had reaped the whirlwind sown by their constant incitements to "ruthless" terror. The two massacres in Kraljevo and Kragujevac had immediate repercussions, especially as the entire Serbian workforce of an airplane factory in Kraljevo producing for the German war effort was among the victims. The OKW was dismayed at this incident, and Nedic also urged that the arbitrary shootings be stopped. Böhme agreed, and Bader ordered all units to cease mass executions until further orders.[144] Meanwhile, Faulmüller and Turner hammered out a new reprisal policy, forthcoming on October 25, which stated: "Arbitrary arrests and shootings of Serbs are driving to the insurgents circles of the population which up to now did not participate in the insurrection, [and so] strengthen the communist resistance. . . . It must be avoided that precisely those elements of the population are seized and shot as hostages who, being nonparticipants in the insurrection, did not flee before the German punitive expedition."[145]

If the massacres at Kraljevo and Kragujevac moved Böhme to ensure that further arbitrary shootings of Serbs did not occur, that was of no help to the incarcerated Jews. If the Germans could conceive that not all Serbs were partisans and that random shooting of "innocent" Serbs would damage German interests, they had no doubt that all Jews were anti-German. And if more care had to be exercised in selecting Serbian hostages, the pressure to find hostages elsewhere was that much greater. Harald Turner, who had previously sought to deport the Jews, best exemplified this attitude in a memorandum of October 26. On the one hand he noted that "the belief in the feeling for justice of the German Wehrmacht must be destroyed if not only people who are *completely* innocent are shot to death but—as occurred in one case—just those men of the village were executed who remained at the place of work waiting for German troops because of their confidence in their own innocence." On the other hand he noted: "As a matter of principle it must be said that the Jews and Gypsies in general represent an element of insecurity and thus a danger to public order and safety. . . . That is why it is a matter of principle in each case to put all Jewish men and all male Gypsies at the disposal of the troops as hostages."[146]

The murder of the remaining male Jews in Serbia began on October 27.[147] Two days later 250 additional Gypsies were arrested in Belgrade to swell the hostage pool.[148] The shooting commando of Lieutenant Hans-Dietrich Walther resumed the executions on October 30. Walther noted in his summary report on "the shooting of Jews and Gypsies": "At first my soldiers were not affected. On the second day, however, it became obvious that one or another did not have the nerve to carry out shootings over a long period of time. It is my personal impression that during the shooting one does not have psychological blocks [keine seelischen Hemmungen]. They set in, however, after several days when one reflects about it on evenings alone [wenn man nach Tagen abends in Ruhe darüber nachdenkt]." A week later, after Walther had had some days to reflect, he was ordered to carry out yet a third execution. Afterward he went to his battalion commander and pleaded release from his assignment because his nerves were finished and he dreamed of the shootings at night. The next execution was given to a different company commander.[149]

After the liquidation of the male Jews and "Gypsies" in Serbia, the reprisal quotas were no longer enforced with the earlier severity. Although 11,345 reprisal shootings were carried out in November and an additional 984 in December, this left the Germans far behind in fulfilling their quota.[150] With random reprisals excluded and the supply of Jews and "Gypsies" exhausted, the quotas simply could not be met. When General Bader replaced Böhme on December 5, he had a statistical study of the reprisal program prepared. It concluded that at least 11,164 reprisal shootings had been carried out as of December 5, 1941, although this figure was low, for the compilers admitted not receiving data from all units (including those units which had carried out the Sabac shootings in mid-October). Calculating German casualties, the report concluded that there was a still a shortfall of 20,174 reprisal executions.[151]

On December 22 Bader issued a lowered reprisal quota, stipulating ratios of 50:1 and 25:1 for dead and wounded, respectively. But still to be taken as reprisal prisoners were those who "because of their attitude and behavior were earmarked to atone for German lives, for example, communists captured without weapons, Gypsies, Jews, criminals, and so forth" (auf Grund ihrer Einstellung und ihres Verhaltens zur Sühne für deutsche Menschenleben bestimmt sind, z.B. nicht mit der Waffe betroffene Kommunisten, Zigeuner, Juden, Verbrecher, u. dergl.).[152] Even after the male Jews and "Gypsies" had been murdered, the Germans could not refrain from including them among the groups who, because of their presumed attitude and behavior, could automatically be counted as reprisal prisoners doomed to death. Thus if the Germans did not fulfill their reprisal quota, it was because insufficient numbers of communists could be found, the political cost of randomly killing Serbs was too high, and the supply of "expendable" Jews and "Gypsies" was exhausted. There is absolutely no reason to believe the quota would not have been met if enough Jews and "Gypsies" had been available.

The mass murder of the male Jews in Serbia was not a conscious part of a European-wide Final Solution to the Jewish question. The killing of the male Jews emerged primarily out of local factors related to the partisan war and the army's reprisal policy. The victims, both Jews and "Gypsies," were convenient and expendable groups whose execution would satisfy the required reprisal quotas without producing undesired political repercussions aggravating the antipartisan struggle. Most important, the army did not operate with the avowed aim of exterminating the entire Jewish population, and thus the women, children, and elderly were not killed.

But at the same time, the massacres in Serbia in the fall of 1941 were an anticipation of the Final Solution, for ultimately the Jews were killed because they were Jews.[153] The mass murder was the culmination of a process in which the German authorities had first singled the Jews out for special persecution in the spring of 1941 and subjected them to disproportionate reprisals and internment in the summer. Once partisan resistance drove the Germans to impose upon themselves the obligation to fulfill the maximum reprisal quota, all Serbs were at risk, but the male Jews were doomed. The German military could conceive of innocent Serbs but not of innocent Jews, hence the totality of the destruction of Jewish men.

Even if local in its origins, this first systematic mass murder of Jews outside Soviet territory had wider implications concerning German preparedness for the Final Solution. Not only on the eastern front but also elsewhere in Europe, the German military viewed the Jews as part of the wider "enemy" against whom "ruthless" measures—including mass murder—were justified. The German Foreign Office, perhaps the elite of the ministerial bureaucracy, proved itself equally accommodating to mass murder. Without orders from above (Ribbentrop had in fact authorized Luther to inquire about deportation), Luther moved on his own initiative to reach an agreement with Heydrich on a "local solution" to the troublesome Jewish problem in Serbia. Such initiative from below obviated the necessity for orders from above in harnessing the Foreign Office to the mass murder of European Jewry. In sending Rademacher and Suhr, Heydrich and Luther together sought to push the German authorities in Serbia into shooting the Jews on the spot. They discovered that they were pushing on an open door, since the executions were already underway by the time the Berlin emissaries arrived. Thus a commonality of interests had emerged between the Wehrmacht, ss, and Foreign Office to kill the male Jews of Serbia even before the Final Solution to murder all the Jews of Europe was in operation. It is no wonder that, when instituted, the European-wide murder program would meet no meaningful resistance from any organized segment of German society.

Eastern Galicia

In Serbia Jews were killed simply because they were Jews. However, the killing was limited to adult males and took place within a framework of large-scale reprisal shootings, not as a conscious first step toward the comprehensive murder of the entire Jewish population. At that time in Serbia it was still expected that the surviving Jewish women, children, and elderly would be expelled eastward. In one other region of Europe to the west of Rosenberg's Occupied Eastern Territories, Eastern Galicia, the mass shooting of Jews also occurred in the fall of 1941. Here too the killing owed a great deal not only to encouragement and approval from above but also to local consensus and initiative. In Eastern Galicia, however, the killing not only reached even greater dimensions than in Serbia but also was more clearly perceived as the first step toward the liquidation of the entire Jewish population.

Eastern Galicia, part of the Austro-Hungarian Empire until 1918 and then Poland until 1939, fell to Stalin in the Nazi-Soviet Non-Aggression Pact. German occupation replaced Soviet occupation in June and July 1941, and approximately half a million Jews—about 10% of the population—came under Nazi control.[154] The capital, Lwow, with 150,000–160,000 Jews at the time of the invasion,[155] became the third largest Jewish community in the Nazi empire after Warsaw and Lodz. On August 1 this region was joined to the General Government of Hans Frank and designated as the district of Galicia.

When the Soviet armies were driven from Eastern Galicia, the Jews there suffered a double blow. First, the native population—predominately Ukrainian—unleashed pogroms against the Jewish communities in Lwow, Tarnopol, and elsewhere. These were often encouraged and always tolerated by the German authorities.[156] Second, Einsatzgruppe C swept through on its way to the Ukraine, and was quickly followed by another ad hoc Einsatzgruppe assembled by Schöngarth from the KdS Dienststellen of Cracow (150 men), Warsaw (50 men), and Lublin (30 men).[157] Both Einsatzgruppen carried out mass executions, aimed above all at the Jewish intelligentsia.[158] As with the Einsatzgruppen in Poland in the fall of 1939, various units of Schöngarth's Einsatzgruppe became stationary, forming the nuclei of the branch offices or Aussendienststellen of the KdS in Lwow under Obersturmbannführer Dr. Herbert Tanzmann. The crucial components of this network were the KdS Aussendienststellen in Tarnopol, Stanislawow, Czortkow, Kolomyja, and Drohobycz, from which most of the local massacres and deportations of Galician Jews would be directed. As in the other districts of the General Government, an SSPF was also appointed, in this case 35-year-old Friedrich Katzmann, who was transferred from Radom.[159]

Following the pogroms and Einsatzgruppen massacres in the summer of

1941, a partial abatement in the murder of Galician Jews set in until the fall. (The major exception was the murder of 1,000 Jews from Stryj on September 1.)[160] Nazi Jewish policy in Galicia was then intensified with the initiation of three programs: the creation of a network of forced labor camps, ghettoization, and a new wave of mass executions.

Ghettoization in Galicia, as earlier in the other districts of the General Government, was more haphazard than systematic. As of late October there was still a general prohibition against constructing more ghettos in the General Government, "because it is hoped that the Jews can be deported out of the General Government in the near future."[161] Nonetheless, in September 1941 the Krieshauptmann in Tarnopol, Gerhard Hager, had ordered the establishment of a ghetto in that city. Implementation of the population transfers was put in the hands of his Judenreferent, none other than Alexander Palfinger, the erstwhile advocate of deliberate attrition in the Lodz and Warsaw ghettos. Permission then seems to have been obtained from Cracow to construct ghettos in Stanislawow and eventually Lwow as well.[162] The process of ghettoizing 12,000 Jews in Tarnopol apparently went slowly, and the ghetto was closed only in early December.[163]

According to Dieter Pohl, "It is no accident that the massacres took place almost simultaneously with the first ghettoizations."[164] In Stanislawow, with a Jewish population of at least 27,500 and possibly over 40,000, the local German authorities (Kreishauptmann Heinz Albrecht and Stadtkommissar Emil Beau) pressed for ghettoization. However, the space they were willing to grant for the envisaged ghetto amounted to only one-sixth of the town's area for over half the town's population.[165] The task of reducing the Jewish population sufficiently to make ghettoization possible lay in the hands of the chief of the Stanislawow Security Police, Hans Krüger.[166]

Krüger had arrived in Galicia with Schöngarth's Einsatzgruppe. Along with 20–30 other officials slated for assignment in the branch offices, he attended a special "model shooting" (Mustererschiessung) put on by Schöngarth in Lwow. He was then dispatched to Stanislawow, where on August 8 he had carried out the execution of some 300 Jewish and 200 Polish intellectuals and professionals. In late September or early October, Katzmann held a meeting in Lwow with Krüger and Tanzmann. According to Krüger's postwar testimony, Katzmann announced that Himmler had ordered large-scale actions and thus the liquidation of the Galician Jews was now to begin. But Krüger also admitted that the first large-scale massacre that he would subsequently carry out had a more specific and immediate goal. "It was not actually intended to make Stanislawow 'free of Jews' in one day. It was much more a matter of decimating the Jews, in order to be able to construct a ghetto in Stanislawow."[167]

In preparation or training for such a large-scale execution–what would be the largest massacre yet carried out by the Nazis in Galicia—Krüger took a team of Security Police, Ukrainian militiamen, and Order Police of Reserve Police Battalion 133 to nearby Nadworna on October 6, 1941, and shot 2,000 Jews.[168] Only nightfall brought a halt to the shooting. Krüger discussed the Nadworna execution with Katzmann, who then ordered a decimation of the Stanislawow Jews, with the remainder to be ghettoized.

Once again mobilizing the local Schupo with its Ukrainian militia, as well as Reserve Police Battalion 133, Krüger carried out the "Bloody Sunday" massacre of Stanislawow Jews on October 12, 1941. The Jews were ordered to assemble, taking their valuables with them. From the Ringplatz, columns of 200–250 Jews at a time were marched to the Jewish cemetery, where Schupo commander Captain Streege had supervised the digging of graves by his Ukrainian militia. The Jews were taken through the cemetery gate, where they were forced to surrender their valuables and undress. They were then led to one of the graves and shot by rotating firing squads. The shooting began at noon. At nightfall Krüger attempted to continue the shooting under the headlights of trucks but finally gave up and allowed the remaining Jews to return to the newly formed ghetto. At least 10,000 Jews were killed on "Bloody Sunday."[169]

But ghetto building in Stanislawow was not the only reason behind Krüger's "Bloody Sunday." The Nadworna and Stanislawow massacres were only the first in a series of large-scale massacres carried out in the southern region of Galicia in the fall of 1941. Just four days after "Bloody Sunday," policemen from the border police post (Grenzpolizei-Posten or GPP) at Tatarow under Krüger's subordinate Ernst Varchim, along with the 3rd company of Reserve Police Battalion 133, which had assisted the "Bloody Sunday" massacre, and a unit of the ubiquitous Ukrainian Hilfspolizei (Hipo or auxiliary police), descended upon Delatyn and shot 1,950 Jews.[170] Varchim's police also carried out several smaller massacres over the next several months to clear his border area of Jews.[171] The Stanislawow Security Police were also at least suspected of having carried out the shooting of 1,000 Jews in Brzezany on December 12, 1941.[172]

Krüger's chief rival for large-scale massacres in Galicia in the fall of 1941 was the Security Police Aussendienststelle at Kolomyja under Obersturmführer Peter Leideritz and his deputy Erwin Gay. Founded in September 1941, it was composed of some 25 German officials and a guard force of 20 ethnic Germans and Ukrainians. Also stationed in Kolomyja was a Schutzpolizei-

Dienstabteilung of Obersturmführer Herbert Härtel, with 25 police officials and 100 Ukrainian militia men.[173]

On October 12, the same day as the events in Stanislawow, Leideritz's men killed several thousand Jews in Kolomyja.[174] Three days later, Leideritz sent Gay to the town of Kossow, some 20 miles from Kolomyja, with instructions to shoot as many Jews as possible. Order Police from Reserve Police Battalion 133 were loaned from Stanislawow, and with their help over 2,000 Jews in Kossow were shot on October 16–17.[175] Following the killing of an additional 800 Jews in Kolomyja itself on November 6,[176] the murderous efforts of Lederitz and his men peaked in December. On December 4–5 Lederitz himself led a commando to Horodenko, where the Kreishauptmann had assembled the Jewish population of 4,000 under the pretext of receiving typhus inoculations. Leideritz conducted the selection, exempting workers and doctors. The remaining 2,600 Jews were shot.[177] Finally, on December 19 and 26, Kolomyja Sipo units orchestrated massacres of 600 and 1,000 Jews in Zabie and Zablatow, respectively.[178]

While Krüger and Leideritz conducted large-scale massacres in the southern areas of the district of Galicia, numerous smaller killings—often aimed at sick and elderly Jews or the intelligentsia—were carried out by the Security Police Aussendienststellen of Tarnopol under Edmund Schöne, of Drohobycz under Franz Wenzel, and of Czortkow under Karl Hildemann.[179] At the end of the year, Tanzmann temporarily suspended the shooting actions.[180]

In addition to gaining approval for the construction of ghettos in Tarnopol and Stanislawow in the fall of 1941, the German occupiers in Galicia also pressed for the ghettoization of the largest Galician Jewish community in the district capital of Lwow. They cited the proverbial shortage of housing and the cultural status of the city, as well as the anomaly that the Jews of Lwow were being treated differently from those of Cracow and Warsaw. An exception to the official policy of the General Government against further ghetto building was once again granted. On November 6, the governor, Dr. Karl Lasch, entrusted sspf Katzmann with transferring some 80,000 Lwow Jews into the Zamarstynow and Kleperow districts, where some 25,000 Jews already lived. The population transfer, ordered on November 8, was to take place between November 12 and December 15.[181] As in Stanislawow, ghettoization was combined with decimation. Access to the ghetto was limited to passage under two railway bridges, where German and Ukrainian policemen seized valuables from the incoming Jews and conducted a selection. As Katzmann later wrote, as the Jews passed through his "sluices" (*Schleusen*), "all the shirking and asocial Jewish rabble were seized and subjected to special treatment" (*das gesamte arbeitsscheue und asoziale jüd. Gesindel erfasst und sonderbehandelt wurde*).[182] Many thousands of Jews were killed in the so-called bridge of death Aktion, and unlike the so-called Intelligenz-Aktion the previous summer, women were for the first time the primary victims.[183] Many thousands of other Jews must also have fled or gone underground, for the Judenrat of Lwow reported a drop in the Jewish population between October and December from 119,000 to 106,000.[184]

Shortly before the December deadline to close the ghetto, with 20,000 Jews still on the "Aryan" side and spotted fever breaking out and threatening to spread through the city, the Germans broke off the ghettoization process they had set in motion. Katzmann, who was in charge of the resettlement, later wrote in his summary report: "It became increasingly apparent that the civil administration was unable even to approach a satisfactory solution to the Jewish question. Because the repeated attempts of the city administration of Lwow, for example, to lodge the Jews in a sealed Jewish quarter failed, this question was also solved by the SSPF in short order. . . . These measures were all the more urgent because large centers of epidemic appeared everywhere in the city in the winter months of 1941."[185] Dieter Pohl, the German historian of the Final Solution in Eastern Galicia, has observed: "Here is demonstrated once again what a grotesque distortion of facts Katzmann submitted to the SS hierarchy in 1943. He himself had been entrusted with the formation of the ghetto in 1941, and this was stopped precisely because it led to a spread of epidemic."[186]

By the end of 1941, therefore, although few Galician Jews were as yet ghettoized, they were no strangers to mass murder. By one estimate, at least 30,000 Galician Jews had been killed in the fall of 1941, and total loss of Jewish life since the German invasion had reached 55,000–65,000.[187] If the dimensions of the unfolding tragedy in Galicia seem clear, the light that these events shed on the overall evolution of Nazi Jewish policy is less so. It is particularly unclear who was primarily responsible for initiating the wave of killing. After the war, the most incriminated executioner from the fall of 1941, Hans Krüger, head of the Stanislawow Security Police, testified in various interrogations to orders from both Katzmann and Tanzmann that in turn allegedly came from Himmler and the RSHA.[188] Katzmann himself, in his self-congratulatory summary report of 1943, boasted that he had seen the solution of the Jewish question as his "most urgent task."[189] But Krüger's testimony was self-exculpatory. And strangely for a man seeking to maximize his own achievements, Katzmann's own report did not even mention the fall 1941 massacres and began its account of "resettlement" in Galicia in April 1942. The two leading scholars on the topic, Dieter Pohl and Thomas Sandkühler, suggest that local authorities, particularly leading figures in the Security Police, played a particularly significant role in initiating the mass killings of fall 1941.[190] Given the consistent use of combined police forces (Sipo, Order Police battalions, Schupo, border police, and Ukrainian militia), Katzmann was clearly deeply involved. It was precisely the coordination of such combined police forces that was, after all, the principal task of the SSPF.

Whatever the relative balance of orders from above and initiative from below, two factors seem clear. On the one hand, the ghettoization and shootings of the fall of 1941 in Galicia were not a uniform policy for the entire district. Ghettoization was limited to special cases—Tarnopol, Stanislawow, and Lwow—for which special exemption to the general prohibition against further ghetto building in the General Government was obtained by district officials. The large-scale massacres were concentrated in the southern region of the district and were carried out above all by just two of the Security Police branch offices—Stanislawow and Kolomyja. In the early massacres the victims seem to have been chosen randomly for the purpose of reducing the overall population. Only later—especially in Horodenko and Lwow—did a consistent pattern of selection, targeting the weak and exempting potential workers, emerge. Large-scale massacres confined to one region of the district, with a shifting pattern of targeting, do not suggest that a comprehensive policy to liquidate all the Jews of Galicia was already underway.

On the other hand, by the fall of 1941 local officials in Galicia did not seem to be in any doubt about the eventual fate awaiting all Jews there. They could relieve their security concerns along the southern border and the housing shortage, as well as potentially overcrowded ghettos, by killing large numbers of Jews. And they could do so knowing that such killings would not only meet with approval from Berlin but constituted the first step in a program of mass murder that they were going to carry out eventually in any case. They were anticipating the future even more consciously than the executioners in Serbia.

INVENTING THE EXTERMINATION CAMP

The "war of destruction" on the eastern front had unleashed an onslaught against Soviet Jewry through the primitive firing-squad methods of the Einsatzgruppen and their many helpers. With the increased targeting of Jewish women and children in August, the crucial step to systematic mass murder had been taken. The enticing prospect of vast spaces in conquered Soviet territory had brought forth a groundswell of pressure from occupation authorities throughout the German empire to commence the long-stalled expulsion of European Jewry. Hitler had initially rejected such deportations until "after the war." Then in mid-September he approved them, at least for Jews from the territories of the Third Reich, before the end of the year. The un-prepared and distressed recipients of these deportations complained vocifer-ously, as did those who were not yet allowed to rid themselves of their unwanted Jews. In several places exhortations to the mass murder of European Jewry anticipated the Final Solution, and in Serbia and Galicia anticipation passed from words to deeds.

Yet another set of developments must be taken into account to complete the picture of the crucial and complex events between August and October 1941—namely, attempts to solve the unprecedented problems posed by the possible extension of systematic mass murder to the European Jews. Just as the Nazi regime was making the transition from selective to total mass murder of Soviet Jewry in mid-summer 1941, Hitler apparently gave the signal (this is admittedly speculative) that some kind of mass murder program should also be prepared for European Jewry for implementation after the Russian campaign. In any case, Heydrich had procured Göring's authorization on July 31 to draft and submit a plan for a "total solution" to the European Jewish question. Given that Hey-drich had been in charge of Jewish emigration and expulsion since January 1939 and that he had already submitted to Göring a plan for the total "resettlement" of European Jewry into the Soviet Union in March 1941, a new authorization for yet another kind of plan would indicate that something new and different was now expected.[191] What Heydrich had procured from Göring was, in effect, authorization to prepare a "feasibility study" for perpetrating mass murder on an unprecedented scale.

But events on Soviet territory had demonstrated that many problems had to be solved. The staggering logistical task of killing even the Soviet Jews by firing squad had required the mobilization of considerable manpower, and the awe-some task had just begun. Two other difficulties also emerged. One was the psychological burden on the killers. As HSSPF Bach-Zelewski claimed to have told a shaken Himmler after the latter had witnessed a relatively small execution in Minsk: "Look at the eyes of the men in this commando, how deeply shaken they are! These men are finished for the rest of their lives. What kind of followers are we training here? Either neurotics or savages!"[192] And finally, the mass executions in Russia were simply much too public. Knowledge of the massacres became widespread among the German troops.[193] They in turn took pictures, wrote home, and spoke to family and friends on leave. Word of the massacres on the Russian front filtered through German society. Given the shortcomings for firing-squad methods on Soviet territory, where proximity to the battlefield and the cover of antipartisan actions helped to mitigate the most serious repercussions, clearly different methods—more efficient, detached, and secret—were needed to extend the killing process to the rest of Europe in what was still envisaged as the postwar period.

By October Nazi innovators had conceptualized one potential, though as yet untried, solution to their problems: the *Vernichtungslager* or extermination camp. Basically, the planners brought together elements of three programs they were already experienced with. The concentration camp setting—in existence since 1933 and expanding rapidly since the outbreak of the war—provided secrecy, especially in eastern Europe far from prewar German boundaries. The gassing technology of the euthanasia program provided a killing method of much greater efficiency and psychological detachment. And finally, the factories of death were to be fed their endless streams of victims by a program of massive uprooting and deportation that would utilize the experiences and personnel— in particular, the HSSPF and Eichmann's RSHA office for "Jewish affairs and evacuations"—of the earlier population resettlement programs.

The actions of these innovators in August and September are difficult to trace in detail. Their actions were not centralized, and they did not leave the kind of paper trail that characterized either the voluminous and wordy protests of German officials in Lodz and Riga or the eager, even impatient, suggestions of Höppner in Poznan and Zeitschel in Paris. Nevertheless, the idea of using poison gas for mass killing beyond the euthanasia program was clearly widespread in the late summer of 1941 and led to local experimentation. By September and October gassing as one possible method for the mass murder of Jews was an idea waiting to be institutionalized.

The first written proposal in this regard seems to have been Rolf Heinz Höppner's letter to "dear comrade Eichmann" of July 16, urging the use of a "quick-acting agent" as the "most humane solution to dispose" of the nonworking Jews of Lodz.[194] The killers on the central Russian front, HSSPF Bach-Zelewski and Einsatzgruppe B commander Arthur Nebe, were not far behind. In early August, Nebe requested a chemist of the Criminal Technical Institute (KTI) to come to Smolensk.[195] On August 16 and 18, just after Himmler's visit to Minsk, Bach-Zelewski asked HSSPF Koppe of the Warthegau to send his itinerant euthanasia killer, Herbert Lange, from Poznan.[196] Lange's Sonderkommando in Poznan had considerable experience in killing mental patients inside a sealed van using bottled carbon monoxide.[197] According to Bach-Zelewski's postwar testimony, another initiative had come from Himmler, who after witnessing the execution in Minsk on August 15 had asked Nebe to consider other killing methods. In response Nebe allegedly suggested the testing of explosives.[198]

There is no evidence that Lange ever visited, but a chemist from the KTI, Dr. Albert Widmann, along with an explosives expert, did visit Nebe and Bach-

Zelewski in Minsk and Mogilev in mid-September 1941.[199] The crime lab chemist Widmann had in fact already conducted experiments in the fall of 1939 and had advised the euthanasia program to use bottled carbon monoxide for its killing operations. Within the KTI, its director Dr. Walter Heess had already mentioned to Widmann, while riding home from work on the underground, that Nebe had suggested the possibility of using engine exhaust instead of bottled gas. The suggestion had been occasioned by Nebe's close brush with death when, returning home from a party after drinking heavily, he had fallen asleep in his garage with the car motor running. Both this earlier Nebe suggestion and his early August request even before Himmler's visit to Minsk would suggest that it was Nebe who initiated the subsequent exhaust gas experiment, but as of mid-August he did so with the knowledge, approval, and encouragement of Himmler.

In any case, a test using explosives on mental patients from the Novinki asylum near Minsk proved most unsatisfactory. The gruesome experiment required two explosions to kill all the test victims locked in a bunker and left parts of bodies strewn about and even hanging from nearby trees. Two gassing tests, one on mental patients from the Novinki asylum and the other in Mogilev, were more successful. The victims were killed in sealed rooms by introducing exhaust gas through hoses from a car and truck parked outside.

The Minsk-Mogilev experiments in killing with exhaust gas did not remain a local experiment for local purposes. In Berlin, Reinhard Heydrich immediately turned to the head of his office for technical affairs within the RSHA (Amt II D), Walter Rauff. Rauff's jurisdiction included all motor vehicles— some 4,000 thousand—of the Security Police. The chief of this motor pool was Friedrich Pradel, who had already organized transportation for the Einsatzgruppen when they were training at Pretzsch. His chief mechanic in the Security Police garage on Prinz Albrecht Strasse was Harry Wentritt. Sometime in September Rauff summoned Pradel to his office and instructed him to ask his chief mechanic if exhaust gas could be directed into a closed truck to kill the passengers. A "more humane method of execution" was needed for the Einsatzgruppen in Russia, Rauff noted.[200] Pradel put the question to Wentritt, likewise explaining that the firing squads in Russia suffered frequent nervous breakdowns and needed a "more humane" method of killing. Pradel informed him that the work would have to be done in Wentritt's garage. Wentritt later claimed that he asked Pradel if there was a way out of having to do this, but Pradel told him—"in a friendly tone"—to think of his wife and children.[201] Rauff then instructed Pradel to consult with Dr. Heess of the KTI on how the proposed gas van should function. After some difficulty, Rauff himself procured five Saurer model truck chassis.[202] Pradel and Wentritt visited the body-making firm of Gaubschat in Berlin and subcontracted them to construct airtight compartments on the RSHA truck chassis. When work on the first chassis was finished, Wentritt brought the converted Saurer, which now looked like a furniture van, to his garage. He inserted a T-joint in the exhaust pipe and bored a two-inch hole in the floor of the rear compartment. A perforated U-shaped pipe was welded on the inside and a nozzle on the outside of the hole. When the T-joint and the nozzle were joined by a pipe and the regular exhaust pipe was capped, exhaust gas was diverted into the rear compartment.[203]

Wentritt drove the prototype to the courtyard of the KTI, where Widmann summoned his young chemists and explained that through adjusting the timing of the ignition, one could maximize the amount of poisonous carbon monoxide in the exhaust. One of his men then donned a gas mask and conducted a measurement of the carbon monoxide that could be produced within the sealed compartment. With this truck, Widmann explained, the firing squads on the eastern front would be spared. Some days later, probably in late October or early November,[204] Dr. Heess drove two of the young chemists who had been present at the recent KTI carbon monoxide measurement to the concentration camp at Sachsenhausen. There they found the gas van amid a group of about thirty SS officers. Forty naked Russians were led from a nearby barracks and locked in the truck, which drove to the crematorium in another part of the camp. After twenty minutes the doors were opened, and the bodies pressed against the doors tumbled out. The pink color of the corpses indicated that death had been caused by poisoning, not suffocation.[205] Firma Gaubschat was thereupon contracted for a total of thirty conversions.[206]

The initiative that led to the development and construction of the gas van may have come from Nebe, and the initial intention may have been to facilitate the Einsatzgruppen killing operations on Soviet territory. Nonetheless, by the time the prototype gas van had been constructed and tested in Berlin under Heydrich's auspices, it was available as one potential solution to SS planners pondering the means for killing the European Jews. Moreover, Heydrich's vans were in fact only one of three different gassing technologies being tested and developed in September and October of 1941. A second involved the testing of Zyklon B in Auschwitz, while the third involved preparations to transfer the technology and personnel of carbon-monoxide gassing (using the newly tested engine exhaust, however, rather than bottled gas) from the euthanasia institutes in Germany to stationary gas chambers in Poland.

According to Auschwitz commandant Rudolf Höss's partially contradictory testimony,[207] either two or three gassing tests took place in Auschwitz in late summer 1941. In one account his assistant Fritzsch used a powerful chemical fumigant, Zyklon B, to gas Russian prisoners of war in the basement cells of Bunker 11, and somewhat later he was present at a test using the crematory of Auschwitz I, after the doors had been made airtight and holes had been punched in the ceiling through which the Zyklon B could be poured.[208] In Höss's second account, Fritzsch conducted a small test in Bunker 11, and then Höss was present at a second, large-scale test in Bunker 11. On this occasion Höss wore a gas mask for protection. Then a third test, with Höss also present, was conducted "soon afterward" in the "old crematory."[209] September 3, 1941, has been reasonably suggested as the date for the large-scale test in Bunker 11. One room in the "old crematory" in the Auschwitz *Stammlager* (Auschwitz I) was then converted into a gas chamber and first tested on September 16.[210] Several further gassings with Zyklon B were conducted later in the year on small contingents of Jews trucked into the camp.[211] These were apparently Jews from the nearby Organisation Schmelt camps, where now for the first time, in the fall of 1941, Jews no longer capable of work were regularly selected and sent to their death in Auschwitz.[212]

As in the case of Nebe's August initiative that led to the Widmann tests, the Zyklon B experiments in Auschwitz were not initially envisaged as part of a search for the means to kill the European Jews, Höss's postwar testimony notwithstanding. Rather, as Robert Jan van Pelt and Karin Orth have persuasively demonstrated, the experimental gassing of the Soviet POWs was part of the extension of euthanasia killing into the concentration camps, known as Aktion 14f13. As part of this program, in late July 575 sick prisoners had been sent from Auschwitz to the euthanasia center at Sonnenstein and gassed. With the closing of the euthanasia centers and the arrival of large numbers of Soviet POWs in August, the Auschwitz camp commanders then experimented with methods to carry out such killings on the spot.[213] But once the old crematory in the Auschwitz *Stammlager* was periodically used for the killing of Jews selected in the Organisation Schmelt camps, the potential of crematories as dual-purpose buildings was an idea that took on a life of its own.

On October 1, 1941, Karl Bischoff was put in charge of Auschwitz construction, with a mandate to design a second large camp at Birkenau for an anticipated 100,000 Soviet prisoners of war. He quickly realized that the existing cremation capacity at Auschwitz would be entirely inadequate and summoned Kurt Prüfer of Topf and Sons, the firm with which the SS had contracted for crematoria at other concentration camps. Meeting on October 21 and 22, 1941, Prüfer and Bischoff designed and contracted for a new crematory of vastly increased capacity, with five three-muffle furnaces, to be located in the *Stammlager*.[214]

Two features of the new crematory's design support the commonsense proposition that the ss engineers and architects were not designing a new crematory that would be less versatile and less capable of being used as a gas chamber than the old one already in dual use. First, the smaller of two underground cellar rooms in the new crematory, in contrast to the rest of the building, was to have an additional forced air ventilation system—one that extracted old air and another that introduced fresh air.[215] Second, the ventilation ducts for this particular cellar, but again in no other parts of the building, were recessed into the wall and covered with concrete. Such a design was both unusual and considerably more expensive. Michael Thad Allen has concluded that "the massively built masonry and concrete ductwork for Morgue 1 would seem to have only one explanation: the ss did not want to take any chances that its victims, in the throes of death and gasping for air, would kick in or pull down fragile tin ducts."[216] Since the special design for the recessed ducts was already present in the refined design drawings of January 1942, the idea of recessed ducts must have already emerged in the fall of 1941 in close conjunction with the idea for the extra feature of the forced air ventilation system.[217] The design of a single new crematory in the *Stammlager* to serve also as a gas chamber was simply an improvement on the existing facilities at Auschwitz, to facilitate existing practices, and does not yet suggest the camp's future role in the Final Solution. But it does indicate how widespread the idea of gassing had become in the fall of 1941.

The third chain of developments was centered in Lublin. Events here can be seen from two perspectives, that of the German occupiers in Poland and that of officials in Berlin. First the perspective from the General Government.

Frank, following his mid-March 1941 meetings with Hitler, was still taking a long-term view. Although the General Government was to become free of Jews "within a reasonable space of time" (*in absehbarer Zeit*), economic decisions relating to the Warsaw ghetto were made in the context of maintaining the ghetto for up to five years. Making the General Government as purely German as the Rhineland was seen as a project that would extend over several decades.[218] As with so many other plans, Frank's timetable shortened under the impact of Germany's initial military success against the Soviet Union. On July 17, 1941, Frank cited Hitler's renewed assurance that "within a reasonable space of time" the Jews would be removed from the General Government, which would thus henceforth serve only as a "kind of transit camp" (*gewissermassen Durchgangs-*

lager.)²¹⁹ Just two days later, Frank proposed to Lammers that the Pripet marshes be added to the General Government, because that currently worthless territory could be made valuable through the productive labor of certain "elements of the population (above all things Jewish)" (*Bevölkerungselemente [vor allen Dingen jüdisch]*).²²⁰ And on July 21 Frank was discussing "the imminent clearing" (*die kommende Räumung*) of the Warsaw ghetto with his chief of public health, Dr. Jost Walbaum.²²¹ At virtually the same moment, Himmler visited SSPF Globocnik in Lublin on July 20, 1941. Globocnik received instructions to build a large concentration camp (Majdanek) and to prepare for German settlement in the Lublin district (particularly the Zamosc region) and the construction of SS and police strongholds further east.²²²

Just as the expectations of quick military victory over the Soviet Union were thwarted, so expectations in the General Government of an "imminent clearing" of the Warsaw ghetto and expulsion of Jews eastward to areas like the Pripet marshes proved futile. The pre-Barbarossa plans to increase the rations of Jewish workers in the ghettos were likewise unrealized. And Globocnik's "Germanization" plans remained on the drawing board. From the local perspective, the bottleneck blocking a solution to these problems was broken by a series of developments in October 1941.²²³ On October 1 Globocnik wrote to Himmler: "Reichsführer! In implementation of your intentions for the Germanization of the district, yesterday I turned over the prepared documentation to Obergruppenführer Krüger and intended that Obergruppenführer Krüger immediately submit these documents to you, Reichsführer." (*Reichsführer! Im Vollzug Ihrer Absichten in der Verdeutschung des Distriktes habe ich gestern Obergruppenführer Krüger die ausgearbeiteten Unterlagen übergeben und wollte SS-Obergruppenführer Krüger diese Unterlagen Ihnen, Reichsführer, sogleich zur Vorlage bringen.*) Globocnik indicated that Krüger shared his sense of urgency because the situation of the Volksdeutsche in the General Government was deteriorating. He also noted that a "consolidation" (*Zusammensiedlung*) of the ethnic Germans was tied to a "removal" (*Entsiedlung*) of the alien populations. Krüger had therefore ordered Globocnik to request an immediate meeting with Himmler.²²⁴

For two hours on the evening of October 13, Globocnik and Krüger met with Himmler.²²⁵ The content of that meeting is not recorded, but two days later Hauptsturmführer Hellmut Müller summarized Globocnik's views. He considered "a general clearing of the entire GG of Jews and also Poles as necessary for the security of the eastern territory. . . . He is full of far-reaching and good plans in this regard" (*die allmähliche Säuberung des gesamten GG. von Juden und auch Polen zwecks Sicherung der Ostgebiete usw. für notwendig. . . . Er steckt in diesem*

Zusammenhang voller weitgehender und guter Pläne).[226] Among the many far-reaching plans proposed by Globocnik that found Himmler's immediate approval, both Dieter Pohl and Bogdan Musial agree, must have been one for the creation of a camp with gas chambers at Belzec. Polish workers at that site began construction work just two weeks later on November 1, 1941.[227]

The notion of killing Jews in the General Government struck a responsive cord among Frank's men, who felt beleaguered on a number of fronts at this moment. On October 13, 1941, the same day as the Himmler-Krüger-Globocnik meeting, Frank had approached Rosenberg about "the possibility of deporting the Jewish population of the General Government into the occupied eastern territories." "For the moment," however, Rosenberg saw "no possibility for the carrying out of such resettlement plans."[228] Two days later, on October 15, Frank began a series of meetings with district authorities in the General Government. The first such meeting was in Warsaw, where the district governor Fischer and the ghetto administrators Auerswald and Bischof gave discouraging reports on the state of the Warsaw ghetto with particular emphasis on the food shortage and looming threat of epidemic.[229] Frank responded by refusing any increase in rations, since "even for the Polish population . . . hardly anything more can be provided."[230] At the same time he agreed to the death penalty for all Jews caught leaving the ghetto.[231] (It was also at this time that Dr. Jost Walbaum addressed a meeting of 100 public health, ss, and military doctors in Bad Krynica, and his statement that "we sentence the Jews in the ghetto to death by hunger or we shoot them" was greeted with stormy applause.)[232]

Continuing his tour of the district capitals, Frank was in Lublin on October 17. Globocnik was back from his Berlin meeting with Himmler and also present in Lublin. Frank and Globocnik clearly conferred, for a few days later, on October 25, Globocnik reported to Himmler on his conversations with Frank at this time.[233] In Lublin as earlier in Warsaw the local authorities pressed for the death penalty for Jews caught outside the ghettos, and the Stadthauptmann of Lublin, Fritz Sauermann, added, "Naturally a clarification of the Jewish question will finally be achieved only when a total deportation of all Jews can be accomplished." Local officials were informed of the forthcoming edict decreeing the death penalty for Jews caught outside the ghettos without authorization.[234] But they also learned of a yet further development. "The Jews—with the exception of indispensable artisans and the like—will be evacuated from Lublin. To begin with, 1,000 Jews will be sent over the Bug River [*über den Bug überstellt werden*]. The ss and Polizeiführer [Globocnik] will be in charge of the implementation. The selection of the Jews to be evacuated will be made by the Stadthauptmann [Sauermann]." To this revelation, Frank personally added the additional news: "In the near future, on the basis of a special assignment of the Führer, I will have much to do here and will thus have the good fortune to appear frequently in Lublin."[235]

In sum, from his October 17 visit to Lublin and meeting with Globocnik, Frank had learned that Hitler had approved clearing the Lublin district of all Jews except indispensable workers, and clearly assumed that he and his civil administration would have a central role to play. Moreover, Frank obviously realized that the alleged deportation over the Bug was a euphemism for killing, since he had no intention of deporting Jews into the district of Galicia and he knew that deportations to Rosenberg's territories were foreclosed. Moreover, he either knew or at least hoped that the looming evacuation of Jews would not be limited to the Lublin district. Four days later, when Frank was in Lwow, the prohibition against further ghetto building was repeated, "because the hope exists, that *in the near future* [italics mine] the Jews can be deported out of the General Government" (*da die Hoffnung besteht, dass die Juden in naher Zukunft aus dem Generalgouvernement abgeschoben werden könnten*).[236] Frank immediately followed his visit to Lwow with a festive reception in Stanislawow on October 22, where just ten days earlier the "Bloody Sunday" massacre had inaugurated the wave of mass executions in the district of Galicia that would continue into December.[237]

Seen from the perspective of the General Government, it is tempting to conclude that the impetus for Hitler and Himmler's approval of a plan for the "evacuation" of Polish Jews and the construction of the Belzec extermination camp was triggered by Globocnik's initiative on October 1 and welcomed by local officials because of the multifaceted crisis facing the General Government. From this point of view, the October developments in the General Government are to be seen as "a kind of special program" arising from local circumstances, motives, and initiatives, quite apart from and preceding any wider decision to kill all the Jews of Europe.[238] But the course of events in September and October must also be traced through the perspective of the center.

In mid-September Hitler had reversed his earlier position of deferring the deportation of Jews from the Third Reich until "after the war" and authorized Himmler to commence with their immediate deportation to temporary internment in Lodz, Riga, and Minsk, with subsequent deportation "further east" the following spring. Did this decision also constitute an answer to the question posed by Rolf-Heinz Höppner concerning the fate of the deportees, "Is it the goal to ensure them a certain level of life in the long run, or shall they be totally eradicated"? Was this deportation program still envisaged within the framework of earlier expulsion plans, or did it represent the Nazi regime's fundamental watershed after which all subsequent decisions were taken and plans were made with the expectation and goal of total eradication? There is a strong convergence of evidence and higher probability for the latter interpretation.

On September 2, 1941, Himmler met with HSSPF Krüger of the General Government and discussed the "Jewish question—resettlement from the Reich."[239] Two days later, Himmler met with the HSSPF of the Warthegau, Wilhelm Koppe, and apparently discussed the possibility of sending 60,000 Reich Jews to Lodz.[240] While Himmler was launching the search for reception areas for deported Reich Jews, the highest officials of the euthanasia program were also becoming active on a new front. On August 24 Hitler had suspended the adult euthanasia program in Germany. Sometime in September, Bouhler and Viktor Brack, the men in the Führer Chancellery in charge of euthanasia, visited Globocnik in Lublin.[241] Back in Berlin, employees of the deactivated euthanasia program sat in the canteen and talked about the transfer of people to Lublin, including the subsequent head of Globocnik's extermination camps in the General Government, Christian Wirth. "I knew police captain Wirth, the administrative head of various euthanasia institutes, who told me in the late summer of 1941, that he . . . was being transferred to a euthanasia institute in the Lublin area" (erzählte mir im Spätsommer 1941, dass er . . . an eine Euthanasie-Anstalt im Raum Lublin versetzt sei.)[242] Another man recalled that it was "clear" that "something similar" to the euthanasia program was starting in Lublin, only this time according to rumor it was to be for the Jews.[243]

The convergence of these two strands of deportation and gassing was dramatically illustrated by the encounter between the ss deportation export Adolf Eichmann and euthanasia functionary Christian Wirth, both of whom had been sent from Berlin to the Lublin district. Sometime in the fall of 1941, according to Eichmann,[244] he was summoned to Heydrich and told: "The Führer has ordered the physical destruction of the Jews. Globocnik has received his relevant instructions from the Reichsführer. Thus Globocnik is supposed to use antitank ditches for that purpose. I want to know what he is doing and how far he has come."[245]

Eichmann was driven from Lublin for an hour and a half or two hours by Globocnik's assistant Hans Höfle until they arrived at a small wooden house on the right-hand side of the road. Eichmann could not remember the name of the place, but it had "a more Polish-sounding name" than Treblinka.[246] "We were received by an Order policeman in rolled up sleeves, who himself apparently had been working by hand. The style of his boots and the cut of his riding breeches indicated that he was an officer. From the introduction I learned that I was dealing with a captain of the Order Police. In the postwar years his name had long ago escaped me. Only through the literature did I remember again. His name was Wirth."[247] Concerning Wirth, Eichmann remembered specifically that he spoke in a coarse voice and southwest dialect.[248]

Wirth led Eichmann and Höfle along a small forest path on the left side of the road. In one version Eichmann said they came to two to three wooden houses "still under construction" (*noch im Bau*).[249] In a second version they arrived at "two small peasant huts standing under the deciduous trees" (*standen unter Laubbäumen zwei kleinere Bauernhäuser*). Wirth explained that he "he had to hermetically seal all the windows and doors" (*hatte er sämtliche Fenster und Türen hermetisch zu verschliessen*). "After the work was completed, Jews would come into the rooms and be killed by exhaust gas from a Russian U-boat engine that would be channeled into these rooms."[250] In yet another version Eichmann added that "these wood structures were in, were in a forest, a deciduous forest, a quite dense deciduous forest, large trees and so in, in full color, their leaves were. . . . It was therefore 1941 in the fall" (*diese Holzhausbauten in einer, in einer Laub, in einer Laubbaumzone gewesen sind, ziemlich dichten Laubbaumzone, grössere Bäume und so im, im vollen Schmuck, ihrer Blätter waren. . . . Das wäre also 1941 im Herbst*).[251]

Eichmann could not remember seeing any working parties.[252] "The motor was not yet there, the installation was not yet in operation."[253] Indeed he did not see anything that was yet identifiable as a camp. But he did remember distinctly that he had gone to Lublin expecting to see preparations for using antitank ditches as a shooting site, and instead this was the first time that he learned of actual preparations for gassing Jews.

There are three key elements to Eichmann's account. He was sent to Poland *after* being told by Heydrich of a basic Hitler decision for the physical destruction of European Jewry. He visited the site of a prospective Globocnik extermination camp near Lublin at the very earliest stage of construction, when the idea of constructing stationary gas chambers and using exhaust gas was just taking shape. And this visit came at the peak of fall colors in 1941, therefore in late September or early October.[254] If Eichmann's account is correct on these counts, then clearly Hitler's decision to deport German Jews in mid-September cannot be distinctly separated from an allegedly later decision for the Final Solution, and the role of the central government in the fall of 1941 was not one of merely reacting passively to unrelated initiatives from the periphery.

As with any detailed eyewitness testimonies after so many years, Eichmann's various accounts differ from one another and are not free of puzzling contradictions with other evidence. In terms of his dating this visit to the fall of 1941, two problems stand out. First, according to the testimony of Josef Oberhauser,

Wirth did not arrive at Belzec until late December 1941.[255] And second, according to the testimony of Stanislaw Kozak and Eustachy Urkainski, construction at Belzec by local Polish workers of the first three wooden barracks, including the future gas chambers, did not begin until November 1.[256] But there is no evidence that precludes Wirth's having been to Lublin before Oberhauser's arrival in October or November. Indeed, given the visit of Bouhler and Brack to the General Government in September, it is not at all unlikely that a representative of the euthanasia program, such as Wirth, would have been present during the earliest stages of testing and planning and then returned later to take command of Belzec when the camp was near completion. And if Eichmann's final testimony is correct, that is, that he saw two small peasant houses in the midst of a thick forest rather than two to three wooden houses under construction, there is yet another puzzle. The site of the Belzec camp, long presumed to be the site of this initial visit, lay alongside the main road and rail line, in sight of the train station and town. The location of the camp and the size of the buildings constructed for it do not at all fit Eichmann's description of two peasant huts deep in the forest.

Can these seeming contradictions be resolved? I would suggest the following scenario. In September Wirth was sent to the Lublin district to create a gassing facility. He first contemplated converting two peasant huts into gas chambers by sealing them hermetically (as Höss was to do with Bunkers 1 and 2 at Birkenau), but then after Eichmann's visit, presumably at the meeting of Himmler, Krüger, and Globocnik on October 13, it was decided to construct the entire camp from scratch next to the rail line for the logistical necessity of handling a continuous flow of transports. In this scenario, Wirth's initial peasant huts in the woods would have formed the basis for some of the "prepared documentation" and "far-reaching and good plans" that Globocnik was eager to submit to Himmler on October 1. The plans were then altered and expanded to meet Himmler's needs and expectations.

In support of this possibility, a number of obscure and seemingly trivial items of evidence are worth noting. In recounting his first visit to Birkenau in the spring of 1942, Eichmann said that he saw "these same huts" (*dieselben Häuschen*) as he had seen in the camp in the woods.[257] The commander of the Gendarmerie in the Lublin district, Ferdinand Hahnzog, also testified to the existence of "a primitive installation, consisting of a hermetically sealed shack hidden deep in the forest across from Galicia near Belzec" (*eine tief im Grenzwalde gegen Galizien bei Belzec verborgene primitive Anlage . . . die aus einem abgedichteten Schuppen bestand*), into which exhaust gas from a truck was piped in a test killing.[258] On two occasions Eichmann also placed his trip to Lublin in a sequence that implied late September. In court he stated that this trip took place "a little while before" his negotiations in Lodz.[259] And in his last account he wrote that the trip occurred "shortly before the order to prepare this first great Jewish deportation."[260] Eichmann said that he met with Heydrich in Berlin, but after September 27 Heydrich was increasingly in Prague.[261] All of this would indicate the existence of an experimental site in the woods near Belzec which Eichmann visited in late September and which formed the basis for an entirely new camp to be constructed by the rail line in Belzec beginning on November 1.

In any case, the problems and contradictions of accepting Eichmann's testimony for a fall visit to Belzec are minor in comparison to asserting that it can be made compatible with a visit in the following winter.[262] By the end of December, according to Kozak, the Polish workers had constructed three large barracks (50 m × 12.5 m, 25 × 12.5 m, and 12 × 8 m), while simultaneously 70 Russian POWs in black uniforms had dug the first large grave (50 m long, 20 m wide, and 6 m deep) connected to the future gas chamber by a narrow rail line. They had also encircled the camp with a thick, barbed wire fence.[263] In short, in any winter visit Eichmann would have encountered a nearly complete camp not remotely similar to anything he described in any of his testimonies.

The credibility of Eichmann's account of a fall visit to Belzec *following* a Hitler decision for the Final Decision must above all be tested against the context of other events in October 1941. Following the Himmler-Krüger-Globocnik two-hour meeting on October 13, which presumably was the occasion of Himmler's approval for the construction of Belzec, and a five-hour Himmler-Heydrich meeting on following day, October 14,[264] within a very short time period there occurred an extraordinary flurry of events that fall into two categories. The first concerned the proliferation of prospective gassing sites. The second reflected a watershed change in the vision of a solution to the Jewish question from expulsion to extermination.

First of all, Belzec was not the only extermination camp being planned, either in the General Government or elsewhere at this time. According to the stationmaster at Sobibor, Jan Piwonski, a group of SS officers arrived there sometime in the fall of 1941 to measure the track and ramp, which indicates that the site of that future extermination camp was also already under consideration.[265] In the neighboring Warthegau, similar events were occurring. Since early 1940 Herbert Lange in Poznan had led a Sonderkommando that had carried out euthanasia killings in East Prussia and the incorporated territories, some through shooting and at least some in a gas van equipped with canisters of bottled carbon monoxide.[266] According to Lange's chauffeur, he drove the Sonderkommando chief around the Warthegau in the fall of 1941, searching for a suitable site for a camp. Lange then drove to Berlin for consultations and returned to a village northwest of Lodz in late October or early November, where a team of SS men and Order Police was assembled from both Lodz and Poznan and a workforce of Poles began renovating and fencing an old villa or Schloss in the center of town. The village was Chelmno.[267] A similar chronology was confirmed by the local Volksdeutsche Amtskommissar. He was away from town toward the end of 1941 when some SS men arrived and investigated the Schloss and other buildings in town. Some days later, after his return, Lange appeared and confiscated various buildings. Lange returned still later with a team of SS men, followed by police, and work on the Schloss began.[268]

It has been argued that the founding of the extermination camp at Chelmno, like Belzec, was primarily a local phenomenon, the product of special approval by Himmler on the initiative of Gauleiter Greiser to reduce the nonworking Jewish population of the Lodz ghetto in order to make the local authorities more amenable to the arrival of the 20,000 Reich Jews and 5,000 "Gypsies" who were being deported there as of mid-October 1941.[269] But the assignment of the euthanasia killer Lange and the dispatch of gas vans and drivers by the motor pool of the RSHA in Berlin indicated the close cooperation and common purpose of Brack and the Führer Chancellery, Heydrich and the RSHA, as well as Himmler and his HSSPF Wilhelm Koppe. Chelmno may have been a local extermination camp for the Warthegau Jews, but its rapid emergence in the fall of 1941 occurred in no small part because the perceptions and desires of local officials there dovetailed perfectly with the visions and goals at the center.

If preparations for the future extermination camps at Belzec and Chelmno were already underway in late October (and at least site selection for the future camp at Sobibor occurred sometime in the fall of 1941), planning (ultimately unrealized) for at least two other extermination camps can also be dated to late October. Just as Chelmno was being constructed near the terminus of the initial deportations to Lodz, two camps were being planned for Mogilev and Riga at the very moment that the second wave of deportations to Minsk and Riga were being prepared. On October 23, the day that Eichmann met with all his deportation experts in Berlin to discuss the impending deportation of 50,000 Reich Jews to these two cities,[270] Himmler was in Mogilev inspecting a factory labor camp of Bach-Zelewski's. According to one witness, Himmler declared that solutions other than shooting would soon be available to kill Jews. According to Bach-Zelewski (who attributed this episode to a later date), Himmler explicitly discussed the construction of gas chambers. By mid-November the Topf company had been commissioned to construct a huge crematorium in Mogilev, and in December the first four-chamber crematorium oven was delivered. The gas chambers were never constructed, and subsequent crematory units were diverted to Auschwitz.[271] Instead, a killing center at Maly Trostinez, closer to Minsk, was created the following spring.

At the same time that Himmler was discussing plans for installing gas chambers in a camp in Mogilev during his visit there on October 23–25, the possibility of establishing gassing facilities in Riga was a topic of conversation in Berlin between officials of the euthanasia program, the Ostministerium, and the RSHA. As noted earlier, on October 24 Reichskommissar Lohse and Generalkommissar Drechsler met with Einsatzkommando leader Rudolf Lange to discuss the arrival of Jewish transports from the Reich. Frustrated by the unilateral action of the SS, Lohse announced that he was going to Berlin the next day to clear up the matter.[272] Two weeks later Lohse was still in Berlin when the head of his political division, Trampedach, urged his intervention to prevent the now imminent Jewish transports. The reply from Berlin informed Trampedach that the Ostministerium had no objections because the camps in Riga and Minsk were only temporary measures. The Jews would be sent "further to the east."[273] What had Lohse learned in Berlin that so completely altered the Ostministerium's attitude to the Jewish transports?

On October 25, the day after Lohse's meeting with Lange and the very day he arrived in Berlin, Ostministerium Jewish expert Erhard Wetzel drafted a letter for his minister, Rosenberg, concerning conversations he had had first with Viktor Brack and then with Eichmann of the RSHA. The letter's recipient was to be none other than Lohse. The time of the meeting was shortly before the successful testing of the prototype gas van in Sachsenhausen but perhaps after the preliminary tests at the KTI.

According to Wetzel, Brack declared himself ready to aid in the construction of "gassing apparatuses" (*Vergasungsapparate*) on the spot in Riga because they were not in sufficient supply in the Reich. They had yet to be built. Brack offered to send his chemist Dr. Kallmeyer to Riga, where he would take care of everything. The procedure in question, Brack warned, was "not without danger," so special protective measures would have to be taken. Thus Lohse should apply through the HSSPF in Riga for Kallmeyer and other personnel.

Eichmann confirmed that Jewish camps were about to be set up in Riga and Minsk to receive German Jews. Following this discussion with Eichmann, Wetzel concluded that those Jews capable of labor would be sent "to the east" later, but under the circumstances there would be no objections "if those Jews who are not fit for work are removed by Brack's device" (*wenn diejenigen Juden, die nicht arbeitsfähig sind, mit den Brackschen Hilfsmitteln beseitigt werden*) in the meantime.[274]

According to Wetzel's postwar testimony, he was summoned on October 23 to a meeting with Brack in the Führer's Chancellery. "Brack said to me . . . he had a task for me. I should inform Minister Rosenberg of the following: He, Brack, had a gassing apparatus that ought to be sent to Riga. The Minister should inform Reichskommissar Lohse of this. Brack told me, the gassing apparatus was intended for the destruction of Jews. During his explanation, Brack told me by the way that it was a question of a Führer order or a mandate of the Führer." Wetzel subsequently sought out Eichmann, with whom he had a "short and substantive conversation" (*ein kurzes und sachliches Gespräch*). He then returned to the Ostministerium and gave a detailed report to Dr. Otto Bräutigam, who said it was a "delicate matter" (*heikle Sache*) that had to be discussed with Leibbrandt. It was Leibbrandt's suggestion to draft a letter for Lohse containing a report on the Brack and Eichmann meetings.[275]

Since Lohse had just arrived in Berlin, presumably Bräutigam and Leibbrandt discussed with him in person the question of Jewish transports to Riga as well as Brack's proposal, and the letter drafted in Rosenberg's name was neither signed nor sent. Apparently, Kallmeyer did not make the trip, and gas vans were not constructed in Riga.[276] Ultimately, gas vans constructed in Berlin were sent instead.

Inevitably, as the invention of the extermination camp passed from conception and experimentation to preparation, other people within the Nazi regime began to receive unmistakable signals from their colleagues in the ss that Nazi Jewish policy had passed a fateful divide. Not expulsion but mass murder awaited the European Jews. Two examples documented in the records of the Foreign Office demonstrate the hints that officials there were receiving by the end of October.

A number of Spanish Jews had been arrested and interned in France, which led the Spanish government to suggest the possibility of evacuating all Spanish Jews (some 2,000) to Spanish Morocco. On October 13, 1941, the Foreign Office Undersecretary Martin Luther urged negotiations in that direction—a position fully in line with the hitherto prevailing policy of achieving a *judenrein* Europe through expulsion. But four days later (and just three days after Heydrich's five-hour meeting with Himmler), Heydrich's rsha informed Luther by telephone of its opposition to the Spanish proposal, since the Spanish government had neither the will nor the experience to guard the Jews effectively in Morocco. "In addition these Jews would also be too much out of the direct reach of the measures for a basic solution to the Jewish question to be enacted after the war." (*Darüber hinaus wären diese Juden aber auch bei den nach Kriegsende zu ergrei-*

fenden Massnahmen zur grundsätzlichen Lösung der Judenfrage dem unmittelbaren Zugriff allzusehr entzogen.) The rejection of deportation to Morocco combined with the mention of a basic solution to be enacted after the war, which removal of the Jews would thwart, indicate that a fundamental shift in Nazi Jewish policy had occurred. Within the SS a *judenfrei* Europe was no longer being pursued through expulsion.[277]

On October 18, 1941, one day after Heydrich informed Luther that the Spanish Jews in France could not be allowed to go to Morocco, Heinrich Himmler made a note on a telephone conversation with Heydrich: "No emigration by Jews to overseas."[278] On October 23, the emigration gates officially closed. Gestapo chief Heinrich Müller dispatched a circular letter to the various agencies and offices of the Sipo-SD announcing Himmler's order that Jewish emigration was to be stopped.[279] If the message had not been clear enough already, Franz Rademacher in the Foreign Office received official confirmation from Eichmann on November 4 that the halt to Jewish emigration did not just apply to the case of Spanish Jews and Morocco, but to all Jews in Europe.[280]

Also in October 1941 Eichmann's associate Friedrich Suhr accompanied the Foreign Office Jewish expert Franz Rademacher to Belgrade to deal with the Jewish question in Serbia. After the fate of the adult male Jews had been settled at a meeting on October 20, Rademacher reported on the women, children, and elderly: "Then as soon as the technical possibility exists within the framework of a total solution to the Jewish question, the Jews will be deported by waterway to the reception camps in the east." (*Sobald dann im Rahmen der Gesamtlösung der Judenfrage die technische Möglichkeit besteht, werden die Juden auf dem Wasserwege in die Auffanglager im Osten abgeschoben.*)[281]

When Rademacher returned to Berlin five days later, he found waiting a letter of October 23 from an old friend, Paul Wurm, foreign editor of *Der Stürmer*. Wurm had been visiting Berlin and had just missed seeing Rademacher, but he had had another interesting conversation, which he hurried to inform Rademacher of in this personal note. "Dear Party Comrade Rademacher! On my return trip from Berlin I met an old party comrade, who works in the east on the settlement of the Jewish question. In the near future many of the Jewish vermin will be exterminated through special measures." (*Auf meine Rückreise aus Berlin traf ich einen alten Parteigenossen, der im Osten an der Regelung der Judenfrage arbeitet. In nächster Zeit wird von dem jüdischen Ungezeifer durch besondere Massnahmen manches vernichtet werden.*)[282] What an extraordinary coincidence that on that very day, October 23, when Wurm encountered visitors from the east to Berlin talking of exterminating Jews through special measures, Eichmann had met in Berlin with his deportation experts, including those from the east, to discuss the impending deportation of 50,000 Reich Jews to Riga and Minsk that would follow the first wave of deportation to Lodz.[283]

In the last days of October, Hitler's own rhetoric before his guests at headquarters, usually veiled in such circumstances, became more candid. For top Nazis seeking affirmation that they had understood Hitler's intentions and "wishes" correctly, he left no ambiguity. On October 17, in the presence of Fritz Sauckel and Fritz Todt, he ruminated about the Germanization of the eastern territories. The native populations were to be treated "as Indians" (als Indianer). They would be "sifted," except for the urban populations that were to be starved. Moreover, "we are getting rid of the destructive Jews entirely" ([d]en destruktiven Juden setzen wir ganz hinaus). Hitler showed no qualms. "I proceed with these matters ice-cold. I feel myself to be only the executor of a will of history."[284] On October 21, during a midday meeting with Bormann, Hitler talked expansively about Christianity and Bolshevism as two versions of the eternal revolutionary Jewish threat. "When we exterminate this plague, then we perform a deed for humanity, the significance of which our men out there can still not at all imagine."[285] And on the night of October 25, he met with Heydrich and Himmler just after the latter's return from Mogilev. He recalled his Reichstag prophecy and blamed the Jews for the German lives lost in both wars. "Let no one say to me: We cannot send them into the swamp. Who then cares about our own people? It is good when the terror precedes us that we are exterminating the Jews. . . . We are writing history anew, from the racial standpoint." (Sage mir keiner: wir können sie doch nicht in den Morast schicken! Wer kümmert sich denn um unsere Menschen? Es ist gut, wenn uns der Schrecken vorangeht, dass wir das Judentum ausrotten. . . . Wir schreiben die Geschichte auch wieder neu: vom Rassestandpunkt aus.)[286]

What kind of scenario can be constructed out of the incomplete, disparate, and sometimes contested evidence? I would suggest the following. In mid-July, during the first peak of victory euphoria, Hitler gave the signal to Himmler and Heydrich to commence with the immediate and comprehensive murder of Soviet Jewry. The transition to implementation followed swiftly over the next four weeks, as Himmler both increased manpower and visited various units in the east to spread the word. At the same time, Hitler also led Himmler and Heydrich to believe he expected proposals concerning the fate of the rest of European Jewry that went beyond the expulsion plans of the previous years. Heydrich moved quickly to get written authorization from Göring both to prepare a new, unprecedented plan, different from what he had submitted to

Göring in March, and to coordinate the activities of the agencies that would be involved. In August, Heydrich, followed by Goebbels, also proposed that deportation of the Reich Jews begin. But Hitler—facing new uncertainty on the eastern front—declared that such deportations would not occur until after the war. By late August, with the conflict over strategy resolved and resumption of the offensive pending, Hitler granted Goebbels's request for a marking decree on August 19. Himmler also met with Hitler on August 20 and may well have come away with the impression that the latter's position on deferring deportations until after the war was not inflexible.

In the last days of August, Eichmann wrote of plans for the Final Solution "now in preparation." His colleague Höppner, after consulting with Eichmann, impatiently awaited the basic Führer decision as to whether deportees should be "totally eradicated." In the first days of September, Himmler met with the two HSSPFs of the General Government and the Warthegau, Krüger and Koppe. He discussed the "Jewish question" in relationship to "resettlement from the Reich" with the former, and the resettlement of 60,000 Reich Jews in Lodz with the latter. On September 16 Himmler met with Hitler and two days later wrote to Greiser about deportations to Lodz and subsequent deportation further east the following spring. On September 22–24 Himmler and Heydrich were again with Hitler, by which time deportations to "camps" in Minsk and Riga were also being planned. Sometime during this same month Bouhler and Brack, with men to spare from the recently suspended adult euthanasia program, visited the General Government, and Christian Wirth informed colleagues that he was heading for Lublin. In my opinion, it is most probable that in mid-September Hitler tentatively approved not only the deportations but also at least in principle the "eradication" of the deportees, though precisely how, when, and where this would take place was still not clear. The capture of Kiev and double encirclement victory at Vyazma and Bryansk created a second peak of victory euphoria that emboldened Hitler further. What had been tentative in mid-September became definite in early October.

I think that it was most probably in late September that Heydrich informed Eichmann of Hitler's decision for the "physical destruction" of the European Jews and dispatched him to Lublin to report on Globocnik's progress. Heydrich knew that Himmler had initiated Globocnik but still thought he was going to use antitank ditches for mass shooting. Instead, Eichmann encountered Wirth in the very earliest stages of sealing two peasant huts in the forest to create gas chambers. This was presumably one of the many "good and far-reaching plans" that Globocnik and Krüger were so anxious to share with Himmler when they requested a meeting on October 1. In the meeting with Globocnik and Krüger on October 13, Himmler must have seized upon the Wirth solution with alacrity. Four days later, after meeting with Globocnik, Frank knew that beginning in Lublin the nonworking Jews of the General Government were going to be deported "over the Bug," that is, killed. And on November 1 construction of two large barracks and the gas chambers began at Belzec next to the rail line, indicating that the modest preparations Eichmann had seen earlier were now being considerably enlarged upon. Belzec was no longer simply to be the site of a Wirth experiment but rather a camp capable of receiving a steady flow of deportation trains. Soon the possibility of a further site at Sobibor (where the train station ramp was measured by investigating ss men) was also being explored.

At the same time that Himmler took up the Belzec project, Heydrich seized upon the Widmann experiments in Belorussia and undertook the mass production of gas vans through the RSHA motor pool in Berlin. By late October the visiting Herbert Lange was promised several of these vans for Chelmno, and on October 23 Brack invited Wetzel to the Führer Chancellery to offer the Ostministerium officials help in constructing similar vans in Riga. On October 23–25 Himmler was in Mogilev, apparently laying the groundwork for the construction of a gas chamber camp there as well. Thus in the last weeks of October, extermination camps were envisioned not only in the Lublin district but also near the three cities that were to receive deportations from the Reich—Chelmno for Lodz, Mogilev for Minsk, and Riga. The idea of gassing Jews had demonstrably been percolating among various Nazis since Höppner's mid-July suggestion and Nebe's August initiatives. In mid-October this idea was eagerly seized upon by Himmler and Heydrich as the answer to their search for an effective mass killing method, a search that had become urgent with Hitler's approval of deportations from the Reich one month earlier, to say nothing of the onset of deportations on October 15.[287]

By October 25 even Germans who were not at the center of these developments—such as Franz Rademacher and Paul Wurm—had become aware of plans for "reception camps" in the east and "special measures" to exterminate "many" of the "Jewish vermin" in the "near future." Moreover, all the Jews of Europe were targeted. On October 17 Heydrich articulated the policy that no Jews should be allowed to escape "the direct reach of the measures for a basic solution to the Jewish question to be enacted after the war." And one day later, October 18, Himmler instructed Heydrich to end all Jewish emigration.

In his superb study of the Nazi persecution of the Jews, Peter Longerich takes a somewhat different approach. He argues that in the fall of 1941 "a concrete plan for the short term, systematic murder" of the Jews did not yet exist, rather only "the climate for the development of such a program or plan."[288] He adds: "In the fall of 1941 the decision for the immediate murder of all European Jews had not yet been taken. In the fall of 1941 the murder of hundreds of thousands, but not millions of human beings was being prepared."[289] Longerich chooses his words carefully, and in a strict sense he is correct. A plan or program for the "immediate" mass murder of "all European Jews" did not yet exist. Over the coming months many important decisions were yet to be taken concerning how, when, where, at what rate, and with what exceptions the task of murdering the European Jews was to be accomplished.

But such an approach underplays the significance of what had happened by the last week in October 1941. Quite simply, the fundamental question concerning the fate of the Jews that had been posed by Höppner on September 3, "Is it the goal to ensure them a certain level of life in the long run, or shall they be totally eradicated," had been answered. The Nazi regime had crossed the key watershed. Until the summer of 1941, the Nazi leadership had envisaged a solution to its self-imposed Jewish question through expulsion and accompanying decimation. By the last week of October, the close circle around Hitler, and gradually others as well, knew what Hitler expected of them and in what general direction they planned to proceed. They were now aware that, whatever the methods and timetable, no European Jews, not even women and children in Belgrade or Spanish Jews in Paris, were to escape the "measures for a basic solution to the Jewish question to be enacted after the war." And the goal of these measures was "physical destruction." The vision was there, the decision had been taken, planning was underway, and implementation was scheduled for a time period characterized as both "the next spring" and "after the war."

9

The Final Solution from Conception to Implementation, October 1941–March 1942

By the end of October 1941 the conception of the Final Solution had taken shape. The Jews of Europe were to be deported to secret camps designed to perpetrate mass murder by poison gas, though other possible methods of killing were not excluded. This program could not get fully underway until the spring of 1942, however, because neither the "factories of death" nor the "supply system"—the administrative and logistical apparatus necessary to deliver the victims—was in place. Between October 1941 and March 1942 the Nazi regime moved to remedy these deficiencies. It was a period, therefore, of initiation, experimentation, and preparation. Nearly 60,000 Jews and "Gypsies" were deported from the Third Reich. Some 6,000 of these deported German Jews were murdered upon arrival before firing squads in Kaunas and Riga. The first extermination camp—equipped with gas vans—began operating in Chelmno, and gas vans were sent to other sites as well, including Semlin (Sajmiste) outside Belgrade in Yugoslavia. Construction of the initial stationary gas chambers at Belzec was completed, and also at Birkenau a peasant hut (Bunker 1) was converted into a gas chamber facility. And finally, awareness of the impending mass murder program spread through the bureaucracy, and an ever increasing array of German governmental agencies was drawn into the destruction process. As a result of this initiation, experimentation, and preparation, the Nazi regime was ready to commence full-scale implementation of the Final Solution in March 1942.

After rejecting earlier proposals to begin deporting German Jews before the end of the war, Hitler not only approved deportations from the Third Reich in mid-September 1941 but pressed for as complete as possible an evacuation by the end of the year. With no extermination camps yet in place, Himmler and Heydrich now faced great difficulties in fulfilling their master's wish. Initially Himmler proposed to Greiser sending 60,000 Jews to Lodz, but quickly had to scale this back to 20,000 Jews and 5,000 "Gypsies."[1] Himmler then focused on reception areas in western Russia, and planned to deport 25,000 Jews to Minsk, 20,000 to Riga, and 5,000 to Kaunas.[2] Ultimately Himmler met neither his deadline nor his quota. These deportations began on October 15, 1941, but extended well beyond the turn of the year, ending only on February 21, 1942. In that time, 59 transports carried more than 58,000 deportees (including 5,000 "Gypsies")—about 17,000 short of the announced goal—out of the Reich to the east.

The first wave of deportations to Lodz was composed of two segments.[3] Between October 15 and November 2, twenty trains carried slightly under 20,000 Jews.[4]

City	Date of departure	Arrival
1. Vienna	15 Oct. 41	16 Oct. 41
2. Prague	16 Oct. 41	17 Oct. 41
3. Luxembourg/Trier	16 Oct. 41	18 Oct. 41
4. Berlin	18 Oct. 41	19 Oct. 41
5. Vienna	19 Oct. 41	20 Oct. 41
6. Frankfurt a.M.	20 Oct. 41	21 Oct. 41
7. Prague	21 Oct. 41	22 Oct. 41
8. Cologne	22 Oct. 41	23 Oct. 41
9. Vienna	23 Oct. 41	24 Oct. 41
10. Berlin	24 Oct. 41	25 Oct. 41
11. Hamburg	25 Oct. 41	26 Oct. 41
12. Prague	26 Oct. 41	27 Oct. 41
13. Düsseldorf	27 Oct. 41	28 Oct. 41
14. Vienna	27 Oct. 41	30 Oct. 41
15. Berlin	29 Oct. 41	29 Oct. 41
16. Cologne	30 Oct. 41	31 Oct. 41
17. Prague	31 Oct. 41	1 Nov. 41
18. Berlin	1 Nov. 41	2 Nov. 41

City	Date of departure	Arrival
19. Vienna	2 Nov. 41	3 Nov. 41
20. Prague	3 Nov. 41	4 Nov. 41

These were followed by five transports of "Gypsies" from Austria.

21. Hartberg	5 Nov. 41	
22. Fürstenfeld	6 Nov. 41	
23. Mattersberg	7 Nov. 41	
24. Rotenturm	8 Nov. 41	
25. Oserwart	9 Nov. 41	

The second wave of deportations was composed of four segments. Between November 8 and 28, seven transports departed for Minsk.

1. Hamburg	8 Nov. 41	11 Nov. 41
2. Düsseldorf	10 Nov. 41	15 Nov. 41
3. Frankfurt a.M.	11 / 12 Nov. 41	17 Nov. 41
4. Berlin	14 Nov. 41	18 Nov. 41
5. Brünn	16 Nov. 41	20 / 21 Nov. 41
6. Hamburg and Bremen	18 Nov. 41	22 Nov. 41
7. Vienna	28 Nov. 41	5 Dec. 41

Between November 17 and 25, five transports departed for Kaunas.

1. Berlin	17 Nov. 41	21 Nov. 41
2. Munich	20 Nov. 41	24 / 25 Nov. 41
3. Frankfurt a.M.	22 Nov. 41	25 Nov. 41
4. Vienna	23 Nov. 41	26 Nov. 41
5. Breslau	23 Nov. 41	28 Nov. 41

Between November 27 and December 15, ten transports departed for Riga.

1. Berlin	27 Nov. 41	30 Nov. 41
2. Nuremberg	29 Nov. 41	2 Dec. 41
3. Stuttgart	1 Dec. 41	4 Dec. 41
4. Vienna	3 Dec. 41	6 Dec. 41
5. Hamburg	6 Dec. 41	9 Dec. 41
6. Cologne	7 Dec. 41	10 Dec. 41
7. Kassel	9 Dec. 41	12 Dec. 41
8. Düsseldorf	11 Dec. 41	13 Dec. 41

City	Date of departure	Arrival
9. Münster/Bielefeld	13 Dec. 41	16 Dec. 41
10. Hanover	15 Dec. 41	18 Dec. 41

And finally, after a three-week pause, another ten transports departed for Riga between January 9 and February 6.

City	Date of departure	Arrival
1. Theresienstadt	9 Jan. 42	12 Jan. 42
2. Vienna	11 Jan. 42	15 Jan. 42
3. Berlin	13 Jan. 42	16 Jan. 42
4. Theresienstadt	15 Jan. 42	19 Jan. 42
5. Berlin	19 Jan. 42	23 Jan. 42
6. Leipzig/Dresden	21 Jan. 42	24 Jan. 42
7. Berlin	25 Jan. 42	30 Jan. 42
8. Vienna	26 Jan. 42	31 Jan. 42
9. Dortmund/Münster	27 Jan. 42	1 Feb. 42
10. Vienna	6 Feb. 42	10 Feb. 42

On a city-by-city basis, the deportations of the first and second waves (not including the "Gypsy" transports) were as follows:

No. of deportations	City of departure
11	Vienna
10	Berlin
5	Prague
4	Hamburg
3 each	Düsseldorf, Cologne, Frankfurt
2 each	Theresienstadt, Münster
1 each	Munich, Luxembourg, Brünn, Breslau, Nuremberg, Stuttgart, Kassel, Hannover, Dortmund, Leipzig, and Dresden

While the first two waves of deportation caught less than 20% of the more than 300,000 Jews living in Germany, Austria, and the Protectorate,[5] the experience gained and the techniques developed were crucial to the implementation of the Final Solution. The problems that the Germans had to solve in carrying out the first two waves of deportations can be broken down into two categories, those concerning departure from Germany and those concerning arrival in the east.

Departure

The departure of the Jews of Germany, Austria, and the Protectorate was a highly centralized operation, in which Adolf Eichmann of the RSHA played the key role. The local organizer of forced emigration from Vienna and Prague before the war, he had been in charge of the ill-fated Nisko experiment in the fall of 1939. The Nisko failure did not damage his career; on the contrary, in December 1939 he was brought to Berlin as Heydrich's "special adviser" for Jewish matters and evacuations. His Sonderreferat R (*Räumungsangelegenheiten*) was soon lodged within Heinrich Müller's Gestapo of Heydrich's RSHA and designated IV D 4, with jurisdiction over emigration and evacuation. In a March 1941 reorganization, Eichmann's office was renamed IV B 4, with jurisdiction over "Jews and evacuations." Although technically ranked as the mere head of a Referat, Eichmann in fact continued to function more as a "special adviser" to Heydrich. He enjoyed his own office at Kurfürstenstrasse 115/116, had his own registry for secret documents, and could submit correspondence directly to Müller without working through his nominal department head, Albert Hartl.[6]

As of March 1941, Eichmann's Referat had 107 employees, about three-quarters of whom were secretaries and file clerks.[7] Clearly the Referat generated enormous amounts of paperwork. Eichmann's deputy was his longtime associate Rolf Günther, who also headed section A of IV B 4, in charge of evacuations. Friedrich Suhr joined the Referat in July 1941 as head of section B for Jews. Suhr's personnel file in fact indicates that his transfer to IV B 4 was for the purpose of becoming the Referent for "the Final Solution of the Jewish question," especially beyond Germany's borders.[8]

Eichmann's reach extended far beyond the Berlin offices of IV B 4 because, in addition to the Central Agencies for Jewish Emigration in Vienna and Prague, he had also established deportation centers staffed with cadres of his own men in the incorporated territories. The Umwandererzentrale in Poznan with a branch office in Lodz became the center of his attempt to deport both Poles and Jews into the General Government. In addition to the Warthegau, each of the other incorporated Gaue had an Eichmann specialist on the spot. But Eichmann's various attempts to set in motion massive deportations of Jews from the Third Reich—from the Nisko experiment to the Madagascar Plan— had been repeatedly frustrated. In mid-March 1941 even the deportation of Poles from the incorporated territories had come to a complete standstill. With Hitler's change of heart in mid-September 1941, Eichmann now raced to meet Himmler's year-end quota of 70,000 Jewish deportees from the Third Reich.

In Vienna and Prague he worked through the Central Agencies for Jewish Emigration that he had created in 1938–39 and that were still staffed with his own men. Within Germany he worked through the regional and district Security Police offices (Stapoleitstellen and Stapostellen). Around the middle of October, Eichmann summoned the specialists for Jewish affairs from these offices to one of several meetings in Berlin devoted to the impending deportations. To a group of 12–15 Jewish specialists from western Germany, he emphasized the need to free up housing due to the Allied bombing.[9] To a group including the Jewish expert from Nuremberg-Fürth, Eichmann noted that the Rhineland had already been partially freed of Jews and read a memorandum that summarized the experiences of the earlier deportations—presumably the first wave of deportations to Lodz. To avoid complications, subsequent transports were to proceed in total compliance with instructions from the RSHA.[10] At least one such meeting, chaired by Eichmann and attended by Franz Abromeit from Danzig, can be dated to October 23, 1941.[11]

The *Personenkreis* or group of people vulnerable to deportation were all those defined as Jews by the 1935 Nuremberg Laws, with four exceptions: Jews living in mixed marriage, working in jobs important to the war economy, or over 60 years were exempted, as were those possessing foreign citizenship other than that of the Soviet Union. Stateless Jews, especially formerly Polish and Luxembourgian citizens, were explicitly included.

To swell the pool of victims, as well as to establish a precedent for later deportations from other countries in Europe, Eichmann asked the Foreign Office if the Croatian and Slovakian Jews living on German territory could be included. Typical of the zealous cooperation that his deportation efforts elicited from the German bureaucracy, Foreign Office Jewish expert Franz Rademacher went beyond minimal compliance with Eichmann's inquiry in two ways. First, the Romanians were approached as well. Second, Rademacher devised a method of exerting pressure to produce the desired assent. Each country was informed that unless it was willing to take its Jews back, it would have to permit their deportation to the east along with the German Jews. Romania expressed no interest in the return of its Jews. Croatia was thankful for their imminent deportation. But the Slovak government fretted over its claim to the property left behind by its Jews "if they are shoved off to the east never to be seen again" (*wenn sie auf Nimmerwiedersehn in den Osten abgeschoben werden*). The Slovaks finally agreed, but only on the condition that their property claims were in no way endangered. Because the issue of legal claims to property then had to be examined within the Foreign Office bureaucracy, Undersecretary Luther could not give Eichmann an affirmative answer until January 10, 1942, much too late for the Romanian, Croatian, and Slovakian Jews to be included in the first wave.[12]

The Slovak government was not the only one interested in the property of deported Jews. Both the RSHA and the Finance Ministry were committed to maximizing the proceeds from the property of deported German Jews.[13] The RSHA issued detailed instructions on the matter. Jews were forbidden to alienate any of their property, and any such transactions after October 15 were retroactively invalidated. Each deportee was to fill out an exhaustive inventory of his or her property that would be surrendered before deportation, whereupon a confiscation order would be served on the deportee by a court official or bailiff (Gerichtsvollzieher). Also, before deportation the Jews were to pay their utility bills and turn off the electricity, gas, and water. Their keys—clearly marked— were to be surrendered, and their apartments sealed upon departure.

In principle, all Jewish property was to go to the Reich through the good offices of the Finance Ministry, which instructed its local officials to zealously guard the ministry's prerogatives. Initially, confiscation was carried out on the basis of 1933 laws providing for the seizure of the property of communists and other enemies of the state. This was bureaucratically clumsy, however, for it required an individual determination for each deportee, often procured through the coerced signing of an unread confession or admission. For many months the Interior Ministry had wrestled with the question of stripping German Jews of their citizenship. Already on January 15, 1941, the Finance Ministry had broached the possibility of combining such legislation with provisions for the automatic forfeiture of property of all such denationalized Jews residing outside Reich boundaries. The Interior Ministry revealed Hitler's agreement in principle to the combined annulment of citizenship and forfeiture of property for all German Jews residing outside the Reich on July 7, 1941. However, it was not until November 25, more than a month after the deportations had begun, that these measures were officially promulgated as the 11th Decree to the Reich Citizenship Law. Included, of course, were Jews who were deported to the incorporated territories, the General Government, and the German-occupied east.[14] German Jews would first lose their citizenship and property and only then their lives.

The RSHA–Finance Ministry partnership to despoil the Jews was not without rivalry and friction. The Finance Ministry instructed its officials to take whatever furniture and other items could be of use to the ministry before selling off the rest. Needy officials were likewise to be provided with housing from the vacated Jewish apartments.[15] The RSHA also wanted to finance the cost of deportation out of Jewish property, which could only be done by extracting it before Finance Ministry confiscation. Thus the RSHA decreed that each deportee was to pay 50 RM into a special account (*Sonderkonto* W) established by the Kultusvereinigung or local Jewish organization in each community. Local police quickly added their own surcharge to the assessment. This proved insufficient, especially since some of the deportees were penniless and unable to pay anything. The RSHA then ordered the Jewish communities to urge propertied deportees to contribute 25% of their liquid assets into the special account before the confiscation procedures took place, both to defray the costs of the deportation and allegedly to finance the welfare obligations of the Reichsvereinigung der Juden.

The RSHA laid down careful specifications concerning what could be taken by the deportees: 100 RM; 50 kilos of luggage in one or two suitcases; bedding and mattresses; plates, bowls, and spoons, but no knives and forks; tools that would be useful in making a new start as pioneers in the east; 14 days of provisions plus 3 days' travel rations. Each transport was also to be equipped by the local Jewish community with stoves, kettles, barbed wire, and window glass. One watch and one wedding ring were allowed, but all other valuables—such as jewelry, cash, securities, savings books, and cameras—were forbidden. To enforce these provisions, the deportees were to be subjected not only to a luggage search but also to a body search.

Almost as soon as the deportations from Germany had been approved in late September 1941, Heydrich reached an agreement with the main office of the Order Police in Berlin on a division of labor. The Security Police would organize the transports, but the task of guarding them would be assumed by the Order Police.[16] Subsequently, before each deportation wave, the local Order Police were instructed to accommodate Security Police requests for the agreed-upon transport guards.[17] Ordinarily, the Orpo provided one officer and 15 men for each transport.[18]

The procurement of trains was another essential task of Eichmann's office. Here the young Austrian Franz Novak emerged as the expert. An early adherent of National Socialism, he had joined the Hitler Youth in 1929 at the age of 16 and the party four years later. Active in the 1934 Putsch attempt, he fled to Germany but returned to Vienna in 1938 and joined the SS. He worked in Eichmann's Central Agency for Jewish Emigration and became a fixture in Eichmann's entourage, following him to Prague and Berlin (and finally to Budapest in 1944). After Eichmann came to Berlin as Heydrich's adviser for both Jewish matters and "evacuations," it was Novak who handled the technical problems of organizing deportation trains "resettling" Poles and Jews from the incorporated territories to the General Government in 1940–41.[19] By the end of the war, Novak had organized at least 260 trains from Germany, Austria, and the Protectorate, at least 147 from Hungary, 87 from Holland, 76 from France, 63 from Slovakia, 27 from Belgium, 23 from Greece, 11 from Italy, 7 from Bulgaria, and 6 from Croatia—more than 707 from western and southern Europe.[20] In the fall of 1941, therefore, Novak was just beginning a process that was to become as routine as it was deadly.

Once the RSHA had determined what trains it needed in the coming months, Rolf Günther or Novak took the request to the Reich Transportation Ministry. Then both central and regional offices of the Reichsbahn would have a role to play.[21] Particularly important for the RSHA was the Operations Division (E II) of the Reichsbahn (initially under Max Leibbrand and after August 1941 under Gustav Dill), which handled scheduling. Within the Operations Division, large shipments (*Massenbeförderung*) were the business of Ministerialdirigent Paul Schnell's Referat 21. Under Schnell, Regierungsrat Otto Stange—Novak's counterpart—prepared the "special trains" (*Sonderzüge*) that ran outside the regular schedule. When Günther and Schnell had come to a general agreement, and Novak and Stange had worked out the details, Reichsbahn officials were then responsible for coordinating the activities of the regional and district offices. Germany was divided into three Generalbetriebsleitungen or regional operations offices (East—Berlin; South—Munich; West—Essen). The preeminent one was in Berlin, for it contained the Main Car Allocation Office and supervised the operations of the Ostbahn in the General Government as well.

Faced with coordinating requests from many sides, officials of the three Generalbetriebsleitungen would meet periodically in conferences to plan out the special train schedule for the next several months. For Jewish transports, two officials in the Generalbetriebsleitung Ost were especially important: Reichsbahnoberinspektor Fähnrich for car assignment and Reichsbahnoberinspektor Bruno Klemm for passenger scheduling. As Raul Hilberg has noted, Jews may have been shipped like cattle but they were booked as passengers.[22] From these conferences, a master plan would emerge. The district offices or Reichsbahndirektionen in which each special train was to originate then had the responsibility of assembling the trains that had been authorized and scheduled.

Novak in the RSHA was also informed of each new master plan. It was his job to inform each regional and district office of the Security Police of the date and quota—usually 1,000 people—of the train it was to fill with Jewish deportees. Each train, therefore, was the product of negotiation and interministerial cooperation. Each train generated large amounts of paperwork, both within the

Transportation Ministry and between Novak and the local Security Police offices. Nonetheless, with 850,000 train cars within the German empire, out of which 130,000 were allocated every day, a single Jewish transport of 10 to 20 cars carrying some 1,000 victims to their deaths was not obtrusive. It was even less so because, as Hilberg has noted, the procurement of each train was "embedded in the regular procedures of allocation" for the entire rolling stock of Europe.[23] However insignificant the initial Jewish transports might have seemed within the overall picture of the daily movement of Europe's rail system, they were nonetheless prepared with great care and even an eye for aesthetic symmetry. How else can one account for the fact that the 25 trains to Lodz, arriving from cities all over the Third Reich, were neatly scheduled to reach their destination on 25 consecutive days, each pulling into the Radegast train station punctually at 11:00 AM![24]

Despite Eichmann's centralized coordination and detailed instructions, a great deal had to be left to the discretion, initiative, and problem-solving abilities of the regional and district Security Police chiefs and their respective Jewish experts. In Berlin, with over 70,000 Jews, and Vienna and Prague, each with about 50,000 Jews, a more-or-less permanent deportation apparatus was created for the many transports that had to be organized. Elsewhere, the transports were occasional, and the deportation apparatus was ad hoc. But everywhere local officials faced the same problems: they had to mobilize and assign manpower; procure facilities as collection centers; design procedures and timetables for selecting, informing, and processing the deportees; and then physically carry out the actual deportations.

While in Vienna and Prague the Central Agencies for Jewish Emigration automatically became the deportation centers, in Berlin a permanent apparatus had to be developed within the Gestapo office of the Stapoleitstelle. (Each Stapoleitstelle was organized as a miniature RSHA, so that the Gestapo office and its Jewish desk were lodged in Abteilung IV.) On October 1 or 2 three leaders of the Jewish community in Berlin were summoned to the Gestapo and informed by Franz Prüfer of the Jewish desk that the resettlement of Berlin Jews was about to begin. The organization of the local Jewish community or Kultusgemeinde would have to help, or otherwise it would be left to the SS and SA, and the Jewish leaders surely knew what that meant, he noted ominously. The first task of the Jewish community administration was to invite the Berlin Jews, on the basis of its lists, to come to the Kultusgemeinde and fill out questionnaires that would subsequently be submitted to the Gestapo. Deportation lists were then compiled and returned to the Kultusgemeinde, which in turn had to inform the selected Jews of their imminent deportation. It was the Kultusgemeinde that issued the detailed property inventory form (to be filled out within three days) and the instructions for closing the apartment and preparing for transport.

At a given time and date, the deportees were to report to the permanent collection center erected in the former synagogue on the Levetzowstrasse. There the deportees usually waited one or two days while the processing was completed. Jewish secretaries did much of the paperwork, and Jewish work groups handled the luggage. Among the approximately 35 Security Police officials extensively involved in Jewish affairs in Berlin, Judenreferat members Franz Prüfer, Gerhard Stübbs, and Max Starck were most prominent in supervising the collection center and delegating work to the Jewish employees of the Kultusgemeinde. When processing was complete, the deportees were then marched or driven in trucks to the train station, usually the Lehrter freight depot, and loaded onto the transport.[25]

Not every local deportation procedure worked well the first time. Perhaps least successful was the deportation from Frankfurt to Lodz of October 20. The Gestapo had drawn up a list of 1,200 names from a card file previously prepared by the Jewish community administration. This list was submitted to the Jewish community on Friday, October 17, with instructions to add supplementary information about the former and present occupations of those on the list. Rumors of deportation spread quickly, which the Kultusgemeinde was ordered to deny. Two days later, at 5:30 on Sunday morning, 250 mobilized SA men assembled to hear an encouraging speech from the local Kreisleiter, Schwebel, and to receive their instructions and assignments from Obersturmbahnführer Poche of the Stapoleitstelle. Teams of SA men then fanned out to their assigned apartments, where the Jews were informed of their immediate deportation. Filling out the lengthy property inventory, preparing the apartment to be sealed, and packing for the trip all had to be done without prior warning or preparation. The SA men and their charges could not leave until Gestapo officials arrived to give their final approval and seal the apartments, but since far too few Gestapo men were available for the task, they often had to wait many hours. Jews did not begin to trickle into the exceptionally conspicuous collection center—the large market hall or Grossmarkthalle, which was unoccupied on Sunday—until early afternoon. Most of the deportees had to march through the city on foot and did not arrive until early evening. The SA men then had to wait with their charges, who advanced through slow-moving lines to be processed. This operation took all night, and the transport only departed the following morning. The postdeportation reports complained that the SA men, who had been up all night, then had to go to work. No one commented, however, on what happened when the delayed deportation proceedings were encountered by workers trying to set up the market early Monday morning.[26]

The lessons learned from such early transports were probably incorporated into Eichmann's orientation of the assembled Gestapo Jewish experts at subsequent orientation meetings in Berlin. Later deportations from other cities, such as Nuremberg, Stuttgart, and Cologne, went much more smoothly. For the November 29 transport from Nuremberg to Riga, Judenreferat head Theodore Grafenberg prepared exhaustively. Notified a full month in advance, Grafenberg sent out two sets of detailed instructions on November 11 and 19.[27] In addition to 500 deportees from Nuremberg, neighboring Fürth was to provide 100 and Würzberg 200. The Upper Franconian cities of Bamberg, Bayreuth, and Coburg were to provide the remaining 200. Grafenberg's own team of police worked in both Nuremberg and Fürth, and a branch office (Aussendienststelle) of the Security Police in Würzburg handled arrangements there. In Bamberg, Bayreuth, and Coburg, Grafenberg worked with the local criminal police (Kripo) through the mayors' offices. In Nuremberg the deportees were selected by the police from the card file of the Jewish community. In Würzberg the police provided the quota, with guidelines, and the Gemeinde was left to compile the list.

On November 23 "evacuation teams" (*Evakuierungsgruppen*) were assembled in each town and given instructions. They then proceeded to notify the Jews, giving them instructions and the property inventory forms. In Würzburg and Upper Franconia the Jews assembled at the collection points on November 26 and were brought to Nuremberg in separate train cars attached to regular trains on November 27. In Nuremberg-Fürth Jewish workers picked up luggage on November 26, and on the following day the deportation teams brought the Jews to the collection center at Camp Langwasser, a barracks adjacent to the annual party rally grounds.

Fifty-five ss men guarded the camp, while the combined deportation teams processed the deportees through four rooms. In the first room, their luggage was searched, then sent off to the train station. In the second, they turned over their property inventories, all valuables and securities, and the 60 RM transportation fee. In the third room, the deportees were subjected to a body search. The secretaries and even the cleaning ladies who worked at the police station were mobilized to body search the female Jews. In the fourth room, the court bailiffs presided over the official confiscation of property, and identity cards were stamped "evacuated." The deportees then passed into the *Sammellager* or collection camp, where they slept on bare floors and awaited deportation. Processing was complete by the late afternoon of November 28, and the transport departed on the afternoon of November 29. This model deportation was officially recorded by the Müller-Nickel film company.

In Stuttgart the head of the Stapoleitstelle, Sturmbannführer Mussgay, was responsible for organizing the deportation of 1,000 Jews from all over Württemberg on December 1. In contrast to Nuremberg, he created a relatively decentralized procedure. The Jewish Kultusvereinigung Württemberg was ordered to compile the list of 1,000 deportees and to send out notifications and property inventory forms, which it did on November 15. Mussgay then sent instructions to the various Landräte in Württemberg, who in turn contacted the mayors of towns from which Jews were to be deported. Local authorities were to collect the property forms by November 25, and to carry out the body and luggage searches, seal the empty apartments, and provide police escort to Stuttgart. There the Jews were collected in the exposition hall of the Reich Garden Show on the Killesberg on November 27 and 28. The transport finally departed on the morning of December 1.[28]

The Stapoleitstelle in Cologne organized three deportations in the fall of 1941, two in late October to Lodz and one in December to Riga. The local Gauleiter was already pressing for the removal of the Cologne Jews, and had sent both the Stapoleitstelle head, Emanuel Schäfer, and Kreisleiter Schaller to Berlin to argue his case. There they learned of the imminent deportations to the east. The Jewish expert of the Gestapo, Jean Brodesser, subsequently attended an Eichmann meeting in Berlin, where he was informed that the first Cologne deportation was scheduled for October 22.

Upon his return to Cologne, Brodesser summoned the head of the Jewish community, Bernhard, who was given 24 hours to prepare a list of 1,000 deportees. When the list was compiled, Bernhard and other officials of the Jewish community had to instruct each deportee to fill out a questionnaire and property inventory and to report punctually on October 21 to the north hall of the exhibition grounds in Deutz across the Rhine from Cologne, where they were kept overnight. Urban police or Schutzpolizei (Schupo) units guarded the exhibition hall, and except for a skeleton crew left at the office, the entire Stapoleitstelle (some 40 Gestapo and 70 Kripo officials as well as the secretaries) was mobilized to carry out the processing for deportation. In addition to the police, finance officials presided over the confiscation of property. Each deportee was forced to sign a confession of communist activity, to provide a legal pretext for confiscation. Officials from the Labor Office were present to collect work books. On October 22 the Jews were taken to the Cologne-Deutz train station, which had been temporarily sealed off. The second and third deportations proceeded in the same manner. What had changed were the expectations of the Jewish deportees. For the first train to Lodz, many had bought tools to make a new start. Before the third to Riga, many took poison.[29]

If somewhat behind schedule and somewhat below the targeted goal of 70,000 Jews, the first two waves of deportation were nonetheless a major success for the Nazi regime. The opportunity to deport significant numbers of Jews—stymied since 1939—had elicited from all levels of the German government not just compliance and cooperation but enthusiasm and initiative. At the highest level the Finance Ministry, Foreign Office, and Transportation Ministry had all been eager participants. At the local level small-town mayors ensured that their handfuls of Jews were included, cleaning ladies collected overtime pay to conduct strip searches of the female deportees, and the German Red Cross expressed profuse gratitude for the perishable foods of deported Jews turned over to its care for charitable distribution.[30]

One element of consensus behind the deportations was the common rush for spoils, especially in response to the housing shortage that would inevitably only worsen under the impact of Allied bombing. The housing shortage was in fact frequently cited at the onset of the deportation program. Gauleiter Karl Kaufmann had appealed directly to Hitler in the wake of the September 15–16, 1941, attack on Hamburg for the deportation of Jews as a means of providing accommodation for the bombing victims. This request had coincided with other proposals reaching Hitler in mid-September and his decision to approve Jewish deportations that fall.[31] Indeed there was a short-lived plan to evacuate at least two trainloads of Hamburg Jews to Hrubieszow in the Lublin district of the General Government, which Frank blocked in early October.[32] In Vienna, Alois Brunner also told Josef Löwenherz on September 30, 1941, that deportations from Germany were beginning in connection with the need for housing due to the bombing attacks.[33] A similar pretext was cited by Eichmann at a meeting of the representatives of the Stapoleitstellen from western Germany.[34] In fact, the bulk of the early deportations left from Berlin, Vienna, and Prague, not from the cities of western Germany most exposed to Allied bombing. Hitler's wish to give priority to these key cities, not a housing shortage aggravated by Allied bombing, was obviously most determinative of deportation priorities. The housing shortage was a useful pretext but not the major cause of the deportations.

Nonetheless, the scramble for housing spoils in response to the deportations was manifested from top to bottom in German society. In late January 1942, Speer fought off a demand by Rosenberg to relinquish recently evacuated Jewish apartments in Berlin to employers of the Ostministerium. He had to keep a large reserve of such apartments in hand, Speer explained, for possible victims of bombing, and his quota had by no means been reached, since the evacuation of the Jews was temporarily halted until spring.[35] In Württemberg the Oberfinanz-präsident rejected requests from the post office and railway for housing for their employees. He did not have enough Jewish apartments even to cover the needs of the police and his own employees.[36] And the Göttingen party bureau reported, "Since the intention to deport the Jews from Göttingen in the near future has already become common knowledge, the district [party] administration has been flooded with applications for flats."[37] A commonly heard complaint was that Jewish property left behind was lining the pockets of party bosses rather than being shared out among those most in need.[38] Whatever the disaffection of the losers in the scramble for spoils, however, the demand for Jewish apartments only increased support for accelerated deportations.

Attitude of the German Population to Deportations and the Final Solution
While the regime overcame many problems in launching the deportation program, one potentially important problem simply did not arise. Among the German population there was virtually no sign of dismay or even interest concerning the deportations. There was no political cost to the popularity of the regime. Three historians—Ian Kershaw, Otto Dov Kulka, and David Bankier—who have carefully examined the elusive evidence concerning the attitude of the German population at large to Nazi Jewish policy during the war (the marking decree and deportations in particular) have reached consensus on some issues and maintained nuanced differences on others.[39] Kulka and Bankier deduce a more specific awareness of the Final Solution among the German people than does Kershaw.[40] Kershaw and Bankier advocate a more critical and less literal reading of the SD reports than does Kulka.[41] Kershaw sees a general "retreat into the private sphere" as the basis for widespread indifference and apathy toward Nazi Jewish policy. Kulka, however, sees a greater internalization of Nazi anti-Semitism among the population at large—particularly concerning the accep-tance of a solution to the Jewish question through some unspecified kind of "elimination"—and thus prefers the more morally weighted terms "passive" or "objective complicity" rather than the more descriptive term "indifference."[42] Bankier emphasizes a greater sense of guilt and shame among Germans, wide-spread denial and repression, and a growing fear over the consequences of impending defeat and a commensurate rejection of the regime's anti-Semitic propaganda.[43]

Despite these differences, all three scholars agree on many issues. Above all, they accept that the fanatical anti-Semitism of the party "true believers" was not identical to the anti-Semitic attitudes of the population at large, and that the anti-Semitic priorities and genocidal commitment of the regime were not shared by "ordinary Germans." Kershaw concludes that while the "depersonalization of the Jew had been the real success story of Nazi propaganda and policy," nonetheless "the 'Jewish Question' was of no more than minimal interest to the vast majority of Germans during the war years. . . . Popular opinion, largely indifferent and infused with a latent anti-Jewish feeling further bolstered by propaganda provided the climate within which spiraling Nazi aggression towards the Jews could take place unchallenged. But it did not provoke the radicalization in the first place."[44] Kershaw summed up his position in the memorable phrase that "the road to Auschwitz was built by hatred, but paved with indifference."[45]

Despite his subsequent critique of Kershaw, Kulka's conclusions are strikingly similar. Surveying the SD reports, he notes that "during the war period the unquestionably dominant feature was the almost total absence of any reference to the existence, persecution and extermination of the Jews—a kind of national conspiracy of silence." The few reactions that were noted were "characterized by a strikingly abysmal indifference to the fate of the Jews as human beings. It seems that here, the 'Jewish Question' and the entire process of its 'solution' in the Third Reich reached the point of almost total depersonalization."[46] "What is known is that the composite picture that the regime obtained from popular-opinion reports pointed toward the general passivity of the population in the face of the persecution of the Jews." While the Jewish question "might not have been high on the list of priorities for the population at large . . . there were sufficient numbers who chose to give the regime the freedom of action to push for a radical 'Final Solution.' "[47]

Bankier notes the "deep-seated anti-Jewish feelings" in German society but likewise concludes "that on the whole the public did not assign anti-Semitism the same importance as the Nazis did. . . . The policy of deportations and mass murder succeeded because the public displayed moral insensibility to the Jews' fate." But Bankier goes beyond moral insensibility and passivity to argue for a growing schism between the people and the regime:

From 1941 onwards, the failure of Nazi promises to materialize drove a wedge between the population and the regime . . . declining hopes of victory and spiraling presentiments of a bitter end issued in a move to distance themselves from propaganda in general and from the Jewish issue in particular. . . . Ordinary Germans knew how to distinguish between an acceptable discrimination . . . and the unacceptable horror of genocide . . . the more the news of mass murder filtered through, the less the public wanted to be involved in the final solution of the Jewish question.[48]

The reaction of the regime indicates that it perceived a less-than-adequate coincidence between its attitudes and those of the population at large. Indeed, the popular reaction to the introduction of marking with the Jewish star displeased Goebbels, who in late 1941 complained that it "has had the opposite effect from what we intended. . . . People everywhere are showing sympathy for them [the Jews]. This nation is simply not yet mature; it's full of all kinds of idiotic sentimentality."[49] In late October Goebbels complained in his diary: "Our intellectuals and high society have once again suddenly discovered their humanitarian feelings for the poor Jews. . . . The Jews need only to send an old lady with a Jewish star to the Kurfürstendamm, and the German Michel is already inclined to forget everything that the Jews have done to us in the past years and decades. . . . It is remarkable what a lack of instinct [*Instinktlosigkeit*] for the Jewish question is even now to be found in our high society and intellectual circles."[50]

The October 4, 1941, issue of the *Stuttgart NS-Kurier* bemoaned that "cases of unsuitable compassion for Jews are not unusual." Goebbels's editorial in *Das Reich* of November 16 condemned the "false sentimentalism" and "pity" displayed toward Jews and shrilly warned: "Whoever takes the part of the Jews has gone over to the side of the enemy in the midst of war."[51] The RSHA responded with a decree of October 24, 1941, that was circulated to local police stations in early November:[52]

Recently it has been repeatedly noticed here that, as in the past, people of German blood maintain friendly relations to Jews and blatantly show themselves with Jews in public. As these people of German blood in question even today display total incomprehension regarding the most elementary principles of National Socialism and their behavior must be seen as contemptuous of official policy, I order that on such occasions the person of German blood is to be taken into temporary custody on educational grounds. The Jew in each case is for the time being to be arrested for incarceration in a concentration camp.

If the introduction of the star elicited at least some short-lived signs of sympathy among some of the German population for the plight of the Jews, to which the regime responded with incredulity, coercion, and propaganda, the deportations were met with near total silence and even an unseemly rush for spoils by others. Nonetheless, in the following years the regime continued to display unease about the extent of popular support for genocide, particularly as both rumor and solid information about the fate of the Jews became more available and widespread within German society in 1942.

A Party Chancellery circular of October 19, 1942, noted that rumors of the "very sharp measures" (*sehr scharfe Massnahmen*) against Jews in the east were widespread, especially because of the talk of soldiers home on leave. Since it was "conceivable" that not all racial comrades were "capable of demonstrating sufficient understanding for the necessity of such measures," the rumors—frequently of an "intentionally tendentious character"—were to be countered. While asserting that solving the Jewish question was an urgent priority for the "existence of the German people" and required "ruthless severity," the circular nonetheless reiterated the camouflage explanation that Jews were being sent to camps for labor or in order to be sent "still further to the east."[53] The following summer, on Hitler's behalf, Martin Bormann circulated instructions that no discussion of a "total solution" to the Jewish question was to take place in public, though mention could be made that Jews were being taken for labor.[54]

Speaking to a group of leading SS officers at Poznan on October 4, 1943, Himmler lauded the "tact" of the SS whereby the murder of the Jews was not spoken about even among themselves. This was "an unwritten and never to be written page of glory in our history" (*ein niemals geschriebenes und niemals zu schreibendes Ruhmesblatt unserer Geschichte*).[55] Himmler was obviously reluctant but ultimately firm about the wisdom of such secrecy. "Later perhaps we can consider whether the German people should be told about this. But I think it is better that we—we together—carry for our people the responsibility . . . and then take the secret with us to the grave."[56]

Ironically, it was precisely the two most prominent spokesmen of the Nazi regime—Joseph Goebbels and Adolf Hitler himself—who on occasion apparently could not resist the urge to speak about the mass murder, especially in reference to Hitler's 1939 "prophecy." Citing the prophecy by its proper date of January 30, Goebbels trumpeted in *Das Reich* on November 16, 1941, that "we are just experiencing the fulfillment of this prophecy" and that Jewry "is now suffering the gradual process of annihilation which it intended for us. . . . It now perishes according to its own precept of 'An eye for an eye and a tooth for a tooth!' "[57] In the May 9, 1943, issue of *Das Reich*, Goebbels returned to the topic. Referring over and over to alleged Jewish plans of "extermination and annihilation" and "total destruction" of the German people, Goebbels repeated once again that Hitler's prophecy was coming to pass with "tremendous certainty and inevitability."[58] Hitler too referred to his 1939 Reichstag prophecy (misdated to September 1 instead of January 30) on numerous occasions during the war, not only in closed gatherings but also in his Berlin Sportspalast speeches on January 30 and September 30, 1942.[59]

Arrival

The organizers of the deportations from the Third Reich had to coordinate not only the departure of the Jewish transports but also their arrival in the east. Here the problems were of a very different nature. In Germany the deporters were trying to develop techniques and methods that would facilitate future deportations as well. In the east reception measures were stopgap improvisations. The extermination camps had been conceived and approved, and several were being constructed. In the meantime the Germans would cope as best they could.

In late September, sometime before the 29th, Eichmann was in Lodz meeting with the Gestapo Jewish expert Gunter Fuchs and possibly with Hans Biebow, who he later claimed had assented to the deportation plans.[60] Despite Uebelhoer's complaints about Eichmann's "Gypsylike horse-trading manners," 25 transports with 19,837 Jews and 5,000 "Gypsies" began arriving. The Lodz ghetto administration adjusted quickly. Earlier, on October 4, Uebelhoer had used Biebow's argument with Himmler that only "if the Lodz ghetto were a pure decimation ghetto" (*[w]äre das Getto Litzmannstadt ein reines Dezimierungsghetto*) could one contemplate a greater concentration of Jews.[61] Now Biebow's assistant Ribbe used the "decimation ghetto" concept in a different way. After a meeting on October 9 between Ribbe and representatives of the Gestapo and Labor Office in Lodz, he recorded: "It was further established that the Lodz ghetto as a pure decimation ghetto [*als reines Dezimierungsgetto*] can give up no Jews, because these are needed for its own employment." When a week later the Poznan Labor Office suggested taking the incoming Jews for work on the Autobahn, Ribbe insisted on first claim to skilled workers and artisans, but in exchange would give up other workers. "Above all things we have a shortage of good German-speaking office workers and particularly good craftsmen," Ribbe explained. "The ghetto administration would first of all undertake a screening and itself employ truly useful labor."[62] Under the impact of the arriving transports and months before the deportations to Chelmno began, therefore, the ghetto administration in Lodz had embraced the idea of screening its Jews to keep the best and get rid of the rest.

At the same time, Biebow and Ribbe felt constrained to personally warn the staff of the ghetto administration against engaging in "absolutely negative criticism" (*absolut negativer Kritik*) or "fully irresponsible prattle" (*völlig unverant-*

wortlichen Redereien) in public places that would be eagerly overheard out of a "humanly understandable lust for sensation" (*menschlich verständliche Sensationslust*). The solution to the Jewish question was "an affair of high politics," and all employees of the ghetto administration had to preserve the strictest secrecy about everything concerning the treatment of the Jewish problem.[63]

While the Lodz ghetto administration was adjusting to the new situation, Eichmann went on to Prague, where Heydrich once again discussed the imminent deportations on October 10. "Temporarily much consideration still had to be shown for the authorities in Litzmannstadt," Heydrich conceded. Thus 50,000 Jews would be sent to Minsk and Riga, where the Einsatzgruppen commanders could place them in camps. "This has already been initiated according to Sturmbannführer Eichmann's information."[64] And, of course, the busy Eichmann was back in Berlin on October 23 and met not only with his deportation experts but also with Wetzel. The latter thereupon concluded that there would be no objection to removing with the help of Brack's "gassing apparatus" those Reich Jews sent to Riga who could not work.[65]

In fact, Brack's "gassing apparatus" was not constructed in Riga, but other solutions had already been considered and were being tried. In late October the Generalkommissariat Weissruthenien was being transferred from the jurisdiction of the HSSPF Center Erich von dem Bach-Zelewski and Nebe's Einsatzgruppe B to that of HSSPF North Friedrich Jeckeln and Stahlecker's Einsatzgruppe A. Hans-Hermann Remmers, the head of a mixed unit of Security Police from various Einsatzkommandos in Minsk during the changeover, received a telephone call from Stahlecker's staff in Riga. A number of transports with German Jews would shortly begin arriving in Minsk, Remmers was told. In order to create room for them in the Minsk ghetto, a large number of Russian Jews would have to be shot. This order for the reduction of the Minsk ghetto did not originate with Stahlecker, since the operation was in fact being coordinated from Berlin.[66] The executions were organized by Remmers and SSPF Carl Zenner and carried out by a combination of Security Police, Order Police, and Ukrainian auxiliaries. A subsequent report noted that "in Minsk a total of 6,624 Jews were shot in the period from November 7 until November 11, 1941." To reach the stipulated goal, another mass execution of 5,000 Minsk Jews was carried out on November 20. The first transport from Hamburg arrived on November 14, followed by six more. The deportees were lodged in the quarter of the ghetto that had just been cleared.[67]

After these first seven transports to Minsk, which had departed the Third Reich between November 8 and 28, no further transports arrived. But the Generalkommissar Weissruthenien, Wilhelm Kube, was troubled even by the presence of the first 6,000–7,000 of the promised 25,000 Reich Jews. They were as susceptible to east European epidemics as "Reich Germans." Certain army and police units had already set upon their property. In the coming months they would probably starve or freeze to death. This disturbed Kube.

> Among these Jews are front veterans with the Iron Cross first and second class, war wounded, half-Aryans, and even a three-quarter Aryan. . . . In repeated official visits to the ghetto I have discovered that among these Jews, who distinguish themselves from Russian Jews in their personal cleanliness, are also skilled workers, who are perhaps five times as productive as Russian Jews. . . .
>
> I am certainly tough and ready to help solve the Jewish question, but human beings who come from our cultural sphere are something other than the native bestial hordes. Should one assign the Lithuanians and Latvians, who are even rejected by the population here, with their slaughter? I could not do it.[68]

Kube asked that "explicit instructions" be given to "take the necessary steps in the most humane way." He seemed to have no doubt about the eventual intended fate of the deported Reich Jews but objected to their being killed in the same manner as *Ostjuden*.[69]

In early January 1942 the distressed Stadtkommissar of Minsk, Wilhelm Janetzke, heard that Berlin intended to send not just 25,000 but 50,000 Jews to Minsk. Going over the heads of Kube and Lohse, he complained directly to Rosenberg that this would be a "catastrophe" due to the lack of food.[70] Lohse chastised Janetzke for not following channels, and told Kube that the RSHA quota for Minsk was still 25,000 Jews. At the moment, even these could not be sent because of transportation difficulties. Once those difficulties were overcome, however, Minsk must reckon upon the arrival of these Jews.[71] Kube defended Janetzke's presentation of the situation in Minsk. One could not suddenly lodge 25,000 people in a city 80% destroyed. Moreover, "because the ground in White Russia is frozen down to the depth of two meters, other possibilities were also not available."[72] In fact, transports to Minsk did not resume until May 1942, when the ground was no longer frozen. Kube's "other possibilities" were then implemented. Unlike the first transports, these subsequent Reich Jews would be murdered upon arrival.

Thus in Lodz the labor potential of the incoming Reich Jews was still valued, although plans were clearly afoot to rid the ghetto of its undesired nonworking population; while in Minsk German officials shot Soviet Jews immediately to make room for the newcomers from the Reich but still felt some inhibitions about the mass murder of the latter. But no such pragmatic calculations or inhibitions troubled the Germans in Kaunas. On November 8 Stahlecker relayed to Lohse's officials in Riga that 5 of the 25 Jewish transports destined for Riga would instead be directed to Kaunas, "to be placed in the ghetto" there (*in das Ghetto in Kauen einzuweisen*). Whether it would be the first five transports or five later ones depended on transportation technicalities, and thus the final decision had not yet been made.[73] On November 20 Lange informed the Reichskommissariat Ostland that indeed the first five transports were being diverted to Kaunas.[74] These five trains departed from Munich, Berlin, Frankfurt, Vienna, and Breslau between November 17 and 23. The men of Karl Jäger's Einsatzkommando 3, the most prolific killers on the entire eastern front, were waiting at the Fort IX execution site. The notorious Jäger report noted succinctly in its five-page list of "executions":

25 Nov. 41 Kaunas-F.IX—1159 male Jews, 1600 female Jews, 175 Jewish children. 2934 (Resettled from Berlin, Munich and Frankfurt a.M.)

29 Nov. 41 Kaunas-F.IX—693 male Jews, 1155 female Jews, 152 Jewish children. 2000 (Resettled from Vienna and Breslau)

These 4,934 victims were a mere fraction of EK 3's incredible tally of 133,346 Jews murdered by the end of November 1941.[75]

These were the first German Jews systematically murdered by the Nazi regime as part of the Final Solution to the European Jewish question. Another threshold had been crossed. Available documentation makes it clear that the decision to send these five transports to Kaunas originated in Berlin and had been under consideration weeks in advance. It does not clarify how, when, why, and by whom the decision was taken to kill these Jews upon arrival at Fort IX rather than incarcerate them in the Kaunas ghetto as had been done earlier in Lodz and Minsk. The events surrounding the fate of the next Jewish transport, which left Berlin on November 27 and arrived in Riga on the night of November 29/30, just one day after the second Kaunas massacre, suggests some tentative conclusions, however.

On November 10 or 11, 1941, Heinrich Himmler personally briefed the newly appointed HSSPF North, Friedrich Jeckeln. According to Jeckeln, Himmler said "that all Jews in the Ostland had to be destroyed to the last man" (*dass alle im Ostland sich befindenden Juden bis zum letzten Mann vernichtet werden müssen*). This had already been accomplished elsewhere in the Ostland, but the Riga ghetto still had to be liquidated. Jeckeln's predecessor, Hans-Adolf Prützmann, had indicated to Himmler that Lohse, the Reichskommissar Ostland, was against this liquidation, but Jeckeln was to carry it out anyhow. "You tell

Lohse, that is my order, which is also the Führer's wish!" (*Sagen Sie dem Lohse, es ist mein Befehl, der auch einem Wunsch des Führers entspricht!*) Lohse in fact had no objections, and Jeckeln gave the order for the liquidation of the Riga ghetto.[76] According to *Ereignismeldung* No. 156 of January 16, 1942, Jeckeln's men, with help from Rudolf Lange's EK 2, shot 10,600 Jews on the so-called *Blutsonntag* or Bloody Sunday of November 30, 1941.[77] According to another report, a second day of executions on December 8 brought the total number of victims to at least 27,800.[78]

It was into this maelstrom that the first Riga transport, having departed Berlin on November 27, arrived, and its deportees were promptly killed on the morning of November 30. For whatever reason, Himmler belatedly attempted to have the Riga transports handled as in Minsk, not as in Kaunas. The deportees were to be temporarily lodged in the space made available by the recent murder of Latvian Jews rather than liquidated upon arrival. At 1:30 PM on November 30, Himmler called from Hitler's headquarters to Heydrich in Berlin and noted in his telephone log: "Jewish transport from Berlin. No liquidation." (*Judentransport aus Berlin. Keine Liquidierung.*)[79] His intervention was too late, since the Berlin Jews had already been shot early that morning before the columns of Jews being marched from the Riga ghetto reached the shooting site at Rumbula.

The following day Himmler discussed "executions in Riga" with Heydrich once again.[80] He also expressed himself quite forcefully to Jeckeln: "The Jews resettled in the Ostland are to be dealt with only according the guidelines given by me or by the RSHA acting on my behalf. I will punish unilateral acts and violations." (*Die in das Gebiet Ostland ausgesiedelten Juden sind nur nach den von mir bezw. vom Reichssicherheitshauptamt in meinem Auftrag gegebenen Richtlinien zu behandeln. Eigenmächtigkeiten und Zuwiderhandlungen werde ich bestrafen.*)[81] Jeckeln was then summoned to Himmler's headquarters, where on December 4, 1941, they again discussed the "Jewish question."[82] Thereafter, the Jews from the remaining 19 transports—9 before Christmas and 10 after—were settled in the Riga ghetto or in the nearby camps of Jungfernhof and Salispils,[83] with two exceptions. The second transport of Czech Jews that departed Theresienstadt on January 15, 1942, was liquidated upon arrival.[84] And the February 10 transport from Vienna was met by a gas van, which was used to murder 700 of its 1,000 deportees.[85]

The evidence is confusing. If the Kaunas killings represented a point at which Himmler had ordered the killing of all subsequent transports, but he then suddenly changed his mind again on November 30, why was he angry at Jeckeln for faithfully carrying out orders that had not yet been rescinded? If the Kaunas killings represented a special case and Jeckeln had no orders to destroy the Berlin transport, how did it even occur to Himmler and Heydrich on November 30 to discuss "no liquidation" of this particular transport? But whatever the confusion concerning the first transport to Riga, several things seem clear. First, Himmler had issued specific guidelines concerning the fate of the deported Reich Jews and emphatically insisted on compliance. There is not the slightest evidence that the killings at Kaunas, carried out on two occasions four days apart and with no repercussions from Himmler, resulted from anything other than his own policy. And second, after November 30, it was again Himmler's policy to incarcerate, not immediately liquidate, the subsequent transports of Reich Jews. It is only speculation, but the repercussions of the Kaunas killings may have given Himmler pause.[86] At this sensitive and increasingly uncertain time in the war, he may have decided to postpone the further killing of Reich Jews until it could be done, as Kube urged, in a more discrete and "humane" way.

Stahlecker, otherwise so proud to list his victims, made no mention of liquidating these transports in his undated summary report of early 1942. Since December, he wrote, 20,000 Jews from the Reich had arrived in Riga and were lodged either in the new camp or in a separate section of the Riga ghetto. "Of the Jews from the Reich only a small portion are capable of work. Some 70–80% are women and children as well as elderly persons incapable of work. The mortality rate is also climbing steadily, as a result of the extraordinarily harsh winter." There was also, of course, the danger of epidemic. "In individual cases infectious Jews were separated and executed under the pretext of being sent to a Jewish old people's home or hospital."[87]

According to Jeckeln, even in late January 1942, Himmler was still expressing uncertainty over how to kill the Reich Jews sent to Riga. He told Jeckeln that more transports would come but "that he had not yet decided in which way they were to be destroyed . . . to be shot in Salispils or to be chased off somewhere into the swamp" (*dass er noch nicht entschieden habe, auf welche Weise die zu vernichten seien . . . in Salispils zu erschiessen oder irgendwo auf dem Sumpf zu jagen*). Jeckeln replied that "shooting would be an easier and quicker death."[88] Jeckeln's preference was heeded. In early February some 2,500 Reich Jews—1,500 from the Riga ghetto and 1,000 in Jungfernhof—were shot; in March another 1,800 were shot at Jungfernhof. Within months of the first deportations, only half the 20,000 Reich Jews sent to Riga remained alive.[89]

In the last months of 1941, the total mass murder of the deported Reich Jews was clearly not yet being implemented. Jews in the Organisation Schmelt camps in Silesia who were no longer capable of work were already being selected and gassed in nearby Auschwitz, and German authorities in Riga were advised that they could do the same there. Six transports from the Reich had been massacred upon arrival in Kaunas and Riga. Most of the deportees, however, were placed in the ghettos of Lodz, Minsk, and Riga. But local German occupation authorities were informed that this was temporary. These undesired deportees were to be "evacuated" yet further east in the spring. Neither Jeckeln in his discussions with Himmler, or the reticent Kube in Minsk, had any doubt about the eventual fate of these Jews. The only questions were how and when the killing would be done, and if it could be done in a more discrete and "humane" way than the brutal and semipublic shooting massacres of Soviet Jews.

INTEGRATING THE BUREAUCRACY INTO THE FINAL SOLUTION

For years the German bureaucracy had been attuned to the notion of a *judenfrei* Germany as the ultimate goal of Nazi Jewish policy. Years of frustration had come to an end and long-held expectations were being realized as the first Jewish transports departed from German cities in mid-October 1941. Thus the commencement of these deportations had elicited ready cooperation from a myriad of local authorities as well as the Transportation Ministry, Finance Ministry, and Foreign Office. But would the German bureaucracy be as eager to participate in a program of systematic mass murder of all European Jewry? Was the rest of the bureaucracy as ready to be part of a consensus on the Final Solution as some elements of the Foreign Office had proved themselves in Serbia? Surely Himmler and Heydrich faced two major doubts in this regard.

First, the ss had long taken a proprietary view toward Nazi Jewish policy, trying to curtail or even eliminate the influence and participation of others. In this Darwinistic struggle of bureaucratic jurisdictional imperialism, the ss had been overwhelmingly successful. Could the fires of enthusiasm for a role in Nazi Jewish policy, in some cases long dampened if not extinguished, be rekindled among the former rivals of the triumphant ss? Would they accept junior partnership in place of their former competition?

Second, the idea of the systematic and total mass murder of European Jewry, unlike that of a *judenfrei* Germany, was not a notion to which the German bureaucracy had been long accustomed. On the contrary, the Final Solution was extraordinarily radical and unprecedented for those sitting behind their desks in Berlin as opposed to those with direct experience in imposing the Nazis' racial imperialism in eastern Europe. The Nazis had long sought to infuse German political culture with an appetite for unfettered violence and a total disregard for humanitarian scruples. The legal and moral norms of pre-Nazi society—what were in fact the centuries-long heritage of the Judeo-Christian and Greco-Roman elements of Western civilization that had fused and evolved from the Middle Ages through the Enlightenment—were anathema to the Nazis. To Hitler these norms and inhibitions were epitomized by the notion of a "Jewish conscience" that had to be extirpated from German consciousness. Accordingly, the German bureaucracy, with its notions of legal authority, proper procedure, and paternalistic responsibility, had long been an object of contempt among the Nazis. Hitler had all too openly proclaimed his scorn for jurists and officials afraid to jump over their own shadows. The bureaucrats occasionally recipro-cated this feeling of contempt, even if all too often out of social snobbery and resentment rather than moral revulsion.

Himmler and Heydrich must have pondered uneasily the question of how the German bureaucracy would respond to the Final Solution. The military had supported Hitler's rearmament and aggression, balked briefly at the atroci-ties in Poland, and then become partners in the "war of destruction" in the Soviet Union. The bureaucracy had been the conduit for the host of "legal" anti-Jewish measures of the 1930s but had shied, like most of German society, from the open violence of Kristallnacht. Would they, like the military, now become partners in the murder of European Jewry? Or would the last shocking quantum leap to systematic mass murder, no matter how bureaucratically orga-nized and implemented, prove too much for German officialdom? In late Octo-ber 1941, despite the numerous "anticipations" of the Final Solution, Himmler and Heydrich could not have been sure of the answers to these questions.

The need to accustom the German bureaucracy to the idea of systematic mass murder is the most probable explanation behind Heydrich's decision in late October to officially inform the ministerial bureaucracy in Berlin about the "war of destruction" Germany had been waging in the Soviet Union. This pro-cess of dissemination can be traced most clearly in the Foreign Office, though presumably a similar process occurred elsewhere as well.

In accordance with Heydrich's orders, on October 30, 1941, Heinrich Müller of the Gestapo sent Foreign Minister Ribbentrop the first five "activity and situation reports" (*Tätigkeits- und Lageberichte*) of the Sipo-SD Einsatzgruppen. The first report, covering events through the end of July, noted "excellent cooperation" with the Wehrmacht. Around Riga "numerous snipers and func-tionaries, mostly Jews, were liquidated" by Einsatzgruppe A. In retaliation for plundering, Einsatzgruppe B had "liquidated a total of 8,000 people. Most of them belonged to the Jewish intelligentsia." In the Ukraine the main activity of Einsatzgruppe C was directed toward "the liquidation of the Jews and Bolsheviks responsible for the bloody terror there." Seven thousand Jews had been seized and shot. Einsatzgruppe D complained that the Hungarian army exhibited "a basic friendliness to Jews and Poles." The Romanians posed a quite different problem. "The Romanians proceed against the Jews without any plans. There would be nothing to complain about the very numerous shootings of Jews if the technical preparations and implementation were not so inadequate. The Romanians leave the executed lying on the spot mostly without burial."[90]

The second report covered events from July 29 to August 14. In the Baltic "the self-cleansing efforts in most places were only slowly getting underway. Through pogroms in Mitau (Jelgava) all 1,550 Jews are now removed." In Belorussia Jews were being ghettoized in many places, but "in Vileyka all the Jews had to be liquidated." In Oshmiany 527 and in Viteklo 332 Jews were liquidated as well. In the western Ukraine 416 Jews had been shot in the last several days. "Jewish pogroms could be launched in only a few places. So, for example, in Tarnopol 600 and in Chorostkov 110 were killed by the population." Furthermore, 400 Jews had been shot in Zhitomir, as were 110 Jews and Bolsheviks in Tschaijachov, 222 Jews in Verditshev, and 146 in Vinnitsa. In Romanian-occupied territory, 682 Jews in Czernowitz (Cernauti), 150 Jews and communists in Hotin (Khotin), 97 Jews in Kekyina, 551 Jews in Kishinev, and 155 Jews in Tighina had been "shot," "liquidated," or "removed" by Einsatzgruppe D in cooperation with the Romanian police.[91]

The third report covered the last half of August, and now Jews were listed in a separate subsection. The report noted ongoing ghettoization of Jews in Kaunas and Belorussia, and four-figure executions in the Ukraine. A large part of the Ukraine had already been made *judenfrei*. However, the Romanians had tried to drive thousands of nonworking Jews into the German sphere; 27,500 had been driven back and 1,265 shot. In Czernowitz and the eastern Dniester region, 1,106 Jews had been "liquidated."[92]

The fourth report covered September 1–15, and noted ongoing executions only in Belorussia.[93] The fifth report, for the last half of September, emphasized the Baltic. "In places in which a markedly intensified propaganda activity was noticed, the Jewish inhabitants were shot. Through these measures, for example, the number of people liquidated by one Sonderkommando reached 75,000. For the same reasons, the Einsatzkommando active in the districts of Rokiskis, Sarasai, Persai, and Prienai reached an execution figure of 85,000 persons. The districts named are free of Jews." This passage was specially marked by an attentive Foreign Office reader. Meanwhile, in Belorussia 1,025 Jews in Yanovichi and 2,278 Jews in Minsk had been executed. In the Ukraine a Sonderkommando had shot 1,668 Jews "who through their filth represented a constant danger of epidemic." It thereby raised its total count to 11,328 Jews as of September 6. Shmielenk had now been made *judenfrei.*[94]

On November 26 Heydrich personally sent Ribbentrop a copy of the next report, for the entire month of October. The section on Ostland Jews dispensed with the sham justifications and rationalizations that had been formulaically attached to the previous reports to justify the mass shootings of Jews. It now bluntly declared: "The male Jews over 16, with the exception of doctors and Jewish council elders, are being executed. This measure is still partly in progress. After the conclusion of the action, there will be only 500 Jewish women and children present in the Ostland." In Belorussia the population complained about the Jews but nonetheless was not ready for pogroms. "For its part the Einsatzgruppe of the Sipo-SD proceeds all the more intensively against the Jews." Therefore, in Belorussia rationalizations were still invoked in describing executions: 165 Jewish "terrorists" in Gorodnia, in Mogilev 337 Jewish women for "especially rebellious behavior" and 113 men for resisting relocation in the ghetto, 321 Jewish "saboteurs" and 118 Jewish "plunderers" in Borisov, 380 Jews in Bobruysk for incitement, all male Jews in Tatarsk for leaving the ghetto, 272 Jewish men and women in Sadrudubs for resistance, 222 Jews in Talka for anti-German propaganda, 996 Jews in Marina Gorka for violating German regulations, 627 Jews in Shklov for sabotage, and all the Jews of the Vitebsk ghetto—some 3,000—for danger of epidemic. In the Ukraine, "as a retaliation measure for setting fire to Kiev, all Jews were arrested and on September 29 and 30, a total of 33,771 Jews were executed." Again this passage was underlined and marked in the margin by a Foreign Office reader. In Zhitomir 3,145 Jews were shot as carriers of Bolshevik propaganda and sabotage; in Cherson 410 Jews as a retaliation measure. But in the end pretenses were again dropped. "The solution to the Jewish question was tackled energetically by the Einsatzgruppe of the Sipo-SD especially in the area of the Dnieper. The territory newly occupied by the commandos was made free of Jews. In the process 4,891 Jews were liquidated."[95]

What was the impact of these reports in attuning and acclimating the recipients to the idea of the mass murder of the Jews? Two factors must be noted. First, the Foreign Office was only one recipient among many. The second report to the Foreign Office was one of 53 copies, the third report one of 80 copies, and the fourth, fifth, and sixth reports one of 100 copies. In October and November Heydrich was veritably flooding the German bureaucracy with information on the massacres taking place on Soviet territory.

Second, the information in the single Foreign Office copy was widely disseminated and understood. The first five were not sent directly to Ribbentrop but to the ss and police liaison desk known as D II under Undersecretary Martin Luther. Although the reports covered all the activities of the Einsatzgruppen, it must have been immediately clear that the information about the Jewish massacres was paramount, for the reports were next sent on to the neighboring Jewish desk, D III, of Franz Rademacher. The first five reports were summarized by Rademacher's assistant, Fritz Gebhard von Hahn. He noted, "An exact overview of the Jews liquidated in all three Reichskommissariate cannot be obtained from the reports." He extrapolated, however, from the examples of EK 2 and 3 in the Baltic, and wrongly concluded that each individual Sonderkommando had on the average liquidated 70,000–80,000 Jews. The result was an over- rather than an underestimate of the number of Jews murdered, but clearly Hahn had not failed to grasp the significance of the reports concerning the intended fate of Soviet Jewry.[96] Undersecretary Luther himself wrote a summary of the sixth report, noting that in the Ostland all male Jews over 16 other than doctors and council members would be executed, and that at the conclusion of the action only 500 Jewish women and children would be left alive. He also noted that 33,000 Jews in Kiev, 3,000 in Vitebsk, and 5,000 east of the Dnieper had been shot. The summary was initialed by State Secretary Weizsäcker the day it was written.

The Luther and Hahn summaries were then submitted through State Secretary Weizsäcker and the head of the political division, Ernst Woermann—both of whom initialed the cover letter—to a number of other divisions and desks in the Foreign Office. From late December through late January the summaries made the rounds. In the end the original reports had been read by at least 5 people and the summaries had been initialed by 16. One can only speculate how many others who did not officially have to initial the circulation sheets either saw or heard of the summaries. Although all the documents were marked *Geheime Reichssache* or "Top Secret," this was one secret meant to be an "open" secret. Officials were to know enough to know what was expected of them when it was their turn to contribute to the Final Solution.

Throughout the following spring the flow of information continued, only now not just summaries but the entire reports were circulated through the Foreign Office. The seventh and eighth reports, each one of 100 copies, covered the months of November and December, respectively, and were sent to the Foreign Office on January 16, 1942. "The Jewish question in the Ostland can be regarded as solved," the seventh report boasted. "Large-scale executions have severely decimated the Jewish population and the remaining Jews were ghettoized." In Gorki 2,200, in Mstislavl 900, and in Lubny 1,865 Jews had been shot. In Mogilev 3,276 Jews had been shot in a large action, and that city was now *judenfrei*. As a result of Jewish actions in Kiev and Zhitomir, 137 truckloads of clothing had been given to the National Socialist Welfare agency. The eighth report made no attempt to disguise the shootings as spontaneous retaliation. "In Rovno the long-planned Jewish action was carried out, in which 15,000 could be shot." Massacres of 5,281 Jews in Bobruysk, 1,113 in Parichi, 835 in Rudnia, and 2,365 near Gomel were also reported. These reports were initialed by 13 officials, including once again State Secretary Weizsäcker and the top-ranking undersecretary, Ernst Woermann.[97]

A ninth report, for January, was not received, but on March 5, 1942, Müller sent the tenth report, for the month of February. It stated succinctly: "Now that the Jewish question in the Ostland can be regarded practically as solved and settled, the clarification of this problem progresses further in the other occupied territories of the east. . . . Again and again, Jews who violate official regulations are seized and shot. To prevent the further spread of epidemic danger, various shootings of Jews were necessary." Luther prepared a summary of this report, which was sent to Weizsäcker and seven others.[98] The eleventh and final report, for the month of April, announced that the Ostland was for the most part *judenfrei* and reported massacres of 3,412 Jews in Minsk, 2,007 in Baranovichi, 1,224 in Artemovsk, and in Rakov 15,000, which made that city *judenfrei*. One thousand "Jews and Gypsies" were also shot in the Crimea. This report was circulated to 16 officials, including Woermann but not Weizsäcker.[99]

While Heydrich was feeding information to the ministerial bureaucracy in Berlin, Himmler did not remain silent. On November 11 he told his masseur Felix Kersten that "the destruction of the Jews is being planned. . . . Now the destruction of the Jews is imminent."[100] Four days later, on November 15, Himmler had a four-hour discussion with Alfred Rosenberg. One topic discussed was the question of relations between Himmler's HSSPF and Rosenberg's Reichskommissaren, especially in regard to the local Jewish experts. It was agreed that the local Jewish experts would hold positions both with the HSSPF and in the political division of the Reichskommissariat in "personal union." Himmler's file note does not reveal further discussion of the Jewish question with Rosenberg.[101]

Three days after this meeting with Himmler, and indeed just five days after Rosenberg's ministry in Berlin had told its officials in Riga that incoming transports of Reich Jews would be sent further east in the spring, Rosenberg gave an extraordinary "confidential" background report to the German press. The reporters were not yet to print the details of what was happening in the east, but they needed sufficient background so that the press could give its treatment the proper "color" (*Farbe*), he explained. Among the topics Rosenberg dealt with was the Jewish question.

At the same time this eastern territory is called upon to solve a question which is posed to the peoples of Europe; that is, the Jewish question. In the east some six million Jews still live, and this question can only be solved *in a biological eradication of the entire Jewry of Europe* [italics mine]. The Jewish question is solved for Germany only when the last Jew has left German territory, and for Europe when not a single Jew lives on the European continent up to the Urals. [. . . *diese Frage kann nur gelöst werden in einer biologischen Ausmerzung des gesamten Judentums in Europa. Die Judenfrage ist für Deutschland erst gelöst, wenn der letzte Jude das deutsche Territoriums verlassen hat, und für Europa wenn kein Jude mehr bis zum Ural auf dem europäischen Kontinent steht.*] That is the task that fate has posed to us. You can imagine that for the implementation of these measures, only those men are assigned who conceive of the question as a historical task, who do not act out of personal hatred, but rather out of this very mature political and historical perspective. The 9th of November 1918 was for us a day of fate and decision. At that time Jewry revealed that it was geared to the destruction of Germany. Thanks only to the Führer and the strength of character of the German nation, they did not succeed. Thus we must be on our guard that a romantic generation in Europe does not again raise up the Jews. For this reason it is necessary to expel them over the Urals or eradicate them in some other way. [. . . *dazu ist es nötig, sie über den Ural zu drängen oder sonst irgendwie zur Ausmerzung.*][102]

If Rosenberg was still unsure exactly how and in what area in the east the Jews of Europe were fated to die, he now knew that a "biological eradication" of all European Jews was the clear goal. And the same can be said for all of those to whom he spoke.

On November 24 Himmler had a long discussion with State Secretary Wilhelm Stuckart of the Interior Ministry. The Interior Ministry had been one of Himmler's major rivals for jurisdiction over Jewish policy, and Himmler's agenda indicates he intended to leave Stuckart in no doubt as to how this rivalry had been resolved: "Jewish questions belong to me." (*Judenfragen gehören zu mir.*)[103] Himmler apparently also told Stuckart much else about the state of Nazi Jewish policy. On December 19, less than a month after this meeting, Stuckart was visited by Interior Ministry Jewish expert Bernhard Lösener at the latter's urgent request. The distressed Lösener related what he had just learned from his colleague, Regierungsrat Werner Feldscher. A reliable acquaintance of Feldscher's had been an eyewitness of the murder of the Berlin Jews in Riga. He had returned to Berlin and described the gruesome event. Lösener told the state secretary that under these circumstances he could no longer work in the Interior Ministry, even if it endangered his past attempts to preserve the category of *Mischlinge* distinct from that of full Jew. Stuckart replied, "The proceedings against the evacuated Jews are based on a decision from the highest authority. You must come to terms with it." (*Das Verfahren gegen die evakuierten Juden beruht auf einer Entscheidung von höchster Stelle. Damit werden Sie sich abfinden müssen.*) He castigated Lösener for being "not dynamic enough" and for sticking too stubbornly to the Nuremberg Laws. Because Lösener had not understood how to maintain the necessary ties with the party and now especially with the ss, "the leadership in the Jewish question always slipped further away" from the Interior Ministry, Stuckart said accusingly. He emphatically insisted that the Jews were to blame for forcing the war upon Germany and thus also for all German casualties. "If we strike back harshly, then one must appreciate the world historical necessity of this harshness and cannot squeamishly ask whether precisely this or that particular deported Jew is personally deserving of the fate that overtakes him."[104]

Growing awareness of the new turn in German policy spread not only among the bureaucrats in Berlin but also abroad. Eichmann summoned his various Jewish experts to Berlin,[105] and presumably his emissary from the Netherlands was less than discrete upon his return. Four reports that had been submitted to the HSSPF by an ardently pro-Nazi and anti-Semitic Dutch collaborator and ss informer made increasingly explicit references to the fate not only of Reich but also of Dutch Jews. On November 20, 1941, the collaborator noted that "the dragging off of all German Jews to Poland" had been ordered, and he vehemently urged that Dutch Jews also be deported as soon as possible, "best of all likewise to Poland." On December 4 he was aware that the deportation of all German Jews, "which means a partial extermination of Jewry" (*was eine teilweise Ausrottung des Judentums bedeute*), would be followed by the deportation of all Dutch Jews in the spring "also to east Poland" (*ebenfalls nach Ost-Polen*). He thus urged the immediate introduction of preparatory measures such as marking, restrictions on movement, and the "starvation of the Jews in the Netherlands." By December 18, 1941, the informant proclaimed that "extermination, destruction, and dragging off of the Jews shall make a revival of the Jews impossible for all time." (*Ausrottung, Vernichtung, und Verschleppung des Judentums sollte für alle Zeiten eine Wiederauferstehung des Judentums unmöglich machen.*)[106] In short, by early

December the Dutch collaborator knew not only that both Reich and Dutch Jews were to be deported to their death but also that the geographical location was now "east Poland."

The intentions of the Nazi regime were increasingly revealed not only unofficially among the lower echelons but also at the highest level. On November 28, 1941, Hitler received the Grand Mufti of Jerusalem in Berlin. Hitler went beyond what he had said in late July to an earlier guest, Marshal Kvaternik of Croatia, in both adding a non-European dimension and explicating the fate that awaited the Jews: "Germany has resolved, step by step, to ask one European nation after the other to solve its Jewish problem, and at the proper time, direct a similar appeal to non-European nations as well." When Germany had defeated Russia and broken through the Caucasus into the Middle East, it would have no further imperial goals of its own and would support Arab liberation, Hitler assured his guest. But Hitler did have one goal. "Germany's objective would then be solely the destruction of the Jewish element residing in the Arab sphere under the protection of British power." (*Das deutsche Ziel würde dann lediglich die Vernichtung des im arabischen Raum unter der Protektion der britischen Macht lebenden Judentums sein.*)[107] In short, Jews were not simply to be driven out of the German sphere but would be hunted down and destroyed even beyond it.

On November 29, 1941, the very day Jäger's SK 3 was murdering the fourth and fifth transports of Reich Jews to Kaunas, and the day before the first transport to Riga would be liquidated by Jeckeln and Lange's men in Riga, Heydrich sent out invitations to a meeting on December 9.[108] Within the ministerial bureaucracy, recipients of the invitation included the state secretaries of Interior, Propaganda, Justice, the Four-Year Plan, and the Ostministerium, as well as Undersecretary of State Luther of the Foreign Office and Ministerialdirektor Kritzinger of the Reich Chancellery. Not included were Finance and Transportation, which were already cooperating frictionlessly in the deportation program. When HSSPF Krüger in the General Government met with Himmler on November 28 and complained about Frank's tendencies to control Jewish policy himself, Heydrich quickly extended State Secretary Josef Bühler an invitation as well.[109]

Heydrich enclosed a copy of Göring's July 31 authorization for him to prepare a plan for a "total solution" to the Jewish question in Europe. He justified the meeting in view of the "extraordinary significance" of the topic and the interest of attaining a common understanding among all the central agencies whose work was connected with this "Final Solution." A common understanding was especially urgent given that Jewish transports had been leaving the Reich continuously since October 15.

The impact of Heydrich's invitation can be traced for at least one of the recipients—Undersecretary Martin Luther. This erstwhile defender of Foreign Office prerogatives against ss encroachment, but Heydrich's partner in murder since their meeting in early October over the Serbian Jews, was the only undersecretary among a plethora of state secretaries from the Berlin ministries to be invited. Heydrich obviously preferred the ambitious and opportunistic Luther to the latter's stodgy and inhibited boss, Weizsäcker.[110] Luther instructed Rademacher to prepare a memorandum of "our wishes and desires" (*unsere Wünsche und Ideen*) for his use at the meeting. Though divided into eight points, the memo basically committed the Foreign Office to influencing other European countries to adopt German-style Jewish legislation and then deport their Jews. These measures were to be carried out "as hitherto[,] on friendly terms with the Gestapo."[111]

On December 5 the Soviet army began its counteroffensive on the edge of Moscow, and on December 7 the Japanese navy attacked Pearl Harbor. On December 11 Germany declared war on the United States. Because of this flurry of sudden and crucial events, claiming the attention of many of the invitees, Heydrich had to postpone the meeting at the last minute.[112] One month later he informed the invitees that the meeting was rescheduled for January 20, 1942.

But while Heydrich's meeting, intended to coordinate the participation of the ministerial bureaucracy and to assert his jurisdiction,[113] was postponed six weeks, another important meeting was not. On December 12, 1941, Hitler hosted the Reichsleiter and Gauleiter, that is the top echelons of the Nazi Party, for a gathering in his private apartment in Berlin. Goebbels recorded the gist of Hitler's lengthy remarks in his diary, including brief comments on the Jews:

> Concerning the Jewish question, the Führer is determined to make a clean sweep. He prophesied to the Jews that if they were once again to cause a world war, the result would be their own destruction. That was no figure of speech. The world war is here, the destruction of the Jews must be the inevitable consequence. This question is to be viewed without sentimentality. It is our duty to have sympathy not for the Jews but only for our own German people. If the German people have now again sacrificed 160,000 dead on the eastern front, then the authors of this bloody conflict must pay for it with their lives.[114]

> (*Bezüglich der Judenfrage ist der Führer entschlossen, reinen Tisch zu machen. Er hat den Juden prophezeit, dass, wenn sie noch einmal einen Weltkrieg herbeiführen würden, sie dabei ihre Vernichtung erleben würden. Das ist keine Phrase*

gewesen. Der Weltkrieg ist da, die Vernichtung des Judentums muss die notwendige Folge sein. Diese Frage ist ohne jede Sentimentalität zu betrachten. Wir sind nicht dazu da, Mitleid mit den Juden, sondern nur Mitleid mit unserem deutschen Volk zu haben. Wenn das deutsche Volk jetzt wieder im Ostfeldzug an die 160.000 Tote geopfert hat, so werden die Urheber dieses blutigen Konflikts dafür mit ihrem Leben bezahlen müssen.)

Once again, Hitler gave no explicit order but made unmistakably clear that his prophecy of January 1939—often referred to in the past—had to be taken utterly literally. Moreover, his statement resolved a possible ambiguity about the timetable for the Final Solution. In the fall of 1941, the anticipated timetable had been expressed in two ways—"after the war" and "next spring." In October these were two ways of expressing the same notion. In December, however, after the Red Army counteroffensive and the American entry into the war, "after the war" and "next spring" were no longer two different expressions for the same timetable, and the conflict between the two had to be resolved. Hitler's remarks made it clear that the Final Solution would go forward "next spring" and would not be delayed until "after the war."

Hitler's remarks also signaled to his inner circle that they in turn could initiate others. After his long meeting with Himmler on November 15, Rosenberg had already proceeded to speak with extraordinary frankness to the German press. His speech, moreover, resonated with Himmler-style rhetoric. Following Hitler's speech, the same scenario was now replayed by Hans Frank. During his visit to Berlin from December 10 to 13, Frank had attended the meeting of party leaders and may have met with Hitler privately.[115] Upon returning to the General Government, Frank addressed a gathering of his district governors and division leaders on December 16. Part of his speech was devoted to the Jewish question. It went well beyond his vague hints of late October and in parts eerily echoed the words he had just heard from Hitler in Berlin.

We must put an end to the Jews, that I want to say quite openly. The Führer once spoke these words: If united Jewry should once more succeed in unleashing a world war, then the peoples who have been incited to this war will not be its only victims, because the Jew in Europe will also have found his end. . . . Before I continue to speak I would ask you to agree with me on the following principle: we want to have compassion only for the German people, otherwise for no one in the whole world. Others have had no compassion for us. As an old National Socialist, I must also say: if the Jewish tribe were to survive the war in Europe, while we had sacrificed our best blood for Europe's preservation, then this war would be only a partial success. Thus vis-à-vis the Jews I will in principle proceed only on the assumption that they will disappear. They must go. I have entered into negotiations for the purpose of deporting them to the east. In January a large meeting will take place in Berlin on this topic, to which I will send State Secretary Dr. Bühler. This meeting will be convened in the Reich Security Main Office by ss-Obergruppenführer Heydrich. In any case a large migration of Jews will be set in motion.

But what is to happen to the Jews? Do you believe that they will be lodged in settlements in the Ostland? In Berlin we were told: why all this trouble; we cannot use them in the Ostland or the Reichskommissariat either; liquidate them yourselves! [*liquidiert sie selber!*] Gentlemen, I must ask you, arm yourselves against any thoughts of compassion. We must destroy the Jews, wherever we encounter them and wherever it is possible [*Wir müssen die Juden vernichten, wo immer wir sie treffen und wo es irgend möglich ist*], in order to preserve the entire structure of the Reich.

Frank had obviously had time to wonder how this was to be accomplished, but apparently he and Bühler had not yet learned enough in Berlin to be able to tell his audience.

One cannot apply previous conceptions to such a gigantic, unique event. In any case we must find a way to achieve our goal. . . . We have an estimated 2.5 million Jews in the General Government, perhaps with the half-Jews and all that that entails some 3.5 million. We cannot shoot these 3.5 million Jews, we cannot poison them, but nonetheless we will take some kind of action that will lead to a successful destruction, and indeed in conjunction with the important measures to be discussed in the Reich. The General Government must become just as free of Jews as the Reich.[116]

Thus Frank at least knew from his conversations in Berlin that the postponed state secretaries' conference would be rescheduled for January to deal with a problem implicit in Hitler's speech, namely, how the Jews were to be killed. These two meetings—one for the party leaders and one for the state secretaries—had originally been scheduled to simultaneously orient their respective audiences from the top ranks of the party and bureaucracy. The latter would now become in one sense a follow-up conference to discuss methods of implementation.

Even as awareness spread in December, both Himmler and Hitler began to exhibit some unease that the increasingly "open secret" might become too open.

On December 14 Himmler met with Viktor Brack, one of the heads of the euthanasia program who was providing personnel for the death camps in Poland. Himmler expressed a sense of urgency: "One must work as quickly as possible if only for reasons of camouflage [*Tarnung*]."[117]

Another party leader who had attended Hitler's gathering was Rosenberg, who met again with Hitler, also on December 14. He discussed with Hitler the draft of a speech he had written before Germany's declaration of war on the United States that apparently threatened dire retaliation against the Jews of eastern Europe in response to "New Yorker Jews" calling for Germany's encirclement.[118] Rosenberg raised the issue with Hitler: "Concerning the Jewish question, I said that now after the decision my remarks over the New York Jews perhaps had to be changed somewhat. I took the viewpoint not to speak of the extermination of the Jews. The Führer approved this attitude and said they had burdened us with this war and had caused the destruction. It should come as no surprise when they above all suffered the consequences."[119] Following Germany's declaration of war on the United States, threats against Jews as a means of deterring their alleged pressure for an American entry into the war was now not only pointless but also counterproductive in drawing attention to the intended extermination program.[120] Within Rosenberg's Ostministerium, there had been long-standing confusion about the totality of the destruction intended. No longer. Four days after Rosenberg's meeting with Hitler, an inquiry from the Reichskommissariat Ostland as to whether all Jews should be liquidated regardless of age, sex, and economic interest was answered from Berlin: "In the meantime clarity on the Jewish question has been achieved through oral discussion: economic interests are to be disregarded on principle in the settlement of this problem."[121]

On December 18 Himmler met with Hitler. The cryptic remark in Himmler's appointment book stated simply: "Jewish question/to be exterminated as partisans" (*Judenfrage | als Partisanen auszurotten*).[122] Most likely, they discussed how the killing of the Jews was to be justified and what were the rules for speaking about it.

By the time Heydrich sent out a new invitation on January 8 for a noon meeting on January 20, this time "with lunch included,"[123] the process of initiation, dissemination, and integration was quite advanced. Dr. Stuckart of the Interior Ministry, Martin Luther of the Foreign Office, Dr. Josef Bühler of the General Government, and Drs. Alfred Meyer and Georg Leibbrandt of the Ostministerium all had direct knowledge of the fundamental change in Nazi Jewish policy that had occurred. Representing the Justice Ministry was State

Secretary Roland Freisler, the subsequent "hanging judge" of the notorious People's Court. Ministerialdirektor Friedrich Wilhelm Kritzinger, reputedly one of the best informed people in Nazi Germany,[124] represented the Reich Chancellery of Heinrich Lammers. Göring, whose authorization to Heydrich had been included in the first invitation, was represented by State Secretary Dr. Erich Neumann. Notably absent from the invitees was Goebbels's state secretary Leopold Gutterer.

Various ss leaders were also in attendance: Heinrich Müller of the Gestapo (who had sent Eichmann to Minsk and Chelmno); Otto Hofmann of the Race and Resettlement Main Office; Dr. Karl Eberhard Schöngarth, BdS in the General Government (who had also led a special Einsatzgruppe into Galicia in July 1941); Dr. Rudolf Lange of Einsatzkommando 2 (who had helped carry out the Riga massacres); Oberführer Gerhard Klopfer, state secretary of Bormann's Party Chancellery; and of course Reinhard Heydrich and his Jewish expert Adolf Eichmann. No less than eight of the fifteen participants held the doctorate. Thus it was not a dimwitted crowd unable to grasp what was going to be said to them. Nor were they going to be overcome with surprise or shock, for Heydrich was not talking to the uninitiated or squeamish.

The meeting took place at a 1914 villa that had been purchased by the ss in 1940 and was located at a fashionable suburban street address, 56/58 Am Grossen Wannsee.[125] Heydrich opened the conference with a long speech, based in large part on materials that Eichmann had compiled for him.[126] In the first part of the speech, Heydrich reiterated his authority from Göring to coordinate—without regard to geographic boundaries—a Final Solution to the Jewish question and reviewed the policy of emigration that had led to the exit of 537,000 Jews from the German sphere until Himmler had forbidden further emigration in the fall of 1941.

Heydrich then made the transition to the second section of his speech. "In place of emigration, the evacuation of the Jews to the east has now emerged, after the appropriate prior approval of the Führer, as a further possible solution." These evacuations (i.e., those to Lodz, Minsk, and Riga) were to be regarded "solely as temporary measures" (*lediglich als Ausweichmöglichkeiten*). However, "practical experiences" (*praktische Erfahrungen*) were already being gathered that would be of great significance for the "imminent" Final Solution of the Jewish question, which would include over 11 million Jews, including those from every corner of Europe, such as England, Turkey, Finland, Portugal, and even Ireland. Heydrich then went on to explain just what he meant by this. The Jews would be utilized for labor in the east.

Separated by sex, the Jews capable of work will be led into these areas in large labor columns to build roads, whereby a large part will doubtless fall away through natural diminution.

The remnant that finally survives all this, because it is undoubtedly a question of the part with the greatest resistance, will have to be treated accordingly, because this remnant, representing a natural selection, must be regarded as the germ cell of a new Jewish reconstruction if released.

(*In grossen Arbeitskolonnen, unter Trennung der Geschlechter, werden die arbeitsfähigen Juden strassenbauend in diese Gebiete geführt, wobei zweifellos ein Grossteil durch natürliche Verminderung ausfallen wird.*

Der allfällig endlich verbleibende Restbestand wird, da es sich bei diesen zweifellos um den widerstandsfähigsten Teil handelt, entsprechend behandelt werden müssen, da dieser, eine natürliche Auslese darstellend, bei Freilassung als Keimzelle eines neuen jüdischen Aufbaues anzusprechen ist.)

Despite the euphemisms—separation of sexes, labor utilization leading to large-scale natural diminution, and finally appropriate treatment of the surviving remnant that could not be released to begin a renewal of the Jewish race—the genocidal implications were totally and unmistakably clear. If most of those attending the conference already knew that Jews were being murdered in large numbers, they now had no further doubts about the intended scope of this murderous policy; it aimed at killing every last Jew in Europe from Ireland to the Urals, and from the Arctic to the Mediterranean.

Heydrich then moved into the third section of his speech, discussing some of the particular problems that would have to be dealt with. He proposed an old people's ghetto to ward off anticipated interventions over individual cases and the sending of Jewish advisers to certain satellite countries to make preparations. But the most complex problem involved the fate of Jews in mixed marriages and their part-Jewish offspring. A major portion of the conference was spent exploring this problem, and it was only at this point that animated discussion began. Heydrich wanted to deport half-Jews—that is, murder them—but to equate quarter-Jews with Germans, provided that neither their appearance nor their behavior was markedly Jewish. Jews in mixed marriage would be either deported to the east or sent to the old people's ghetto on a case-by-case basis, depending on the anticipated effect on German relations. Stuckart of the Interior Ministry pressed for compulsory sterilization of the half-Jews rather than deportation, while Hofmann proposed giving the half-Jews a choice between deportation and sterilization. To avoid endless administrative problems over mixed marriages, Stuckart also proposed compulsory divorce. These issues were not resolved and were the subject of two further conferences in March and October 1942.

Thereafter the discussion became quite freewheeling and unstructured. As Eichmann—who was sitting in the corner and supervising the stenotypists—described it at his trial in Jerusalem: "The first part where everyone was quiet and listened to the various lectures, and then in the second part, everyone spoke out of turn and people would go around, butlers, adjutants, and would give out liquor. Well, I don't want to say that there was an atmosphere of drunkardness there. It was an official atmosphere, but nevertheless it was not one of those stiff, formal, official affairs where everyone spoke in turn. But people just talked at cross vertices."[127]

Neumann asked that Jews important to the war economy not be deported until they could be replaced, and Heydrich concurred. Bühler on the other hand urged that the Final Solution begin in the General Government, because there was no transportation problem there and most of the Jews were already incapable of work. "He had only one request, that the Jewish question in this region be solved as quickly as possible." At this point the protocol notes cryptically: "Finally there was a discussion of the various types of possible solutions. . . ." (*Abschliessend wurden die verschiedenen Arten der Lösungsmöglichkeiten besprochen. . . .*)

On Heydrich's instructions, Eichmann did not include the details of this part of the meeting in the protocol, but in Jerusalem he testified as follows: " . . . these gentlemen were standing together, or sitting together, and were discussing the subject quite bluntly, quite differently from the language which I had to use later in the record. During the conversation they minced no words about it at all . . . they spoke about methods of killing, about liquidation, about extermination." At this point, of course, the Germans were still unsure about methods. The experiments in killing technology then underway, the "practical experiences" that were being gathered at this moment, could not yet be assumed to be adequate to the scale of killing that was going to be required.[128] Obviously the murderous use of Jewish labor was included.[129] But Bühler's comments also show that the participants were well aware that most of the Jews were not capable of physical labor and that another, more immediate fate—whatever the killing method—awaited them.

Heydrich closed the conference with a plea for the cooperation of all the participants. Eichmann estimated that the whole meeting had taken between one and one and a half hours. Not everyone left immediately, however. Some stood around in small groups "to discuss the ins and outs of the agenda and also of certain work to be undertaken afterward." In these more intimate circumstances, Heydrich "gave expression to his great satisfaction" and allowed himself a glass of cognac, although it was unusual for him to drink in front of others. He had cause for satisfaction. As Eichmann recalled, Heydrich "more than anybody else [had] expected considerable stumbling blocks and difficulties." Instead he had found "an atmosphere not only of agreement on the part of the participants, but more than that, one could feel an agreement which had assumed a form which had not been expected." Not only had the state secretaries of the ministerial bureaucracy not made difficulties, they were committed and enthusiastic about doing their part in the Final Solution.

A number of Final Solution conferences, involving lower-ranking officials, would be held in the wake of the Wannsee Conference. The first of these was convened in the Ostministerium on January 29, 1942, just nine days later. At issue were the definition of a Jew and the appropriateness of the concept of *Mischlinge* in the eastern occupied territories. According to Dr. Leibbrandt, head of Rosenberg's political division, the Nuremberg Laws provided no adequate model for a definition because the documentary proof of ancestry was unavailable. Likewise, there was no need to preserve the legal position of half-Jews as in Germany. In the east half-Jews were "racially just as undesirable as full Jews," for no German "touch of blood" (*Bluteinschlag*) had to be taken into consideration. Thus the Ostministerium proposed that anyone of former Russian citizenship or who was stateless be defined as a Jew if he admitted to being a Jew; if he was recognized by the Jewish community as a Jew; if his membership to Jewry resulted from some other circumstance; or if he had one parent defined as a Jew by one of the above three criteria.[130]

The conference, under the chairmanship of Dr. Otto Bräutigam, was attended by a total of 17 representatives from the SS, Four-Year Plan, Interior Ministry, Party Chancellery, and Foreign Office, as well as the Ostministerium. The SS successfully intervened to expand the application of the definition of Jew from people who were stateless or former Soviet citizens to anyone who normally resided in the eastern occupied territories. Lösener of the Interior Ministry raised the *Mischlinge* issue. Speaking as if all the participants surely knew, he observed that the conference of January 20 had decided that first-degree *Mischlinge* would be sterilized. (In fact Heydrich had sent out 30 copies of the protocol just three days earlier.) In the interest of a unified European definition of Jew, Lösener suggested desisting from equating full Jews with half-Jews in the east. Dr. Wetzel cryptically replied that "as a result of the awaited solution of the Jewish question, political danger from the equalization of half-Jews from the eastern territories was not to be expected." In short, Lösener's fear of two conflicting definitions of half-Jews was groundless, for after the Final Solution no half-Jews would exist in the east.[131]

Lösener was not the only bureaucrat invoking the Wannsee Conference. On February 10, 1942, Rademacher reminded the head of the Foreign Office colonial desk, Bielfeld, of the files on the Madagascar Plan that Rademacher had sent to him in August 1940. At that time Madagascar was to be demanded from the French in the peace treaty. The situation had now changed, he noted. "The war against the Soviet Union has in the meantime created the opportunity to use other territories for the Final Solution. Accordingly, the Führer has decided that the Jews will not be shoved off to Madagascar but rather to the east. Madagascar no longer needs to be earmarked for the Final Solution."[132] When the head of the political division, Woermann, asked about the authority for Rademacher's important memo, Rademacher turned to Luther. Rademacher explained that he had sent the memo to Bielfeld on the basis of new developments, as Heydrich had explained them to Luther. He requested that Luther inform Woermann of his discussion with Heydrich. Luther replied, "I have answered the inquiry personally."[133]

There was one major exception to the accelerating initiation and integration of the bureaucracy into the Final Solution—Goebbels's Propaganda Ministry. No representative of the Propaganda Ministry had attended either the Wannsee Conference or the Ostministerium conference in January. The participants of the Wannsee Conference had been sent copies of the protocol on January 26. It would appear that Goebbels received an expurgated version only much later. He noted in his diary entry of March 7, 1942: "I read a detailed report from the SD and police regarding the Final Solution of the Jewish question. A vast number of new significant points emerge from it. The Jewish question must now be solved within a pan-European framework. There are more than 11 million Jews still in Europe. They will have to be concentrated later, to begin with, in the east; possibly an island, such as Madagascar can be assigned to them after the war."[134] But Goebbels's exclusion was the exception. By March 1942 awareness of the Final Solution had penetrated deeply albeit unevenly into the German bureaucracy, where for the most part this awareness evoked a ready willingness to contribute—in Rosenberg's words—to the "historic task" that "fate has posed" to Nazi Germany.

THE GASSING BEGINS

At the Wannsee Conference Heydrich noted that "practical experiences" were being gathered for the purpose of implementing the Final Solution. Of the two extermination camps with gassing facilities under construction by early November—Chelmno and Belzec—the first was already in operation and the second was nearing completion and initial testing. At a third site, Auschwitz-Birkenau, key decisions were about to be made. The Germans would not be in doubt much longer about the killing capacity of the newly invented extermination camps.

Chelmno

From 1939 to 1941 Himmler had loaned ss personnel to the euthanasia program, which had been lodged in the Führer Chancellery. Now he was going to collect his debts by taking back his ss personnel experienced in gassing and borrowing some of Viktor Brack's men was well. These men would be one of the major sources of manpower for the new extermination camps. One example was Herbert Lange, who had previously led a Sonderkommando to kill mentally ill patients in the incorporated territories.[135]

In the fall of 1941 Lange had driven around the Warthegau, seeking an appropriate site for his extermination camp, which he found in the small village of Chelmno some 55 kilometers northwest of Lodz. He then drove to Berlin for discussions, returned to Chelmno in late October or early November, and began confiscating various buildings in the village. In the postwar version of HSSPF Wilhelm Koppe, upon Lange's return from Berlin, he meet with Koppe and informed him of a new task—the "evacuation" of the Jews of the Warthegau, which Koppe immediately understood to mean killing. Himmler's adjutant, Brandt, also telephoned Koppe from Berlin to explain that the "testing of Brack's gas" (*die Erprobung der Brackschen Gase*) was planned for the Warthegau.[136] One may reasonably doubt whether Koppe's role was as passive as he later portrayed it, but the dating and language of the account ring true. On October 23 Wetzel and Brack were discussing the possibility of employing "Brack's helper" (*Brackschen Hilfsmittel*) in Riga, so such phrases were quite in vogue at that time.

Koppe henceforth provided the manpower for Lange's Sonderkommando. Some 10–15 ss men from Poznan and Lodz were assigned to Lange through the Sipo-SD Inspector (IdS), Hermann Damzog.[137] Koppe also met with the commander of the Order Police (BdO) in the Warthegau, Oskar Knofe, and asked for a unit of policemen as well.[138] A force of some 80 Orpo men was always in Chelmno, as Knofe rotated men from the police battalion in Lodz for duty at the extermination camp.[139] But if the personnel were supplied by HSSPF Koppe and his Sipo-SD and Orpo commanders, Lange's instructions came from Himmler in Berlin and to some extent from Gauleiter Arthur Greiser, to whom Himmler apparently delegated considerable authority.[140] The men of the Sonderkommando were paid their daily bonus from a special fund of Greiser's Reichsstatthalterei, that is, Greiser's state office rather than his party office of Gauleiter.[141]

Lange's Sonderkommando traveled from Poznan to Chelmno in early November, accompanying what was presumably the original gas van of the 1940 euthanasia actions which was equipped with bottled carbon monoxide. Along the way the men from Poznan stopped in a forest outside Kazimierz Biskupi just north of Konin. Here some 3,000 Jews from the towns of Zagorow, Gradziec, and Rzgow had already been killed in a shooting action in October.[142] According to one of the Polish prisoners who was repeatedly detailed to Sonderkommando Lange throughout the war, a gas van killing action was now carried out in the forest over two days in November, after which the men went directly on to Chelmno.[143]

At the end of the month, the Sonderkommando took the gas van to the labor camp at Bornhagen (Kozminek), where the Jews of the Kalisz region had been ghettoized in 1940. On November 26, 1941, the camp commandant, Ferdinand Göhler, summoned the camp inmates and told them that the young were to go to a children's home and the elderly to a sanatorium. Those selected were locked in the synagogue. Accompanied by SS men, a large truck in the shape of furniture van, with its insides covered with sheet metal, backed up to the synagogue. It was tightly packed with 70–80 Jews, and from within the cab the driver activated the gas flow before driving away. The process was repeated for a number of days, including a special "children's resettlement" on November 30. On some days the truck made more than one trip. With each day, greater force had to be applied to drive the Jews to the square, where the names of the day's victims were read. When the action was finished, some 700 Jews had been taken away in the mysterious truck. The graves of the victims were exhumed in the nearby forest after the war.[144]

Chelmno was a small town of about 250 people. Volhynian Germans had been resettled there on the larger farms, but most of the population was still Polish. The Sonderkommando proceeded to create an extermination camp in the middle of the town, centered around the Schloss or villa and its surrounding park, which dominated the little community. The operation of the camp was in no way concealed from the inhabitants of the town. Initially the villa grounds were surrounded merely by wire. Only after killing operations had been under-way for at least a month was a board fence put up to block the view.[145]

On December 8, 1941, one day before the Wannsee Conference had origi-nally been scheduled, the gassing began at Chelmno itself.[146] At first Jews were rounded up by the local Gendarmerie in nearby communities and brought to Chelmno in a fleet of trucks and buses driven by civilian drivers.[147] One truck at a time was allowed to enter the villa compound through a large gate. The Jews climbed down from the truck or bus and heard a pacifying speech telling them they had to be disinfected before they could be sent to work in Germany. The Jews then entered the main room of the Schloss, where they undressed and registered their valuables under the supervision of a permanent team of seven Polish prisoners. They then descended into the cellar of the Schloss and up a ramp into a waiting gas van. The doors of the van were closed, and the gassing took place immediately. The van then left the compound and drove four kilome-ters north of the village and turned off into the "forest camp" or *Waldlager*.

From the first transports, Jews were selected for three work teams. The smallest was the craftsman commando of 8–10 prisoners. The Schloss com-mando of some 15 prisoners collected and sorted clothing from the undressing room. By far the largest work commando, of at least 30 Jews, worked in the *Waldlager*. It had the terrible job of unloading and cleaning the trucks, and placing the bodies in large mass graves.[148]

Within the small German Sonderkommando, virtually every member had his own specialized job. Some of the Orpo men also took on specialized func-tions and became part of the permanent staff. Most of the Order Police were, like the Jews, divided into three groups. One was the guard detachment in charge of accompanying the Jews to the camp. The second was the Schloss detachment, which guarded the main compound. The third was the *Waldlager* detachment, which guarded the forest burial ground.

Between December 8, 1941, and January 15, 1942, 6,400 Jews from Kowale Panski, Kolo, Bugaj, Dabie, Izbica Kujawska, and Klodawa were murdered at Chelmno.[149] Also in early January 1942, 4,400 Gypsies who had been deported from Austria in October 1941 and were still alive in the "Gypsy camp" within the ghetto were sent to Chelmno and gassed.[150]

It is probable that sometime in January two additional gas vans—designed to kill by diverting exhaust gas into the sealed compartment of the truck—arrived from Berlin.[151] Their origin and make are uncertain. Though agreeing that they were definitely converted from foreign models, one driver remembered them as Dodges, another as Renaults. In Berlin, Walter Rauff of the RSHA technical division was producing Saurer and Opel-Blitz models of gas vans through the

Sipo garage of Friedrich Pradel and a private contractor, Firma Gaubschat. It is probable that the Chelmno vans were part of this same production process, for the designs of the airtight compartment and the exhaust hookup were identical to those of the other gas vans, and at least one Chelmno driver was dispatched through the Berlin motor pool in the same way as drivers were sent to the RSHA-produced gas vans operating with the Einsatzgruppen in the Soviet Union.[152]

Sometime during this earliest phase, the peripatetic Eichmann inspected the killing procedures in Chelmno. Most probably this visit came in January, for the gas van he saw in operation already used exhaust gas, not bottled carbon monoxide. In his postwar testimony, he claimed to have been so sickened that he forgot to time the operation with his stopwatch. Nor could he accept the invitation of the gas van driver to peer through the peek hole into the rear compartment to witness the death agonies of the victims.[153]

On January 16, just four days before the Wannsee Conference, the first trainload of Jews left Lodz for Kolo, from which they were subsequently taken by truck and bus to the nearby Chelmno extermination camp. Chelmno was ready to begin the task for which it had primarily been constructed—the murder of the Lodz ghetto Jews.

Belzec

Construction of a second extermination camp, at Belzec in the district of Lublin, began at the same time as that in Chelmno.[154] In technology and personnel it was the most direct heir of the euthanasia institutes, employing stationary gas chambers and carbon monoxide. However, as at Chelmno, the carbon monoxide was produced in engine exhaust and not delivered in chemically pure form from steel bottles as at the euthanasia institutes. Belzec thus represented another variant in gassing technology and extermination camp design.

Belzec had been one of Globocnik's notorious Jewish work camps in 1940, built almost directly on the demarcation line to provide labor for the construction of fortifications. This camp was dissolved in the fall of 1940. One year later, three SS officers returned to Belzec and demanded a labor contingent of 20 Poles. The individual laborers, who were selected by the local Polish administration and "well paid" for their efforts, began their work on November 1.[155] Josef Oberhauser, a former employee of the euthanasia program, was also assigned to Globocnik in Lublin in October 1941 and first visited Belzec that fall—before there was any extermination camp there—to clear away military equipment.[156]

The Polish workers put up three buildings, the smallest of which was 12 meters by 8 meters. It was divided into three equal rooms, the insides of which were lined with sheet metal. Sand was poured between the inner and outer wall boarding. Each of the three rooms also had an inner and outer door. These doors were very strong, opened outward, had rubber seals, and could be locked with heavy crossbars from the outside. Pipes ran under the floors into each room. Work was supervised by a handsome, blond, 20-year-old ethnic German carpenter from Katowice, who carried around a set of plans. He laughed when the Poles asked him what the building was intended for. The Poles finished on December 22 and were released from their work.[157]

In December Oberhauser returned to Belzec with building materials and a team of ex-Soviet POWs in black uniforms. They were Ukrainians who had been recruited from German POW camps and trained at an SS camp at Trawniki, also in the Lublin district, to work for their new German masters. The Ukrainians built a ramp on the north side of the three-room building, the side with the outside doors, and then built a small rail line into the nearby field, where they dug a large hole 2 meters deep, 20 meters wide, and 50 meters long. They also strung barbed wire around the camp and planted a screen of fir and spruce trees.[158] The young ethnic German supervising the construction was much less reticent with Oberhauser and showed him the plans for the gas chamber facility.[159] Also in December, Christian Wirth returned to Belzec and took command. Oberhauser became his liaison to SSPF Globocnik in Lublin.

After the Polish workers had been let go, Jewish workers were brought in from Lubzcza and Mosty Male. Watchtowers and more buildings were constructed in January.[160] Also after Christmas, Dr. Helmut Kallmeyer, the chemist whom Viktor Brack had wanted to send to Riga to construct gassing facilities in late October but who claimed never to have made the trip, was dispatched to Lublin. He waited to be assigned work, but was eventually told that no chemist was needed and sent home.[161] In February the 150 Jewish workers were killed in the first test of the gas chambers.[162] Wirth then told the German officer in charge of the Ukrainians to telephone Globocnik and inform him that Wirth and his commando were going back to Berlin. All else would be arranged there. When Globocnik sent Oberhauser to investigate, he found neither prisoners nor Wirth's team.[163]

Wirth's sudden departure without Globocnik's knowledge or approval would indicate that he did not yet consider Globocnik his direct superior and that some tensions had arisen because of this.[164] After "negotiations" in Berlin, the terms of Wirth's subordination to Globocnik must have been established. Wirth returned in early March with a camp commando composed almost entirely of former euthanasia personnel. The first transports of Jews from Galicia arrived on March 15 or 16 and from the Lublin ghetto on March 17, 1942. Full-scale killing was ready to began at the Belzec extermination camp.

Birkenau

In addition to testing Zyklon B, first in Bunker 11 and then in the old crematory in the Auschwitz Stammlager in August/September 1941, Rudolph Höss had other major projects on his agenda. He was expecting the arrival of large numbers of Soviet POWs, and had been charged by Himmler with creating a large camp at Birkenau to accommodate 100,000 of them. Construction began in October 1941. At the same time, the SS's crematorium expert, the engineer Kurt Prüfer of the company Topf and Sons, arrived in Auschwitz to plan construction of a new large crematorium, which was to be located not in Birkenau but rather in the Stammlager.[165]

By early 1942, however, it was relatively evident that large numbers of Soviet POWs would never reach the camp planned for them at Birkenau. If they were still alive, they were to be sent to the Reich for labor. But gradually another task began to loom increasingly large for what had become "a site in search of a mission." Already in the fall of 1941, Jews deemed no longer fit to work in the Organisation Schmelt camps had been sent to Auschwitz in small numbers and gassed in the old crematory. On February 15, 1942, a small transport of elderly Silesian Jews arrived in Auschwitz from Beuthen and was taken to the old crematory in the Stammlager to be gassed and cremated—an operation that required suspension of the normal routine of the Stammlager.[166] If Auschwitz-Birkenau was now to take on the same role for Silesia as Chelmno was already performing for the Warthegau, that is, to kill the nonworking Jews, changes had to be made.

On February 27 Hans Kammler, the head of SS construction, visited Auschwitz and approved plans in which the large new crematorium was to be located in the northwest corner of Birkenau rather than in the Stammlager. At the same time, the peasant hut called the "red house" and located in the birch woods just beyond the northwest corner of the camp was being converted into the gas chamber designated Bunker 1. As Robert Jan van Pelt has argued, it is highly unlikely that these two developments were unrelated.[167] Sometime around March 20, 1942, Jews from East Upper Silesia were gassed in Bunker 1 for the first time, and their bodies were buried in the nearby meadow.[168] Birkenau had begun its fateful career as an extermination camp, although the large-scale liquidation in Bunker 1 of Jewish transports from Silesia would not begin until May.[169]

Semlin

In addition to Chelmno, Belzec, and Birkenau, yet a fourth, albeit improvised and temporary, site for the gassing of Jews was established by the Germans in the town of Semlin (Sajmiste) on Croatian territory across the Sava River from Belgrade in early 1942. In the fall of 1941, firing squads of the Wehrmacht and Police Battalion 64 had killed virtually all the adult male Jews and "Gypsies" in Serbia. Beginning in December 1941, the women, children, and elderly Jews and "Gypsies" of Belgrade were interned in a camp established on the Semlin fair grounds. Internees from elsewhere in Serbia followed. Living in large unheated exhibition pavilions, underfed, and subjected to hard physical labor, the prisoners suffered grievously during the harsh winter.[170]

As the Jews and "Gypsies" were being interned in December 1941, the Foreign Office plenipotentiary Felix Benzler urged that they be deported as soon as possible, and Luther held out the prospect of the following spring at the earliest.[171] At the Wannsee Conference, however, Heydrich did not foresee early deportations from Serbia, since he contemplated combing Europe from west to east. In any case, the Jewish women, children, and elderly interned in Semlin—whom the military would not shoot to fill their reprisal quotas—were "extraordinarily burdensome" (ausserordentlich lästig) to local German authorities but ranked very low on Berlin's list of priorities.[172] At the very same time, the motor pool of the RSHA in Berlin was producing gas vans that had been designed to lighten the burden of killing women and children. Though the details of the process remain unclear, the decision to send a gas van to Semlin in the spring of 1942 to kill the interned Jewish women, children, and elderly must have been close to self-evident.

The head of the military administration, Harald Turner, wrote to Himmler's adjutant Karl Wolff on April 11, 1942: "Already some months ago I had all the available Jews shot and all Jewish women and children concentrated in a camp and at the same time, with the help of the SD, procured a 'delousing truck' [Entlausungswagen] that will finally clear the camp in some 14 days to 4 weeks."[173] Turner was at that time embattled over his position and seeking Wolff's help.[174] One must suspect that his boastful claim to having procured a gas van was as exaggerated as his claim to primary responsibility for having had the male Jews shot.

The commander of the Security Police in Belgrade, Emanuel Schäfer, had previously commanded an Einsatzgruppe in Poland in 1939. After being transferred to the Stapoleitstelle in Cologne, he had dispatched three Jewish transports from that city in late 1941. In January 1942 Heydrich sent him to Belgrade. Testifying after the war, Schäfer gave a straightforward account. Gestapo chief Heinrich Müller simply sent him a cryptic telegram announcing the arrival of a "special truck" with a "special assignment" for a Jewish action in Serbia, leaving Schäfer in no doubt about what was intended. A large-model Saurer gas van with two drivers arrived in early March.[175]

The "Gypsies" were released from the Semlin camp.[176] The Final Solution—in contrast to the reprisal shootings—was not yet meant for them. Then, for some two months, every morning and two or three afternoons each week, excepting Sundays and holidays, the gas van arrived at the gates of the Semlin camp and was loaded with close to a hundred Jews. It crossed the one surviving span of the Sava River bridge, where the driver then stopped and redirected the exhaust gas into the sealed compartment. The van then drove through downtown Belgrade to the Avala shooting range southeast of the city. Here seven Serbian prisoners, guarded by four policemen of Reserve Police Battalion 64, emptied the dead Jews into a mass grave. On May 10, 1942, the van made its last deadly trip.[177] By then some 8,500 Jews had perished in Semlin, perhaps some 7,300 in the gas van and the rest from the harsh conditions and executions.[178]

One of the most remarkable features of the Semlin camp and gassing was its public nature. The camp itself was in full view from the heights of Belgrade across the river. In late 1943, when the Germans had begun to worry, the new German ambassador proposed (in vain) moving the Semlin camp because its continuing existence "before the eyes of the people of Belgrade was politically intolerable for reasons of public feelings."[179] And the van itself drove through the middle of Belgrade as the gassing took place. Certainly the German officials involved were not reluctant to draw attention to their accomplishment. On May 29 the Foreign Office Jewish expert Franz Rademacher wrote: "The Jewish question in Serbia is no longer acute." And Schäfer boasted "with pride" that "Belgrade was the only great city of Europe that was free of Jews."[180]

Conclusion

HITLER AND THE DECISION-MAKING PROCESS IN NAZI JEWISH POLICY, SEPTEMBER 1939–MARCH 1942

In the five weeks between September 18 and October 25, 1941, events had moved rapidly. Hitler had reversed his earlier decision not to permit the deportation of Jews from the Third Reich until after the war and instead sought the unrealizable goal of a *judenfrei* Germany by the end of the year. The sites of the first extermination camps were selected. The testing of various methods of killing by poison gas were conducted. Jewish emigration from the Third Reich was forbidden. And the first 11 Jewish transports had departed for Lodz as a temporary holding station. The vision of the Final Solution—a program aimed at murdering every last Jew in the German grasp—had crystallized in the minds of the Nazi leadership and was henceforth being turned into reality.

If the last pieces in the decision-making process came together quickly in the end, this fateful cluster of decisions itself was the climax of a long process stretching over a period of 25 months from September 1939 to October 1941. The commitment to some kind of final solution to the Jewish question had been inherent in Nazi ideology from the beginning. Thus Nazi Jewish policy had evolved through a series of final solutions, which first envisaged a *judenfrei* Germany through emigration and then a *judenfrei* Europe through expulsion. This process of radicalization culminated in 1941 in the ultimate Final Solution of systematic mass murder. Jewish policy could evolve no further in concept. It remained only to be implemented through action.

What was Hitler's role in this fateful evolution? As the ultimate embodiment of Nazi ideology as well as the constant inciter and mobilizer of the party faithful, Hitler had certainly legitimized and prodded the ongoing search for final solutions. His obsession with the Jewish question ensured that the Nazi commitment would not slacken, that the search for a solution *one way or another* to this self-imposed problem would not fade away into obscurity or be indefinitely postponed. No leading Nazi could prosper who did not appear to take the Jewish question as seriously as Hitler did himself. Thus Hitler, simply by his existence, exerted a continuing pressure on the political system, which induced a competition among the faithful and ambitious to advance ever more radical proposals and to carry out Jewish policy in an ever more brutal and comprehensive manner. For many—the "true believers"—this commitment to the Final Solution was a deeply felt conviction. For the unquestioning loyalists, it was a matter of completely identifying with Hitler. For eugenicists and planning experts, it was the opportunity to realize an agenda of their own that overlapped with that of Hitler. For technicians of many sorts, it was a chance to display their skills. And for countless others, it was a cynical exercise in political careerism, opportunism, and accommodation. In the end the results were the same. The commitment to some kind of final solution permeated the entire regime, and acceptance of such a priority on the part of the regime characterized much of the German population at large.

But Hitler's role was also more immediate. From September 1939 to October 1941 he was an active and continuing participant in the decision-making process. Indeed, not a single significant change in Nazi Jewish policy occurred without his intervention and approval. Two basic conclusions can be drawn about this participation. The first concerns Hitler's mode of operation. To make his wishes known, he would give signals in the form of relatively vague and inexplicit statements, exhortations, and prophecies. Others, especially Himmler, responded to these signals with extraordinary alacrity and sensitivity, bringing to Hitler more specific guidelines for his approval. The classic example is Himmler's May 1940 memorandum on the treatment of alien populations in the east. On occasion, not only guidelines but quite concrete proposals—such as those for marking German Jews or commencing deportations from particular cities in the Reich to particular destinations in the east—were submitted to Hitler as well. If one continuity above all others emerges in this regard, it is the close and sympathetic relationship between Hitler and Himmler during this period. If one wants to know what Hitler was thinking, one should look at what Himmler was doing.

A second rather consistent pattern is the chronological correlation between victory and radicalization, indicating that the emergence of the Final Solution was influenced and shaped not only by Hitler's enduring obsession with the Jewish question but also by the changing circumstances and the periods of elation and victory euphoria in which the Third Reich found itself. Let us briefly review this chronological pattern.

Hitler had indicated in his January 30, 1939, Reichstag speech that the outbreak of war would have fateful consequences, leading to the destruction of the Jews in Europe. He thus communicated to his followers, or at least to the more astute among them, that his expectations would be radicalized in wartime. Himmler did not disappoint. In mid-September, in the flush of victory over Poland, the Reichsführer-ss submitted proposals for the demographic reorganization of eastern Europe, including the Lublin reservation for Polish Jews, which Hitler approved. In March 1940 Hitler indicated his disenchantment with the plan for the Lublin reservation, however, and the opposition of Göring and Frank threatened Himmler's wider demographic design for the quick "Germanization" of the incorporated territories. In May 1940, after the decisive breakthrough in France, Himmler submitted his memorandum on the treatment of the alien populations in the east, with the prospect of sending the Jews to Africa. Hitler deemed the memorandum "very good and correct." In the following month, with the victory over France assured, Hitler embraced the Madagascar Plan, which had been initiated in the Foreign Office and immediately co-opted by Heydrich.

With the imminent expansion of the war into the Soviet Union, Hitler again signaled new expectations. On at least four occasions between February 26 and March 30, 1941, he set the tone for a "war of destruction" against Jewish Bolshevism. Not just the ss but also the military and economic planners immediately sought to cast his ideological pronouncements into specific policies, such as the ss-Wehrmacht agreement on Einsatzgruppen activities in the war zone, the *Kommissarbefehl*, and the plan to deprive large areas of the Soviet Union of a subsistence-level food supply. In mid-July, with the stupendous early victories of the Barbarossa campaign, Hitler urged an acceleration in the murder campaign, to create a "Garden of Eden" in the east from which Germany would never withdraw. He also indicated that the time had now come to approach every country in Europe with the demand for the removal of every last Jew. Shortly thereafter, Heydrich procured authorization to prepare and submit a "total solution" to the European Jewish question. In September the Germans encircled Leningrad and captured Kiev, and in early October they resumed the march on Moscow and won the stunning double encirclement victory at Vyazma and Bryansk. Victory by the end of the year still seemed attainable, and a mood of euphoria reminiscent of midsummer again permeated the Führer's headquarters. Also in mid-September Hitler reversed his earlier deferral of deportations until "after the war." In October the deportations began, and further Jewish emigration from the Continent was forbidden. In the same weeks various gassing experiments were conducted, and German commandos ap-

pear
natic
and
N
peak
temp
destr
Eurc
Augr
and
an ea
B
abru
plies
Red
road
Sovi
comr
ria o
Hitle
and
cling
reacl

drich on the telephone about the Jewish question and Krüger'
tion in the General Government as state secretary for se
parted for Cracow and Lublin. There Himmler had
Krüger, and Globocnik on March 13 and 14, on the
from Lublin and Galicia to Belzec. And on March
dinner with the recently returned Himmler, w
to the Führer as well. This was just hours
begun to operate full-time.[3] Ten days l
his diary:

The Jews in the General G
evacuated to the east. Th
here more precisely,
judgment is being
deserved. The
world war
governm
tion

Jewry and then of Germany itself.

That October 1941 was not only the fateful watershed in Nazi Jewish policy but also a crucial military turning point on the eastern front can be seen in hindsight. Such a perspective was not, of course, available to the Nazi leadership at the time. The Nazi regime would continue doggedly to pursue military victory, which would elude them, as well as preparations for a genocide of the European Jews that would prove all too successful. In regard to the latter, Hitler continued to incite his followers and legitimize the policy of mass murder. On December 12, 1941, he met with the party leadership and made it clear that the entry of the United States into the war would not delay implementation of the Final Solution. In the month following the Wannsee Conference he made numerous comments, both public and private, about the fate of the Jews that exceeded in frequency and vitriol even his comments of the preceding months.[2]

On March 10, 1942, Hitler had dinner with Himmler, who also gave a postdinner presentation. On March 11, 12, and 13, Himmler spoke with Hey-

s enhanced posi-
urity and then de-
meetings with Frank,
ve of the first deportations
17, Hitler had both lunch and
no made yet another presentation
after the gas chambers at Belzec had
ter, on March 27, Goebbels reported in

overnment, beginning in Lublin, are now being
is is a pretty barbaric procedure, not to be described
nd of the Jews themselves not much will remain. . . . A
carried out against the Jews that, indeed barbaric, is fully
prophecy that the Führer made about them for causing a new
s beginning to come true in a most terrible manner. . . . No other
ment and no other regime would have the strength to solve this ques-
comprehensively. Here, too, the Führer is the unflinching champion and
pokesman of a radical solution[4]

In the long evolution of Nazi Jewish policy to the Final Solution, Hitler had
been of course not only "champion and spokesman" but also the necessary and
pivotal decision maker.

GERMANS AND THE FINAL SOLUTION

During the Kristallnacht pogrom in November 1938, aside from
the frustrated party activists who had finally been allowed their day in the
streets, most Germans were (to borrow Saul Friedländer's term) "onlookers"
who disapproved of the violent and destructive attack upon German Jews and
their property. For most Germans the disapproval was not triggered by any
sense of solidarity with Germany's beleaguered Jews or principled opposition to
their being deprived of both their rights and property by legal and administrative processes. The nature of the pogrom, with its wanton destruction of property, the burning of houses of worship, and the flaunting of public violence,
rather than the persecution of the Jews itself, was the most disturbing aspect of
Kristallnacht for most "ordinary" Germans.[5]

Nevertheless, the largely negative public reaction to Kristallnacht begs the
vital question. If "ordinary" Germans still shied from the breaking of shop
windows, the torching of synagogues, and the beating of Jews in the streets of

Germany in 1938, why were they willing just three years later to begin murdering Jews en masse in eastern Europe. In terms of public violence, there was no comparison. The firing squad executions left the killers saturated in the blood of their victims, and even deportation from the Third Reich to the faraway death camps involved pathetic processions of elderly Jews and waves of suicides. And on Polish territory the deportations would soon be characterized by widespread and highly visible ghetto-clearing operations that were mounted with tremendous ferocity and left the streets lined with corpses. How in three brief years had "ordinary" Germans been transformed from "onlookers" squeamish and disapproving of vandalism, arson, and assault into "willing executioners" who could perpetrate mass murder with unfettered violence?

Change in time and place was vitally important. After September 1939 Germany was at war, which in turn created a vast German empire in eastern Europe. Even though the initial popular reaction to the outbreak of war was one of apprehension rather than enthusiasm,[6] almost no one in Germany was prepared to engage in dissident, critical, or nonconformist behavior in this regard. It would be no exaggeration to state that the single greatest consensus in the political culture of German society (and scarcely unique to Germany) was the obligation to do one's duty and support one's country in time of war. This consensus was not invented by the Nazis, but it served them well. War in general meant the suspension of critical stance, the temporary erasure of the distinction between loyalty to country and loyalty to regime, the acceptance of demands for sacrifice and toughness, the predisposition to see the world as divided between friends and enemies, and the expectation that terrible things will inevitably happen paradoxically combined with the tendency to dismiss reports of such as exaggerated enemy propaganda.

Indeed, the Nazi leadership was well aware that war would create a propitious situation for carrying out policies that were inexpedient if not unthinkable in peacetime. As Göring alerted the assembled Nazi leaders in the wake of Kristallnacht: "If in some foreseeable future an external conflict were to happen, it is obvious that we in Germany would also think first and foremost of carrying out a big settling of accounts with the Jews."[7] Hitler in turn made this expectation quite public in his Reichstag "prophecy" of January 30, 1939, that world war would mean "the destruction of the Jewish race in Europe." And Jews were not the only Nazi target whose vulnerability was vastly intensified by the outbreak of war, as Hitler's order for the mass murder of mentally and physically handicapped Germans in the fall of 1939 clearly shows.

The conquest and partition of Poland in September 1939 was a major step in the creation of Nazi Germany's east European empire and offered a propitious site for various policies of racial imperialism. As the terms of the Treaty of Brest-Litovsk, the Freikorps campaigns, and the almost total rejection of the Versailles Treaty demonstrate, refusal to accept the verdict of World War I and unquenched imperial aspirations in eastern Europe underpinned by notions of German racial and cultural superiority were broadly held sentiments in German society. They provided more common ground between the bulk of the German population and the Nazi regime than did anti-Semitism.

In short, wartime Poland offered a time and place where Germans would be more transformed by what they saw and did between 1939 and 1941 than they had been by their experience of the domestic dictatorship in 1933–39. Just as the decision-making process leading to the Final Solution was incremental and influenced by the intoxicating euphoria of success on the one hand and the frustration of impasse and dashed expectations on the other, so was the process of adaptation among the perpetrators. An unbroken chain of victories not just in Poland but also in Scandinavia, France and the Low Countries, and the Balkans extended German control over the Continent. But it was in Poland above all that Germans were exhorted to behave as the master race over inferior native populations and where they encountered in massive numbers the strange and alien *Ostjuden* so different from assimilated, middle-class German Jews. Here the corrupting process of racial imperialism could be launched most easily.

In Germany the regime attempted to keep the mass murder of the mentally and physically handicapped relatively secret. Not so for racial imperialism in Poland. There was little reticence over the arrest and murder of the Polish leadership and intelligentsia, and the roundups of Poles for either expulsion or labor were even more open. The degradation rituals and public torments aimed against Polish Jews were especially visible. The flood of measures for marking, expropriation, forced labor, and segregation and the heightened incidence of impoverishment, starvation, and disease that so disproportionately afflicted Polish Jewry accelerated the vicious circle of dehumanization and further persecution.

Committed to Germany's proclaimed mission of racial empire building in the east, German occupiers in Poland soon accepted and indeed advocated the notion that when they were done remaking the demographic map of eastern Europe, no Jews would remain. The Jews in Poland, far more than the relatively small and constantly declining number of assimilated Jews in Germany, posed a problem to be solved. Mass expulsion—what we now call "ethnic cleansing" but what the Nazis euphemistically called "resettlement"—first to Lublin, then to Madagascar, and finally further east was the imagined panacea. It was but one aspect of a wider demographic revolution the Nazis intended to engineer, but it proved illusory. The reality was overcrowded, disease-ridden, impoverished ghettos of Polish Jews who could be concentrated but not expelled. The Nazis' self-imposed problem had both worsened and become further rather than closer to solution.

German colonial administrators in Poland differed on interim measures: some favored an intensified attrition of the Jewish population through starvation while others preferred the productive use of Jewish labor to cover the cost of food, reduce the threat of epidemic, and contribute to the war economy. But virtually no Germans in Poland—whether they were city administrators dealing with food and housing shortages, public health officials facing epidemics, policemen combating the black market, economists and military contractors exploiting the territory, or urban and landscape designers and "demographic engineers" planning "aesthetic" German settlements—envisaged a long-term Jewish future there. The goal that all Jews would disappear was widely accepted before the means of systematic mass murder were chosen, but German policies had created "untenable circumstances" (*unhaltbare Verhältnisse*)[8] and "an impossible situation" (*ein unmöglicher Zustand*)[9] for which it would be increasingly easy to mobilize consensus for a radical solution.

The decisive leap from disappearance through expulsion to disappearance through systematic mass murder was first taken, however, not in Poland but rather in the Soviet Union. Added to the existing context of racial imperialism and "untenable circumstances" were the crusade against Bolshevism and the "war of destruction." According to measures planned not only by the ss but also by military leaders, economists, and civil administrators, millions in the Soviet Union were fated to die through mass execution, starvation, and expulsion. One pattern was already clear. In the past wherever the Nazis carried out mass executions, Jews were shot in disproportionate numbers; wherever food was scarce, Jews starved first; and wherever people were deported, the Germans never conceived of any Jews being left behind. For example, as Henry Friedlander has shown for the "euthanasia" program, selected German handicapped were killed after screening, but all of the German Jewish handicapped were killed indiscriminately without selection.[10] These tendencies would inevitably be intensified by the identification of Jews and Bolsheviks that was not only embedded in Nazi ideology but also widely held by conservatives throughout Europe. In short, even before the invasion German intentions for the Soviet Union had genocidal implications for Soviet Jews that transcended what Polish Jewry had yet suffered.

By the spring of 1942, two million Soviet prisoners of war had perished, and millions of other Soviet citizens had starved or been shot. When these victims are added to the 70,000–80,000 German mentally and physically handicapped, the Polish intelligentsia, the reprisal victims, and many others who had also been killed by then, the capacity of the Nazi regime to mobilize Germans to kill even non-Jews by the millions is evident. In these cases anti-Semitism was not even a relevant much less sufficient motivation. These dead were almost invariably victims of Nazi racial imperialism, which devalued the lives of whole categories of people in addition to Jews.

When, in the context of racial imperialism, "war of destruction," and crusade against Bolshevism, Germans were willing to kill millions of others, they were also willing to kill *all* Soviet Jews. In late 19th-century Germany, Shulamit Volkov has written, Jews had become a "cultural code" for democracy and socialism, capitalism and free enterprise, internationalism, and cultural experimentation. In Poland they had also become a symbol for the "untenable circumstances" of disease, overcrowding, black marketeering, filth, and starvation. By 1941 on Soviet territory the Jews had become a code word for Bolshevism, Asiatic threat, and partisan resistance in what was conceived of as an all-or-nothing war between implacable racial and ideological enemies.

German anti-Semitism was not static but intensified with the changing historical context. In the 1930s growing enthusiasm for Hitler and the Nazi regime was due primarily to the restoration of political order, the return of economic prosperity, and the revival of national grandeur. There was no similar popular acclamation for the persecution of German Jews, but likewise no solidarity with the victims, who were increasingly isolated and deprived of their rights and property by a succession of legal and administrative measures. As of 1938, aside from a minority of party activists, most Germans were not yet ready or willing to visit physical violence upon their Jewish neighbors but neither were they interested in coming to their defense.

With the outbreak of war and the commencement of racial empire building, first in Poland but above all on Soviet territory, that situation changed. Two vicious circles were set in motion. For the decision makers at the top, each victory and territorial expansion was a setback in solving their self-imposed Jewish problem, as the number of Jews within the German sphere swelled inexorably. For the occupiers in the east, each measure taken brought a solution no closer but instead contributed to "untenable circumstances" (or at best a precarious stabilization) that dehumanized the Jews yet further and at the same time disposed the German occupiers to expect and advocate yet more radical measures. The solution to the Jewish problem through the eventual disappearance of the Jews—sometime, somehow—was taken for granted.

Within the context of the murderous "war of destruction" against the Soviet

Union, the leap from disappearance of the Jews "sometime, somehow" to "mass murder now" was taken in the summer of 1941. Once underway on Soviet territory, this ultimate or Final Solution beckoned to the Nazi regime as a solution for the rest of Europe's Jews as well. Already in the midst of committing mass murder against millions of Jews and non-Jews on Soviet territory, "ordinary" Germans would not shrink from implementing Hitler's Final Solution for the Jews of Europe as well.

Notes

1. Background

1. For understanding the formation and dynamic of medieval anti-Semitism, I am especially indebted to Gavin Langmuir, "Prolegomena to Any Present Analysis of Hostility against the Jews," and "From Anti-Judaism to Antisemitism."

2. Robert Chazan, "Medieval Antisemitism," pp. 54–55; Leon Poliakov, *The History of Anti-Semitism from the Time of Christ to the Court Jews*, pp. 41–72.

3. Langmuir, "From Anti-Judaism to Antisemitism," p. 291.

4. Langmuir, "Prolegomena," pp. 154–57.

5. Steven Katz, *The Holocaust in Historical Context*, vol. 1, chap. 7.

6. The basic work to which I am indebted on the relationship between modernization and racial anti-Semitism is Peter Pulzer, *The Rise of Political Anti-Semitism in Germany and Austria*.

7. For the emergence of racism: George Mosse, *Toward the Final Solution: A History of European Racism*.

8. George Mosse, *The Crisis of German Ideology*; Fritz Stern, *The Politics of Cultural Despair*; Jeffrey Herf, *Reactionary Modernism: Technology, Culture and Politics in Weimar and the Third Reich*.

9. Hans-Ulrich Wehler, *The German Empire*; James Retallack, "Social History with a Vengeance? Some Reactions to H-U Wehler's 'Das Kaiserreich' "; Roger Fletcher, "Recent Developments in the West German Historiography: The Bielefeld School and Its Critics." This approach has been challenged by Geoff Eley and David Blackbourn, who question the whole notion of a failed or missing bourgeois-liberal revolution in 19th-century Germany, and assert that a bourgeois-liberal transformation of the country simply came about in a gradual though pervasive manner despite the failure of 1848.

10. Daniel Jonah Goldhagen, *Hitler's Willing Executioners: Ordinary Germans and the Holocaust*, pp. 419, 444.

11. John Weiss, *Ideology of Death: Why the Holocaust Happened in Germany*.

12. Shulamit Volkov, "Antisemitism as a Cultural Code"; See also Pulzer, *The Rise of Political Antisemitism in Germany and Austria*.

13. Uriel Tal, *Christians and Jews in Germany: Religion, Politics, and Ideology in the Second Reich, 1870–1914*, esp. pp. 121–59, 223–59.

14. Saul Friedländer, *The Years of Persecution, 1933–1939*, vol. 1 of *Nazi Germany and the Jews*, esp. pp. 73–112.

15. Tal, *Christians and Jews in Germany*, pp. 300–301.

16. Richard S. Levy, *The Downfall of the Anti-Semitic Political Parties in Imperial Germany*, p. 4.

17. William Sheridan Allen, *The Nazi Seizure of Power*, p. 84.

18. Ian Kershaw, "The Persecution of the Jews and German Public Opinion in the Third Reich"; Kershaw, *Popular Opinion and Political Dissent in the Third Reich: Bavaria 1933–1945*; Kershaw, *The Hitler "Myth": Image and Reality in the Third Reich*; and Kershaw, "German Popular Opinion and the 'Jewish Question,' 1933–1943: Some Further Reflections." Otto Dov Kulka, " 'Public Opinion' in Nazi Germany and the 'Jewish Question' "; and Kulka and Aron Rodrigue, "The German Population and the Jews in the Third Reich: Recent Publications and Trends in Research on German Society and the 'Jewish Question'." David Bankier, "The Germans and the Holocaust: What Did They Know"; Bankier, *The Germans and the Final Solution: Public Opinion under Nazism*; and Bankier, ed., *Probing the Depths of German Antisemitism: German Society and the Persecution of the Jews, 1933–1941*. See also Marlis Steinert, *Hitler's War and the Germans*; Lawrence D.

Stokes, "The German People and the Destruction of the European Jews"; Walter Laqueur, *The Terrible Secret: Suppression of the Truth about Hitler's "Final Solution"*; Sarah Gordon, *Hitler, Germans, and the "Jewish Question"*; Robert Gellately, *The Gestapo and German Society: Enforcing Racial Policy, 1933–1945*; Ursula Büttner, "Die deutsche Bevölkerung und die Judenverfolgung 1933–1945." In contrast, see Michael Kater, "Everyday Anti-Semitism in Prewar Nazi Germany."

19. Friedländer, *The Years of Persecution*, pp. 298, 327–28.

20. Peter Longerich, *Politik der Vernichtung: Eine Gesamtdarstellung der nationalsozialistische Judenverfolgung*, pp. 23–226, provides an excellent study of the interaction of Nazi activism, government policy, and public attitudes.

21. Eberhard Jäckel, *Hitler's Weltanschauung*.

22. Uwe Dietrich Adam, *Judenpolitik im Dritten Reich*, pp. 339–40.

23. Raul Hilberg, *The Destruction of the European Jews* (1961 ed.), p. 639.

2. Poland, Laboratory of Racial Policy

1. The most conservative estimate of 1.68 million is found in Frank Golchewski, "Polen," p. 426. The German demographer Burgdörfer estimated 1.8 million Polish Jews in the German sphere in 1940. Politisches Archiv des Auswärtigen Amtes (hereafter cited as PA), Inland II AB 35 / 2, Burgdörfer Gutachten, July 17, 1940. Yisrael Gutman, *The Jews of Warsaw: Ghetto, Underground, Revolt*, p. 11, estimates 2 million, as does Hilberg, *The Destruction of the European Jews*, p. 189. Philip Friedman, "The Extermination of the Polish Jews during the German Occupation, 1939–1945," pp. 212–13, estimates 1.835 million; Martin Broszat, *Nationalsozialistische Polenpolitik 1939–1945*, p. 67, estimates 1.9 million; Yehuda Bauer, *American Jewry and the Holocaust*, p. 69, estimates 1.8–1.9 million.

2. Gutman, *The Jews of Warsaw*, p. 11.

3. Adam, *Judenpolitik im Dritten Reich*, pp. 233–36.

4. For an exceptionally insightful analysis of the initial confrontation of Germans with *Ostjudentum* accompanying the conquest of Poland, see Bodgan Musial, *Deutsche Zivilverwaltung und Judenverfolgung im Generalgouvernement: Eine Fallstudie zum Distrikt Lublin 1939–1944*, pp. 183–88.

5. Broszat, *NS Polenpolitik*, p. 67.

6. The connection between 19th-century European imperialism and 20th-century totalitarianism was of course a crucial insight of Hannah Arendt, *The Origins of Totalitarianism*. The point has also been made more recently by Sven Lindqvist, *"Exterminate All the Brutes."* For a study of the explicit connection between German colonial and Nazi race and population policies, see Annegret Ehmann, "From Colonial Racism to Nazi Population Policy: The Role of the So-Called Mischlinge"; and Woodruff D. Smith, *The Ideological Origins of Nazi Imperialism*.

7. This suggestive phrase comes from Hans Mommsen, "Die Realisierung des Utopischen: Die 'Endlösung der Judenfrage' im 'Dritten Reich.'"

8. *Nazi Conspiracy and Aggression* (Washingon DC, 1946) (hereafter cited as NCA), 3:665 (1014-PS: Unsigned notes on Hitler's second speech, August 22, 1939, from the OKW files). Winfried Baumgart, "Zur Ansprache Hitlers vor den Führern der Wehrmacht am 22.

August 1939," explains why this document probably contains the original notes of Admiral Wilhelm Canaris, the head of military intelligence (Abwehr), and is thus to be preferred over various other accounts of Hitler's remarks later written up from memory or reworked from notes taken at the time. General Halder's war diary conveyed the same sentiments: "Goal: destruction of Poland—elimination of its living force. It is not a question of reaching a certain line or new boundary but the destruction of the enemy. . . . The means do not matter. The victor will never be questioned whether his reasons were justified. It is not a question whether our side is right but only of victory." Franz Halder, *Kriegstagebuch: Tägliche Aufzeichnungen des Chefs des Generalstabes des Heeres 1939–1942*, 1:25. A more apocalyptic version, smuggled to the British presumably with the purpose of persuading them to stand by Poland, attributed to Hitler the following: "Genghis Khan had millions of women and children killed by his own will and with a gay heart. History sees only in him a great state builder. What weak western civilization thinks about me does not matter. . . . I have sent to the East my 'Death head Units' with the order to kill without mercy all men, women, and children of the Polish race or language. Only in such a way will we win the vital space that we need. Who still talks nowadays of the extermination of the Armenians." NCA, 7:753 (L-3).

9. Hans Umbreit, *Deutsche Militärverwaltungen 1938/39: Die militärische Besetzung der Tschechoslowakei und Polen*, pp. 71, 74–75.

10. Alexander B. Rossino, *Hitler Strikes Poland: Blitzkrieg, Ideology, and Atrocity*, pp. 5–8, 23–27; and Rossino, "Destructive Impulses: German Soldiers and the Conquest of Poland."

11. Helmut Krausnick and Hans-Heinrich Wilhelm, *Die Truppe des Weltanschauungskrieges*, p. 34. At a meeting in his apartment on July 5, 1939, Heydrich initially envisaged four Einsatzgruppen under Meisinger, Damzog, Schäfer, and Streckenbach, totaling 2,000 men. United States Holocaust Memorial Museum Archives (hereafter cited as USHMMA), RG 15.007m (RSHA files, Main Commission for the Investigation of Crimes against the Polish Nation, RG 362), reel 11, file 154, pp. 4–6. Einsatzgruppe I under Streckenbach centered its activities around Cracow and southern Poland. Einsatzgruppe II under Schäfer was headquartered first in Czestochowa and then Radom. Einsatzgruppe III under Fischer was headquartered in Lodz. Einsatzgruppe IV under Beutel moved through West Prussia and Bydgoszcz to East Prussia and Bialystok. Einsatzgruppe V under Damzog operated out of East Prusia toward Warsaw. Einsatzgruppe VI under Naumann was centered in Poznan. The Einsatzgruppe z.b.V., first under von Woyrsch and then Rasch operated primarily in Upper Silesia and also briefly in Tarnow. The routes of march can be found in the daily reports of Sonderreferat "Unternehmen Tannenberg" of the Sipo from September 6 to October 6, 1939. USHMMA, RG 15.007m, reel 2, files 1 and 2.

12. For the Einsatzgruppen personnel, see Zentralstelle der Landesjustizverwaltungen in Ludwisburg (hereafter cited as ZStL), "Einsatzgruppen in Polen: Einsatzgruppen der Sicherheitspolizei, Selbstschutz und andere Formationen" (hereafter cited as "EG in Polen"), 1:31–76, 84–95, and 2:10–17. A copy is in the Yad Vashem Archives (hereafter cited as YVA), O-4/51/1–2. For the cohort of intellectuals in Heydrich's RSHA, see Michael Wildt, *Generation des Unbedingten: Das Führungskorps des Reichssicherheitshauptamtes*.

13. YVA, O/53/49/345–51: Richtlinien für den auswärtigen Einsatz der Sicherheitspolizei und SD, undated.

14. Eduard Wagner, *Der Generalquartiermeister: Briefe und Tagebuch Eduard Wagners*, p. 103.

15. Krausnick and Wilhelm, *Die Truppe des Weltanschauungskrieges*, p. 40; Wagner, *Der Generalquartiermeister*, pp. 103–4.

16. Helmuth Groscurth, *Tagebücher eines Abwehroffiziers 1938–40*, p. 201 (Privattagebuch, September 8, 1939).

17. Groscurth, *Tagebücher*, p. 202 (Privattagebuch, September 9, 1939).

18. NCA, 5:769 (3047-PS: notes by Lahousen from diary of Canaris).

19. A military court imposing a three-year sentence on a SS man for murdering 50 Jews noted: "Being a SS man, the sight of the Jews brought out in him very strongly his resentment of the anti-German attitude of Jewry; thus he acted with youthful recklessness and quite spontaneously." It should be noted, however, that General von Küchler, with Brauchitsch's approval, refused to confirm the three-year sentence as too lenient. NCA, Suppl. A, pp. 869–70 (D-421).

20. Rossino, *Hitler Strikes Poland*, pp. 59–74; Krausnick and Wilhelm, *Die Truppe des Weltanschauungskrieges*, pp. 57, 62.

21. Groscurth, *Tagebücher*, p. 360 (Doc. Nr. 13: Tippelskirch to Brauchitsch, September 17, 1939). According to Krausnick and Wilhelm, *Die Truppe des Weltanschauungskrieges*, p. 44, the Himmler order was issued on September 3. As Krausnick notes (p. 50), the army itself, in the face of ongoing resistance and unrest behind the lines, had simplified its procedures for dealing with insurgents, providing for quick justice through "drumhead courts martial" and immediate execution without appeal. Nonetheless, the Einsatzgruppen procedures of mass shootings without any pretense of judicial procedure went considerably beyond this. For overall relations between Einsatzgruppe II and the 10th Army, see Rossino, *Hitler Strikes Poland*, pp. 83–86.

22. Groscurth, *Tagebücher*, p. 209. On the von Woyrsch Einsatzgruppe, see Alexander Rossino, "Nazi Anti-Jewish Policy during the Polish Campaign: The Case of Einsatzgruppe von Woyrsch"; and *Hitler Strikes Poland*, pp. 80–82.

23. Wagner, *Der Generalquartiermeister*, p. 134.

24. Halder, *Kriegstagebuch*, 1:79.

25. Wagner, *Der Generalquartiermeister*, p. 134.

26. National Archives microfilm (hereafter cited as NA), T175/239/2728228–31. Conference of Heydrich's division heads, September 19, 1939 (copy in YVA, JM 4542).

27. Halder, *Kriegstagebuch*, 1:82.

28. Klaus-Jürgen Müller, *Das Heer und Hitler: Armee und nationalsozialistische Regime 1933–40*, p. 667 (Doc. Nr. 45: Brauchitsch to army commanders, September 21, 1939).

29. Groscurth, *Tagebücher*, pp. 361–62 (Doc. Nr. 14: Groscurth memo on verbal orientation from Major Radke, September 22, 1939).

30. Groscurth, *Tagebücher*, p. 209 (Privattagebuch, September 23, 1939), p. 277 (Diensttagebuch, September 23, 1939).

31. Groscurth, *Tagebücher*, p. 362 (Doc. Nr. 14: Groscurth memo on verbal orientation from Major Radke, September 22, 1939).

32. Wagner, *Der Generalquartiermeister*, p. 135.

33. Rossino, *Hitler Strikes Poland*, pp. 58–87, documents the extent to which, occasional

protests against "excesses" and "indiscipline" aside, the military welcomed and relied upon the Einsatzgruppen actions against presumed security threats.

34. Müller, *Das Heer und Hitler*, p. 434.

35. Müller, *Das Heer und Hitler*, p. 9.

36. Ironically, General List of the 14th Army requested its return to the demarcation line, on the grounds that its "alleged" abuses had been "exaggerated" and its "ruthless" clearing of "bands, guerrillas, and plunderers" was "extraordinarily successful" and "in the interest of the troops." Rossino, *Hitler Strikes Poland*, p. 101.

37. Wagner, *Der Generalquartiermeister*, p. 130.

38. Umbreit, *Deutsche Militärverwaltungen*, pp. 85–86, 107. Even earlier, Heydrich had assured his division heads that the military government in Poland would be ended and replaced by a civilian administration as soon as hostilities were over. Conference of Heydrich's division chiefs, September 7, 1939, NA, T175/239/2728499–502.

39. Wagner, *Der Generalquartiermeister*, p. 137; Umbreit, *Deutsch Militärverwaltungen*, p. 98.

40. Umbreit, *Deutsche Militärverwaltungen*, pp. 107–9.

41. Robert Koehl, RKFDV: *German Resettlement and Population Policy, 1939–45*, pp. 50–53.

42. Norman Rich, *The Establishment of the New Order*, vol. 2 of *Hitler's War Aims*, p. 73; *Trials of the War Criminals before the Nuernberg Military Tribunals* (hereafter cited as TWC), 4:718–20 (EC-410).

43. Broszat, *NS Polenpolitik*, pp. 29–30.

44. Umbreit, *Deutsche Militärverwaltungen*, p. 98.

45. Umbreit, *Deutsche Militärverwaltungen*, p. 114.

46. Harold Deutsch, *The Conspiracy against Hitler in the Twilight War*, p. 71.

47. Müller, *Das Heer und Hitler*, p. 437.

48. Umbreit, *Deutsche Militärverwaltungen*, p. 107.

49. Halder, *Kriegstagebuch*, 1:98.

50. Broszat, *NS Polenpolitik*, p. 30.

51. Müller, *Das Heer und Hitler*, p. 437.

52. Groscurth, *Tagebücher*, p. 218 (Privattagebuch, October 16, 1939).

53. *Trials of the War Criminals before the International Military Tribunal* (hereafter cited as IMT), 26:379–80 (864-PS: notes prepared by Wagner for Keitel, October 17, 1939).

54. IMT, 26:378–79, 381–83. These portions of 864-PS are made up of three documents: Keitel's notes, Wagner's notes of Keitel's recapitulation, and the OKW summary based on Keitel's notes written down three days later by Col. Gause. Two other accounts of Hitler's statements at this conference are found in Groscurth, *Tagebücher*, p. 381 (Doc. Nr. 24: unsigned memorandum of October 18, 1939); and Halder, *Kriegstagebuch*, 1:107 (entry of October 18, 1939).

55. Groscurth, *Tagebücher*, p. 298 (Diensttagebuch, October 18, 1939).

56. NA microfilm, T175/239/2728499–502. Conference of Heydrich's division heads, September 7, 1939.

57. NA microfilm, T175/239/2728513–15. Conference of Heydrich's division heads, September 14, 1939.

58. NA microfilm, T175/239/2728524–28. Conference of Heydrich's division heads and Einsatzgruppen leaders, September 21, 1939.

59. NCA, 6:97–101 (3363-PS: Heydrich Schnellbrief to Einsatzgruppen leaders, September 21, 1939).

60. Groscurth, *Tagebücher*, p. 362 (Doc. Nr. 14: Groscurth memorandum on verbal orientation by Major Radke, September 22, 1939).

61. Müller, *Das Heer und Hitler*, pp. 671–72 (Doc. Nr. 47: Heydrich to Einsatzgruppen leaders, September 30, 1939).

62. Krausnick and Wilhelm, *Die Truppe des Weltanschauungskrieges*, p. 75 (Manstein Document WB-2752 cited).

63. NA microfilm, T175/239/2728534. Conference of Heydrich's division heads, October 3, 1939.

64. Broszat, *NS Polenpolitik*, p. 15.

65. Alfred Rosenberg, *Das politische Tagebuch*, p. 81. Heydrich was likewise aware that the target area of Jewish deportation was no longer the region east of Cracow and north of the Slovak border, but now the Lublin area between the Vistula and Bug. On September 29 he informed his division heads that "in the area behind Warsaw and around Lublin a 'Nature Protection Area' or 'Reichs-Getto' will be created, in which all political and Jewish elements that must be resettled from the future German provinces will be lodged." NA microfilm, T175/239/2828531–32. Conference of Heydrich's division heads, September 29, 1939.

66. Götz Aly, *"Final Solution": Nazi Population Policy and the Murder of the European Jews*, pp. 4–9. See also Götz Aly and Susanne Heim, *Architects of Annihilation: Auschwitz and the Logic of Destruction*; Michael Burleigh, *Germany Turns Eastward: A Study of Ostforschung in the Third Reich*; Burleigh, "Die Stunde der Experten"; Hans Mommsen, "Umvolkungspläne des Nationalsozialismus und der Holocaust."

67. Umbreit, *Deutsche Militärverwaltungen*, p. 166.

68. Szymon Datner, *55 Dni/1.IX-25.X.1939. Wehrmachtu W Polsce*, pp. 114–17. Army Group South to 8th, 10th, and 14th Armies, September 20, 1939, cited in "EG in Polen," 1:151. According to Czeslaw Madajczyk, *Die Okkupationspolitk Nazideutschlands in Polen 1939–1945*, p. 28, of the 764 executions that took place between September 1 and October 26, 1939, 311 were organized by the Wehrmacht. Madajczyk estimates that 20,000 people perished in these executions. Krausnick and Wilhelm, *Die Truppe des Weltanschauungskrieges*, pp. 42–46. The Einsatzgruppe reports compiled by Sonderreferat Unternehmen Tannenberg contain almost no reports or useful statistics concerning executions. USHMMA, RG 15.007m, reel 1, files 1 and 2.

69. Wlodzimierz Jastrzebski, *Der Bromberger Blutsonntag: Legende und Wirklichkeit*, p. 168, claims that, according to German figures from December 1939, 103 ethnic Germans lost their lives in Bydgoszcz in early September, but that that figure was subsequently inflated. Madajczyk, *Die Okkupationspolitik Nazideutschlands in Polen*, p. 10, estimates that about 150 ethnic Germans perished in Bydgoszcz on September 3, and ethnic German losses reached a total of about 300 before the Polish army withdrew. Both Polish historians emphasize that the killing was triggered when ethnic Germans in Bydgoszcz attempted a "diversionary" action against Polish troops.

70. Tadeuz Esman and Wlodzimierz Jastrzebski, eds., *Pierwsze Miesiace Okupacji Hitlerowskiej W Bydgoszcz* (hereafter cited as *Bydgoszcz*), pp. 9–11 (excerpts from the war diary of Rear Army Area 580, September 9–11, 1939). Datner (*55 Dni*, pp. 114–17) records considerably higher figures for Bydgoszcz than found in these documents: 2,177 executions through September 10, and 5,755 by October 25. No useful numbers are contained in the report of Einsatzgruppe IV, which merely noted that "counter-measures are underway." USHMMA, RG 15.007m, 2/1/34 (Sonderreferat Unternehmen Tannenberg, report of September 9, 1939).

71. NCA, Suppl. A, pp. 869–70 (D-421); Halder, *Kriegstagebuch*, 1:67.

72. Groscurth, *Tagebücher*, p. 203 (Privattagebuch, September 11, 1939).

73. Umbreit, *Deutsche Militärverwaltungen*, p. 167; Krausnick and Wilhelm, *Die Truppe des Weltanschauungskriegs*, pp. 81–82.

74. Groscurth, *Tagebücher*, p. 363 (Doc. Nr. 14: Groscurth memorandum on verbal orientation by Major Radke, September 22, 1939).

75. Groscurth, *Tagebücher*, p. 209 (Privattagebuch, September 23, 1939).

76. "EG in Polen," 2:162 (Commandant in Wloclawek to 8th Army, September 25, 1939).

77. USHMMA, RG 15.007m, 2/1/14, 40–41, 82 (reports of September 7, 10, and 15, 1939).

78. USHMMA, RG 15.007m, 2/2/34, 50, 55 (reports September 24, 27, and 28, 1939).

79. USHMMA, RG 15.007m, 2/1/76 (report of September 14, 1939).

80. Krausnick and Wilhelm, *Die Truppe des Weltanschauungskrieges*, pp. 70–71; Rossino, *Hitler Strikes Poland*, p. 97.

81. Rossino, *Hitler Strikes Poland*, p. 119. Madajczyk, *Okkupationspolitik Nazideutschlands in Polen*, p. 18, notes the expulsion not only of 2,000 young male Jews from Silesia and 4,000 Jews (by the Wehrmacht) from Tarnobrzeg but also of 20,000 Jews from the Rzeszow/Jaroslaw region.

82. Krausnick and Wilhelm, *Die Truppe des Weltanschauungskrieges*, p. 71; and Dieter Pohl, *Von der "Judenpolitik" zum Judenmord: Der Distrikt Lublin des Generalgouvernements 1939–1944*, p. 56. On the basis of Polish sources, Pohl estimates the number of Jewish victims of German terror in Poland before the end of 1939 at 7,000 (p. 25), as does Bogdan Musial, *Deutsche Zivilverwaltung und Judenverfolgung im Generalgouvernement*, p. 106.

83. Jastrzebski, *Der Bromberger Blutsonntag*, argues vigorously against the German claim, made both at the time and in the postwar period, that Polish troops and villagers in rage and panic assaulted the ethnic German community, and instead argues for the thesis that the ethnic Germans attempted a military diversion.

84. Broszat estimates 4,000–5,000 in NS *Polenpolitik*, p. 47. The first German "Whitebook" claimed 5,800 before this was quickly multiplied tenfold for purposes of propaganda and incitement. C. F. Rütter et al., eds., *Justiz und NS-Verbrechen. Sammlung deutscher Strafurteile wegen nationalsozialistischer Tötungsverbrechen, 1945–1966* (hereafter cited as JNSV), 21:12.

85. On the Selbstschutz, see "EG in Polen," 1:164–81, 2:43–119; Umbreit, *Deutsche Militärverwaltungen*, 176–81; JNSV, 21:13–14; and esp. Christian Jansen and Arno Weckbecker, *Der "Volksdeutsche Selbstschutz" in Polen 1939/40*.

86. "EG in Polen," 2:163 (Alvensleben to Daluege, October 7, 1939).

87. *Bydgoszcz*, p. 53 (Einsatzkommando Situation Report, October 14, 1939).

88. NA microfilm, T175/239/2728535–37. Conference of Heydrich's division heads, October 14, 1939.

89. *Bydgoszcz*, pp. 61–62 (Oebsger-Röder memorandum, undated).

90. *Bydgoszcz*, pp. 58–60 (Einsatzkommando Situation Report, October 20, 1939).

91. *Bydgoszcz*, pp. 75–77 (Lölgen Report, October 24, 1939).

92. *Bydgoszcz*, p. 60 (Einsatzkommando Situation Report, October 20, 1939), p. 97 (Abromeit Report, November 14, 1939), p. 100 (Einsatzkommando Situation Report, November 17, 1939).

93. *Bydgoszcz*, p. 67 (Einsatzkommando Situation Report, November 2, 1939).

94. *Bydgoszcz*, p. 80 (Lölgen Report, November 4, 1939).

95. *Bydgoszcz*, p. 62 (Oebsger-Röder memorandum, undated), pp. 86–87 (Einsatzkommando Situation Report, November 9, 1939).

96. *JNSV*, 21:15–16, and 15:714–20.

97. "EG in Polen," 2:62, 93–94.

98. USHMMA, RG 15.007m, 11/153/1–2 (Bericht betr: Massnahmen der Bezirksverwaltung Pelpin gegen den Selbstschutz, October 24, 1939).

99. *Bydgoszcz*, p. 61 (Oebsger-Röder memorandum, undated). Jansen and Weckbecker, *Der "Volksdeutsche Selbstschutz,"* pp. 155–56, 211–29, estimate 20,000–30,000 Selbstschutz victims overall, with two-thirds of them in Danzig–West Prussia and another tenth in counties in which Selbstschutz units from Danzig–West Prussia operated. Of the 359 mass shootings in which they can identify Selbstschutz participation, 348 were in West Prussia. They note that the recent estimate of the Polish scholar Tadeuz Kur of 51,000 includes shootings in which Selbstschutz participation was not clearly established. Madajczyk, *Okkupationspolitik Nazideutschlands in Polen*, p. 12, states that in September alone the total number of executions in Danzig and Pomerania was 11,000 out of a total of 16,000 for all Poland.

100. *IMT*, 36:302 (305-EC).

101. *Bydgoszcz*, p. 60 (Einsatzkommando Situation Report, October 20, 1939), p. 92 (Lölgen Report, November 10, 1939), p. 97 (Abromeit Report, November 15, 1939), p. 100 (Einsatzkommando Situation Report, November 17, 1939).

102. For three such cases, see *JNSV*, 19:647–53, 20:9–10, 22:397–412.

103. Datner et al., eds., "Wysiedlanie Ludnosci Z Ziem Polskich Wcielonych Do Rzesy," *Biuletyn Glownej Komisji Badania Zbrodni Hitlerowskich W Polsce* 12 (hereafter cited as *Biuletyn* 12), pp. 22–31 (Rapp report, December 18, 1939). YVA, O-53/49/442–44 (private letter of Adolf Freuer, April 12, 1943).

104. Umbreit, *Deutsche Militärverwaltung*, p. 98.

105. Nuremberg Document (hereafter Nbg. Doc.) NO-1073, (affidavit of Otto Rasch, June 16, 1943); Nbg. Doc. NO-1074 (affidavit of Friedrich Schlegel, June 3, 1943, and Kaltenbrunner to SS judge, February 11, 1943). The indescribably wretched conditions at the Soldau camps became the center of an SS investigation after an epidemic broke out in August 1941 that killed six guards and forced the evacuation of the camp.

106. Madajczyk, *Okkupationspolitik Nazideutschlands in Polen*, p. 17. Madajczyk credits relative Nazi "restraint" here to the desire to restore Silesian economic production quickly.

107. Hans Frank, *Das Diensttagebuch des deutschen Generalgouverneurs in Polen 1939–1945*, p. 104 (interview with Kleiss, February 6, 1940).

108. IMT, 29:372 (2233-PS, Abteilungleitersitzung, March 8, 1940), p. 386 (Conference with Wille, Weh and Sage, February 19, 1940), p. 432 (Radom Arbeitstagung, February 25, 1940), p. 439 (Kreis- und Stadthauptmann's conference, March 4, 1940).

109. Frank, *Diensttagebuch*, pp. 209–12 (Polizeisitzung, May 30, 1940).

110. Musial, *Deutsche Zivilverwaltung und Judenverfolgung im Generalgouvernement*, p. 106.

3. The Search for a Final Solution through Expulsion

1. When I wrote the initial draft of this chapter and briefly summarized it in my article "Nazi Resettlement Policy and the Search for a Solution to the Jewish Question, 1939–1941" (1986), the only book-length study of Nazi resettlement policy, focusing on the repatriation of the ethnic Germans, was Robert Koehl, *German Resettlement and Population Policy, 1939–45*. Since then a number of important scholarly studies have appeared, including Aly, *"Final Solution"*; Rolf-Dieter Müller, *Hitlers Ostkrieg und die deutsche Siedlungspolitik*; Mommsen, "Umvolkungspläne des Nationalsozialismus und der Holocaust"; and Isabel Heinemann, *"Rasse, Siedlung, deutsches Blut": Das Rasse- & Siedlungshauptamt der SS und die rassenpolitische Neuordnung Europas*.

2. Gutman, *The Jews of Warsaw*, p. 17, estimates that 300,000 Jews crossed the demarcation line before it was closed in December 1939, as does Golchewski, "Polen," p. 426. Yehuda Bauer has a lower estimate of 200,000–250,000 (*American Jewry and the Holocaust*, p. 69).

3. This question was first raised by Seev Goshen, "Eichmann und die Nisko-Aktion im Oktober 1939," p. 80.

4. For the most recent studies of Eichmann, see Hans Safrian, *Die Eichmann-Männer*; Yaacov Lozowick, *Hitler's Bureaucrats: The Nazi Security Police and the Banality of Evil*; and Irmtrud Wojak, *Eichmanns Memoiren: Ein kritischer Essay*.

5. YVA, O/53/93/283, Eichmann Vermerk, October 6, 1939. This document and many of those referred to below have been printed in the unpaginated pamphlet, Rudolf Iltis, ed., *Nazi-Dokumente Sprechen*. The basic studies of the Nisko episode are Goshen, "Eichmann und die Nisko-Aktion"; Jonny Moser, "Nisko: The First Experiment in Deportation"; H. G. Adler, *Der verwaltete Mensch: Studien zur Deportation der Juden aus Deutschland*, pp. 126–40; and Safrian, *Die Eichmann-Männer*, pp. 68–86. Goshen attributes a high degree of private initiative to Eichmann, suggesting that he concocted his orders from Müller out of some vague verbal assent that he construed as he wished. Goshen doubts Müller even authorized Eichmann to actually begin deportations (p. 84).

6. YVA, O/53/93/194–97, Dannecker Vermerk, October 11, 1939, on conference of October 9, 1939.

7. YVA, O/53/93/258–59, R. Günther Vermerk on conference of October 9, 1939,

with Knobelsdorf; and 284, R. Günther Vermerk on conference of October 10, 1939, with Wagner.

8. Eichmann Trial Document T-1135, Löwenherz memorandum, October 10, 1939.

9. Gerhard Botz, *Wohnungspolitik und Judendeportation in Wien 1938 bis 1945*, pp. 164–86 (Doc. VII: Becker memorandum, October 11, 1939).

10. YVA, O/53/93/223–24, Memorandum of October 17, 1939, on Eichmann-Ebner-Becker meeting of October 16, 1939; and 206, Vermerk for Eichmann of October 18, 1939.

11. YVA, O/53/93/211, Eichmann to R. Günther, October 15, 1939; and 218, R. Günther Vermerk, October 16, 1939.

12. YVA, O/53/93/289, Braune to Wagner, October 13, 1939; 299–300, Eichmann to Nebe, October 16, 1939; and 227–9, R. Günther-Braune FS-Gespräch, October 18, 1939.

13. YVA, O/53/93/225–26, Günther to Eichmann, October 18, 1939; 245, Vermerk of October 21, 1939; and 307, Günther Vermerk, October 1939. See also Herbert Rosenkranz, *Verfolgung und Selbstbehauptung: Die Juden in Österreich 1938–1945*, pp. 216–17, for the deportations from Austria.

14. Iltis, ed., *Nazi-Dokumente Sprechen*, I. Zehngut testimony.

15. Adler, *Der verwaltete Mensch*, p. 135.

16. Adler, *Der verwaltete Mensch*, 138–39; Iltis, ed., *Nazi-Dokumente Sprechen*, I. Zehngut testimony.

17. YVA, O/53/93/235–38, R. Günther Tagesbericht, October 19, 1939; 220, undated R. Günther telegram; and 244, R. Günther Vermerk, October 21, 1939.

18. YVA, O/53/93/249–50, R. Günther Vermerk, October 24, 1939.

19. Rosenkranz, *Verfolgung und Selbstbehauptung*, p. 217.

20. YVA, O/53/93/262–64, Novak to Brunner, November 3, 1939, and Sonderreferat-Zentrale Stelle in Mährisch Ostrau to R. Günther, November 3, 1939. Adler, *Der verwaltete Mensch*, pp. 134–35. These Prague Jews were eventually allowed to emigrate via Slovakia in 1940. Bauer, *American Jewry and the Holocaust*, p. 360.

21. YVA, O/53/93/256–57, Brunner to Eichmann, October 28, 1939.

22. Goshen, "Eichmann und die Nisko-Aktion," p. 96.

23. Goshen, "Eichmann und die Nisko-Aktion," pp. 92–93.

24. Umbreit, *Deutsche Militärverwaltungen*, p. 110.

25. Frank, *Diensttagebuch*, p. 82 (entry of December 20, 1939).

26. YVA, O/53/93/256–57, Brunner to Eichmann, October 28, 1939.

27. Goshen's theory that Eichmann was operating totally beyond Berlin's knowledge and had not been reporting to Müller is also contradicted by Rolf Günther's observation that the Müller stop order must have crossed with Eichmann's last report. O-53/93/220, undated R. Günther telegram.

28. NCA, 6:116 (3398-PS, Seyss-Inquart to Himmler, November 4, 1939); and Botz, *Wohnungspolitik und Judendeportation in Wien*, p. 196 (Doc. X, Himmler to Bürckel, November 9, 1939).

29. Umbreit, *Deutsche Militärverwaltungen*, p. 218.

30. Koehl, *RKFDV*, p. 61p; Rich, *The Establishment of the New Order*, p. 73; TWC, 4:958–60 (Nbg. Doc. NO-2676: Himmler to Supreme Reich Authorities, November 10, 1939).

31. Tatiana Berenstein et al., eds., *Faschismus, Getto, Massenmord: Dokumentation über Ausrottung und Widerstand der Juden in Polen während des zweiten Weltkrieges* (hereafter cited as *FGM*), pp. 42–43. Nbg. Doc. NO-4059 (General Orders and Directives of RKFDV, undated, signed by Creutz). YVA, JM 21/1, Frank Tagebuch: Streckenbach report of October 31, 1939. For Himmler's order that Jews of the General Government would be moved from west to east of the Vistula the following year: USHMMA, RG 15.005m, 2/104/15 (Müller, RSHA, to EG VI in Posen, November 8, 1939).

32. *Documente Occupationis Teutonicae* (hereafter cited as *DOT*), 5:2–28 (NO-3732: RPA Memorandum, "Die Frage der Behandlung der Bevölkerung der ehemaligen polnischen Gebiete nach rassenpolitischen Gesichtspunkten," November 25, 1939, by E. Wetzel and G. Hecht); Heinrich Himmler, "Denkschrift Himmlers über die Behandlung der fremdvölkischen im Osten (May 1940)" (Nbg. Doc. NO-1880).

33. *IMT*, 30:95 (2278-PS: Seyss-Inquart report on trip to Poland, November 17–22, 1939).

34. *FGM*, p. 46 (Frank speech in Radom, November 25, 1939). The full text of this speech can be found in YVA, O-53/99/442–63.

35. *Die Tagebücher von Joseph Goebbels*, Teil I: *Aufzeichnungen 1924–1941*, 3:604, 612, 628, 658 (entries of October 10 and 17, November 2, and December 5, 1939). For an English edition of this period of the diaries: *The Goebbels Diaries, 1939–1941*.

36. Umbreit, *Deutsche Militärverwaltungen*, pp. 217–18.

37. Nbg. Doc. NO-4613: Himmler to Lorenz, Heydrich, Greifelt, Forster, Greiser, October 11, 1939. YVA, O-53/59/342 (Damzog to Jäger, October 26, 1939); *DOT*, 8:3 (excerpt from Lagebericht, November 5, 1939); YVA, JM 3582 (Bethke to Derichsweiler, November 4, 1939, microfilmed from the Bundesarchiv, R 75/3b).

38. There are two reports of this conference: *Biuletyn* 12, pp. 11F–14F; and Frank, *Diensttagebuch*, pp. 60–61.

39. YVA, JM 3582 (Rapp report, January 26, 1940).

40. USHMMA, RG 15.015m (Records of the Umwandererzentrale Posen), 1/95/4–7 (Rapp draft, November 10, 1939).

41. USHMMA, RG 15.005m, 2/99/1–5 (Koppe circular, November 12, 1939). An excerpt is reprinted in *FGM*, pp. 43–47.

42. YVA, JM 3582 (Rapp report, January 26, 1940, with list of regulations). USHMMA, RG 15.015m, 2/107/1–35 (protocols of conferences of November 17 and 23, 1939).

43. YVA, JM 3582 (Sonderbefehl über die Heranziehung der jüdischen Ältestenräte bei der Evakuierung der Juden, November 24, 1939).

44. "EG in Polen," 2:117.

45. *Die Tagebücher von Joseph Goebbels I*, 3:654 (entry of November 30, 1939).

46. USHMMA, RG 15.015m, 2/104/1 (Müller to Naumann, December 26, 1939).

47. USHMMA, RG 15007m, 8/94/1 (Müller, RSHA IV, to Sandberger, Einwandererzentralestelle Gotenhafen, November 8, 1939).

48. YVA, O/53/68/639–41 (Polizeisitzung in Danzig, November 15, 1939) and 642–3 (conference of November 20, 1939); JM 3582 (Hildebrandt speech of November 26, 1939, in Bydgoszcz).

49. *Biuletyn* 12, pp. 15F–18F (Heydrich to HSSPF Krakau, Breslau, Posen, Danzig,

November 28, 1939, and Heydrich to Krüger, Streckenbach, Koppe, and Damzog, November 28, 1939).

50. *Biuletyn* 12, pp. 22F–31F, and USHMMA RG 11.001m (Osobyi Fond 500, Opis 1, file 88), 1/88/185–202 (Rapp report of December 18, 1939); YVA, JM 3582, and USHMMA, RG 15.015m, 3/208/1–12 (Rapp report of January 26, 1940).

51. *Biuletyn* 12, pp. 37F–39F (Eichmann remarks at conference of January 4, 1940); Nbg. Doc. NO-5150 (Sipo-SD summary report of November 15, 1940). However, the Final Report of the "third short-range plan" (3. *Nahplan*) refers to the December 1939 evacuations as the "resettlement of politically leading Polish intelligentsia and to some extent Jews." YVA, JM 3582 (microfilmed from Bundasarchiv, R 75/8).

52. USHMMA, RGI 15.015m, 4/235/22 (Richter report, n.d.). According to Theo Richmond, *Konin: A Quest*, p. 84, the number of Jewish deportees from Konin on December 1, 1939, was 1,080.

53. USHMMA, RG 15.015m, 3/218/13–14 (undated report of Richter).

54. USHMMA, RG 15.015m, 3/218/27–35 (Richter report, December 16, 1939).

55. USHMMA, RG 15.015m, 4/235/12 and 22 (Landrat Konin to Koppe, November 17, 1939, and Richter report, n.d.).

56. USHMMA, RG 15.015m, 4/243/17–19 (Landrat of Kreis Schroda to Koppe, December 12, 1939).

57. USHMMA, RG 15.015m, 4/243/15 (Richter report, n.d.).

58. USHMMA, RG 15.004m, 1/2/1 (EK 11, Aussenstelle Ciechocinek, to Bürgermeister of Alexandrow, November 14, 1939).

59. YVA, JM 3581 (RSHA II/112 an den Leiter II im Hause, December 19, 1939, microfilmed from the Bundesarchiv, R 58/544).

60. YVA, JM 3581 (Müller to all Staatspolizeileitstellen, December 21, 1939, and Heydrich to Sipo-SD in Krakau, Breslau, Posen, Danzig, and Königsberg, December 21, 1939). Eichmann knew of these decisions two days earlier, when he informed the head of the Austrian Jewish community, Dr. Löwenherz, that there would be no further transports from Austria to Poland and that he had been placed in charge of Jewish emigration and would now work in Berlin as well as Prague and Vienna. Eichmann Trial document T-1139 (Löwenherz memorandum, December 19, 1939).

61. USHMMA, RG 15.007m, 8/101/13 (Heydrich circular, December 22, 1939).

62. USHMMA, RG 15.015m, 2/97/1–7 (2. Nahplan, December 21, 1939).

63. Aly, *"Final Solution,"* p. 23.

64. *Biuletyn* 12, pp. 37F–39F (Abromeit Vermerk of January 8, 1940, on conference of January 4, 1940).

65. Aly, *"Final Solution,"* p. 54 n. 41. Aly notes that few Jews lived in these pre-1918 territories because most of them, out of fear of Polish anti-Semitism, had exercised the option in 1919/20 to move within postwar German boundaries.

66. Regarding suspicion of German-speaking Poles claiming to be *Volksdeutsche*, see *Bydgoszcz*, pp. 56–60 (SD Lagebericht from Bydgoszcz, October 20, 1939); and DOT 8:24 (Rapp report, December 18, 1939). On Rapp's subsequent defensiveness about selecting out *Volksdeutsche*, see YVA, JM 3582 (Rapp report of January 26, 1940). For complaints from the General Government about *Volksdeutsche* having been deported: YVA, JM 3582

(Koppe to Greiser and Rapp, January 4, 1940). For Himmler's restrictive orders: Nbg. Doc. NO-5411 (Creutz to Koppe, January 18, 1940); and *Biuletyn* 12, pp. 44F–45F (Vermerk of Eichmann-Seidl conversation, January 22–23, 1940). On economic disruption: *DOT*, 8:32–33 (Gendarmerie report from Landkreis Schrimm, January 22, 1940); and YVA, JM 3582 (Lodz Aussenstelle to Rapp, January 15, 1940).

67. *Biuletyn* 12, pp. 37F–39F (Abromeit Vermerk of January 8, 1940, on conference of January 4, 1940); *FGM*, pp. 48 and 53 (reports of Gschliesser and Wächter); *DOT*, 8:37–38 (report of Mattern).

68. *Die Tagebücher von Joseph Goebbels I*, 4:19 and 21 (entries of January 20 and 23, 1940).

69. USHMMA, RG 15.015m, 2/107/40 (Rapp Vermerk, December 2, 1939).

70. USHMMA, RG 15.015m, 2/101/5 (police report, December 3, 1939), and 3/166/1 (Petzel order, February 3, 1940).

71. *IMT*, 36:328–31 (Nbg. Doc. 344-EC: excerpt of report "Deutsche Rüstungswirtschaft in Polen, 1939/40"); and Nbg. Doc. 302-2-EC (excerpt from unidentified document).

72. *IMT*, 26:210–12 (661-PS: Presentation for German Academy of Law, January 1940).

73. Frank, *Diensttagebuch*, pp. 93–97 (Abteilungsleitersitzung, January 19, 1940).

74. USHMMA, RG 15.015m, 1/7/1, 10–14 (Strickner instruction for composing the evacuation list, January 6, 1940; Blank to Rapp, November 20, 1940).

75. USHMMA, RG 15.015m, 2/114/9 (Damzog to Rapp, January 12, 1940) and 3/197/10 (HSSPF Posen to SD-Abschnitt Lodz, January 12, 1940).

76. USHMMA, RG 15.015m, 2/114/12–14 (Döring to Rapp, January 9, 1940, and Jahr Vermerk, January 9, 1940).

77. USHMMA, RG 15.015m, 3/218/36–39, 49 (KdSchupo Sonderbefehl, January 23, 1940; Amt für Balteneinsatz, Aussenstelle Lodz, Tagesberichte Nr. 2 and 3, January 23, 1940, and Tagesbericht Nr. 6, January 25, 1940).

78. USHMMA, RG 15.015m, 1/96/8–10 (Koppe circular, January 20, 1940).

79. Valdis O. Lumans, *Himmler's Auxiliaries: The Volksdeutsche Mittelstelle and the German Nationalities of Europe, 1933–1945*, pp. 161–64.

80. USHMMA, RG 15.015m, 1/96/12–13 (Krumey report, January 30, 1940, on Leipzig Fahrplanbesprechung of January 26–27, 1940).

81. Aly, *"Endlösung,"* pp. 113–14.

82. For general decisions and policies concerning the use of Polish labor in 1939–40, see Ulrich Herbert, *Fremdarbeiter: Politik und Praxis des "Ausländer-Einsatzes" in der Kriegswirtschaft des Dritten Reiches*, pp. 67–90.

83. USHMMA, RG 15.015m, 2/146/1 (Gestapo, Berlin, to Döring, Posen, January 5, 1940).

84. USHMMA, RG 15.015m, 2/146/9–15 (Report on meeting of January 11, 1940).

85. *Biuletyn* 12, pp. 66F–75F (NO-5322: Conference of January 30, 1940); USHMMA, RG 15.015m, 2/109/1–3 (Rapp Vermerk, February 1, 1940).

86. *IMT*, 36:300–306 (EC-305: Karinhall conference, February 12, 1940). Concerning the ethnic Germans in the Lublin district designated to become the *Judenreservat*, Frank had proposed their removal on November 1, 1939, and Himmler had approved by mid-

December. Frank, *Diensttagebuch*, p. 56; USHMMA, RG 15.015m, 2/115/2 (Frank to Greiser, December 14, 1939).

87. Frank, *Diensttagebuch*, pp. 131 and 146–47 (Sitzung des Reichsverteidigungsausschuss, Warsaw, March 2, 1940, and Dienstversammlung der Kreis- und Stadthauptmänner des Distrikts Lublin, March 4, 1940). The military representative at the March 2 conference in Warsaw apparently gained the impression that the deportation of the Jews was not imminent, since he recorded, "The Jewish question poses no immediate danger." Nbg. Doc. 300-EC (Aktenvermerk über die Sitzung des RVA in Warschau, March 2, 1940).

88. YVA, JM 3582 (Gestapo Hohensalza to IdS Posen, July 17, 1940). USHMMA, RG 15.015m, 1/96/22 (Fahrplan of Zwischenplan).

89. USHMMA, RG 15.015m, 1/96/16–17 (Hagelstein report, January 31, 1940), 18–19 (Koppe circular, February 1, 1940), 20–21 (Rapp circular, February 6, 1940), and 28–29 (Rapp circular, February 26, 1940).

90. USHMMA, RG 15.015m, 3/97/16 (Rapp to Eichmann, February 3, 1940), 3/97/19–20 (Rapp to Streckenbach and Eichmann, February 15, 1940), and 1/96/27 (Rapp to Aussenstellen, February 15, 1940).

91. USHMMA, RG 15.015m, 1/96/35–36 (Rapp to Regierungspräsident of Kalisch), and 3/153/1 (Oberbürgermeister of Posen to Koppe and Rapp, March 5, 1940).

92. USHMMA, RG 15.015m, 1/97/25–27 (Rapp to Eichmann, March 7, 1940; Aktenvermerk, March 11, 1940), and 3/203/1 (Eichmann to Rapp, March 13, 1940).

93. Frank, *Diensttagebuch*, p. 153 (entry of March 12, 1940).

94. YVA, O/53/48/650–52 (Umwandererzentrale Abschlussbericht 1940).

95. USHMMA, RG 15.015m, 2/129/1 (Barth to Rapp, March 7, 1940).

96. USHMMA, RG 15.105m, 3/155/2 (Posen to Umwandererzentralstelle-Dienststelle Litzmannstadt, date illegible). These Jews must have been deported from towns other than the city of Konin itself, for this deportation is not mentioned in Richmond, *Konin*.

97. USHMMA, RG 15.026m, 11/14/27–29 (report of Jüdische Gemeinde Krakau, May 20, 1940).

98. USHMMA, RG 15.015m, 3/228/1 (Kreisweise Aufstellung of Poles deported from the Warthegau).

99. USHMMA, RG 15.015m, 1/96/37–38 (Rapp to Eichmann, March 7, 1940).

100. Adler, *Der verwaltete Mensch*, p. 140, gives a figure of 1,200. Longerich, *Politik der Vernichtung*, pp. 161, 654, estimates over 1,100. The Sipo-SD records (*IMT*, 31:283–94: 2916-PS) claim 1,000.

101. PA: Unterstaatssekretär—Judenfrage, DBN Bern, February 16, 1940, on report in *Neue Züriche Zeitung* (NG-1530), and Weizsäcker to Ref. D, February 16, 1940; Inland II AB 42/2, excerpt from *Politiken* of Copenhagen, February 16, 1940.

102. Aly, "*Final Solution,*" p. 60, has shown that this was in fact a limited measure to obtain housing in Stettin for returning Baltic Germans.

103. PA, Inland II AB 42/2: Bielefeld and Neuwirth to Weizsäcker, February 17, 1940, and Schumburg to Müller, February 20, 1940.

104. The Reich Chancellery version is Nbg. Doc. NG-2490, printed in Adler, *Der verwaltete Mensch*, pp. 144–45. The Foreign Office version is in PA, Inland II AB 42/2.

105. PA, Inland II AB 42/2, Schumburg to Weizsäcker, March 21, 1940.

106. PA, Inland IIg 173, Notiz of March 29, 1940; Schumberg to Weizsäcker, March 29, 1940; Notiz of April 2, 1940; Schumburg to Weizsäcker, April 2, 1940; and Göring telegram of March 23, 1940 (T120/K774/K205691–96).

107. FGM, pp. 53–54 (Berlin conference of April 1, 1940).

108. Frank, Diensttagebuch, p. 158 (entry of April 5, 1940) and p. 204 (entry of May 19, 1940); Dokumenty i Materialy Do Dziejow Okupacji Niemieckiej W Polsce (hereafter cited as DiM), vol. 3: Getto Lodzkie, pp. 168–69 (Regierungspräsident to officials of Bezirk Lodz and Kalisch, May 8, 1940).

109. USHMMA, RG 15.015m, 2/130/4–5 (Rapp report on meeting of February 4, 1940); 2/131/3–35 (reports of Haussmann and Burket on meetings with Landräte).

110. USHMMA, RG 15.015m, 2/130/7–9 (report on Kr. Tureck, February 6, 1940).

111. USHMMA, RG 15.015m, 2/109/3–6 (Doerksen to Rapp, February 8, 1940).

112. USHMMA, RG 15.015m, 2/130/26–32 (Koppe Merkpunkte, March 2, 1940).

113. For the three-camp system: USHMMA, RG 15.015m, 2/109/16–17 (Barth to Rapp, April 1, 1940) and 2/130/43–49 (Rapp to Aussenstellen, April 1, 1940) and 58–61 (Rapp to Aussenstellen, April 19, 1940). For the criteria to screen out people of possible German origin: USHMMA, RG 15.015m, 3/198/6–7 (Rapp to Aussenstellen, February 29, 1940), and 3/214/1 (Seidel Aktenvermerk, March 19, 1940).

114. USHMMA, RG 15.015m, 3/184/11 (Internierungslager Glowno, Aktennotiz, March 30, 1940) and 3/228/1 (Kreisweise Aufstellung of Poles deported from the Warthegau).

115. USHMMA, RG 15.015m, 2/130/73–75 (Rapp Aktenvermerk, April 20, 1940). The Umwandererzentralstelle in Lodz had reported to Rapp on April 17 that only 72 out of 994 Poles scheduled to be processed on April 13–14 had actually been taken into custody. In any case, the Poles should be left in peace until the harvest was complete, and meanwhile "strangers" should disappear from the villages where farms were to be taken over. USHMMA, RG 15.015m, 3/190/7–8 (Krumey to Rapp, April 17, 1940).

116. USHMMA, RG 15.015m, 2/130/81–82 (Himmler to Greifelt, May 10, 1940).

117. USHMMA, RG 15.015m, 1/49/1 (Eichlich, RSHA III B, to Höppner, Umwanderer-zentralstelle Posen, May 22, 1940).

118. Documents on German Foreign Policy (hereafter cited as DGFP), Series D, 8:912–13 (Hewel memorandum on conversation of Hitler and Colin Ross, March 12, 1940).

119. FGM, p. 109 (Schön report, January 20, 1941).

120. IMT, 31:283–85 (2916-PS: excerpt from "Der Reichsführer SS. Reichskommissar für die Festigung deutschen Volkstums [printed in December 1940], including Himmler order of May 9, 1940).

121. USHMMA, RG 15.015m, 4/215/2–3 (Himmler to HSSPF Ost, Nordost, Weichsel, Warthe, Südost, May 20, 1940).

122. Himmler, "Denkschrift Himmlers über die Behandlung der fremdvölkischen im Osten," ed. Helmut Krausnick, pp. 196–98.

123. Himmler, "Denkschrift Himmlers," pp. 195–96 (Himmler memorandum, May 28, 1940).

124. NA microfilm, T175/122/266598ff. (Himmler memorandum, June 24, 1940).

125. Frank, Diensttagebuch, pp. 210, 216 (Polizeisitzung, May 30, 1940).

126. Biuletyn 12, pp. 94F–95F (R. Günther to Höppner, July 1, 1940).

127. Nbg. Doc. NG-1627 (Frank to Lammers, June 25, 1940).

128. *Biuletyn* 12, pp. 96F–97F (Vermerk on Höppner-IV D 4 discussion, July 9, 1940).

129. This could not easily be done without the pioneering work of Klaus-Jürgen Müller, *Das Heer und Hitler*, and the excellent editing of the Groscurth papers by Helmut Krausnick and Harold Deutsch, *Tagebücher eines Abwehroffiziers 1938–1940*.

130. Deutsch, *The Conspiracy against Hitler in the Twilight War*, pp. 73–77.

131. Deutsch, *The Conspiracy against Hitler*, pp. 195–236; Groscurth, *Tagebücher*, pp. 223–24 (Privattagebuch, November 1 and 5, 1939).

132. Groscurth, *Tagebücher*, pp. 409–11 (Doc. Nr. 37: Bock to Forster, November 17, 1939).

133. IMT, 35:88–91 (D-419: Report of General Petzel, November 23, 1939, forwarded to OKW by OKH).

134. Helmut Stief, "Ausgewählte Briefe von Generalmajor Helmut Stief," p. 300 (letter of November 21, 1939).

135. Groscurth, *Tagebücher*, pp. 426–27 (Doc. Nr. 43: Blaskowitz to OKH, November 27, 1939).

136. Gerhard Engel, *Heeresadjutant bei Hitler: 1938–43. Aufzeichnungen des Majors Engel*, ed. von Kotze, p. 68. As the editor notes, Engel's dating of November 18 for Hitler's dismissal of the report is possibly mistaken, since Engel apparently did not date these notes until after the war. Richard Giziowski, *The Enigma of General Blaskowitz*, pp. 172–73, assumes that there were two Blaskowitz memoranda in November, one of November 17 and a second of November 27.

137. Groscurth, *Tagebücher*, p. 234 (Privattagebuch, December 10, 1939). For the general policy and effect of Hitler's bribery of his generals, see Norman Goda, "Black Marks: Hitler's Bribery of His Senior Officers during World War II."

138. Groscurth, *Tagebücher*, p. 236 (Privattagebuch, December 10, 1939). The same list of reasons was given by Halder to Gördeler. Ulrich von Hassell, *The Von Hassell Diaries, 1938–1944*, pp. 89–90 (entry of December 5, 1939).

139. Giziowski, *The Enigma of General Blaskowitz*, pp. 176–80. This report does not survive.

140. Groscurth, *Tagebücher*, p. 238 (Privatagebuch, December 19, 1939).

141. Müller, *Das Heer und Hitler*, p. 442; and Klaus-Jürgen Müller, ed., "Zu Vorgeschichte und Inhalt der Rede Himmlers vor der höheren Generalität am 13. März 1940 in Koblenz," p. 103.

142. Groscurth, *Tagebücher*, p. 241 (Privattagebuch, January 13, 1940).

143. Müller, *Das Heer und Hitler*, p. 443; Giziowski, *The Enigma of General Blaskowitz*, p. 199.

144. Müller, "Zu Vorgeschichte und Inhalt der Rede Himmlers," p. 109 (Tippelskirch Tagebuch, January 23, 1940). The indignation over Brauchitsch's weak attitude to the ss seems to have been fueled as much by a Himmler directive encouraging ss men to father children out of wedlock during the war to compensate for the anticipated loss of German blood as by the atrocities in Poland. Groscurth, *Tagebücher*, pp. 427–30 (Doc. Nr. 44: List to Heeresgruppe A, November 28, 1939; Leeb to Brauchitsch, November 30, 1939; Bock to Brauchitsch, December 5, 1939).

145. Müller, "Zu Vorgeschichte und Inhalt der Rede Himmlers," p. 110 (Tippelskirch Tagebuch, January 23, 1940).

146. Müller, "Zu Vorgeschichte und Inhalt der Rede Himmlers," p. 111 (Tippelskirch Tagebuch, February 2, 1940).

147. Groscurth, *Tagebücher*, p. 247 (Privattagebuch, February 2 and 14, 1940).

148. Groscurth, *Tagebücher*, p. 247 (Privattagebuch, February 2, 1940).

149. Halder, *Kriegstagebuch*, 1:183–40 (entry of February 5, 1940).

150. Müller, "Zu Vorgeschichte und Inhalt der Rede Himmlers," p. 111 (Tippelskirch Tagebuch, February 5, 1940).

151. Nbg. Doc. NOKW-1799 (Brauchitsch to army and army group commanders and OberOst, concerning the army and the SS, February 7, 1940).

152. Groscurth, *Tagebücher*, pp. 247–48 (Privattagebuch, February 2 and 14, 1940).

153. Nbg. Doc. NO-3011 (Notes for presentation to Brauchitsch at Spala on February 15, 1940, including Ulex report of February 2, 1940). Now printed in Giziowski, *The Enigma of General Blaskowitz*, pp. 483–504.

154. Müller, *Das Heer und Hitler*, p. 675 (Doc. Nr. 50: Mackensen to Brauchitsch, February 14, 1940).

155. Müller, "Zu Vorgeschichte und Inhalt der Rede Himmlers," pp. 112–13 (Tippelskirch Tagebuch, February 20, 1940).

156. Müller, *Das Heer und Hitler*, pp. 673–74 (Doc. Nr. 49: Vortragsnotiz Radke, March 4, 1940, about Wolff's telephone call).

157. Krausnick and Wilhelm, *Die Truppe des Weltanschauungskrieges*, p. 105.

158. Müller, "Zu Vorgeschichte und Inhalt der Rede Himmlers," pp. 95–96, 108.

159. Wagner, *Der Generalquartiermeister*, p. 182 (entry of June 15, 1940). This final "conversion" of the generals in the wake of the victory in France has been most effectively discussed by Krausnick, *Die Truppe des Weltanschauungskrieges*, pp. 110–12.

160. Giziowski, *The Enigma of General Blaskowitz*, pp. 213, 221; Deutsch, *The Conspiracy against Hitler*, p. 188.

161. *TWC*, 13:1208 (NOKW-1531: Küchler order of July 22, 1940).

162. Magnus Brechtken, *"Madagaskar für die Juden": Antisemitische Idee und politische Praxis*, pp. 31–79. On the British anti-Semites: Louis W. Bondy, *Racketeers of Hatred*, pp. 131–38; and J. E. Morrel, "Arnold Leese—Fascist and Antisemite." See also Philip Friedman, "The Lublin Reservation and the Madagascar Plan: Two Aspects of Nazi Jewish Policy during the Second World War," p. 166; Leni Yahil, "Madagascar—Phantom of a Solution for the Jewish Question," pp. 319–20; and Hans Jansen, *Madagaskar-Plan. Die beabsichtigte Deportation der europäischen Juden nach Madagaskar*.

163. Yahil, "Madagascar," pp. 321–22.

164. Yahil, "Madagascar," pp. 317–18; Eugene Hevesi, "Hitler's Plan for Madagascar"; Brechtken, *"Madagaskar für die Juden,"* pp. 81–164.

165. For Streicher, Schacht, Göring, Rosenberg, and Ribbentrop, see Yahil, "Madagascar," pp. 320–21, 323, 332. For Frank: *IMT*, 26:210–22 (661-PS).

166. Yahil, "Madagascar," p. 321.

167. On Rademacher's background, see Christopher R. Browning, *The Final Solution and the German Foreign Office*, pp. 29–30.

168. PA, Inland II AB 347/3, Rademacher memorandum "Gedanken über die Arbeit und Aufgaben des Ref. D III, June 3, 1940." A synopsis of this memorandum is Nbg. Doc. NG-5764. Rademacher confusedly attributed his inspiration on Madagascar to the "old Dutch anti-Semite Beamish," whose pamphlet from the 1920s he found in the files of Referat Deutschland. PA, Inland IIg 177, Rademacher memorandum of August 30, 1940 (T120/1512/ 372050–52), and Staatsarchiv Nürnberg, Zz 431, Nr. 1, Rademacher affidavit, July 20, 1948. It is thus unclear whether Rademacher meant the Englishman Beamish, the Dutch-sounding pseudonym van Winghene of Georg de Pottere, or perhaps both. An article in *Der Stürmer* in September 1938 also attributed the idea of Madagascar as the ideal area of Jewish resettlement to a Dutch brochure. USHMMA, RG 11.001, 9/672/2 (clipping from *Der Stürmer*).

169. Galeazzo Ciano, *The Ciano Diaries 1939–43*, pp. 265–66; Paul Schmidt, *Hitler's Interpreter*, p. 178.

170. Klaus Hildebrand, *Vom Reich zum Weltreich: Hitler, NSDAP, und koloniale Frage 1919–1945*, pp. 651–52.

171. PA, Inland IIg 177: Heydrich to Ribbentrop, June 24, 1940 (T120/1512/372047); and Rademacher's handwritten note on his synopsis of June 3, 1940 (T120/1512/372108).

172. Frank, *Diensttagebuch*, p. 248 (entry of July 10, 1940).

173. Frank, *Diensttagebuch*, pp. 252 and 258 (Abteilungsleitersitzung, July 12, and entry of July 25, 1940).

174. *The Warsaw Diary of Adam Czerniakow* (hereafter cited as *Czerniakow Diary*), p. 169 (entry of July 1, 1940).

175. FGM, p. 110 (excerpt from Schön report, January 20, 1941). The Kreishauptmann of Minsk Mazowiecki, also reported that the construction of a ghetto there was "already begun in June . . . but was stopped again in July upon orders from above." FGM, p. 96 (report of Kreishauptmann of Minsk Mazowiecki, October 11, 1940).

176. YVA, JM 814, Situation Report of Kreishauptmann of Krysnystaw, September 10, 1940.

177. Frank, *Diensttagebuch*, pp. 261–63 (entry of July 31, 1940).

178. Eichmann's claim to have originated the idea, only to see others meddle and claim it for their own, is in fact precisely contrary to the actual sequence of events. *The Trial of Adolf Eichmann: Record of the Proceedings in the District Court of Jerusalem* (hereafter cited as *Eichmann Trial*), 4:1396, 1609, 1616, 7:137, 8:278. Magnus Brechtken has now also documented Göring's role in soliciting preparatory memoranda for the Madagascar Plan as well: *"Madagaskar für die Juden,"* pp. 254–59.

179. *Akten zur deutschen auswärtigen Politik* (hereafter cited as ADAP), Series D, 10:92–94 (Rademacher memorandum, Die Judenfrage im Friedensvertrage, July 3, 1940); PA, Inland, IIg 177, Plan zur Lösung der Judenfrage, July 2, 1940 (T120/1512/372104–5).

180. PA, Inland II AB 35/2, Burgdörfer Gutachten, July 17, 1940 (T120/3071/ D612577–80); Inland IIg 177, Schumacher Gutachten, August 2, 1940, and excerpt from *Meyer's Lexicon* (T120/1512/372099–102, 372096–97). On Burgdörfer, see Götz Aly and Karl Heinz Roth, *Die Restlose Erfassung: Volkszählen, Identifizieren, Aussondern im Nationalsozialismus*, pp. 36–37.

181. PA, Inland IIg 177, Rademacher memorandum "Gedanken über die Gründung

einer intereuropäischen Bank für die Verwertung des Judenvermögens in Europa," August 12, 1940 (T120/1512/372106–7).

182. *ADAP*, D, 10:389 (Luther to Rademacher, August 15, 1940).

183. Esriel Hildesheimer, *Jüdische Selbstverwaltung unter dem NS-Regime: Der Existenz-kampf der Reichsvertretung und Reichsvereinigung der Juden in Deutschland*, pp. 186–87.

184. Eichmann Trial Document T-1143 (Löwenherz memorandum, July 3, 1940).

185. PA, Inland IIg 177: Dannecker to Rademacher, August 15, 1940, and "Reichssi-cherheitshauptamt: Madagaskar Projekt" (T120/1512/372053–54 and 372056–71).

186. The Foreign Office statistics of Burgdörfer claimed 4.9 million Jews for all of Europe in comparison to the RSHA figure of 4 million in the German sphere alone, because Burgdörfer estimated fully 1 million fewer Jews in the Third Reich and the General Government than did the SS.

187. PA, Inland IIg 177, Rademacher memorandum "Bisherige Entwicklung des Madagaskar-Plans des Referats D III," August 30, 1940 (T120/1512/372050–52).

188. Bernhard Lösener, "Als Rassereferent im Reichsministerium des Innern," p. 296. Lösener's memoir is now also available in *Legislating the Holocaust: The Bernhard Loesener Memoirs and Supporting Documents*.

189. Yahil, "Madagascar," p. 327.

190. This conclusion is shared by Brechtken, *"Madagaskar für die Juden,"* p. 295.

191. *IMT*, 29:104 (1918-PS: Himmler speech at Metz).

192. For Lorraine: Nbg. Doc. NO-5150 (overview of evacuations to November 15, 1940, compiled by the Chief of Sipo-SD). For Alsace: Akten der Partei-Kanzlei der *NSDAP*, 101 23821 (Chef der Zivilverwaltung im Elsass, April 22, 1941, to Bormann, on census of February 15, 1941). In addition to 3,259 Jews, among those deported from Alsace were 2,381 in mixed marriages, 171 professional criminals, 672 "Gypsies," 738 drunkards and prostitutes, 161 homosexuals, 1,797 foreigners from enemy countries, and—without clari-fying the distinction between them—935 "inner" Frenchmen, 1,626 "patois" French, and 12,504 pro-French Alsatians.

193. *Eichmann Trial*, 7:141 and 145. The following sources also suggest that the initia-tive came from the Gauleiter: Lösener, "Als Rassereferent," p. 295; and PA, Inland IIg 189, anonymous report over the deportation of German Jews to southern France, printed in *Dokumente über die Verfolgung der jüdischen Bürger in Baden-Württemberg durch das Na-tionalsozialistische Regime 1933–1945* (hereafter cited as *Dokumente Baden-Württemberg*), 2:242–43. The same conclusion is reached by Jacob Toury, "Die Entstehungsgeschichte des Austreibungsbefehle gegen die Juden der Saarpfalz und Baden 22/23. Oktober 1940—Camp de Gurs."

194. Lösener, "Als Rassereferent," p. 295; *Dokumente Baden-Württemberg*, p. 238 (Re-port of Gendarmerie-Einzelposten in Malsch, October 24, 1940).

195. *Dokumente Baden-Württemberg*, pp. 236–37 (Merkblatt für eingesetzten Beamten).

196. *Dokumente Baden-Württemberg*, p. 239 (Report of Gendarmerie-Posten Walldorf, October 23, 1940).

197. PA, Inland IIg 189, Heydrich to Luther, October 29, 1940 (printed in *Dokumente Baden-Württemberg*, p. 241); *Eichmann Trial*, 4:142–44; Adler, *Der verwaltete Mensch*, p. 158.

198. PA, Inland IIg 189, Welck to Foreign Office, October 28, 1940 (printed in *Dokumente Baden-Württemburg*, p. 244).

199. PA, Inland IIg 189, Heydrich to Luther, October 29, 1940; *ADAP*, D, 11:376 (Todenhöfer to Luther and Ribbentrop, October 31, 1940).

200. PA, Inland IIg 189, anonymous report, October 30, 1940.

201. PA, Inland IIg 189, Rademacher to Luther, November 21, 1940 (printed in *Dokumente Baden-Württemburg*, pp. 245–46).

202. PA, Inland IIg 189, Hencke to Foreign Office, November 19, 1940 (printed in *Dokumente Baden-Württemburg*, pp. 244–45).

203. PA, Inland IIg 189, Note of Grote, November 20, 1940 (T120/K773/K204464).

204. PA, Inland IIg 189: Sonnleithner to Weizsäcker and Wörmann, November 22, 1940 (printed in *Dokumente Baden-Württemburg*, pp. 246–47); Luther to Kramarz, November 25, 1940 (T120/K773/K204472); Rademacher to Hencke at Weisbaden, December 7, 1940 (T120/K773/K204624). Adler, *Der verwaltete Mensch*, pp. 162–65.

205. PA, Inland II AB 132/79: Hencke to Foreign Office, November 30, 1940; report of chief of military administration, Bordeaux, December 18, 1940.

206. PA, Inland II AB 132/79: Welck to Foreign Office, December 21, 1940 and February 14, 1941.

207. PA, Inland II AB 132/79, Chief Sipo-SD (IV D 4) to Luther, February 28, 1941.

208. PA, Inland II AB 132/79, Note of OKH, May 13, 1941.

209. PA, Inland II AB 132/79: Welck to Foreign Office, June 4, 1941; IV D 4 to D III, July 9, 1941.

210. USHMMA, RG 15.015m, 3/227/2 (statistical report of the 2. Nahplan) and 3/228/ 1–2 (Wolhynienaktion trains).

211. USHMMA, RG 15.015m, 3/213/13–14 (Aussenstelle Gostynin to UWZ Posen, May 25, 1940).

212. *DOT*, 8:62 (Lodz Gestapo report, July 25, 1940).

213. USHMMA, RG 15.015m, 3/169/3–4 (Höppner Aktenvermerk, June 18, 1940).

214. USHMMA, RG 15.015m, 3/147/1–110 (UWZ Posen-Police Battalion 44 correspondence, September 7–December 13, 1940).

215. USHMMA, RG 15.015m, 2/143/9–10 (Höppner to Eichmann, November 15, 1940).

216. Bundesarchiv Berlin (hereafter cited as BA), R 20/51/3–7 (activity report of Police Battalion 101, May 5, 1940–April 7, 1941).

217. USHMMA, RG 15.015m, 3/201/1–2 (UWZ Litzmannstadt to Eichmann, November 3, 1940).

218. USHMMA, RG 15.015m, 2/143/9–10 (Höppner to Eichmann, November 15, 1940).

219. USHMMA, RG 15.015m, 3/220/1 (Aussenstelle Nessau to UWZ Litzmannstadt, May 24, 1940). The repatriated ethnic Germans, if they were able to find out in advance what Polish farms were being allotted to them, could not resist going to see them for themselves, thus also giving the Poles advance warning. USHMMA, RG 15.004, 1/3/12 (Landrat Hermmansbad, February 27, 1941, to Amtskommissare and Gendarmerieposten).

220. USHMMA, RG 15.015m, 2/134/4 and 6 (SD report to Döring, September 23, 1940, and enclosure); 9 (Seidel Aktenvermerk, n.d.); 11–12, 14 (Höppner Aktenvermerken, October 5, 8, and 17, 1940); 20 (Döring to Ansiedlungsstab Litzmannstadt, November 3,

1940); 21 (SD-Aussenstelle Obornik report, November 23, 1940); 24–25 (Höppner to Döring, December 11, 1940); 28 (Aussenstelle Altburgund to UMZ Posen, June 25, 1941).

221. USHMMA, RG 15.015m, 3/195/4–5 (SD-Hauptaussenstelle Posen to SD-Leitabschnitt Posen, October 19, 1940, with Höppner marginalia); 6 (unknown SS-Obersturmbannführer to Regierungspräsident Hohensalza), and 7 (Landrat Hohensalza to Regierungspräsident, September 16, 1940). Aly, *"Final Solution,"* p. 123.

222. USHMMA, RG 15.015m, 3/151/2 (Höppner to Medizinalrat Dr. Gundermann, April 4, 1941).

223. USHMMA, RG 15.015m, 3/214/6–7 (Bilharz to UWZ Posen and Litzmannstadt, May 24, 1940).

224. USHMMA, RG 15.015m, 2/121/4 (Bilharz Aktenvermerk, June 17, 1940) and 7–8 (Höppner to Ehlich and Eichmann, June 28, 1940).

225. USHMMA, RG 15.015m, 2/121/10 (Günther to Höppner, July 1, 1940) and 2/125/1 (Höppner to Krumey, June 14, 1940).

226. USHMMA, RG 15.015m, 1/121/16 (Höppner to Damzog, Eichmann, and Krumey, July 18, 1940), and 1/122/4 (Höppner Aktenvermerk, December 5, 1940). This plan of a vast military training area in Konin was revived and then postponed once again in 1941. USHMMA, RG 15.015m, 2/122 (miscellaneous correspondence).

227. Frank, *Diensttagebuch*, p. 56 (entry of November 1, 1940); USHMMA, RG 15.105m, 2/115/2 (Frank to Greiser, December 14, 1939).

228. USHMMA, RG 15.015m, 2/115/3 (UWZ Posen Aktenvermerk, May 25, 1940).

229. USHMMA, RG 15.015m, 2/115/11–12 (Seidel Aktenvermerk, June 27, 1940), 17–25 (Höppner to Ehlich and Eichmann, June 28, 1940) and 25–26 (Krumey Aktenvermerk, June 28, 1940).

230. USHMMA, RG 15.015m, 2/115/28–29 (Günther to Höppner, July 1, 1940, and Höppner Aktenvermerk, July 3, 1940).

231. USHMMA, RG 15.015m, 2/115/35 (IV D 4 Vermerk, July 9, 1940).

232. USHMMA, RG 15.015m, 2/115/38 (conference of Ansiedlungsstab, Posen, July 12, 1940), 40–41 (Höppner to Eichmann and Ehlich, July 12, 1940), and 50 (Krumey Aktenvermerk, August 21, 1940).

233. USHMMA, RG 15.015m, 3/228/3 (Aufstellung der Cholmer Aktion).

234. YVA, O/53/66/305–7 (train lists from BA, R 75/9a); Gerhard Eisenblätter, "Grundlinien der Politik des Reiches gegenüber dem Generalgouvernement, 1939–1945," p. 188; and Aly, *"Endlösung,"* p. 183. (Aly mistakenly states that the deportations of the Litauer Aktion were from West rather than East Prussia.) For Mlawa, see also USHMMA, RG 15.015m, 2/124/2 (Krumey to Ehlich, November 12, 1940); and YVA, O-53/66/301 (Krumey to Eichmann, December 6, 1940). For the Litauer Aktion, see also USHMMA, RG 15.015m, 2/142/3, 5–7, 11–12 (miscellaneous correspondence).

235. IMT, 39:426–29 (USSR-172: Bormann Aktenvermerk on Hitler discussion of October 2, 1940).

236. *Biuletyn* 12, p. 113F (Höppner to Eichmann and Ehlich, November 5, 1940).

237. Frank, *Diensttagebuch*, p. 302 (entry of November 6, 1940).

238. Frank, *Diensttagebuch*, p. 327 (entry of January 15, 1941).

239. NCA, 4:592 (1950-PS: Lammers to Shirach, December 3, 1940).

240. Frank, *Diensttagebuch*, p. 309 (entry of December 2, 1940).

241. YVA, O/53/66/231 (Eichmann to Höppner, Krumey, Abromeit, Schlegel, and Riedel, December 12, 1940).

242. Frank, *Diensttagebuch*, p. 327 (conference of January 15, 1941). USHMMA, RG 15.015m, 3/199/4–6 (Vermerk on conference of January 8, 1941, Posen, January 10, 1941) and 8–9 (Höppner Aktenvermerk on Fahrplankonferenz of January 16, 1941, Posen, January 17, 1941). *Biuletyn* 12, p. 127F (Krumey to Eichmann, January 6, 41). YVA, JM 3582, Abschlussbericht 1941. The Warthegau quota was 330,000.

243. For the Warthegau: USHMMA, RG 15.015m, 3/227/1 (Kreisweise Aufstellung der . . . aus dem Warthegau ausgesiedelten Polen).

244. Frank, *Diensttagebuch*, p. 326 (conference of January 15, 1941).

245. YVA, JM 3582, Abschlussbericht 1941.

246. YVA, O/53/68/682–83 (Report on conference on Jewish evacuation in Danzig–West Prussia, February 19, 1941). According to Emmanuel Ringelblum, *Notes from the Warsaw Ghetto*, p. 136, the Danzig transport brought 2,000 Jews to Warsaw. According to Wlodzimierz Jastrzebski, "Nazi Deportations of Polish and Jewish Population from Territories Incorporated into the Third Reich," this Danzig transport took 319 Jews.

247. Eichmann Trial Document T-1147 (Löwenherz memorandum February 1, 1941); Rosenkranz, *Verfolgung und Selbstbehauptung*, pp. 261–62.

248. PA, Inland II AB 42/2: anonymous letter of February 15, 1941 (T120/5772H/E420853), and Rademacher to RSHA, February 20 and May 21, 1941.

249. Bundesarchiv-Militärarchiv Freiburg (hereafter cited as BA-MA), RH 20-17/83: AOK 17 to OKH Gen.Qu., February 14, 1941; MiG to AOK 17, February 14, 1941; Abwehrstelle b. Mbfh im GG to OKW Amt Aus/Abw, February 17, 1941; AOK 17 to OKH, March 3, 1941; Bühler to Stülpnagel, March 11, 1941. I am grateful to Dr. Jürgen Förster for sharing these documents with me.

250. YVA, JM 3583 (Günther to Höppner, Krumey, Abromeit, Brunner, February 21, 1941); *Biuletyn* 12, pp. 134F–135F (Eichmann to Höppner, Krumey, Abromeit, Schlegel, February 27, 1941).

251. *Biuletyn* 12, pp. 138F–139F (Müller to Königsberg, Gotenhafen, Posen, Lodz, Wien, March 15, 1941).

252. Frank, *Diensttagebuch*, pp. 336–38 (Regierungssitzung of March 25 and entry of March 26, 1941); IMT, 29:492 (Nbg. Doc. 2233-PS: Regierungssitzung of March 25, 1941).

253. Engel, *Heeresadjutant bei Hitler*, pp. 94–95.

254. Richard Breitman, in *The Architect of Genocide: Himmler and the Final Solution*, is the most eloquent advocate of this position—namely, that Hitler and Himmler, operating in a conspiratorial manner not openly reflected in the documentation, reached a "fundamental" or "basic" decision in the early months of 1941, and that subsequent decisions should be seen merely as decisions of "implementation."

255. Brechtken, *"Madagaskar für die Juden,"* pp. 278–83.

256. USHMMA, RG 15.015m, 3/168/8–14 (Chef der Sicherheitspolizei und des SD, IV D 6, October 30, 1940, an alle Staatspolizei[leit]stellen).

257. Bernhard Lösener, "Als Rassereferent," p. 296.

258. Götz Aly and Susanne Heim, eds., *Bevölkerungsstruktur und Massenmord: Neue*

Dokumente zur deutschen Politik der Jahre 1938–1945, pp. 24–27 (Eichmann summary "submitted to the RFSS," December 4, 1940); Aly, *"Final Solution,"* pp. 124–26. For much of what follows concerning yet a third expulsion plan for Jews after Lublin and Madagascar, I am deeply indebted to the pioneering research and scholarship of Götz Aly.

259. Aly, *"Final Solution,"* p. 126.

260. Cited in Serge Klarsfeld, *Vichy-Auschwitz: Die Zusammenarbeit der deutschen und französischen Behörden bei der "Endlösung der Judenfrage" in Frankreich,* pp. 361–63.

261. PA, Inland II AB 80–41 Sdh. III, Bd. 1, Heydrich to Luther, February 5, 1941.

262. PA, Inland II AB 80–41 Sdh. III, Bd. 1, Streckenbach to Luther, February 14, 1941.

263. Cited in Aly, *"Final Solution,"* p. 172. This document is from the Moscow Special Archives 500/3/795.

264. Aly, "Final Solution," p. 173.

265. *Die Tagebücher von Joseph Goebbels I,* 4:543 (entry of March 18, 1941).

266. NA microfilm, T81/676/548604–5 (Propaganda Ministry memorandum Eva-kuierung der Juden aus Berlin, March 21, 1941). Printed in Adler, *Der verwaltete Mensch,* pp. 152–53.

267. *Die Tagebücher von Joseph Goebbels I,* 4:547 (entry of March 22, 1941).

268. NA microfilm, T81/676/5485642 (Tiessler note, April 21, 1941).

269. NA microfilm, T81/676/5485631 (Reischer of Party Chancellery to Tiessler, May 24, 1941).

270. Frank, *Diensttagebuch,* pp. 335–39 (entries of March 25 and 26, 1941, and Re-gierungssitzung of March 25, 1941).

271. Lösener, "Als Rassereferent," p. 296.

272. TWC, 1:732 (testimony of Viktor Brack, May 1947). Nbg. Doc. NO-203 (Brack to Himmler, March 28, 1941) and NO-204 (Tiefenbacher to Brack, May 12, 1941). For con-flicting interpetations of the episode and Brack's testimony, see Richard Breitman, "Plans for the Final Solution in Early 1941," pp. 486–87; and Philippe Burrin, *Hitler and the Jews,* p. 92. The fact that Brack's reply is documented supports the veracity of this part of his testimony. Unlike Breitman, I do not find at all credible Brack's apologetic explanation for this incriminating document that he followed up on Himmler's request to study the pos-sibility of X-ray sterilization as a lesser evil to already well-known "plans to exterminate the Jews" that Brack allegedly opposed.

273. *Biuletyn* 12, pp. 90F–91F (Aktenvermerk of Höppner on discussion with Eich-mann, June 6, 1940).

274. Groscurth, *Tagebücher,* p. 381 (Doc. Nr. 24: unsigned memorandum of October 18, 1939); IMT, 39:426–29 (USSR-172): Bormann Aktenvermerk of statement of Hitler, October 2, 1940). For a similar statement to the western Gauleiters: Aly, *"Final Solution,"* pp. 99–100.

4. The Polish Ghettos

1. NA microfilm, T175/239/2728524–28. Conference of Heydrich's division heads and Einsatzgruppen leaders, September 21, 1939.

2. DOT, 6:532–36 (Nbg. Doc. 3363-PS: Heydrich Schnellbrief, September 21, 1939).

3. Müller, *Das Heer und Hitler*, pp. 671–72 (Doc. Nr. 47: Heydrich to Einsatzgruppen leaders, September 30, 1939).

4. For a recent study that shares many of my views about German ghettoization policy in Poland as reflected in the Lublin district, see Musial, *Deutsche Zivilverwaltung und Judenverfolgung im Generalgouvernement*, pp. 126–45.

5. Umbreit, *Deutsche Militärverwaltungen*, p. 205.

6. Umbriet, *Deutsche Militärverwaltungen*, p. 209.

7. *Biuletyn* 12, pp. 11F–14F (Conference of November 8, 1939).

8. Berlin Document Center (hereafter cited as BDC): Greiser Pers. Akten, Besuchs-Vermerk of the Staff of the Führer's deputy, January 11, 1940. I am grateful to Dr. Hans Umbreit for a copy of this document.

9. *FGM*, pp. 78–81 (Rundschreiben of Uebelhoer to party and police authorities, December 10, 1939).

10. *FGM*, pp. 78–81 (Rundschreiben of Uebelhoer to party and police authorities, December 10, 1939).

11. *DiM*, 3:35–37 (Schäfer orders of February 8, 1940) and 3:74–75 (Schiffer to Rumkowski, April 30, 1940).

12. *DOT*, 8:57–58 (undated document of Reichsjustizamt).

13. Philip Friedman, "The Jewish Ghettos of the Nazi Era," p. 72. An earlier ghetto was unsuccessfully attempted at Piotrkow, and the first permanent ghetto was established in Tuliszkow in December 1939 or January 1940.

14. YVA, O-6/79 (Report of Statistical Office of Lodz on the Jewish population in 1940). Lucjan Dobroszycki, "Introduction," *The Chronicle of the Lodz Ghetto, 1941–1944*, p. xxxix.

15. YVA, O/53/116/726 (Report of Gendarmerieposten Hinterberg, March 14, 1940).

16. *FGM*, p. 109 (Schön report of January 20, 1941); Frank, *Diensttagebuch*, p. 286 (Schwender report, October 8, 1940); Jürgen Stroop, *The Stroop Report*, pp. 1–2; Dobroszycki, "Introduction," *Chronicle of the Lodz Ghetto*, p. xxxix.

17. Czeslaw Madajczyk, *Polityka III-Rzeszy w okupowanej Polsce*, 1:245; Bauer, *American Jewry and the Holocaust*, p. 69.

18. *FGM*, p. 81 (Rundschreiben of Uebelhoer to party and police authorities, December 10, 1939).

19. *DiM*, 3:168–69 (conference of April 1, 1940, and Baur to Landräte, May 8, 1940).

20. Frank, *Diensttagebuch*, pp. 261–63 (entry of July 31, 1940).

21. YVA, JM 799/202 (Report to Regierungspräsident, April 6, 1940).

22. YVA, JM 799/209 (Vermerk of conferences of April 26 and 27, 1940); O-58/78/296–97 (Rumkowski to Marder, April 6, 1940). *DiM*, 3:74–75 (Oberbürgermeister to Rumkowski, April 30, 1940).

23. YVA, JM 800/387–89 (Vermerk by Dr. Nebel of conference of May 27, 1940).

24. YVA, JM 800/395 (Biebow Aktennotiz of May 28, 1940); JM 799/196 (Biebow Aktennotiz of conference of June 6, 1940).

25. Dobroszycki, "Introduction," pp. xli–xlii.

26. YVA, JM 798, Activity report for July 1940.

27. YVA, JM 799/193 (Palfinger Aktennotiz July 16, 1940).

28. YVA, JM 798, Activity report for August 1940.

29. YVA, JM 800/217–20 (Marder to Reich Trustee for labor, Posen, August 21, 1940), 227–28 (Marder to Regierungspräsident, September 10, 1940), and 239 (Aktennotiz, September 17, 1940); JM 798, undated memo, "Beschäftigung von Juden durch Privatunternehmungen."

30. YVA, JM 798, Auditor's report of February 1941.

31. YVA, JM 798, Activity report for September 1940.

32. YVA, JM 798, Auditor's report of February 1941.

33. *DiM*, 3:102–4 (conference of October 18, 1940).

34. YVA, O/53/78/76–82 (Palfinger's "critical report" of November 7, 1940). Elsewhere Palfinger elaborated on what he meant about "total indifference" to a "dying out of the Jews" as long as "the concomitant effects leave the public interest of the German people untouched." Concerning diseases he noted: "Tuberculosis and other noninfectious children's diseases, as well as other sicknesses that result in a rapid rise in the death statistics, do not interest the German authorities." The only exceptions were epidemics that threatened to spread from the Jews to the civilian population. YVA, JM 799/174 (Palfinger Aktennotiz, October 30, 1940).

35. *DiM*, 3:177–79 (Marder to Uebelhoer, July 4, 1941).

36. YVA, O/53/78/76–82 (Palfinger's "critical report" of November 7, 1940); *DiM*, 3:256–57 (Biebow to Marder, November 12, 1940).

37. YVA, JM 799/167–68 (Ribbe to Marder, November 22, 1941).

38. *Czerniakow Diary*, pp. 87, 90 (entries of November 4–5, 1939); Gutman, *The Jews of Warsaw*, p. 49.

39. YVA, JM 1112 (Auerswald report "Zwei Jahre Aufbauarbeit Distrikt Warschau: Juden im Distrikt Warschau").

40. Frank, *Diensttagebuch*, p. 59 (entry of November 7, 1939).

41. *Czerniakow Diary*, pp. 98, 101, 117 (entries of December 9 and 20, 1939; February 14, 1940).

42. YVA, O/53/49/83–86 (Schön personnel questionnaire) and 90 (Fischer order, January 23, 1940).

43. *FGM*, pp. 108–9 (Schön report, January 20, 1941).

44. *FGM*, p. 109 (Schön report, January 20, 1941).

45. YVA, O-53/102/391–99. ("Halbjahres Bericht" of Dr. Kreppel, Abt. Innere Verwaltung, Warschau Distrikt, May 14, 1940).

46. *Czerniakow Diary*, pp. 134–40, 148 (entries of April 4, 6, 8, 10, and May 10, 1940).

47. *FGM*, p. 109 (Schön report, January 20, 1941).

48. Frank, *Diensttagebuch*, pp. 227–39 (Wirtschaftstagung, June 6–7, 1940).

49. *FGM*, p. 110 (Schön report, January 20, 1941).

50. YVA, JM 814: Lambrecht report, September 3, 1940, and report of division of Internal Administration, September 4, 1940. *FGM*, p. 110 (Schön report, January 20, 1941).

51. *IMT*, 29:406 (2233-PS); Frank, *Diensttagebuch*, p. 281 (Abteilungleiterssitzung, September 12, 1940).

52. *Czerniakow Diary*, p. 182 (entry of August 9, 1940).

53. Ringelblum, *Notes from the Warsaw Ghetto*, pp. 75, 90; YVA, JM 814, October Situation Report of Warsaw District, November 15, 1940.

54. *FGM*, p. 111 (Schön report, January 20, 1941); Frank, *Diensttagebuch*, p. 343 (Fischer speech at conference of April 3, 1941).

55. Musial, *Deutsche Zivilverwaltung und Judenverfolgung im Generalgouvernement*, pp. 129–30, documents how the combination of German anti-Semitism and notions of "beautification" (*Verschönerung*) were important motives for ghettoization in other parts of the General Government as well.

56. YVA, JM 1112 (Auerswald report: "Zwei Jahre Aufbauarbeit"); O-53/48/792–816 (Schön report, January 20, 1941). An article in the journal *Ostland* of May 15, 1941, entitled "The Jewish Residence Areas in the General Government," offered the following reasons for ghettoization: (1) sanitary considerations, i.e., the Jews, accustomed to filth, provided a breeding ground for "filth diseases" (*Schmutzkrankheiten*) against which other, more sanitary people had less resistance; (2) political considerations, i.e., to remove the Jewish influence on Poles in order to effectively combat the black market. The article posed but left open the question whether ghettoization was a "final solution" (*endgültige Lösung*) to the Jewish question or only a provisional one until the "complete removal" of the Jews was "practical." USHMMA, RG 15.031, 13/129/91–95.

57. YVA, JM 1112 (Auerswald "Two-year report" of September 26, 1941).

58. YVA, O/53/48/792–816 (Schön report, January 20, 1941).

59. *Czerniakow Diary*, pp. 194 and 197 (entries of September 5 and 13, 1940).

60. Frank, *Diensttagebuch*, pp. 286–87 (Schwender report, October 8, 1940).

61. YVA, JM 1112 (Auerswald "Two-year report" of September 26, 1941); *Czerniakow Diary*, pp. 201–9 (entries of September 25, 27, and 28, and October 2, 10, 12, and 20, 1940).

62. Gutman, *The Jews of Warsaw*, p. 60.

63. *FGM*, p. 112 (Schön report, January 20, 1941).

64. Gutman, *The Jews of Warsaw*, p. 63. YVA, JM 814, February Situation Report of Warsaw District, March 10, 1941.

65. Ringelblum, *Notes from the Warsaw Ghetto*, p. 158.

66. YVA, O/53/48/792/792–816 (Schön report, January 20, 1941).

67. YVA, O/53/48/792/792–816 (Schön report, January 20, 1941), compared with YVA, JM 814, October Situation Report of Warsaw District, November 15, 1940.

68. YVA, JM 1113, Conference of December 2, 1940.

69. *Czerniakow Diary*, p. 223 (entry of December 4, 1940).

70. YVA, JM 1113, Czerniakow letters of December 30, 1940, and January 8, 1941.

71. Frank, *Diensttagebuch*, p. 328 (conference of January 15, 1941).

72. *Czerniakow Diary*, p. 394 (Appended document: conference of February 3, 1941). YVA, O-53/105/III/760–68 (Hagen report, July 7, 1941).

73. Frank, *Diensttagebuch*, p. 336 (Regierungssitzung, March 25, 1941).

74. Frank, *Diensttagebuch*, p. 334 (entry of March 22, 1941); YVA, JM 10016, "Die Wirtschaftsbilanz des jüdischen Wohnbezirks in Warschau," March 1941; Isaiah Trunk, *Judenrat: The Jewish Councils in Eastern Europe under Nazi Occupation*, p. 287. For a very different interpretation of the Gater memorandum and the events surrounding it, see Götz

Aly and Susanne Heim, "Die Ökonomie der 'Endlösung': Menschenvernichtung und wirtschafliche Neuordnung." The entire document has now been published in Aly and Heim, eds., *Bevölkerungsstruktur und Massenmord*, pp. 74–138. For my critique of the initial Aly/Heim interpretation, see Christopher R. Browning, "German Technocrats, Jewish Labor, and the Final Solution," in *The Path to Genocide*, pp. 59–76. Aly and Heim's more recent account in *Vordenker der Vernichtung*, pp. 312–30, at least acknowledges a conflict between Emmerich and Gater on the one hand and Palfinger and Schön on the other and thus comes somewhat closer to my interpretation.

75. Frank, *Diensttagebuch*, p. 337 (entry of March 25, 1941).

76. Frank, *Diensttagebuch*, pp. 343–46 (conference of April 3, 1941). That Fischer was simply trying to allay interference from Cracow and was a strong advocate of Schön and Palfinger's attritionist policies can be seen from his statement quoted by Philip Friedman: "The Jews will disappear because of hunger and need, and nothing will remain of the Jewish question but a cemetery." In "The Jewish Ghettos of the Nazi Era," p. 69.

77. Archivum Panstwowe m. st. Warszawy, Der Kommissar für den jüdischen Wohn-bezirk in Warschau, Nr. 125, Palfinger Aktennotiz, April 7, 1941.

78. DOT, 6:556 (Verordnung über den jüdischen Wohnbezirk in Warschau vom April 19, 1941).

79. That Czerniakow, in contrast to Rumkowski in Lodz, did not let such titles and positions go to his head is witnessed by his sardonic comment: "I was named the mayor. Together with the King of Croatia." *Czerniakow Diary*, p. 238 (entry of May 19, 1941).

80. Frank, *Diensttagebuch*, pp. 354–55 (entry of April 9, 1941).

81. Frank, *Diensttagebuch*, pp. 359–62 (conference of April 19, 1941).

82. Aly and Heim, *Vordenker der Vernichtung*, p. 324.

83. YVA, JM 1112, Bischof Aktenvermerk on discussion with Fischer, April 30, 1941.

84. YVA, O/53, 49/103–4 (personnel questionnaire of Auerswald).

85. YVA, JM 1112, Bischof Aktenvermerk, May 8, 1941.

86. *Czerniakow Diary*, pp. 230–46 (entries of May 5, 6, 8, 12, and 21 and June 3, 1941). The baneful influence of the lame duck Palfinger was not entirely at an end, however. On June 3 Czerniakow noted: "I asked Bischof about purchasing food on the free market; he agreed, then asked Palfinger, who said it would be an 'insult to authority.' Bischof with-drew consent, as he did on another issue after consulting Palfinger." *Czerniakow Diary*, pp. 245–46.

87. By German statistics of July 1940, the district of Radom contained 310,000 Jews, Lublin 250,000 and Cracow 200,000, in comparison to Warsaw's 610,000 and 550,000 in the incorporated territories. *FGM*, p. 86.

88. The successive waves of uprooting and resettlement in the Lublin district are traced by Musial, *Deutsche Zivilverwaltung und Judenverfolgung im Generalgouvernement*, pp. 127–44. A graphic example of this constant flux of the Jewish population is the city of Zamosc in the Lublin district. According to the chairman of the Jewish council there, Mieczyslaw Garfinkel, of a prewar Jewish population of 12,000–14,000, all but 3,000 fled to the Soviet zone. They were immediately replaced, however, by Jews from neighboring villages as well as 8,000 Jews from the incorporated territories. In April and May 1942, 4,500 Jews were deported to Belzec, and replaced with 3,000 Jews from the Protectorate and Germany. The

Jews residing in Zamosc, almost entirely different from the prewar population, were finally murdered in the fall of 1942. YVA, O-53/95/198–202.

89. Frank, *Diensttagebuch*, p. 165 (entry of April 12, 1940).

90. YVA, O/53/85/738 (Cracow to Gendarmerie Lublin, August 2, 1940) and 752 (Lublin department for population and welfare to Kreishauptleuten, August 9, 1940). USHMMA, RG 15.026m, 1/14/23 (draft, Generalgouverneur to district heads, May 1940); 24 (Bekanntmachung des Stadthauptmanns betr. Abwanderung von Juden, n.d.); and 42–43 (Generalgouverneur to district heads, May 25, 1940).

91. USHMMA, RG 15.025, 1/14/27–29 (report of Jüdische Gemeinde Krakau, May 20, 1940).

92. USHMMA, RG 15.026m, 1/14/68–70 (Ragger report on meeting with Frank, August 2, 1940).

93. USHMMA, RG 15.026m, 1/14/38 (Schmid to Krüger, July 23, 1940); and 44–45 (Ragger, BuF, to Obmann des Judenrates Krakau, July 25, 1940). For the Office of Population and Welfare, see Aly and Heim, *Architects of Annihilation*, pp. 130–36.

94. USHMMA, RG 15.026m, 1/14/51–53 (Ragger report, July 26, 1940, on meeting of July 24, 1940).

95. USHMMA, RG 15.026m, 1/14/68–70 (Ragger report on meeting with Frank, August 2, 1940).

96. USHMMA, RG 15.026m, 1/14/79–81 (Ragger report on meeting of August 19, 1940).

97. USHMMA, RG 15.026m, 1/14/82–83 (Ragger Aktennotiz, August 20, 1940).

98. USHMMA, RG 15.026m, 1/14/86–90 (Bieberstein to Stadthauptmann Krakau, August 22, 1940).

99. USHMMA, RG 15.026m, 1/14/100 (statistical summary of resettled Jews by September 1, 1940). YVA, JM 814, Division of Internal Administration's summary of Situation Reports, Cracow, September 30, 1940.

100. YVA, JM 814, Situation Report of Kreis Krakau-Land, September 8, 1940.

101. YVA, JM 814, Situation Report of Kreis Jaslo, August 29, 1940.

102. YVA, JM 814, Situation Report of Kreis Tarnow, August 31, 1940.

103. YVA, JM 814, Situation Report of Kreis Opatow, September 7, 1940.

104. YVA, JM 814: Situation Reports of Krasnystaw, September 10, 1940; Rzeszow, August 30 and October 30, 1940; Neu Sandez, October 29, November 29, and December 30, 1940; Sokolow-Wengrow, February 1941; and Cracow summaries of Situation Reports, December 10, 1940 and January 7, 1941.

105. USHMMA, RG 15.026m, 1/14/94–99 (Aktenvermerk and report on meeting of October 2, 1940).

106. USHMMA, RG 15.026m, 1/14/101–3 (Wächter to Schmid, November 21, 1940). YVA, JM 814, Situation Report of Krakau-Land, November 8, 1940.

107. YVA, JM 814, Situation Report of Cracow District, January 27, 1941 (Wächter to Bühler). USHMMA, RG 15.026m, 1/14/113–15 (KdO Krakau, Einsatzbefehl, November 27, 1940).

108. YVA, JM 814: Situation Reports of Zamosc, December 8, 1940; Lublin-Land, December 9, 1940; Krakau-Land, January 10, 1941; Neu Sandez, December 31, 1940; Lublin District, January 8, 1941 (Zörner to Bühler).

109. YVA, JM 814, Situation Report of Cracow District, March 13, 1941 (Wächter to Bühler).

110. YVA, O/53/85/743 (Kreishauptmann Lublin-Land to Lublin department for population and welfare, February 27, 1941), 747 (Kreishauptmann of Lublin-Land to President of JSS Cracow, February 14, 1941), and 989 (Kreishauptmann of Lublin-Land to Lublin department for population and welfare, February 3, 1941); and JM 814, Lublin District Situation Report, March 6, 1941.

111. FGM, pp. 120, 122 (Wächter orders of February 27 and March 3, 1941).

112. Helge Grabitz and Wolfgang Scheffler, *Letzte Spuren*, pp. 283–84; Pohl, *Von der "Judenpolitik" zum Judenmord*, pp. 86–87.

113. YVA, JM 814, Situation Report of Busko, January 11, 1940. Ringelblum, *Notes from the Warsaw Ghetto*, pp. 105, 132.

114. YVA, JM 814, Situation Report of city of Radom, February 1941. According to Philip Friedman, "The Jewish Ghettos of the Nazi Era," p. 73, the Radom ghetto ultimately contained 14,000 Jews.

115. FGM, pp. 124–25 (order of Stadthauptmann of Kielce, Drechser, March 31, 1941) and 127 (report of Kreishauptmann of Opatow, Ritter); YVA, JM 1489, Bekanntmachung of the Czestochowa ghetto, April 9, 1941; USHMMA, RG 15.031m, 13/129/5 (Stadtkommissar Skarzysko-Kamienna, to Distriktchef Radom, April 8, 1941); Friedman, "The Jewish Ghettos," p. 73.

116. USHMMA, RG 15.031m, 13/129/1–4 (Stadhauptmann to Kreishauptmann Kielce, January 23, 1940, and replies, January 27 and 31, 1941).

117. USHMMA, RG 15.031m, 13/129/10 (Abt. I to BuF, Radom, May 5, 1941).

118. USHMMA, RG 15.031m, 13/129/52 (Kreishauptmann to Stadthauptmann Kielce, July 3, 1941), and 88 (Stadtverwaltung Checiny to Kreishauptmann Kielce, August 8, 1941).

119. According to Pohl, *Von der "Judenpolitik" zum Judenmord*, p. 67, several ghettos had already been created in the Lublin district on local initiative: Pulawy in December 1939 and Krasnystaw in August 1940. The ghettoization of Piaski was ordered in December 1940, and it became the first sealed ghetto in the Lublin district in the spring of 1941. Musial, *Deutsche Zivilverwaltung und Judenverfolgung im Generalgouvernement*, p. 131.

120. BA-MA, RH 20-17/83: AOK 17 to OKH, March 3, 1941, and Bühler to Heydrich, copy to Stülpnagel, March 11, 1941. I am indebted to Dr. Jürgen Förster for copies of these documents.

121. Frank, *Diensttagebuch*, p. 338 (Regierungssitzung, March 25, 1941).

122. YVA, O/53/85/720–22 (Aktenvermerken of March 9 and 12, 1941); FGM, p. 121 (Vermerk of chairman of JSS in Cracow, March 12, 1941).

123. YVA, O/53/85/999–1001 (announcement of ghettoization in Lublin); FGM, pp. 123–24 (Aktenvermerk of March 31, 1941). Friedman, "The Jewish Ghettos," p. 73.

124. YVA, O/53/85/1011 (Standortarzt Miedzyrzec to Sipo Aussendienststelle Radzyn, April 12, 1941).

125. YVA, O/53/82/465 (Lublin department of population and welfare to Cracow, February 6, 1942).

126. Musial, *Deutsche Zivilverwaltung und Judenverfolgung im Generalgouvernement,* p. 143.

127. Friedman, "The Jewish Ghettos," p. 74.

128. *FGM,* p. 68 (Uebelhoer decree of November 14, 1939); *DiM,* 3:23 (Uebelhoer decree of December 11, 1939).

129. *FGM,* p. 66 (Frank decree of November 23, 1939); YVA, O-53 / 102 / 331–39 (Kreppel's Halbjahresbericht, May 14, 1940).

130. Umbreit, *Deutsche Militärverwaltungen,* p. 206; *FGM,* p. 200 (report of Warsaw Jewish council) and p. 203 (Frank decree of October 26, 1939).

131. Trunk, *Judenrat,* pp. 62–64.

132. *FGM,* p. 71 (Frank decree of November 28, 1939).

133. YVA, O / 53 / 102 / 331–39 (Kreppel's Halbjahresbericht, May 14, 1940).

134. Heinemann, *"Rasse, Siedlung, deutsches Blut,"* pp. 212–14; Rich, *The Establishment of the New Order,* p. 73; Trunk, *Judenrat,* p. 63. For a good summary of Nazi measures against Jewish property, see Trunk, pp. 61–71; and Hilberg, *The Destruction of the European Jews,* pp. 239–49.

135. Hilberg, *The Destruction of the European Jews,* p. 241.

136. *FGM,* p. 165 (decree of the chief of the civil administration, September 6, 1939) and p. 166 (order of the chief of the civil administration, September 15, 1939).

137. On the gold rush mentality and behavior of the German occupiers in Poland, see esp. Musial, *Deutsche Zivilverwaltung und Judenverfolgung im Generalgouvernement,* pp. 188–92.

138. YVA, O / 53 / 66 / 309–44 (summary and protocol of meeting of November 23, 1939, in Posen).

139. *DiM,* 3:54–59 (meeting of January 16, 1940).

140. *DiM,* 3:38–44 (decree of Schäfer, February 8, 1940).

141. *DiM,* 3:63–64 (Uebelhoer to Schäfer, Janaury 10, 1940; and Schäfer order, January 17, 1940).

142. *DiM,* 3:67–68 (Regierungspräsident Kalisch, March 4, 1940, to the Landräte and Oberbürgermeister in Kalisch and Lodz).

143. *DiM,* 3:70–71 (decrees of Oberbürgermeister of Litzmannstadt, April 15 and 16, 1940).

144. *DiM,* 3:92–94 (Bracken memorandum, May 19, 1940).

145. *DiM,* 3:96–98 (Richter memorandum for conference on August 28, 1940).

146. *DiM,* 3:100–101 (Zirpins memorandum, October 23, 1940).

147. YVA, JM 814, Situation Report of Krasnystaw, September 10, 1940.

148. Hilberg, *The Destruction of the European Jews,* p. 240.

149. *FGM,* p. 203 (decree of October 26, 1939).

150. *FGM,* p. 200 (Jewish council report for October 7, 1939–December 31, 1940); *Czerniakow Diary,* p. 84 (entry of October 20, 1939).

151. *Czerniakow Diary,* pp. 109–10 (entry of January 15, 1940); Trunk, *Judenrat,* p. 72.

152. Frank, *Diensttagebuch,* p. 77 (Abteilungsleitersitzung, December 8, 1939).

153. *Czerniakow Diary,* p. 112 (entry of January 28, 1940); YVA, JM 1113 (Czerniakow report of February 18, 1940, and Dengel to Kulski, January 7 and February 16, 1940).

154. Frank, *Diensttagebuch*, p. 105 (Kleiss interview, February 6, 1940).

155. *Biuletyn* 12, pp. 66F–75F (NO-5322: conference of January 30, 1940); Halder, *Kriegstagebuch*, 1:184 (entry of February 5, 1940). Rolf-Dieter Müller, *Hitlers Ostkrieg und die deutsche Siedlungspolitik*, pp. 20–22, points out that Himmler was seeking a military and economic legitimization for deporting Jews into the General Government over the growing opposition of Frank and the military there. As part of his rapprochement with Himmler at Koblenz in March 1940, Brauchitsch accepted the plan over the opposition of Blaskowitz, who subsequently resigned.

156. Gutman, *The Jews of Warsaw*, p. 23; Frank, *Diensttagebuch*, p. 217 (entry of May 30, 1940).

157. YVA, O/53/85/967–70 (SSPF Lublin guidelines for the use of Jewish forced labor, May 8, 1940). In reality, of course, various German agencies in Lublin had no compunction about entering the Jewish quarter and brutally seizing labor whenever they wished. On the eve of Heydrich's visit to Lublin in mid-June to inspect the newly installed branch office of the Einwandererzentralstelle that was organizing the Volhynian Aktion, the staff of the branch office entered the Jewish quarter on June 11 to seize workers to unload office furniture. One of the staff, Unterscharführer Eichner, fired several shots "allegedly in the air" (*angeblich in die Luft*) to stop a fleeing Jew, and a Jewish woman standing at her window was killed. The investigators concluded that because there were a number of other groups in the quarter hunting down Jewish workers at that time from whom "shots were fired repeatedly," it could not be proven with certainty that Eichner's shots were the cause of death. USHMMA, RG 15.034m, 6/68/3–11 (reports dating from June 12 to July 8, 1940).

158. *IMT*, 29:448–56 (2233-PS: Polizeisitzung of May 30, 1940).

159. Frank, *Diensttagebuch*, pp. 230–32, 239 (Wirtschaftstagung, June 6–7, 1940).

160. It was not just the civil authorities who expressed such sentiments. A week earlier the commander of the Sipo-SD in the General Government, Bruno Streckenbach, had stated: "In the end one cannot starve them." Frank, *Diensttagebuch*, p. 216 (Polizeisitzung, May 30, 1940).

161. YVA, O/53/79/94–95 (Krüger to Frauendorfer, June 13, 1940).

162. *DOT*, 6:568–72 (Frauendorfer circular, July 5, 1940).

163. *Czerniakow Diary*, p. 148 (entry of May 10, 1940).

164. YVA, JM 814, Situation Report of Pulawy, September 7, 1940.

165. YVA, JM 814, Situation Report of Jaslo, October 31, 1940.

166. *FGM*, p. 217 (Situation Report of Miechow, October 4, 1940).

167. YVA, JM 814, Situation Report of Czestochowa, September 14, 1940.

168. *FGM*, p. 215 (Sitzung of Labor Division, Cracow, August 6, 1940).

169. For the role of the civil administration in the struggle over Jewish forced labor in the Lublin district, see esp. Musial, *Deutsche Zivilverwaltung und Judenverfolgung im Generalgouvernement*, pp. 164–70.

170. Müller, *Hitlers Ostkrieg und die deutsche Siedlungspolitik*, p. 22. In the end only 13 kilometers of worthless antitank ditches were dug before the military turned its attention to preparing offensive staging areas instead of defensive fortifications.

171. YVA, O/53/79/96 (Globocnik to Jache, July 15, 1940); *FGM*, p. 213 (Globocnik to Schmidt, July 30, 1940).

172. YVA, O/53/79/197–98 (Hecht Vermerk, July 23, 1940).

173. YVA, O/53/79/99 (Jache Vermerk, July 23, 1940).

174. YVA, JM 2700, Cracow conference on Jewish labor, August 6, 1940.

175. YVA, O/53/79/102 (Ramm Vermerk to Jache and Hecht on discussion with Globocnik, Wendt, and Hofbauer, August 8, 1940).

176. YVA, O/53/79/129 (Lerch to Ramm, August 19, 1940).

177. YVA, O/53/79/116–17 (Zamosc labor office report on event of August 13–14, 1940), 118–19 (Ramm Vermerk, August 15, 1940).

178. YVA, O/53/79/110–14 (Damrau to Frank, August 16, 1940).

179. YVA, O/53/79/141–42 (Ramm to Globocnik, August 19, 1940), 137 (Ramm Vermerk to Jache and Hecht, August 20, 1940), 130 (Labor Division to Globocnik, August 20, 1940), 136 (Ramm Vermerk to Jache and Hecht, August 20, 1940), 140 (Globocnik to Labor Division, August 23, 1940), and 138 (Labor Division to Globocnik, August 24, 1940).

180. YVA, O/53/79/133 (Ramm to Gschliesser, August 20, 1940), and 132 (Ramm to Frauendorfer, August 20, 1940); FGM, p. 216 (Situation Report of September 7, 1940, of Abteilung Innere Verwaltung, Distrikt Lublin).

181. YVA, O/53/79/142 (Hecht Vermerk, September 6, 1940).

182. YVA, JM 2700, Vermerke of October 21 and November 15, 1940.

183. FGM, p. 218 (Aktenvermerk of November 28, 1940).

184. YVA, JM 1113, Activity Report of Warsaw Jewish council, November 29–December 5, 1940. FGM, p. 216 (excerpt of August report of Fischer) and pp. 218–21 (excerpts from reports on the Lublin work camps).

185. YVA, JM 2700, undated note to Labor Division Cracow. See also FGM, p. 217 (October report of Zörner, November 6, 1940); YVA, O-53/79/150–51 (Jache to Frauendorfer, October 10, 1940).

186. DiM, vol. 1: Obozy, pp. 220–21 (Bevölkerungswesen und Fürsorge, Innere Verwaltung, Lublin, to Föhl, BuF, Cracow, October 21, 1940).

187. YVA, JM 814, Situation Reports of Warsaw, January 25, 1941 (Hummel) and Lublin, January 8, 1941 (Zörner); JM 1113, Activity report of Warsaw Jewish council, December 27, 1940–January 2, 1941.

188. Musial, Deutsche Zivilverwaltung und Judenverfolgung im Generalgouvernement, pp. 165–68.

189. YVA, O/53/105/II/415–17 (Wielikowski report, June 30, 1940).

190. Ringelblum, Notes from the Warsaw Ghetto, pp. 154, 158–63, 170–71; Czerniakow Diary, pp. 226–27, 229–30 (entries of April 26 and 29, and May 5, 1941).

191. YVA, O/53/105/II/339–41 (Wielikowski report, May 10, 1941).

192. YVA, O/53/105/II/342–45 (Meissner report, May 14, 1941).

193. YVA, O/53/105/II/351–52 (undated, unsigned memorandum from Auerswald's files).

194. YVA, O/53/105/II/346 (Goebel letter, May 19, 1941).

195. YVA, O/53/105/II/337 (Mohns to Auerswald, May 13, 1941). Czerniakow Diary, p. 231 (entry of May 8, 1941).

196. YVA, O/53/105/II/363–64 (Auerswald Vermerk, May 23, 1941).

197. YVA, O/53/105/II/366–67 (Meissner report, June 30, 1941).

198. YVA, O/53/105/II/414–16 (Wielikowski report, June 30, 1941).

199. *Czerniakow Diary*, p. 256 (entry of July 8, 1941).

200. YVA, O/53/105/II/402 (Auerswald Aktennotiz, July 16, 1941).

201. YVA, JM 1112, Auerswald report, September 26, 1941; and JM 3462, Monthly report for October 1941 of Labor Division branch office for Jewish District (Hoffmann).

202. YVA, JM 3462, Hoffmann report for August 1941; O-53/105/II/712–15 (Hoffman report on Jewish labor, undated, but from context the report is for September).

203. YVA, JM 3462, conference on Jewish labor of March 20, 1942.

204. YVA, JM 3462, Frauendorfer to district Labor Divisions, June 25, 1942.

205. Gutman, *The Jews of Warsaw*, pp. 63–65.

206. Ringelblum, *Notes from the Warsaw Ghetto*, pp. 157, 184, 206. Trunk estimates that Warsaw was officially supplied with 10% of its nutritional needs, and in Lodz workers got 65% and nonworkers 45–58% of their minimal needs. Trunk, *Judenrat*, p. 105.

207. *DiM*, 3:241–42 (Palfinger protocol of conference of October 24, 1940).

208. YVA, O/53/78/70–74 (conference of November 9, 1940).

209. YVA, O/58/78/296–97 (Rumkowski to Marder, April 6, 1940) and 237–41 (Rumkowski memorandum, November 23, 1940).

210. *DiM*, 3:74–75 (Oberbürgermeister to Rumkowski, April 30, 1940).

211. YVA, O/53/78/137–39 (Gettoverwaltung memorandum, March 24, 1943). *DiM*, 3:114–16 (Biebow to Treuhandstelle Posen, March 26, 1942).

212. YVA, JM 798, Activity report of February 1941; JM 800/148 (Aktennotiz of March 10, 1941).

213. YVA, JM 798, Activity reports of March, April, and May 1941.

214. YVA, JM 798, Activity reports of October and December 1940.

215. Dobroszycki, *Chronicle of the Lodz Ghetto*, p. 46 (entry of April 11, 1941).

216. YVA, O/53/78/137–39 (Gettoverwaltung memorandum, March 24, 1943). *DiM*, 3:177–79 (Marder to Uebelhoer, July 4, 1941) and 3:243–45 (Biebow to Fuchs, March 4, 1942).

217. YVA, O/53/78/137–39 (Gettoverwaltung memorandum, March 24, 1943).

218. Trunk, *Judenrat*, p. 84.

219. Trunk, *Judenrat*, pp. 76, 282–83.

220. YVA, JM 798, Auditor's report of Rechnungshof of February 1941. *DiM*, pp. 177–79 (Marder to Uebelhoer, July 4, 1941).

221. *DiM*, 3:151–53 (Biebow to Ventski, February 8, 1943).

222. Trunk, *Judenrat*, p. 91.

223. YVA, JM 798, Activity report for November 1940.

224. YVA, JM 798, Activity report for December 1940.

225. Dobroszycki, *Chronicle of the Lodz Ghetto*, pp. 9, 21 (entries of January 14 and March 1, 1941).

226. YVA, JM 798, Activity report for November 1940.

227. YVA, JM 800/160–61 (Aktenvermerk of conference of January 14, 1941).

228. YVA, JM 798, Activity report for February 1941.

229. YVA, JM 798, Auditor's report for February 1941. This document has recently been

published in Aly and Heim, eds., *Bevölkerungsstruktur und Massenmord*, pp. 39–73. For commentary, see Aly and Heim, *Architects of Annihilation*, pp. 189–91.

230. YVA, JM 798, Activity reports for March and April 1941. The improvement in food supplies was reflected in Dobroszycki, *Chronicle of the Lodz Ghetto*, pp. 26, 30 (entries of March 3 and 5, 1941).

231. YVA, JM 800/82–83 (Posen conference of June 7, 1941), and 94 (Aktennotiz, June 11, 1941).

232. YVA, JM 798, Activity report for August 1941.

233. *DiM*, 3:243–45 (Biebow to Fuchs, March 4, 1942).

234. YVA, O/53/78/242–43 (Stadtmedizinalrat to Ventzki, June 15, 1942).

235. *DiM*, 3:245–48 (Biebow to Ventzki, April 19, 1943, and Ventzki Aktenvermerk). Once again the Lodz public health officer joined Biebow's petition for increased ghetto food supplies. YVA, O-53/78/244 (Stadtmedizinalrat to Ventzki, April 24, 1943).

236. NA microfilm, T-501/214/269 (monthly report of Kommandantur Warsaw, May 20, 1941, to militiary commander of the General Government).

237. YVA, JM 1112, Auerswald report, September 26, 1941. Ringelblum, *Notes from the Warsaw Ghetto*, pp. 191–92; Gutman, *The Jews of Warsaw*, pp. 63–65.

238. *Czerniakow Diary*, pp. 239, 256, 269 (entries of May 21, July 7, and August 19, 1941).

239. YVA, JM 1112, Transferstelle report of October 8, 1941. Archivum Panstwowe m. st. Warszawy, Der Kommissar für den jüdischen Wohnbezirk in Warschau, Nr. 132, speeches by Max Bischof, Heinz Auerswald, and Ludwig Fischer, October 15, 1941.

240. YVA, JM 21/4 (Frank Tagebuch, October 15, 1941).

241. YVA, JM 1112, Transferstelle report of November 8, 1941.

242. *Czerniakow Diary*, p. 295 (entry of November 1, 1941).

243. YVA, JM 1112, Transferstelle reports of December 6, 1941, and January 7, 1942.

244. YVA, JM 1112, Auerswald Two-Year Report, September 26, 1941.

245. YVA, JM 1112, Auerswald Two-Year Report, September 26, 1941.

246. *Czerniakow Diary*, p. 248 (entry of June 13, 1941).

247. YVA, JM 1112, Auerswald Two-Year Report, September 26, 1941.

248. *FGM*, pp. 127–28 (Auerswald circular, September 18, 1941).

249. YVA, JM 3462, Amtsarzt Hagen to Leist, September 22, 1941.

250. *Czerniakow Diary*, pp. 285–86 (entries of October 4 and 6, 1941).

251. *FGM*, pp. 128–29 (Frank decree of October 15, 1941). YVA, JM 21/4 (Frank Tagebuch, October 15, 1941).

252. YVA, O/53/145/75–78 (Arbeitstagung der Abt. Gesundheitswesen, October 13–16, 1941).

253. Hilberg, *The Destruction of the European Jews*, p. 224; Christopher R. Browning, "Genocide and Public Health: German Doctors and Polish Jews, 1939–41."

254. *Czerniakow Diary*, pp. 296, 299–301 (entries of November 6, 17, and 21, 1941).

255. YVA, O/53/101, Hummel's monthly reports to Bühler in Cracow from December 1941 to July 1942. In December 1941, 1,971 new cases of spotted fever were reported. This dropped to 784 in February 1942 and to a mere 67 in July 1942.

256. *Czerniakow Diary*, p. 330 (entry of February 26, 1942). Ringelblum, *Notes from the*

Warsaw Ghetto, p. 234. I am more comfortable with Gutman's evaluation of Auerswald (*The Jews of Warsaw*, pp. 97, 99) than with Trunk's more negative one (*Judenrat*, pp. 294–98). Trunk bases his characterization of Auerswald as "a successfully indoctrinated Nazi functionary who strictly abided by popular National Socialist slogans about the Jews" in large part on the unsavory rhetoric of his report "Zwei Jahre Aufbauarbeit im Distrikt Warschau: Die Juden im Distrikt Warschau." Trunk does not note, however, that Auerswald's initial report, of September 26, 1941, both sober and critical, was rejected by the Cracow authorities as "unsuitable" for inclusion in a series of essays celebrating two years of Frank's rule in Poland. Auerswald was told to produce something more fitting for the occasion. See the correspondence concerning these two reports in YVA, JM 1112.

257. YVA, JM 814, Hummel's February Situation Report to Bühler, March 10, 1941.

258. YVA, JM 1112, Auerswald Two-Year Report, September 26, 1941.

259. YVA, JM 3462, Hoffmann reports of October and November 1941.

260. YVA, JM 1112, Auerswald Two-Year Report, September 26, 1941.

261. YVA, JM 1112, Auerswald Two-Year Report, September 26, 1941.

262. YVA, JM 3462, Hoffmann reports of October and November 1941.

263. *Czerniakow Diary*, p. 401 (appended document: Auerswald to Medeazza, November 24, 1941).

264. YVA, JM 1112, Auerswald Vermerk, March 4, 1942.

265. Gutman, *The Jews of Warsaw*, p. 75; Trunk, *Judenrat*, pp. 78–81.

266. YVA, JM 1112, Transferstelle report of January 7, 1942.

267. YVA, JM 1112, Transferstelle reports of December 6, 1941, and January 7, 1942.

268. Archivum Panstwowe m. st. Warszawy, Der Kommissar für den jüdischen Wohnbezirk in Warschau, Nr. 132, speech by Max Bischof, October 15, 1941.

269. Christian Streit, *Keine Kameraden: Die Wehrmacht und die sowjetischen Kriegsgefangenen 1941–1945*; Ulrich Herbert, "Arbeit und Vernichtung: Ökonomischer Interesse und Primat der 'Weltanschauung' in Nationalsozialismus"; Herbert, *Fremdarbeiter*, esp. pp. 137–49.

270. YVA, JM 3462, Conference of March 20, 1942, on Jewish labor.

271. YVA, JM 3462, Hoffmann reports of April and May 1942 and Czerniakow report (No. 65) of May 1942.

272. YVA, O-53/101, Hummel's monthly reports to Bühler for January through May, and bimonthly report of June/July 1942.

273. Frank, *Diensttagebuch*, p. 510 (Polizeisitzung, June 18, 1942).

274. YVA, JM 1113, Mohns to Leist, January 11, 1941.

275. *Czerniakow Diary*, p. 402 (appended document: Auerswald to Medeazza, November 24, 1941).

276. Trunk, *Judenrat*, p. 61.

277. Musial, *Deutsche Zivilverwaltung und Judenverfolgung im Generalgouvernement*, pp. 174–78, effectively analyzes the "vicious circle" created by German measures. However, because Musial focuses on the Lublin district but not Lodz and Warsaw, he does not consider the issue of ghetto maintenance in his excellent study.

278. Even after the liquidation of the Warsaw ghetto, Auerswald did not attempt to rewrite with hindsight what he considered to be the successes of his term as commissioner

of the Jewish district in order to make it appear as if he had prepared for and contributed to the subsequent mass murder. "Achievements of the Agency: simplification of the boundaries, construction of the wall, maintenance of peace (in May 1941 the Higher ss and Police Leader feared the outbreak of hunger revolts!), construction of an essentially satisfactorily functioning Jewish communal administration, improvement of the hygienic situation in the interest of combating epidemic (decline of spotted fever), and—together with the Transferstelle—prevention of an initially feared economic failure (employment of a large number of skilled workers in armaments industries)." YVA, O-53/49/132 (Auerswald report on his activities in Warsaw, undated but after January 1943).

279. Gutman, *The Jews of Warsaw*, p. 71.

280. *Czerniakow Diary*, p. 402 (appended document: Auerswald to Medeazza, November 24, 1941).

5. Germany and Europe

1. Wolf Gruner, "Die NS-Judenverfolgung und die Kommunen: Zur wechselseitigen Dynamisierung von zentraler und lokaler Politik 1933–1941," p. 121.

2. Konrad Kwiet, "Nach dem Pogrom: Stufen der Ausgrenzung," p. 602.

3. Raul Hilberg, *The Destruction of the European Jews*, p. 157.

4. Wolf Gruner, *Die Geschlossene Arbeitseinsatz deutscher Juden: Zur Zwangsarbeit als Element der Verfolgung 1938–1943*, pp. 108, 127.

5. Marion Kaplan, *Between Dignity and Despair: Jewish Life in Nazi Germany*, p. 153.

6. Gruner, "Die NS-Judenverfolgung und die Kommunen," p. 109.

7. Adler, *Der verwaltete Mensch*, p. 44.

8. Wolf Gruner, *Zwangsarbeit und Verfolgung: Österreichische Juden im NS-Staat*, pp. 222–23.

9. Gruner, "Die NS-Judenverfolgung und die Kommunen," pp. 117–19, and *Die Geschlossene Arbeitseinsatz deutscher Juden*, pp. 249–62.

10. Kaplan, *Between Dignity and Despair*, p. 155.

11. Joseph Walk, *Das Sonderrecht für die Juden im NS-Staat*, pp. 304–36, 320, 326, 345, 360, 364.

12. For the systematic expropriation of Jewish property, see Helmut Genschel, *Die Verdrängung der Juden aus der Wirtschaft im Dritten Reich*; Avraham Barkai, *From Boycott to Annihilation: The Economic Struggle of German Jews, 1933–1943*; Frank Bajohr, *"Aryanisation" in Hamburg: The Economic Exclusion of Jews and the Confiscation of Their Property in Nazi Germany*; and Peter Hayes and Irmtrud Wojack, eds., *"Arisierung" im Nationalsozialismus: Volksgemeinschaft, Raub und Gedächtnis*.

13. Adam, *Judenpolitik im Dritten*, p. 266.

14. Hilberg, *The Destruction of the European Jews*, p. 149.

15. Walk, *Das Sonderrecht für die Juden im NS-Staat*, pp. 355, 361, 371.

16. Adam, *Judenpolitik im Dritten Reich*, p. 260.

17. Kaplan, *Between Dignity and Despair*, pp. 150–51; Walk, *Das Sonderrecht für die Juden im NS-Staat*, pp. 312, 314, 316.

18. Hilberg, *The Destruction of the European Jews*, p. 151.

19. Hilberg, *The Destruction of the European Jews*, pp. 146–47; Gruner, *Der Geschlossene Arbeitseinsatz deutscher Juden*, pp. 151–59, 194–204.

20. Walk, *Das Sonderrecht für die Juden im NS-Staat*, pp. 308, 319.

21. Eric A. Johnson, *Nazi Terror: The Gestapo, Jews, and Ordinary Germans*, pp. 355–58, 382–95. On denunciation, see Robert Gellately, *The Gestapo and German Society: Enforcing Racial Policy, 1933–1945*, pp. 160–64, 192–96.

22. The debate over the citizenship status of German Jews is discussed in detail in the following: Adam, *Judenpolitik im Dritten Reich*, pp. 292–302; Adler, *Der verwaltete Mensch*, pp. 496–505; and most recently Cornelia Essner, *Die 'Nürnberger Gesetze' oder die Verwaltung Rassenwahns 1933–1945*. Martin Dean, "The Development and Implementation of Nazi Denaturalization and Confiscation Policy up to the Eleventh Decree to the Reich Citizenship Law," pp. 226–34.

23. Cited in Adler, *Der verwaltete Mensch*, p. 496.

24. Cited in Adam, *Judenpolitik im Dritten Reich*, p. 300.

25. Walk, *Das Sonderrecht für die Juden im NS-Staat*, pp. 307–8.

26. Walk, *Das Sonderrecht für die Juden im NS-Staat*, pp. 363–64, 366, 372, 374, 383.

27. Konrad Kwiet, "Forced Labour of German Jews in Nazi Germany," p. 392; Adler, *Der verwaltete Mensch*, pp. 208–9.

28. Gruner, *Der Geschlossene Arbeitseinsatz deutscher Juden*, p. 114.

29. Werner Best memorandum, March 1, 1939, of Interior Ministry meeting, February 28, 1939, printed in Kwiet, "Forced Labour of German Jews in Nazi Germany," pp. 408–10.

30. Gruner, *Zwangsarbeit und Verfolgung*, pp. 133–36.

31. Gruner, *Der Geschlossene Arbeitseinsatz deutscher Juden*, pp. 116–22.

32. Gruner, *Der Geschlossene Arbeitseinsatz deutscher Juden*, pp. 133–39; Dieter Maier, *Arbeitseinsatz und Deportation: Die Mitwirkung der Arbeitsverwaltung bei der nationalsozialistischen Judenverfolgung in den Jahren 1938–1945*, pp. 71–76.

33. Gruner, *Der Geschlossene Arbeitseinsatz deutscher Juden*, pp. 162–63.

34. Gruner, *Zwangsarbeit und Verfolgung*, pp. 166–67, 189, 192.

35. Wolf Gruner, "Juden bauen die 'Strassen des Führers.' Zwangsarbeit und Zwangsarbeitslager für nichtdeutsche Juden im Altreich 1940 bis 1943/44," pp. 789–91, 800.

36. Gruner, "Juden bauen die 'Strassen des Führers,' " p. 792.

37. Nbg. Doc. NG-363 (Syrup to Landesarbeitsämter, March 14, 1941), cited in Adler, *Der verwaltete Mensch*, p. 211.

38. NA microfilm, T81/676/548604–5 (Propaganda Ministry memorandum Evakuierung der Juden aus Berlin, March 21, 1941), printed in Adler, *Der verwaltete Mensch*, pp. 152–53.

39. *Die Tagebücher von Joseph Goebbels I*, 4:547 (entry of March 22, 1941).

40. Cited in Gruner, "Juden bauen die 'Strassen des Führers,' " p. 793.

41. Adler, *Der verwaltete Mensch*, p. 212.

42. Maier, *Arbeitseinsatz und Deportation*, p. 235.

43. Gruner, *Der Geschlossene Arbeitseinsatz deutscher Juden*, pp. 148–60.

44. For two studies that place the persecution and murder of the "Gypsies" within the wider context of Nazi racism and genocide, see Henry Friedlander, *The Origins of Nazi*

Genocide: From Euthanasia to the Final Solution; and Michael Burleigh and Wolfgang Wippermann, *The Racial State: Germany 1933–1945*. The two most detailed and invaluable studies of the Nazi persecution of the "Gypsies" are Guenter Lewy, *The Nazi Persecution of the Gypsies*; and Michael Zimmermann, *Rassenutopie und Genozid: Die nationalsozialisitsche "Lösung der Zigeunerfrage."* See also Zimmermann, "The National Socialist 'Solution of the Gypsy Question': Central Decisions, Local Initiatives, and Their Interrelation."

45. Henry Friedlander (*The Origins of Nazi Genocide*, p. 248) estimates 30,000–35,000 Sinti in Germany and 4,000 Sinti and 8,000 Roma in Austria. Guenter Lewy (*The Nazi Persecution of the Gypsies*, pp. 15, 56) estimates 26,000 "Gypsies" in Germany and 11,000 in Austria.

46. Zimmerman, *Rassenutopie und Genozid*, pp. 381–83.

47. While I appreciate the careful distinctions that Guenter Lewy makes and share most of his conclusions, I do not share his narrow approach to the concept of genocide, whereby he argues that there was no "intent" to destroy the "Gypsies" as a group, because each measure of the Nazi persecution of the "Gypsies," in and of itself, was not part of a single plan or general program to realize that goal. Lewy, *The Nazi Persecution of the Gypsies*, pp. 221–24. I do think there was an intent, in the form of an amorphous consensus, among the Nazi leadership that the German and Austrian "Gypsies" should cease to exist as a cultural and racial group, and the cumulative measures to achieve this consensual goal—deportation, incarceration, slave labor under lethal conditions, sterilization, and outright murder in gas chambers—resulted in the death of the clear majority of the target group. However imprecise the notion of destruction "in part" of the genocide convention may be, surely the fate of the German and Austrian "Gypsies" passes this threshold, and the lack of a single, unified general plan or program does not mean that this result was not intended. I would agree that German policies toward the "Gypsies" outside the Third Reich, however murderous, did not constitute genocide.

48. Friedlander, *The Origins of Nazi Genocide*, pp. 249–52; Lewy, *The Nazi Persecution of the Gypsies*, pp. 24–26.

49. Zimmerman, *Rassenutopie und Genozid*, p. 370.

50. Lewy, *The Nazi Persecution of the Gypsies*, pp. 39–41.

51. Friedlander, *The Origins of Nazi Genocide*, pp. 254–55; Lewy, *The Nazi Persecution of the Gypsies*, pp. 20–23.

52. Lewy, *The Nazi Persecution of the Gypsies*, p. 42; Burleigh and Wippermann, *The Racial State*, p. 116.

53. Lewy, *The Nazi Persecution of the Gypsies*, pp. 43–47; Friedlander, *The Origins of Nazi Genocide*, p. 253.

54. Lewy, *The Nazi Persecution of the Gypsies*, pp. 47–49.

55. Burleigh and Wippermann, *The Racial State*, pp. 120–21, citing Himmler's circular on "the Fight against the Gypsy Nuisance," December 8, 1938.

56. NA microfilm, T175/239/2728524–28. Conference of Heydrich's division heads and Einsatzgruppen leaders, September 21, 1939.

57. Groscurth, *Tagebücher*, p. 362 (Doc. Nr. 14: Groscurth memorandum on verbal orientation by Major Radke, September 22, 1939).

58. YVA, O/53/93/289, Braune to Wagner, October 13, 1939; 299–300, Eichmann to Nebe, October 16, 1939; and 227–29, R. Günther-Braune FS-Gespräch, October 18, 1939.

59. IMT, 26:381 (864-PS).

60. Heydrich express letter, October 17, 1939, printed in Reinhard Rürup, ed., *Topography of Terror: Gestapo, SS and Reichssicherheitshauptamt on the "Prinz-Albrecht-Terrain": A Documentation*, pp. 126–27.

61. Zimmermann, *Rassenutopie und Genozid*, p. 170; Lewy, *The Nazi Persecution of the Gypsies*, p. 68.

62. Zimmermann, *Rassenutopie und Genozid*, pp. 170–71; Lewy, *The Nazi Persecution of the Gypsies*, p. 71.

63. *Biuletyn* 12, pp. 66F–75F (NO-5322: conference of January 30, 1940).

64. Zimmermann, *Rassenutopie und Genozid*, p. 172.

65. Detailed descriptions are provided in Zimmermann, *Rassenutopie und Genozid*, pp. 173–84; Lewy, *The Nazi Persecution of the Gypsies*, pp. 72–81.

66. Frank, *Diensttagebuch*, p. 262.

67. Zimmermann, *Rassenutopie und Genozid*, p. 200.

68. Zimmermann, *Rassenutopie und Genozid*, p. 186; Lewy, *The Nazi Persecution of the Gypsies*, p. 77.

69. Erika Thurner, *National Socialism and Gypsies in Austria*; Zimmermann, *Rassenutopie und Genozid*, pp. 201–7, 218–22; Lewy, *The Nazi Persecution of the Gypsies*, pp. 107–11.

70. Zimmermann, *Rassenutopie und Genozid*, pp. 214–17; Lewy, *The Nazi Persecution of the Gypsies*, pp. 81–82.

71. Zimmermann, *Rassenutopie und Genozid*, pp. 195–98; Lewy, *The Nazi Persecution of the Gypsies*, pp. 94–95. The military wavered on the issue of *Ziguenermischlinge* in 1943 but reasserted its ban in 1944.

72. Lewy, *The Nazi Persecution of the Gypsies*, pp. 90–93, 100.

73. Zimmerman, *Rassenutopie und Genozid*, p. 210.

74. On the historical relationship between social Darwinism, racism, and eugenics in Germany, see Paul Weindling, *Health, Race and German Politics between National Unification and Nazism, 1870–1945*.

75. Henry Friedlander, *The Origins of Nazi Genocide*, p. 15. The bibliography on eugenics and the Nazi murder of the handicapped is immense. I am particularly indebted to Henry Friedlander's masterful work for both its scope of research and acuity of analysis.

76. Stefan Kühl, *The Nazi Connection: Eugenics, American Racism, and German National Socialism*, pp. 77–84.

77. Friedlander, *The Origins of Nazi Genocide*, pp. 16–20.

78. Ulf Schmidt, "Kriegsausbruch und 'Euthanasie': Neue Forschungsergebnisse zum 'Knauer Kind' im Jahre 1939," *"Euthanasie" und die aktuelle Sterbehilfe-Debatte*, p. 127 (for a shorter, English version of this article, see "Reassessing the Beginning of the 'Euthanasia' Programme"); Friedlander, *The Origins of Nazi Genocide*, p. 39; Michael Burleigh, *Death and Deliverance: "Euthanasia" in Germany, 1900–1945*, p. 97.

79. Schmidt, "Kriegsausbruch und 'Euthanasie,'" pp. 117–23.

80. Friedlander, *The Origins of Nazi Genocide*, p. 43.

81. Friedlander, *The Origins of Nazi Genocide*, pp. 62–63.

82. Schmidt, "Kriegsausbruch und 'Euthanasie,'" pp. 123–24.

83. Schmidt, "Kriegsausbruch und 'Euthanasie,'" p. 131, places this meeting in September, as does Volker Riess, *Die Anfänge der Vernichtung "lebensunwerten Lebens" in den Reichsgauen Danzig-Westpreussen und Wartheland 1939/40*, pp. 45–46. Burleigh, *Death and Deliverance*, pp. 111–12, places it before July. Friedlander, *The Origins of Nazi Genocide*, p. 63, gives no date.

84. Riess, *Anfänge der Vernichtung*, pp. 45–46.

85. Riess, *Anfänge der Vernichtung*, pp. 24–25.

86. Riess, *Anfänge der Vernichtung*, pp. 28, 119–50.

87. Riess, *Anfänge der Vernichtung*, p. 171.

88. Riess, *Anfänge der Vernichtung*, pp. 152–53.

89. Riess, *Anfänge der Vernichtung*, pp. 29–36, 120, 135–36, 142, 143–48, 153, 156–57, 169.

90. Riess, *Anfänge der Vernichtung*, pp. 53–88; Ernst Klee, *"Euthanasie" im NS-Staat: Die "Vernichtung lebesunwerten Lebens,"* pp. 95–98.

91. Riess, *Anfänge der Vernichtung*, pp. 243–57, 266–71.

92. Riess, *Anfänge der Vernichtung*, pp. 285–89.

93. Riess, *Anfänge der Vernichtung*, pp. 298–304.

94. Riess, *Anfänge der Vernichtung*, pp. 306–7, 311–16, 321–22.

95. Riess, *Anfänge der Vernichtung*, pp. 330–39.

96. Friedlander, *The Origins of Nazi Genocide*, pp. 139–40; Riess, *Anfänge der Vernichtung*, pp. 348–52.

97. Riess, *Anfänge der Vernichtung*, p. 355.

98. Friedlander, *The Origins of Nazi Genocide*, pp. 40–61.

99. Friedlander, *The Origins of Nazi Genocide*, pp. 64–85.

100. Friedlander, *The Origins of Nazi Genocide*, pp. 86–110.

101. Friedlander, *The Origins of Nazi Genocide*, pp. 270–83.

102. Klee, *"Euthanasie" im NS-Staat*, pp. 345–55; Friedlander, *The Origins of Nazi Genocide*, pp. 142–49.

103. Friedlander, *The Origins of Nazi Genocide*, pp. 106–7.

104. Klee, *"Euthanasie" im NS-Staat*, pp. 333–40; Friedlander, *The Origins of Nazi Genocide*, pp. 111–16. Klee gives primary credit to the protest of churchmen, while Friedlander argues that "the protest of the churches lagged behind public outrage" (p. 116).

105. Friedlander, *The Origins of Nazi Genocide*, pp. 150–63; quotation from p. 151.

106. Gerald Reitlinger, *The Final Solution: The Attempt to Exterminate the Jews of Europe, 1939–1945*, pp. 123–33.

107. Raul Hilberg, *The Destruction of the European Jews* (1961 ed.), mentions "euthanasia" only on one page (p. 561). The revised and expanded edition (1985) discusses the connection between "euthanasia" and the Final Solution on pp. 872–83 and 894–95.

108. Michael Burleigh and Wolfgang Wippermann, *The Racial State: Germany, 1933–1945*.

109. For the role of the German Foreign Office in Nazi Jewish policy, see Christopher R. Browning, *The Final Solution and the German Foreign Office*. For the nazification of Foreign

Office personnel, see Hans-Jürgen Döscher, *Das Auswärtiges Amt im Dritten Reich. Diplomatie im Schatten der "Endlösung."*

110. Aly, *"Final Solution,"* p. 125.

111. Aly, *"Final Solution,"* p. 134.

112. PA, Inland II AB 45/1a: German embassy Bern to AA, forwarding IRC inquiry of September 27, 1939; Lischka to Ref. D, October 14, 1939; and German consulate Geneva to AA, November 16, 1939. For the history of the International Committee of the Red Cross and the Holocaust, see Jean-Claude Favez, *The Red Cross and the Holocaust.*

113. PA, Inland II AB 54/2: Lischka to AA, November 14, 1939, and Ref. D note to Ref. Kult.

114. PA, Inland II AB 45/1a: Woermann note, September 30, 1939; and Müller to AA, October 17, 1939.

115. PA, Inland II AB 45/1a: Müller to AA, May 21, 1940; and Luther to D III, May 27, 1940.

116. PA, Inland II AB 45/1a, Rademacher memo, July 10, 1940; and Inland II AB 47/2, Reichsstelle für das Auswanderungswesen to Security Police, June 29, 1940.

117. PA, Inland II AB 45/2, Weintz (RF-SS) to D III, September 25, 1940.

118. PA, Inland II AB 45/1a: German consulate Kovno to AA, February 8, 1940; Krause (RF-SS) to Rödiger (AA), March 26, 1940, and Machule (RF-SS) to Rödiger, July 15, 1940.

119. PA, Inland II AB 45/1a: Eichmann to Rademacher, September 4, 1940; Legal Division to Rademacher, September 17, 1940; and Rademacher to Security Police, September 20, 1940.

120. PA, Pressburg 332/2: Wisliceny to German consulate in Pressburg, March 15, 1941; and Eichmann to AA, March 26, 1941.

121. PA, Inland IIg 182, Schellenberg circular, May 20, 1941 (Nbg. Doc. NG-3104). Both the ominous phrase "in view of the doubtless imminent final solution" and the policy of blocking Jewish emigration from non-German territory had been standard since the previous fall. Moreover, the document is clearly about maximizing the increasingly tenuous possibility of continued wartime emigration of Jews from the Third Reich via Spain and Portugal—a policy that would not be reversed until October 1941. This document is not, as some historians (for example Krausnick and Breitman) have suggested, about some fateful change in German policy.

122. For German aims and policies in France, see Eberhard Jäckel, *Frankreich in Hitlers Europa. Die deutsche Frankreichpolitik im Zweiten Weltkrieg*; and Hans Umbreit, *Der Militärbefehlshaber in Frankreich 1940–1944.* For the Vichy regime, see Robert Paxton, *Vichy France: Old Guard and New Order.*

123. Ulrich Herbert, *Best: Biographischen Studien über Radikalismus, Weltanschauung und Vernunft 1903–1989*, pp. 251–54.

124. Michael R. Marrus and Robert O. Paxton, *Vichy France and the Jews*, pp. 6, 78; Klarsfeld, *Vichy-Auschwitz*, p. 32; John P. Fox, "German Bureaucrat or Nazified Ideologue? Ambassador Otto Abetz and Hitler's Anti-Jewish Policies 1940–44," p. 183. Fox rightly notes the Nazi ties and ideological commitment of the Abetz embassy but generalizes from this as if it were typical, when in fact the Abetz case is rather exceptional in this regard.

125. Klarsfeld, *Vichy-Auschwitz*, pp. 36–37, 47–50.

126. *DGFP*, D, 10:484, No. 345 (Luther memorandum, August 15, 1940).

127. PA, Inland IIg 189, Abetz to Ribbentrop, August 20, 1940 (T120/K773/K204577; Nbg. Doc. NG-4893).

128. Herbert, *Best*, p. 263; Klarsfeld, *Vichy-Auschwitz*, pp. 356–59 (Best Vermerk, August 19, 1940; Mahnke Vermerk, August 22, 1940; and Storz Vermerk, n.d.).

129. Herbert, *Best*, p. 263; Fox, "German Bureaucrat," p. 186.

130. PA, Inland IIg 189, Rademacher Vermerk, August 31, 1940 (T120/K773/K204571).

131. PA, Inland IIg 189, Luther to Paris, September 28, 1940 (T120/K773/K204565–66).

132. PA, Inland IIg 189, Heydrich to Luther, September 20, 1940 (T120/K773/K204567–68). Printed in Klarsfeld, *Vichy-Auschwitz*, p. 360.

133. PA, Inland IIg 189, Schleier to AA, October 9, 1940.

134. Herbert, *Best*, pp. 264–65.

135. Cited in Marrus and Paxton, *Vichy France and the Jews*, p. 13.

136. Marrus and Paxton, *Vichy France and the Jews*, pp. 3–9, 76.

137. Herbert, *Best*, p. 264.

138. PA, Inland II AB 61/4, Bargen to AA, November 11, 1940; Serge Klarsfeld and Maxime Steinberg, eds., *Die Endlösung der Judenfrage in Belgien*, pp. 11–12 (Sonderbericht: Das Judentum in Belgien, January 31, 1942); Maxime Steinberg, "The Judenpolitik in Belgium within the West European Context: Comparative Observations," p. 200.

139. Klarsfeld, *Vichy-Auschwitz*, pp. 361–65 (Dannecker memorandum, January 21, 1941; Mahnke Vermerk, February 3, 1941; and Abetz to Thomas, February 14, 1941).

140. PA, Inland II AB 80–41 Sdh. III, Bd. 1: Heydrich to Luther, February 5, 1941; and Streckenbach to Luther, February 14, 1941.

141. Marrus and Paxton, *Vichy France and the Jews*, pp. 81–83 (on the founding of the CGQJ) and pp. 88–95 (on Vallat); Fox, "German Bureaucrat," pp. 187, 193–94.

142. Klarsfeld, *Vichy-Auschwitz*, pp. 366–67 (Best to MBH, April 4, 1941).

143. Marrus and Paxton, *Vichy France and the Jews*, pp. 96–97; Herbert, *Best*, pp. 306–7.

144. *DGFP*, D, 12:228, No. 127 (Abetz to AA, March 6, 1942).

145. Herbert, *Best*, p. 308.

146. Marrus and Paxton, *Vichy France and the Jews*, pp. 98–104.

147. Marrus and Paxton, *Vichy France and the Jews*, pp. 108–9.

148. For the German occupation regime in the Netherlands: Gerhard Hirschfeld, *Nazi Rule and Dutch Collaboration: The Netherlands under German Occupation*; Werner Warmbrunn, *The Dutch under German Occupation, 1940–45*; Konrad Kwiet, *Reichskommissariat Niederlande: Versuch und Scheitern nationalsozialistischer Neuordnung*.

149. Michael Marrus and Robert Paxton, "The Nazis and Jews in Occupied Western Europe, 1940–1944," p. 175.

150. Jacob Presser, *The Destruction of the Dutch Jews*, pp. 16–25; Bob Moore, *Victims and Survivors: The Nazi Persecution of the Jews in the Netherlands, 1940–1945*, pp. 54–56, 190–94.

151. Presser, *The Destruction of the Dutch Jews*, p. 31; Moore, *Victims and Survivors*, pp. 56–57, 194–96; Guus Meershoek, "The Amsterdam Police and the Persecution of the Jews," pp. 284–87. For explicit comparisons, see Ron Zeller and Pim Griffioen, "Judenverfolgung in den Niederlanden und in Belgien während des Zweiten Weltkrieges. Eine vergleichende Analyse"; and J. C. H. Bloom, "The Persecution of the Jews in the Netherlands: A Comparative Western European Perspective."

152. Presser, *The Destruction of the Dutch Jews*, pp. 33–35; Moore, *Victims and Survivors*, pp. 196–99.

153. Hilberg, *The Destruction of the European Jews*, pp. 571–78.

154. Meershoek, "The Amsterdam Police," p. 287.

155. Presser, *The Destruction of the Dutch Jews*, pp. 45–57; Moore, *Victims and Survivors*, pp. 66–73; Meershoek, "The Amsterdam Police," p. 287, suggests that the strike was more like a "riot."

156. Cited in Joseph Michmann, "Planning for the Final Solution against the Background of Developments in Holland in 1941," pp. 150–53, 161. See also Johannes Houwink ten Cate, "Heydrich's Security Police and the Amsterdam Jewish Council."

157. Michmann, "Planning for the Final Solution," pp. 162–65; Moore, *Victims and Survivors*, pp. 73–77.

158. Michmann, "Planning for the Final Solution," pp. 167–69; Leni Yahil, "Methods of Persecution: A Comparison of the 'Final Solution' in Holland and Denmark," p. 181; Houwink ten Cate, "Heydrich's Security Police and the Amsterdam Jewish Council," pp. 387–89.

159. Meershoek, "The Amsterdam Police," pp. 287–95.

160. Klarsfeld and Steinberg, eds., *Die Endlösung der Judenfrage in Belgien*, pp. 12–13 (Sonderbericht: Das Judentum in Belgien, January 31, 1942); Steinberg, "The Judenpolitik in Belgium," pp. 200–201, 207; Zeller and Griffioen, "Judenverfolgung in den Niederlanden und in Belgien," part 1, pp. 43–48; Hilberg, *The Destruction of the European Jews*, pp. 602–5.

161. Hilberg, *The Destruction of the European Jews*, p. 722; Rich, *The Establishment of the New Order*, p. 65.

162. Jelinek, "Slovakia's Internal Policy and the Third Reich," pp. 242–45; and Jelinek, "Storm-Troopers in Slovakia: The Rodobranna and the Hlinka Guard," pp. 108–9.

163. DGFP, D, 9:420–22, No. 309 (Woermann memorandum, May 23, 1940).

164. DGFP, D, 9:537–40, No. 407 (Killinger report, June 9, 1940).

165. DGFP, D, 10:345–48, No. 248 (Berghof meeting, July 28, 1940).

166. DGFP, D, 10:375–76, No. 263 (Ribbentrop to Killinger, July 29, 1940).

167. PA, Luther Handakten, vol. 32: Luther to Killinger, October 15, 1940 (T120/4442/E086040–41).

168. DGFP, D, 10:269, No. 205 (Bernhard memorandum, July 22, 1940).

169. Leni Yahil, *The Holocaust: The Fate of European Jewry, 1932–1945*, pp. 180–81; Martin Broszat, "Das deutsch-slowakische Verhältnis 1939/40 und seine Rückwirkung auf die slowakische Judenpolitik," pp. 221–29.

170. Martin Broszat, "Das deutsch-ungarische Verhältnis und die ungarische Juden-

politik in den Jahren 1938–41," pp. 184–87; Randolph Braham, *The Politics of Genocide*, 1:118–25.

171. Braham, *The Politics of Genocide*, 1:128–34.

172. *DGFP*, D, 5:366, No. 272 (meeting of Hitler and Csaky, January 16, 1939).

173. Braham, *The Politics of Genocide*, 1:144–45; Broszat, "Das deutsch-ungarische Verhältnis," p. 191.

174. *IMT*, 35:435 (Nbg. Doc. 737-D: meeting of Ribbentrop, Teleki, and Csaky, April 29, 1939).

175. Braham, *The Politics of Genocide*, 1:148–54.

176. Braham, *The Politics of Genocide*, 1:173.

177. Braham, *The Politics of Genocide*, 1:177.

178. Radu Ioanid, *The Holocaust in Romania: The Destruction of the Jews and Gypsies under the Antonescu Regime, 1940–1944*, pp. 17–18.

179. Max Münz, "Die Verantwortlichkeit für die Judenverfolgungen im Ausland während der national-sozialistischen Herrschaft," pp. 137–41.

180. *DGFP*, D, 10:69, No. 67 (Killinger report, June 30, 1940), and 10:308–9, 316, No. 233–34 (Ribbentrop and Hitler meetings with Gigurtu, July 26, 1940).

181. Ioanid, *The Holocaust in Romania*, pp. 19–23, 25; Martin Broszat, "Das dritte Reich und die rumänische Judenpolitik," pp. 114–16; Hilberg, *The Destruction of the European Jews*, pp. 761–62.

182. Hilberg, *The Destruction of the European Jews*, p. 761.

183. Hilberg, *The Destruction of the European Jews*, p. 763; Ioanid, *The Holocaust in Romania*, pp. 23–31; Münz, "Die Verantwortlichkeit," pp. 149–50.

184. Ioanid, *The Holocaust in Romania*, pp. 52–61.

185. Broszat, "Die dritte Reich und die rumänische Judenpolitik," pp. 123–25.

186. Frederick B. Chary, *The Bulgarian Jews and the Final Solution, 1940–1944*, pp. 35–41. See also S. Fauck, "Das deutsch-bulgarische Verhältnis 1939–1944 und seine Rückwirkung auf die bulgarische Judenpolitik," pp. 46–49; Oren Nissan, "The Bulgarian Exception: A Reassessment of the Salvation of the Jewish Community," pp. 85–88, 92–93; Tzvetan Todorov, *The Fragility of Goodness: Why Bulgaria's Jews Survived the Holocaust*, pp. 3–6; Hans-Joachim Hoppe, "Bulgarien," pp. 278–82.

6. Preparing for the "War of Destruction"

1. For my analysis of and participation in this historiographical debate over the past two decades, see Christopher R. Browning, *Fateful Months: Essays on the Emergence of the Final Solution*, pp. 8–38; *The Path to Genocide: Essays on Launching the Final Solution*, pp. 86–121; and *Nazi Policy, Jewish Workers, German Killers*, pp. 26–57.

2. The most emphatic advocate of an explicit continuity thesis is Peter Longerich, *Politik der Vernichtung*.

3. Streit, *Keine Kameraden*, pp. 127, 356; Alfred Streim, *Die Behandlung sowjetischer Kriegsgefangener im "Fall Barbarossa,"* pp. 74–93. For several examples (among many) of recent support for the Streit-Streim thesis, see Peter Longerich, "Vom Massenmord zur

'Endlösung.' Die Erschiessungen von jüdischen Zivilisten in den ersten Monaten des Ostfeldzuges im Kontext des nationalsozialistischen Judenmords"; Ralf Ogorreck, *Die Einsatzgruppen und die "Genesis der Endlösung"*; Christian Gerlach, *Krieg, Ernährung, Völkermord*, pp. 58–81. For a dissenting view: Goldhagen, *Hitler's Willing Executioners*, pp. 148–53; Breitman, *Architecht of Genocide*, pp. 162–66.

4. The scholarly literature on the "war of destruction" has grown enormously in recent years. I am particularly indebted to the following fundamental studies: Hans-Adolf Jacobsen, "Kommissarbefehl und Massenexekutionen sowjetischer Kreigsgefangener"; Andreas Hillgruber, "Die 'Endlösung' und das deutsche Ostimperium als Kernstück des rassenideologischen Programms des Nationalsozialismus"; Streit, *Keine Kameraden*; Krausnick and Wilhelm, *Die Truppe des Weltanschauungskrieges*; Helmut Krausnick, "Kommissarbefehl und 'Gerichtsbarkeiterlass Barbarossa' in neuer Sicht"; and esp. the contributions of Jürgen Förster in *Germany and the Second World War*, vol. 4: *The Attack on the Soviet Union*.

5. Halder, *Kriegstagebuch*, 2:49.

6. *Kriegstagebuch des Oberkommandos der Wehrmacht 1940–1941* (hereafter cited as KTB OKW), 1:203–9, 237 (entries of December 5 and 18, 1940).

7. KTB OKW, 1:257–58 (entry of January 9, 1941).

8. Rolf-Dieter Müller, "From Economic Alliance to a War of Colonial Exploitation," p. 153; and Jürgen Förster, "Operation Barbarossa as a War of Conquest and Annihilation," pp. 481–82.

9. KTB OKW, 1:341–42 (entry for March 3, 1941).

10. Halder, *Kriegstagebuch*, 2:303 (entry of March 5, 1941).

11. Jacobsen, "Kommissarbefehl," pp. 198–201 (Doc. Nr. 1: Richtlinien auf Sondergebieten zur Weisung Nr. 21, March 13, 1941, signed by Keitel).

12. Halder, *Kriegstagebuch*, 2:311 (entry for March 13, 1941: "Conference Wagner-Heydrich. Police matters . . ." [*Besprechung Wagner-Heydrich: Polizeifrage . . .*]).

13. Halder, *Kriegstagebuch*, 2:320 (entry of March 17, 1941).

14. Jacobsen, "Kommissarbefehl," pp. 202–5 (Doc. Nr. 2 [NOKW-256]: draft of March 26, 1941; and Doc. Nr. 3 [NOKW-2080]: Regelung des Einsatzes der Sicherheitspolizei und des SD im Verbande des Heeres, April 28, 1941).

15. Krausnick and Wilhelm, *Die Truppe des Weltanschauungskrieges*, p. 135 (citin~~g~~ ~~th~~ original manuscript but not the published memoirs of Walter Schellenberg).

16. Krausnick and Wilhelm, *Die Truppe des Weltanschauungskrieges*, p. 125.

17. Jacobsen, "Kommissarbefehl," pp. 198–201 (Doc. Nr. 1: Keitel order of M~~ay~~ 1941).

18. Halder, *Kriegstagebuch*, 2:336–37 (entry of March 30, 1941).

19. Jacobsen, "Kommissarbefehl," p. 207 (Doc. Nr. 5: Müller to OKW, M~~~~ [NOKW-209]). For details on the preparation of these decrees, see esp. Krausn~~ick, "Kom~~missarbefehl und 'Gerichtsbarkeitserlass Barbarossa' "; Streit, *Keine Kamera~~den*, pp. 4~~3–50; and Förster, "Operation Barbarossa as a War of Conquest," pp. 496–513.

20. KTB OKW, 1:344 (entry of March 4, 1941) and 1:349 (entry of March 8, ~~1941~~).

21. Quoted in Streit, *Keine Kameraden*, pp. 37–38.

22. Halder, *Kriegstagebuch*, 2:399 (entry of May 6, 1941).

23. Jacobsen, "Kommissarbefehl," pp. 208–10 (Doc. Nr. 5: Draft of Barbarossa-Gerichtsbarkeitserlass of May 6, 1941).

24. Cited in Streit, *Keine Kameraden*, pp. 40–41.

25. Jacobsen, "Kommissarbefehl," pp. 216–18 (Doc. Nr. 8: Gerichtsbarkeitserlass Barbarossa, signed by Keitel, May 13, 1941).

26. Jacobsen, "Kommissarbefehl," pp. 211–12 (Doc. Nr. 6: draft of Kommissarbefehl forwarded from Warlimont to Jodl, May 12, 1941 [Nbg. Doc. PS-1471]).

27. Jacobsen, "Kommissarbefehl," pp. 213–14 (Doc. Nr. 7: Warlimont memorandum, May 12, 1941).

28. Jacobsen, "Kommissarbefehl," pp. 225–27 (Doc. Nr. 12: Kommissarbefehl, June 6, 1941 [Nbg. Doc. NOKW-1076]).

29. Förster, "Operation Barbarossa as a War of Conquest," p. 506; Streit, *Keine Kameraden*, p. 44.

30. Förster, "Operation Barbarossa as a War of Conquest," p. 520.

31. Streit, *Keine Kameraden*, p. 59.

32. Jacobsen, "Kommissarbefehl," pp. 221–22 (Doc. Nr. 10: Brauchitsch order of May 24, 1941 [Nbg. Doc. NOKW-3357]).

33. Jacobsen, "Kommissarbefehl," p. 229 (Doc. Nr. 13: Brauchitsch order of June 8, 1941 [Nbg. Doc. NOKW-1076]).

34. Förster, "Operation Barbarossa as a War of Conquest," pp. 494–95.

35. Förster, "Operation Barbarossa as a War of Conquest," p. 495.

36. Förster, "Operation Barbarossa as a War of Conquest," pp. 504, 508–9; Streit, *Keine Kameraden*, p. 42.

37. Förster, "Operation Barbarossa as a War of Conquest," p. 509.

38. Förster, "Operation Barbarossa as a War of Conquest," pp. 505–6, 511; Streit, *Keine Kameraden*, p. 43.

39. Förster, "Operation Barbarossa as a War of Conquest," pp. 511.

40. Jacobsen, "Kommissarbefehl," pp. 223–24 (Doc. Nr. 11: Richtlinien für das Verhalten der Truppe in Russland, June 4, 1941 [Nbg. Doc. NOKW-1692]).

41. The conclusions that follow have been reached, with considerable unanimity, by Streit, *Keine Kameraden*, pp. 50–61; Krausnick and Wilhelm, *Die Truppe des Weltanschauungskrieges*, pp. 111–15, 122–26, 134; and Förster, "Operation Barbarossa as a War of Conquest," pp. 519–21.

42. Krausnick and Wilhelm, *Die Truppe des Weltanschauungskrieges*, pp. 127–33.

43. Breitman, *Architect of Genocide*, p. 148.

44. On Streckenbach, see Michael Wildt, "Der Hamburger Gestapochef Bruno Streckenbach. Eine Nationalsozialistische Karriere."

45. Ralf Ogorreck, "Die Einsatzgruppen der Sicherheitspolizei und des Sicherheitsdienstes im Rahmen der 'Genesis der Endlösung,'" pp. 151–56. This chapter was not included in the published version of Ogorreck's thesis, *Die Einsatzgruppen und die "Genesis der Endlösung."*

46. Klaus-Michael Mallmann, "Die Türöffner der 'Endlösung.' Zur Genesis des Genozids," pp. 457–58.

47. Ogorreck, "Die Einsatzgruppen der Sicherheitspolizei," pp. 157–58.

48. Mallmann, "Die Türöffner der 'Endlösung,' " p. 456.

49. Peter Klein, introduction to *Die Einsatzgruppen in der besetzten Sowjetunion 1941 / 42. Die Tätigkeits- und Lageberichte des Chefs der Sicherheitspolizei und des SD*, p. 22. Klaus-Michael Mallmann, "Menschenjagd und Massenmord: Das neue Instrument der Einsatzgruppen und kommandos 1938–1945," p. 304.

50. Nbg. Doc. L-180: Stahlecker Report, Anlage 1a, October 15, 1941.

51. The numbers varied over time. Einsatzgruppe B had 655 men at the start of the campaign. Christian Gerlach, "Einsatzgruppe B," in Klein, *Die Einsatzgruppen in der besetzten Sowjetunion*, p. 52. Einsatzgruppe C varied between 700 and 800. Dieter Pohl, "Einsatzgruppe C," in Klein, *Die Einsatzgruppen in der besetzten Sowjetunion*, p. 71. Einsatzgruppe D comprised approximately 500–600 men. Krausnick and Wilhelm, *Die Truppe des Weltanschuauungskrieges*, p. 147.

52. The term "energetic ruthlessness" comes from Jürgen Matthäus, "Antisemitism as an Offer—Ideological Indoctrination of the SS- and Police Corps during the Holocaust," paper presented at the Lessons and Legacies Conference, Minneapolis, November 2002. For recent scholarship on the SS ideological elite, see Herbert, *Best*; Jens Banach, *Heydrichs Elite. Das Führerkorps der Sicherheitspolizei und des SD 1936–1945*; Michael Wildt, *Generation des Unbedingten. Das Führerkorps des Reichssicherheitshauptamtes*; and George Browder, *Hitler's Enforcers: The Gestapo and the SS Security Service in the Nazi Revolution*. On the branch office Gestapo chiefs, most of whom rotated through the Einsatzgruppen at some point in the war, and the Gestapo ethos, see Mallmann, "Die Türöffner der 'Endlösung,' " pp. 456–63; and Gerhard Paul, "Ganz normale Akademiker: Eine Fallstudie zur regionalen staatspolizeilichen Funktio̶n̶s̶e̶l̶i̶t̶e̶."

53. Krausnick and Wilhelm, *Die Truppe des Weltanschauungskrieges*, p. 148; Ogorreck, "Die Einsatzgruppen der Sicherheitspolizei," p. 152.

54. Ogorreck, *Die Einsatzgruppen*, pp. 56–58.

55. Ogorreck, *Die Einsatzgruppen*, pp. 106–9.

56. Hans-Heinrich Wilhelm, *Die Einsatzgruppe A der Sicherheitspolizei und des SD 1941 / 42*, pp. 17–18.

57. Andrej Angrick, "Einsatzgruppe D," in Klein, *Die Einsatzgruppen in der besetzten Sowjetunion 1941 / 42*, p. 88.

58. Ogorreck, *Die Einsatzgruppen*, pp. 48–49.

59. For the most important and authoritative example, see Krausnick and Wilhelm, *Die Truppe des Weltanschauungskrieges*, pp. 150–72.

60. Ogorreck, *Die Einsatzgruppen*, pp. 47–109, esp. 95–96, provides the most thorough compilation of the various testimonies on this issue.

61. Streim, *Die Behandlung sowjetischer Kriegsgefangener im "Fall Barbarossa,"* pp. 74–93. The other historian who early on rejected the notion of a preinvasion comprehensive killing order was Streit, *Keine Kameraden*, pp. 127, 356. For the ensuing exchanges between Krausnick and Streim, see Helmut Krausnick, "Hitler und die Befehle an die Einsatzgruppen im Sommer 1941"; and Alfred Streim, "Zur Eröffung des allgemeinen Judenvernichtungsbefehls gegenüber den Einsatzgruppen"; Streim, "The Tasks of the Einsatzgruppen"; and the Krausnick-Streim exchange in the *Simon Wiesenthal Center Annual*. As

part of the debate, see also Yaacov Lozowick, "Rollbahn Mord: The Early Activities of Einsatzgruppe C"; and Roland Headland, "The Einsatzgruppen: The Question of Their Initial Operations."

62. For example, see Longerich, "Vom Massenmord zur 'Endlösung'"; Ogorreck, *Die Einsatzgruppen*; Gerlach, *Krieg, Ernährung, Völkermord*, pp. 56–81; Mallmann, "Die Türöffner der 'Endlösung,'" pp. 437–47. For a dissenting opinion to the general trend toward accepting the Streim thesis: Goldhagen, *Hitler's Willing Executioners*, pp. 148–53.

63. Cited in Ogorreck, *Die Einsatzgruppen*, pp. 104–6.

64. Klein, *Die Einsatzgruppen in der besetzten Sowjetunion*, p. 319 (Heydrich to Einsatzgruppen chiefs, June 29, 1941).

65. Klein, *Die Einsatzgruppen in der besetzten Sowjetunion*, pp. 324–28 (Heydrich to HSSPF Jeckeln, v.d. Bach, Prützmann, and Korsemann, July 2, 1941).

66. For Schulz, see Wildt, *Generation des Unbedingten*, pp. 561–70, 779–84.

67. Ogorreck, *Die Einsatzgruppen*, pp. 83, 98.

68. BA, R 19/336, Daluege presentation over the manpower and war activities of the Orpo, February 1–4, 1942; Longerich, *Politik der Vernichtung*, pp. 308–9; Georg Tessin, Norbert Kannapin, and Brün Meyer, *Waffen-ss und Ordnungspolizei im Kriegseinsatz 1939–1945*, pp. 629–38. For an excellent review of the historiography of the Order Police and the Final Solution, see Klaus-Michael Mallmann, "Vom Fussvolk der 'Endlösung.' Ordnungspolizei, Ostkrieg und Judenmord." For Daluege's meetings with Himmler in preparation for Order Police participation in Barbarossa, see Richard Breitman, *Official Secrets*, pp. 36–37.

69. Tessin, Kannapin, and Meyer, *Waffen-ss und Ordnungspolizei*, pp. 534–37.

70. Edward B. Westermann, " 'Friend and Helper': German Uniformed Police Operations in the General Government, 1939–1941," pp. 643–61; Tessin, Kannapin, and Meyer, *Waffen-ss und Ordnungspolizei*, pp. 559, 629–30.

71. Georg Tessin, "Die Stäbe und Truppeneinheiten der Ordnungspolizei," pp. 24, 49.

72. Longerich, *Politik der Vernichtung*, pp. 306–7; Tessin, Kannapin, and Meyer, *Waffen-ss und Ordnungspolizei*, p. 538.

73. BA, R 19/336, Manpower of the Order Police, July 20, 1940.

74. Christopher R. Browning, *Ordinary Men: Reserve Police Battalion 101 and the Final Solution in Poland*, pp. 41–42, 44–48.

75. Edward B. Westermann, " 'Ordinary Men' or 'Ideological Soldiers'? Police Battalion 310 in Russia, 1942," esp. pp. 47–53; Longerich, *Politik der Vernichtung*, pp. 306–8.

76. Tessin, Kannipin, and Meyer, *Waffen-ss und Ordnungspolizei*, pp. 629–38; Longerich, *Politik der Vernichtung*, pp. 308–9. For case studies of some of these 300-level battalions, see Westermann, " 'Ordinary Men' or 'Ideological Soldiers'?"; Konrad Kwiet, "From the Diary of a Killing Unit"; Andrej Angrick et al., " 'Da hätte man schon ein Tagebuch führen müssen.' Das Polizeibataillon 322 und die Judenmorde im Bereich des Heeresgruppe Mitte während des Sommers und Herbstes 1941"; Klaus-Michael Mallmann, "Der Einstieg in den Genozid. Das Lübecker Polizeibatallion 307 und das Massaker in Brest-Litovsk Anfang Juli 1941"; Stefan Klemp, "Kölner Polizeibatallione in Osteuropa: Die Polizeibatallione 69, 309, 319 und die Polizeireservekompanie Köln"; Winfried Nachtwei, " 'Ganz normale Männer.' Die Verwicklung von Polizeibataillonen aus dem Rheinland

und Westfalen in den nationalsozialistischen Vernichtungskrieg"; Heiner Lichtenstein, *Himmlers grüne Helfer. Die Schutz- und Ordnungspolizei im "Dritten Reich"*; Lichtenstein, "Ein Lügenwirr—Der Wuppertaler Prozess gegen Angehörige des Polizeibatallions 309."

77. Acording to Tessin, Kannapin, and Meyer, *Waffen-ss und Ordnungspolizei*, pp. 635–37, Police Battalions 303, 304, 307, 309, 311, and 314 were all stationed in occupied Poland before Barbarossa, while 316, 317, 318, and 320 served in the Protectorate.

78. Ludwig Eiber, ed., " ' . . . ein bisschen die Wahrheit.' Briefe eines Bremer Kaufmanns von seinem Einsatz beim Reserve-Polizeibattalion 105 in der Sowjetunion"; Goldhagen, *Hitler's Willing Executioners*, pp. 191–94, for RPB 65. For the investigation of the especially lethal Reserve Police Battralion 45 in the Ukraine, see ZStL, II 204 AR-Z 1251/65.

79. Edward B. Westermann, "Himmler's Uniformed Police on the Eastern Front: The Reich's Secret Soldiers, 1941–1942."

80. BA, R 19/336, Daluege Vortrag on the manpower of the Order Police in 1941, February 1–4, 1942.

81. Browning, *Ordinary Men*, pp. 47–48.

82. Westermann, " 'Ordinary Men' or 'Ideological Soldiers'?," pp. 48–51. Westermann's figures do not separate NCOs and rank and file for party membership, so a direct statistical comparison cannot be made.

83. BA, R 19/308: Guidelines for training of police battalions, January 23, 1940.

84. BA, R 19/308: RFSS/CDP memo for the training of reserve police battalions, December 12, 1940.

85. BA, R 19/308: Guidelines for carrying out the ideological training of the Order Police during the war, June 2, 1940.

86. *Mitteilungsblätter für die weltanschauliche Schulung der Ordnungspolizei*, appearing every ten days, and *Schriftenreihe für die Weltanschauliche Schulung der Ordnungspolizei*, published 4–6 times per year, can be found in BA: R 19: RD 18/15-1, RD 18/15-2, RD 18/16, RD 18/19, RD 18/41, and RD 18/42.

87. Beginning in late 1941, with pamphlets such as "One Goal of This War: Europe Free of Jews" ("Ein Ziel dieses Krieges: Das judenfrei Europa"), the explicit anti-Semitic focus of these Order Police indoctrination materials sharpens considerably.

88. For these conclusions I am particularly indebted to the recent presentations at the Lessons and Legacies Conference, Minneapolis, November 2002, of Edward B. Westermann, "Ideology and Organizational Culture: Creating the Police Soldier, 1933–45"; and Jürgen Matthäus, "Antisemitism as an Offer." See also Matthäus et al., *Ausbildung Judenmord? "Weltanschauliche Erziehung" von SS, Polizei, und Waffen-SS im Rahmen der "Endlösung"*; Matthäus, "Ausbildung Judenmord? Zum Stellenwert der 'weltanschaulichen Erziehung' von SS und Polizei im Rahmen der 'Endlösung,' "; Matthäus, " 'Warum wird über das Judentum geschult?' Die ideologische Vorbereitung der deutschen Polizei auf den Holocaust"; and Matthäus, "An vorderster Front. Voraussetzungen für die Beteiligung der Ordnungspolizei an der Shoah."

89. YVA, TR-10/823, Judgment against Buchs and others, Landgericht Wuppertal, 12 Ks 1/67, pp. 29–30.

90. YVA, O/53/127, War Diary of Police Battalion 322, entries of June 6 and July 2, 1941.

91. Eiber, " ' . . . ein bisschen die Wahrheit,' " p. 67.

92. Yehoshua Büchler, "Kommandostab Reichsführer-SS: Himmler's Personal Murder Brigades in 1941," esp. pp. 13–15. For the Waffen-SS in general: Bernd Wegner, *Hitlers politische Soldaten. Die Waffen-SS 1939–1945: Leitbild, Struktur und Funktion einer nationalsozialistischen Elite.*

93. Bettina Birn, *Die Höheren SS- und Polizeiführer: Himmlers Vertreter im Reich und in den besetzten Gebieten*, pp. 10–12, 61–75, 331, 337, 339, 342.

94. Jacobsen, "Kommissarbefehl," pp. 184–85 (Doc. No. 9 [Nbg. Doc. NOKW-2079]: Himmler Memorandum, May 21, 1941).

95. Birn, *Die Höheren SS- und Polizeiführer*, pp. 363–99.

96. Aly and Heim, *Architects of Annihilation*; Koehl, RKFDV.

97. Rolf-Dieter Müller, "From Economic Alliance to a War of Colonial Exploitation," pp. 150–54.

98. Note on a conference of state secretaries, May 2, 1941, Nbg. Doc. 2718-PS, IMT, 31:84–85. Christian Gerlach, *Kalkulierte Morde. Die deutsche Wirtschafts- und Vernichtungspolitik in Weissrussland 1941 bis 1944*, pp. 46–47, presents a different interpretation of this document; see also Gerlach, "Die Ausweitung der deutschen Massenmorde in den besetzten sowjetischen Gebieten im Herbst 1941. Überlegungen zur Vernichtungspolitik gegen Juden und sowjetische Kriegsgefangene," in *Krieg, Ernährung, Völkermord*, pp. 10–84; Longerich, *Politik der Vernichtung*, p. 298; Aly, *"Final Solution,"* p. 185; Streit, *Keine Kameraden*, p. 63.

99. So far, there is no political biography of Rosenberg; on his role as party ideologue, see Fritz Nova, *Alfred Rosenberg: Nazi Theorist of the Holocaust*. On April 20, 1941, Rosenberg was appointed Bevollmächtigter für die zentrale Bearbeitung der Fragen des osteuropäischen Raumes (plenipotentiary for the central preparation of questions concerning the east European region).

100. Secret file note Heydrich (CdS B Nr. 3795/41) to Müller ("also for the information of Eichmann" [*auch zur Unterrichtung Eichmann*]), Schellenberg, Streckenbach, Filbert (for Jost), Ohlendorf ("only for personal, very confidential information" [*nur zur persönlichen, streng vertraulichen Information*]), March 26, 1941, Special Archive Moscow (hereafter cited as SAM) 500-3-795, fols. 140–45, extracts printed in Klein, *Die Einsatzgruppen in der besetzten Sowjetunion*, pp. 367–68; Aly, *"Final Solution,"* p. 172.

101. See *Der Dienstkalender Heinrich Himmlers 1941/42* (hereafter cited as DKHH), ed. Peter Witte et al., p. 119 n. 10.

102. Speech of Rosenberg at opening of Institut für die Erforschung der Judenfrage at Frankfurt am Main, March 28, 1941, BA NS 15/271.

103. Rosenberg diary entry, April 2, 1941, quoted from Robert M. W. Kempner, *SS im Kreuzverhör. Die Elite, die Europa in Scherben schlug*, p. 226.

104. Cited in Robert Kempner, *Eichmann und Komplizen*, p. 97.

105. Rosenberg Denkschrift 1 "betr. UdssR," April 2, 1941, Nbg. Doc. 1017-PS, IMT, 26:547–54.

106. Rosenberg diary entry, April 11, 1941, quoted from Kempner, *SS im Kreuzverhör*, p. 226.

107. Rosenberg memo "Allgemeiner Aufbau und Aufgaben einer Dienststelle für die zentrale Bearbeitung der Fragen des osteuropäischen Raumes," April 29, 1941, Nbg. Doc. 1024-PS, *IMT*, 26:560–66.

108. Rosenberg instructions for Reichskommissare Ukraine and "Ostland," May 7/8, 1941, Nbg. Doc. 1028-PS, 1029-PS, *IMT*, 26:567–76, partly printed in Norbert Müller, ed., *Die faschistische Okkupationspolitik in den zeitweilig besetzten Gebieten der Sowjetunion (1941–1944)*, pp. 128–32. Reichskommissare with regional subagencies (General-, Gebietskommissare) were originally planned for "Ostland" comprising the Baltic States and parts of Belorussia, Ukraine, Russia, and the Caucasus; because of the stalemate on the front, only Ostland and Ukraine became Reichskommissariate. See Timothy P. Mulligan, *The Politics of Illusion and Empire: German Occupation Policy in the Soviet Union, 1942–43*, pp. 123–35; Theo J. Schulte, *The German Army and Nazi Policies in Occupied Russia*, pp. 53–68.

109. On May 12/13, 1941, Warlimont and Jodl noted the discrepancy between the OKH's draft of the *Kommissarbefehl*, which called for the execution of leading political functionaries and commissars (*"Politische Hoheitsträger und Leiter [Kommissare] sind zu beseitigen"*), and Rosenberg's "Denkschrift 3," which targeted "higher and highest functionaries only" (*nur hohe und höchste Funktionäre zu erledigen*). In view of an anticipated decision by Hitler, Jodl recommended glossing over the army's intended measures as reprisals. Nbg. Doc. 884-PS, *IMT*, 26:406–8. Some of the "Barbarossa orders" are reprinted in facsimile in *Verbrechen der Wehrmacht. Dimensionen des Vernichtungskrieges 1941–1944*, pp. 43–55.

110. See Förster, "Operation Barbarossa as a War of Conquest," pp. 488–89; Gerlach, *Kalkulierte Morde*, p. 46 n. 60. Rosenberg claimed he had frequent conferences with representatives of the Ministry of Economics, the Wirtschaftsführungsstab Ost, and others before the war. Report by Rosenberg, June 28, 1941, Nbg. Doc. 1039-PS, *IMT*, 26:584–92.

111. Rosenberg, "Allgemeine Instruktion für alle Reichskommissare in den besetzten Ostgebieten," May 8, 1941, Nbg. Doc. 1030-PS, *IMT*, 26:576–80.

112. Wirtschaftsstab Ost, Gruppe La, Wirtschaftspolitische Richtlinien für Wirtschaftsorganisation Ost, Gruppe Landwirtschaft, May 23, 1941, Nbg. Doc. 126-EC, *IMT*, 36:135–57, partly printed in N. Müller, *Die faschistische Okkupationspolitik*, pp. 135–43. See also Gerlach, *Kalkulierte Morde*, pp. 48–51; Longerich, *Politik der Vernichtung*, pp. 298–99; Christoph Dieckmann, "Der Krieg und die Ermordung die litauischen Juden," p. 310. The Wirtschaftsstab Ost, subordinated to the Wirtschaftsführungsstab Ost under the direct control of Göring and led by his state secretary Körner in conjunction with, among others, Backe and General Thomas of the OKW's Wehrwirtschafts- und Rüstungsamt, was established to coordinate economic measures in the east. It comprised several groups (Führungsgruppe, Gruppe La, Gruppe W, Gruppe M) for different aspects of the economy in the occupied Soviet Union, where it supervised the work of other economic agencies, three Wirtschaftsinspektionen (economic inspectorates) at the Befehlshaber des rückwärtigen Heeresgebietes (commander of the rear army areas) and the Wirtschaftskommandos at the

Sicherungsdivisionen (economic commandos at the security divisions) (see Richtlinien für die Führung der Wirtschaft in den neubesetzten Ostgebieten [Grüne Mappe], Teil 1 [2. Auflage]: Aufgaben und Organisation der Wirtschaft, July 1941, Nbg. Doc. 472-EC, *IMT*, 36:542–45; Raul Hilberg, *The Destruction of the European Jews*, pp. 355–57.

113. Nbg. Doc. 126-EC, *IMT*, 36:140.

114. Nbg. Doc. 126-EC, *IMT*, 36:156.

115. Nbg. Doc. 126-EC, *IMT*, 36:138–40.

116. Nbg. Doc. 126-EC, *IMT*, 36:148–51.

117. Nbg. Doc. 126-EC, *IMT*, 36:146.

118. Nbg. Doc. 126-EC, *IMT*, 36:145.

119. Nbg. Doc. 126-EC, *IMT*, 36:146–47.

120. In line with his stress on German economic planning as a driving force for the treatment of the population in the occupied Soviet territories, Christian Gerlach claims that the document represents a "plan for destruction by hunger approved by Hitler." Gerlach, *Kalkulierte Morde*, p. 51; see also his "Die Ausweitung der deutschen Massenmorde," p. 17. While economic factors clearly influenced German politics, Gerlach's interpretation goes, in our opinion, too far. In regard to this specific document, he overlooks the vagueness of the reference to "higher authorities" and the exceptions provided for in the guidelines. In general, Gerlach tends to overstate the importance of prewar plans for the living conditions of the local population which, as shown in his excellent case study on Belorussia, seemed to be determined by the course of events following the German occupation.

121. Nbg. Doc. 126-EC, *IMT*, 36:142–43, 153–54.

122. Christian Streit, *Keine Kameraden*, pp. 62–82.

123. Rolf-Dieter Müller, "From Economic Alliance to a War of Colonial Exploitation, p. 181.

124. Rosenberg dairy entry, June 1, 1941, see Kempner, *SS im Kreuzverhör*, p. 226.

125. *Die Tagebücher von Joseph Goebbels I*, 4:705 (entry of June 20, 1941). This was only one of several occasions on which Goebbels, hearing about the misfortunes of the Jews, invoked the fulfillment of Hitler's prophecy. *Die Tagebücher von Joseph Goebbels*, Teil II, 1:269 (entry of August 19, 1941), and 3:561 (entry of March 23, 1942).

126. Frank, *Diensttagebuch*, pp. 386, 389 (entries of July 17 and 27, 1941). Even in mid-October 1941, Frank was still looking for a place in the east to resettle his Jews. *Dienst-tagebuch*, p. 413 (entry of October 14, 1941, on a discussion with Rosenberg on October 13).

127. Burrin, *Hitler and the Jews*, p. 100; Aly, *"Final Solution,"* p. 175.

128. Speech by Rosenberg "vor den engsten Beteiligten am Ostproblem," Nbg. Doc. 1058-PS, *IMT*, 26:610–27. The Kempner papers, Archive of the United States Holocaust Memorial Museum (USHMMA), Nuremberg box #4, contain handwritten notes dated June 6, 1941, for this speech.

129. Aly and Heim, *Architects of Annihilation*, pp. 253–55.

130. This meeting has now been dated to June 12–15, 1941, according to DKHH, pp. 172–74. For Bach-Zelewski's testimony dating it to March 1941, see *JNSV*, vol. 20 (Nr. 580, LG München II 1 Ks 1/64), p. 413 (trial of Karl Wolff). At his even earlier testimony at Nuremberg, Bach-Zelewski merely said that it took place early in 1941. *IMT*, 4:482–88.

131. Dietrich Eichholz, "Der 'Generalplan Ost.' Über eine Ausgeburt imperialistischer Denkart und Politik," p. 256 (Doc. Nr. 2: Meyer to Himmler, July 15, 1941); Breitman, *The Architect of Genocide*, p. 168.

132. Breitman, *The Architect of Genocide*, pp. 177, 184–86.

133. Helmut Heiber, ed., "Der Generalplan Ost," pp. 300, 308, 313 (Doc. Nr. 2: Stellungnahme und Gedanken zum Generalplan Ost des Reichsführer ss, by Wetzel, April 27, 1942).

134. Czeslaw Madajczyk, "Generalplan Ost." For the burgeoning literature on Generalplan Ost, see also Madayczyk, "Was the Generalplan Ost Synchronous with the Final Solution?"; Rolf-Dieter Müller, *Hitlers Ostkrieg und die deutsche Siedlungspolitik*, pp. 94–110; Aly and Heim, *Architects of Annihilation*, pp. 253–82; and Mechtild Rössler and Sabine Schleiermacher, eds., *Der "Generalplan Ost": Hauptlinien der nationalsozialistischen Planungs- und Vernichtungspolitik*.

135. Burrin, *Hitler and the Jews*, pp. 99, 196, is the first scholar to note these implications.

136. Safrian, *Die Eichmann-Männer*, pp. 23–36.

137. See R.-D. Müller, *Hitlers Ostkrieg und die deutsche Siedlungspolitik*, pp. 25–39; quotation from OKW / AWABW Sied., Merkblatt Nr. 1 über die Ansiedlung von Wehrmachtsangehörigen in den neu eingegliederten Ostgebieten, May 16, 1941, in *Hitlers Ostkrieg*, pp. 142–46, on p. 143. Von Leeb and von Rundstedt, the commanders of Army Groups North and South, both received a check for over 250,000 RM from Hitler on the occasion of their 65th birthdays, on September 5 and December 12, 1941, respectively. See Gert R. Ueberschär and Winfried Vogel, *Dienen und Verdienen. Hitlers Geschenke an seine Eliten*, pp. 151, 157.

138. Nbg. Doc. 126-EC, *IMT*, 36:154–55.

139. See Birn, *Die Höheren ss- und Polizeiführer*, pp. 331, 337, 339, 342, 391–95.

140. See Breitman, *Official Secrets*, pp. 39–40; Matthäus, " 'Warum wird über das Judentum geschult?,' " p. 110.

141. See Mommsen, "Hitlers Stellung im nationalsozialistischen Herrschaftssystem."

142. Werner Jochmann, ed., *Monologe im Führerhauptquartier 1941–1944*, p. 82 (entry for October 14, 1941).

7. Operation Barbarossa and the Onset of the Holocaust

1. Historiography on the German war against the Soviet Union has benefited immensely in the last ten years from regional and local case studies as well as from in-depth research into German crimes committed against Jews, POWs, and other groups regarded as "enemies of the Reich." In developing my argument, I am especially indebted to Christopher Browning, who invited me to contribute to this book, and to the many other scholars referred to in the notes.

2. Longerich, *Politik der Vernichtung*, p. 418; Hilberg, *The Destruction of the European Jews*, p. 341; Streit, *Keine Kameraden*, pp. 105, 128. Lack of reliable sources make a more precise estimate impossible.

3. The classical monograph studies are Alexander Dallin, *German Rule in Russia, 1941–*

1945: A Study of Occupation Policies; Gerald Reitlinger, *The House Built on Sand: The Conflicts of German Policy in Russia, 1939–1945*. More recently and with special focus on the murder of the Jews in the occupied Soviet Union, Hilberg, *The Destruction of the European Jews*, pp. 271–390; Leni Yahil, *The Holocaust: The Fate of European Jewry, 1932–1945*, pp. 253–305; Wolf Kaiser, ed., *Täter im Vernichtungskrieg. Der Überfall auf die Sowjetunion und der Völkermord an den Juden*.

4. Hans Mommsen, "The Realization of the Unthinkable: The 'Final Solution of the Jewish Question' in the Third Reich."

5. Ian Kershaw, *Hitler 1889–1936: Hubris*, pp. 246–48; from a different perspective, Eberhard Jäckel, *Hitler's Weltanschauung: A Blueprint for Power*, pp. 32–38.

6. So far, no systematic study of the German "eastern experience" in occupied Poland or the Soviet Union has been undertaken. For important elements, see Aly and Heim, *Architects of Annihilation*, pp. 115–129; Hans-Heinrich Wilhelm, "Motivation und 'Kriegsbild' deutscher Generale und Offiziere im Krieg gegen die Sowjetunion." Crucial for understanding the historical framework is Michael Burleigh, *Germany Turns Eastward*. For the impact of World War I, see Vejas G. Liulevicius, *War Land on the Eastern Front: Culture, National Identity, and German Occupation in World War I*.

7. Steven E. Aschheim, *Brothers and Strangers: The East European Jew in German and German Jewish Consciousness, 1800–1923*, pp. 139–56; Jürgen Matthäus, "German Judenpolitik in Lithuania during the First World War."

8. Peter Jahn, " 'Russenfurcht' und Antibolschewismus: Zur Entstehung und Wechselwirkung von Feindbildern," pp. 47–56; "bandits" quoted from Colonel General Hoepner, May 2, 1941, on p. 49. See also Jürgen Förster, "The German Army and the Ideological War against the Soviet Union."

9. Meeting with "General zu besonderer Verfügung beim Oberbefehlshaber des Heeres" Müller in Warsaw, June 11, 1941, quoted from Förster, "Operation Barbarossa as a War of Conquest," pp. 502–3. On Müller, see ibid., p. 499. For army leaders, see Andreas Hillgruber, "Das Russland-Bild der führenden deutschen Militärs vor Beginn des Angriffs auf die Sowjetunion," pp. 125–28.

10. The nature of the conservative merging of anti-Semitism, anticommunism, and geopolitical stereotypes has so far not been analyzed in detail. For some of its elements, see Jahn, "Russenfurcht," pp. 47–50; Kai-Uwe Merz, *Das Schreckbild. Deutschland und der Bolschewismus 1917 bis 1921*, pp. 402–12, 432–48.

11. Hilberg, *The Destruction of the European Jews*, pp. 90–91; Kershaw, *Hitler 1889–1936*, pp. 517–18. In general, see Michael Geyer, "Etudes in Political History: Reichswehr, NSDAP, and the Seizure of Power"; Manfred Messerschmidt, *Die Wehrmacht im NS-Staat. Zeit der Indoktrination*.

12. Quoted in Förster, "Operation Barbarossa as a War of Conquest," pp. 512–13.

13. Allgemeines Wehrmachtsamt Abt. Inland, Schulungshefte für den Unterricht über nationalsozialistische Weltanschauung und nationalpolitische Zielsetzung, Heft 5/1: Der Jude in der deutschen Geschichte, quoted from Messerschmidt, *Die Wehrmacht im NS-Staat*, p. 354.

14. Christian Gerlach, "Männer des 20. Juli und der Krieg gegen die Sowjetunion."

15. Omer Bartov, *The Eastern Front, 1941–1945: German Troops and the Barbarization of Warfare*, pp. 76–105. For the SS, police, and Waffen-SS, see Matthäus et al., *Ausbildungsziel Judenmord?*

16. Rossino, "Destructive Impulses"; Matthäus et al., *Ausbildungsziel Judenmord?*, pp. 31–32.

17. Manfred Weissbecker, " 'Wenn hier Deutsche wohnten . . .' Beharrung und Veränderung im Russlandbild Hitlers und der NSDAP," pp. 30–33. See also Brauchitsch guidelines for the "weltanschauliche Erziehung" of army soldiers and officers of October 7, 1940, with no mention of "Jewish Bolshevism" because of the German-Soviet pact (in Förster, "Operation Barbarossa as a War of Conquest," p. 514).

18. Bartov, *The Eastern Front*, pp. 12–21.

19. See Edward Shils and Morris Janowitz, "Cohesion and Disintegration in the Wehrmacht in World War II," p. 368.

20. Quoted from Streit, *Keine Kameraden*, pp. 34–35.

21. Hitler monologue, September 17 / 18, 1941, from *Monologe im Führerhauptquartier*, pp. 61–64.

22. Order by Colonel General Hoepner, Panzergruppe 4, May 2, 1941, quoted from Förster, "Operation Barbarossa as a War of Conquest," p. 520. See also Mallmann, "Die Türöffner der 'Endlösung.' "

23. Drafts by "General zu besonderer Verfügung beim ObdH" Müller, May 6, 1941, Nbg. Doc. 877-PS, IMT, 26:401–6.

24. "Erlass über die Ausübung der Gerichtsbarkeit im Gebiet 'Barbarossa' und über besondere Massnahmen der Truppe," May 13, 1941, partly printed in N. Müller, *Die faschistische Okkupationspolitik*, pp. 132–34.

25. Meeting of I c officers, May 24, 1941, Nbg. Doc. NOKW-486.

26. OKW / WPr "Richtlinien für das Verhalten der Truppe in Russland," May 19, 1941; quoted from N. Müller, *Die faschistische Okkupationspolitik*, pp. 134–35.

27. OKW / WFSt "Weisungen für die Handhabung der Propaganda im Fall 'Barbarossa,' " "Mitteilungen für die Truppe" issued on or after June 22, quoted in Förster, "Operation Barbarossa as a War of Conquest," pp. 515–16.

28. Chef OKW (Keitel) "Richtlinien für die Behandlung politischer Kommissare," June 6, 1941, BA-MA RW 4 / v.578, partly printed in N. Müller, *Die faschistische Okkupationspolitik*, pp. 145–46. The order was distributed on June 8 by the OKH, in writing only up to army level, further down orally. See Förster, "Operation Barbarossa as a War of Conquest," p. 510; Longerich, *Politik der Vernichtung*, pp. 300–301.

29. OKW Abt. Kriegsgefangene, June 16, 1941, BA-MA RW 4 / v.578, quoted in Förster, "Operation Barbarossa as a War of Conquest," pp. 486–87. Streit, *Keine Kameraden*, pp. 74–75, argues that the lack of provisions for reports to the central registration office, the Wehrmachtsauskunftsstelle, was based on the expectation of an exceptionally high death rate among the POWs, and that the absence of any mention of Jews implied the existence of a "special order."

30. Browning, *Ordinary Men*. For a different interpretation based on preconceived notions about the quality of German anti-Semitism, see Goldhagen, *Hitler's Willing Executioners*.

31. See Birn, *Die Höheren SS- und Polizeiführer*, pp. 363–95; Breitman, *Official Secrets*, pp. 38–40.

32. See Jens Banach, *Das Führerkorps der Sicherheitspolizei und des SD 1936–1945*; George C. Browder, *Hitler's Enforcers: The Gestapo and the SS Security Service in the Nazi Revolution*.

33. Konrad Kwiet, "Erziehung zum Mord—Zwei Beispiele zur Kontinuität der deutschen 'Endlösung der Judenfrage.' "

34. Kershaw, *The "Hitler Myth,"* p. 4.

35. Kwiet, "Erziehung zum Mord," pp. 446–48. In general on ideological indoctrination in the SS and police, see Matthäus et al., *Ausbildungsziel Judenmord?*, p. 692. For the deployment of Security Police trainees from the "Führerschule" Charlottenburg, see Andrej Angrick, "Die Einsatzgruppe D. Struktur und Tätigkeit einer mobilen Einheit der Sicherheitspolizei und des SD in der deutsch besetzten Sowjetunion," pp. 202–3; Mallmann, "Die Türöffner der 'Endlösung.' "

36. RSHA IV (N) 950/41, May 22, 1941, based on a repoort by Stapostelle Tilsit III E5d68/41g, May 16, 1941. Central State Archive (CSA) Vilnius 1173-1-7, fol. 24. See also Michael MacQueen, "Nazi Policy toward the Jews in the Reichskommissariat Ostland, June–December 1941: From White Terror to Holocaust in Lithuania"; MacQueen, "The Context of Mass Destruction: Agents and Prerequisites of the Holocaust in Lithuania."

37. See Krausnick and Wilhelm, *Die Truppe des Weltanschauungskrieges*, pp. 36–51.

38. CdS I B 1 (Heydrich), "Richtlinien für den Einsatz der Sicherheitspolizei und des SD in Norwegen," April 14, 1940, SAM 500-5-3, fol. 2.

39. OKH order re: deployment of Sipo/SD in Balkan war, April 2, 1941, BA-MA RH 31-I/v.23. For the Balkan campaign, see Browning, *Fateful Months*, pp. 39–56.

40. The following description of events in Garsden is based on the court verdict by Landgericht Ulm, August 29, 1958, printed in *JNSV*, vol. 15, no. 465, pp. 53–61. See also Konrad Kwiet, "Rehearsing for Murder: The Beginning of the Final Solution in Lithuania in June 1941"; Dieckmann, "Der Krieg und die Ermordung der litauischen Juden," pp. 295–99; Jürgen Matthäus, "Jenseits der Grenze."

41. *JNSV*, 15:61.

42. See, e.g., Helmut Krausnick, who based his assumption that an order for the killing of all Jews had been issued before the war on the testimony of Böhme and the other defendants in the Ulm trial (Krausnick and Wilhelm, *Die Truppe des Weltanschauungskrieges*, pp. 162–63). Stahlecker was killed in early 1942 in an antipartisan action. Heydrich delivered the eulogy at his funeral service (see BA, RD 81/1: *Die Deutsche Polizei*, April 15, 1942, pp. 113–14).

43. Stapostelle Tilsit to RSHA IV (Müller), July 1, 1941, SAM 500-1-758, fols. 2–5; partly printed in Wolfgang Benz, Konrad Kwiet, and Jürgen Matthäus, eds., *Einsatz im "Reichskommissariat Ostland." Dokumente zum Völkermord im Baltikum und in Weissrussland 1941–1944*, pp. 73–74.

44. Ereignismeldung (EM) 26, July 18, 1941, printed in Yitzhak Arad, Shmuel Krakowski, and Shmuel Spector, eds., *The Einsatzgruppen Reports: Selections from the Dispatches of the Nazi Death Squads' Campaign against the Jews in Occupied Territories of the Soviet Union, July 1941–January 1943*, p. 36.

45. Quotes from postwar investigations by Landgericht Wuppertal in Longerich, *Die Politik der Vernichtung*, pp. 345–48. See also Gerlach, *Kalkulierte Morde*, pp. 542–43; Browning, *Ordinary Men*, pp. 11–13; Klaus-Michael Mallmann, Volker Riess, and Wolfram Pyta, eds., *Deutscher Osten 1939–1945. Der Weltanschauungskrieg in Photos und Texten*, pp. 70–77.

46. See Hilberg, *The Destruction of the European Jews*, pp. 291–334.

47. Since the late 1980s most historians agree on the absence of such a plan. See Christopher R. Browning, "Beyond 'Intentionalism' and 'Functionalism': The Decision for the Final Solution Reconsidered," in *The Path to Genocide*, pp. 88–101.

48. Tätigkeitsbericht Kommandostab RF-SS, July 17, 1941, USHMMA RG 48.004m, reel 1 (MHA Prague KdoS RF-SS). See also Gerlach, *Kalkulierte Morde*, p. 555.

49. See Breitman, *Architect of Genocide*, pp. 168–70; Pohl, "Einsatzgruppe C," p. 72.

50. See Angrick et al., " 'Da hätte man schon ein Tagebuch führen müssen,' " p. 331.

51. The administrative status of the occupied area differed according to its proximity to the front line and the speed of the German advance. Once the fighting units of the Army Groups North, Center, and South had moved on, the rear area was first declared a "rear operation area" (*rückwärtiges Armeegebiet*), later, after the Wehrmacht had pushed further east, a "rear army area" (*rückwärtiges Heeresgebiet*). In each army group, the commander for the rear army area (Befehlshaber rückwärtiges Heeresgebiet Nord, Mitte, Süd) had at his disposal three security divisions (Sicherungsdivisionen) and an Order Police regiment. As outlined in the planning stages of Operation Barbarossa, the occupied territory was earmarked for transfer to the civil administration as part of Rosenberg's Ostministerium, established in mid-July 1941. The German failure to crush the Red Army resulted in a dual system of occupation, the western part subordinated to civilian commissioners (Reichskommissariate Ostland and Ukraine) while the eastern part remained under military administration. The Einsatzgruppen of the Security Police and the SD as well as the HSSPF operated in both areas, relying heavily on Order Police battalions. In the western parts, the Einsatzgruppen became stationary agencies attached to the office of the Reichskommissar (as Befehlshaber der Sicherheitspolizei und des SD, BdS) or the Generalkommissar (as Kommandeur der Sicherheitspolizei und des SD, KdS); in the east they remained mobile. See Krausnick and Wilhelm, *Die Truppe der Weltanschauungskrieges*, pp. 285–89.

52. Angrick et al., " "Da hätte man schon ein Tagebuch führen müssen,' " p. 334.

53. The date of this massacre, which is not explicitely mentioned in the war diary of Police Battalion 322, remains unclear; see Angrick et al., " 'Da hätte man schon ein Tagebuch führen müssen,' " pp. 333–36; Gerlach, *Kalkulierte Morde*, p. 543; Browning, *Nazi Policy*, pp. 120–21. Also on Police Battalion 322: Kwiet, "From the Diary of a Killing Unit." For some of Daluege's trips to the east, see Breitman, *Official Secrets*, pp. 47–48, 261 n. 8.

54. Matthäus et al., *Ausbildungsziel Judenmord?*, p. 77. Gerlach, "Einsatzgruppe B," p. 56, raises the question whether the visits by Himmler, Heydrich, and Daluege were signs of insecurity over the course of action. For a different interpretation, see again Browning, *Nazi Policy* pp. 120–21.

55. Angrick et al., " 'Da hätte man schon ein Tagebuch führen müssen,' " pp. 335–36.

56. Polizeiregiment Mitte Ia (Montua) to Polizeibatallione 307, 316, 322, July 11, 1941,

MHA Prague SS.-Pol.Rgt. karton 1; printed in Benz et al., *Einsatz im "Reichskommissariat Ostland,"* pp. 75–76. See also Browning, *Ordinary Men*, pp. 13–14; Matthäus et al., *Ausbildungsziel Judenmord?*, pp. 74–75.

57. For examples, see Arad et al., *The Einsatzgruppen Reports*, pp. 9, 14–15, 46, 69–70, 78.

58. *Verbrechen der Wehrmacht*, pp. 78–83.

59. Bartov, *The Eastern Front*, pp. 107–19; Christian Gerlach, "Verbrechen deutscher Fronttruppen in Weissrussland 1941–1944. Eine Annäherung"; Streit, *Keine Kameraden*; Streit, "The German Army and the Policies of Genocide."

60. Report by Xaver Dorsch to Rosenberg, July 10, 1941, Nbg. Doc. 022-PS, IMT, 25:81–83; printed in Paul Kohl, *"Ich wundere mich, dass ich noch lebe." Sowjetische Augenzeugen berichten*, p. 220.

61. Gerlach, *Kalkulierte Morde*, pp. 506–10.

62. KTB IV. Armeekorps, July 2, 1941, quoted from Pohl, *Nationalsozialistische Judenverfolgung in Ostgalizien 1941–1944*, p. 70.

63. Panzergruppe 4 (Hoepner) to OKH, July 12, 1941, BA-MA AOK 17/14499/51, quoted in Streit, *Keine Kameraden*, p. 124.

64. EM 14, July 6, 1941; EM 21, July 13, 1941, EM 24, July 16, 1941, partly printed in Arad et al., *The Einsatzgruppen Reports*, pp. 10–12, 22–24, 27–33; Situation Report EK 1b, July 1, 1941, SAM 500-1-756, fols. 4–6. For Galicia, see Pohl, *Judenverfolgung in Ostgalizien*, pp. 59–69. Bogdan Musial, *"Konterrevolutionäre Elemente sind zu erschiessen." Die Brutalisierung des deutsch-sowjetischen Krieges im Sommer 1941* overstates German behavior as reactive.

65. Browning, *Nazi Policy*, pp. 118–21, stresses that these killings in Brest, following the "course of events in nearby Bialystok," resulted from orders given by Daluege and Schenckendorff, as testified to after the war by members of Police Battalion 307. Gerlach, *Kalkulierte Morde*, pp. 547, notes that on this point the witness statements widely disagree. See also Mallmann, "Der Einstieg in den Genozid."

66. EM 19, July 11, 1941, quoted from Arad et al., *The Einsatzgruppen Reports*, pp. 17–18.

67. For Minsk, see Gerlach, *Kalkulierte Morde*, pp. 523–24.

68. Benz et al., *Einsatz im "Reichskommissariat Ostland,"* pp. 122–23; Gerlach, *Kalkulierte Morde*, pp. 525–26. The first central order by the OKH regarding ghettoization was issued on August 19, 1941 (no copy survived); according to a directive by the commander of the rear army area north, this order did not present ghettoization as a pressing task for the military and advised coordination with the HSSPF (Benz et al., *Einsatz im "Reichskommissariat Ostland,"* p. 123).

69. In accordance with the Hedyrich-Wagner cooperation agreement, the Wehrmacht and Einsatzgruppen were in regular contact. Heydrich preferred to appoint as liaison Einsatzgruppen officers who knew their Wehrmacht counterparts from before the beginning of Operation Barbarossa, as in the case of the leaders of Einsatzgruppe A and B (Stahlecker and Nebe) operating in the areas of the commander of the rear army area north and center (von Roques and Schenckendorff). Krausnick and Wilhelm, *Die Truppe des Weltanschauungskrieges*, pp. 222–26; Gerlach, *Kalkulierte Morde*, p. 544; *Verbrechen der Wehrmacht*, p. 85.

70. Margers Vestermanis, "Ortskommandantur Libau. Zwei Monate deutscher Besatzung im Sommer 1941"; with stronger emphasis on the role of the German Navy, Hans-Ludger Borgert, "Die Kriegsmarine und das Unternehmen 'Barbarossa' " (I thank Jürgen Förster for a copy of this article).

71. Report by EG B (Nebe) to RSHA for period June 23 to July 13, printed in Klein, *Die Einsatzgruppen*, pp. 375–85. For the murder of Jews from the Minsk ghetto in August/September see Gerlach, *Kalkulierte Morde*, pp. 567–69.

72. Pohl, *Judenverfolgung in Ostgalizien*, pp. 71–73; similarly, Pohl, "Einsatzgruppe C," p. 73. A security police unit of the BdS Krakau deployed in Eastern Poland (later referred to as "Einsatzgruppe z.b.V.") reported 1,726 executions since July 2, 1941. See Krausnick and Wilhelm, *Die Truppe des Weltanschauungskrieges*, pp. 180–81, 186; Dieter Pohl, "Hans Krüger and the Murder of the Jews in the Stanislawow Region (Galicia)"; Gerlach, *Kalkulierte Morde*, pp. 540–41.

73. Gerlach, "Einsatzgruppe B," p. 62.

74. Gerlach, "Die Ausweitung der deutschen Massenmorde," in *Krieg, Ernährung, Völkermord*, p. 58.

75. Quoted from Eiber, " '. . . ein bisschen die Wahrheit,' " p. 71.

76. Report by 295 Inf.Div/Ic, July 3, 1941, BA-MA RH 26-295/16, fol. 60. The pogrom lasted until July 7; it cost the lives of about 2,000 victims and was assisted if not instigated by SK 4b and the German Feldgendarmerie (see Pohl, *Judenverfolgung in Ostgalizien*, pp. 62–63).

77. EK 3, "Gesamtaufstellung der im Bereiche des EK 3 bis jetzt durchgeführten Exekutionen," September 10, 1941, USHMMA RG 11.001m, reel 183 (SAM 500-1-25), entries for June/July. See also EM 54, August 16, 1941, in Arad et al., *The Einsatzgruppen Reports*, pp. 90–91.

78. Pohl, *Judenverfolgung in Ostgalizien*, pp. 64–65.

79. Pol.Rgt. Mitte Ia to Pol.Btl. 307, 316, 322, NSKK-Komp. Berlin, Stuttgart, Nürnberg, 27 July 1941, MHA Prague Pol.Rgt.

80. Gerlach, *Kalkulierte Morde*, p. 277; Pohl, "Einsatzgruppe C," p. 74.

81. Quoted from Eiber, " '. . . ein bisschen die Wahrheit,' " p. 73.

82. Hilberg, *The Destruction of the European Jews*, pp. 318–20. As an example: "Gesamtaufstellung der im Bereich des EK 3 bis zum 1. Dezember 1941 durchgeführten Exekutionen," 1 December 1941, partly printed in Yitzhak Arad, Yisrael Gutman, and Abraham Margaliot, eds., *Documents on the Holocaust: Selected Sources on the Destruction of the Jews of Germany and Austria, Poland, and the Soviet Union*, pp. 398–400, in which Jäger describes the process as a mere "organizational problem." For accounts by survivors of mass executions or eyewitnesses, see ibid., pp. 421–25, 427–30; Peter Longerich, ed., *Die Ermordung der europäischen Juden: Eine umfassende Dokumentation des Holocaust*, pp. 127–29, 146–48.

83. See examples in Benz et al., *Einsatz im "Reichskommissariat Ostland,"* pp. 85, 92–93; Arad et al., *Documents on the Holocaust*, p. 388.

84. See Hilberg, *The Destruction of the European Jews*, pp. 317–20; Knut Stang, *Kollaboration und Massenmord. Die litauische Hilfspolizei, das Rollkommando Hamann und die Ermordung der litauischen Juden*, pp. 257–67.

85. Report by Wirtschaftsstab Ost, July 16, 1941, BA-MA RW 31/66, fols. 11–12, quoted

in Pohl, *Judenverfolgung in Ostgalzien*, pp. 46–47. Nevertheless, owing to the lack of expert laborers, Jews had to be brought back to work in the Drohobycz oil refinery. See Thomas Sandkühler, *"Endlösung" in Galizien: Der Judenmord in Ostpolen und die Rettungsiniativen von Berthold Beitz, 1941–1944*, pp. 314–15.

86. See reports by Wirtschaftsstab Ost, July 14, 1941, BA-MA RW 31/11 (quoted in Aly, *"Final Solution,"* p. 190); July 15, 1941, CSA Riga P70-2-52, fol. 202 (quoted in Dieckmann, "Der Krieg und die Ermordung der litauischen Juden," p. 299). This was the case in Riga; see report Wirtschaftskommando Riga to Wirtschaftsinspektion Nord, July 21, 1941, Nbg. Doc. PS-579.

87. Report re meeting of army officers at Amtschef OKW Wehrwirtschafts- und Rüstungsamt (Thomas), July 31, 1941, partly printed in N. Müller, *Die faschistische Okkupationspolitik*, pp. 178–80. For examples of anti-Jewish orders, see Benz et al., *Einsatz im "Reichskommissariat Ostland,"* pp. 119–21.

88. Report by Wirtschaftsstab Ost for June 22 to July 5, July 10, 1941, BA-MA RW 31/66, fol. 2.

89. Report by German official (Sonderführer Schröter) re Belorussia, July 12, 1941, YIVO Occ E3a-2. For lack of an alternative, the same reasoning was applied by most Jewish councils in the ghettos; see Raul Hilberg, "The Ghetto as a Form of Government"; Isaiah Trunk, *Judenrat*, pp. 400–413.

90. CdS Amtschef IV (Heydrich) to EG, June 29, 1941, partly printed in Arad et al., *Documents on the Holocaust*, pp. 377–78.

91. CdS (Heydrich) to leaders of Einsatzgruppen, July 1, 1941, printed in Klein, *Die Einsatzgruppen*, pp. 321–22. Gerlach, "Einsatzgruppe B," p. 53, points out that Heydrich's preference for a speedy advance left even less time for large-scale killing actions.

92. Heydrich to HSSPF, July 2, 1941; partly printed in Longerich, *Die Ermordung der europäischen Juden*, pp. 116–18.

93. Mommsen, "The Realization of the Unthinkable," pp. 99–100. According to a postwar statement by an Einsatzgruppen officer, the Ereignismeldungen were designed to subject the government offices to the dynamic of the escalating killing process ("Regierungsstellen sturmreif schiessen"; quoted from Longerich, *Politik der Vernichtung*, p. 314).

94. Copy of radio message by RSHA IV A 1 b (Müller) to Einsatzgruppen, August 1, 1941, USHMMA RG 11.001m, reel 183 (SAM 500-1-25, fol. 416).

95. CdS (Heydrich) to leaders of Einsatzgruppen, July 4, 1941, quoted from Klein, *Die Einsatzgruppen*, pp. 329–30.

96. See, e.g., Pol.Rgt. Mitte Ia to Pol.Btl. 307, 316, 322, NSKK-Komp. Berlin, Stuttgart, Nürnberg, 27 July 1941, MHA Prague Pol.Rgt.; Funkspruch by Sonderzug "Heinrich" (Grothmann) to 1. SS-Brigade (Herrmann) via HSSPF Russland-Süd (Jeckeln), August 11, 1941, BA NS 33/312, fol. 26; Kommandostab RF-SS (Knoblauch) to HSSPF Russland-Süd (Jeckeln), August 12, 1941, BA NS 33/312, fol. 23. For communication problems between the SS leadership and the units at the eastern periphery, see Breitman, *Official Secrets*, pp. 56–57.

97. See Breitman, *Official Secrets*, pp. 91–93. Breitman quotes a speech by Winston Churchill of August 24, 1941, in which he refers to the killings in Russia as "methodical,

merciless butchery" unprecedented in European history since the Mongol invasion. See also Breitman, *Architect of Genocide*, p. 179.

98. CdS directive to security police agencies, September 3, 1941 (printed in Benz et al., *Einsatz im "Reichskommissariat Ostland,"* pp. 68–69). For the temporary stop of "Aktion T 4" see Friedlander, *The Origins of Nazi Genocide*, p. 111.

99. Hitler monologue, September 17/18, 1941, in *Monologe im Führerhauptquartier*, pp. 61–64.

100. See Klaus Latzel, *Deutsche Soldaten—nationalsozialistischer Krieg? Kriegserlebnis, Kriegserfahrung 1939–1945* (quotation: direction by Reichspressechef for German press, July 5, 1941, p. 180).

101. See Walter Manoschek, ed., *"Es gibt nur eines für das Judentum: Vernichtung." Das Judenbild in deutschen Soldatenbriefen 1939–1944*, based on a small selection from about 50,000 letters contained in the "Sammlung Sterz" held at the Bibliothek für Zeitgeschichte in Stuttgart. Among 739 letters evaluated, Martin Humburg, *Das Gesicht des Krieges. Feldpostbriefe von Wehrmachtssoldaten aus der Sowjetunion 1941–1944*, pp. 197–205, counts only 15 that mention Jews, while derogatory remarks about primitive conditions were much more frequent. For letters by Wehrmacht soldiers, see *Verbrechen der Wehrmacht*, pp. 629–36. For photographic images, see Sybil Milton, "The Camera as a Weapon: Documentary Photography and the Holocaust"; on wartime photography, see Bernd Hüppauf, "Der entleerte Blick hinter der Kamera"; Alexander B. Rossino, "Eastern Europe through German Eyes: Soldiers' Photographs 1939–42"; Nechama Tec and Daniel Weiss, "The Heroine of Minsk: Eight Photographs of an Execution," pp. 322–30. More research based on private photographic or written sources is needed to arrive at a fuller picture of German perceptions about the east and their change over time.

102. Humburg, *Das Gesicht des Krieges*, pp. 152–55; in general, see Bartov, *The Eastern Front*.

103. Quoted from Hamburg Institute for Social Research, ed., *The German Army and Genocide: Crimes against War Prisoners, Jews, and Other Civilians in the East, 1939–1944*, p. 82; also in Manoschek, *"Es gibt nur eines für das Judentum,"* p. 33. For the pogroms in Tarnopol, see also *Verbrechen der Wehrmacht*, pp. 100–108.

104. File memorandum regarding discussion between Hitler, Rosenberg, Lammers, Keitel, and Göring, July 16, 1941, Nbg. Doc. 221-L, IMT, 38:86–88, emphases in the original. Lammers testified after the war that Bormann, the likely author of the memorandum, expressed his strong bias against Rosenberg in phrasing the document (TWC, 12:1329–30).

105. Compare Rosenberg's instructions for a RK Ukraine and a RK Ostland, May 7/8, 1941, Nbg. Doc. 1028-PS, 1029-PS, IMT, 26:567–76.

106. Rosenberg diary entry, July 16, 1941, USHMMA Kempner papers, Nuremberg box #4. The fate of the original diary after it was partly translated for the Nuremberg trial proceedings is unknown; a segment was published in 1956 by Hans-Günther Seraphim as *Das politische Tagebuch Alfred Rosenbergs 1935/36 und 1939/40*.

107. Nbg. Doc. 221-L, IMT, 38:91, emphasis in the original.

108. Nbg. Doc. 221-L, IMT, 38:92, emphasis in the original.

109. Rosenberg diary entry, July 16, 1941, USHMMA Kempner papers, Nuremberg box #4, emphasis in the original. See also diary entry of Otto Bräutigam of July 16, 1941, in Braütigam, "Aus dem Kriegstagebuch des Diplomaten Otto Bräutigam," pp. 136–37.

110. Browning, *The Path to Genocide*, pp. 111, 113.

111. Kommandostab RF-SS Ic Tätigkeitsbericht Nr. 7, July 28, 1941, USHMMA RG 48.004m, reel 1 (MHA Prague KdoS RF-SS).

112. Diary entry of von Leeb for July 8, 1941, quoted from Jürgen Förster, "Securing 'Living Space,'" p. 1206.

113. See letter from Lammers to Rosenberg, July 18, 1941, transmitting "Decree of the Führer on the Appointment of Armed Forces Commanders in the Newly Occupied Eastern Territories," June 25, 1941; "Decree of the Führer on the Economy in the Newly Occupied Eastern Territories," June 29, 1941; "Decree of the Führer concerning the Administration of the Newly Occupied Eastern Territories"; and "First Decree of the Führer on the Introduction of the Civil Administration in the Newly Occupied Eastern Territories," Nbg. Doc. NG-1280, *TWC*, 12:1298–1303; "Führer Decree concerning Police Security within the Newly Occupied Eastern Territories," July 17, 1941, Nbg. Doc. NG-1688, *TWC*, 12:1303–4.

114. Nbg. Doc. 710-PS, *IMT*, 26:266–67.

115. Reichskommissariat Ostland was formed on July 25 and at that time comprised parts of Lithuania and Latvia. The area of Vilnius and the remaining parts of Lithuania were added on August 1, Latvia and parts of Belorussia on September 1, and Estonia on December 5, 1941. Reichskommissariat Ukraine was formed on September 1 and enlarged on October 20 and November 15, 1941, to cover the area west of the river Dnieper. See Förster, "Securing 'Living Space,'" pp. 1238–40; Scheffler, "Einsatzgruppe A," p. 47 n. 25; Pohl, "Einsatzgruppe C," p. 81.

116. Raul Hilberg, *Perpetrators, Victims, Bystanders: The Jewish Catastrophe, 1933–1945*.

117. Heydrich to Einsatzgruppen, June 29, 1941, partly printed in Longerich, *Die Ermordung der europäischen Juden*, pp. 118–19.

118. Nechama Tec's *When Light Pierced the Darkness: Christian Rescue of Jews in Nazi-Occupied Poland* is important for much more than the Polish case.

119. EK 3, "Gesamtaufstellung der im Bereiche des EK 3 bis jetzt durchgeführten Exekutionen," September 10, 1941 USHMMA RG 11.001m, reel 183 (SAM 500-1-25), fols. 104–7, partly printed in Reinhard Rürup, ed., *Erobern und Vernichtung. Der Krieg gegen die Sowjetunion 1941–1945. Eine Dokumentation*, pp. 118–20; "Gesamtaufstellung der im Bereich des EK 3 bis zum 1. Dezember 1941 durchgeführten Exekutionen," December 1, 1941, USHMMA RG 11.001m, reel 183 (SAM 500-1-25), fols. 104–17, partly printed in Arad et al., *Documents of the Holocaust*, pp. 398–400. See also Dina Porat, "The Holocaust in Lithuania: Some Unique Aspects." Christoph Dieckmann, Freiburg, is preparing a detailed study on German occupation policy in Lithuania.

120. Andrew Ezergailis, *The Holocaust in Latvia, 1941–1944: The Missing Center*, pp. 173–202; Robert Waite, "Kollaboration und deutsche Besatzungspolitik in Lettland 1941 bis 1945," pp. 218–22; Katrin Reichelt, "Kollaboration und Holocaust in Lettland, 1941–

1945." While Einsatzgruppe A was unable to instigate pogroms in Vilnius, Lithuanian auxiliary policemen assisted a unit of Einsatzgruppe B in killing between 4,000 to 5,000 Jews in that city by July 20, 1941 (Gerlach, "Einsatzgruppe B," p. 56).

121. Pohl, "Einsatzgruppe C," p. 72; Pohl, *Judenverfolgung in Ostgalizien*, pp. 60–62; Andrzej Zbikowski, "Local Anti-Jewish Pogroms in the Occupied Territories of Eastern Poland, June–July 1941."

122. There is no systematic study on collaboration in the occupied Soviet Union. For some aspects, see Gerhart Hass, "Deutsche Okkupationsziele und die Kollaboration in den besetzten Gebieten der Russischen Föderativen Sowjetrepublik 1941–44"; Stang, *Kollaboration und Massenmord*; Martin Dean, *Collaboration in the Holocaust: Crimes of the Local Police in Belorussia and Ukraine, 1941–1944*. According to Andrew Ezergailis, *The Holocaust in Lativa*, p. 173, the Latvian Arays commando killed at least 26,000 Jews by the end of the German occupation.

123. Nbg. Doc. L–221, TWC, 12:1292.

124. For Latvia, see Waite, "Kollaboration und deutsche Besatzungspolitik in Lettland," p. 218; for Lithuania, Yitzhak Arad, *Ghetto in Flames: The Struggle and Destruction of the Jews in Vilna in the Holocaust*, pp. 35–38.

125. JNSV, 15:26–27; MacQueen, "Nazi Policy toward the Jews in the Reichskommissariat Ostland," pp. 96–97.

126. For prewar domestic politics in Lithuania, see Michael MacQueen, "The Context of Mass Destruction."

127. LAF leaflet, March 19, 1941, quoted from B. Baranauskas, K. Ruksenas, E. Rozauskas, eds., *Documents Accuse*, pp. 123–24.

128. MacQueen, "The Context of Mass Destruction," pp. 35–37.

129. Statements by von Bischoffshausen and Röder, quoted from Ernst Klee, Willi Dressen, and Volker Riess, eds., *"The Good Old Days": The Holocaust as Seen by Its Perpetrators and Bystanders*, pp. 28, 33. On the pogroms in Kaunas, see also Mellmann et al., *Deutscher Osten*, pp. 61–69.

130. Quoted from Pohl, *Judenverfolgung in Ostgalizien*, p. 61; Förster, "Securing 'Living Space,'" p. 1227. After about 2,000 (predominantly male) Jews had lost their lives, the German Stadtkommandant stopped the Lwow pogroms on July 2 (Pohl, *Judenverfolgung in Ostgalizien*, p. 61).

131. Report Ortskommandantur Drohobycz to Feldkommandantur 676 in Sambor, 8 July 1941, SAM 1275-3-661, fols. 1–3.

132. Diary entry of von Leeb, July 8, 1941, quoted from Förster, "Securing 'Living Space,'" p. 1206.

133. Report GFP-Gruppe 711 (with 454th Security Division), July 7, 1941, quoted from Pohl, *Judenverfolgung in Ostgalizien*, p. 58.

134. See, e.g., the letter by "Franzl" quoted in Hamburg Institute, *The German Army and Genocide*, p. 82; Manoschek, *"Es gibt nur eines für das Judentum,"* pp. 31, 34, 39, 51.

135. Situation Report EK 1b to RSHA-Eingangsstelle, EG I [sic], July 1, 1941, SAM 500-1-756, fols. 4–6. See also EM 8 and 14, partly printed in Arad et al., *The Einsatzgruppen Reports*, pp. 1, 10–12. Despite the use of the term "Konzentrationslager" by the military

and the Security Police, there was no such camp in Kaunas in 1941. German and Lithuanian police used Forts IV, VII, and IX in Kaunas for executions.

136. On the historiographical value of Einsatzgruppen reports, i.e., reports from individual units and the edited Ereignismeldungen and Tätigkeits- und Lageberichte, see Ronald Headland, *Messages of Death: A Study of the Reports of the Einsatzgruppen of the Security Police and the Security Service, 1941–1943*, pp. 177–204; Krausnick and Wilhelm, *Die Truppe des Weltanschauungskrieges*, pp. 333–47; Klein, *Die Einsatzgruppen*, pp. 9–11.

137. Appeal by Lithuanian military commander, June 28, 1941, CSA Vilnius 1444-1-8, fol. 37a.

138. Scheffler, "Einsatzgruppe A," p. 19.

139. CdS (Heydrich) to Einsatzgruppen, "Einsatzbefehl Nr. 2" (Abschrift), July 1, 1941, USHMMA, RG 11.001m, reel 183 (SAM 500-1-25).

140. Latvian "Perkonkrusts," quoted from Waite, "Kollaboration und deutsche Besatzungspolitik in Lettland," p. 218.

141. Report by Einsatzgruppe A for the period October 16, 1941, to January 31, 1942 (so-called second Stahlecker report), n.d. (early 1942), Nbg. Doc. PS-2273, *IMT*, 30:71–80.

142. Gerlach, "Einsatzgruppe B," p. 56.

143. Kommandostab RF-SS Ia 11/7/41/geh., copy of telex AOK 9 Ic/AO Nr. 1963/41 geh, June 25, 1941, to XXXXII. ak, USHMMA RG 48.004M, reel 1 (MHA Prague Kdos RF-SS).

144. MacQueen, "Nazi Policy toward the Jews in the Reichskommissariat Ostland," pp. 97–98; Stang, *Kollaboration und Massenmord*, pp. 153–71.

145. Nbg. Doc. 221-L, *TWC*, 12:1292.

146. RF-SS to HSSPF in Russia, SSPF Lublin (Globocnik), July 25, 1941, NA, T 454, reel 100, frames 699–700; see also MacQueen, "Nazi Policy toward the Jews in the Reichskommissariat Ostland," p. 99.

147. While opposing the formation of military units in the Baltic States and in Ukraine, Hitler agreed to the expansion of the Schutzmannschaft in early 1942 (Himmler to Jeckeln, January 27, 1942, NA, T 175, reel 127, frame 2654001).

148. "Osteinsatz Polizei," BDC O 464; report by Daluege, January 1943, Nbg. Doc. NO-285; Browning, *Ordinary Men*, p. 24. See also Richard Breitman, "Himmler's Police Auxiliaries in the Occupied Soviet Territories." For Belorussia, see Bernhard Chiari, *Alltag hinter der Front. Besatzung, Kollaboration und Widerstand in Weissrussland 1941–1944*, pp. 160–94; Gerlach, *Kalkulierte Morde*, pp. 202–7; for Ukraine, see Frank Golchewski, "Organe der deutschen Besatzungsmacht," pp. 173–96; for Galicia, see Pohl, *Judenverfolgung in Ostgalizien*, pp. 92–93.

149. Directive by commander of the rear army area north (von Roques), August 3, 1941, printed in Benz et al., *Einsatz im "Reichskommissariat Ostland,"* p. 86.

150. According to a report by the HSSPF North, the Latvian Schutzmannschaft in early August in the city of Riga alone comprised 2,799 men, most of them deployed in the 13 police precincts. Waite, "Kollaboration und deutsche Besatzungspolitik in Lettland," pp. 225–26.

151. Report by Gebietskommissar Mitau to Generalkommissar Lettland, August 12, 1941, printed in Benz et al., *Einsatz im "Reichskommissariat Ostland,"* p. 88. For the ac-

tivities of Latvian auxiliary police units in July/August, see Waite, "Kollaboration und deutsche Besatzungspolitik in Lettland," pp. 221–24.

152. Chiari, *Alltag hinter der Front*, p. 172.

153. EM 67, August 29, 1941, quoted from Gerlach, *Kalkulierte Morde*, p. 203. In areas under military occupation, the term Ordnungsdienst was used; where the civil administration had taken over, local police men were referred to as Schutzmänner. For the different types of non-German police units, see Breitman, "Himmler's Police Auxiliaries in the Occupied Soviet Territories."

154. Kohl, *"Ich wundere mich,"* pp. 207–9.

155. According to Gerlach, *Kalkulierte Morde*, p. 204, in late 1941 there were 3,680 Schutzmänner in the Generalkommissariat Weissruthenien. For the involvement of local policemen in the "second killing wave" and antipartisan warfare, see ibid., pp. 697–705; Dean, *Collaboration in the Holocaust*; Jürgen Matthäus, " 'Reibungslos und planmässig.' Die zweite Welle der Judenvernichtung im Generalkommissariat Weissruthenien (1942–1944)." Klaus-Michael Mallmann is preparing a detailed study on the role of the Order Police during the Holocaust.

156. For Lithuania, see MacQueen, "The Context of Mass Destruction," pp. 38–39; for Latvia, see Waite, "Kollaboration und deutsche Besatzungspolitik in Lettland"; for Estonia, see Birn, "Collaboration in the East."

157. For Belorussia, see Chiari, *Alltag hinter der Front*, pp. 96–159; Gerlach, *Kalkulierte Morde*, pp. 530–31; also Gerlach, "Einsatzgruppe B," p. 53; for the militia in Ukraine, see Pohl, "Einsatzgruppe C," pp. 79–80. Further research on other areas is needed to arrive at a more coherent picture on the role of the auxiliary administration.

158. See Dieckmann, "Der Krieg und die Ermordung der litauischen Juden," p. 298.

159. EK 3, "Gesamtaufstellung der im Bereiche des EK 3 bis jetzt durchgeführten Exekutionen," September 10, 1941, USHMMA RG 11.001m, reel 183 (SAM 500-1-25), fols. 104–7 (entries for August 13 to 31, and September 9, 1941).

160. Scheffler, "Einsatzgruppe A," pp. 32, 35.

161. For examples, see Pohl, "Einsatzgruppe C," p. 80.

162. Hilberg, *The Destruction of the European Jews*, pp. 304–5; Pohl, *Judenverfolgung in Ostgalizien*, p. 50; Klein, *Die Einsatzgruppen*, pp. 119–20, 140, 218.

163. Ioanid, *The Holocaust in Romania*, pp. 38–43.

164. USHMMA RG 25.004m, reel 16 (Romanian Intelligence Service), quoted from Ioanid, *The Holocaust in Romania*, pp. 91–92. See also the important articles by Jean Ancel: "The Romanian Way of Solving the 'Jewish Problem' in Bessarabia and Bukovina, June–July 1941"; "Antonescu and the Jews," in *Yad Vashem Studies*; and "Antonescu and the Jews," in *The Holocaust and History*.

165. Presidium of the Council of Ministers, Ministry of National Propaganda, June 19, 1941, quoted from Matatias Carp, ed., *Holocaust in Rumania: Facts and Documents on the Annihilation of Rumania's Jews, 1940–1944*, p. 170.

166. Ioanid, *The Holocaust in Romania*, p. 93.

167. Hilberg, *The Destruction of the European Jews*, p. 771. Jean Ancel estimates that at least 100,000 Jews had been murdered by the Romanians by the end of August 1941. "Antonescu and the Jews," *The Holocaust and History*, p. 468.

168. Ioanid, *The Holocaust in Romania*, pp. 94–96.

169. Ioanid, *The Holocaust in Romania*, pp. 63–90, quotation on p. 80; Carp, *Holocaust in Rumania*, pp. 141–69; Angrick, "Einsatzgruppe D," in *Die Einsatzgruppen*, pp. 90–91.

170. Note on meeting with I c officer of 11th Army, July 16, 1941, quoted from Angrick, "Einsatzgruppe D," in *Die Einsatzgruppen*, p. 93. For the murder of Jews in Romanian-occupied Transnistria by ethnic German units (Volksdeutscher Selbstschutz) under the direction of Himmler's Volksdeutsche Mittelstelle, see Angrick, "The Escalation of German-Rumanian Anti-Jewish Policy," pp. 229–34.

171. Angrick, "Einsatzgruppe D," in *Die Einsatzgruppen*, pp. 93–95; Angrick, "The Escalation of German-Rumanian Anti-Jewish Policy," p. 209; Angrick, "Die Einsatzgruppe D. Struktur und Tätigkeit," pp. 93–97.

172. Streit, *Keine Kameraden*, p. 83.

173. CdS "Einsatzbefehl Nr. 8," July 17, 1941 (Richtlinien über die Säuberung der Gefangenenlager, in denen Sowjetrussen untergebracht sind), printed in Klein, *Die Einsatzgruppen*, pp. 331–40. The order did not refer directly to the treatment of Jewish POWs beyond their identification. See Reinhard Otto, *Wehrmacht, Gestapo und sowjetische Kriegsgefangene im deutschen Reichsgebiet*, pp. 48–58. Streit, *Keine Kameraden*, p. 93, interprets the order as "the last radicalization of persecuting enemies in the context of the ideological orders developed since March 1941" (*letzte Radikalisierung der Gegnervernichtung im Rahmen der seit März 1941 entwickelten weltanschaulichen Befehle*). See also Aly, *"Endlösung,"* p. 293.

174. Hitler monologue, August 1, 1941, quoted from *Monologe im Führerhauptquartier*, pp. 50–51. See also the protocol of the meeting of army officers at Amtschef OKW Wehrwirtschafts- und Rüstungsamt (Thomas) on July 31, 1941, where participants expressed the impossibility of administering the entire area ("Wir können nicht das ganze Land verwalten") and envisaged mass starvation ("Grosse Gebiete werden sich selbst überlassen bleiben müssen [verhungern]") (partly printed in N. Müller, *Die faschistische Okkupationspolitik*, pp. 178–80).

175. According to Hitler's "Weisung Nr. 33a" of July 23, 1941, the terror against the civilian population had to be increased to destroy "any inclination toward recalcitrance" (partly printed in N. Müller, *Die faschistische Okkupationspolitik*, pp. 182–83). See also order OKH/Gen.z.b.V.b. ObdH (Müller), July 25, 1941 (partly printed in ibid., pp. 168–71); Streit, *Keine Kameraden*, pp. 106–8.

176. See examples in Förster, "Securing 'Living Space,'" pp. 1208–11; Benz et al., *Einsatz im "Reichskommissariat Ostland,"* pp. 84–86. The Security Police received orders to prevent "the gathering of onlookers, even if they are officers of the Wehrmacht" during mass executions (order RSHA IV to Einsatzgruppen, August 30, 1941, printed in Benz et al., p. 69).

177. Sicherungsdivision Ic, July 28, 1941, BA-MA RH 26-221/70, quoted from Förster, "Securing 'Living Space,'" pp. 1206–7; for other units, see pp. 1037–38. The 221st Security Division was deployed in the Bialystok area, which was incorporated into Eastern Prussia on August 1, 1941.

178. Order by AOK 6, July 19, 1941, in Bernd Boll and Hans Safrian, "Auf dem Weg nach Stalingrad. Die 6. Armee 1941/42," p. 268; order by Befehlshaber rückwärtiges Heeres-

gebiet Süd, August 16, 1941, in Truman Anderson, "Die 62. Infanterie-Division. Repressalien im Heeresgebiet Süd, Oktober bis Dezember 1941," p. 300; order by Kommandant in Weissruthenien (von Bechtolsheim), October 10, 1941, partly printed in Benz et al., *Einsatz im "Reichskommissariat Ostland,"* p. 77; order by 281st Security Division, August 11, 1941, in ibid., pp. 86–87.

179. Gerlach, *Kalkulierte Morde*, pp. 870–84. For the development of the partisan movement, see John Armstrong, ed., *Soviet Partisans in World War II*; Leonid D. Grenkevich, *The Soviet Partisan Movement, 1941–1944: A Critical Historiographical Analysis*; Kenneth D. Slepyan, " 'The People's Avengers': Soviet Partisans, Stalinist Society and the Politics of Resistance, 1941–1944."

180. Jürgen Förster, "Das andere Gesicht des Krieges: Das 'Unternehmen Barbarossa' als Eroberungs- und Vernichtungskrieg," pp. 155–57; Ruth Bettina Birn, "Zweierlei Wirklichkeit? Fallbeispiele zur Partisanenbekämpfung im Osten"; Büchler, "Kommandostab Reichsführer-ss"; Lozowick, "*Rollbahn Mord.*" Martin Cüppers, Berlin, is preparing a Ph.D. study on the Kommandostab.

181. Matthäus et al., *Ausbildungsziel Judenmord?*, pp. 97–99.

182. KdoS RF-SS Ia "Betr.: Einsatz von Truppen zur Befriedung des 'rückwärtigen Heeresgebietes' und des 'Gebietes der politischen Verwaltung,' " July 6, 1941; "Merkblatt über Beurteilung der Lage, Entschlussfassung und Befehlsgebung," July 19, 1941, USHMMA RG 48.004m, reel 1 (MHA Prague KdoS RF-SS).

183. *DKHH*, p. 186 n. 18; Pohl, *Judenverfolgung in Ostgalizien*, p. 65.

184. Förster, "Securing 'Living Space,' " p. 1194.

185. KdoS RF-SS, Activity report, July 23, 1941, USHMMA RG 48.004m, reel 1 (MHA Prague KdoS RF-SS).

186. Birn, "Zweierlei Wirklichkeit?," p. 280.

187. KdoS RF-SS Ic, Activity report for July 20–27, 1941, July 28, 1941, USHMMA RG 48.004m, reel 1 (MHA Prague KdoS RF-SS).

188. KdoS RF-SS Ia, Activity report for July 20–27, 1941, July 31, 1941, USHMMA RG 48.004m, reel 1 (MHA Prague KdoS RF-SS).

189. ss-Kav.Rgt. 1 Ia (Fegelein) "Regimentsbefehl Nr. 42," July 27, 1941, NA, T-175 Roll 109; see also Benz et al., *Einsatz im "Reichskommissariat Ostland,"* pp. 75–76.

190. "Kommandosonderbefehl" Himmler, July 28, 1941, partly printed in N. Müller, *Die faschistische Okkupationspolitik*, pp. 175–77.

191. Gerlach, *Kalkulierte Morde*, p. 559; KdoS RF-SS Ia, Activity report for July 28 to August 3, 1941, August 6, 1941, USHMMA RG 48.004m, reel 1 (MHA Prague KdoS RF-SS).

192. Gerlach, *Kalkulierte Morde*, pp. 565–66.

193. Order by Befehlshaber rückwärtiges Heeresgebiet Süd, July 29, 1941, BA-MA RH 22/170; Förster, "Securing 'Living Space,' " pp. 1200, 1208; Pohl, *Judenverfolgung in Ostgalizien*, p. 60.

194. ss-Brigade Ia, Activity report for July 27–30, 1941, July 30, 1941, printed in *Unsere Ehre heisst Treue: Kriegstagebuch des Kommandostabes Reichsführer ss. Tätigkeitsberichte der 1. und 2. ss-Inf.-Brigade, der 1. ss-Kav.-Brigade und von Sonderkommandos der ss*, pp. 95–96; Longerich, *Die Ermordung der europäischen Juden*, p. 131. See also KdoS RF-SS Ia, Activity report for July 28 to August 3, 1941, August 6, 1941, USHMMA RG 48.004m, reel 1. Accord-

ing to Dieter Pohl, "Schauplatz Ukraine: Der Massenmord an den Juden im Militärverwaltungsgebiet und im Reichskommissariat 1941–1943," p. 139, Jeckeln had issued an
order to the 1st SS-Brigade that called for the execution of all persons supporting the
"Bolshevist system."

195. Gerlach, *Kalkulierte Morde*, p. 559; DKHH, p. 186 n. 23.

196. SS-Kav.Rgt. 2 Reit.Abt., August 1, 1941, 10:00 AM, BA-MA RS 4/441; quoted in
Gerlach, *Kalkulierte Morde*, p. 560; Christian Gerlach, "Deutsche Wirtschaftsinteressen,
Besatzungspolitik und der Mord an den Juden in Weissrussland, 1941–1943, p. 278.

197. SS-Kav.Rgt. 1 Reit.Abt. (Lombard) Abteilungsbefehl Nr. 28, August 1, 1941 (6:30
PM), BA-MA RS 4/441.

198. Gerlach, *Kalkulierte Morde*, p. 560.

199. SS-Kav.Rgt. 2 Reit.Abt. (Magill), August 12, 1941, printed in *Unsere Ehre heisst
Treue*, pp. 229–30.

200. KdoS RF-SS Ic, Situation Report, August 12, 1941; Activity report for August 4–10,
August 13, USHMMA RG 48.004m, reel 1 (MHA Prague KdoS RF-SS).

201. Gerlach, *Kalkulierte Morde*, pp. 563–64. The Einsatzgruppe z.b.V. which had been
sent in from Cracow was also involved in the murder of Jews in Sluzk, Brest, Bialystok,
Vilnius, and the Minsk area. Büchler, "Kommandostab Reichsführer-SS," p. 13.

202. KdoS RF-SS Ia, Activity report for July 28 to August 3, 1941, August 6, 1941;
Activity report for August 4–10, August 13, USHMMA RG 48.004m, reel 1 (MHA Prague
KdoS RF-SS); 1. SS-Brigade Ia, Activity report for August 3–6, 1941, August 6, 1941;
Activity report for August 6–10, 1941, August 10, 1941, printed in *Unsere Ehre heisst Treue*,
pp. 98–99, 101–5. Subordinated to the 6th Army since August 6, the 1st SS-Brigade with its
SS-Infantry Regiments 8 and 10 was involved in "cleansing actions" (see ibid., p. 24).

203. Birn, "Zweierlei Wirklichkeit?," pp. 278–80.

204. KdoS RF-SS Ia/Ic, Kommandobefehl Nr. 42, November 11, 1941, USHMMA RG
48.004m, reel 1 (MHA Prague KdoS RF-SS).

205. SS-Kav. Brigade 1 (Fegelein) to HSSPF Russia Center, "Betr.: Zu Abschlussmeldung
für den RF-SS," August 13, 1941, USHMMA RG 48.004m, reel 1 (MHA Prague, KdoS RF-SS),
printed in *Unsere Ehre heisst Treue*, pp. 214–16.

206. Longerich, *Politik der Vernichtung*, p. 368 ("neue Dimension"); Gerlach, *Kalkulierte Morde*, p. 562 ("neue Qualität des Mordens").

207. Pohl, "Hans Krüger," p. 244.

208. The claim that Jeckeln, during his visit to Himmler on August 12, 1941, received an "order for the expansion of the killing actions" (Gerlach, "Deutsche Wirtschaftsinteressen," p. 278; also Gerlach, *Kalkulierte Morde*, p. 638; Pohl, "Einsatzgruppe C," p. 67
n. 37, p. 85 n. 18; Pohl, "Schauplatz Ukraine," p. 143) or pressed for more radical measures
against Jews (DKHH, pp. 70–71, 191) is, in my view, not substantiated by the available
documentation. On August 11, 1941, Himmler's aide Grothmann had sent a radio message
to the commander of the 1st SS-Brigade, SS-Brigadier General Herrmann, stating the
Reichsführer's dissatisfaction with the frequency of reports ("RF-SS ist sehr ungehalten über
mangelhaften Eingang von Einsatzmeldungen"), especially in light of the more regular
reports from the SS-Cavalry Brigade (BA NS 33/312, fol. 26). One day later, Kommandostab
leader Knoblauch radioed to Jeckeln that Himmler expected an immediate report regard-

ing the activities of the 1st ss-Brigade (BA NS 33/312, fol. 23). There is no evidence that it was the number of executions, as opposed to the frequency of reports, that caused Himmler's dissatisfaction (see *Unsere Ehre heisst Treue*, pp. 26–27, 35, 149). While it remains unclear what Himmler told Jeckeln on August 12, his instructions were interpreted by some of his subordinates as a license or order to kill women and children. Other units of the Kommandostab, most notably the 2nd ss-Brigade, were not involved in the cleansing sweeps performed by the ss-Cavalry Brigade and the 1st ss-Brigade (see ibid., pp. 21–33; Mellmann et al., *Deutscher Osten*, pp. 143–48).

209. Gerlach, *Kalkulierte Morde*, pp. 719–21.

210. Browning, *The Path to Genocide*, p. 111; Browning, *Fateful Months*, p. 59.

211. DKHH, pp. 193 (with wrong reference to Lombard), 195. According to the editors, the execution took place in either Smolevichi or Smilovichi (ibid., p. 195 n. 14).

212. Ogorreck, *Die Einsatzgruppen*, pp. 179–83 (quotation from the leader of EK 8, Bradfisch, p. 181). Even in Bradfisch's statement, the reference to Hitler is not clear. According to Bradfisch, Himmler claimed to have received an order from Hitler; at the same time, the Reichsführer talked quite superfluously if a Hitler order had existed about the destruction of the Jews as a "war aim" (*Kriegsziel*) and a "necessity of state" (*Staatsnotwendigkeit*).

213. Gerlach, *Kalkulierte Morde*, pp. 646–48.

214. DKHH, p. 195 n. 15; Gerlach, "Failure of Plans for an ss Extermination Camp in Mogilev, Belorussia," p. 65.

215. EK 3, "Gesamtaufstellung," September 10, 1941, USHMMA RG 11.001m, reel 183 (SAM 500-1-25), in which EK 3 reported the execution of 3,200 "Jews, Jewesses and Jewish children" (*Juden, Jüdinnen und J-Kinder*) in Rokiskis.

216. See Gerlach, "Einsatzgruppe B," p. 57; Gerlach, *Kalkulierte Morde*, p. 641. Compare Ogorreck, *Die Einsatzgruppen*, p. 181, who claims that Himmler issued such an order on August 15.

217. Despite widespread agreement among historians on the existence of a triangular, mutually reinforcing, relation between general guidelines, initiatives from below, and coordination efforts from above (Longerich, *Politik der Vernichtung*, pp. 369, 372; Browning, *Nazi Policy*, p. 126), the specific character of this relation remains open to debate. According to conventional wisdom, Hitler at some stage in the course of 1941 arrived at a decision that in the form of an order, directive, or at least declaration of intent drove the anti-Jewish measures adopted at the periphery as well as the development toward the "Final Solution"; thus, the focus of the interpretation is usually on the role of the center. Local and regional studies like those by Christian Gerlach and Dieter Pohl as well as the work of Götz Aly and Hans Safrian have greatly contributed to a shift toward stressing the role of the periphery (see Browning, *Nazi Policy*, pp. 26–57).

218. "Die Zivilverwaltung in den besetzten Ostgebieten" (so-called Braune Mappe), part I: Reichskommissariat Ostland, n.d. (summer 1941), BA R43II/685a (partly printed in Benz et al., *Einsatz im "Reichskommissariat Ostland,"* pp. 33–37, quotation on pp. 33–34); part II: Reichskommissariat Ukraine, CSA Moscow 7021-148-183.

219. In Kaunas on July 29 Himmler seems to have met with Lohse and the commander

of the Order Police (KdO) for Lithuania, but not with his most successful murderers in the area, Jäger and Stahlecker (according to the not fully intact *Dienstkalender*, the Reichsführer did not meet with the latter in the entire period from the beginning of Operation Barbarossa to Stahlecker's death in early spring 1942). Two days later, Himmler visited Lohse and Prützmann en route to Baranovichi (see *DKHH*, pp. 188 n. 20, 189 n. 23).

220. Protocol (probably by Alfred Meyer) of "Besprechung über die politische und wirtschaftliche Lage im Ostland in der Sitzung bei Reichsminister Rosenberg," August 1, 1941, BA R 6/300, fols. 1–5. The meeting was convened by Rosenberg to discuss the currency issue; quotes from ibid., fol. 4v (cf. Dieckmann, "Der Krieg und die Ermordung der litauischen Juden," pp. 320, 327).

221. "Besprechung," BA R 6/300, fol. 4.

222. Reichskommissar Ostland II (Lohse) to HSSPF, August 2, 1941, printed in Benz et al., *Einsatz im "Reichskommissariat Ostland,"* pp. 38–42.

223. See report by Generalkommissar in Latvia to Reichskommissar Ostland, October 20, 1941, printed in N. Müller, *Die faschistische Okkupationspolitik*, pp. 205–7, noting that at the time of the arrival of the civil administration in Riga "the most necessary and urgent measures" against the Jews (registration, marking, forced labor duty, appointment of a Jewish council, and preparations for creating a ghetto) had already been taken.

224. See EG A (Stahlecker) to RSHA II, July 21, 1941, and October 6, 1941, according to which the concentration camp was designed to house the remaining approximately 25,000 Riga Jews (USHMMA RG 11.001m5, reel 75 [SAM 504-2-8]). While Stahlecker might have favored the model of the "Zwangsarbeitslager für Juden" established by Globocnik and Friedrich Katzmann in 1940/41 in the General Government (see Dieter Pohl, "Die grossen Zwangsarbeitslager der SS- und Polizeiführer für Juden im Generalgouvernement 1942–1945"), the RSHA agreed only to the creation of an "extended police prison" (*erweitertes Polizeigefängnis*) administered by the Security Police (RSHA II C 3 to EG A, August 4, 1941, USHMMA, RG 11.001m5, reel 75 ([SAM 504-2-8]; see also Longerich, *Politik der Vernichtung*, p. 396).

225. Draft response letter by Stahlecker regarding Lohse's "preliminary guidelines," August 6, 1941 (two copies with handwritten annotations from different authors), partly printed in Benz et al., *Einsatz im "Reichskommissariat Ostland,"* pp. 42–46. The last passage quoted was inserted in handwriting. Browning, *The Path to Genocide*, p. 110, interprets Stahlecker's reference to "Jewish reserve areas" as a "cover story."

226. See EK 3, "Gesamtaufstellung," September 10, 1941, December 1, 1941, USHMMA RG 11.001m, reel 183 (SAM 500-1-25); Activity reports by Einsatzgruppe A until October 15, 1941, and January 31, 1942 USHMMA RG 11.001m, reel 14 (SAM 500-1-93, 500-1-91) EG A (Tschierschky) to EK 3, August 4, 1941, printed in Benz et al., *Einsatz im "Reichskommissariat Ostland,"* p. 42.

227. The leader of RSHA Amt VI (SD-Ausland), Walter Schellenberg, testified after the war that "Stahlecker was a man who, no matter what type of work he did, always made a stage play out of it" (interrogation, November 14, 1945, NA, T-1139 reel 52, frame 1021).

228. See EM 52, August 14, 1941, re Einsatzgruppe C, printed in Arad et al., *The Einsatzgruppen Reports*, p. 87.

229. Quoted from Benz et al., *Einsatz im "Reichskommissariat Ostland,"* p. 76.

230. Reichskommissar Ostland to Generalkommissare, August 18, 1941, partly printed in Benz et al., *Einsatz im "Reichskommissariat Ostland,"* pp. 46–47. While giving in on the issue of anti-Jewish policy, the civil administration insisted that the police had no right to interfere in economic matters. Reichsministerium (Meyer) to Reichskommissar Ostland, August 23, 1941, USHMMA RG 11.001m, reel 183 (SAM 500-1-25, fol. 423).

231. Stahlecker to Einsatzkommandos, August 29, 1941, printed in Benz et al., *Einsatz im "Reichskommissariat Ostland,"* pp. 47–48.

232. EK 3, "Gesamtaufstellung," September 10, 1941, December 1, 1941, USHMMA RG 11.001m, reel 183 (SAM 500-1-25); Benz et al., *Einsatz im "Reichskommissariat Ostland,"* pp. 87–94.

233. EK 3, "Gesamtaufstellung," December 1, 1941, USHMMA RG 11.001m, reel 183 (SAM 500-1-25); letter GK Lettland to KdS Lettland, March 12, 1942, printed in Benz et al., *Einsatz im "Reichskommissariat Ostland,"* p. 55. See also EM 54, Nbg. Doc. NO-2849.

234. EK 3, "Gesamtaufstellung," December 1, 1941, USHMMA RG 11.001m, reel 183 (SAM 500-1-25). The murder of persons described as "mentally ill" (*Geisteskranke*) was reported for August 22 in Aglona (544 persons including 48 children).

235. "Generalkommissariat Weissruthenien" was an artificially created administrative entity that resembled Belorussia only partly in its pre- and postwar borders. Under German occupation, the area of Volhynia-Podolia became part of the Ukraine; in the east, the territory of the Generalkommissariat extended barely beyond Minsk (see Gerlach, *Kalkulierte Morde*, pp. 160–65). Kube's clashes with the Security Police regarding the Jewish question, especially his concern about German Jews deported to Minsk, have at times been overestimated. During a conversation in 1942 with a representative of Martin Bormann's Party Chancellery, Kube admitted to have given "ca. 3 to 5" candies to Jewish children during an execution by the SD in the Minsk ghetto, which he disapproved because of its public character. Despite complaints by the Security Police about a strained relationship with the civil administration, Kube backed their demands for more personnel to be deployed in the countryside. Beauftragter des Reichsleiters Bormann im OKW / Stab z.b.V. Generalleutnant von Unruh (Albert Hoffmann) to Bormann, "Bericht Nr.4 Weissruthenien / Minsk" (Zweitschrift), May 26, 1942, USHMMA Kempner papers, Nuremberg box #4.

236. See KdoS RF-SS SS-Kav. Brigade Ia (Fegelein), September 19, 1941, "Abschlussmeldung der SS-Kav.Brigade über Befriedung der Prypec-Sümpfe." On the second Pripet sweep, see Gerlach, *Kalkulierte Morde*, pp. 606–8.

237. Krausnick and Wilhelm, *Die Truppe des Weltanschauungskrieges*, pp. 247–48; Gerlach, *Kalkulierte Morde*, p. 566; Benz et al., *Einsatz im "Reichskommissariat Ostland,"* pp. 76–77.

238. OKW / WFSt / Abt. L (IV / Qu), September 12, 1941, quoted from Gerlach, *Kalkulierte Morde*, p. 604. Bechtolsheim transmitted the OKH guideline of October 25 regarding partisan warfare to the battalions in late November: Kommandant in Weissruthenien, order no. 24, November 24, 1941, USHMMA RG 53.002m, reel 2 (CSA Minsk 378-1-698, fol. 32).

239. ObdH / GenStdH / Ausb.Abt.(Ia) "Richtlinien für Partisanenbekämpfung," October 25, 1941: "The enemy must be *completely destroyed*. Constant decision making over the

life and death of captured partisans or suspects is hard even for the most thick-skinned soldier. One must act. Those act right who, while totally subordinating their possible personal sentiments, set to work ruthlessly and unmercifully." USHMMA RG 48.004m, reel 1 (MHA Prague KdoS RF-SS), emphasis in the original.

240. Report by Kommandant in Weissruthenien Abt. Ia, October 16, 1941, USHMMA RG 53.002m, reel 2 (CSA Minsk 378-1-698, fol. 11b); report by Wehrmachtsbefehlshaber Ostland Abt.Ia, November 10, 1941, BA-MA RH 26-707/2.

241. Gerlach, *Kalkulierte Morde*, pp. 587–88, 593, 639.

242. "Merkblatt" 339th Infantry Division, November 11, 1941, quoted from Gerlach, *Kalkulierte Morde*, pp. 605. For the course and wider context of the killing of Jews in Belorussia, see ibid., pp. 596–605, 870–84. On the persecution of "Gypsies," which according to Gerlach was less based on racial categories and less systematic than in the case of the Jews, see pp. 1063–67.

243. Order No. 24 by Kommandant in Weissruthenien (von Bechtolsheim), November 24, 1941, printed in Benz et al., *Einsatz im "Reichskommissariat Ostland,"* p. 78.

244. Gerlach, *Kalkulierte Morde*, pp. 609, 628.

245. Baranauskas et al., *Documents Accuse*, pp. 105–9. Similar to the structure established for the Security Police in the area under civil administration, the Order Police in the Ostland was commanded by the Befehlshaber der Ordnungspolizei (BdO), police general Jedicke. The 3rd company of Reserve Police Battalion 11 had been in charge of guarding the Kaunas ghetto (see Browning, *Ordinary Men*, p. 18).

246. Reports by Kommandant in Weissruthenien Abt. Ia, October 10 and 16, 1941, USHMMA RG 53.002m, reel 2 (CSA Minsk 378-1-698, fols. 4, 11). In its report, Reserve Police Battalion 11 claims that 1,300 "Jews, Communists and anti-German elements" were killed by its 2nd and 4th company in conjunction with two Schutzmannschaft companies (Jedicke to Lohse, October 25, 1941, USHMMA RG 22.001 Folder 18 [CSA Minsk 651-1-1, fol. 4). A GFP outpost had been established in Minsk in mid-September (see Abwehrstelle Ostland, September 12, 1941, SAM 1369-1-29, fol. 345).

247. Gerlach, *Kalkulierte Morde*, pp. 612–13. While Reserve Police Battalion 11 was discharged by Bechtolsheim on November 6, its Lithuanian Schutzmänner remained in Belorussia.

248. Carl to Kube, October 30, 1941, printed in Browning, *Ordinary Men*, pp. 19–23. See also Benz et al., *Einsatz im "Reichskommissariat Ostland,"* pp. 137–38.

249. Wehrmachtsbefehlshaber Ostland Abt. Ia to Reichskommissar Ostland, October 17, 1941, SAM 1369-1-29, fol. 358.

250. Kommandant in Weissruthenien Abt. Ia, order no. 24, November 24, 1941, USHMMA RG 53.002m, reel 2 (CSA Minsk 378-1-698, fol. 32), emphasis in the original.

251. Mordechai Altshuler, "Escape and Evacuation of Soviet Jews at the Time of the Nazi Invasion," pp. 94–97 (Ukraine).

252. Pohl, "Einsatzgruppe C," pp. 73–74.

253. With the crossing of the Juznyi Bug, AOK 11 and Einsatzgruppe D operated outside the Romanian sphere of interest agreed upon between the two governments. See Angrick, "Einsatzgruppe D," in *Die Einsatzgruppen*, p. 97.

254. Boll and Safrian, "Auf dem Weg nach Stalingrad," pp. 270–73; Wendy Lower, "Nazi Colonial Dreams: German Policies and Ukrainian Society in Zhytomyr," pp. 138–40 (I thank Wendy Lower for a copy of her thesis).

255. See the compilation by Browning, *Ordinary Men*, p. 17; Pohl, "Einsatzgruppe C," p. 78.

256. Boll and Safrian, "Auf dem Weg nach Stalingrad," pp. 275–81 (quotations from Groscurth, *Tagebücher*).

257. Angrick, "The Escalation of German-Rumanian Anti-Jewish Policy," pp. 210–29; Randolph Braham, "The Kamenets Podolsk and Delvidek Massacres"; Klaus-Michael Mallmann, "Der qualitative Sprung im Vernichtungsprozess"; Mallman et al., *Deutscher Osten*, pp. 85–87.

258. Longerich, *Politik der Vernichtung*, p. 377–79. In 1941, according to Pohl, "Schauplatz Ukraine," p. 152, the six police battalions deployed in the Ukraine under the HSSPF murdered considerably more Jews than Einsatzgruppen C and D.

259. EM 106, October 7, 1941, quoted from Arad et al., *The Einsatzgruppen Reports*, p. 174.

260. Pohl, "Schauplatz Ukraine," p. 146; Lower, "Nazi Colonial Dreams," pp. 141–42.

261. Hilberg, *The Destruction of the European Jews*, p. 302; Pohl, "Schauplatz Ukraine," pp. 147–49; Boll and Safrian, "Auf dem Weg nach Stalingrad," pp. 279–81.

262. The overall death toll for Ohlendorf's Einsatzgruppe reported in early October was 35,782; see EM 101, 103, October 2/4, 1941, in Arad et al., *The Einsatzgruppen Reports*, pp. 168–69; Angrick, "Einsatzgruppe D," in *Die Einsatzgruppen*, p. 98.

263. Postwar statement by EK 11a chief Paul Zapp; see DKHH, p. 225 n. 6. Ogorreck, *Die Einsatzgruppen*, p. 207 n. 117, quotes other accounts by perpetrators dating from the 1960s according to which on this occasion Himmler repeated an order for the killing of all Jews first given to Ohlendorf in August (see also Angrick, "Einsatzgruppe D," *Die Einsatzgruppen*, pp. 94, 98, 100). In addition to their obvious exculpatory function, the credibility of such accounts is greatly diminished by Ohlendorf's defense strategy during his trial in 1947/48 (see Browning, *Fateful Months*, pp. 17–19).

264. Hilberg, *The Destruction of the European Jews*, pp. 292, 306–7; Angrick, "Einsatzgruppe D. Struktur und Tätigkeit," pp. 199–202, with different approximations of the number of victims. Ioanid, *The Holocaust in Romania*, p. 182, estimates that at least 25,000 Jews were killed in Odessa in late October. Ancel, "Antonescu and the Jews," *The Holocaust and History*, p. 470, provides the figure of 5,000 in the city itself and 20,500 in nearby Dalnic.

265. Angrick, "Die Einsatzgruppe D. Struktur und Tätigkeit," pp. 216–41; Angrick, "Einsatzgruppe D," in *Die Einsatzgruppen*, pp. 101–2.

266. EM 145, December 12, 1941, printed in Arad et al., *The Einsatzgruppen Reports*, p. 256.

267. Report by 454. Sich.Div./VII, September 23, 1941, quoted from Pohl, "Schauplatz Ukraine," p. 145.

268. Förster, "Securing 'Living Space,'" pp. 1211–13; printed in N. Müller, *Die faschistische Okkupationspolitik*, pp. 203–4.

269. *Verbrechen der Wehrmacht*, pp. 89–90.

270. In addition to Jeckeln, HSSPF z.b.V. Gerret Korsemann was at that time also in Ukraine, waiting for his deployment in the Caucasus region, which had not yet been occupied. Korsemann seems to have been involved in the murder of Jews on Rovno in early November 1941 (see Pohl, "Schauplatz Ukraine," pp. 147, 144).

271. Pohl, "Schauplatz Ukraine," pp. 154–63; Hilberg, *The Destruction of the European Jews*, pp. 368–89; Yahil, *The Holocaust*, pp. 442–49.

272. Shmuel Spector, *The Holocaust of the Volhynian Jews, 1941–1944*, pp. 118–20, with descriptions of so-called open, i.e., unfenced, ghettos.

273. Hermann Kaienburg, "Jüdische Arbeitslager an der 'Strasse der SS.'" For the Galician part of the project, see Pohl, *Judenverfolgung in Ostgalizien*, pp. 338–42.

274. Pohl, "Schauplatz Ukraine," p. 156; Müller, *Hitlers Ostkrieg und die deutsche Siedlungspolitik*, pp. 161–67.

275. According to postwar estimates by a German court, approximately 25,000 Jewish forced laborers involved in the construction of Durchgangsstrasse IV were shot. Most of them had been brought in from Rumanian-controlled Transnistria and Ukrainian towns in the vicinity of the construction site. Kaienburg, "Jüdische Arbeitslager an der 'Strasse der SS,'" pp. 25–26.

276. See report on a conference at the OKW Wehrwirtschafts- und Rüstungsamt, July 31, 1941, printed in N. Müller, *Die faschistische Okkupationspolitik*, pp. 178–80.

277. On September 16, 1941, Göring stressed that in the occupied east only those parts of the population who worked for the Germans were to be fed. Streit, *Keine Kameraden*, p. 143.

278. In late September low-level military administrators in southern Ukraine complained about the prevailing "organized chaos" (*Organisation der Unordnung*), adding that "the higher economic offices can hardly be reached by the lower ones and that the latter lack clear guidelines." Report by FK 676 in Perwomaisk to Befehlshaber rückwärtiges Heeresgebiet Süd Abt. VII, September 21, 1941, SAM 1275-3-661, fol. 21.

279. Pohl, "Schauplatz Ukraine," p. 155. A similar argument for Belorussia is presented by Gerlach, *Kalkulierte Morde*, pp. 574–85, and "Wirtschaftsinteressen"; and for Lithuania by Dieckmann, "Die Krieg und die Ermordung der litauischen Juden."

280. See Wirtschaftsstab Ost, "Besondere Anordnung Nr. 44," November 4, 1941, printed in N. Müller, *Die faschistische Okkupationspolitik*, pp. 212–14.

281. Stadtkommissar Brest (Burat) to Generalkommissar Wolhynien-Podolien, November 11, 1941, quoted from Browning, "German Killers," p. 129. Until the beginning of November, the 17,000 Jews in Brest had at least officially received the same rations as non-Jews but suffered ever increasing food shortages thereafter (pp. 130–33). Under German occupation, the region of Brest was incorporated into the Reichskommissariat Ukraine. On Brest, see also Yehuda Bauer, *Rethinking the Holocaust*, pp. 153–62.

282. Report by FK 676 in Perwomaisk to Befehlshaber rückwärtiges Heeresgebiet Süd Abt. VII, September 21, 1941, SAM 1275-3-661, fol. 23. See also reports by Ortskommandantur Drohobycz, July 8, 1941; FK 676 to 444th Security Division, Befehlshaber rückwärtiges Heeresgebiet Süd Abt. VII, July 10, 30, September 9, 21, 1941, SAM 1275-3-661, fols. 2, 4, 15–16, 21, 30–31.

283. Gerlach, *Kalkulierte Morde*, p. 806; Streit, *Keine Kameraden*, p. 132 (death rate

among Soviet POWs for June–September 1941 ca. 0.3% per day). In the second half of September, Einsatzgruppe B executed an average of 419 persons per day (Gerlach, "Einsatzgruppe B," p. 62; Gerlach, *Kalkulierte Morde*, p. 279 n. 50). Einsatzgruppe A reported almost twice that number: EK 3, "Gesamtaufstellung," December 1, 1941, USHMMA RG 11.001m, reel 183 (SAM 500-1-25).

284. See Streit, *Keine Kameraden*, pp. 132–35; Otto, *Wehrmacht, Gestapo und sowjetische Kriegsgefangene*, pp. 271–72; Gerlach, *Kalkulierte Morde*, pp. 806–23; Gerlach, *Krieg, Ernährung, Völkermord*, p. 46.

285. Zimmermann, *Rassenutopie und Genozid*, pp. 259–76; Benz et al., *Einsatz im "Reichskommissariat Ostland,"* pp. 77–79.

286. EM 86, September 17, 1941, quoted from Arad et al., *The Einsatzgruppen Reports*, p. 137.

287. EM 133, November 14, 1941, BA R 58/219 (see also Arad et al., *The Einsatzgruppen Reports*, p. 236).

288. See report by Rüstungsinspektion Ukraine (Seraphim) to Chef WiRueAmt, December 2, 1941, which addresses some of the economic repercussions of mass murder and raises the question "who is actually supposed to produce economic value" in the east (Nbg. Doc. 3257-PS, IMT, 32:71–75).

289. Both selections were accompanied by large-scale murder actions with varying ratios of victims and temporary survivors, in Kaunas in late October (9,200 out of ca. 30,000 ghetto inmates), in Berdichev in mid-September (ca. 4,000 out of 20,000). Jäger argues that in Kaunas workers were selected with their families to increase productivity: EK 3, "Gesamtaufstellung," December 1, 1941, USHMMA RG 11.001m, reel 183 (SAM 500-1-25).

290. Browning, *Ordinary Men*, pp. 184–86.

291. Browning, *Nazi Policy,* pp. 166–67; Jürgen Matthäus, "What About the 'Ordinary Men'? The German Order Police and the Holocaust in the Occupied Soviet Union," pp. 138–39.

292. Letter by Walter Mattner, October 10, 1941, quoted from Gerlach, *Kalkulierte Morde*, pp. 588–89, who cites a source compilation by Tuvia Friedman. See also Mallmann et al., *Deutscher Osten*, pp. 27–28. According to Gerlach, Polizeisekretär Mattner was at least at a later stage a member of an Order Police office (SS- und Polizeistandortführer) in Mogilev. In 1947 and 1964 Mattner's case was investigated by Viennese courts, but it did not end in a conviction (I thank Winfried Garscha, Vienna, for this information).

293. KdoS RF-SS Ia/Ic, Kommandobefehl Nr. 42, November 18, 1941, USHMMA RG 48.004m, reel 1 (MHA Prague KdoS RF-SS).

294. KdoS RF-SS Ia/Ic "Betr.: Verhalten der Truppe im Ostraum," November 18, 1941, USHMMA RG 48.004m, reel 1 (MHA Prague KdoS RF-SS). The order had been issued in conjunction with Müller's Gestapo office in the RSHA: see KdoS RF-SS Ic 206/41, December 10, 1941, "Tätigkeitsbericht Nr. 24," USHMMA RG 48.004m, reel 1.

295. Gerlach, *Kalkulierte Morde*, p. 589. The frequency with which Hitler's "prophecy" was reiterated by himself and others was in large part thanks to Goebbels's propaganda machine, which, e.g., included it in the anti-Semitic film *Der ewige Jude*. Hans Mommsen, "Hitler's Reichstag speech of 30 January 1939"; Longerich, *Politik der Vernichtung*, pp. 428–29. The local Wehrmacht command in Krivoj Rog (Ukraine) reported in mid-

October, along with the fact that police units were making the city "free of Jews," that the only German film on show in the local cinemas was *Der ewige Jude*. Report OK 253 to FK 246, October 15, 1941, SAM 1275-3-665.

296. "Mitteilungsblätter für die weltanschauliche Schulung der Ordnungspolizei," Folge 27, December 1, 1941, see Browning, *Ordinary Men*, p. 179; Matthäus, "Ausbildungsziel Judenmord," p. 692.

297. The German press in the east played a particularly important role in propagating images of normalcy; see, e.g., *Deutsche Zeitung im Ostland*, published in Riga from August 5, 1941. For the eastern experience of Germans in Belorussia, see also Chiari, *Alltag hinter der Front*, pp. 72–95, 308–9.

298. Beauftragter des Reichsleiters Bormann im OKW / Stab z.b.V. Generalleutnant von Unruh (Albert Hoffmann) to Bormann, "Bericht Nr. 4 Weissruthenien / Minsk" (Zweitschrift), May 26, 1942, USHMMA Kempner papers, Nuremberg box #4.

299. Statement Edith Sch., January 10, 1961, Staatsanwaltschaft Koblenz 9 Ks 2/62, vol. 42, fol. 6380; similarly in vol. 29, fol. 4340 (Ulrich Fr.); vol. 47, pp. 7058–67 (Ruth Z.); vol. 48, fol. 7193–202 (Ryszard Sch.).

300. Statement Irma Sch., March 29, 1961, Staatsanwaltschaft Koblenz 9 Ks 2/62, vol. 48, fol. 7126–35. A gas van driver brought his 14-year-old son from Germany to Trostinez, where he became an office boy but, according to his father, never saw any atrocities being committed (statement Karl G., April 2, 1961, ibid., vol. 71, fol. 10590–99; vol. 73, fol. 10845–46). For Trostinez, see Kohl, *"Ich wundere mich,"* pp. 91–103; Gerlach, *Kalkulierte Morde*, pp. 768–71.

301. Statement Karl v.d.G., April 10, 1961, Staatsanwaltschaft Koblenz 9 Ks 2/62, vol. 49, fol. 7350–55.

302. For the German postwar perception of the Third Reich, see Norbert Frei, *Vergangenheitspolitik. Die Anfänge der Bundesrepublik und die NS-Vergangenheit*; Norbert Frei and Sybille Steinbacher, eds., *Beschweigen und Bekennen. Die deutsche Nachkriegsgesellschaft und der Holocaust*.

303. See Longerich, *Politik der Vernichtung*, pp. 426, 429.

304. On the memo by Carltheo Zeitschel, see Aly, *"Final Solution,"* p. 219; Safrian, *Die Eichmann-Männer*, pp. 110–11.

305. Speech by Heydrich, October 2, 1941, quoted from Miroslav Karny, Jaroslava Milotova, Margita Karna, eds., *Deutsche Politik im "Protektorat Böhmen und Mähren" unter Reinhard Heydrich*, pp. 107–22.

306. Notes on a meeting between Heydrich and Alfred Meyer et al., October 4, 1941, BA NS 19/1734, fols. 2–7 (in fols. 6–7). On October 26 Himmler commented extensively on the notes, but did not touch on the Jewish question (fols. 9–12).

307. Note on a conversation with Rosenberg by Chef des SS-Hauptamtes (Berger) to Himmler, October 10, 1941, NA, T 175 reel 22, frames 2525944–46. Later, SS General Berger acted as Himmler's liaison officer to Rosenberg (see DKHH, p. 668).

308. See Safrian, *Die Eichmann-Männer*, pp. 121–22.

309. Protocol of a meeting regarding "Lösung der Judenfragen," October 10, 1941, quoted from USHMMA RG 48.005m, reel 3 (CSA Prague), printed in Karny et al., *Deutsche*

Politik im "Protektorat," pp. 137–41, emphasis in the original; see also Adler, *Der verwaltete Mensch*, pp. 87–88; Safrian, *Die Eichmann-Männer*, pp. 124–25; Aly, *"Final Solution,"* pp. 229–30.

310. Press announcement by Heydrich, October 10, 1941, quoted from Eva Schmidt-Hartmann, "Tschechoslowakei," p. 361 n. 28.

311. According to the protocol of the October 10 meeting, evacuation from the "temporary collection camps" was to have the effect of "drastically decimating" the Jewish population in the Protectorate (USHMMA RG 48.005m, reel 3, fol. 79).

312. Hitler, *Monologe im Führerhauptquartier 1941–1944*, p. 82 (entry of October 14, 1941).

313. Gerlach, *Kalkulierte Morde*, p. 651; Gerlach, *Krieg, Ernährung, Völkermord*, p. 62.

314. Draft letter by Stahlecker, August 6, 1941, partly printed in Benz et al., *Einsatz im "Reichskommissariat Ostland,"* pp. 42–46.

315. File note BdS Riga/EG A II (Lange), October 1, 1941; BdS/EG A (Stahlecker) to RSHA II, October 6, 1941, USHMMA RG 11.001m5, reel 75 (SAM 504-2-8); see also Longerich, *Politik der Vernichtung*, p. 459.

316. Note from Generalkommissar in Latvia (Drechsler), October 20, 1941, about visit from Stahlecker on October 11, 1941, YIVO Occ E3–29. In a meeting on October 24, 1941, with representatives of the civil administration, the KdS Latvia, Lange, pressed his point by referring to an order by Heydrich (note from Reichskommissar Ostland, October 27, 1941, YIVO Occ E3–30).

317. Report from Gebietskommissar Libau to Generalkommissar Lettland, October 11, 1941, printed in Benz et al., *Einsatz im "Reichskommissariat Ostland,"* pp. 92–93. See also Borgert, "Die Kriegsmarine und das Unternehmen 'Barbarossa,'" p. 61.

318. Bräutigam, "Aus dem Kriegstagebuch," p. 148.

319. Nbg. Doc. 082-PS, quoted from Streit, *Keine Kameraden*, p. 341 n. 95.

320. DKHH, p. 235.

321. Activity report by Einsatzgruppe A until October 15, 1941; partly printed in N. Müller, *Die faschistische Okkupationspolitik*, pp. 204–5.

322. Longerich, *Politik der Vernichtung*, pp. 448–49.

323. See note from Reichskommissar Ostland, October 27, 1941, YIVO Occ E3–30. According to the note, Lange stated that virtually nothing had been done so far regarding the construction of the camp near Riga.

324. DKHH, p. 245.

325. See Nbg. Doc. 3921-PS, IMT, 33:535–36. Wolf Gruner, "Die NS-Judenverfolgung und die Kommunen," p. 75, claims that Hitler was directly involved in selecting the deportation sites. If this was indeed the case, he took no interest in what was to happen with the deportees after arrival.

326. See, e.g., the complaint by the Gebietskommissar in Slutsk dated October 30, 1941 to Generalkommissar Lohse that found its way to Rosenberg's office, quoted in Browning, *Ordinary Men*, pp. 19–23.

327. Longerich, *Politik der Vernichtung*, p. 442.

328. Draft letter from Wetzel to Lohse "Betr.: Lösung der Judenfrage," October 25,

1941, Nbg. Doc. NO-365. See also Friedlander, *The Origins of Nazi Genocide*, pp. 211–12.

329. Browning, *Fateful Months*, pp. 57–68; Gerlach, *Kalkulierte Morde*, pp. 764–67. A file kept by Nebe's aide, SS-Obersturmbannführer Engelmann, confirms postwar statements that already in early August a chemist of the RSHA's Criminal Technical Institute was ordered to Smolensk by Einsatzgruppe B commander Nebe (Engelmann to KdS Warschau, August 8, 1941, BA ZR 7, fol. 120). See also Gerlach, *Kalkulierte Morde*, pp. 648–49. In mid-December 1941, Nebe informed his successor as Einsatzgruppe B commander that two "special vehicles" were about to be sent to the East. (Nebe to Naumann, December 12, 1941, BA ZR 7, fol. 165).

330. File note from Trampedach, November 7, 1941, quoted from Safrian, *Die Eichmann-Männer*, p. 147.

331. BdS/EG A (Lange) to RK Ostland, November 8, 1941, YIVO Occ E3-31; KdS in Latvia to Gebietskommissar Dünaburg, November 11, 1941, printed in Benz et al., *Einsatz im "Reichskommissariat Ostland,"* p. 94. On November 7 the Jewish community in Berlin on order of the Gestapo sent out notifications to those Jews who were to be deported to Kaunas (CSA Vilnius 1390-3-67, fols. 1–7).

332. Telegram RK Ostland II (Trampedach) to RmfdbO, Lohse, November 9, 1941, YIVO Occ E3-32. Jeckeln and Prützmann had exchanged positions at the end of October.

333. Telegram from Reichsministerium für die besetzten Ostgebiete (Leibbrandt) to RK Ostland, November 9, 1941, YIVO Occ E3-32.

334. Twenty-five thousand deportees were scheduled for Riga. As construction work had only begun in Salaspils, transports were to be sent to Jungfernhof. The first five transports originally scheduled for Riga had to be rerouted to Kaunas (BdS/EG A [Lange] to RK Ostland, November 8, 1941, YIVO Occ E3-31).

335. Gerlach, *Kalkulierte Morde*, pp. 624–26.

336. Statement by Friedrich Jeckeln, December 14, 1945 (protocol in German), USHMMA Accession Number 1996.A510 (KGB Archive collection). There is no reference to a meeting with Jeckeln on this day in Himmler's appointment books (*DKHH*, pp. 258–59).

337. EM 151, January 5, 1942, in Arad et al., *The Einsatzgruppen Reports*, p. 269.

338. See EK 3, "Gesamtaufstellung," December 1, 1941, USHMMA RG 11.001m, reel 183 (SAM 500-1-25), according to which 4,934 Jews from Berlin, Munich, Frankfurt, Vienna, and Breslau were murdered in Kaunas on November 25 and 29, 1941.

339. EM 155, January 11, 1942, in Arad et al., *The Einsatzgruppen Reports*, p. 277; Safrian, *Die Eichmann-Männer*, p. 153. The action in Riga increased the tension between the Security Police and the Stadtkommissar, who had planned to extract further assets from the ghetto on December 1; see Scheffler, "Einsatzgruppe A," p. 40.

340. Safrian, *Die Eichmann-Männer*, p. 154.

341. Radio messages from Himmler to Jeckeln, December 1, 1941, Public Record Office HW 16/32, GPD 471 No. 2, quoted from Gerlach, *Krieg, Ernährung, Völkermord*, p. 95; see also *DKHH*, p. 278.

342. File note by Lösener on a meeting with State Secretary Stuckart, December 26, 1941, quoted from Wilhelm Lenz, ed., "Die Handakten von Bernhard Lösener, 'Rassereferent' im Reichsministerium des Innern," p. 697.

343. Letter from Lohse to Reichsministerium für die besetzten Ostgebiete, November 15, 1941, quoted from Kurt Pätzold and Erika Schwarz, *Tagesordnung: Judenmord*, pp. 95–96.

344. File note from Rosenberg, November 11, 1941, quoted from DKHH, p. 262 n. 46.

345. Heydrich to Rosenberg, January 10, 1942, YIVO Occ E4–22; Himmler to Berger, October 9, 1942, BA NS 19/1704; Benz et al., *Einsatz im "Reichskommissariat Ostland,"* pp. 51–61.

346. Wehrmachtsbefehlshaber Ostland (Braemer) to RK Ostland, November 20, 1941, YIVO Occ E3–34; printed in N. Müller, *Die faschistische Okkupationspolitik*, pp. 225–26.

347. Karny et al., *Deutsche Politik im "Protektorat,"* p. 130.

348. Hilberg, *The Destruction of the European Jews*, pp. 353–54; Gerlach, *Krieg, Ernährung, Völkermord*, p. 97. According to Gerlach, Kube's protests against the deportation of "Mischlinge" and German Jews with war decorations did not have an impact on the temporary stop to deportations (p. 100).

349. Aly, *"Final Solution,"* pp. 342–47, 361; Gerlach, "Failure of Plans for an SS Extermination Camp in Mogilev, Belorussia," pp. 60–64; Breitman, *Official Secrets*, pp. 75–76. In a document compiled in mid-November, the Erfurt-based company Topf & Söhne, provider of the Auschwitz crematoria ovens, hints at an even larger project by referring to the planned and "extremely urgent" construction of about 25 crematoria facilities ordered by Himmler "for prisoner camps in the East." RFSS, ca. 25 Krematoriumsanlagen für Gefangenenlager im Osten-äusserst dringlich!, Topf an Industrie- und Handelskammer Erfurt, November 3, 1941, Topf company papers held by Jean-Claude Pressac. I am grateful to Mr. Pressac for showing me this document.

350. See for Lithuania, EK 3, "Gesamtaufstellung," December 1, 1941, USHMMA RG 11.001m, reel 183 (SAM 500-1-25); for Latvia, report by Generalkommissar in Latvia, November 20, 1941, partly printed in Benz et al., *Einsatz im "Reichskommissariat Ostland,"* pp. 126–28, 138–41; for Estonia being reported "free of Jews," see "Tätigkeits- und Lagebericht" No. 9 until January 31, 1941, partly printed in ibid., p. 104.

351. See note (by Lohse?), November 28, 1941, YIVO Occ E3–32; notes by Lohse, November 26, December 1, 1941 ("IIa: Nichts mehr zu veranlassen"), YIVO Occ E3–26. See also Safrian, *Die Eichmann-Männer*, p. 149.

352. Leibbrandt to Lohse, December 4, 1941, "Betr.: Lösung der Judenfrage," BA R 90/146, quoted from Gerlach, *Krieg, Ernährung, Völkermord*, p. 95 n. 30.

353. Letter from Kube to Lohse, December 16, 1941, YIVO Occ E3–36; see Hilberg, *The Destruction of the European Jews*, p. 354.

354. Reichsministerium für die besetzten Ostgebiete I (Bräutigam) to RK Ostland, December 18, 1941, YIVO Occ E3–28, printed in Pätzold and Schwarz, *Tagesordnung: Judenmord*, p. 96.

355. DKHH, pp. 283–84. For a report by an Order Police officer regarding the deportation of German Jews from the Rhineland to Riga in December 1941, see Pätzold and Schwarz, *Tagesordnung: Judenmord*, pp. 97–98.

356. SS order by Himmler, December 12, 1941, quoted from Benz et al., *Einsatz im "Reichskommissariat Ostland,"* pp. 28–29. Kwiet, "Erziehung zum Mord," pp. 449–52, stresses the importance of this document.

357. Heydrich speech, October 2, 1941, cited in Karny et al., *Deutsche Politik im "Protektorat,"* pp. 107–22.

358. Already in early August, British intelligence analysts observed on the basis of the intercepted German execution reports that the HSSPF "stand somewhat in competition with each other as to their 'scores'" (quoted in Breitman, *Official Secrets*, p. 92).

359. See fragmentary report by EK 2 (Lange), no date (early 1942), BA R 70 Sowjetunion / 20: "The goal, of which EK 2 had a vague notion from the beginning, was a radical solution of the Jewish problem through the execution of all Jews." (*Das Ziel, das dem EK 2 von Anfang an vorschwebte, war eine radikale Lösung des Judenproblems durch die Exekution aller Juden.*) See also EK 3 (Jäger), "Gesamtaufstellung," December 1, 1941, USHMMA RG 11.001m, reel 183 (SAM 500-1-25, fol. 115).

8. From War of Destruction to the Final Solution

1. *Die Tagebücher von Joseph Goebbels I*, 4:740 (entry of July 8, 1941).

2. *Die Tagebücher von Joseph Goebbels II*, 1:30, 33 (entry of July 9, 1941). Just several days earlier, Hitler had proclaimed that "Bolshevism must be destroyed" and Moscow as its center "will disappear from the face of the earth." Werner Jochmann, ed., *Monologe im Führerhauptquartier 1941–1944*, p. 39.

3. Cited in Martin Broszat, "Hitler and the Genesis of the Final Solution: An Assessment of David Irving's Thesis," p. 88.

4. IMT, 38:86–94 (Nbg. Doc. 221-L: conference, July 16, 1941).

5. Büchler, "Kommandostab Reichsführer-SS"; Prague Military Archives, Kommandostab-RFSS, sig. Ia 12 / 1, Kr. 10 (manpower strength of the units under the Kommandostab-RFSS, July 1, 1941).

6. Police Battalion 322 was transferred to von dem Bach-Zelewski on July 23, 1941, for "impending tasks." YVA, O-53 / 27 / 53, war diary entry, July 23, 1941.

7. BA-MA, R 19 / 326: Himmler to HSSPFs, July 25, 1941.

8. For the police battalions: BDC, O 464, Osteinsatz Polizei, "Die im Osten eingesetzten Stäbe." For the auxiliary police: Nbg. Doc. NO-285 (Daluege report of January 1943).

9. DKHH, pp. 181, 183.

10. DKHH, p. 189.

11. BA-MA, RS 3–8 / 36: Himmler order of July 30, 1941, to SS Cavalry Regiment 2, August 1, 1941. See also JNSV, vol. 20, No. 570 (LG Braunschweig 2 Ks 1 / 63), p. 44.

12. YVA, O / 53 / 144 / 409–10 (Tschierschky to Stahlecker, August 5, 1941); Benz et al., *Einsatz im "Reichskommissariat Ostland,"* p. 42 (Tschierschky to Jäger, August 4, 1941); and YVA, O-53 / 144 / 412 (Stahlecker to Heydrich, October 8, 1941).

13. Historical State Archives, Riga: "Betriff: Entwurf über die Aufstellung vorläufiger Richtlinien für die Behandlung der Juden im Gebiet des Reichskommissariates Ostland, August 6, 1941, Nowosselje," signed by Stahlecker. I am grateful to Professor Gerald Fleming for giving me a copy of this document. Now printed in Hans Mommsen, ed., *Herrschaftsalltag im Dritten Reich*, pp. 467–71, and in Benz et al., *Einsatz im "Reichskommissariat Ostland,"* p. 41–46.

14. YVA, O / 53 / 141 / 30–38 (Jäger report, December 1, 1941).

15. *DKHH*, p. 186.

16. ZStL, II 204 AR-Z 1251/65 (LG Regensburg Ks 6/70, judgment against Engelbert Kreuzer), pp. 11–15, 33–35.

17. *DKHH*, p. 191; Landgericht Köln, 24 Ks 1/52, 3:747–55 (testimony of Erwin Schulz, February 3, 1953). For the career of Erwin Schulz, see Wildt, *Generation des Unbedingten*, pp. 561–78. In his affidavit of May 26, 1947 (Nbg. Doc. NO-3644), Schulz dated this meeting with Rasch and the dissemination of the Jeckeln order to around July 25, 1941. For an analysis of the collected testimonies of Schulz (including less precise dating to early or mid-August), see Ogorreck, *Die Einsatzgruppen*, pp. 190–91. For the text of Schulz's letter to Lucius Clay asking for clemency, see Hans-Heinrich Wilhelm, ed., *Rassenpolitik und Kriegführung. Sicherheitspolizei und Wehrmacht in Polen und der Sowjetunion*, pp. 220–27.

18. Arad et al., *The Einsatzgruppen Reports*, p. 158 (No. 94, September 24, 1941).

19. *DKHH*, pp. 192–96.

20. Browning, *Fateful Months*, pp. 59–60.

21. Ogorreck, *Die Einsatzgruppen*, p. 183, cites the testimony of an SS man: "On the day after Himmler's visit we were told that he had ordered that now not only men but also women and children, that is, the entire Jewish population, was to be seized. We were told that if left alive the young ones could later take revenge. From this day on, then, women and children of every age were also shot." The transition to the shooting of Jewish children in Belorussia was neither so immediate nor so comprehensive as this testimony suggests, but the testimony nevertheless supports the notion that the issue of shooting Jewish women and children was broached by Himmler during his visit.

22. YVA, O-53/127, war diary of Police Battalion 322 (entries of August 31 and September 1, 1941).

23. Headland, *Messengers of Death*; Breitman, *Official Secrets*, p. 56.

24. Klein, *Die Einsatzgruppen*, p. 342 (Müller to Einsatzgruppen A, B, C, D, August 1, 1941).

25. *Unsere Ehre heisst Treue*, pp. 219–38; and more fully the records from the Prague Military Archive available on microfilm, USHMMA, RG 48.004m.

26. *DKHH*, p. 191 n. 4.

27. YVA, O/53/128/242–75 and O-53/86/14–62; Breitman, *Official Secrets*, p. 63.

28. Ogorreck, *Die Einsatzgruppen*, pp. 204–6.

29. Arad et al., *The Einsatzgruppen Reports*, p. 43 (No. 31, July 23, 1941). In EM 52 of August 14, 1941, a segment presumably based on a report from Ohlendorf written several days earlier noted that "until the final solution of the Jewish question for the entire continent is achieved, the superfluous Jewish masses can be excellently employed and used for cultivating the vast Pripet swamps, the northern Dnieper swamps as well as those of the Volga." Arad et al., *The Einsatzgruppen Reports*, p. 87. This, of course, dates from before Ohlendorf's mid-August visit to Heydrich in Berlin.

30. Arad et al., *The Einsatzgruppen Reports*, p. 137 (No. 86, September 17, 1941).

31. Eiber, " ' . . . ein bisschen die Wahrheit,' " pp. 71, 73.

32. *ADAP*, D, vol. 12/2, appendix 3, p. 838 (memo of Hewel on conversation of Hitler with Keitel and Kvaternik, July 22, 1941).

33. BDC, SS officer file for Friedrich Suhr.

34. *IMT*, 26:266–7 (710-PS). In one account Eichmann claimed that he drafted this Göring authorization on Heydrich's instruction, and it was then submitted for Göring's signature. Eichmann, *Ich Adolf Eichmann. Ein historischer Zeugenbericht*, p. 479. In another account, while still assuming the initiative came from Heydrich, Eichmann admitted, "In any case, how Heydrich received this authorization I do not know." BAK, All. Proz. 6/199, "Meine Memoiren" manuscript pp. 112–13. As Eberhard Jäckel has noted, according to Göring's appointment book, Heydrich had scheduled a one-hour meeting with Göring on the early evening of July 31, 1941, during which time the authorization could have been submitted for Göring's signature. The fact that the document was not written on Göring's letterhead but rather on a plain sheet of paper, Jäckel notes, further strengthens the suspicion that it was drafted by Heydrich. Eberhard Jäckel and Jürgen Rohwer, eds., *Der Mord an den Juden im Zweiten Weltkrieg: Entschlussbildung und Verwirklichung*, p. 15.

35. PA, Inland IIg 177, Heydrich to Ribbentrop, June 23, 1940; Browning, *The Final Solution and the German Foreign Office*, pp. 19, 38.

36. The interpretation of Götz Aly, *"Final Solution,"* p. 172, that the July 31 document was only a written confirmation—necessary to strengthen Heydrich's hand vis-à-vis others—to submit an expulsion plan for which he had already obtained approval in March 1941 is unpersuasive. Heydrich did not need a written document from Göring to submit a "draft" for a plan that had already been approved by Hitler and Göring months earlier.

37. See the suggestive subtitle—"Es ist des Führers Wünsch"— of Gerald Fleming's *Hitler und die Endlösung*.

38. Lösener, "Als Rassereferent," pp. 302–3.

39. NA microfilm, T81/676/5485740–56 (Propaganda Ministry memorandum for Reichminister Goebbels, August 17, 1941). This memorandum is cited extensively in Adler, *Der verwaltete Mensch*, pp. 50–51.

40. *Die Tagebücher von Joseph Goebbels II*, 1:265–66, 269, 278 (entries of August 19 and 20, 1941). By mid-August Antonescu's forces had killed many Jews in Bessarabia and were trying to expel the remaining Bessarabian Jews over the Dniester River into Transnistria.

41. For the Interior Ministry: Lösener, "Als Rassereferent," p. 305. For the Foreign Office: PA, Inland IIg 172: Rademacher memorandum, August 21, 1941; Luther note, August 22, 1941; and Luther memorandum, August 22, 1941 (T120/K796/K210292–93 and K210277–78).

42. Lösener, "Als Rassereferent," pp. 305–7.

43. PA, Inland IIg 172: Rademacher memorandum, September 8, 1941; and Luther to Ribbentrop, September 11, 1941 (T120/K796/K210175–76 and K210266–68).

44. In this episode as elsewhere in his new biography, Ian Kershaw portrays Hitler's role in actual decision making on Jewish policy as more passive, simply assenting to pressures and proposals from others. *Hitler 1936–1945: Nemesis*, pp. 461–95. In sharp contrast, Tobias Jersak, "Die Interaktion von Kriegsverlauf und Judenvernichtung: Ein Blick auf Hitlers Strategie im Spätsommer 1941," portrays Hitler as making decisions entirely on his own and sees the mid-August signing of the Atlantic Charter as the exact point at which he gave up expectation of a Blitzkrieg victory over the Soviet Union and ordered the Final Solution as an "alternative."

45. The pivotal role of American entry into the war in activating Hitler's January 1939

prophecy concerning the consequences of a "world war" for European Jews is argued by a number of scholars, esp. L. J. Hartog, *Der Befehl zum Judenmord: Hitler, Amerika, und die Juden*; and Gerlach, "Die Wannsee-Konferenz." Jersak has argued the same connection, but dated to the Atlantic Charter rather than Pearl Harbor, in "Die Interaktion von Kriegs-verlauf und Judenvernichtung."

46. *DKHH*, p. 198.

47. Cited in Adalbert Rückerl, *Nationalsozialistische Vernichtungslager im Spiegel deut-scher Strafprozesse: Belzec, Sobibor, Treblinka, Chelmno*, pp. 256–57.

48. PA, Inland II AB 47/1, Eichmann to D III, August 28, 1941.

49. USHMMA, RG 15.007m, 8/103/45–62 (Höppner Aktenvermerk, September 2, 1941, and Höppner to Ehlich and Eichmann, September 3, 1941). The Aktenvermerk is printed in Czeslaw Madajczyk, ed., *Vom Generalplan Ost zum Generalsiedlungsplan*, Anlage Nr. 3, pp. 392–96.

50. Klarsfeld, *Vichy-Auschwitz*, pp. 367–68 (Zeitschel to Abetz, August 22, 1942).

51. PA, Inland II AB 65/4, Benzler to Foreign Office, August 14, 1941.

52. *ADAP*, D, vol. 13/1, pp. 378, 386 (Veesenmayer and Benzler to Foreign Office, September 8 and 10, 1941); PA, Inland IIg 194, Benzler to Foreign Office, September 12, 1941 (T120/K773/K205193).

53. PA, Inland IIg 194, Rademacher marginalia, September 13, 1941, on Benzler to Foreign Office, September 12, 1941.

54. Bräutigam, "Aus dem Kriegstagebuch," pp. 144–45. See also Adler, *Der verwaltete Mensch*, pp. 176–77.

55. Ulrich Herbert, "Die deutsche Militärverwaltung und die Deportation der fran-zösischen Juden," pp. 435–36, 443–44.

56. Klarsfeld, *Vichy-Auschwitz*, p. 32 (Zeitschel to Abetz, September 10, 1941). Peter Witte, "Two Decisions Concerning the 'Final Solution to the Jewish Question': Deporta-tions to Lodz and Mass Murder in Chelmno," pp. 327–28. I am very indebted to Witte's masterful reconstruction of the events of September 14–18, 1941.

57. Witte, "Two Decisions," pp. 324–25.

58. Landgericht Köln, 24 Ks 3/53, 2:366–67 (testimony of Jean Brodesser).

59. *DKHH*, pp. 200–203.

60. *DKHH*, p. 205, esp. n. 19.

61. Witte, "Two Decisions," pp. 328–29; *DKHH*, pp. 210–12.

62. Witte, "Two Decisions," p. 325.

63. NA microfilm, T175/54/2568695: Himmler to Greiser, September 18, 1941.

64. YVA, O-53/85/1036: Türk to KHM Hrubieszow, October 7, 1941.

65. Burrin, *Hitler and the Jews*, p. 123; Witte, "Two Decisions," p. 325.

66. The struggle over strategy can be traced in the appendixes of *KTB* OKW, pp. 1029–68. See also Ernst Klink, "The War against the Soviet Union until the Turn of 1941/1942," pp. 569–94; and Gerhard Weinberg, *A World at Arms: A Global History of Word War II*, pp. 269–70.

67. *Die Tagebücher von Joseph Goebbels II*, 1:261 (entry of August 19, 1941).

68. Alan Clark, *Barbarossa: The Russian-German Conflict, 1941–45*, p. 155.

69. *KTB* OKW, 2:661.

70. *Die Tagebücher von Joseph Goebbels II*, 1:480–82, 485 (entry of September 24, 1941).

71. Klink, "The War against the Soviet Union," pp. 664–65.

72. *Die Tagebücher von Joseph Goebbels II*, 2:49–50 (entry of October 4, 1941).

73. Koeppens's note of October 7, 1941, printed in Karny et al., *Deutsche Politik im "Protektorat,"* Doc. No. 25, pp. 129–31. On September 29, 1941, Eichmann had informed colleagues of the Umwandererzentrale (UMZ) in Lodz that Soviet territory was being considered as a "provisional alternative" (*vorläufige Ausweichmöglichkeit*) to receive expellees, but "we should wait until the transportation situation improves." For the moment, no decision could be taken concerning the resumption of resettlement actions. Aly, *"Final Solution,"* p. 351. According to Hitler's adjutant, Gerhard Engel, allegedly Hitler met with Himmler, Heydrich, Keitel, and Jodl on October 2, 1941, and at this meeting Himmler reported on the deportation of Jews and mentioned Riga, Reval, and Minsk in particular. Hitler also allegedly authorized Himmler to carry out the deportation of Jews from Salonika, where he feared a disastrous intermingling of Jews and Levantines. Engel, *Heeresadjutant bei Hitler*, 111. The dating in Engel is unreliable. Philippe Burrin, in *Hitler and the Jews*, pp. 171–72, points out that Himmler was in the Ukraine at that time and did not return until October 5, 1941. Burrin assumes, quite plausibly, that this meeting took place later.

74. *Die Tagebücher von Joseph Goebbels II*, 2:73 (entry of October 7, 1941). According to Klink, "Agreement about the favorable situation was general." Klink, "The War against the Soviet Union," p. 675. According to Andreas Hillgruber, Hitler exuded a "spirit of total victory" (*voller Siegesstimmung*) reminiscent of mid-July. Hillgruber, ed., *Staatsmänner bei Hitler: Vertrauliche Aufzeichnungen über Unterredungen mit Vertretern des Auslandes 1939–41*, p. 626.

75. Karny et al., *Deutsche Politik im "Protektorat,"* Doc. No. 24 (undated position paper), pp. 128–29.

76. Heydrich had been busy in the previous week. As Burrin, *Hitler and the Jews*, pp. 123–24, has noted, seven Parisian synagogues were bombed on the night of October 2. When the investigation by the German military led to the German Security Police in Paris, Heydrich candidly admitted responsibility. He explained he had given permission "only from the moment when, at the highest level, Jewry had been forcefully designated as the culpable incendiary in Europe, one which must definitively disappear from Europe." On October 4 Heydrich had met with Alfred Meyer of the Ostministerium and bemoaned that businesses wanting to keep Jewish labor "would reduce to naught the plan for a total resettlement of the Jews out of the territories occupied by us."

77. Notes on conference of October 10, 1941, in Prague, printed in H. G. Adler, *Theresienstadt 1941–1945: Das Anlitz einer Zwangsgemeinschaft*, Doc. 46b, pp. 720–22.

78. For the end of resistance at Vyazma and Bryansk, see *KTB* OKW, 2:702, 708.

79. Centre de Documentation Juive Contemporaine, Doc. V-16 (Zeitschel to Dannecker, October 8, 1941), copy in YVA, O-53/136/2275–76.

80. Frank, *Diensttagebuch*, p. 413 (entry of October 14, 1941).

81. *DiM*, 3:184 (excerpt of monthly report of June 6, 1941), pp. 188–93 (Biebow to

Landrat Wolun, September 2, 1941; Greiser to Uebelhoer, September 11, 1941; Ventzki to Uebelhoer, September 16, 1941; Polizeidirektor to Reichsbahndirektion Posen, September 20, 1941).

82. NA microfilm, T175/54/2568671–94 (Ventzki to Uebelhoer, September 24, 1941) and 2568668–70 (Uebelhoer to Himmler, October 4, 1941).

83. NA microfilm, T175/54/2568662–63 (Himmler to Uebelhoer, October 10, 1941).

84. NA microfilm, T175/54/2568653–54 (Uebelhoer to Himmler, October 9, 1941).

85. NA microfilm, T175/54/2568648–49 (Thomas to Himmler, October 11, 1941).

86. NA microfilm, T175/54/2568651 (Himmler to Uebelhoer, October 11, 1941).

87. NA microfilm, T175/54/2568645–47 (Heydrich to Himmler, October 19, 1941).

88. NA microfilm, T175/54/2568641–43 (Greiser to Himmler, October 28, 1941; and Himmler to Greiser, November 10, 1941).

89. Hilberg, *The Destruction of the European Jews*, pp. 351–52 (citing YIVO doc. Occ E3–29: Drechsler to Lohse, October 20, 1941, and unsigned note, October 21, 1941).

90. YVA, JM 3435 (YIVO Berlin Collection Occ E3-30): RK Ostland Vermerk, October 27, 1941, initialed by Wetzel).

91. YVA, JM 3435: Lange to RK Ostland, November 8, 1941.

92. YVA, JM 3435: Trampedach to Ostministerium and Lohse, November 9, 1941.

93. YVA, JM 3435: Leibbrandt to RK Ostland, November 13, 1941.

94. YVA, JM 3435: Wehrmachtbefehlshaber Ostland, November 20, 1941, to RK Ostland; Trampedach to RK Ostland, January 13, 1942. Field Marshal von Bock commanding the Army Group Center apparently also protested against using scarce transport for the resettlement of thousands of Jews at the high point of preparations for the decisive battle for Moscow and during an ongoing provisioning crisis aggravated by bad weather. Krausnick and Wilhelm, *Die Truppe des Weltanschauungskrieges*, p. 585. There is no record of a response to this protest, however.

95. Gerlach, "Die Wannsee-Konferenz," p. 13.

96. The following is a summary of studies already published in Browning, *The Final Solution and the German Foreign Office*, pp. 56–67; and *Fateful Months*, pp. 39–56.

97. On Turner's career, see Christopher R. Browning, "Harald Turner und die Militärverwaltung in Serbien 1941–1942," pp. 352–53.

98. Landgericht Köln 24 Ks 1/52 (hereafter cited as Schäfer trial), 2:397–8 (testimony of Alexander F.). BA-MA): RW 40/4: entry of July 5, 1941; and Anlage 33, report of July 22, 1941 (Nbg. Doc. NOKW-1091). Nbg. Doc. NO-2942 (report of Chef der Sipo-SD, July 19, 1941). American Military Tribunal (hereafter cited as AMT), Case VII, transcript, p. 917 (testimony of Georg Kiessel).

99. BA-MA, RH 26-104/8, Anlage 156 (Verfügung über Vorbeugungs- und Sühnemassnahmen).

100. BA-MA, RH 40/4, Anlage 61, Ehrmann report, August 1, 1941. PA, Staatssekretär-Jugoslawien, Bd. 3, Benzler to Foreign Office, August 1, 1941. Nbg. Doc. NOKW-1661 (Kiesel to Tippelskirch, August 9, 1941) and Nbg. Doc. NOKW-551 (OKW daily report of August 11, 1941).

101. BA-MA: RW 40/4, entry of July 22, 1941, and Anlage 33, Gravenhorst to 65th Corps, July 21, 1941; 40411/7, Bader to List, August 28, 1941.

102. BA-MA, RW 40/4: entries of July 24 and 29, 1941; and Anlage 48, List to Danckelmann, July 29, 1941.

103. PA, Staatskretär-Jugoslawien, Bd. 3, Benzler to Foreign Office, July 23 and August 1, 1941; Inland IIg 401, Benzler to Foreign Office, August 8, 1941. BA-MA: RW 40/4, Anlage 45, report of Feldkommandantur 816 for July 12–27, 1941, and Anlage 59, Ic report of Picht for July; 14 749/18, reports of Wehrmachtverbindungsstelle, July 31 and August 8, 1941 (Nbg. Doc. NOKW-1114); 40411/6, Bader report of August 23, 1941.

104. Paul Hehn, *The German Struggle against Yugoslav Guerrillas in World War II: German Counter-Insurgency in Yugoslavia, 1941–1943*, pp. 28–29 (citing the Wisshaupt report).

105. PA, Staatssekretär-Jugoslawien, Bd. 3, Benzler to Foreign Office, July 23, 1941. BA-MA: RW 40/4, Anlage 35, Kiessel to List, July 23, 1941; RH 25-104/9, Anlage 116, Jost report, July 30, 1941; Anlage 179g, Borowski to 65th Corps, August 9, 1941, and Anlage 180, Stobbe to 704th division, August 7, 1941; RW 40/5, entry of August 9, 1941; RH 26-114/3, August summary.

106. PA: Staatssekretär-Jugoslawien, Bd. 3, Benzler to Foreign Office, July 23, August 8, 12, 27, and 28, 1941; and Inland II AB 65/4, Benzler to Foreign Office, August 14, 1941. BA-MA, RW 40/4, Anlage 35, Kiessel to List, July 23, 1941; Anlage 45, report of FK 816 for July 12–27, 1941; and Anlage 59, Ic report of Picht for July; RW 40/5, entry of August 2, 1941, Anlage 1, Danckelmann to List, August 2, 1941, Anlage 2, Danckelmann to OKH, August 3, 1941, Anlage 40, Danckelmann to OKW, August 14, 1941, Anlage 111, report of I c Fetz, August 21–31, 1941, Anlage 114, report of Ia Kogard for August 1941; RW 40/184, Turner report, July 10, 1941; RW 40/185, Turner report, August 10, 1941; RW 40/186, Turner report, September 6, 1941. BA, NS 19/1730, Danckelmann to List, September 3, 1941. Hehn, *German Struggle*, p. 28.

107. Hehn, *German Struggle*, pp. 29–30, 34–35.

108. BA-MA: 14 749/5, Anlage 58, List to Danckelmann and Bader, September 4, 1941 (Nbg. Doc. NOKW-453); RW 40/11, Anlage 7, List to Danckelmann, September 5, 1941 (Nbg. Doc. NOKW-625).

109. On List, see (*a*) his testimony before the American Military Tribunal, transcript, pp. 3148ff., 3321ff., 9605ff.; (*b*) his pretrial interrogations, Nürnberg Staatsarchiv (hereafter cited as NStA), Rep. 502, VI , L 65; (*c*) the account of his chief of staff, Hermann Foertsch, Institut für Zeitgeschichte, Zz 37; and (*d*) List Defense Documents, NStA, Rep. 501, VII, Le, vols. 2–10.

110. NStA, List Defense Document 35 (affidavit of Angelo Roncalli).

111. NStA, List Defense Documents 23 (affidavit of Franz Halder) and 134 (affidavit of Konrad Rudolf).

112. AMT, Case VII, transcript, pp. 3427–29.

113. Hehn, *German Struggle*, p. 31.

114. PA, Staatssekretär-Jugoslawien, Bd. 4, Benzler to Foreign Office, September 12, 1941. BA-MA, 40/11: Anlage 31, Danckelmann to 65th Corps, September 12, 1941; and Anlage 33, daily report of September 12, 1941.

115. Hehn, *German Struggle*, pp. 37–39; AMT, Case VII, p. 4158 (Foertsch testimony).

116. On Böhme, see Nbg. Doc. NOKW-876, 1560, and 1041; and NStA, Rep. 502, VI B 110.

117. BA-MA 17 729.4: Anlage 11, Kewisch report, September 21, 1941; and Anlage 17, Turner to Böhme, September 21, 1941 (NOKW-892).

118. BA-MA, 17 729.4: Anlage 20, Böhme order of September 22, 1941 (Nbg. Doc. NOKW-183); Anlage 22, Böhme order of September 23, 1941 (Nbg. Doc. NOKW-194); 17 729.9, Anlage 17, Pemsel to Turner and 342nd div., September 27, 1941 (Nbg. Doc. NOKW-193).

119. BA-MA, 17 729.9, Anlage 31, Böhme order and message to the troops, September 25, 1941 (Nbg. Doc. NOKW-1048).

120. M. Jovanovic, "Wir packen, wir auspacken. Tragnica Sudbina Jevreja-Isbeglica U Sapcu 1941." Hinghofer had ordered that the evacuation be carried out "with the greatest severity and without false sense of pity" (*mit allergrösster Schärfe und ohne falsch verstandenes Mitleid*). BA-MA, 15 365.14, Schuster to Ia, October 1, 1941.

121. BA-MA, 15 365.7: Krogh to regiments, September 29, 1941;, and Ia to IR 699, September 28, 1941.

122. BA-MA: 15 365.16, summary for September 24–October 9, 1941; 15 365.3, entry of October 7, 1941; 17 7129.4, Anlage 80, Böhme to 342nd div., October 7, 1941.

123. BA-MA: 17 1729.2, entries of October 2 and 3, 1941; RH 26-114/3, October summary. AMT, Case VII, transcript, pp. 8433–34 (testimony of Topola survivor, Johann Kerbler).

124. BA-MA, 17 7129.2, entry of October 2, 1941. As Walter Manoschek, *"Serbien ist Judenfrei." Militärbesatzungspolitik und Judenvernichtung in Serbien 1941/42*, pp. 82–83, has now proven, Böhme was fully aware that the initial report that the bodies of the German troops killed at Topola had been mutilated was false, but he did nothing to counter the mutilation "legend" that served his purposes.

125. BA-MA, 17 729.9, Anlage 48, excerpt from Keitel order of September 16, 1941 (Nbg. Doc. NOKW-258).

126. BA-MA, 17 729.8, Anlage 24, Faulmüller draft order to Turner and 342nd division, October 4, 1941, with Faulmüller marginal note (Nbg. Doc. NOKW-192). No written order was signed by Böhme; instead, the order was transmitted verbally by Faulmüller. On October 8, Faulmüller as quartermaster was granted jurisdiction over reprisal measures. BA-MA, 17 1729.8, entry of October 8, 1941.

127. BA-MA, 17 729.8, Anlage 28, List to Böhme, October 4, 1941 (Nbg. Doc. NOKW-203); 17 729.2, entry of October 5, 1941.

128. BA-MA, 17 1729.9, Anlage 48, Böhme order, nr. 2848/1g, October 10, 1941 (Nbg. Doc. NOKW-891 and 557).

129. AMT, Case VII, transcript, p. 3370.

130. Jovanovic, "Wir packen, wir auspacken," pp. 245–79.

131. BA-MA, 17 729.9, Anlage 64, Liepe report, October 13, 1941 (Nbg. Doc. NOKW-497). Landgericht Kassel, 3 Js 11/66, Ermittlungsverfahren gegen Walter Liepe, contains detailed testimony about the executions.

132. BA-MA: 15 367.7, Treustedt note, October 8, 1941, and 342nd Ia, nr. 13/41g, October 8, 1941; 17 7129.9, Anlagen 12 and 17, Pemsel to Turner, October 25 and 27, 1941 (Nbg. Doc. NOKW-183 and 193), Anlage 100, Turner to Böhme, October 25, 1941 (Nbg. Doc. NOKW-561), Anlage 159, Böhme to List, October 20, 1941. Nbg. Doc. NO-3156 (Sipo-SD report, October 9, 1941). Jewish History Museum, Belgrade, 24–3-1/6-1 (testimony of Milorad Jelsic, February 20, 1945).

133. Nbg. Doc. NO-5810 (Turner to Hildebrandt, October 17, 1941).

134. PA, Inland II AB 65/4, Benzler to Foreign Office, August 14, 1941; Inland IIg 194, Benzler to Foreign Office, September 12, 1941. *ADAP*, D, vol. 13/1, pp. 378, 386.

135. PA, Inland IIg 194, Rademacher marginalia, September 13, 1941, on Benzler to Foreign Office, September 12, 1941.

136. PA, Inland IIg 194, Luther to Belgrade, September 16, 1941.

137. PA, Inland IIg 194, Benzler to Ribbentrop, September 28, 1941.

138. PA, Inland IIg 194, Luther to Ribbentrop, October 2, 1941.

139. PA, Inland IIg 194, Büro RAM to Luther, October 3, 1941.

140. PA, Inland IIg 194, Luther to Belgrade, October 4, 8, and 15, 1941.

141. *ADAP*, D, vol. 13/2, pp. 570–72 (Rademacher report, October 25, 1941). The following account of Rademacher's trip is based on this report and Landgericht Nürnberg-Fürth, 2 Ks 3/53, pp. 53–58.

142. BA-MA, RH 26-117/3, entries of October 15–17, 1941.

143. BA-MA: RH 26-104/16, Anlage 486c, König report of October 27, 1941 (Nbg. Doc. NOKW-904); RW 40.12, Bischofshausen report of October 20, 1941 (Nbg. Doc. NOKW-387); RH 26-104/13, König report of September 20, 1941.

144. BA-MA: 17 729.9, Anlagen 80 and 81, Faulmüller to IR 749, October 21, 1941, and Pemsel to 65th corps, October 22, 1941; 17 729.2, entry of October 22, 1941; RH 26-104/14, Anlage 53, Bader order of October 24, 1941.

145. BA-MA: 17 729.8, entries of October 23 and 24, 1941; 17 729.9, Anlage 97, Böhme order, nr. 3208/41, October 25, 1941 (Nbg. Doc. NOKW-562).

146. Nbg. Doc. NOKW-802 (Turner to FK, KK, October 26, 1941).

147. BA-MA: RH 26-104/15, Reg. 734 to Div. 704, October 28, 1941 (Nbg. Doc. NOKW-906); RH 26-104/4, entry of October 27, 1941.

148. BA-MA, RW 40.12, Anlage 56, Kogard to Böhme, October 29, 1941.

149. BA-MA, RH 26-104/16, Walther report, November 1, 1941 (Nbg. Doc. NOKW-905). Landgericht Konstanz, 12 Js 823/62, Ermittlungsverfahren gegen Hans-Dietrich Walther, 1:215–59 (interrogation of Walther).

150. BA-MA: 17 729.4, Anlagen 253, 288, and 329, and RW 40/14, Anlagen 12, 26, and 44 (10-day reports for November 10, 20, and 30, 1941, and December 10, 20, 30, 1941).

151. BA-MA, RW 40/2, Aktennotiz of December 20, 1941 (Nbg. Doc. NOKW-474). The report shows that 68% of the shootings had been carried out by army units and 32% by Turner's military administration, i.e., the Sipo-SD Einsatzgruppe and the 64th Reserve Police Battalion.

152. BA-MA, RW 40/14: Anlage 29, Bader to Verwaltungsstab, December 22, 1941; and Anlage 26, Supplement Nr. 3 to 10-day report of December 20, 1941 (Nbg. Doc. NOKW-840).

153. Walter Manoschek, *"Serbien ist Judenfrei,"* disagrees with my characterization of the murder of the male Jews in Serbia as a prelude to or anticipation of the Final Solution. The difference seems to be one of definition, not a conceptual inability on my part to give due status to local events not determined by central policy, as he alleges. Manoschek in effect defines as the Final Solution the killing of Jews solely because they were Jews. Here, as in my discussion of the killing of Soviet Jews the previous summer, I have considered the key criterion to be the intention to kill *all* Jews, including women and children.

154. The most comprehensive studies of the Final Solution in Eastern Galicia are Dieter Pohl, *Nationalsozialistische Judenverfolgung in Ostgalizien 1941–1944*; and Thomas Sandkühler, *"Endlösung" in Galizien*. Pohl (pp. 43–45) estimates that 540,000 Jews fell into German hands in Galicia. Golchewski, "Polen," p. 445, estimates 500,000.

155. Tatiana Berenstein, "Eksterminacja Ludnosci Zydowskiej W Dystrikcie Galicja" (hereafter cited as Berenstein, "Galicja"), table 1; YVA, TR-10/696, Ks 5/65 LG Sttugart, Judgment against Rudolf Röder, Anton Löhnert, and others (hereafter cited as Röder/Löhnert Judgment), p. 19; Philip Friedman, "The Destruction of the Jews of Lwow," p. 244.

156. For the Ukrainian pogroms and German complicity, see Pohl, *Judenverfolgung in Ostgalizien*, pp. 54–67.

157. YVA, TR-10/518, StA Stuttgart 12 Js 1403/61, Indictment of Paul Raebel, Hermann Müller, and others (hereafter Raebel/Müller Indictment), pp. 94–95.

158. Pohl, *Judenverfolgung in Ostgalizien*, pp. 67–74; Sandkühler, *"Endlösung" in Galizien*, pp. 114–22.

159. Pohl, *Judenverfolgung in Ostgalizien*, pp. 83–93; Sandkühler, *"Endlösung" in Galizien*, pp. 80–85.

160. YVA, TR-10/1116, Polizeidirektion Wien to Staatsanwaltschaft Wien, November 18, 1947, summarizing witness testimony. Aharon Weiss, "Stry," *Encyclopedia of the Holocaust*, gives a date of "early September." Berenstein, "Galicja," table 10, records a massacre of 800 Jews in Stryj in either September or October.

161. Frank, *Diensttagebuch*, p. 436 (Regierungssitzung, October 21, 1941).

162. Pohl, *Judenverfolgung in Ostgalizien*, pp. 141, 154–58.

163. Raebel/Müller Indictment, p. 100; Aharon Weiss, "Ternopol," *Encylopedia of the Holocaust*, p. 1458.

164. Pohl, *Judenverfolgung in Ostgalizien*, p. 141.

165. Pohl, *Judenverfolgung in Ostgalizien*, p. 157. This lowest estimate is from Berenstein, "Galicya," table 9. Aharon Weiss, "Stanislawow," *Encyclopedia of the Holocaust*, estimates a Jewish population of 40,000. Sandkühler, *"Endlösung" in Galizien*, p. 149, gives the highest estimate of 42,000.

166. For Krüger and the following events under his command, see YVA, TR-10/785, LG Münster 5 Ks 4/65, Judgment against Hans Krüger (hereafter cited as Krüger Judgment), pp. 82–84, 100–106, 139–42, 197–205; Pohl, *Judenverfolgung in Galizien*, pp. 143–47; Pohl, "Hans Krüger and the Murder of the Jews in the Stanislawow Region"; Sandkühler, *"Endlösung" in Galizien*, pp. 149–52; and Elisabeth Freundlich, *Die Ermordung einer Stadt names Stanislau: NS-Vernichtungspolitik in Polen 1939–1945*.

167. Cited in Pohl, *Judenverfolgung in Ostgalizien*, p. 144.

168. Berenstein, "Galicja," table 9, estimates 2,000. The minimal estimate of the Stuttgart court in Krüger Judgment, p. 142, is 1,200.

169. Berenstein, "Galicja," table 9; Pohl, *Judenverfolgung in Ostgalizien*, p. 147, and Sandkühler, *"Endlösung" in Galizien*, p. 152, estimate 10,000–12,000.

170. Pohl, *Judenverfolgung in Ostgalizien*, p. 145.

171. Krüger Judgment, pp. 332, 381, 388, 391.

172. Raebel/Müller Indictment, p. 134; Berenstein, "Galicja," table 2.

173. YVA, TR-10/831, 2 Js 50/66 StA Darmstadt, Indictment of Herbert Härtel, Erwin Gay, and others (hereafter Härtel/Gay Indictment), pp. 177–81.

174. Sandkühler, *"Endlösung" in Galizien,* p. 153, gives an estimate of 1,200 victims. Aharon Weiss, "Kolomyia," *The Encyclopedia of the Holocaust,* claims 3,000. However, neither Berenstein nor German court records indicate a large-scale killing action in Kolomyja at this time.

175. Härtel/Gay Indictment, pp. 203–5; Berenstein, "Galicja," table 6.

176. Weiss, "Kolomyia"; Berenstein, "Galicja," table 6. Weiss also notes a massacre of 3,000 Jews in Kolomyja on October 12, 1941, but neither Berenstein nor the court records refer to a massacre of such magnitude.

177. Härtel/Gay Indictment, pp. 219–20; Berenstein, "Galicja," table 6; Pohl, *Judenverfolgung in Ostgalizien,* p. 149; Sandkühler, *"Endlösung" in Galizien,* p. 154.

178. Härtel/Gay Indictment, pp. 191, 223; Berenstein, "Galicja," table 6; Pohl, *Judenverfolgung in Ostgalizien,* p. 149.

179. Pohl, *Judenverfolgung in Ostgalizien,* p. 149; various tables of Berenstein, "Galicja."

180. Pohl, *Judenverfolgung in Ostgalizien,* p. 150.

181. For the murderous but less than unsuccessful ghettoization of Lwow, see Pohl, *Judenverfolgung in Ostgalizien,* pp. 158–62.

182. *IMT,* 37:393 (Nbg. Doc. 018-L: Katzmann report to Krüger, June 30, 1943).

183. Friedman, "The Destruction of the Lwow Jews," p. 263.

184. Pohl, *Judenverfolgung in Ostgalizien,* p. 158; Berenstsein, "Galicja," table 1.

185. *IMT,* 37:393 (Katzmann report).

186. Pohl, *Judenverfolgung in Ostgalizien,* p. 160.

187. Pohl, *Judenverfolgung in Ostgalizien,* p. 151. Sandkühler, *"Endlösung" in Galizien,* p. 148, gives a lower estimate of 20,000 victims for the fall massacres.

188. Pohl, *Judenverfolgung in Ostgalizien,* pp. 140, 142–43.

189. *IMT,* 37:392 (Katzmann report).

190. Pohl, *Judenverfolgung in Ostgalizien,* pp. 140–44; Sandkühler, *"Endlösung" in Galizien,* pp. 137–41.

191. For a very different view: Aly, *"Final Solution,"* p. 200.

192. Cited in Hilberg, *The Destruction of the European Jews,* p. 332. For his general discussion of the psychological repercussions, see pp. 327–34.

193. Hilberg, *The Destruction of the European Jews,* pp. 323–27.

194. Cited in Rückerl, *NS-Vernichtung im Spiegel deutscher Strafprozze,* pp. 256–57.

195. Engelmann to KdS Warschau, August 8, 1941, cited above, chap. 7, n. 329.

196. *DKHH,* p. 195 n. 15, citing British wireless intercepts.

197. Browning, *Fateful Months,* p. 59. For more detail, see Volker Riess, *Die Anfänge der Vernichtung "lebensunwerten Lebens" in den Reichsgauen Danzig-Westpreussen und Wartheland 1939/40,* pp. 273–353.

198. Hilberg, *The Destruction of the European Jews,* pp. 332–33.

199. For Widmann's September experiments, see Landgericht Hannover, 2 Ks 2/65, Strafverfahren gegen Pradel und Wentritt (hereafter Pradel/Wentritt trial), 2:95–102 (Zentralstelle to StA Hannover, March 29, 1960); 8:224–25 (testimony of Walter S.); 11:127–28 (Widmann testimony); 14:120 (testimony of Helmut H.). ZStL, 439 AR-Z

18a/60 (Ermittlungsverfahren gegen Dr. August Becker, StA Stuttgart, 13 Js 328/60), pp. 79–80 (Widmann testimony). Mathias Beer, "Die Entwicklung der Gaswagen beim Mord an den Juden," pp. 407–8, dates Widmann's trip from September 13 to September 21, 1941. Christian Gerlach, "Failure of Plans for an ss Extermination Camp in Mogilev," p. 65, is the first scholar to argue for a gassing test in Mogilev shortly before the September 18 gassing test at Novinki, at which Widmann may no longer have been present. See also Gerlach, *Kalkulierte Morde*, pp. 646–49.

200. Pradel/Wentritt trial, 5:251–54, 261–62, and 14:103 (Pradel testimony); and 12:153–61 (Rauff testimony).

201. Pradel/Wentritt trial, 4:69–75, 5:207–9, 6:72–75 (Wentritt testimony).

202. Pradel/Wentritt trial, 5:521–24 (Pradel testimony).

203. Pradel/Wentritt trial, 4:69–76 (Wentritt testimony); 14:137 (judgment).

204. Beer, "Die Entwicklung der Gaswagen," p. 411, dates the Sachsenhausen test to November 3, 1941.

205. Pradel/Wentritt trial, 8:221–22 (testimony of Helmut H.); 9:16–19, 14:118 (testimony of Theodor L.).

206. BA, R 58/71, Vermerk of Sipo-SD II D 3, June 23, 1942.

207. For the most penetrating analysis of the Höss testimony, see Karin Orth, "Rudolf Höss und die 'Endlösung der Judenfrage.' Drei Argumente gegen deren Datierung auf den Sommer 1941." She is very persuasive in demonstrating his confusion in matters of dating and chronology. Because he telescoped events of 1941 and 1942, his claim that Himmler told him of a Hitler order for the destruction of the European Jews in the summer of 1941 in particular is not credible.

208. Rudolf Höss, *Death Dealer: The Memoirs of the SS Kommandant at Auschwitz*, pp. 29–30:

While I was away on camp-related business, Captain Fritzsch, on his own initiative, employed a gas for the killing of these Russian POWs. He crammed the Russians into the individual cells in the basement [of Block 11] and while using gasmasks he threw the Zyklon gas in the cells. . . . During Eichmann's next visit I reported all this to him, about how the Zyklon B was used, and we decided that for the future mass annihilations we would use this gas. The killing of the above-mentioned Russian POWs using Zyklon B was continued, but no longer in Block 11 because it took at least two days to air out the building. We therefore used the morgue of the crematory as the gassing facility. The doors were made airtight, and we knocked some holes in the ceiling through which we could throw in the gas crystals. But I remember only one transport of nine hundred Russian POWs who were gassed there.

209. Höss, *Death Dealer*, pp. 155–56:

While I was on an official trip, my second in command, Camp Commander Fritzsch, experimented with gas for these killings. He used a gas called Zyklon B. . . . When I returned Fritzsch reported to me about how he had used the gas. We used it again out in the basement of Block 11. I viewed the killings wearing a gas mask for protection. . . . I remember well and was much more impressed by the gassing of nine hundred Russians which occurred *soon afterwards* [italics mine] in the old crematory because the use of Block 11 caused too many problems. While the unloading took place, several holes were simply punched from above through the earth and concrete ceiling of the mortuary.

210. Danuta Czech, *Kalendarium der Ereignisse im Konzentrationslager Auschwitz-Birkenau 1939–1945*, pp. 115–19, 122, concludes that the first gassing by Fritzsch took place in late August, and the second gassing that was observed by Höss occurred on September 3, with the bodies being removed from Bunker 11 on September 4. This test involved 600 Russian POWs and some 250 sick inmates. She bases this conclusion on witness statements and the fact that the Bunker Register indicates that no new prisoners were admitted between August 31 and September 5. Without providing a further source or rationale, Czech suggests September 16 as the date for the first gassing in the "old crematory." See also Eugen Kogon, Hermann Langbein, and Adalbert Rückerl, eds., *Nazi Mass Murder: A Documentary History of the Use of Poison Gas*, pp. 145–46; ZStL, IV 402 AR-z 37/58 (LG Frankfurt 4 Ks 2/63), Sonderband 16, p. 2475 (testimony of Edward Pys); Franziszek Piper, "Gas Chambers and Crematoria," p. 157, 177; Stanislaw Klodzinski, "Die erste Vergasung von Häftlingen und Kriegsgegfangenen im Konzentrationslager Auschwitz."

211. ZStL, IV 402 AR-z 37/58: Sonderband 6, p. 970 (testimony of Hans Stark); Sonderband 16, pp. 2469–70 (testimony of Edward Pys); and Judgment (Frankfurt 4 Ks 2/63, p/242). One witness, Hans Stark, gave October 1941 as the date for the gassing of small groups of Jews trucked into Auschwitz. Since Stark was on leave from Auschwitz from December 1941 through March 1942, he could not have been confusing events from the fall of 1941 with those of early 1942. Moreover, his testimony about experimental gassing in the old crematory of the Auschwitz Stammlager in October 1941 took the interrogators by surprise and was in no way the result of their leading the witness. The testimony is, therefore, quite credible. Hans Aumeier testified that the gassing of small groups of Jews (50–80) occurred in November or December 1942, but presumably he meant 1941. See Expert Opinion of Robert Jan van Pelt, Irving vs. Penguin Books and Deborah Lipstadt, citing PRO WO 208/4661, p. 261 (Van Pelt does not include this part of Aumeier's testimony in the published version, *The Case for Auschwitz: Evidence from the Irving Trial*). Bernd C. Wagner, "Gerüchte, Wissen, Verdrängung: Die IG Auschwitz und das Vernichtungslager Birkenau," p. 234. Jean-Claude Pressac, with Robert Jan van Pelt, "The Machinery of Mass Murder at Auschwitz," pp. 209, 242–43. Citing Jan Sehn, Pressac gives December 1941 as the date of the first gassing in the old crematorium. He does not explain why he does not accept the evidence cited by others for the earlier date.

212. Sybille Steinbacher, *"Musterstadt" Auschwitz: Germanisierungspolitik und Judenmord in Ostoberschlesien*, pp. 276–77.

213. Robert Jan van Pelt and Deborah Dwork, *Auschwitz: 1290 to the Present*, pp. 279–83, 292–93; Orth, "Rudolf Höss und die 'Endlösung der Judenfrage,'" pp. 49–51.

214. Robert Jan van Pelt, "A Site in Search of a Mission," pp. 118, 139. Pressac, "The Machinery of Mass Murder at Auschwitz," pp. 198–99.

215. Michael Thad Allen, "The Devil in the Details: The Gas Chambers of Birkenau, October 1941," pp. 199–201; Pressac, "The Machinery of Mass Murder at Auschwitz," pp. 200–201; Jean-Claude Pressac, *Les Crématoires d'Auschwitz*, pp. 26–30.

216. Allen, "The Devil in the Details," p. 201.

217. Drawing 1173, January 15, 1942, and drawing 934, January 27, 1942, reproduced in Jean-Claude Pressac, *Auschwitz: Technique and Operation of the Gas Chambers*, pp. 357–58.

218. Frank, *Diensttagebuch*, pp. 335–36, 338–39 (March 25 and 26, 1941).

219. Frank, *Diensttagebuch*, p. 386 (July 17, 1941).

220. Cited in Aly, *"Final Solution,"* p. 175 (Frank to Lammers, July 19, 1941).

221. Frank, *Diensttagebuch*, p. 389 (July 21, 1941).

222. Breitman, *The Architect of Genocide*, pp. 184–86.

223. For the following reconstruction of events in the General Government, I am very indebted to two authors in particular, even if I do not share all of their conclusions: Dieter Pohl, *Von der "Judenpolitik" zum Judenmord*, pp. 89–111; and Bogdan Musial, *Deutsche Zivilverwaltung und Judenverfolgung im Generalgouvernement*, pp. 193–215.

224. Globocnik to Himmler, October 1, 1941, cited in Musial, *Deutsche Zivilverwaltung und Judenverfolgung*, pp. 203–4.

225. *DKHH*, p. 233.

226. Nbg. Doc. NO-5875: Hellmut Müller report, October 15, 1941, printed in *TWC*, 4:864–86.

227. Kogon et al., *Nazi Mass Murder*, p. 107 (testimony of Stanislaw Kozak).

228. Frank, *Diensttagebuch*, p. 413 (Aktennotiz of Frank-Rosenberg meeting on October 13, 1941).

229. Archivum Pastwowe mj. St. Warszawy, Der Kommissar für den jüdischen Wohnbezirk, Nr. 132, speeches by Max Bischof, Heinz Auerswald, and Ludwig Fischer, October 15, 1941.

230. YVA, JM 21 / 4 (Frank Tagebuch, October 15, 1941).

231. *FGM*, pp. 128–29 (Frank decree of October 15, 1941).

232. YVA, O / 53 / 145 / 57–265 (Arbeitstagung der Abteilung Gesundheitswesen i. d. Regierung in Bad Krynica, October 13–16, 1941).

233. *DKHH*, p. 246 (entry of October 25, 1941, and n. 79).

234. Frank, *Diensttagebuch*, pp. 427–28 (Regierungssitzung in Lublin and Anlage, October 17, 1941).

235. Cited in Musial, *Deutsche Zivilverwaltung und Judenverfolgung*, pp. 196–98. Musial found these remarks in hitherto unpublished sections of the Frank Tagebuch.

236. Frank, *Diensttagebuch*, p. 436 (Regierungssitzung in Lwow, October 21, 1941).

237. Frank, *Diensttagebuch*, p. 441 (entry of October 21, 1941).

238. Musial, *Deutsche Zivilverwaltung und Judenverfolgung*, pp. 193, 200, in support of Gerlach, "Die Wannsee-Konferenz." See also Longerich, *Politik der Vernichtung*.

239. *DKHH*, pp. 201–2.

240. *DKHH*, p. 205, esp. n. 19.

241. Burrin, *Hitler and the Jews*, p. 127.

242. Affidavit of Hans Bodo Gorgass, February 23, 1947 (Nbg. Doc. NO-3010), cited by Helmut Krausnick in *Der Mord an den Juden im Zweiten Weltkrieg*, pp. 139–40.

243. ZStL, 8 AR-Z 252 / 59, 5:925–30 (testimony of Hans-Joachim B.).

244. There are now at least six different Eichmann testimonies. (1) In 1957 he gave an interview to the Dutch journalist Willem Sassen, and made his own corrections to the

transcripts of the interview (BAK, All. Proz. 6/95–111). Two published versions, based on the Sassen interviews, were compiled by others: *Ich Adolf Eichmann. Ein historischer Zeugenbericht*, ed. Rudolf Aschenauer; and "Eichmann Tells His Own Damning Story," *Life Magazine*. (2) In his prison cell, before he had seen any of the documentation in the hands of the prosecution, Eichmann prepared a 127-page handwritten account of his life that he entitled "Meine Memoiren," completed on June 16, 1960. The original is in the Israeli State Archives (hereafter ISA). Copies are available at the Yad Vashem Archives and the ZStL. It was published serially in *Die Welt* between August 11 and September 3, 1999. (3) Beginning in late May 1960, Eichmann was interrogated extensively in Israel, especially by Avner Less. The interrogations have been published in *Eichmann Trial*, vols. 7–8. A copy is available in BAK, All. Proz. 6/1–6). Excerpts from the transcripts of these interrogations have also been published: Jochen von Lang, ed., *Eichmann Interrogated: Transcripts from the Archives of the Israeli Police*. (4) In preparation for his trial, Eichmann met with his attorney, Robert Servatius, and prepared various timelines, dated March 28, 1961, and notes that are in the Servatius Nachlass (BAK, All. Proz. 6/169). (5) He gave extensive testimony in court in June 1961, published in English translation in *Eichmann Trial*, vol. 4. The transcript of Eichmann's testimony in the original German and with a somewhat different English translation is in BAK, All. Proz. 6/11–83. (6) In the spring of 2000, the ISA made available in typescript Eichmann's 485-page posttrial handwritten account entitled "Götzen" (false gods or idols) and dated September 1961. Unlike "Meine Memoiren," "Götzen" makes frequent reference to court documentation and is complemented by an additional 620 pages of drafts and notes. Historiographical examination of the various Eichmann testimonies can be found in Irmtrud Wojack, *Eichmanns Memoiren: Ein kritischer Essay*; and Christian Gerlach, "The Eichmann Interrogations in Holocaust Historiography." See also Christopher R. Browning, "Perpetrator Testimony: Another Look at Adolf Eichmann."

245. ISA, "Götzen," part 1, p. 119.

246. *Eichmann Trial*, 7:169–74, 180 (Eichmann pretrial interrogation).

247. ISA, "Götzen," part 1, p. 121.

248. *Eichmann Trial*, 7:169–74.

249. YVA, Eichmann, "Meine Memoiren," p. 97.

250. ISA, "Götzen," part 1, p. 122.

251. *Eichmann Trial*, 7:174 (Eichmann pretrial interrogation). Eichmann damaged his case by admitting to a fall trip to Belzec, for he thereby was admitting that he had clearly known the fate of the Jews he was deporting in the fall of 1941. To mitigate the damage, he thus claimed that in the first wave of deportations he had sent the Jews to Lodz, rather than Riga and Minsk, to avoid sending them to their deaths, but that thereafter he was never given a choice of destination. The suggestion that Eichmann's dating his trip to Belzec in the fall instead of winter was a defense strategy fails on two counts: insofar as he had a defense strategy, it was to push dates back, thus making it more plausible that he had not been to Auschwitz until the spring of 1942 (contra Höss), and such an admission was against his interest and very damaging to his case.

252. ISA, "Götzen," part 1, p. 122.

253. *Eichmann Trial*, 7:400.

254. On October 9, 1941, Goebbels records in his diary that further north in Berlin the

leaves had already turned brown and were falling. *Die Tagebücher von Joseph Goebbels II*, 2:84 (entry of October 9, 1941).

255. ZStL, 8 AR-Z 252/59, 9:1680 (Oberhauser testimony of December 12, 1962).

256. ZStL, 8 AR-Z 252/9, 6:1119–20 (testimony of Eustachy Urkainski, October 11, 1945), and pp. 1129–32 (testimony of Stanislaw Kozak, October 14, 1945). See also Kogon et al., *Nazi Mass Murder*, pp. 107–9.

257. *Eichmann Trial*, 7:372–73 (Eichmann pretrial interrogation).

258. Cited in Musial, *Deutsche Zivilverwaltung und Judenverfolgung*, pp. 205–6. Hahnzog dated this to the spring, not the fall, of 1941.

259. *Eichmann Trial*, 4:1416 (Eichmann trial testimony). Eichmann had already returned from his trip to Lodz on September 29, for it was on that date that he reported in Berlin on the alleged agreement of the Lodz authorities to accept 20,000 Jews and 5,000 "Gypsies." NA microfilm, T175/54/2568653–54 (Uebelhoer to Himmler, October 9, 1941).

260. ISA, "Götzen," part 1, pp. 144–45.

261. According to Dr. Charles Sydnor Jr., Heydrich was in Berlin from late on September 24 until the afternoon of September 27, when he departed for Prague to take up his position as acting Reichsprotektor. He was again in Berlin on October 4.

262. Peter Witte, "Auf Befehl des 'Führers,' " and Gerlach, "Die Wannsee-Konferenz," pp. 30–31, suggest a winter date. Wojack, *Eichmanns Memoiren*, p. 183, proposes a March 1942 date.

263. Kogon et al., *Nazi Mass Murder*, pp. 107–9 (testimony of Stanislaw Kozak).

264. DKHH, pp. 233–34.

265. ZStL, 298 AR 64–71 (Staatsanwalt Hamburg, 147 Js 43/69, investigation of Streibel), 2:442 (testimony of Jan Piwonski). Musial, *Deutsche Zivilverwaltung und die Judenverfolgung*, p. 208.

266. Browning, *Fateful Months*, p. 59; Henry Friedlander, *The Origins of Nazi Genocide*, pp. 136–40; Riess, *Anfänge der Vernichtung*, pp. 330–39, 348–52.

267. ZStL, V 203 AR-Z 69/59 (Urteil, Landgericht Bonn, 8 Ks 2/63), pp. 24 and 92; 203 AR-Z 69/59, 4:624–43, and 6:961–89 (testimony of Walter Burmeister). Part of Burmeister's testimony can be found in Kogon et al., *Nazi Mass Murder*, pp. 76–77. I am unpersuaded by Peter Klein's argument that Chelmno was founded in July rather than in the fall of 1941, because Walter Burmeister's subsequent citation for service in the Sonderkommando Lange gave his service time as "July 1941–5.4.1943." Klein, "Die Rolle der Vernichtungslager Kulmhof (Chelmno), Belzec und Auschwitz-Birkenau in den frühen Deportationsverbreitungen," p. 475.

268. ZStL, 203 AR-Z 69/59, 7:1288–93 (testimony of Konrad S.). In the same volume see the corroborating testimony of Nelli L., Herbert W., Adele F., and Erhard M., all Volksdeutsche inhabitants of Chelmno. Also Kogon et al., *Nazi Mass Murder*, pp. 80–83.

269. Ian Kershaw, "Improvised Genocide? The Emergence of the 'Final Solution' in the 'Warthegau' "; Longerich, *Politik der Vernichtung*, pp. 451–52.

270. YVA, O/53/76/110–11 (Abromeit Vermerk, October 24, 1941, on meeting in Berlin on October 23, 1941).

271. Gerlach, "Failure of Plans for an SS Extermination Center in Mogilev," pp. 60–64,

and *Kalkulierte Morde*, pp. 650–53; Ogorreck, "Die Einsatzgruppen der Sicherheitspolizei," pp. 280, 289. See also Breitman, *Official Secrets*, pp. 74–75; Aly, *"Final Solution,"* pp. 223–25; Pressac, "The Machinery of Mass Murder at Auschwitz," pp. 201, 208; Pressac, *Les Crématoires d'Auschwitz*, pp. 31–40. Himmler's trip to Mogilev can now be reliably dated from DKHH, pp. 245–46.

272. YVA, JM 3435: Wetzel memorandum of October 27, 1941.

273. YVA, JM 3435: Trampedach to Ostministerium and Lohse, November 9, 1941; Leibbrandt to RK Ostland, November 13, 1941.

274. Nbg. Doc. NO-365: draft letter, Rosenberg to Lohse, initialed by Wetzel, October 25, 1941. A second version of Wetzel's draft, in Wetzel's handwriting, is Nbg. Doc. NO-996 and NO-997. In this version Rosenberg stated that he had no objection to proposals concerning the Jewish question contained in a report from Lohse of October 4. However, he was sending Lohse the record of Wetzel's conversations with Brack and Eichmann; he asked Lohse "to infer the particulars concerning the current state of the matter" (*das Nähere über den Stand der Angelegenheit zu entnehmen*). Copies of the letter were to be sent to Brack and Eichmann. The difficulty in procurement and production of the gas van in the desired numbers is confirmed by testimony in the gas van (Pradel / Wentritt) trial and by surviving documents of the automotive section (II D 3) of the RSHA: BA, R 58/871.

275. ZStL, VI 420 AR-Z 1439/65 (Wetzel testimony, September 20, 1961). I am grateful to Prof. Dr. Helmut Krausnick for drawing my attention to this testimony.

276. ZStL, 18 AR-Z 252/59, Landgericht Munich I, 1 Js 278/60 (hereafter cited as Belzec trial), 5:974–75 (Kallmeyer to his attorney, June 18, 1960).

277. PA, Pol.Abt. III 246, Luther memoranda of October 13 and 17, 1941.

278. DDHK, p. 238 (entry of October 18, 1941).

279. Eichmann Trial Document T/1209, cited in Adler, *Der verwaltete Mensch*, pp. 29–30.

280. PA, Inland II AB 46/2 I: Huene to D III, November 12, 1941, and Rademacher note, November 14, 1941.

281. ADAP, D, vol. 13/2, pp. 570–72. Rademacher report, October 25, 1941. Rademacher's reference to transport by waterway to the "reception camps in the east" would suggest a Danube–Black Sea route and hence that sites somewhere on Soviet territory were being considered. The possibility of water routes for deporting Jews in relation to the projected Mogilev camp is considered by Aly, *"Final Solution,"* pp. 223–25, and Gerlach, "Failure of Plans for an SS Extermination Camp in Mogilev," pp. 60–78.

282. PA, Inland II AB 59/3, Wurm to Rademacher, October 23, 1941.

283. YVA, O/53/76/110–11 (Abromeit Vermerk, October 24, 1941, on meeting in Berlin on October 23, 1941).

284. Jochmann, *Monologe im Führerhauptquartier*, pp. 90–91 (entry of October 17, 1941). Also emphasizing the radical turn in Hitler's rhetoric at this time is Saul Friedländer, "Ideology and Extermination: The Immediate Origins of the Final Solution," esp. pp. 35–41.

285. Jochmann, *Monologe im Führerhauptquartier*, pp. 96–99 (entry of October 21, 1941).

286. Jochmann, *Monologe im Führerhauptquartier*, p. 106 (entry of October 25, 1941).

Christian Gerlach perceptively points out that the phrase about sending the Jews into the swamp had both a figurative and a literal meaning for Hitler and Himmler. Himmler had used the expression during the massacre of Jews in the Pripet marshes, and now Hitler used it just after Himmler's return from Mogilev. Gerlach, *Kalklulierte Morde*, p. 653.

287. Klein, "Die Rolle der Vernichtungslager Kulmhof (Chelmno), Belzec und Auschwitz-Birkenau," makes just the opposite argument, namely, that the early history of these three camps indicates that they were local responses to the prospect of deportation and not evidence of the vision of a European-wide extermination program at this time. He does not consider the contemporaneous considerations of gassing in Sobibor, Mogilev, and Riga.

288. Longerich, *Politik der Vernichtung*, pp. 440, 448.

289. Longerich, *Politik der Vernichtung*, p. 456.

9. The Final Solution from Conception to Implementation

1. NA microfilm, T175/54/2568695 and 2568671–94 (Himmler to Greiser, September 18, 1941, and Ventzki to Uebelhoer, September 24, 1941).

2. IMT, 33:534–35 (3921-PS: Daluege to IdOs (Inspectorates of the Order Police), October 24, 1941; YVA, JM 3435, Lange to RK Ostland, November 8, 1941).

3. The first major attempt to analyze the deportations from Germany by breaking them down by time and destination is Henry Friedlander, "The Deportations of the German Jews: Post-War Trials of Nazi Criminals." My reconstruction of the deportations from Germany, Austria, and the Protectorate is based on the following sources: For Berlin, the Bovensiepen indictment (Berlin 1 Js 69/65), pp. 224–331, in YVA, TR-10/622. For Vienna, International Tracing Service (hereafter ITS), Arolson, transportation list summary, in YVA, BD 23/6. For Prague, YVA, JM 807 (Gestapo compilations of individual transports arriving in Lodz, and plan of Judentransport arrivals). For Hamburg and Bremen, ITS lists in YVA, BD 23/4; Andreas Röpcke and Günther Rohdenburg, eds., *"Es geht tatsächlich nach Minsk": Texte und Materialien zur Erinnerung an die Deportation von Bremer Juden am 18.11.41 in das Vernichtungslager Minsk*; and *Hamburger jüdische Opfer des Nationalsozialismus: Gedenkbuch*, p. xix. For Düsseldorf, ITS lists in YVA, BD 23/4; JNSV, vol. 5, Nr. 148 (Düsseldorf 8 Ks 19/49), p. 5; and Holger Berschel, *Bürokratie und Terror: Das Judenreferat der Gestapo Düsseldorf 1935–1945*, p. 363. For Cologne, JNSV, vol. 12, Nr. 403a (Köln 24 Ks 3/53), p. 581; Dieter Corbach, *6:00 Uhr ab Messe Köln-Deutz: Deportationen 1938–1945*; and *Die jüdische Opfer des Nationalsozialismus aus Köln: Gedenkbuch*, pp. 536–37. For Frankfurt, see Commission for Researching the History of the Frankfurt Jews, ed., *Dokumente zur Geschichte der Frankfurter Juden 1933–1945*, Doc. Nr. XIV/15, pp. 323–24; JNSV, vol. 6, Nr. 207 (Frankfurt/M. 51 Ks 1/50), p. 378; ITS lists, YVA, BD 23/5; and Adolf Diamant, *Deportationsbuch der von Frankfurt am Main aus gewaltsam verschickte Juden in den Jahren 1941 bis 1944*. For Munich, ITS materials in YVA, BD 23/3. For Nuremberg, JNSV, vol. 11, Nr. 363 (Nürnberg-Fürth Ks 1/51), p. 190, and vol. 4, Nr. 138 (Würzberg KLs 63/48), p. 483. For Dresden and Leipzig, Adolf Diamant, *Chronik der Juden in Dresden*, pp. 446–47. For Stuttgart, Paul Sauer, ed., *Die Schicksal der jüdischen Bürger Baden-Württemburg während der nationalsozialistischen Verfolgungszeit*, pp. 282–307; and JNSV, vol. 22, Nr. 615 (Stutt-

gart Ks 35 / 50), pp. 761–62. For Kassel, Beate Kleinert and Wolfgang Prinz, eds., *Namen und Schicksal der Juden Kassels 1933–45*. For Münster, *JNSV*, vol. 17, Nr. 503 (Münster 6 Ks 1 / 55), p. 93; and Giesela Möllenhoff, and Rita Schlautmann-Overmeyer, *Jüdische Familien in Münster 1918–1945*, Teil 2.2, pp. 836–48. For Hannover, Zvi Asaria, *Die Juden in Niedersachsen*, p. 52. For Breslau, Karol Jonca, "Deportations of German Jews from Breslau 1941–1944 as Described in Eyewitness Testimony." For Dortmund, Ernst Pfeiffer, *Die Juden im Dortmund*, p. 69. For deportations from (as well as deportations to) Theresienstadt, Zdenek Lederer, *Getto Theresienstadt*, pp. 250–63. For arrivals in Lodz, including the Gypsy transports and the Luxemburg transport, see YVA, JM 807, plan of Judentransport und Zigeunertransport arrivals. A somewhat different plan for the "Gypsy" transports is found in YVA, O-51 / 63 / 4 (Butennop, KdO Wien, October 24, 1941, to various units). For arrivals in Minsk, including Brünn, *JNSV*, vol. 19, Nr. 552 (Koblenz 9 Ks 2 / 62), p. 190 (which concluded that 6,963 Jews were deported in this wave). For arrivals in Riga and Kaunas, including the Breslau and Dortmund transports, Gertrude Schneider, *Journey into Terror: Story of the Riga Ghetto*, pp. 148, 155.

4. *DiM*, 3:203–5 (Erfahrungsbericht, November 13, 1941). This document lists 5,000 deportees each from Vienna and Prague, 4,187 from Berlin, 2,007 from Cologne, 1,113 from Frankfurt, 1,034 from Hamburg, 984 from Düsseldorf, and 512 from Luxemburg, for a total of 19,837.

5. For Germany, 166,000, according to statistics of the Reichsvereinigung der deutschen Juden, August 1941, in Commission for Researching the History of the Frankfurt Jews, *Dokumente zur Geschichte der Frankfurter Juden*, pp. 474–75. For the Protectorate, 88,000, according to Heydrich's statement at the Prague conference of October 10, 1941, in Adler, *Theresienstadt*, pp. 720–22. For Vienna, 50,000, according to Propaganda Ministry statistics in NA, T81 / 675 / 5485696.

6. ZStL, 415 AR 1310 / 63 (hereafter Investigation of Bosshamer), E 5, Bd. III, pp. 53, 71, 109. Especially important for Eichmann and his Referat are Safrian, *Die Eichmann-Männer*; and Yaacov Lozowick, *Hitler's Bureaucrats: The Nazi Security Police and the Banality of Evil*.

7. Investigation of Bosshamer, pp. 112, 117.

8. Investigation of Bosshamer, p. 127; BDC, Friedrich Suhr file (copy in YVA).

9. Landgericht Köln, 24 Ks 3 / 53, Hauptakten, 2:367–69 (testimony of Jean Brodesser).

10. *JNSV*, vol. 11, Nr. 363, p. 189. No copy of Eichmann's first set of instructions has survived, but both their content and date can be ascertained from the instructions of the Stapostelle Nürnberg-Fürth to its branch office or Aussendienststelle in Würzburg. Eichmann Trial Document T / 1277, "Organisationweisung zur Durchführung der Juden Evakuierung an 29.11.41," signed by Grafenberg, November 11, 1941, in "Judendeportationen aus dem Reichsgebiet," vol. 2, Anl. 5. This is a collection compiled to provide German prosecutors with basic documents concerning the deportation of German Jews. Most of the documents come from the surviving Gestapo records in Düsseldorf and Würzburg. A copy of this collection is in YVA as O-4 / 52. The other key documents in the collection for the organization of the fall 1941 deportations are: Anl. 2, "Richtlinien zur technischen Durchführung der Evakuierung von Juden nach Ostland" (Eichmann Trial Document T / 1275); Anl. 3, RSHA "Richtlinien für Behandlung des Vermögens," December 3, 1941 (Eichmann

Trial Document T/1283); and Anl. 6, Staatspolizei Nürnberg-Fürth to Aussendienststelle Würzburg, November 19, 1941 (Eichmann Trial Document T/1276). For studies based on the Düsseldorf documents, see Berschel, *Bürokratie und Terror*; Berschel, "Polizeirou-tiniers und Judenverfolgung. Die Bearbeitung von 'Judenangelegenheiten' bei der Stapo-Leitstelle Düsseldorf"; Michael Zimmerman, "Die Gestapo und die regionale Organi-sation der Judendeportationen. Das Beispiel der Stapo-Leitstelle Düsseldorf." See also *Dokumente Baden-Württemberg*, Nr. 462, pp. 272–75 (Staatspolizei Stuttgart to Landräte and Polizeidirektoren, November 18, 1941), and Nr. 482, pp. 304–6 (Heydrich to all Staatspolizei[leit]stellen, November 27, 1941).

11. YVA, O/53/76/110–11 (Abromeit Vermerk, October 24, 1941, on meeting in Berlin on October 23, 1941, concerning the Führerbefehl to evacuate 50,000 Jews). This meeting was also attended by the "Jewish expert" from the Gestapo in Kiel. Gerhard Paul, " 'Betr.: Evakuierung von Juden.' Die Gestapo als regionale Zentralinstitution der Judenverfolgung," p. 510.

12. PA: Inland IIg 174, Rademacher to Luther, October 27, 1941; Rademacher through Luther to Weizsäcker, October 29, 1941; Killinger to Foreign Office, November 13, 1941; Kasche to Foreign Office, November 21, 1941; Luther to Eichmann, January 10, 1942; and Gesandtschaft Pressburg 312/5, Ludin to Foreign Office, December 2 and 4, 1941. (T 120/703/261459–60, 261455, 261447, and 261442; K1655/K403488–90).

13. For the most thorough analysis of property measures, see Hilberg, *The Destruction of the European Jews*, pp. 471–81; and Adler, *Der verwaltete Mensch*, pp. 489–644.

14. Adler, *Der verwaltete Mensch*, pp. 496–500.

15. Nbg. Doc. NG-4905 (Finance Ministry to Oberfinanzpräsidenten, November 4, 1941), printed in Adler, *Der verwaltete Mensch*, pp. 506–9. See also Hilberg, *The Destruction of the European Jews*, pp. 478–79.

16. YVA, O/51/63/6 (Bomhard memorandum on the evacuation of the Jews, October 4, 1941).

17. IMT, 33:534–36 (3921-PS: Daluege to Inspectors of the Order Police, October 27, 1941. YVA, O-51/63/4 (Butennop, KdO Wien, October 24, 1941, to local Orpo units).

18. For the most graphic and detailed description by an Orpo officer, see the report of the Orpo commander, Salitter, of a transport from Düsseldorf to Riga in December 1941, printed in Schneider, *Journey into Terror*, pp. 195–211. See also Andreas Determann, "Wegbegleiter in den Tod. Zur Funktion bei der Deportationen jüdischer Bürger in den Osten."

19. YVA, TR-10/622 (Novak indictment: Wien 15 St 1416/61, 4–5, 34–35). Kurt Pät-zold and Erika Schwarz, *"Auschwitz war für mich nur ein Bahnhof." Franz Novak—der Transportoffizier Adolf Eichmanns*.

20. For Germany, Austria, and the Protectorate, see n. 3 of this chapter. For the other countries, YVA, TR-10/835 (indictment of Ganzenmüller: Düsseldorf, 8 Js 430/67, 177–78). Local deportations, such as within the General Government or from various parts of the Protectorate to Theresienstadt, did not have to be organized by the RHSA in Berlin, but could be arranged by local Security Police and railway officials.

21. For the organization and procedure of the Reichsbahn, see Raul Hilberg, *Sonderzüge*

nach Auschwitz (Mainz: Dumjahn, 1981), and *The Destruction of the European Jews*, pp. 409–16; and YVA, TR-10/835 (Ganzenmüller indictment, 94–109, 141–43).

22. Hilberg, *The Destruction of the European Jews*, p. 411.

23. Hilberg, *The Destruction of the European Jews*, p. 412.

24. YVA, JM 805 (undated plan for Judentransport and Zigeunertransport arrivals). In fact the trains were always between 60 and 470 minutes late, with unloading often not beginning until dark, as the German police in Lodz complained. *DiM*, 3:203–5 (Erfahrungsbericht, November 13, 1941).

25. Adler, *Theresienstadt*, pp. 782–83 (testimony of Martha Mosse); YVA, TR-10/662 (Bovensiepen indictment, 26 and 145–55). In Vienna, Alois Brunner informed Dr. Löwenherz of the impending deportations to Lodz one day earlier on September 30, 1941. Safrian, *Die Eichmann-Männer*, p. 120.

26. Commission for Researching the History of the Frankfurt Jews, *Dokumente zur Geschichte der Frankfurter Juden*, Doc. Nr. XIV.1 (testimony of Lina Katz), and XIV.2.A–E. (reports of various SA units), pp. 507–14.

27. "Judendeportationen aus dem Reichsgebiet," vol. 2, Anlage 5 and 6; *JNSV*, vol. 4, Nr. 138, pp. 482–89, and Nr. 140a, pp. 529–40; and vol. 11, Nr. 363, pp. 189–95.

28. See the documents in *Dokumente Baden-Württemberg*, pp. 268–309, esp. Nr. 462 (Mussgay to Landräte and Polizeidirektoren, November 18, 1941).

29. Landgericht Köln, 24 Ks 3/53, Hauptakten, 1:20–21 (testimony of E. Schäfer); 41–5 (Moritz Goldschmidt), 50–3 (Aloysia Nussbaum), 103 (Frowein), 189–91 (Jakob Marx); II, 220 (Hubert Götz), 362–75 (Jean Brodesser); III, 422–8 (Schäfer). For a study of the Gestapo in Cologne and Krefeld, see Johnson, *Nazi Terror*. For all Cologne deportations, see Dieter Corbach, *6:00 Uhr ab Messe Köln-Deutz*.

30. "Judendeportationen aus dem Reichsgebiet," Anlage 53 (German Red Cross Düsseldorf, to Gestapo Düsseldorf, May 4, 1942).

31. Witte, "Two Decisions," pp. 324–25.

32. YVA, O-53/85/1036: Türk to KHM Hrubieszow, October 7, 1941.

33. Eichmann Document T-1151: Löwenherz report on meeting with Brunner, September 30, 1941.

34. Landgericht Köln, 24 Ks 3/53, 2:367 (testimony of Jean Brodesser).

35. Nbg. Doc. 1738-PS: Speer to Rosenberg, January 26, 1942.

36. *Dokumente Baden-Württemberg*, pp. 308–9 (Doc. Nr. 485: report of Oberfinanzpräsident to RM der Finanzen, February 12, 1942).

37. Cited in Kulka, " 'Public Opinion' in Nazi Germany," 26:35. For the number of "material beneficiaries" from the despoilment, deportation, and murder of the Jews, see Frank Bajohr, *"Aryanisation" in Hamburg: The Economic Exclusion of Jews and the Confiscation of Their Property in Nazi Germany*, pp. 277–82. For the role of Albert Speer and city planning in the seizure of Jewish apartments, see Susanne Willems, *Der entsiedelte Jude. Albert Speers Wohungsmarktpolitik für den Berliner Hauptstadtbau*.

38. Kershaw, *Popular Opinion and Political Dissent in the Third Reich*, p. 363; Bankier, *The Germans and the Final Solution*, pp. 132, 134.

39. Kershaw, "The Persecution of the Jews and German Public Opinion"; Kershaw,

Popular Opinion and Political Dissent, pp. 358–72; Kershaw, "German Popular Opinion and the 'Jewish Question,' 1939–1943"; Kershaw, *The "Hitler Myth,"* pp. 230–52; Kulka, " 'Public Opinion' in Nazi Germany"; Kulka and Rodrigue, "The German Population and the Jews in the Third Reich"; Bankier, *The Germans and the Final Solution*, esp. pp. 101–38. In addition to these three historians, others have also dealt with the topic. Sarah Gordon, *Hitler, Germans, and the "Jewish Question,"* perceives an even greater gap between the German people and the regime. In contrast, Michael Kater, "Everyday Anti-Semitism in Prewar Nazi Germany," feels there has been too great a tendency to downplay the popular manifestations of anti-Semitism within the German population.

Most recently, Daniel Jonah Goldhagen, *Hitler's Willing Executioners* has made the most sweeping generalizations of any historian about pervasive anti-Semitism in pre-Nazi German society and popular enthusiasm for persecution and genocide during the Nazi regime. Goldhagen begins his book with a conceptual model of anti-Semitism that includes a continuum of attitudes along two axes: the degree of negativity attached to Jews on the one hand and the degree of importance attached to the issue on the other. Ian Kershaw articulated just such an approach years earlier when he argued that Germans became both more hostile to and less concerned about Jews during the war. Yet Goldhagen attacks Kershaw's thesis of "indifference" as underconceptualized. Saul Friedländer's new book, *Nazi Germany and the Jews*, is sympathetic to the Kershaw-Kulka-Bankier interpretation. The work and conclusions of Kershaw, Kulka, and Bankier were anticipated in many ways by Lawrence D. Stokes, "The German People and the Destruction of the European Jews."

40. Kulka, " 'Public Opinion' in Nazi Germany," 26:36; Bankier, *The Germans and the Final Solution*, pp. 101–15. Also arguing for widespread wartime awareness of the fate of the Jews among the Germans is Eric Johnson, *Nazi Terror*, pp. 433–59.

41. Bankier, *The Germans and the Final Solution*, p. 117; Kershaw, "German Popular Opinion," p. 373.

42. Kulka and Rodrigue, "The German Population and the Jews," pp. 430–35.

43. Bankier, *The Germans and the Final Solution*, pp. 114–15, 137, 140, 146, 151–52.

44. Kershaw, "The Persecution of the Jews," pp. 281, 288.

45. Kershaw, *Popular Opinion and Political Dissent*, p. 277.

46. Kulka, " 'Public Opinion' in Nazi Germany," 26:43–44.

47. Kulka and Rodrigue, "The German Population and the Jews," p. 435.

48. Bankier, *The Germans and the Final Solution*, pp. 155–56, 151–52.

49. Albert Speer, *Spandau: The Secret Diaries*, p. 260.

50. *Die Tagebücher von Joseph Goebbels II*, 2:193–95 (entry of October 28, 1941).

51. Bankier, *The Germans and the Final Solution*, pp. 127–28.

52. Bankier, *The Germans and the Final Solution*, p. 127; Kershaw, "Persecution and German Popular Opinion," p. 283. For the copy circulated by the Kattowitz Staatspolizeistelle, see USHMMA, RG 15.033m, reel 6, file 210, p. 71, Geheime Staatspolizei Kattowitz, November 4, 1941, Rundverfügung.

53. NCA, 5:945–46 (English); and Kurt Pätzold, ed., *Verfolgung, Vertreibung, Vernichtung*, pp. 351–53 (German): Nbg. Doc. 3244-PS: Party Chancellery circular, October 9, 1942.

54. Arad et al., *Documents on the Holocaust*, p. 342 (Nbg. Doc. NO-2710: Party Chancellery circular, July 11, 1943, on treatment of the Jewish question).

55. *IMT*, 29:145 (Nbg. Doc. 1919-PS: Himmler speech to the ss leaders at Posen, October 4, 1943).

56. Quoted in Jeremy Noakes, "No Ordinary People."

57. Cited in Hans-Heinrich Wilhelm, "The Holocaust in NS-Rhetoric," p. 105.

58. Wilhelm, "The Holocaust in NS-Rhetoric," pp. 108–13.

59. Andreas Hillgruber, "Die ideologisch-dogmatische Grundlage der nationalsozialistischen Politik der Ausrottung der Juden in den besetzten Gebieten der Sowjetunion und ihre Durchführung 1941–1944."

60. NA microfilm, T175/54/2568653–55 (Uebelhoer to Himmler, October 9, 1941).

61. NA microfilm, T175/54/2568668–70 (Uebelhoer to Himmler, October 4, 1941).

62. YVA, JM 800 (Aktennotizen by Ribbe on meetings of October 9 and 16, 1941).

63. YVA, JM 806 (circular to all ghetto administration employees, October 20, 1941, signed by Biebow and Ribbe).

64. Adler, *Theresienstadt*, pp. 720–22 (protocol of Prague meeting, October 10, 1941).

65. Nbg. Doc. NO-365 (Wetzel draft for Lohse, October 25, 1941).

66. Eichmann's role in these November executions is unclear. In Prague on October 10, 1941, Heydrich had stated that Eichmann was handling the question of the reception of the deported Reich Jews directly with the Einsatzgruppen commanders. In Eichmann's initial account, he said that after his trip to Globocnik in Lublin, he was sent "later that year" to Minsk, where 5,000 Jews were being shot. He arrived late, saw the last group of Jews (including women and children) undress and jump into large pit, where they were shot. He recalled that a women held up her child in desperation before being hit. Since the weather was very cold, he was wearing an ankle-length leather coat, which was splattered with "bits of brains" that his chauffeur had to help him remove. See "Eichmann Tells His Own Damning Story." During his interrogation, the story was somewhat changed. Eichmann now dated the Minsk trip to early 1942 after his visit to Chelmno. The pit was full of corpses when he witnessed the last round of shooting and the killing of one women in particular. And he recalled driving back through Lwow, where an ss officer showed him another mass grave, from which blood was spurting like a "geyser." *Eichmann Trial*, 4:181, 210–15. He again dated the Minsk trip to the winter of early 1942 in the timeline he drew up with his defense attorney, Servatius. He specifically noted the "child" and that he had been wearing a winter coat. BA, All. Proz. 6/169, Zeitplan 1942. Christian Gerlach, the expert on German occupation policy in Belorussia, concludes that Eichmann witnessed a shooting of women and children within the ghetto on March 2–3, 1942, not in the fall of 1941. Gerlach, *Kalkulierte Massenmord*, pp. 693–94. Irmtrud Wojack, *Eichmanns Memoiren*, pp. 171–72, accepts the November 1941 date. I believe that the November 1941 date for Eichmann's trip to Minsk, in conjunction with assuring reception of the transports from Germany, is most likely, in part because it most logically fits his role at that time and in part because the March 2–3, 1942, date is highly improbable, since Eichmann was back in Berlin on March 4 conducting a meeting.

67. *JNSV*, vol. 17, Nr. 512 (judgment against Remmers and Zenner, Koblenz 9 Ks 1/61), pp. 510–13; Gerlach, *Kalkulierte Massenmord*, pp. 624–26.

68. YVA, JM 3455 (Kube to Lohse, December 16, 1941).

69. Gerlach has pointed out that Kube was asking for explicit instructions because

he would not order the murder of German Jews on his own authority. "Die Wannsee-Konferenz," p. 17.

70. YVA, JM 3455 (Janetzke to Rosenberg, January 5, 1942).

71. YVA, JM 3455 (Lohse, RK Ostland, to Kube, GK Minsk, January 27, 1942).

72. YVA, JM 3455 (Kube to Lohse, February 6, 1942).

73. YVA, JM 3435 (Lange to RK Ostland, November 8, 1941).

74. YVA, JM 3435 (Lange to RK Ostland, November 20, 1941).

75. YVA, O/53/141/4378–86 (Jäger report of EK 3, Kovno, December 1, 1941).

76. Krausnick and Wilhelm, *Die Truppe des Weltanschauungskrieges*, pp. 565–68. For the complete Jeckeln interrogation, see YVA, O/53/144/395–402. This alleged Himmler-Jeckeln meeting is not recorded in the Himmler *Dienstkalendar*.

77. Arad et al., *The Einsatzgruppen Reports*, p. 280 (EM No. 156, January 16, 1942).

78. Arad et al., *The Einsatzgruppen Reports*, p. 277 (EM No. 155, January 11, 1942); Schneider, *Journey into Terror*, pp. 12–14. Andrew Ezergailis, *The Holocaust in Latvia*, pp. 239–70, provides the most detailed account. He estimates that close to 24,000 Latvian Jews and 1,000 German Jews were killed at Rumbula on these two days. About 5,000 Latvian Jews (not 2,600 as reported in EG No. 155) were held back for labor.

79. *DKHH*, p. 278.

80. *DKHH*, p. 280.

81. Public Record Office, London HW 16/32, intercept of Himmler to Jeckeln, December 1, 1941. This intercept was first cited by Richard Breitman, who was a pioneer in the use of British intercepts as a source for Holocaust history. *Official Secrets*, p. 83.

82. *DKHH*, p. 284.

83. *DKHH*, pp. 283–84; Broszat, "Hitler und die Genesis der Endlösung," pp. 760–61; Hilberg, *The Destruction of the European Jews*, p. 353; Ezergailis, *The Holocaust in Latvia*, p. 253; Schneider, *Journey into Terror*, pp. 23–30.

84. Adler, *Theresienstadt*, p. 799.

85. Safrian, *Die Eichmann-Männer*, pp. 180–81.

86. On the complications caused by the Kaunas and Riga shootings, see Gerlach, "Die Wannsee-Konferenz," pp. 13, 15–16; and Gerald Fleming, *Hitler and the Final Solution*, pp. 78–90.

87. *IMT*, 30:79–80 (2273-PS: undated Stahlecker summary report of early 1942).

88. Krausnick and Wilhelm, *Die Truppe des Weltanschauungskrieges*, p. 568. The Himmler *Dienstkalendar* has gaps in late January and early February. After December 4, 1941, the next Himmler-Jeckeln meeting on record is March 20, 1942.

89. Safrian, *Die Eichmann-Männer*, pp. 180–81.

90. PA, Inland IIg 431, Tätigkeits- und Lagebericht Nr. 1 (T120/465/226362–404). All the Tätigkeits- und Lageberichte have now been published and annotated in Peter Klein, ed., *Die Einsatzgruppen in der besetzten Sowjetunion 1941/42*, pp. 111–315.

91. PA, Inland IIg 431, Tätigkeits- und Lagebericht Nr. 2 (T120/465/226405–41).

92. PA, Inland IIg 431, Tätigkeits- und Lagebericht Nr. 3 (T120/465/226442–87).

93. PA, Inland IIg 431, Tätigkeits- und Lagebericht Nr. 4 (T120/465/226488–526).

94. PA, Inland IIg 431, Tätigkeits- und Lagebericht Nr. 5 (T120/465/226527–60).

95. PA, Inland IIg 431, Tätigkeits- und Lagebericht Nr. 6 (T120/465/226562–601).

96. PA, Inland IIg 431, Hahn summary report, December 10, 1941 (T120/465/226354–60).

97. PA, Inland IIg 431, Tätigkeits- und Lageberichte Nr. 7 and 8 and circulation sheets (T120/465/226657–95, 226697–720).

98. PA, Inland IIg 431, Tätigkeits- und Lagebericht Nr. 10, and Luther summary (T120/465/226722–42, 226744–48).

99. PA, Inland IIg 431, Tätigkeits- und Lagebericht Nr. 11 and circulation sheet (T120/465/226750–75, 226777).

100. Felix Kersten, *The Kersten Memoirs, 1940–1945*, p. 119.

101. Nbg. Doc. NO-5329: Himmler file note of November 15, 1941, on conversation with Rosenberg. *DKHH*, p. 262.

102. PA, Pol. XIII, VAA Berichte, Rosenberg speech, November 18, 1941 (T120/339/198808–21).

103. *DKHH*, pp. 273–74.

104. Lösener memorandum, December 26, 1941, on his December 19, 1941, conversation with Stuckart, printed in Lenz, ed., "Die Handakten von Bernhard Lösener," pp. 684–99. Lenz points out some telling discrepancies concerning Stuckart between this Lösener memorandum, written at the time, and his postwar account, "Als Rassereferent im Reichsministerium des Innern," pp. 310–11. Only the former relates Stuckart's own justification for the murder of the Jews, although both versions affirm Stuckart's claim that it was based on an order from the highest authority, i.e., Hitler. Lösener's postwar Nuremberg court testimony is now reprinted in *Legislating the Holocaust: The Bernhard Loesener Memoirs and Supporting Documents*, pp. 111–52.

105. Höss dates a meeting of Eichmann's deputies from all over Europe to November 1941, which may be a rare occasion on which his dating is correct. *Death Dealer*, p. 29.

106. Rijksinstituut voor Oorlogsdocumentatie, HSSPF 25 A–B: reports of Denis H., November 20 and December 4, 11, and 18, 1941. I am very grateful to Thomas Sandkühler for drawing my attention to these documents and to Peter Romijn for sending copies to me.

107. *ADAP*, D, vol. 13/2, no. 515, pp. 718–21 (Schmidt memorandum, November 30, 1941, on the conversation between Hitler and the Grand Mufti, November 28, 1941). Another version of Hitler's assurance to the Grand Mufti, made by Grobba, was less specific. At the moment of Arab liberation, "Germany had no interest there other than the destruction of the power protecting the Jews" (*die Vernichtung der das Judentum protegierenden Macht*). See David Yisraeli, *The Palestine Problem in German Politics, 1889–1945*, p. 310. I am indebted to Dan Michman for this reference.

108. An example can be seen in the invitation to "dear party comrade Luther" in the Foreign Office: PA, Inland IIg 177, Heydrich to Luther, November 29, 1941 (T120/1512/372043–44).

109. Concerning the Bühler invitation, see "A Preparatory Document for the Wannsee 'Conference,' " with comment by Yehoshua Büchler and Richard Breitman. *DKHH*, p. 277.

110. On the relations between Heydrich and Luther, and Luther and Weizsäcker, see Browning, *The Final Solution and the German Foreign Office*.

111. PA, Inland IIg 177, Luther marginalia on Heydrich invitation, Rademacher cover letter of December 8, 1941, and memo "Wünschen und Ideen" (T120/1512/372040–42).

112. PA, Inland IIg 177, Rademacher marginalia of December 8, 1941; and Heydrich to Luther, January 8, 1942 (T120/1512/372039). Hans Safrian, in contrast to the view I have been presenting, argues that the postponement was due to the collapse of any last illusions about quick victory in the Soviet Union following the Soviet counteroffensive, and that Heydrich and others now needed time to adjust their thinking and develop new plans, including an alternative to expulsion beyond the Urals. Safrian, *Die Eichmann-Männer*, p. 169.

Christian Gerlach, "Die Wannsee-Konferenz," has argued that the Wannsee Conference as originally scheduled was to deal only with issues related to the deportation of German Jews, whose ultimate fate was as yet undecided. He argues that Hitler announced the basic decision to kill all European Jews only on December 12, 1941, and hence the rescheduled conference eventually took place under significantly altered circumstances. What he interprets as Hitler's basic decision, I see as an official initiation of party leaders to a decision taken several months earlier.

113. Eichmann stated that Heydrich had two (actually three) reasons for holding the conference: (1) to secure the cooperation (*Mitarbeit*) of the invitees; (2) to indulge his vanity and make clear his jurisdiction. *Eichmann Trial*, All. Proz. 6/1, p. 239. See also Eberhard Jäckel, "On the Purpose of the Wannsee Conference," pp. 39–49.

114. *Die Tagebücher von Joseph Goebbels II*, 2:498–99 (entry of December 13, 1941).

115. *IMT*, 12:68–69 (Bühler testimony); Frank, *Diensttagebuch*, p. 459n.

116. Frank, *Diensttagebuch*, pp. 457–58 (Regierungsitzung, December 16, 1941).

117. For the date of the Himmler-Brack meeting: DKHH, p. 290. For the views Himmler expressed at that time: Nbg. Doc. NO-205 (Brack to Himmler, June 23, 1942).

118. Gerlach, "Die Wannsee-Konferenz," pp. 24–25. Gerlach notes that it is unclear from the manuscript whether it is the original or the corrected version or even whether Rosenberg actually delivered the speech at all.

119. *IMT*, 27:270 (1517-PS: Rosenberg-Hitler meeting, December 14, 1941).

120. Gerlach, "Die Wannsee-Konferenz," p. 24, argues that the phrase "now after the decision" refers to an alleged decision by Hitler on December 12 to murder all the Jews of Europe, not to declare war on the United States, on the grounds that there was no reason to drop the threat against Jews in connection with the declaration of war.

121. *IMT*, 32:437 (3666-PS: Bräutigam to Lohse, December 18, 1941).

122. DKHH, pp. 293–94.

123. PA, Inland IIg 177, Heydrich to Luther, January 8, 1942 (T120/1512/372039).

124. Hans Mommsen, "Aufgabenkreis und Verantwortlichkeit des Staatssekretärs der Reichskanzlei Dr. Wilhelm Kritzinger," esp. pp. 380, 396.

125. For recent studies, see Mark Roseman, *The Villa, the Lake, the Meeting: Wannsee and the Final Solution*; Longerich, *Politik der Vernichtung*, pp. 466–72; Gerlach, "Die Wannsee-Konferenz"; Jäckel, "On the Purpose of the Wannsee Conference," pp. 39–49; and Pätzold and Schwarz, *Tagesordnung: Judenmord*, summarized in Kurt Pätzold, "Die Wannsee-Konferenz—zu ihrem Platz in der Geschichte der Judenvernichtung"; Wolfgang Scheffler, "Die Wannsee-Konferenz und ihre historische Bedeutung."

126. The only surviving copy of the Wannsee Protocol is found in PA, Inland IIg 177

(T120/1512/372024–28). A facsimile copy can be found in Robert Kempner, *Eichmann und Komplizen*, pp. 133–47.

127. This and subsequent citations from Eichmann's court testimony are cited from Raul Hilberg, ed., *Documents of Destruction*, pp. 99–106. A slightly different English version can be found in *The Trial of Adolf Eichmann*, 4:1422–23, 1826–27.

128. Two weeks after the Wannsee Conference, in a speech in Prague on February 4, 1942, to an audience of German occupation functionaries, Heydrich referred to the Arctic camps of the Soviet Union as a "future ideal homeland for the 11 million Jews out of Europe" (*zukünftig ideales Heimatland der 11 Millionen Juden aus Europa*). Quoted in Karny et al., *Deutsche Politik im "Protektorat,"* p. 229. I do not think this statement should be taken literally.

129. Hermann Kaienburg, "Jüdische Arbeitslager an der 'Strasse der SS,'" pp. 19–20; and Thomas Sandkühler, "Judenpolitik und Judenmord im Distrikt Galizien, 1941–1942," p. 136, both point out that the D 4 Jewish slave labor camps being created for road construction in Galicia bore an eerie semblance to Heydrich's remarks at the Wannsee Conference concerning the decimation of Jewish labor through road construction. Thus his remarks in this regard should not be dismissed as mere camouflage language.

130. PA, Inland IIg 179: Leibbrandt to Foreign Office, January 22, 1942, with draft legislation and explanations (T120/5117/E295649–68).

131. PA, Inland IIg 179, Protocol of Ostministerium conference of January 29, 1942 (T120/5117/E295643–47).

132. PA, Inland IIg 177, Rademacher to Bielfeld, February 10, 1942. Printed in *ADAP*, E, 1:403.

133. PA, Inland IIg 177: Woermann to Rademacher, February 14, 1942; Rademacher to Luther, February 24, 1942; with Luther marginalia, February 26, 1942 (T120/3910H/E050132–33).

134. *Die Tagebücher von Joseph Goebbels II*, 3:431.

135. For "euthanasia" in the Warthegau, see Riess, *Anfänge der Vernichtung*, pp. 273–353.

136. ZStL, 203 AR-Z 69/59 (hereafter cited as the Chelmno trial), 1:138–39 (Koppe interrogation).

137. ZStL, Ordner Nr. 350, Bild 530–1 (Damzog to Krumey, December 18, 1941; Krumey Vermerk, January 6, 1942).

138. Chelmno trial, 3:459–63 (Knofe interrogation).

139. For rotation, see Chelmno trial, 3:411–21 (Theodore Malzmüller), and 7a:1193–98 (Heinz Schattner).

140. For the confused chain of command, see the discussion in Rückerl, *NS-Vernichtungslager*, pp. 251–53. For an interpretation that leans heavily toward seeing the development of the Chelmno death camp more as a local improvisation rather than the local reflection of basic policy decisions at the center, see Kershaw, "Improvised Genocide?"

141. Rückerl, *NS-Vernichtungslager*, p. 264. Florian Freund, Bertrand Perz, and Karl Stuhlpfarrer, "Das Ghetto in Litzmannstadt (Lodz)," pp. 27–28, emphasize a Himmler-Greiser agreement in late October 1941 as the way out of the local difficulties posed by

Hitler's decision to deport Jews from the Third Reich and Himmler's decision to send these deportees to Lodz.

142. Danuta Dabrowska, "Zaglada Skupisk Zydowskich W 'Kraju Warty' W Okresie Okupacji Hitlerowskiej," table 13; Dobroszycki, "Introduction," *Chronicle of the Lodz Ghetto*, p. liv.

143. Patrick O. Montague, "The Chelmno Death Camp," unpublished manuscript, pp. 2, 4. According to another witness, who dated the action to mid-November, on the first day Jews were literally boiled alive in slaked lime in one burial pit, and on the following day a second burial pit was filled with the bodies of Jews killed in the gas van. Richmond, *Konin: A Quest*, pp. 479–80.

144. *JNSV*, vol. 7, Nr. 231b (LG Stuttgart 3 Ks 31/49), pp. 217–33.

145. In postwar testimony two ethnic Germans who were schoolchildren in Chelmno claimed that before the wood fence was built around the Schloss in January 1942 they had been able to find a vantage point from which they could see the gas vans back up to the Schloss and hear the screams of the victims. Even after the fence was built, children in the schoolhouse across from the camp personnel's quarters could see each morning the drunk and naked nurses from the hospital in nearby Warthebrücken lying in the street after the previous night's orgy. Eventually the German school was moved to another town, to which the children were driven in an ss vehicle. Chelmno trial: 4:550–62 (Fritz Ismer), and 624–43 (Walter Burmeister); 7a:1262–65 (Nelli Löhrko), 1266–69 (Else Semmler), 1270–77 (Herbert Wauer), and 1281–86 (Erhard Michelson).

146. This date is given by the postwar Polish report, cited in Chelmno trial, 1:38. Without explaining the discrepancy, the judgment of the Bonn Landgericht (8 Ks 3/62, p. 36) gives December 5 as the starting date, as does Rückerl, NS-*Vernichtungslager*, p. 288.

147. Judgment, LG Bonn 8 Ks 3/62, p. 27.

148. For the killing procedure, see Rückerl, NS-*Vernichtungslager*, pp. 268–76; Chelmno Trial, 4:517–49 (Gustav Laabs); 4:624–43, 6:961–89 (Walter Burmeister); 5:872–83, 6:1046–72 (Kurt Möbius); and Montague, "The Chelmno Death Camp," pp. 30–94.

149. Chelmno trial, 1:83 (Dr. Pieh to Zentrale Stelle, November 6, 1959); and Dabrowska, "Zaglada Skupisk Zydowskich W 'Kraju Warty,'" pp. 163, 169 (tables 7 and 12); Montague, "The Chelmno Death Camp," pp. 17–20.

150. Chelmno trial, 4:550–62 (Fritz Ismer); Dobroszycki, *Chronicle of the Lodz Ghetto*, pp. 107–8. Over 600 Gypsies had died in November and December in Lodz.

151. I am grateful to Patrick Montague, "The Chelmno Death Camp," pp. 51–53, for persuasively documenting that the gassing at Chelmno began with Lange's old van using bottled carbon monoxide. As to when this original van was phased out and the two new vans—whatever their make—and eventually an additional large Sauer van arrived from Berlin, the postwar testimony is unclear. The testimony of a Polish mechanic whom Montague cites (p. 56) would indicate the presence of the new-model vans using exhaust gas in January 1942, although Montague himself argues for a much later date of March–April (p. 55).

152. Pradel/Wentritt trial, 4:117, 7:52–54, 8:227–28 (testimony of Gustav Laabs); 7:200–202 (testimony of Walter Burmeister); 9:193–94 (testimony of Fritz Ismer). Judg-

ment, LG Bonn, 8 Ks 3/63, pp. 27, 92. According to Artur Eisenach, Lange's trucks were purchased in Leipzig. See Eisenach, "Operation Reinhard: Mass Extermination of the Jewish Population in Poland," p. 97. But the November 2, 1942, bill from Motoren-Heyne in Leipzig to Bothmann was for delivery of a diesel motor (*FGM*, pp. 282–83). Thus the date is too late and the object delivered was only a motor, not a van. On the development and production of the gas van, see Browning, *Fateful Months*, pp. 57–67; and Matthais Beer, "Die Entwicklung der Gaswagen."

153. *Eichmann Trial*, 7:174–77 (Eichmann's pretrial interrogation); "Eichmann Tells His Own Damning Story"; "Meine Memoiren," pp. 105–7; ISA, Eichmann posttrial memoirs, part 1, pp. 126–28, in which he states "it must have been January" when Müller ordered him to inspect Chelmno.

154. For published histories of the camp, see Michael Tregenza, "Belzec—Das Vergessene Lager des Holocaust"; Yitzhak Arad, *Belzec, Sobibor, Treblinka: The Operation Reinhard Death Camps*; and Rückerl, NS-*Vernichtungslager*.

155. Tregenza, "Belzec," pp. 247–48.

156. Belzec trial, 1:133 (Oberhauser BDC RUSHA file, wife's letter of October 9, 41); 6:1037 (Oberhauser testimony, September 15, 1960).

157. Belzec trial, 6:1129–32, 1195 (testimony of Stanislaw Kozak); 1117–18 (Eustachy Urkainski); 6:1222 (Edward Ferens).

158. Belzec trial, 6:1129–32 (Kozak); and 6:1156 (Jan Glab).

159. Belzec trial, 9:1681 (Oberhauser, December 12, 1960). Tregenza, "Belzec," p. 247, identifies the ethnic German supervisor merely as "Edward L."

160. Belzec trial, 6:1129–32 (Kozak).

161. Belzec trial, 5:974–75 (Kallmayer to Dr. Stahmer, June 18, 1960).

162. According to Tregenza, "Belzec," pp. 248–49, there were two tests of the gas chambers in February 1942, the first with Zyklon B and the second with bottled carbon monoxide. Among the victims of the second test were German-Jewish psychiatric patients deported from Germany and local Jews from Piaski and Izbica. Only then was a Soviet tank motor installed to produce carbon monoxide from exhaust gas.

163. Belzec trial, 4:656–60 (Oberhauser, February 26, 1960), and 763–65 (Oberhauser, April 20, 1960); 9:1683–84 (Oberhauser, December 12, 1962). Oberhauser's testimony of 1960 clearly dates Wirth's abrupt return to Berlin to February 1942, at a time when he was bringing building materials and the initial Jewish workforce had just been killed. I view his 1962 testimony putting this episode in April and May very skeptically, for Oberhauser was then clearly falsifying the chronology to give the impression that until August 1942—i.e., for the period for which he was on trial—only a small number of test gassings were being carried out in Belzec in a single gas chamber capable of holding 100 people. The testimony of the Polish villagers, based on what they learned from the Ukrainian guards, dates the test gassing of the Jewish workers to February 1942. Belzec trial, 6:1126 (Mieczyslaw Kudyba), 1150 (Michal Kusmierczak), and 6:1158 (Jan Glab). Although the Munich court judgment and Rückerl, NS-*Vernichtungslager*, pp. 136–37, as well as Arad in *Belzec, Sobibor, Treblinka*, pp. 72–73, accept the dating of Oberhauser's 1962 testimony, placing Wirth's departure in April/May, I do not.

164. Rückerl, *NS-Vernichtungslager*, pp. 136–37.

165. Pressac, "The Machinery of Mass Murder at Auschwitz," p. 199; van Pelt, "A Site in Search of a Mission," p. 139.

166. Van Pelt, "A Site in Search of a Mission," p. 145; Czech, *Kalendarium*, p. 174–75. The description of a gassing in the old crematory by Pery Broad, vaguely dated to early 1942, seems to fit this event. Jadwiga Bezwinska and Danuta Czech, eds., *KL Auschwitz Seen by the SS*, pp. 174–77.

167. Van Pelt, "A Site in Search of a Mission," pp. 145–46. Without explanation or evidence, Jean-Claude Pressac asserts that Bunker 1 was not selected, converted, and put into operation until May 1942. Pressac, "The Machinery of Mass Murder," p. 212. Robert Jan van Pelt and Deborah Dwork have made a subsequent argument that the decision to construct Bunker 1 and a large crematorium concurrently and next to each other in one corner of Birkenau was triggered by the opportunity to bring not only Slovak Jewish workers to Auschwitz but also their nonworking families at a profit of 500 RM per head for the Germans. In their view, Himmler and Eichmann pursued the possibility of deporting entire Slovak Jewish families only after the mid-February gassing of Silesian Jews in the Stammlager and Kammler's subsequent, improved technological solution for killing the nonworking Slovak Jews in Birkenau. *Auschwitz: 1270 to the Present*, pp. 301–4. I think this interpretation overemphasizes the role of the Slovak Jews and underemphasizes that of the Silesian Jews in the minds of the decision makers. Between May 5 and June 17, 20,000 Silesian Jews were deported to Birkenau to be gassed. In August 1942 another 10,000–13,000 Silesian Jews were gassed in Auschwitz. Sybille Steinbacher, *"Musterstadt" Auschwitz*, p. 286. See also YVA, BD 23/5 (lists of ITS Arolsen) and USHMMA, RG 15.030M, microfiche 1, Nachverzeichnis aller aus Beuthen O/S ausgesiedelten Juden; and Avihu Ronen, English summary of "The Jews of Zaglembie during the Holocaust," p. 11. In contrast, only the last 8 of 57 Slovak transports in 1942, carrying 7,700 out of the total of 58,000 deportees, were family transports to Birkenau subjected to selection and gassing. For the lists of Slovak transports, see Yehoshua Büchler, "The Deportation of Slovakian Jews to the Lublin District of Poland in 1942," p. 166; and Büchler, "First in the Vale of Affliction: Slovakian Jewish Women in Auschwitz, 1942," pp. 308, 320. In short, in 1942 Birkenau was central to the gassing of Silesian Jews but only peripheral to that of Slovakian Jews.

168. Czech, *Kalendarium*, pp. 186–87. Czech does not explain the source for this precise date. Hilberg, "Auschwitz and the 'Final Solution,'" p. 85, accepts the month of March for Bunker 1. Piper, "Gas Chambers and Crematoria," is the most cautious and concludes, "Insufficient source material does not allow us to determine the exact date of bringing bunker 1 into operation" (p. 178).

169. Reconstructing the chronology of Auschwitz in the fall of 1941 and spring of 1942 has been dependent on the analyses of the construction plans by Pressac and van Pelt because the testimonies of especially Höss and to some extent Eichmann are confused, contradictory, self-serving, and not credible. By Höss's account, Eichmann visited him shortly after a meeting with Himmler in the summer of 1941. Allegedly, Eichmann explained that only gas was suitable because of the difficulties already experienced in the east with both shooting (which Eichmann described as "mowing down") and gas vans using

exhaust gas. He also spoke of plans for roundups all over Europe. According to Höss, he and Eichmann then selected the farmhouse northwest of the planned section III of Birkenau as the future gas chamber, even though a suitable gas had not yet been found. Only after attending a Berlin conference of Eichmann's deportation experts from various European countries in November 1941, i.e., months later, did he and Fritzsch conduct the Zyklon B experiments. Gassing of Silesian Jews then began at the latest in January 1942, and after the first transport Eichmann brought Himmler's orders to extract gold teeth and cut women's hair. Höss, *Death Dealer*, pp. 28–32, 157. It would appear that Höss both exaggerated Eichmann's role and reversed the sequence of his visit(s) on the one hand and the first testing of Zyklon B on the other. Eichmann admitted a trip to the Lublin district in the fall of 1941 (during the peak of bright autumn colors and still warm weather), as well as witnessing a gassing at Chelmno in January and a shooting massacre at Minsk after the weather had turned cold (probably November 1941).

None of these events would have been known without Eichmann's own confession, and he certainly had no motive to make them up. But Eichmann was furious about Höss's account of his role at Auschwitz and adamantly denied it. He considered the issue so important, as he wrote in a note to Servatius, his defense attorney, "because I must prove Höss the arch liar, that I had nothing at all to do with him and his gas chambers and his death camp." (*Weil ich den Erzlügner Höss beweisen musste, dass ich mit ihm und seinen Gaskammern und seinen Tötungslager überhaupt nichts zu tun gehabt habe.*) BA, All. Proz. 6/169, Servatius papers including Eichmann's notes and timeline. According to Eichmann's various accounts, he did not visit Auschwitz until the spring of 1942, when Höss showed him the facilities for gassing with "tablets" (*Tabletten*) that looked like "cardboard coasters" (*Pappedeckeln*, also referred to by Eichmann as *runde Pappsachen*) in "the same little houses" (*dieselben Häuschen*) as he had seen in the camp in the woods beyond Lublin. He remembered distinctly the "remarkable blossoms" (*besondere Blumenfälle*) and "a special profusion of flowers" (*eine besohndere Blumenfülle*), so according to Eichmann his first Auschwitz visit must have taken place in the "peak of spring" (*Hochfrühjahrszeit*). See "Meine Memoiren," p. 102; *Eichmann Trial*, 7:218, 363, 372–76, 380–84, 394; ISA, "Götzen," part 1, pp. 163–66. His visit was presumably around the time of the early May gassing of Jews from East Upper Silesia. Höss too remarked on the memorable incongruity of gassing taking place beneath the "budding fruit trees of the farm" (*Death Dealer*, p. 159). Insofar as Eichmann's testimony was distorted by considerations of defense strategy and personal pique, it was clearly to move dates back, not forward, and above all to minimize his role at Auschwitz.

170. On the gassing of Jews at the Semlin camp, see Browning, *Fateful Months*, pp. 68–85; Menachem Shelach, "Sajmiste Extermination Camp in Serbia."

171. *ADAP*, D, vol. 13/2, p. 580 (Luther Vermerk, December 9, 1941).

172. Landgericht Hannover, 2 Ks 2/65, Pradel/Wentritt trial, 12:238 (Schäfer testimony).

173. BDC, Turner ss-file (Turner to Wolff, April 11, 1942).

174. Browning, "Harald Turner und die Militärverwaltung in Serbien."

175. Schäfer trial, 2:199–204, 331–34, 342–44. Pradel/Wentritt trial, 8:55–57, 12:238–39 (Schäfer testimonies).

176. Shelach, "Sajmiste," pp. 248, 258.

177. Browning, *Fateful Months*, pp. 79–83.

178. Shelach, "Sajmiste," pp. 255–56, estimates over 8,000 deaths from gassing alone (including 500 in the Jewish hospital in Belgrade), execution of 500 men before the arrival of the gas van, and about 10% attrition among the winter inmates from the terrible conditions.

179. Nbg. Doc. NOKW-1421, Felber to Meyszner, December 24, 1943.

180. PA, Pol. IV (348), Rademacher memorandum, May 29, 1942. Schäfer trial, 2:353 (testimony of Dr. R.).

10. Conclusion

1. On October 4 Goebbels reported Hitler's prediction that if the weather held the Soviet army would be demolished within 14 days. *Die Tagebücher von Joseph Goebbels II*, 2:50. Subsequently he reported that weather had begun to turn on October 9 (p. 83) Nevertheless, on October 10, the day of the Prague conference, Goebbels wrote: "The Führer judges the situation entirely optimistically. He is of the opinion that one can no longer speak of Soviet resistance worthy of the name" (p. 87). Despite the reports of increasing difficulties on the eastern front by October 15, according to Goebbels, Hitler viewed the situation more favorably than the generals. He still thought that military actions would be concluded in November (p. 117). By the end of October Goebbels was resigned to the fact that further progress on the front was "almost impossible," and they would have to begin again in the spring (pp. 204, 209). Yet even on November 10 Hitler still expressed the view that "the Soviet Union was already beaten" and hoped within four weeks to encircle Moscow, reach the Volga, and cut off the Caucasus. Germany could then go into winter quarters and resume the offensive in the spring (pp. 262–63).

2. On January 25, 1942, Hitler had guests for lunch, including Himmler and Lammers. Knowing full well that Jewish emigration had been banned, he cynically proclaimed: "The Jew must get out of Europe. . . . I only say he must go. If he croaks in the process, I can't help it. I see only one thing: total extermination, if they don't go voluntarily." (*Der Jude muss aus Europa heraus. . . . Ich sage nur, er muss weg. Wenn er dabei kaputtgeht, da kann ich nicht helfen. Ich sehe nur eines: die absolute Ausrottung, wenn sie nicht freiwillig gehen.*) Jochmann, *Monologe im Führerhauptquartier*, p. 229.

In his public address at the Sportpalast in Berlin in January 30, 1942, he openly invoked his misdated Reichstag prophecy of January 1939: "We are clear that the war can only end either with the extermination of the Aryan peoples or the disappearance of Jewry from Europe. I already stated on September 1, 1939, in the German Reichstag—and I refrain from over-hasty prophecies—that this war will not come to an end as the Jews imagine, with the extermination of the European-Aryan peoples, but that the result of this war will be the annihilation of Jewry. For the first time the old Jewish law will now be applied: an eye for an eye, a tooth for a tooth." *Hitler: Reden und Proklamationen 1932–1945*, II/2, pp. 1828–29.

On February 15, 1942, Goebbels recorded: "The Führer once again expressed his opinion, that he is determined to ruthlessly clear the Jews out of Europe. Here one may in no way lapse into sentimentality. The Jews have earned the catastrophe that they meet with today. With the destruction of our enemies, they will also meet with their own destruction. We must accelerate this process with a cold ruthlessness, and thereby we perform an incalculable service for humanity that has suffered from and for thousands of years been tortured by the Jews." *Die Tagebücher von Joseph Goebbels II*, 3:320–21.

Again on February 22, 1942, with Himmler as his dinner guest, Hitler exclaimed: "The same battle that Pasteur and Koch had to wage must be waged by us today. Countless illnesses have their cause in one bacillus: the Jews! . . . We will recover our health when we eliminate the Jews." Jochmann, *Monologe im Führerhauptquartier*, p. 293.

On February 24, 1942, Hitler addressed the "old fighters" of the party and declared that "my prophecy will find its fulfillment, that not Aryan humanity but rather the Jew will be destroyed through this war. No matter what comes of this war or how long it may last, this will be its ultimate result." Domarus, *Hitler: Reden und Proklamationen*, II/2, p. 1844.

For an assessment of Hitler's role during these months, see also Kershaw, *Hitler 1936– 1645: Nemesis*, pp. 487–95.

3. DKHH, pp. 375–81.

4. *Die Tagebücher von Joseph Goebbels II*, 3:561 (entry of March 27, 1942).

5. Friedländer, *The Years of Persecution*, p. 298. For the general consensus among historians on this issue over the years, see Marlis Steinert, *Hitler's War and the Germans*, p. 37; Stokes, "The German People and the Destruction of the European Jews," pp. 174–75; Sarah Gordon, *Hitler, Germans, and the "Jewish Question,"* pp. 175–80; Kulka, " 'Public Opinion' in Nazi Germany," pp. 135–44; Kershaw, "The Persecution of the Jews and German Popular Opinion," pp. 275–81; Bankier, *The Germans and the Final Solution*, pp. 85–88.

6. Steinert, *Hitler's War and the Germans*, p. 50.

7. Friedländer, *The Years of Persecution*, p. 287.

8. Herbert, "Die deutsche Militärverwaltung und die Deportation der französischen Juden," pp. 444–45.

9. Greiser's expression in Frank, *Diensttagebuch*, p. 261 (entry of July 31, 1940).

10. Friedlander, *The Origins of Nazi Genocide*, pp. 263–83.

Bibliography of Published and Secondary Sources

DOCUMENT COLLECTIONS

Akten zur deutschen auswärtigen Politik, 1918–1945. Series D, 1937–1945, vols. 10, 13/2. Series E, vol. 1. Göttingen: Vandenhoeck & Ruprecht.

Aly, Götz, and Susanne Heim, eds. *Bevölkerungsstruktur und Massenmord: Neue Dokumente zur deutschen Politik der Jahre 1938–1945.* Vol. 9 of *Beiträge zur nationalsozialistischen Gesundheits- und Sozialpolitik.* Berlin: Rotbuch Verlag, 1991.

Arad, Yitzhak, Yisrael Gutman, and Abraham Margoliot, eds. *Documents on the Holocaust: Selected Sources on the Destruction of the Jews of Germany and Austria, Poland, and the Soviet Union.* Jerusalem: Yad Vashem, 1981.

Arad, Yitzhak, Shmuel Krakowski, and Shmuel Spector, eds. *The Einsatzgruppen Reports: Selections from the Dispatches of the Nazi Death Squads' Campaign against the Jews in Occupied Territories of the Soviet Union July 1941–January 1943.* New York: Holocaust Library, 1989.

Baranauskas, B., K. Ruksenas, and E. Rozauskas, eds. *Documents Accuse.* Vilnius: Gintaras, 1970.

Benz, Wolfgang, Konrad Kwiet, Jürgen Matthäus, eds. *Einsatz im "Reichskommissariat Ostland." Dokumente zum Völkermord im Baltikum und in Weissrussland 1941–1944.* Berlin: Metropol, 1998.

Berenstein, Tatiana, Artur Eisenbach, Bernard Mark, and Adam Rutkowski (of the Jewish Historical Institute, Warsaw), eds. *Faschismus, Getto, Massenmord: Dokumentation über Ausrottung und Widerstand der Juden in Polen während des zweiten Weltkrieges.* Berlin [East]: Rütten & Loening, 1960.

Bezwinska, Jadwiga, and Danuta Czech, eds. *KL Auschwitz Seen by the SS.* New York: H. Fertig, 1984.

Carp, Matatias, ed. *Holocaust in Rumania: Facts and Documents on the Annihilation of Rumania's Jews, 1940–1944.* Budapest: Primor Publishing Company, 1994.

Commission for Researching the History of the Frankfurt Jews, ed. *Dokumente zur Geschichte der Frankfurter Juden 1933–1945.* Frankfurt/M.: Kramer, 1963.

Datner, Szymon, Janusz Gumkoswki, and Kazimierz Leszczynski, eds. "Wysiedlanie Ludnosci z ziem Polskich Wcielonych Do Rzesy." *Biuletyn Glownej Komisji Badania Zbrodni Hitlerowskich W Polsce,* vol. 12. Warsaw: Wydawnictwo Prawnicze, 1960.

Dobroszycki, Lucjan, ed. *The Chronicle of the Lodz Ghetto, 1941–1944.* New Haven: Yale University Press, 1984.

Documente Occupationis Teutonicae. Poznan, 1949.

Documents on German Foreign Policy. Series D, vols. 5, 8–10. Washington DC: Government Printing Office, 1949–83.

Dokumente über die Verfolgung der jüdischen Bürger in Baden-Württemberg durch das nationalsozialistische Regime, 1933–1945. Ed. Paul Sauer. Stuttgart: Kohlhammer, 1965.

Dokumenty i Materialy Do Dziejow Okupacji Niemieckiej W Polsce. Ed. Centrala Zydowska Komisja Historyczna w Polsce. Vol. 1: *Obozy* (Lodz, 1946). Vol. 3: *Getto Lodzkie* (Warsaw, 1946).

Esman, Tadeuz, and Wlodzimierz Jastrzebski, eds. *Pierwsze Miesiace Okupacji Hitlerowskiej W Bydgoszcz.* Bydgoszcz, 1967.

Hamburg Institute for Social Research, ed. *The German Army and Genocide: Crimes against War Prisoners, Jews, and Other Civilians in the East, 1939–1944.* New York: I. B. Tauris, 1999.

Heiber, Helmut, ed. "Der Generalplan Ost." *Vierteljahrshefte für Zeitgeschichte* 6 (1958), pp. 281–325.

Hilberg, Raul, ed. *Documents of Destruction.* Chicago: Quadrangle, 1971.

Hillgruber, Andreas, ed. *Staatsmänner bei Hitler: Vertrauliche Aufzeichnungen über Unterredungen mit Vertretern des Auslandes 1939–41.* Frankfurt/M., 1967.

Iltis, Rudolf, ed. *Nazi-Dokumente Sprechen.* Prague: Kirchenzentralverlag, 1965.

Jochmann, Werner, ed. *Monologe im Führerhauptquartier 1941–1944: Die Aufzeichungen Heinrich Heims.* Hamburg: Albrecht Knaus Verlag, 1980.

"Judendeportationen aus dem Reichsgebiet." Unpublished documentary collection compiled by Zentrale Stelle der Landesjustizverwaltungen Ludwigsburg.

Karny, Miroslav, Jaroslava Milotova, and Margita Karna, eds. *Deutsche Politik im "Protektorat Böhmen und Mähren" unter Reinhard Heydrich.* Berlin: Metropol, 1997.

Klarsfeld, Serge. *Vichy-Auschwitz: Die Zusammenarbeit der deutschen und französischen Behörden bei der "Endlösung der Judenfrage" in Frankreich.* Nördlingen: Delphi Politik, 1989.

Klarsfeld, Serge, and Maxime Steinberg, eds. *Die Endlösung der Judenfrage in Belgien.* New York and Paris: Beate Klarsfeld Foundation, n.d.

Klee, Ernst, Willi Dressen, and Volker Riess, eds. *"The Good Old Days": The Holocaust as Seen by Its Perpetrators and Bystanders.* New York: Free Press, 1991. Originally published as *"Schöne Zeiten." Judenmord aus der Sicht der Täter und Gaffer.* Frankfurt/M.: Fischer, 1988.

Klein, Peter, ed. *Die Einsatzgruppen in der besetzten Sowjetunion 1941/42. Die Tätigkeits- und Lageberichte des Chefs der Sicherheitspolizei und des SD.* Berlin: Edition Hentrich, 1997.

Kleinert, Beate, and Wolfgang Prinz, eds. *Namen und Schicksal der Juden Kassels 1933–45.* Kassel: Magistrat der Stadt Kassel-Stadtarchiv, 1980.

Kogon, Eugen, Hermann Langbein, and Adalbert Rückerl, eds. *Nazi Mass Murder: A Documentary History of the Use of Poison Gas.* New Haven: Yale University Press, 1993. Originally published as *Nationalsozialistische Massentötungen durch Giftgas.* Frankfurt: S. Fischer, 1983.

Kohl, Paul, ed. *"Ich wundere mich, dass ich noch lebe." Sowjetische Augenzeugen berichten.* Gütersloh: Güterlohsloher Verlagshaus Gerd Mohn, 1990.

Krausnick, Helmut, ed. "Denkschrift Himmlers über die Behandlung der Fremdvölkischen im Osten." *Vierteljahrshefte für Zeitgeschichte* 5/2 (1957), pp. 194–98.

Kriegstagebuch des Oberkommandos der Wehrmacht 1940–1941. Ed. Percy Schramm; annotated by Hans-Adolf Jacobsen. Frankfurt: Bernard & Graefe, 1965.

Lang, Jochen, von. *Eichmann Interrogated: Transcripts from the Archives of the Israeli Police.* New York: Farrar, Strauss, and Giroux, 1983.

Lenz, Wilhelm, ed. "Die Handakten von Bernhard Lösener, 'Rassereferent' im Reichsministerium des Innern." *Archiv und Geschichte. Festschrift für Friedrich P. Kahlenberg*, ed. Klaus Oldenhage et al., pp. 684–99. Düsseldorf: Droste, 2000.

Longerich, Peter, ed. *Die Ermordung der europäischen Juden: Eine umfassende Dokumentation des Holocaust.* Munich: Piper, 1989.

Madajczyk, Czeslaw, ed. *Vom Generalplan Ost zum Generalsiedlungsplan.* Munich: Saur, 1994.

Manoschek, Walter, ed. *"Es gibt nur eines für das Judentum: Vernichtung." Das Judenbild in deutschen Soldatenbriefen 1939–1944.* Hamburg: Hamburger Edition, 1995.

Matthäus, Jürgen, Konrad Kwiet, Jürgen Förster, and Richard Breitman, eds. *Ausbildungsziel Judenmord? "Weltanschauliche Erziehung" von SS, Polizei und Waffen-SS im Rahme der "Endlösung."* Frankfurt: Fischer, 2003.

Müller, Klaus-Jürgen, ed. "Zu Vorgeschichte und Inhalt der Rede Himmlers vor der höheren Generalität am 13. März 1940 in Koblenz." *Vierteljahrshefte für Zeitgeschichte* 18/1 (1970), pp. 95–120.

Müller, Norbert, ed. *Die faschistische Okkupationspolitik in den zeitweilig besetzten Gebieten der Sowjetunion (1941–1944).* Berlin: Deutscher Verlag der Wissenschaft, 1991.

Nazi Conspiracy and Aggression. 8 vols. and 2 supp. Washington DC, 1946–58.

Pätzold, Kurt, ed. *Verfolgung, Vertreibung, Vernichtung.* Leipzig: Verlag Philipp Reclam, 1984.

"A Preparatory Document for the Wannsee 'Conference,'" with comment by Yehoshua Büchler and Richard Breitman. *Holocaust and Genocide Studies* 9/1 (1995), pp. 121–29.

Röhr, Werner, ed. *Die faschistische Okkupationspolitik in Polen (1939–1945).* Berlin: VEB Deutschen Verlag der Wissenschaft, 1989.

Röpcke, Andreas, and Günter Rodhenburg, eds. *"Es geht tatsächlich nach Minsk": Texte und Materialen zur Erinnerung an die Deportation von Bremer Juden am 18.11.41 in das Vernichtungslager Minsk.* Bremen: Staatsarchiv Bremen, 1992.

Rürup, Reinhard, ed. *Der Krieg gegen die Sowjetunion 1941–1945. Eine Dokumentation.* Berlin: Argon Verlag, 1991.

——. *Topography of Terror: Gestapo, SS and Reichssicherheitshauptamt on the "Prinz-Albrecht-Terrain": A Documentation.* Berlin: Verlag Willmuth Arenhövel, 1989.

Rütter, C. F., et al., eds. *Justiz und NS-Verbrechen. Sammlung Strafurteile wegen nationalsozialistischer Tötungsverbrechen 1945–1966.* 20 vols. Amsterdam: University Press of Amsterdam, 1968–81.

Sauer, Paul, ed. *Die Schicksal der jüdischen Bürger Baden-Württemburg während der nationalsozialistischen Verfolgungszeit.* Stuttgart: Kohlhammer, 1963.

The Trial of Adolf Eichmann: Record of the Proceedings in the District Court of Jerusalem. Jerusalem: State of Israel, Ministry of Justice, 1992–95.

Trials of the Major War Criminals before the Nuernberg Military Tribunals. 42 vols. Nuremburg, 1947–49.

Trials of War Criminals before the Nuernberg Military Tribunals. 15 vols. Washington DC, 1947–49.

Unsere Ehre heisst Treue: Kriegstagebuch des Kommandostabes Reichsführer SS. Tätigkeitsberichte der 1. und 2. SS-Inf.-Brigade, der 1. SS-Kav.-Brigade und von Sonderkommandos der SS. Vienna: Europa Verlag, 1965, 1984.

Verbrechen der Wehrmacht. Dimensionen des Vernichtungskrieges 1941–1944. Ed. Hamburger Institut für Sozialforschung. Hamburg: Hamburger Edition, 2002.

Wilhelm, Hans-Heinrich, ed. *Rassenpolitik und Kriegführung. Sicherheitspolizei und Wehrmacht in Polen und der Sowjetunion.* Passau: Wissenschaftsverlag Robert Rothe, 1991.

MEMOIRS, DIARIES, LETTERS, SPEECHES, PERSONAL ACCOUNTS

Bräutigam, Otto. "Aus dem Kriegstagebuch des Diplomaten Otto Bräutigam." Ed. H. D. Heilmann. *Biedermann und Schreibtischtäter. Materialien zur deutschen Täter-Biographie*, vol. 4: *Beiträge zur nationalsozialistischen Gesundheits- und Sozialpolitik.* Berlin: Rotbuch Verlag, 1987.

Ciano, Galeazzo. *The Ciano Diaries 1939–43.* Garden City, New York: Doubleday, 1946.

Czerniakow, Adam. *The Warsaw Diary of Adam Czerniakow.* Ed. Raul Hilberg, Stanislaw Staron, and Josef Kermisz. New York: Stein and Day, 1969.

Eiber, Ludwig, ed. " '. . . ein bisschen die Wahrheit': Briefe eines Bremer Kaufmanns von seinem Einsatz beim Reserve-Polizeibataillon 105 in der Sowjetunion 1941." *1999: Zeitschrift für Sozialgeschichte des 20. und 21. Jahrhunderts* 1 (1991), pp. 58–83.

Eichmann, Adolf. "Eichmann Tells His Own Damning Story," *Life Magazine*, November 28, 1960, and December 5, 1960.

——. *Ich Adolf Eichmann. Ein historischer Zeugenbericht.* Ed. Rudolf Aschenauer. Leoni am Starnberger See: Druffel Verlag, 1980.

Engel, Gerhard. *Heeresadjutant bei Hitler: 1938–43. Aufzeichnungen des Majors Engel.* Ed. Hildegard von Kotze. Stuttgart: DVA, 1974.

Frank, Hans. *Das Diensttagebuch des deutschen Generalgouverneurs in Polen 1939–1945.* Ed. Werner Präg and Wolfgang Jacobmeyer. Stuttgart: DVA, 1975.

Goebbels, Joseph. *The Goebbels Diaries 1939–1941.* Ed. Fred Taylor. New York: Putnam, 1983.

——. *The Goebbels Diaries 1942–1943.* Ed. Louis Lochner. New York, 1948.

——. *Die Tagebücher von Joseph Goebbels: Sämtliche Fragmente.* Ed. Elke Fröhlich. Teil I, *Aufzeichnungen 1924–1941*, 9 vols. Teil II, *Diktate 1941–1945*, 15 vols. Munich: Saur, 1987.

Groscurth, Helmuth. *Tagebücher eines Abwehroffiziers 1938–1940.* Ed. Helmut Krausnick and Harold Deutsch. Stuttgart: DVA, 1970.

Halder, Franz. *Kriegstagebuch: Tägliche Aufzeichnungen des Chefs des Generalstabes des Heeres 1939–1942.* Ed. Hans Adolph Jacobsen. Stuttgart: DVA, 1962.

Hassell, Ulrich von. *The Von Hassell Diaries, 1938–1944.* London: H. Hamilton, 1948.

Himmler, Heinrich. *Der Dienstkalender Heinrich Himmlers 1941/42.* Ed. Peter Witte et al. Hamburg: Christians, 1999.

——. *Geheimreden 1933 bis 1945 und andere Ansprachen.* Ed. Bradley F. Smith and Agnes Petersen. Frankfurt/M.: Propyläen, 1974.

——. *Reichsführer!: Briefe an und von Himmler.* Ed. Helmut Heiber. Stuttgart: DVA, 1968.

Hitler, Adolf. *Hitler: Reden und Proklamationen 1932–1945.* Ed. Max Domarus. 4 vols. Wiesbaden: Löwit, 1973.

Höss, Rudolf. *Death Dealer: The Memoirs of the SS Kommandant at Auschwitz.* Ed. Steven Paskuly. New York: Da Capo Press, 1996.

Kersten, Felix. *The Kersten Memoirs, 1940–1945.* New York: Macmillan, 1957.

Klemperer, Victor. *I Will Bear Witness: A Diary of the Nazi Years.* New York: Random House, 1998.

Lösener, Bernhard. "Als Rassereferent im Reichsministerium des Innern." *Vierteljahrshefte für Zeitgeschichte* 9 / 3 (1961), pp. 264–313.

———. *Legislating the Holocaust: The Bernhard Loesener Memoirs and Supporting Documents.* Ed. Karl Schleunes. Boulder: Westview Press, 2001.

Ringelblum, Emmanuel. *Notes from the Warsaw Ghetto: The Journal of Emmanuel Ringelblum.* Ed. Jacob Sloan. New York: Schocken, 1974.

Rosenberg, Alfred. *Das politische Tagebuch Alfred Rosenbergs.* Ed. Hans-Günther Seraphim. Göttingen: Musterschmidt, 1956.

Speer, Albert. *Spandau: The Secret Diaries.* New York: Macmillan, 1976.

Stief, Helmut. "Ausgewählte Briefe von Generalmajor Helmut Stief." Ed. Hans Rothfels. *Vierteljahrshefte für Zeitgeschichte* 2 / 3 (1954), pp. 291–305.

Stroop, Jürgen. *The Stroop Report: The Jewish Quarter in Warsaw Is No More.* Ed. Sybil Milton. New York: Pantheon Books, 1979.

Wagner, Eduard. *Der Generalquartiermeister: Briefe und Tagebuch Eduard Wagners.* Ed. Elisabeth Wagner. Munich, 1963.

SECONDARY SOURCES

Adam, Uwe Dietrich. *Judenpolitik im Dritten Reich.* Düsseldorf: Droste, 1972.

Adler, H. G. *Theresienstadt 1941–1945: Das Antlitz einer Zwangsgemeinschaft.* 2nd ed. Tübingen: J. C. B. Mohr, 1960.

———. *Der verwaltete Mensch: Studien zur Deportation der Juden aus Deutschland.* Tübingen: J. C. B. Mohr, 1974.

Allen, Michael Thad. *The Business of Genocide: The SS, Slave Labor, and the Concentration Camps.* Chapel Hill: University of North Carolina Press, 2002.

———. "The Devil in the Details: The Gas Chambers of Birkenau, October 1941." *Holocaust and Genocide Studies* 16 / 2 (2002), pp. 189–216.

Allen, William Sheridan. *The Nazi Seizure of Power: The Experience of a Single German Town, 1922–1945.* Rev. Ed. New York: F. Watts, 1984.

Altschuler, Mordechai. "Escape and Evacuation of Soviet Jews at the Time of the Nazi Invasion." *The Holocaust in the Soviet Union: Studies and Sources on the Destruction of the Jews in Nazi-Occupied Territories of the USSR, 1941–45,* ed. Lucjan Dobroszycki and John Gurock, pp. 77–104. New York: M. E. Sharpe, 1993.

Aly, Götz. *"Final Solution": Nazi Population Policy and the Murder of the European Jews.* London: Arnold, 1999. Originally published as *"Endlösung": Völkerverschiebung und der Mord an den europäischen Juden.* Frankfurt / M.: S. Fischer, 1995.

Aly, Götz, and Susanne Heim. *Architects of Annihilation: Auschwitz and the Logic of Destruction.* London: Weidenfels and Nicolson, 2002. Originally published as

Vordenker der Vernichtung. Auschwitz und die Pläne für eine neue europäische Ordnung. Hamburg: Hoffmann and Campe, 1991.

——. "Die Ökonomie der 'Endlösung': Menschenvernichtung und wirtschaftliche Neuordnung." *Beiträge zur Nationalsozialistischen Gesundheits- und Sozialpolitik*, vol. 5: *Sozialpolitik und Judenvernichtung: Gibt es eine Ökonomie der Endlösung?*, pp. 7–90. Berlin: Rotbuch Verlag, 1987.

Aly, Götz, and Karl Heinz Roth. *Die Restlose Erfassung: Volkszählen, Identifizieren, Aussondern im Nationalsozialismus.* Berlin: Rotbuch, 1984.

Ancel, Jean. "Antonescu and the Jews." *The Holocaust and History: The Known, the Unknown, the Disputed, and the Reexamined*, ed. Michael Berenbaum and Abraham J. Peck, pp. 463–79. Bloomington: Indiana University Press, 1998.

——. "Antonescu and the Jews." *Yad Vashem Studies* 23 (1993), pp. 213–80.

——. "The Romanian Way of Solving the 'Jewish Problem' in Bessarabia and Bukovina, June–July 1941." *Yad Vashem Studies* 19 (1988), pp. 185–232.

Anderson, Truman. "Die 62. Infantrie-Division. Repressalien im Heeresgebiet Süd, Oktober bis Dezember 1941." *Vernichtungskrieg. Verbrechen der Wehrmacht 1941–1945*, ed. Hannes Heer and Klaus Naumann, pp. 297–314. Hamburg: Hamburger Edition, 1995.

Angrick, Andrej. "Einsatzgruppe D." *Die Einsatzgruppen in der besetzten Sowjetunion. Die Tätigkeits- und Lageberichte des Chefs der Sicherheitspolizei und des SD*, ed. Peter Klein, pp. 88–110. Berlin: Edition Hentrich, 1997.

——. "Die Einsatzgruppe D. Struktur und Tätigkeit einer mobilen Einheit der Sicherheitspolizei und des SD in der deutsch besetzten Sowjetunion." Ph.D. dissertation, Technische Universität Berlin, 1999.

——. "The Escalation of German-Rumanian Anti-Jewish Policy after the Attack on the Soviet Union." *Yad Vashem Studies* 26 (1998), pp. 203–38.

Angrick, Andrej, and Martina Voigt, Silke Ammerschubert, Peter Klein. " 'Da hätte man schon ein Tagebuch führen müssen.' Das Polizeibatallion 322 und die Judenmorde im Bereich der Heeresgruppe Mitte während des Sommers und Herbstes 1941." *Die Normalität des Verbrechens. Bilanz und Perspektiven der Forschung zu den nationalsozialistischen Gewaltverbrechen*, ed. Helge Grabitz, Klaus Bästlein, and Johannes Tuchel, pp. 325–85. Berlin: Hentrich Edition, 1994.

Arad, Yitzhak. "Alfred Rosenberg and the 'Final Solution' in the Occupied Soviet Territories." *Yad Vashem Studies* 13 (1979), pp. 263–86.

——. *Belzec, Sobibor, Treblinka: The Operation Reinhard Death Camps.* Bloomington: Indiana University Press, 1987.

——. *Ghetto in Flames: The Struggle and Destruction of the Jews in Vilna in the Holocaust.* New York: Ktav Publishing House, 1982.

Arendt, Hannah. *Eichmann in Jerusalem: A Report on the Banality of Evil.* New York: Penguin Books, 1964.

——. *The Origins of Totalitarianism.* New York: Harcourt Brace, 1951.

Armstrong, John, ed. *Soviet Partisans in World War II.* Madison: University of Wisconsin Press, 1964.

Asaria, Zvi. *Die Juden in Niedersachsen.* Leer: Rautenberg, 1979.

Ascheim, Steven E. *Brothers and Strangers: The East European Jew in German and German Jewish Consciousness, 1800–1923.* Madison: University of Wisconsin Press, 1982.

Bajohr, Frank. *"Aryanisation" in Hamburg: The Economic Exclusion of Jews and the Confiscation of Their Property in Nazi Germany.* New York: Berghahn, 2002.

Banach, Jens. *Heydrichs Elite. Das Führerkorps der Sicherheitspolizei und des SD 1936–1945.* Paderborn: Schönigh, 1998.

Bankier, David. *The Germans and the Final Solution: Public Opinion under Nazism.* New York: Oxford University Press, 1992.

——. "The Germans and the Holocaust: What Did They Know." *Yad Vashem Studies* 20 (1990), pp. 69–98.

——, ed. *Probing the Depths of German Antisemitism: German Society and the Persecution of the Jews, 1933–1941.* New York: Berghahn Books, 2000.

Barkai, Avraham. *From Boycott to Annihilation: The Economic Struggle of German Jews, 1933–1943.* Hanover: University Press of New England, 1989.

Bartov, Omer. *The Eastern Front, 1941–1945: German Troops and the Barbarization of Warfare.* New York: St. Martin's, 1986.

Bauer, Yehuda. *American Jewry and the Holocaust.* Detroit: Wayne State University Press, 1981.

——. *Rethinking the Holocaust.* New Haven: Yale University Press, 2001.

Baumgart, Winfred. "Zur Ansprache Hitlers vor den Führern der Wehrmacht am 22. August 1939." *Vierteljahrshefte für Zeitgeschichte* 16 (1968), pp. 120–49.

Beer, Mathais. "Die Entwicklung der Gaswagen beim Mord an den Juden." *Vierteljahrshefte für Zeitgeschichte* 35/3 (1987), pp. 403–17.

Berenstein, Tatiana. "Eksterminacja Ludnosci Zydowskiej W Dystrikcie Galicja." *Biuletyn Zydowskiego Instytutu Historycznego* 61 (1967), pp. 3–58.

Berschel, Holger. *Bürokratie und Terror: Das Judenreferat der Gestapo Düsseldorf 1935–1945.* Essen: Klartext, 2001.

——. "Polizeiroutiniers und Judenverfolgung. Die Bearbeitung von 'Judenangelegenheiten' bei der Stapo-Leitstelle Düsseldorf." *Die Gestapo im Zweiten Weltkrieg. "Heimatfront" und besetztes Europa,* ed. Gerhard Paul and Klaus-Michael Mallmann, pp. 155–78. Darmstadt: Primus, 2000.

Birn, Ruth Bettina. "Collaboration in the East: The Case of the Estonian Security Police." Forthcoming.

——. *Die Höheren SS- und Polizeiführer. Himmlers Vertreter im Reich und in den besetzten Gebieten.* Düsseldorf: Droste, 1986.

——. "Revising the Holocaust." *Historical Journal* 40/1 (1997), pp. 195–215.

——. "Zweierlei Wirklichkeit? Fallbeispiele zur Partisanenbekämpfung im Osten." *Zwei Wege nach Moskau. Vom Hitler-Stalin-Pakt zum "Unternehmen Barbarossa,"* ed. Bernd Wegner, pp. 275–90. Munich: Piper, 1991.

Blackbourn, David, and Geoff Eley. *The Peculiarities of German History: Bourgeois Society and Politics in Nineteenth-Century Germany.* New York: Oxford University Press, 1984.

Bloom, J. C. "The Persecution of the Jews in the Netherlands: A Comparative Western European Perspective." *European History Quarterly* 19 (1989), pp. 333–51.

Boll, Bernd, and Hans Safrian. "Auf dem Weg nach Stalingrad. Die 6. Armee 1941/42."

Vernichtungskrieg. Verbrechen der Wehrmacht 1941–1945, ed. Hannes Heer and Klaus Naumann, pp. 260–96. Hamburg: Hamburger Edition, 1995.

Bondy, Louis W. *Racketeers of Hatred: Julius Streicher and the Jews-Baiters International.* London: N. Wolsey, 1946.

Borgert, Hans-Ludger. "Die Kriegsmarine und das Unternehmen 'Barbarossa.'" *Mitteilungen des Bundesarchivs* 1 (1999), pp. 52–66.

Botz, Gerhard. *Wohnungspolitik und Judendeportation in Wien 1938 bis 1945: Zur Funktion des Antisemitismus als Ersatz nationalsozialistischer Sozialpolitik.* Vienna: Geyer, 1975.

Braham, Randolph. "The Kamenets Poldolsk and Delvidek Massacres." *Yad Vashem Studies* 9 (1973), pp. 133–56.

———. *The Politics of Genocide.* Vol. 1. New York: Columbia University Press, 1981.

Brechtken, Magnus. *"Madagaskar für die Juden": Antisemitische Idee und politische Praxis.* Munich: Oldenbourg, 1997.

Breitman, Richard. *The Architect of Genocide: Himmler and the Final Solution.* New York: Knopf, 1991.

———. "Himmler's Police Auxiliaries in the Occupied Soviet Territories." *Simon Wiesenthal Center Annual* 7 (1990), pp. 23–29.

———. *Official Secrets: What the Nazis Planned, What the British and Americans Knew.* New York: Knopf, 1998.

———. "Plans for the Final Solution in Early 1941." *German Studies Review* 17/3 (1994), pp. 483–93.

Broszat, Martin. "Das deutsch-slowakische Verhältnis 1939/40 und seine Rückwirkung auf die slowakische Judenpolitik." *Gutachten des Instituts für Zeitgeschichte*, 1:221–29. Munich: Institut für Zeitgeschichte, 1958.

———. "Das deutsch-ungarische Verhältnis und die ungarische Judenpolitik in den Jahren 1938–41." *Gutachten des Instituts für Zeitgeschichte*, 1:183–200. Munich: Institut für Zeitgeschichte, 1958.

———. "Das dritte Reich und die rumänische Judenpolitik." *Gutachten des Instituts für Zeitgeschichte*, 1:102–83. Munich: Institut für Zeitgeschichte, 1958.

———. "Hitler and the Genesis of the Final Solution: An Assessment of David Irving's Theses." *Yad Vashem Studies* 13 (1979), pp. 73–125. Originally published as "Hitler und die Genesis der 'Endlösung.' Aus Anlass der Thesen von David Irving." *Vierteljahrshefte für Zeitgeschichte* 25/4 (1977), pp. 739–75.

———. *Nationalsozialistische Polenpolitik 1939–1945.* Stuttgart: DVA, 1961.

Browder, George. *Hitler's Enforcers: Gestapo and the SS Security Service in the Nazi Revolution.* New York: Oxford University Press, 1996.

Browning, Christopher R. *Fateful Months: Essays on the Emergence of the Final Solution.* New York: Holmes & Meier, 1985.

———. *The Final Solution and the German Foreign Office.* New York: Holmes & Meier, 1978.

———. "Genocide and Public Health: German Doctors and Polish Jews, 1939–41." *Holocaust and Genocide Studies* 3/1 (1988), pp. 21–36.

———. "Harald Turner und die Militärverwaltung in Serbien 1941–1942." *Verwaltung contra Menschenführung im Staat Hitlers*, ed. Dieter Rebentisch and Karl Teppe, pp. 351–73. Göttingen: Vandenhoeck & Ruprecht, 1986.

——. *Nazi Policy, Jewish Workers, German Killers.* New York: Cambridge University Press, 2000.

——. "Nazi Resettlement Policy and the Search for a Solution to the Jewish Question, 1939–1941." *German Studies Review* 9/3 (1986), pp. 497–519.

——. *Ordinary Men: Reserve Police Battalion 101 and the Final Solution in Poland.* New York: HarperCollins, 1992.

——. *The Path to Genocide: Essays on Launching the Final Solution.* New York: Cambridge University Press, 1992.

——. "Perpetrator Testimony: Another Look at Adolf Eichmann." *Postwar Testimony and Holocaust History.* Madison: University of Wisconsin Press, 2003.

Büchler, Yehoshua. "The Deportation of the Slovakian Jews to the Lublin District of Poland in 1942." *Holocaust and Genocide Studies*, 6/2 (1991), pp. 151–66.

——. "First in the Vale of Affliction: Slovakian Jewish Women in Auschwitz, 1942." *Holocaust and Genocide Studies*, 10/3 (1996), pp. 299–325.

——. "Kommandostab Reichsführer-ss: Himmler's Personal Murder Brigades in 1941." *Holocaust and Genocide Studies* 1/1 (1986), pp. 11–25.

Burleigh, Michael. *Death and Deliverance: "Euthanasia" in Germany, 1900–1945.* New York: Cambridge University Press, 1994.

——. *Germany Turns Eastward: A Study of Ostforschung in the Third Reich.* New York: Cambridge University Press, 1988.

——. "Die Stunde der Experten." *Der "Generalplan Ost": Hauptlinien der nationalsozialistischen Planungs- und Vernichtungspolitik*, ed. Mechtild Rössler and Sabine Schleiermacher, pp. 346–50. Berlin: Akademie Verlag, 1993.

Burleigh, Michael, and Wolfgang Wippermann. *The Racial State: Germany, 1933–1945.* New York: Cambridge University Press, 1991.

Burrin, Philippe. *Hitler and the Jews: The Genesis of the Holocaust.* London: Edward Arnold, 1994.

Büttner, Ursula. "Die deutsche Bevölkerung und die Judenverfolgung 1933–1945." *Die Judenverfolgung im Dritten Reich*, ed. Ursula Büttner, pp. 67–88. Hamburg: Christians, 1992.

Chary, Frederick B. *The Bulgarian Jews and the Final Solution, 1940–1944.* Pittsburgh: University of Pittsburgh Press, 1972.

Chazan, Robert. "Medieval Anti-Semitism." *History and Hate: The Dimensions of Anti-Semitism*, ed. David Berger, pp. 49–61. Philadelphia: Jewish Publication Society, 1986.

Chiari, Bernhard. *Alltag hinter der Front. Besatzung, Kollaboration und Widerstand in Weissrussland 1941–1944.* Düsseldorf: Droste, 1998.

Clark, Alan. *Barbarossa: The Russian-German Conflict, 1941–45.* New York: Signet Edition, 1966.

Corbach, Dieter. *6:00 Uhr ab Messe Köln-Deutz: Deportationen 1938–1945.* Cologne: Scriba, 1999.

Corni, Gustavo. *Hitler's Ghettos: Voices from a Beleaguered Society, 1939–1944.* New York: Oxford University Press, 2002.

Czech, Danuta. *Kalendarium der Ereignisse im Konzentrationslager Auschwitz-Birkenau 1939–1945.* Hamburg: Rowohlt, 1989.

Dabrowska, Danuta. "Zaglada Skupisk Zydowskich W 'Kraju Warty' W Okresie Okupacji Hitlerowskiej." *Biuletyn Zydowskiego Instytutu Historycznego* 13–14 (1955), pp. 122–84.

Dallin, Alexander. *German Rule in Russia, 1941–1945: A Study of Occupation Policies.* London: Macmillan, 1957.

Datner, Szymon. *55 Dni / 1.IX-25.x.1939. Wehrmachtu W Polsce.* Warsaw: Ministerstwa Obrony Narodowej, 1967.

Dawidowicz, Lucy. *The War against the Jews.* New York: Holt, Reinhart, and Winston, 1975.

Dean, Martin. *Collaboration in the Holocaust: Crimes of the Local Police in Belorussia and Ukraine, 1941–1944.* New York: St. Martin's, 2000.

——. "The Development and Implementation of Nazi Denaturalization and Confiscation Policy up to the Eleventh Decree to the Reich Citizenship Law." *Holocaust and Genocide Studies* 16 / 2 (2002), pp. 217–42.

Determann, Andreas. "Wegbegleiter in den Tod. Zur Funktion bei der Deportationen jüdischer Bürger in den Osten." *Villa ten Hompel: Sitz der Ordnungspolizei im Dritten Reich*, ed. Alfons Kenkmann, pp. 28–53. Münster: Agenda Verlag, 1996.

Deutsch, Harold. *The Conspiracy against Hitler in the Twilight War.* Minneapolis: University of Minnesota Press, 1968.

Diamant, Adolf. *Chronik der Juden in Dresden.* Darmstadt: Agora, 1973.

——. *Deportationsbuch der von Frankfurt am Main aus gewaltsam verschickten Juden in den Jahren 1941 bis 1944.* Frankfurt / M.: Jüdische Gemeinde Frankfurt, 1984.

Dieckmann, Christoph. "Der Krieg und die Ermordung der litauischen Juden." *Nationalsozialistische Vernichtungspolitik 1939–1945. Neue Forschungen und Kontroversen*, ed. Ulrich Herbert, pp. 292–329. Frankfurt: Fischer, 1998.

Döscher, Hans-Jürgen. *Das Auswärtige Amt im Dritten Reich. Diplomatie im Schatten der "Endlösung."* Berlin: Siedler, 1987.

Ehmann, Annegret. "From Colonial Racism to Nazi Population Policy: The Role of the So-Called Mischlinge." *The Holocaust and History: The Known, the Unknown, the Disputed, and the Reexamined*, ed. Michael Berenbaum and Abraham J. Peck, pp. 115–33. Bloomington: Indiana University Press, 1998.

Eichholz, Dietrich. "Der 'Generalplan Ost'. Über eine Ausgeburt imperialistischer Denkart und Politik." *Jahrbuch für Geschichte* 26 (1982), pp. 217–74.

Eisenach, Artur. "Operation Reinhard: Mass Extermination of the Jewish Population in Poland." *Polish Western Affairs* 3 / 1 (1962), pp. 80–124.

Eisenblätter, Gerhard. "Grundlinien der Politik des Reiches gegenüber dem Generalgouvernement, 1939–1945." Ph.D. Dissertation, Frankfurt / M., 1969.

Essner, Cornelia. *Die "Nürnberger Gesetze" oder die Verwaltung des Rassenwahns 1933–1945.* Paderborn: Schönigh, 2002.

Ezergailis, Andrew. *The Holocaust in Latvia, 1941–1944: The Missing Center.* Riga and Washington DC: Historical Institute of Latvia, 1996.

Fauck, S. "Das deutsch-bulgarische Verhältnis 1939–1944 und seine Rückwirkung auf die bulgarische Judenpolitik." *Gutachten des Instituts für Zeitgeschichte*, 2:46–59. Stuttgart: DVA, 1966.

——. "Das deutsch-slowakische Verhältnis 1941–43 und seine Rückwirkung auf die slowakische Judenpolitik." *Gutachten des Instituts für Zeitgeschichte*, 2:61–73. Stuttgart: DVA, 1966.

Favez, Jean-Claude. *The Red Cross and the Holocaust.* Cambridge: Cambridge University Press, 1999.

Fleming, Gerald. *Hitler and the Final Solution.* Berkeley and Los Angeles: University of California Press, 1984. Originally published as *Hitler und die Endlösung. "Es ist des Führers Wunsch."* Wiesbaden: Limes Verlag, 1982.

Fletcher, Roger. "Recent Developments in West German Historiography: The Bielefeld School and Its Critics." *German Studies Review* 7 / 3 (1984), pp. 451–80.

Förster, Jürgen. "Das andere Gesicht des Krieges: Das 'Unternehmen Barbarossa' als Eroberungs- und Vernichtungskrieg." *"Unternehmen Barbarossa." Zum historischen Ort der deutsch-sowjetischen Beziehungen von 1933 bis Herbst 1941*, ed. Roland G. Foerster, pp. 151–62. Munich: Oldenbourg, 1993.

——. "The German Army and the Ideological War against the Soviet Union." *The Policies of Genocide: Jews and Soviet Prisoners of War in Nazi Germany*, ed. Gerhard Hirschfeld, pp. 15–29. Boston: Allen & Unwin, 1986.

——. "Hitler's Decision in Favour of the War against the Soviet Union." *Germany and the Second World War*, vol. 4: *The Attack on the Soviet Union*, pp. 13–51. Oxford: Clarendon Press, 1998. Originally published as "Hitlers Entscheidung für den Krieg gegen die Sowjetunion." *Das Deutsche Reich und der Zweite Weltkrieg*, vol. 4: *Der Angriff auf die Sowjetunion*, ed. Militärgeschichtliches Forschungsamt, pp. 3–37. Stuttgart: DVA, 1983.

——. "Operation Barbarossa as a War of Conquest and Annihilation." *Germany and the Second World War*, 4:481–521. Originally published as "Das Unternehmen 'Barbarossa' als Eroberungs- und Vernichtungskrieg." *Das Deutsche Reich und der Zweite Weltkrieg*, 4:413–47.

——. "Operation Barbarossa in Historical Perspective." *Germany and the Second World War*, 4:1245–55. Originally published as "Das Unternehmen 'Barbarossa'—eine historische Ortsbestimmung." *Das Deutsche Reich und der Zweite Weltkrieg*, 4:1079–88.

——. "Securing 'Living-Space.'" *Germany and the Second World War*, 4:1189–244.

Fox, John P. "German Bureaucrat or Nazified Ideologue? Ambassador Otto Abetz and Hitler's Anti-Jewish Policies 1940–44." *Powers, Personalities and Policies: Essays in Honour of Donald Cameron Watt*, ed. Michael Graham Fry. London: Frank Cass, 1992.

Frei, Norbert. *Vergangenheitspolitik. Die Anfänge der Bundesrepublik und die NS-Vergangenheit.* Munich: Beck, 1996.

Frei, Norbert, and Sybille Steinbacher, ed. *Beschweigen und Bekennen. Die deutsche Nachkriegsgesellschaft und der Holocaust.* Göttigen: Wallstein Verlag, 2001.

Freund, Florian, Bertrand Perz, and Karl Stuhlpfarrer. "Das Ghetto in Litzmannstadt (Lodz)." *"Unser einziger Weg ist Arbeit." Das Getto in Lodz 1940–1944; eine Ausstellung des Jüdischen Museums Frankfurt am Main.* Vienna: Löcker Verlag, 1990.

Freundlich, Elizabeth. *Die Ermordung einer Stadt names Stanislau: NS-Vernichtungspolitik in Polen 1939–1945.* Vienna: Bundesverlag, 1986.

Friedlander, Henry. "The Deportations of the German Jews: Post-War Trials of Nazi Criminals." *Leo Baeck Institute Yearbook* 29 (1984), pp. 201–26.

——. *The Origins of Nazi Genocide: From Euthanasia to the Final Solution.* Chapel Hill: University of North Carolina Press, 1995.

Friedländer, Saul. "Ideology and Extermination: The Immediate Origins of the Final Solution." *Lessons and Legacies V: The Holocaust and Justice,* ed. Ronald Smelser, pp. 31–48. Evanston: Northwestern University Press, 2002.

——. *The Years of Persecution.* Vol. 1 of *Nazi Germany and the Jews.* New York: HarperCollins, 1997.

Friedman, Philip. "The Destruction of the Jews of Lwow." *Roads to Extinction: Essays on the Holocaust,* pp. 244–321. Philadelphia: Jewish Publication Society, 1980.

——. "The Extermination of the Polish Jews during the German Occupation, 1939–1945." *Roads to Extinction: Essays on the Holocaust,* pp. 211–43. Philadelphia: Jewish Publication Society, 1980.

——. "The Jewish Ghettos of the Nazi Era." *Roads to Extinction: Essays on the Holocaust,* pp. 59–87. Philadelphia: Jewish Publication Society, 1980.

——. "The Lublin Reservation and the Madagascar Plan: Two Aspects of Nazi Jewish Policy during the Second World War." *YIVO Annual of Jewish Social Studies* 8 (1953), pp. 151–77.

Furet, François, ed. *Unanswered Questions: Nazi Germany and the Genocide of the Jews.* New York: Schocken, 1989.

Gellately, Robert. *Backing Hitler: Consent and Coercion in Nazi Germany.* New York: Oxford University Press, 2001.

——. *The Gestapo and German Society: Enforcing Racial Policy, 1933–1945.* New York: Oxford University Press, 1990.

Genschel, Hermann. *Die Verdrängung der Juden aus der Wirtschaft im Dritten Reich.* Göttingen: Musterschmidt, 1966.

Gerlach, Christian. "Deutsche Wirtschaftsinteressen, Besatzungspolitik und der Mord an den Juden in Weissrussland, 1941–1943." *Nationalsozialistische Vernichtungspolitik. Neue Forschungen und Kontroversen,* ed. Ulrich Herbert, pp. 263–91. Frankfurt/M.: Fischer, 1998.

——. "The Eichmann Interrogations in Holocaust Historiography." *Holocaust and Genocide Studies* 15/3 (2001), pp. 428–52.

——. "Einsatzgruppe B." *Die Einsatzgruppen in der besetzten Sowjetunion. Die Tätigkeits- und Lageberichte des Chefs der Sicherheitspolizei und des SD,* ed. Peter Klein, pp. 52–70. Berlin: Edition Hentrich, 1997.

——. "Failure of Plans for an SS Extermination Camp in Mogilev, Belorussia." *Holocaust and Genocide Studies* 7/1 (1997), pp. 60–78.

——. *Kalkulierte Morde. Die deutsche Wirtschafts- und Vernichtungspolitik in Weissrussland 1941 bis 1944.* Hamburg: Hamburger Edition, 1999.

——. *Krieg, Ernährung, Völkermord.* Hamburg: Hamburger Edition, 1998.

——. "Männer des 20. Juli und der Krieg gegen die Sowjetunion." *Vernichtungskrieg. Verbrechen der Wehrmacht 1941–1945,* ed. Hannes Heer and Klaus Naumann, pp. 427–46. Hamburg: Hamburger Edition, 1995.

———. "Verbrechen deutscher Fronttruppen in Weissrussland 1941–1944. Eine Annäherung." *Wehrmacht und Vernichtungspolitik. Militär im nationalsozialistischen System*, ed. Karl Heinrich Pohl, pp. 89–114. Göttingen: Vandenhoeck & Ruprecht, 1999.

———. "Die Wannsee-Konferenz, das Schicksal der deutschen Juden und Hitlers politische Grundsatzentscheidung, alle Juden Europas zu ermordern." *Werkstattgeschichte* 18/6 (1997), pp. 7–44. In English: "The Wannsee Conference, the Fate of the German Jews, and Hitler's Decision in Principle to Exterminate All European Jews." *Journal of Modern History* 70 (1998), pp. 759–812.

Geyer, Michael. "Etudes in Political History: Reichswehr, NSDAP, and the Seizure of Power." *The Nazi Machtergreifung*, ed. Peter Stachura, pp. 101–23. London: Allen & Unwin, 1983.

Giziowski, Richard. *The Enigma of General Blaskowitz*. New York: Hippocrene Books, 1997.

Goda, Norman. "Black Marks: Hitler's Bribery of His Senior Officers." *Journal of Modern History* 72 (June 2000), pp. 413–52.

Golchewski, Frank. "Organe der deutschen Besatzungsmacht: Die ukrainischen Schutzmannschaften." *Die Bürokratie der Okkupation. Strukturen der Herrschaft und Verwaltung im besetzten Europa*, ed. Wolfgang Benz, Johannes Houwink ten Cate, and Gerhard Otto, pp. 173–96. Berlin: Metropol, 1998.

———. "Polen." *Dimension des Völkermords: Die Zahl der jüdischen Opfer des Nationalsozialismus*, ed. Wolfgang Benz, pp. 411–97. Munich: Oldenbourg, 1991.

Goldhagen, Daniel J. *Hitler's Willing Executioners: Ordinary Germans and the Holocaust*. New York: Knopf, 1996.

Gordon, Sarah. *Hitler, Germans, and the "Jewish Question."* Princeton: Princeton University Press, 1984.

Goshen, Seev. "Eichmann und die Nisko-Aktion im Oktober 1939." *Vierteljahrshefte für Zeitgeschichte* 29/1 (1981), pp. 1–30.

Grabitz, Helge, Klaus Bästlein, and Johannes Tuchel, eds. *Die Normalität des Verbrechens: Bilanz und Perspektiven der Forschung zu den nationalsozialistischen Gewaltverbrechen*. Berlin: Edition Hentrich, 1994.

Grabitz, Helge, and Wolfgang Scheffler. *Letzte Spuren: Ghetto Warschau, SS-Arbeitslager Trawniki, Aktion Erntefest: Fotos und Dokumente über Opfer des Endlösungswahns im Spiegel der historischen Ereignisse*. Berlin: Edition Hentrich, 1988.

Grenkevich, Leonid D. *The Soviet Partisan Movement, 1941–1944: A Critical Historiographical Analysis*. London: Frank Cass, 1999.

Gross, Jan Tomasz. *Polish Society under German Occupation, 1939–1944*. Princeton: Princeton University Press, 1979.

Gruner, Wolf. *Die Geschlossene Arbeitseinsatz deutscher Juden: Zur Zwangsarbeit als Element der Verfolgung 1938–1943*. Berlin: Metropol, 1997.

———. "Juden bauen die 'Strassen des Führers.' Zwangsarbeit und Zwangsarbeitslager für nichtdeutsche Juden im Altreich 1940 bis 1943/44." *Zeitschrift für Geschichtswissenschaft* 44/9 (1996), pp. 789–808.

———. "Die NS-Judenverfolgung und die Kommunen: Zur wechselseitigen Dynamisierung von zentraler und lokaler Politik 1933–1941." *Vierteljarhshefte für Zeitgeschichte* 48/1 (2000), pp. 75–126.

——. *Zwangsarbeit und Verfolgung: Österreichische Juden im NS-Staat.* Innsbruck: Studien Verlag, 2000.

Gutman, Yisrael. *The Jews of Warsaw: Ghetto, Underground, Revolt.* Bloomington: Indiana University Press, 1982.

Gutman, Israel [Yisrael], and Gideon Greif, eds. *The Historiography of Genocide of the Jews: Proceedings of the Fifth Yad Vashem International Conference.* Jerusalem: Yad Vashem, 1988.

Haas, Gerhart. "Deutsche Okkupationsziele und die Kollaboration in den besetzten Gebieten der Russischen Föderativen Sowjetrepublik 1941–44." *Okkupation und Kollaboration (1938–1945): Beiträge zu Konzepten und Praxis der Kollaboration in der deutschen Okkupationspolitik,* ed. Werner Röhr, suppl. vol. 1, pp. 273–91. Berlin: Hüthig, 1994.

Hamburger jüdische Opfer des Nationalsozialismus: Gedenkbuch. Ed. Staatsarchiv der Freien und Hansestadt Hamburg. Hamburg: Verlagsdruckerei Schmidt, 1995.

Hartog, L. J. *Der Befehl zum Judenmord: Hitler, Amerika, und die Juden.* Bodenheim: Syndikat Buchgesellschaft, 1997.

Hayes, Peter, and Irmtrud Wojack, eds. *"Arisierung" im Nationalsozialismus: Volksgemeinschaft, Raub und Gedächtnis.* Frankfurt: Campus Verlag, 2000.

Headland, Roland. "The Einsatzgruppen: The Question of Their Initial Operations." *Holocaust and Genocide Studies* 4/4 (1989), pp. 401–12.

——. *Messengers of Murder: A Study of the Reports of the Einsatzgruppen of the Security Police and the Security Service, 1941–1943.* Rutherford NJ: Farleigh Dickenson University Press, 1992.

Heer, Hannes, and Klaus Naumann, ed. *Vernichtungskrieg. Verbrechen der Wehrmacht 1941–1945.* Hamburg: Hamburger Edition, 1995.

Hehn, Paul. *The German Struggle against Yugoslav Guerrillas in World War II: German Counter-Insurgency in Yugoslavia, 1941–1943.* New York: Columbia University Press, 1979.

Heinemann, Isabel. *"Rasse, Siedlung, deutsches Blut": Das Rasse- & Siedlungshauptamt der SS und die rassenpolitische Neuordnung Europas.* Göttingen: Wallstein Verlag, 2003.

Herbert, Ulrich. "Arbeit und Vernichtung: Ökonomischer Interesse und Primat der 'Weltanschauung' in Nationalsozialismus." *Ist der Nationalsozialismus Geschichte? Zu Historisierung und Historikerstreit,* ed. Dan Diner, pp. 198–236. Frankfurt: Fischer, 1987.

——. *Best: Biographischen Studien über Radikalismus, Weltanschauung und Vernunft 1903–1989.* Bonn: Dietz, 1996.

——. "Die deutsche Militärverwaltung und die Deportation der französischen Juden." *Von der Aufgabe der Freiheit,* ed. Christian Jansen, Lutz Niethmammer, und Bernd Weisbrod. Berlin, 1996.

——. *Fremdarbeiter: Politik und Praxis des "Auslander-Einsatzes" in der Kriegswirtschaft des Dritten Reiches.* Bonn: Dietz Verlag, 1985.

———, ed. *Nationalsozialistische Vernichtungspolitik. Neue Forschungen und Kontroversen.* Frankfurt/M.: Fischer, 1998.

Herf, Jeffrey. *Reactionary Modernism: Technology, Culture and Politics in Weimar and the Third Reich.* New York: Cambridge University Press, 1984.

Hevesi, Eugene. "Hitler's Plan for Madagascar." *Contemporary Jewish Record* 5 (1941), pp. 381–95.

Hilberg, Raul. "Auschwitz and the 'Final Solution.'" *Anatomy of the Auschwitz Death Camp*, ed. Yisrael Gutman and Michael Berenbaum, pp. 81–92. Bloomington: Indiana University Press, 1998.

———. *The Destruction of the European Jews.* Chicago: Quadrangle, 1961. Rev. ed., New York: Holmes & Meier, 1985.

———. "The Ghetto as a Form of Government." *APPSS Annals* 450 (1980), pp. 98–112.

———. *Perpetrators, Victims, Bystanders: The Jewish Catastrophe, 1933–1945.* New York: HarperCollins, 1992.

———. *Sonderzüge nach Auschwitz.* Mainz: Dumjahn, 1981.

Hildebrand, Klaus. *Vom Reich zum Weltreich: Hitler, NSDAP, und koloniale Frage 1919–1945.* Munich: W. Fink, 1969.

Hildesheimer, Esriel. *Jüdische Selbstverwaltung unter dem NS-Regime. Der Existenzkampf der Reichsvertretung und Reichsvereinigung der Juden in Deutschland.* Tübingen: J. C. B. Mohr, 1994.

Hillgruber, Andreas. "Die 'Endlösung' und das deutsche Ostimperium als Kernstück des rassenideologischen Programms des Nationalsozialismus." *Vierteljahrshefte für Zeitgeschichte* 20/2 (1972), pp. 133–53.

———. "Die ideologisch-dogmatische Grundlage der nationalsozialistischen Politik der Ausrottung der Juden in den besetzten Gebieten der Sowjetunion und ihre Durchführung 1941–1944." *German Studies Review* 2/2 (1979), pp. 263–96.

———. "Das Russland-Bild der führenden deutschen Militärs vor Beginn des Angriffs auf die Sowjetunion." *Das Russlandbild im Dritten Reich*, ed. Hans-Erich Volkmann, pp. 125–40. Cologne: Böhlau, 1994.

Hirschfeld, Gerhard. *Nazi Rule and Dutch Collaboration: The Netherlands under German Occupation.* New York: Berg, 1988.

———, ed. *The Policies of Genocide: Jews and Soviet Prisoners of War in Nazi Germany.* Boston: Allen & Unwin, 1986.

Höhne, Heinz. *Order of the Death's Head: The Story of Hitler's SS.* New York: Ballantine, 1971.

Hoppe, Hans-Joachim. "Bulgarien." *Dimension des Völkermords. Die Zahl der jüdischen Opfer des Nationalsozialismus*, ed. Wolfgang Benz, pp. 275–310. Munich: Oldenbourg, 1991.

Houwink ten Cate, Johannes. "Heydrich's Security Police and the Amsterdam Jewish Council." *Dutch Jewish History* 3 (1993), pp. 384–86.

Humburg, Martin. *Das Gesicht des Krieges. Feldpostbriefe von Wehrmachtssoldaten aus der Sowjetunion 1941–1944.* Opladen: Westdeutscher, 1998.

Hüppauf, Bernd. "Der entleerte Blick hinter der Kamera." *Vernichtungskrieg. Verbrechen der Wehrmacht 1941–1945*, ed. Hannes Heer and Klaus Naumann, pp. 504–27. Hamburg: Hamburger Edition, 1995.

Ionid, Radu. *The Holocaust in Romania: The Destruction of the Jews and Gypsies under the Antonescu Regime, 1940–1944*. Chicago: Ivan R. Dee, 2000.

Jäckel, Eberhard. *Frankreich in Hitlers Europa. Die deutsche Frankreichpolitik im Zweiten Weltkrieg*. Stuttgart: DVA, 1966.

——. *Hitlers Herrschaft*. Stuttgart: DVA, 1986.

——. *Hilter's Weltanschauung: A Blueprint for Power*. Middletown CT: Wesleyan University Press, 1972.

——. "On the Purpose of the Wannsee Conference." *Perspectives on the Holocaust: Essays in Honor of Raul Hilberg*, pp. 39–49. Boulder CO: Westview Press, 1995.

Jäckel, Eberhard, and Jürgen Rohwer, eds. *Der Mord an den Juden im Zeiten Weltkrieg: Entschlussbildung und Verwirklichung*. Stuttgart: DVA, 1985.

Jacobsen, Hans Adolph. "Kommissarbefehl und Massenexekutionen sowjetischer Kriegsgefangener." *Anatomie des SS-Staates*, 2:161–278. Freiburg: Walter Verlag, 1965.

Jahn, Peter. " 'Russenfurcht' und Antibolschewismus: Zur Entstehung und Wechselwirkung von Feindbildern." *Erobern und Vernichten. Die Krieg gegen die Sowjetunion*, ed. Peter Jahn and Reinhard Rürup, pp. 47–56. Berlin: Argon, 1991.

Jansen, Christian, and Arno Weckbecker. *Der "Volksdeutsche Selbstschutz" in Polen 1939/40*. Munich: Oldenbourg, 1992.

Jansen, Hans. *Madagaskar-Plan. Die beabsichtigte Deportation der europäischen Juden nach Madagaskar*. Munich: Herbig, 1997.

Jastrzebski, Wlodzimierz. *Der Blomberger Blutsonntag: Legende und Wirklichkeit*. Poznan: Westinstitut, 1990.

——. "Nazi Deportations of Polish and Jewish Population from Territories Incorporated into the Third Reich." Paper presented at the Warsaw Conference on Nazi Genocide in Poland and in Europe, April 14–17, 1983.

Jelinek, Yeshayahu. "Slovakia's Internal Policy and the Third Reich." *Central European History* 4/3 (1971), pp. 242–70.

——. "Storm-Troopers in Slovakia: The Rodobranna and the Hlinka Guard." *Journal of Contemporary History* 6/3 (1971), pp. 97–120.

Jersak, Tobias. "Die Interaktion von Kriegsverlauf und Judenvernichtung: Ein Blick auf Hitlers Strategie im Spätsommer 1941." *Historische Zeitschrift* 268/2 (April 1999), pp. 311–49.

Johnson, Eric. *Nazi Terror: The Gestapo, Jews, and Ordinary Germans*. New York: Basic Books, 1999.

Jonca, Karol. "Deportations of German Jews from Breslau 1941–1944 as Described in Eyewitness Testimony." *Yad Vashem Studies* 25 (1996), pp. 275–306.

Jovanovic, M. "Wir packen, wir auspacken. Tragnica Sudbina Jevreja-Isbeglica U Sapcu 1941." *Zbornik* 4 (1979), pp. 245–79.

Die jüdische Opfer des Nationalsozialismus aus Köln: Gedenkbuch. Ed. NS-Dokumentationszentrum der Stadt Köln. Cologne: Böhlau Verlag, 1995.

Kaienburg, Hermann. "Jüdische Arbeitslager an der 'Strasse der SS.'" *1999: Zeitschrift für Sozialgeschichte des 20. und 21. Jahrhunderts* 1 (1996), pp. 13–39.

Kaiser, Wolf, ed. *Täter im Vernichtungskrieg. Der Überfall auf die Sowjetunion und der Völkermord an den Juden*. Berlin: Propyläen, 2002.

Kaplan, Marion. *Between Dignity and Despair: Jewish Life in Nazi Germany*. New York: Oxford University Press, 1998.

Kater, Michael. "Everyday Anti-Semitism in Prewar Nazi Germany." *Yad Vashem Studies* 16 (1984), pp. 129–59.

Katz, Steven. *The Holocaust in Historical Context*. Vol. 1. New York: Oxford University Press, 1991.

Kempner, Robert M. W. *Eichmann und Komplizen*. Zurich: Europa Verlag, 1961.

——. *ss im Kreuzverhör. Die Elite, die Europa in Scherben schlug*. 2nd ed. Nördlingen: Delhi Politik, F. Greno, 1987.

Kershaw, Ian. "German Popular Opinion and the 'Jewish Question.' 1939–1943: Some Further Reflections." *Die Juden in Deutschland: Leben unter nationalsozialistischer Herrschaft*, ed. Wolfgang Benz, pp. 365–85. Tübingen: J. C. B. Mohr, 1986.

——. *Hitler 1889–1936: Hubris*. New York: W. W. Norton, 1998.

——. *Hitler 1936–1945: Nemesis*. New York: W. W. Norton, 2000.

——. *The "Hitler Myth": Image and Reality in the Third Reich*. New York: Oxford University Press, 1987.

——. "Improvised Genocide? The Emergence of the 'Final Solution' in the 'Warthegau.'" *Transactions of the Royal Historical Society*, 6th ser., 2 (1992), pp. 51–78.

——. "The Persecution of the Jews and German Public Opinion in the Third Reich." *Leo Baeck Institute Yearbook* 26 (1981), pp. 261–89.

——. *Popular Opinion and Political Dissent in the Third Reich: Bavaria 1933–1945*. New York: Oxford University Press, 1983.

Klee, Ernst. *"Euthanasie" im NS-Staat: Die "Vernichtung lebensunwerten Lebens."* Frankfurt: S. Fischer, 1983.

Klein, Peter. "Die Rolle der Vernichtungslager Kulmhof (Chelmno), Belzec und Auschwitz-Birkenau in den frühen Deportationsvorbereitungen." *Lager, Zwangsarbeit und Deportation. Dimensionen der Massenverbrechen in der Sowjetunion und in Deutschland, 1933 bis 1945*, ed. Dittmar Dahlmann and Gerhard Hirschfeld, pp. 459–81. Essen: Klartext Verlag, 1999.

Klemp, Stefan. "Kölner Polizeibatallione in Osteuropa: Die Polizeibatallione 69, 309, 319 und die Polizeireservekompanie Köln." *Wessen Freund und wessen Helfer? Die Kölner Polizei im Nationalsozialismus*, ed. Harald Buhlan and Werner Jung, pp. 277–98. Cologne: Emons Verlag, 2000.

Klink, Ernst. "The War against the Soviet Union until the Turn of 1941 / 1942." *Germany and the Second World War*, vol. 4: *The Attack on the Soviet Union*, pp. 525–763. Oxford: Clarendon Press, 1998. Originally published as "Die Krieg gegen die Sowjetunion bis zur Jahreswende 1941 / 42." *Das Deutsche Reich und der Zweite Weltkrieg*, vol. 4: *Der Angriff auf die Sowjetunion*. Stuttgart: DVA, 1983.

Klodzinski, Stanislaw. "Die erste Vergasung von Häftlingen und Kriegsgefangenen im Konzentrationslager Auschwitz." *Die Auschwitz-Hefte: Texte der polnischen Zeitschrift "Przeglad Lekarski" über historische, psychische und medizinische Aspekte des Lebens und*

Sterbens in Auschwitz, ed. Hamburger Institut für Sozialforschung, 1:261–75. Weinheim: Beltz Verlag, 1987.

Koehl, Robert. *Black Corps: The Structure and Power Struggles of the Nazi SS*. Madison: University of Wisconsin Press, 1983.

——. *RKFDV: German Resettlement and Population Policy, 1939–45*. Cambridge MA: Harvard University Press, 1957.

Köhler, Thomas. "Anstiftung zu Versklavung und Völkermord. 'Weltanschauliche Schulung' durch Literatur. Lesestoff für Polizeibeamte während des 'Dritten Reiches.'" *Im Auftrag. Polizei, Verwaltung und Verwantwortung*, ed. Alfons Kenkmann and Christoph Spicher, pp. 130–56. Essen: Klartext, 2001.

Krausnick, Helmut. "Hitler und die Befehle an die Einsatzgruppen im Sommer 1941." *Der Mord an den Juden im Zweiten Weltkrieg. Entschlussbildung und Verwirklichung*, ed. Eberhard Jäckel and Jürgen Rohwer, pp. 88–106. Stuttgart: DVA, 1985.

——. "Kommissarbefehl und 'Gerichtsbarkeiterlass Barbarossa' in neuer Sicht." *Vierteljahrshefte für Zeitgeschichte* 25 / 4 (1977), pp. 682–738.

——. "The Persecution of the Jews." *Anatomy of the SS State*. New York: Walker, 1968.

Krausnick, Helmut, and Alfred Streim. Exchange in *Simon Wiesenthal Center Annual* 6 (1989), pp. 311–47.

Krausnick, Helmut, and Hans-Heinrich Wilhelm. *Die Truppe des Weltanschauungskrieges: Die Einsatzgruppen des Sicherheitspolizei und des SD, 1938–1942*. Stuttgart: DVA, 1981.

Kühl, Stefan. *The Nazi Connection: Eugenics, American Racism, and German National Socialism*. New York: Oxford University Press, 1994.

Kulka, Otto Dov. " 'Public Opinion' in Nazi Germany and the 'Jewish Question.'" *Jerusalem Quarterly* 25 (Fall 1982), pp. 121–44; 26 (Winter 1982), pp. 34–45.

Kulka, Otto Dov, and Aron Rodrigue. "The German Population and the Jews in the Third Reich: Recent Publications and Trends in Research on German Society and the 'Jewish Question.'" *Yad Vashem Studies* 16 (1984), pp. 421–35.

Kwiet, Konrad. "Erziehung zum Mord—Zwei Beispiele zur Kontinuität der deutschen 'Endlösung der Judenfrage.'" *Geschichte und Emanzipation*, ed. Michael Grüttner, Rüdiger Hachtmann, and Heinz-Gerhard Haupt, pp. 435–57. Frankfurt: Campus Verlag, 1999.

——. "Forced Labour of German Jews in Nazi Germany." *Leo Baeck Institute Yearbook* 36 (1991), pp. 389–410.

——. "From the Diary of a Killing Unit." *Why Germany?*, ed. John Milfull, pp. 75–90. Oxford: Berg, 1992.

——. "Nach dem Pogrom: Stufen der Ausgrenzung." *Die Juden in Deutschland 1933–1945: Leben unter nationalsozialistischer Herrschaft*, ed. Wolfgang Benz, pp. 545–659. Munich: Beck, 1988.

——. "Rehearsing for Murder: The Beginning of the Final Solution in Lithuania in June 1941." *Holocaust and Genocide Studies* 12 / 1 (1998), pp. 3–26.

——. *Reichskommissariat Niederlande: Versuch und Scheitern nationalsozialistischer Neuordnung*. Stuttgart: DVA, 1968.

Langmuir, Gavin. "From Anti-Judaism to Antisemitism." *History, Religion, and Antisemitism*, pp. 275–305. Berkeley: University of California Press, 1990.

——. "Prolegomena to Any Present Analysis of Hostility against the Jews." *The Nazi Holocaust*, ed. Michael Marrus, 2:133–71. Westport CT: Meckler, 1989.

Laqueur, Walter. *The Terrible Secret: Suppression of the Truth about Hitler's "Final Solution."* New York: Penguin Books, 1980.

Latzel, Klaus. *Deutsche Soldaten—nationalsozialistischer Krieg? Kriegserlebnis, Kriegserfahrung 1939–1945.* Paderborn: Schönigh, 1998.

Lederer, Zdenek. *Getto Theresienstadt.* London: E. Goldston, 1953.

Levy, Richard S. *The Downfall of the Anti-Semitic Political Parties in Imperial Germany.* New Haven: Yale University Press, 1975.

Lewy, Guenter. *The Nazi Persecution of the Gypsies.* New York: Oxford University Press, 2000.

Lichtenstein, Heiner. *Himmlers grüne Helfer. Die Schutz- und Ordnungspolizei im "Dritten Reich."* Cologne: Bund Verlag, 1990.

——. "Ein Lügenwirr—der Wuppertaler Prozess gegen Angehörige des Polizeibattalions 309." *Wessen Freund und wessen Helfer? Die Kölner Polizei im Nationalsozialismus*, ed. Harald Buhlan and Werner Jung, pp. 619–32. Cologne: Emons Verlag, 2000.

Lindquist, Sven. *"Exterminate All the Brutes."* New York: New Press, 1996.

Liulevicius, Vejas G. *War Land on the Eastern Front: Culture, National Identity, and Occupation in World War I.* Cambridge: Cambridge University Press, 2000.

Longerich, Peter. *Politik der Vernichtung: Eine Gesamtdarstellung der nationalsozialistischen Judenverfolgung.* Munich: Piper, 1998.

——. *The Unwritten Order: Hitler's Role in the Final Solution.* Charleston SC: Tempus, 2001.

——. "Vom Massenmord zur 'Endlösung.' Die Erschiessungen von jüdischen Zivilisten in den ersten Monaten des Ostfeldzuges im Kontext des nationalsozialistischen Judenmords." *Zwei Wege nach Moskau: Vom Hitler-Stalin-Pakt zum "Unternehmen Barbarossa,"* ed. Bernd Wegner, pp. 251–74. Munich: Piper, 1991.

Lower, Wendy. "Nazi Colonial Dreams: German Policies and Ukrainian Society in Zhytomir." Ph.D. dissertation, American University, 1999.

Lozowick, Yaacov. *Hitler's Bureaucrats: The Nazi Security Police and the Banality of Evil.* New York: Continuum, 2002.

——. "*Rollbahn Mord*: The Early Activities of Einsatzgruppe C." *Holocaust and Genocide Studies* 2/2 (1987), pp. 221–42.

Lumans, Valdis O. *Himmler's Auxiliaries: The Volksdeutsche Mittelstelle and the German Nationalities of Europe, 1933–1945.* Chapel Hill: University of North Carolina Press, 1993.

MacQueen, Michael. "The Context of Mass Destruction: Agents and Prerequisites of the Holocaust in Lithuania." *Holocaust and Genocide Studies* 12/1 (1998), pp. 27–48.

——. "Nazi Policy toward the Jews in the Reichskommissariat Ostland, June–December 1941: From White Terror to Holocaust in Lithuania." *Bitter Legacy: Confronting the Holocaust in the USSR*, ed. Zvi Gitelman, pp. 91–103. Bloomington: Indiana University Press, 1997.

Madajczyk, Czeslaw. "Generalplan Ost." *Polish Western Affairs* 3/2 (1962), pp. 391–442.

———. *Die Okkupationspolitik Deutschlands in Polen 1939–1945*. Berlin: Akademie Verlag, 1987.

———. *Polityka III-Rzeszy w okupowanej Polsce*. Warsaw: Panstwowe Wydawn Naukowe, 1970.

———. "Was Generalplan Ost Synchronous with the Final Solution?" *The Shoah and the War*, ed. Asher Cohen, Yehoyakim Cochavi, and Yoah Gelber, pp. 145–60. New York: Peter Lang, 1992.

Maier, Dieter. *Arbeitseinsatz und Deportation: Die Mitwirkung der Arbeitsverwaltung bei der nationalsozialistischen Judenverfolgung in den Jahren 1938–1945*. Berlin: Edition Hentrich, 1994.

Mallmann, Klaus-Michael. "Der Einstieg in den Genozid. Das Lübecker Polizeibatallion 307 und das Massaker in Brest-Litovsk Anfang Juli 1941." *Archiv für Polizeigeschichte* 1999, pp. 82–88.

———. "Menschenjagd und Massenmord: Das neue Instrument der Einsatzgruppen und -kommandos 1938–1945." *Die Gestapo im Zweiten Weltkrieg: "Heimatfront" und besetztes Europa*, ed. Gerhard Paul and Klaus-Michael Mallmann, pp. 291–316. Düsseldorf: Primus, 2000.

———. "Der qualitative Sprung im Vernichtungsprozess. Das Massaker von Kamenez-Podolsk Ende August 1941." *Jahrbuch für Antisemitismusforschung* 10 (2001), pp. 239–64.

———. "Die Türöffner der 'Endlösung.' Zur Genesis des Genozids." *Die Gestapo im Zweiten Weltkrieg: "Heimatfront" und besetztes Europa*, ed. Gerhard Paul and Klaus-Michael Mallmann, pp. 437–63. Darmstadt: Primus, 2000.

———. "Vom Fussvolk der 'Endlösung.' Ordnungspolizei, Ostkrieg und Judenmord." *Tel Aviver Jahrbuch für deutsche Geschichte* 16 (1997), pp. 355–91.

Mallmann, Klaus-Michael, Volker Riess, and Wolfram Pyta, eds. *Deutscher Osten 1939–1945. Der Weltanschauungskrieg in Photos und Texten*. Darmstadt: Wissenschaftliche Buchgesellschaft, 2003.

Manoschek, Walter. *"Serbien ist Judenfrei." Militärbesatzungspolitik und Judenvernichtung in Serbien 1941 / 42*. Munich: Oldenbourg, 1993.

Marrus, Michael, and Robert O. Paxton. "The Nazis and Jews in Occupied Western Europe, 1940–1944." *Unanswered Questions: Nazi Germany and the Genocide of the Jews*, ed. François Furet. New York: Schocken, 1989.

———. *Vichy France and the Jews*. New York: Schocken, 1981.

Matthäus, Jürgen. "Antisemitism as an Offer—Ideological Indoctrination of the ss and Police Corps during the Holocaust." Paper presented at the Lessons and Legacies Conference, Minneapolis, November 2002.

———. "An vorderster Front. Voraussetzungen für die Beteiligung der Ordnungspolizei an der Shoah." *Die Täter der Shoah. Fanatische Nationalsozialisten oder ganz normale Deutsche?*, ed. Gerhard Paul, pp. 137–66. Göttingen: Wallstein Verlag, 2002.

———. "Ausbildungsziel Judenmord? Zum Stellenwert der 'weltanschaulichen Erziehung' von ss und Polizei im Rahmen der 'Endlösung.'" *Zeitschrift für Geschichtswissenschaft* 8 (1999), pp. 673–99.

———. "German Judenpolitik in Lithuania during the First World War." *Leo Baeck Institute Yearbook* 43 (1998), pp. 155–74.

———. "Jenseits der Grenze: Die ersten Massenerschiessungen von Juden in Litauen (Juni–August 1941)." *Zeitschrift für Geschichtswissenschaft* 2 (1996), pp. 101–17.

———. " 'Reibungslos und planmässig.' Die zweite Welle der Judenvernichtung im Generalkommissariat Weissruthenien (1942–1944)." *Jahrbuch für Antisemitismusforschung* 4 (1995), pp. 254–74.

———. " 'Warum wird über das Judentum geschult?' Die ideologische Vorbereitung der deutschen Polizei auf den Holocaust." *Die Gestapo im Zweiten Weltkrieg: "Heimatfront" und besetztes Europa*, ed. Gerhard Paul and Klaus-Michael Mallmann, pp. 100–124. Darmstadt: Primus, 2000.

———. "What About the 'Ordinary Men'? The German Order Police and the Holocaust in the Occupied Soviet Union." *Holocaust and Genocide Studies* 10 (1996), pp. 138–50.

Matthäus, Jürgen, and Konrad Kwiet, Jürgen Förster, and Richard Breitman. *Ausbildungsziel Judenmord? "Weltanschauliche Erziehung" von SS, Polizei, und Waffen-SS im Rahmen der "Endlösung."* Frankfurt/M.: Fischer Taschenbuch Verlag, 2003.

Mayer, Arno. *Why Did the Heavens Not Darken? The "Final Solution" in History*. New York: Pantheon Books, 1989.

Meershoek, Guus. "The Amsterdam Police and the Persecution of the Jews." *The Known, the Unknown, the Disputed, and the Reexamined*, ed. Michael Berenbaum and Abraham J. Peck, pp. 284–300. Bloomington: Indiana University Press, 1998.

Merz, Kai-Uwe. *Das Schreckensbild. Deutschland und der Bolschewismus 1917 bis 1921*. Berlin: Propyläen, 1995.

Messerschmidt, Manfred. *Die Wehrmacht im NS-Staat. Zeit der Indoktrination*. Hamburg: R. v. Deckers Verlag, G. Schenk, 1969.

Michmann, Joseph. "Planning for the Final Solution against the Background of Developments in Holland in 1941." *Yad Vashem Studies* 17 (1986), pp. 145–80.

Milton, Sybil. "The Camera as a Weapon: Documentary Photography and the Holocaust." *Simon Wiesenthal Center Annual* 1 (1984), pp. 45–68.

Möllenhoff, Gisela, and Rita Schlautmann-Overmeyer. *Jüdische Familien in Münster 1918–1945*. Münster: Verlag Westfälisches Dampfboot, 2001.

Mommsen, Hans. "Aufgabenkreis und Verantwortlichkeit des Staatssekretärs der Reichskanzlei Dr. Wilhelm Kritzinger." *Gutachten des Instituts für Zeitgeschichte*, 2:369–98. Stuttgart: DVA, 1966.

———, ed. *Herrschaftsalltag im Dritten Reich*. Düsseldorf: Droste, 1988.

———. "Hitler's Reichstag Speech of 30 January 1939." *History and Memory* 9 (1997), pp. 147–61.

———. "Hitlers Stellung im nationalsozialistischen Herrschaftssystem." *Der "Führerstaat": Mythos und Realität*, ed. Gerhard Hirschfeld and Lothar Kettenacker, pp. 43–72. Stuttgart: DVA, 1981.

———. "Die Realisierung des Utopischen: Die 'Endlösung der Judenfrage' im 'Dritten Reich.' " *Geschichte und Gesellschaft* 9 (Autumn 1993), pp. 381–420.

———. "The Realization of the Unthinkable: The 'Final Solution of the Jewish Question' in the Third Reich." *The Politics of Genocide: Jews and Soviet Prisoners of War in Nazi Gemany*, ed. Gerhard Hirschfeld, pp. 73–92. London: Allen & Unwin, 1986.

——. "Umvolkungspläne des Nationalsozialismus und der Holocaust." *Die Normalität des Verbrechens: Bilanz und Perspektiven der Forschung zu den nationalsozialistischen Gewaltverbrechen*, pp. 68–84. Ed. Helge Grabitz, Klaus Bästlein, and Johannes Tuchel. Berlin: Edition Hentrich, 1994.

Montague, Patrick O. "The Chelmno Death Camp." Unpublished manuscript.

Moore, Bob. *Victims and Survivors: The Nazi Persecution of the Jews in the Netherlands, 1940–1945*. London: Arnold, 1997.

Morrel, J. E. "Arnold Leese—Fascist and Antisemite." *Wiener Library Bulletin*, new ser., no. 17 (1969), pp. 32–36.

Moser, Jonny. "Nisko: The First Experiment in Deportation." *Simon Wiesenthal Center Annual* 2 (1985), pp. 1–30.

Mosse, George. *The Crisis of German Ideology*. New York: Grosset and Dunlap, 1964.

——. *Toward the Final Solution: A History of European Racism*. New York: HarperCollins, 1978.

Mosse, George, and Bela Vago, eds. *Jews and Non-Jews of Eastern Europe*. New York: Wiley, 1974.

Müller, Klaus-Jürgen. *Das Heer und Hitler. Armee und nationalsozialistisches Regime 1933–40*. Stuttgart: DVA, 1969.

Müller, Rolf-Dieter. "The Failure of the Economic 'Blitzkrieg Strategy.'" *Germany and the Second World War*, vol. 4: *The Attack on the Soviet Union*, pp. 1070–1188. Oxford: Clarendon Press, 1998. Originally published as "Das Scheitern der wirtschaftlichen 'Blitzkriegstrategie.'" *Das Deutsche Reich und der Zweite Weltkrieg*, vol. 4: *Der Angriff auf die Sowjetunion*, ed. Militärgeschichtliches Forschungsamt, pp. 936–1029. Stuttgart: DVA, 1983.

——. "From Economic Alliance to a War of Colonial Exploitation." *Germany and the Second World War*, 4:118–224. Originally published as "Von Wirschaftsallianz zum kolonialen Ausbeutungskrieg." *Das Deutsche Reich und der Zweite Weltkrieg*, 4:98–189.

——. *Hitlers Ostkrieg und die deutsche Siedlungspolitik*. Frankfurt/M.: S. Fischer, 1991.

——. "The Mobilization of the German Economy for Hitler's War Aims." *Germany and the Second World War*, vol. 5/1: *Organization and Mobilization of the German Sphere of Power*, pp. 405–786. Oxford: Clarendon Press, 2000. Originally published as "Die Mobilisierung der deutschen Wirtschaft für Hitlers Kriegführung." *Das Deutsche Reich und der Zweite Weltkrieg*, vol. 5/1: *Organisation und Mobilisierung des deutschen Machtbereiches*, pp. 349–689. Stuttgart: DVA, 1988.

Mulligan, Timothy P. *The Politics of Illusion and Empire: German Occupation Policy in the Soviet Union, 1942–43*. New York: Praeger, 1988.

Münz, Max. "Die Verantwortlichkeit für die Judenverfolgungen im Ausland während der national-sozialistischen Herrschaft." Ph.D. dissertation, Frankfurt/M., 1958.

Musial, Bogdan. *Deutsche Zivilverwaltung und Judenverfolgung im Generalgouvernement: Eine Fallstudie zum Distrikt Lublin 1939–1944*. Wiesbaden: Harrassowitz, 1999.

——. *"Konterrevolutionäre Elemente sind zu erschiessen." Die Brutalisierung des deutsch-sowjetischen Krieges im Sommer 1941*. Munich: Propyläen, 2000.

Nachtwei, Winfried. " 'Ganz normale Männer.' Die Verwicklung von Polizeibatallionen aus dem Rheinland und Westfalen in den nationalsozialistischen Vernichtungskrieg." *Villa ten Hompel: Sitz der Ordnungspolizei im Dritten Reich*, ed. Alfons Kenkmann, pp. 54–77. Münster: Agenda Velag, 1996.

Newman, Leonard, and Ralph Erber, eds. *Understanding Genocide: The Social Psychology of the Holocaust.* New York: Oxford University Press, 2002.

Nissan, Oren. "The Bulgarian Exception: A Reassessment of the Salvation of the Jewish Community." *Yad Vashem Studies* 3 (1966), pp. 83–106.

Noakes, Jeremy. "No Ordinary People." *Times Literary Supplement*, June 7, 1996, p. 10.

Nova, Fritz. *Alfred Rosenberg: Nazi Theorist of the Holocaust.* New York: Hippocrene Books, 1986.

Ogorreck, Ralf. "Die Einsatzgruppen der Sicherheitspolizei und des Sicherheitsdienstes im Rahmen der 'Genesis der Endlösung': Ein Betrag zur Entschlussbildung der 'Endlösung der Judenfrage' im Jahre 1941." Ph.D. dissertation, Berlin, 1992.

———. *Die Einsatzgruppen und die "Genesis der Endlösung."* Berlin: Metropol, 1996.

Orth, Karin. "Rudolf Höss und die 'Endlösung der Judenfrage.' Drei Argumente gegen deren Datierung auf den Sommer 1941." *Werkstattgeschichte* 18 (1997), pp. 45–57.

Otto, Reinhard. *Wehrmacht, Gestapo und sowjetische Kriegsgefangene im deutschen Reichsgebiet.* Munich: Oldenbourg, 1998.

Pätzold, Kurt. "Von Vertreibung zum Genozid. Zur den Ursachen, Treibkräften, und Bedingungen der antijüdischen Politik des faschistischen deutschen Imperialismus." *Faschismusforschung: Positionen, Probleme, Polemik* ed. Dietrich Eichholtz and Kurt Grossweiler. Cologne: Pahl-Rugenstein Verlag, 1980.

———. "Die Wannsee-Konferenz—zu ihrem Platz in der Geschichte der Judenvernichtung." *Faschismus und Rassismus: Kontroversen um Ideologie und Opfer*, ed. Werner Röhr, pp. 257–90. Berlin: Akademie Verlag, 1992.

Pätzold, Kurt, and Erika Schwarz. *"Auschwitz war für mich nur ein Bahnhof." Franz Novak—der Transportoffizier Adolf Eichmanns.* Berlin: Metropol, 1994.

———. *Tagesordnung: Judenmord. Die Wannsee-Konferenz am 20. Januar 1942: Eine Dokumentation zur Organisation der "Endlösung."* Berlin: Metropol, 1992.

Paul, Gerhard. " 'Betr.: Evakuierung von Juden.' Die Gestapo als regionale Zentralinstitution der Judenverfolgung." *Menora und Hakenkreuz. Zur Geschichte der Juden in und aus Schleswig-Holstein, Lübeck, und Altona (1918–1998)*, ed. Gerhard Paul and Miriam Gillis-Carlebach, pp. 491–520. Neumünster: Wachholtz Verlag, 1998.

———. "Ganz normale Akademiker: Eine Fallstudie zur regionalen staatspolizeilichen Funktionselite." *Die Gestapo: Mythos und Realität*, ed. Gerhard Paul and Klaus-Michael Mallmann, pp. 236–54. Darmstadt: Wissenschaftliche Buchgesellschaft, 1995.

———, ed. *Die Täter der Shoah. Fanatische Nationalsozialisten oder ganz normale Deutsche?* Göttingen: Wallstein Verlag, 2002.

Paul, Gerhard, and Klaus-Michael Mallmann, ed. *Die Gestapo im Zweiten Weltkrieg. "Heimatfront" und besetztes Europa.* Darmstadt: Primus, 2000

Paxton, Robert. *Vichy France: Old Guard and New Order.* New York: Knopf, 1972.

Pelt, Robert Jan van. *The Case for Auschwitz: Evidence from the Irving Trial*. Bloomington: Indiana University Press, 2002.

——. "A Site in Search of a Mission." *Anatomy of the Auschwitz Death Camp*, ed. Yisrael Gutman and Michael Berenbaum, pp. 93–156. Bloomington: Indiana University Press, 1994.

Pelt, Robert Jan van, and Deborah Dwork. *Auschwitz: 1290 to the Present*. New York: Norton, 1996.

Pfeiffer, Ernst. *Die Juden im Dortmund*. Dortmund: Harpa, 1986.

Piper, Franciszek. "Gas Chambers and Crematoria." *Anatomy of the Auschwitz Death Camp*, ed. Yisrael Gutman and Michael Berenbaum, pp. 157–82. Bloomington: University of Indiana Press, 1998.

Pohl, Dieter. "Einsatzgruppe C." *Die Einsatzgruppen in der besetzten Sowjetunion. Die Tätigkeits- und Lageberichte des Chefs der Sicherheitspolizei und des SD*, ed. Peter Klein, pp. 71–87. Berlin: Edition Hentrich, 1997.

——. "Die grossen Zwangsarbeitslager der SS- und Polizeiführer für Juden im Generalgouvernement 1942–1945." *Die nationalsozialistischen Konzentrationslager. Entwicklung und Struktur*, ed. Ulrich Herbert, Karin Orth, and Christoph Dieckmann, 1:415–38. Göttingen: Wallstein, 1998.

——. "Hans Krüger and the Murder of the Jews in the Stanislawow Region (Galicia)." *Yad Vashem Studies* 26 (1998), pp. 239–64.

——. *Nationalsozialistische Judenverfolgung in Ostgalizien 1941–1944: Die Organisierung und Durchführung eines staatlichen Massenverbrechens*. Munich: Oldenbourg, 1996.

——. "Schauplatz Ukraine: Der Massenmord an den Juden im Militärverwaltungsgebiet und im Reichskommissariat 1941–1943." *Ausbeutung, Vernichtung, Öffentlichkeit. Studien zur nationalsozialistischen Verfolgungspolitik*, ed. Norbert Frei, Sybille Steinbacher, and Bernd C. Wagner, pp. 135–73. Munich: Saur, 2000.

——. *Von der "Judenpolitik" zum Judenmord: Der Distrikt Lublin des Generalgouvernements 1939–1944*. Frankfurt / M.: Peter Lang, 1993.

Poliakov, Leon. *Harvest of Hatred*. Philadelphia: Jewish Publication Society, 1954.

——. *The History of Anti-Semitism from the Time of Christ to the Court Jews*. New York: Schocken, 1974.

Porat, Dina. "The Holocaust in Lithuania: Some Unique Aspects." *The Final Solution: Origins and Implementation*, ed. David Cesarani, pp. 159–74. London: Routledge, 1994.

Pressac, Jean-Claude. *Auschwitz: Technique and Operation of the Gas Chambers*. New York: Beate Klarsfeld Foundation, 1989.

——. *Les Crématoires d'Auschwitz*. Paris: CRNS Editions, 1993.

Pressac, Jean-Claude, with Robert Jan van Pelt. "The Machinery of Mass Murder at Auschwitz." *Anatomy of the Auschwitz Death Camp*, ed. Yisrael Gutman and Michael Berenbaum, pp. 183–245. Bloomington: Indiana University Press, 1998.

Presser, Jacob. *The Destruction of the Dutch Jews*. New York: Dutton, 1969.

Pulzer, Peter. *The Rise of Political Anti-Semitism in Germany and Austria*. New York: John Wiley, 1964.

Reichelt, Katrin. "Kollaboration und Holocaust in Lettland, 1941–1945." *Täter im Vernichtungskrieg. Der Überfall auf die Sowjetunion und der Völkermord an den Juden*, ed. Wolf Kaiser, pp. 110–24. Berlin: Propyläen, 2002.

Reitlinger, Gerald. *The Final Solution: The Attempt to Exterminate the Jews of Europe, 1939–1945*. New York: Perpetua Edition, 1961.

———. *The House Built on Sand: The Conflicts of German Policy in Russia, 1941–1945*. New York: Viking Press, 1960.

Retallack, James. "Social History with a Vengeance? Some Reactions to H.-U. Wehler's 'Das Kaiserreich.'" *German Studies Review* 7/3 (1984), pp. 423–50.

Rich, Norman. *The Establishment of the New Order*. Vol. 2 of *Hitler's War Aims*. New York: Norton, 1974.

Richmond, Theo. *Konin: A Quest*. New York: Pantheon Books, 1995.

Riess, Volker. *Die Anfänge der Vernichtung "lebensunwerten Lebens" in den Reichsgauen Danzig-Westpreussen und Wartheland 1939/40*. Frankfurt: Peter Lang, 1995.

Röhr, Werner, ed. *Okkupation und Kollaboration (1938–1945): Beiträge zu Konzepten und Praxis der Kollaboration in der deutschen Okkupationspolitik*. Berlin: Hüthig, 1994.

Ronen, Avihu. "The Jews of Zaglembie during the Holocaust." Ph.D. thesis, Tel Aviv University, 1989, in Hebrew with English summary.

Roseman, Mark. *The Villa, the Lake, the Meeting: Wannsee and the Final Solution*. London: Allen Lane, 2002.

Rosenkranz, Herbert. *Verfolgung und Selbstbehauptung: Die Juden in Österreich 1938–1945*. Munich: Herold, 1978.

Rossino, Alexander. "Destructive Impulses: German Soldiers and the Conquest of Poland." *Holocaust and Genocide Studies* 11/3 (1997), pp. 351–65.

———. "Eastern Europe through German Eyes: Soldiers' Photographs 1939–42." *History of Photography* 23 (1999), pp. 313–21.

———. *Hitler Strikes Poland: Blitzkrieg, Ideology, and Atrocity*. Lawrence: University of Kansas Press, 2003.

———. "Nazi Anti-Jewish Policy during the Polish Campaign: The Case of Einsatzgruppe von Woyrsch." *German Studies Review* 24/1 (2001), pp. 35–54.

Rössler, Mechtild, and Sabine Schleiermacher, eds. *Der "Generalplan Ost": Hauptlinien der nationalsozialistischen Planungs- und Vernichtungspolitik*. Berlin: Akademie Verlag, 1993.

Rückerl, Adalbert. *Nationalsozialistische Vernichtungslager im Spiegel deutscher Strafprozesse: Belzec, Sobibor, Treblinka, Chelmno*. Munich: Deutscher Taschenbuch Verlag, 1977.

Safrian, Hans. *Die Eichmann-Männer*. Vienna: Europaverlag, 1993.

Sandkühler, Thomas. *"Endlösung" in Galizien: Der Judenmord in Ostpolen und die Rettungsinitiativen von Berthold Beitz, 1941–1944*. Bonn: Dietz, 1996.

———. "Judenpolitik und Judenmord im Distrikt Galizien, 1941–1942." *Nationalsozialistische Vernichtungspolitik, 1939–1945: Neue Forschungen und Kontroversen*, ed. Ulrich Herbert, pp. 122–47. Frankfurt/M.: Fischer, 1998.

Scheffler, Wolfgang. "Einsatzgruppe A." *Die Einsatzgruppen in der besetzten Sowjetunion.*

Die Tätigkeits- und Lageberichte des Chefs der Sicherheitspolizei und des SD, ed. Peter Klein, pp. 29–51. Berlin: Edition Hentrich, 1997.

——. "Die Wannsee-Konferenz und ihre historische Bedeutung." *Erinnern für die Zukunft: Ansprache und Vorträge zur Eröffnung der Gedankstätte*, pp. 17–34. Berlin: Gedankstätte Haus der Wannseekonferenz, 1992.

——. "Zur Entstehungsgeschichte der 'Endlösung.' " *Aus Politik und Zeitgeschichte*, B/43/82 (November 30, 1982), pp. 3–10.

Schleunes, Karl. *The Twisted Road to Auschwitz*. Urbana: University of Illinois Press, 1970.

Schmidt, Paul. *Hitler's Interpreter*. New York: Macmillan, 1951.

Schmidt, Ulf. "Kriegsausbruch und 'Euthanasie': Neue Forschungsergebnisse zum 'Knauer Kind' im Jahr 1939." *"Euthanasie" und die aktuelle Sterbehilfe-Debatte*, ed. Andreas Frewer and Clemens Eickhoff. Frankfurt: Campus Verlag, 2000.

——. "Reassessing the Beginning of the 'Euthanasia' Program." *German History* 17/4 (1999), pp. 543–50.

Schmidt-Hartmann, Eva. "Tschechoslowakei." *Dimension des Völkermords: Die Zahl der jüdischen Opfer des Nationalsozialismus*, ed. Wolfgang Benz, pp. 353–79. Munich: Oldenbourg, 1991.

Schneider, Gertrude. *Journey into Terror: Story of the Riga Ghetto*. New York: Ark House, 1979.

Schulte, Theo. *The German Army and Nazi Policies in Occupied Russia*. Oxford: Berg, 1989.

Shelach, Menachem. "Sajmiste Extermination Camp in Serbia." *Holocaust and Genocide Studies* 2/2 (1987), pp. 243–60.

Shils, Edward, and Morris Janowitz. "Cohesion and Disintegration in the Wehrmacht in World War II." *Center and Periphery: Essays in Macrosociology*, ed. Edward Shils, pp. 345–83. Chicago: University of Chicago Press, 1975.

Slepyan, Kenneth D. " 'The People's Avengers': Soviet Partisans, Stalinist Society, and the Politics of Resistance, 1941–1944." Ph.D. dissertation, University of Michigan, 1994.

Smith, Woodruff D. *The Ideological Origins of Nazi Imperialism*. New York: Oxford University Press, 1986.

Spector, Shmuel. *The Holocaust of the Volhynian Jews, 1941–1944*. Jerusalem: Yad Vashem, 1990.

Stang, Klaus. *Kollaboration und Massenmord. Die litauische Hilfspolizei, das Rollkommando Hamann und die Ermordung der litauischen Juden*. Frankfurt: Peter Lang, 1996.

Steinbacher, Sybille. *"Musterstadt" Auschwitz: Germanisierungspolitik und Judenmord in Ostoberschlesien*. Munich: Saur, 2000.

Steinberg, Maxime. "The Judenpolitik in Belgium within the West European Context: Comparative Observations." *Belgium and the Holocaust: Jews, Belgians, Germans*, ed. Dan Michman, pp. 199–221. Jerusalem: Yad Vashem, 1998.

Steinert, Marlis. *Hitler's War and the Germans*. Athens: Ohio University Press, 1977.

Stern, Fritz. *The Politics of Cultural Despair*. Berkeley: University of California Press, 1961.

Steur, Claudia. "Eichmanns Emissäre. Die 'Judenberater' in Hitlers Europa." *Die Gestapo im Zweiten Weltkrieg. "Heimatfront" und besetztes Europa*, ed. Gerhard Paul and Klaus-Michael Mallmann, pp. 403–36. Darmstadt: Primus, 2000.

——. *Theodor Dannecker—ein Funktionär der "Endlösung."* Essen: Klartext, 1997.

Stokes, Lawrence D. "The German People and the Destruction of the European Jews." *Central European History* 6/2 (1973), pp. 167–91.

Streim, Alfred. *Die Behandlung sowjetischer Kriegsgefangener im "Fall Barbarossa."* Karlsruhe: C. F. Müller, 1981.

——. "The Tasks of the Einsatzgruppen." *Simon Wiesenthal Center Annual* 4 (1987), pp. 309–28.

——. "Zur Eröffnung des allgemeinen Judenvernichtungsbefehls gegenüber den Einsatzgruppen." *Der Mord an den Juden im Zweiten Weltkrieg: Entschlussbildung und Verwirklichung*, ed. Eberhard Jäckel and Jürgen Rohwer, pp. 107–19. Stuttgart: DVA, 1985.

Streit, Christian. "The German Army and the Policies of Genocide." *The Policies of Genocide: Jews and Soviet Prisoners of War in Nazi Germany*, ed. Gerhard Hirschfeld, pp. 1–14. Boston: Allen & Unwin, 1986.

——. *Keine Kameraden: Die Wehrmacht und die sowjetischen Kriegsgefangenen 1941–1945.* 1st ed., Stuttgart: DVA, 1978. 3rd ed., with rev. introduction. Bonn: Dietz, 1997.

Tal, Uriel. *Christians and Jews in Germany: Religion, Politics, and Ideology in the Second Reich, 1870–1914.* Ithaca NY: Cornell University Press, 1975.

Tec, Nechama. *When Light Pierced the Darkness: Christian Rescue of Jews in Nazi-Occupied Poland.* New York: Oxford University Press, 1986.

Tec, Nechama, and Daniel Weiss. "The Heroine of Minsk: Eight Photographs of an Execution." *History of Photography* 23 (1999), pp. 322–30.

Tessin, Georg. "Die Stäbe und Truppeneinheiten der Ordnungspolizei." *Zur Geschichte der Ordnungspolizei 1939–1945.* Koblenz, 1957.

Tessin, Georg, Norbert Kannapin, and Brün Meyer. *Waffen-SS und Ordnungspolizei im Kriegseinsatz 1939–1945.* Osnabrück: Biblio Verlag, 2000.

Thurner, Erika. *National Socialism and Gypsies in Austria.* Tuscaloosa: University of Alabama Press, 1998.

Todorov, Tzvetan. *The Fragility of Goodness: Why Bulgaria's Jews Survived the Holocaust.* Princeton: Princeton University Press, 1999.

Toury, Jacob. "Die Entstehungsgeschichte des Austreibungsbefehls gegen die Juden der Saarpfalz und Baden 22/23. Oktober 1940—Camp de Gurs." *Jahrbuch des Instituts für Deutsche Geschichte*, Beihefte 10 (1986), pp. 435–64.

Tregenza, Michael. "Belzec—das vergessene Lager des Holocaust." *"Arisierung" im Nationalsozialismus. Volksgemeinschaft, Raub und Gedächtnis*, ed. Peter Hayes and Irmtrud Wojack, pp. 241–67. Frankfurt: Campus Verlag, 2000.

Trunk, Isaiah. *Judenrat: The Jewish Councils in Eastern Europe under Nazi Occupation.* New York: Stein and Day, 1972.

Ueberschär, Gert, and Winfried Vogel. *Dienen und Verdienen. Hitlers Geschenke an seine Eliten.* Frankfurt: S. Fischer, 1999.

Uhlig, Heinrich. "Der verbrecherische Befehl." *Vollmacht des Gewissens. Der militärische Widerstand gegen Hitler im Krieg*, 2:287–410. Frankfurt/M.: Alfred Metzner Verlag, 1965.

Umbreit, Hans. *Deutsche Militärverwaltungen 1938/39: Die militärische Besetzung der Tschechoslowakei und Polen*. Stuttgart: DVA, 1977.

——. *Der Militärbefehlshaber in Frankreich 1940–1944*. Boppard: H. Boldt, 1968.

Vestermanis, Margers. "Ortskommandantur Libau. Zwei Monate deutscher Besatzung im Sommer 1941." *Vernichtungskrieg. Verbrechen der Wehrmacht 1941–1945*, ed. Hannes Heer and Klaus Naumann, pp. 241–59. Hamburg: Hamburger Edition, 1995.

Volkmann, Hans-Erich, ed. *Das Russlandbild im Dritten Reich*. Cologne: Böhlau, 1994.

Volkov, Shulamit. "Antisemitism as a Cultural Code." *Leo Baeck Institute Yearbook* 23 (1978), pp. 25–46.

Wagner, Bernd C. "Gerüchte, Wissen, Verdrängung: Die IG Auschwitz und das Vernichtungslager Birkenau." *Ausbeutung, Vernichtung, Öffentlichkeit: Neue Studien zur nationalsozialistischen Lagerpolitik*, ed. Norbert Frei, Sybille Steinbacher, and Bernd C. Wagner, pp. 231–48. Munich: Saur, 2000.

Waite, Robert. "Kollaboration und deutsche Besatzungspolitik in Lettland 1941 bis 1945." *Okkupation und Kollaboration (1938–1945): Beiträge zu Konzepten und Praxis der Kollaboration in der deutschen Okkupationspolitik*, ed. Werner Röhr, suppl. vol. 1, pp. 217–37. Berlin: Hüthig, 1994.

Walk, Joseph. *Das Sonderrecht für die Juden im NS-Staat*. 2nd ed. Heidelberg: C. F. Müller, 1989.

Waller, James. *Becoming Evil: How Ordinary People Commit Genocide and Mass Killing*. New York: Oxford University Press, 2002.

Warmbrunn, Werner. *The Dutch under German Occupation, 1940–45*. Stanford: Stanford University Press, 1963.

Wegner, Bernd. *Hitlers politische Soldaten. Die Waffen-SS 1933–1945: Leitbild, Struktur und Funktion einer nationalsozialistischen Elite*. Paderborn: Schönigh, 1982.

Wehler, Hans-Ulrich. *The German Empire*. Leamington Spa UK, Dover NH: Berg, 1985.

Weinberg, Gerhard. *Germany, Hitler, and World War II: Essays in Modern German and World History*. New York: Cambridge University Press, 1995.

——. *A World at Arms: A Global History of World War II*. New York: Cambridge University Press, 1994.

——. *World in the Balance: Behind the Scenes of World War II*. Hanover: University Press of New England, 1981.

Weindling, Paul. *Health, Race and German Politics between National Unification and Nazism, 1870–1945*. Cambridge: Cambridge University Press, 1989.

Weiss, Aharon. "Kolomyia." *Encyclopedia of the Holocaust*, ed. Israel Gutman, p. 813. New York: Macmillan, 1990.

——. "Stanislawow." *Encyclopedia of the Holocaust*, ed. Israel Gutman, p. 1408. New York: Macmillan, 1990.

——. "Stry." *Encyclopedia of the Holocaust*, ed. Israel Gutman, p. 1418. New York: Macmillan, 1990.

——. "Ternopol." *Encyclopedia of the Holocaust*, ed. Israel Gutman, p. 1458. New York: Macmillan, 1990.

Weiss, John. *Ideology of Death: Why the Holocaust Happened in Germany*. Chicago: Ivan R. Dee, 1996.

Weissbecker, Manfred. " 'Wenn hier Deutsche wohnten?' Beharrung und Veränderung im Russlandbild Hitlers und der NSDAP." *Das Russlandbild im Dritten Reich*, ed. Hans-Erich Volkmann, pp. 9–54. Cologne: Böhlau, 1994.

Welzer, Harald. "Wer waren die Täter? Anmerkungen zur Täterforschung aus sozialpsychologischer Sicht." *Die Täter der Shoah. Fanatische Nationalsozialisten oder ganz normale Deutsche?*, ed. Gerhard Paul, pp. 237–53. Göttingen: Wallstein Verlag, 2002.

Westermann, Edward B. " 'Friend and Helper': German Uniformed Police Operations in the General Government, 1939–1941." *Journal of Military History* 58 (October 1994), pp. 643–61.

——. "Himmler's Uniformed Police on the Eastern Front: The Reich's Secret Soldiers, 1941–1942." *War in History* 3/3 (1996), pp. 309–29.

——. "Ideology and Organizational Culture: Creating the Police Soldier, 1933–45." Paper presented at the Lessons and Legacies Conference, Minneapolis, November 2002.

——. " 'Ordinary Men' or 'Ideological Soldiers'? Police Battalion 310 in Russia, 1942." *German Studies Review* 21/1 (1998), pp. 43–66.

Wildt, Michael. *Generation des Unbedingten: Das Führungskorps des Reichssicherheitshauptamtes*. Hamburg: Hamburger Edition, 2002.

——. "Der Hamburger Gestapochef Bruno Streckenbach. Eine nationalsozialistische Karriere." *Hamburg in der NS-Zeit. Ergebnisse neuerer Forschungen*, ed. Frank Bajohr, pp. 93–123. Hamburg: Ergebnisse Verlag, 1995.

Wilhelm, Hans-Heinrich. *Die Einsatzgruppe A der Sicherheitspolizei und des SD 1941/42*. Frankfurt/M.: Peter Lang, 1996.

——. "The Holocaust in NS-Rhetoric." *Yad Vashem Studies* 16 (1984), pp. 95–127.

——. "Motivation und 'Kriegsbild' deutscher Generale und Offiziere im Krieg gegen die Sowjetunion." *Erobern und Vernichten. Der Krieg gegen die Sowjetunion*, ed. Peter Jahn and Reinhard Rürup, pp. 153–82. Berlin: Argon, 1991.

Willems, Susanne. *Der entsiedelte Jude. Albert Speers Wohungsmarktpolitik für den Berliner Hauptstadtbau*. Berlin: Hentrich, 2002.

Witte, Peter. "Auf Befehl des 'Führers.' " *Die Welt*, August 27, 1999.

——. "Two Decisions Concerning the 'Final Solution to the Jewish Question': Deportations to Lodz and Mass Murder in Chelmno." *Holocaust and Genocide Studies* 9/3 (1995), pp. 318–45.

Wojack, Imtrud. *Eichmanns Memoiren: Ein kritischer Essay*. Frankfurt/M.: Campus, 2002.

Yahil, Leni. *The Holocaust: The Fate of European Jewry, 1932–1945*. New York: Oxford University Press, 1990.

——. "Madagascar—Phantom of a Solution for the Jewish Question." *Jews and Non-Jews in Eastern Europe*, ed. George Mosse and Bela Vago, pp. 315–34. New York: Wiley, 1974.

——. "Methods of Persecution: A Comparison of the 'Final Solution' in Holland and Denmark." *The Nazi Holocaust*, ed. Michael Marrus, 4:169–90. Westport CT: Meckler, 1989.

Yisraeli, David. *The Palestinian Problem in German Politics, 1889–1945*. Ramat-Gan: Bar-Ilan University, 1974.

Zbikowski, Andrzej. "Local Anti-Jewish Pogroms in the Occupied Territories of Eastern Poland, June–July 1941." *The Holocaust in the Soviet Union: Studies and Sources on the Destruction of the Jews in Nazi-Occupied Territories of the USSR, 1941–45*, ed. Lucjan Dobroszycki and John Gurock, pp. 173–79. New York: M. E. Sharpe, 1993.

Zeller, Ron, and Pim Griffioen. "Judenverfolgung in den Niederlanden und in Belgien während des Zweiten Weltkrieges. Eine vergleichende Analyse." *1999: Zeitschrift für Sozialgeschichte des 20. und 21. Jahrhunderts*, part 1: (1996), pp. 30–54; part 2: (1997), pp. 29–48.

Zentrale Stelle der Landesjustizverwaltungen Ludwigsburg. "Einsatzgruppen in Polen: Einsatzgruppen der Sicherheitspolizei, Selbstschutz und andere Formationen in der Zeit vom 1. September bis Frühjahr 1940." 2 vols. Ludwigsburg, 1962–63.

Zimmerman, Michael. "Die Gestapo und die regionale Organisation der Judendeportationen. Das Beispiel der Stapo-Leitstelle Düsseldorf." *Die Gestapo: Mythos und Realität*, ed. Gerhard Paul and Klaus-Michael Mallmann, pp. 357–72.

——. "The National Socialist 'Solution of the Gypsy Question': Central Decisions, Local Initiative, and Their Interrelation." *Holocaust and Genocide Studies* 15/3 (2001), pp. 412–27.

——. *Rassenutopie und Genozid: Die nationalsozialistische "Lösung der Zigeunerfrage."* Hamburg: Christians, 1996.

Index

215, 245–53, 296–97; and Jewish labor allocation, 149; lack of German manpower in, 278; Lebensraum concept transformed by, 108, 110; local authorities deciding matters of policy, 284, 294, 295, 308, 504n217, 509n278; military preparations for, 215–24; occupied Soviet territory, December 1941, *246*; and onset of the Holocaust, June–December 1941, 244–308, 431–33; Order Police in, 224, 225, 229–34; pogroms during, 268–77; policing the occupied area, 273–75; preparing for, 213–43; second peak of victory euphoria and fate of European Jewry, 314–30, 371, 426; ss in, 216–17, 221, 222, 224–34; toward the Final Solution, August–December 1941, 277–94; from war of destruction to the Final Solution, 309–73; the Wehrmacht in, 215–24, 249–51

Barbarossa-*Erlass* (*Kriegsgerichts-barkeiterlass*), 219, 220, 221, 227

Bartov, Omer, 264

Battalion for the Defense of National Labor (Lithuania), 273

Batz, Rudolph, 121, 226, 227

Bauer, Yehuda, 115–16, 437n1, 444n2

Baumgart, Winfried, 437n8

Beamish, Henry Hamilton, 81, 453n168

Beau, Emil, 348

Beaune-la-Rolande camp, 201

Bechtolsheim, Gustav, Freiherr von, 288, 289, 290, 506n238

Becker, August, 188, 191

Behrens, Captain, 255, 256

Belaja Cerkov, 291, 299

Belev, Aleksandr, 212

Belgium: anti-Jewish measures of, 200, 205; German military administration in, 194; trains deporting Jews from, 382; treatment of Jews in occupied, 205

Belgrade, 340, 341, 373, 374, 422, 423

Belorussia: in activity reports from the east, 400, 401; auxiliary police units in, 274, 310; Brest Litovsk, 259–60, 295, 493n65, 509n281; as "catchment" area for unsocial elements, 240; death toll by end of 1941, 289; and Generalkommissariat Weissruthenien, 506n235; German guidelines on treatment of civilians in, 238; German occupation in World War I, 247; ghettoization in, 400; Himmler visits in mid-August 1941, 283; Jews killed in Brest, 259–60, 493n65; Jews seen as driving force behind resistance in, 333; local collaborators in, 274–75; in "Ostland," 237, 486n108; pattern of killing, September–October 1941, 288–90; Pinsk, 282, 283; pogroms absent in, 273, 274; Vitebsk, 289, 401, 402. *See also* Minsk; Mogilev

Belzec, 419–22; extermination camp constructed at, 360, 361, 362–65, 371–72, 374; labor camp at, 146, 148, 182, 419

Bendorf-Sayn, 192

Bene, Otto, 202

Benzler, Felix, 334, 336, 337, 340, 341, 342, 343, 422

Berdichev, 292, 297, 510n289

Berenstein, Tatiana, 524n160, 524n165, 525n176

Bereska-Kartuska, 281

Berger, Gottlob, 31

Berlin: Gypsies of, 180, 181. *See also* Berlin Jews

Berlin Jews: deportation to the east of, 329, 383–84; execution of deportees to Riga, 305, 396, 405, 538n78; Goebbels on deportation of, 104–5, 177, 320, 327, 328; Hitler blocking evacuation of Jews of, 105; population of, 383

Bernburg, 191, 192

Bessarabia: Bessarabian Jews in Romania, 210, 517n40; ethnic Germans in, 62, 99; Nazi-Soviet Non-Aggression Pact on, 211; violence against Jews in, 276

Besser, Colonel, 311
Best, Werner, 16, 198–200, 201
Bialystok, 255–56, 257, 259, 260, 278, 310
Biebow, Hans: and deportations to Lodz
  ghetto, 330, 331, 392; and economy of
  Lodz ghetto, 120, 153, 154, 155; and
  food supply for Lodz ghetto, 117, 118–
  19, 156, 157–58
Bielfeld (Foreign Office colonial desk), 415
Binding, Karl, 185
Birkenau, 357, 364, 374, 421, 544n167
Bischof, Max, 129–30, 159–60, 162, 164,
  360, 462n86
Bischoff, Karl, 357–58
Blackbourn, David, 436n9
Black Death, 3
Blaskowitz, Johannes, 29, 74–75, 76, 77–
  78, 79
Blobel, Paul, 226, 291, 292
"Bloody Sunday" (Bydgoszcz), 17
"Bloody Sunday" (Riga), 396
"Bloody Sunday" (Stanislawow), 349, 361
Blume, Walter, 226, 227
Bobelis, Colonel, 273
Bobruysk, 289, 403
Bock, Fedor von, 73, 75, 221, 289, 520n94
Bock, Max, 73–74
Böhmcker, Heinrich, 203, 204
Böhme, Franz, 337–39, 340, 343, 344, 345
Böhme, Hans-Joachim, 252, 254–55, 263,
  491n42
Boll, Bernd, 291
Bolsheviks. *See* communists
Boris (king of Bulgaria), 212
Borisov, 289
Bormann, Martin, 101, 174, 186, 265,
  309, 370, 391
Bornhagen (Kozminek), 417
Bouhler, Philipp, 185, 186, 189, 190, 362,
  364, 371
Brack, Viktor: and Chelmno, 416; in
  euthanasia program, 190; in extermi-
  nation camp development, 304, 362,
  364, 366, 367, 368, 371, 372, 393,

531n274; Himmler expressing urgency
  to, 410; in Madagascar Plan, 88; and
  mass sterilization of Jews, 106,
  458n272
Bradfisch, Otto, 226, 227, 504n212
Braemer, Walter, 29, 288, 289, 290, 303,
  306, 333
Brandenberg, 191, 192
Brandt, Karl, 185, 186, 189, 190
Brauchitsch, Walther von: on the army
  and the Einsatzgruppen in Poland, 18,
  20, 21, 439n19; on the army and the
  Einsatzgruppen in Russia, 217, 228;
  asks to give up military administration
  of Poland, 24; calling for merciless
  action against Soviet Jews, 288,
  506n239; crisis of confidence in, 73,
  76, 451n44; *Disziplin-Erlass* of, 221;
  on French Jewish property, 199;
  Groscurth sacked by, 76; and
  Heydrich's Polish measures, 26–27,
  43; Himmler invited to address army
  commanders by, 78–79; Himmler
  offers Jewish labor to, 76, 142, 145,
  466n155; Hitler explains his policy on
  the Poles to, 18–19, 26; Mackensen's
  letter on atrocities to, 78; marriage to
  ardent Nazi, 75; meets with Himmler
  on January 24, 1940, 76; and military
  jurisdiction in Russia, 221–22;
  November 1939 western offensive
  opposed by, 73, 80; as shielding the
  army, 80; as unreceptive to objections
  to atrocities, 72–73, 76, 77
Bräutigam, Otto, 303, 307, 324, 326, 368,
  414
Breitman, Richard, 263, 458n272, 495n97,
  538n81
Brest Litovsk, 259–60, 295, 493n65,
  509n281
Britain. *See* Great Britain
Brodesser, Jean, 386
Bromberg (Bydgoszcz), 17, 29, 31, 32, 33,
  441n69

544n169; Belzec visited by, 362–65, 371, 372, 528n244, 529n251, 530n259; bureaucracy of, 378–79; central coordination of deportations under, 54; Chelmno inspected by, 419; complaints about deportations of, 55, 56; in departure of German Jews, 378, 383; on deportation of Jews from Baden-Saarpfalz, 90–91; on deportation of Jews to Soviet territory, 519n73; on deportation of Schneidemühl Jews, 65; and deportations to Lodz, 331, 332; in emigration of Austrian Jews, 37, 82; on expulsion of Jews from Germany's European economic sphere, 195; on expulsion to "a territory yet to be determined," 102–3; and extermination camp development, 354, 362–65, 367, 368, 370, 371; on gassing Soviet Jews, 304; and Goebbels on expelling Jews from Berlin, 104, 105; Heydrich recommends guidelines on Jewish question of, 306; and Heydrich's expanded authority for Jewish question on July 31, 1941, 517n34; and Höppner's proposal to deport Warthegau Jews, 321, 322; on Hungarian Jews transiting through Germany to Portugal, 197; and the intermediate plan, 63; at interministerial meeting on deportation in January 1940, 53, 55; lecturing at police schools, 252; and Madagascar Plan, 82, 85, 86–87, 88, 453n178; on marking German Jews, 319; meetings on deportation of German Jews of, 379, 385; meets with Heydrich about Jewish policy in Poland, 26, 37; meets with Jewish experts in Berlin, 405, 539n105; and Minsk executions of November 1941, 537n66; new manpower for in July 1941, 315; and the Nisko plan, 36–43, 181, 378; at October 10, 1941, meeting in Prague on deportations, 301; other priorities

intervening in deportation plans of, 108; on pragmatic selection of deportees, 107; *Referat* for Jews and Evacuation under, 59; on Serbian Jews, 323, 325, 341–42; on the small role of the Jews in deportations of 1940, 102; as special assistant to Heydrich, 52, 54, 378, 447n60; at Wannsee Conference, 411, 413, 414, 540n113; at Zentralstelle für jüdische Auswanderung, 37, 378, 379, 381

Eichner, Unterscharführer, 466n157

Eicke, Theodor, 176

Eimann Wachsturm, 31, 186–87

Einsatzgruppen: activity reports sent to Foreign Office by Heydrich, 399–403; commissars to be turned over to, 220; cooperation with the army, 217, 224, 260, 280, 426, 493n69; in Galicia, 347; Heydrich's directive to, 252–53; in ideological war, 251; in killing of Soviet Jews, 255, 256, 259, 260, 261, 262, 263, 276, 283, 288, 289, 290–93, 296, 303, 308, 313, 316; mentally ill killed by, 186, 187, 188, 189; in occupation of Poland, 16, 17–18, 19, 21, 27, 28–30, 110, 438n11; preparation for Barbarossa, 224–29; regular reports to Heydrich from, 312; in Serbia, 334; sizes of units of, 482n51; in system of occupation in the east, 492n51; as unable to control their auxiliaries, 274; in western campaign, 198

Einsatzkommando (EK), 16, 225

Einwandererzentralstelle (EWZ), 52

Eisenach, Artur, 543n152

Eisenlohr, Ernst, 195

Eley, Geoff, 436n9

emigration: of Austrian Jews after the Anschluss, 37, 82; of German Jews, 195–96; Heydrich as in charge of, 83, 87; Himmler halting, 369; Himmler on European Jews', 69; Nazis blocking non-German Jewish, 196–97

Emmerich, Walter, 109, 126, 127–28
Engel, Gerhard, 519n73
Engelmann, ss–Obersturmbannführer, 513n329
Eppstein, Paul, 86–87
Ereignismeldungen, 263, 313
Estonia: German guidelines on treatment of civilians in, 238; refugees after Soviet annexation, 269
ethnic Germans: Bessarabian Germans, 62, 99; Bukovinian Germans, 62, 99; center shifting to the Warthegau, 52; Cholmer Germans, 96–97, 108, 112, 241; competing for Polish property, 94, 445n219; Dobrudja Germans, 99; educated Poles trying to pass as, 55; Himmler as in charge of resettling, 22, 42, 43, 46, 48, 139; Lithuanian Germans, 62, 99, 102; measures to prevent deportation of, 66; Polish Jews transferred to make room for, 43–54, 106–7, 359; repatriation from Soviet Union, 22, 27, 43, 44, 46, 234; settling as priority over Jewish expulsion, 108; settling in former Polish territory, 27, 94–97, 106, 107. *See also* Baltic Germans; Polish ethnic Germans; Volhynian Germans
eugenics movement, 184–85, 425
Europe: Nazi sphere of influence in, 193–212. *See also* Czechoslovakia; European Jews; Germany; Poland; southeastern Europe; Soviet Union; western Europe
European Jews: adversarial relations with Christians, 1–5; in Eastern Europe, 4; emancipation of, 4; emigration halted by Nazis, 369; expulsions of, 4; extension of systematic mass murder to, 353; Germans blocking emigration of, 196–97, 476n121; in German sphere of influence, 194; Himmler on emigration of, 69; Hitler approves eradication of, 371; Madagascar Plan for, 81–89;

Marxism (Bolshevism) associated with, 5, 8, 217, 224, 247–48, 296, 334, 432; population in March 1942, 415; Rademacher's proposal of intra-European bank to administer assets of, 86, 88; second peak of victory euphoria and fate of, 314–30, 371, 426–27; seen as enemies of Germany, 11–12; stereotypes of, 3, 5; as symbols of "social losers'" frustrations, 3, 5. *See also* German Jews; Jewish question; Polish Jews; Slovakian Jews; Soviet Jews
euthanasia, 184–93; Hitler orders stopping of, 264; of Jews, 431; personnel in extermination program, 304, 362, 416, 420; technology used in extermination camps, 354, 357
evacuation teams (*Evakuierungsgruppen*), 385
Der ewige Jude (film), 510n295
executions: becoming daily routine, 278; in Bialystok, 255–56, 257, 258; controlled escalation of, 263; by Einsatzgruppen in Poland, 28–29; "execution tourism," 261; in Garsden, 253–55; of Gypsies, 296; Himmler and Heydrich discuss on October 14, 1941, 303; Himmler on spiritual care of executioners, 300; Himmler witnessing, 283, 312, 313, 353; Keitel on plans for Polish, 17; mass executions, 303–4, 353–54; methods other than shooting sought, 283; Müller requests halt in, 287; number of Poles executed by end of 1939, 35; regulations on military participation in, 278; standardized method adopted, 261; in Upper Silesia in September 1939, 34
exhaust gas, 355–56, 363
expiation tax, 173
expulsion policy, 36–110; Barbarossa and, 239; Cracow deportations, 131–34; curbing of deportation plans, January–February 1940, 54–63; as element of

extermination camps, 354; in evolution of Final Solution, 424; expulsions, September 1939–April 1941, 112; for German Jews in the Reich, 27, 39, 45, 47, 54, 65, 169, 318, 319, 323–30, 361–62, 374–98; versus ghettoization, 36, 112–13, 165, 166, 168; Himmler's proposal for racial organization of eastern Europe, 67–70; Hitler losing faith in, 68; as implying decimation of Jewish population, 213; insurmountable problems of, 35, 430–31; Jewish question still envisioned in terms of in June 1941, 253; Jews of Baden-Saarpfalz deported to France, 89–92; last spasms of, fall 1940–spring 1941, 89–110; mass murder replacing, 368–69, 431; Nisko plan, 36–43, 112, 181, 378; as postponed until after the war, 54, 60, 102, 318, 321, 371, 424; racial theories underlying, 44; Rosenberg on, 232; for settlement of Baltic Germans, 47–53; for settlement of Volhynian Germans, 65–67; settling ethnic Germans as priority over, 108; Stettin deportations, 64–65, 100, 108, 112; to "a territory yet to be determined," 101–6, 200. *See also* Madagascar Plan

extermination camps: Birkenau, 357, 364, 374, 421, 544n167; Chelmno, 312, 366, 372, 374, 416–19, 530n267, 542n145; development of, 352–53; as not an accident, 316; Semlin (Sajmiste), 374, 421–23, 546n178; Sobibor, 365, 366, 372, 426. *See also* Belzec

Ezergailis, Andrew, 538n78

Fähnrich, Reichsbahnoberinspektor, 382
Faninger, Major, 341
Faulmüller, Hans, 338–39, 344, 522n126
Fegelein, Hermann, 280, 283, 288
Felber, Hans, 113–14
Feldscher, Werner, 405
Filbert, Alfred, 226, 227

Final Solution to the Jewish Question: ambiguity about timing of, 408; attitude of German population to, 8–9, 10, 388–92, 428–33; August 15, 1941, as caesura in, 283; auxiliary police units in, 277; background of, 1–11; Barbarossa and onset of the Holocaust, June–December 1941, 244–308; careerism, opportunism, and accommodation in, 425; from conception to implementation, October 1941–March 1942, 374–423; core killing squads of, 310; as crystallizing in minds of Nazi leaders, 424; debate over decision-making process in, 213–14; division of labor in, 298; escalating murder of Soviet Jews opening way for, 224; euthanasia in evolution of, 193; as evolving, 424; expulsion seen as, 36–110, 315, 430–31; first peak of victory euphoria and, 309–14, 426; German imperialism in the east and, 14, 28; Heydrich as responsible for planning, 200; Heydrich's expanded authority for Jewish question in July 1941, 315–16; Heydrich's feasibility study for, 277, 315–16, 330, 353, 370, 406, 426; Heydrich's Jewish desk's note on, 52; Himmler's speech of October 1943 on, 263; Hitler and the decision-making process, 424–28; Hitler's prophecy of January 1939, 11, 209, 299–300, 319, 320, 321, 370, 391–92, 407, 408, 425–26, 429, 510n295, 517n45, 546n2; implied genocide evolving into, 214; integrating bureaucracy into, 398–415; Jewish emigration blocked pending, 196, 197, 476n121; local initiative in evolution of, 284, 294, 295, 308, 504n217, 509n278; Madagascar Plan seen as, 81, 88; mass murders of Serbian Jews as anticipation of, 346, 523n153; mind-set of low-ranking perpetrators, 298–99; murder of Soviet

Final Solution (*continued*)
Jews in evolution of, 245; no general orders issued for, 305, 313; October 1941 as watershed in, 313, 318, 354, 427; ordinary men in, 297–98; Ost-ministerium conference of January 1942, 414–15; passing the threshold to, August–December 1941, 277–94; Poland as laboratory for, 12–35; problem of evidence on, 317; second peak of victory euphoria and fate of European Jewry, 314–30, 426; Suhr made Referent for, 315; turning point in decision-making of mid-July 1941, 267; victory and radicalization of, 425–27, 420; Wannsee Conference, 306, 317, 406–7, 410–14, 415, 540n112, 540n113; from war of destruction to the, 309–73

Firma Gaubschat, 356, 419

First Crusade, 3

First ss Brigade, 233, 256, 261, 279, 282, 310, 312

Fischböck, Hans, 202, 204

Fischer, Ludwig: and Jewish labor, 142, 143; marking decree of, 138; as Warsaw district governor, 109; and Warsaw ghetto, 121, 122, 123, 127–28, 129, 130, 159, 360, 462n76

Fitzner (military administrator), 39

Fletcher, Roger, 436n9

Flurbereinigung (fundamental cleansing), 14, 18, 20, 34, 181

forced labor: "destruction through work," 294; Frank ordering, 138, 141; by German Jews, 175, 176, 177; Gypsies subjected to, 183; Hitler limiting use in Reich, 178; in Lohse's plan for the east, 285; in occupied Soviet Union, 294, 509n275; in Poland, 141–45; in Rosenberg's vision of occupied Soviet Union, 236; by Serbian Jews, 335; in Stahlecker's plan for the east, 286

Forster, Albert, 22, 23, 31, 33, 48, 61, 74, 186

fortifications, 145, 146, 149, 419

Fort VII: Poznan, 188, 189; Kaunas, 287

IV B 4, 378

Fox, John P., 476n124

France: Alsace and Lorraine lost by, 89, 193, 197; to cede Madagascar to Germany, 85, 101, 415; French Revolution, 4, 5; German military administration in northern, 194, 197; Hitler's victory over, 79, 80, 81, 426; Jews from Baden and Saarpfalz deported to, 89–92; Luxembourg Jews infiltrate, 92–93; Parisian synagogue bombings, 519n76; partition of, 197; relatively small Jewish population in, 194; request to deport Jews from, 324, 329, 330; resettlement of Jews to Madagascar considered by, 81; Spanish Jews interned in, 368, 373; trains deporting Jews from, 382; treatment of Jews in, 197–205. *See also* Vichy government

Frank, Hans: address to district governors of December 16, 1941, 408–9; on annexing Pripet marshes to General Government, 239, 359; Austrian Jews sent to General Government of, 98, 99; on Barbarossa and decimation of European Jewry, 239; as chief of military administration in Poland, 22, 109; complete independence from army wanted by, 23, 24; Cracow Jews deported by, 131–32; on death penalty for leaving ghetto, 160, 360; on deportation of German Jews to Poland, 326; on deportation of Jews east of the Vistula, 45; on deportation of Lodz Jews, 114; on deportation potential of General Government, 56–57; eastern Galicia added to government of, 347; and extermination camp development, 358–59, 360–61, 372; and forced Jewish labor, 138, 141, 142, 146, 147;

Hamburg Jews blocked by, 387; and Himmler's memo on racial reorganization, 70, 71; and Himmler's Polish resettlement plans, 54, 59, 61, 62, 63–64, 65, 67–68, 71, 95, 98, 101, 107, 126, 426, 448n86; on Hitler's views on Germanization, 105; on Jewish councils, 138; and Jewish property, 141; on killing Poles, 34–35; Krüger's complaint about, 406; liquidating Polish intelligentsia, 71; and Madagascar Plan, 82, 83–84, 85, 88; on Nisko plan, 42; piratical policy in Poland, 56; on provisioning Jews, 159; on repatriating ethnic Germans, 96; in resettlement schedule agreement for 1940, 93; self-sufficient Warsaw ghetto economy approved by, 105–6, 127, 129; trusteeship of Polish property of, 139; on Warsaw ghetto, 122

Frankfurt, 384

Franz, Major, 311

Frauendorfer, Max, 109, 143–44, 145, 151

Freisler, Roland, 29, 411

French Revolution, 4, 5

Friedlander, Henry, 185, 192, 193, 431, 474n75, 532n3

Friedländer, Saul, 7, 10, 428, 536n39

Friedman, Philip, 437n1, 462n76

Fuchs, Gunter, 392

Fuchs, Wilhelm, 334, 343

fundamental cleansing (*Flurbereinigung*), 14, 18, 20, 34, 181

Fürth, 385

Gabrovski, Petur, 212

Galen, Clemens August, Graf von, 192

Galicia: "Bloody Sunday" in, 349, 361; death toll by August 1941, 260; Drohobycz (Drogobych), 261, 271, 350; ethnic Germans in, 58; ghettoization in, 348, 350, 352; Kolomyja, 349–50, 352; mass murder of Jews in eastern, 347–52; political control in occupied, 278;

Stanislawow, 347, 348–49, 350, 352, 361; Tarnopol, 347, 348, 350, 352, 400; Ukrainians murder Jews in, 268. *See also* Lwow

Garsden (Gargzdai), 253–55, 256, 258

Garwin, Mieczyslaw, 462n88

gas chambers: at Belzec, 360, 363, 364, 419, 543n162, 543n163; at Birkenau, 374; development of, 354–58; as element of extermination camps, 354; Himmler on construction of, 366; mentally ill killed by, 188–89, 191, 193, 354; for Mogilev, 307, 372; for Soviet Jews, 304

gas vans: at Chelmno, 366, 372, 374, 417, 418–19, 542n151, 543n152; engine exhaust testing, 354–56, 367; for killing mental patients, 188–90, 365; for killing Soviet Jews, 304; mass production of, 372; as preferred to shooting women and children, 312, 422; for Riga, 368, 396, 416; at Semlin, 422, 423

Gater, Rudolf, 126, 127, 128, 130, 461n74

Gaubschat company, 356, 419

Gaus, Friedrich, 91

Gay, Erwin, 349, 350

Gdynia (Gotenhafen), 46–47, 60

Gekrat, 191

General Government. *See* Poland

Generalkommissariat Weissruthenien, 288, 306, 393, 506n235

Generalplan Ost, 97, 240, 241

General Union of French Jews, 201, 205

genocide: in Belorussia, 289; and Heydrich's Wannsee Conference speech, 412; selective mass murder transformed into, 278, 292; war of destruction against Soviet Union implying, 213–14

Gerlach, Christian: on camps for communists, 302; on declaration of war against U.S., 540n120; on Eichmann and November 1941 killings, 537n66;

Great Britain: (*continued*)
Order Police code broken by, 263; permitting German Jews to emigrate to Palestine, 195–96; resettlement of Jews to Madagascar considered by, 82

Greece: German occupation of, 194, 334, 336; relatively small Jewish population in, 194; Salonika, 519n73; trains deporting Jews from, 382

Greifelt, Ulrich, 48–49, 67, 325

Greiser, Arthur: and Chelmno, 366, 417; as chief administrator of Poznan, 22; and deportation of Jews to the east, 325, 326, 330, 332, 375; deportations of Jews from Warthegau by, 61, 65; and Himmler, 56; and Lodz ghetto, 114, 116, 118; and Madagascar Plan, 84–85, 88, 93; on marking of Jews, 138; Polish Jews provided for work in Germany by, 177; on provisioning Jews, 158, 159; "Three-Ex System" of, 34

Grodno, 262

Groscurth, Helmuth, 17, 24, 73, 75, 76–77

Gross, Walter, 232

Grossmann, Prof. Dr. and ss–Oberführer, 186

Gruner, Wolf, 169, 512n325

Gschliesser, Dr., 146

Guderian, Heinz, 327, 328

guerrillas, 219, 222

Gumbinnen, 247

Günther, Hans, 39, 40

Günther, Rolf: and Baden-Saarpfalz deportations, 91; in deportations of German Jews, 382; in deportations of Polish Jews, 95–96, 100; as Eichmann's deputy, 378; and Nisko plan, 37, 39, 40, 41, 445n27

Gutman, Yisrael, 167, 444n2, 470n256

Gutterer, Leopold, 104, 318, 320, 411

Gypsies, 178–84; at Chelmno, 418; criteria for identifying, 180; deportation from Baden-Saarpfalz, 89; deportation from Austria, 302, 376; deportation from Germany, 181–83, 374, 375; deportation to Lodz, 330, 331, 366, 392; expulsion from German Poland, 26, 27, 35, 40, 57, 60, 63, 65; killing in occupied Soviet Union, 296; killing of Belorussian, 288, 289, 507n242; killing of Polish, 32; killing of Serbian, 340, 341, 344, 345, 346; no systematic killing of, 179, 473n47; persecution of, 169; at Semlin, 422, 423; Serbian anti-Jewish measures applied to, 335; stereotypes of, 178, 179

Hadamar, 191, 192

Hagen, Herbert, 92, 198

Hagen, Wilhelm, 126, 160

Hager, Gerhard, 348

Hahn (Gendarmerie Hauptwachtmeister of Pelplin), 33

Hahn, Dr. (adviser for police affairs in Slovakia), 208

Hahn, Fritz Gebhard von, 402

Hahnzog, Ferdinand, 364

Halder, Franz: on the army and the Einsatzgruppen, 18, 20, 21, 27; and Barbarossa, 215, 216, 218; on coup against Hitler, 73; Groscurth on collapse of, 24; November 1939 western offensive opposed by, 73, 80; on plan to exterminate Polish people, 17, 20, 21, 23; on the situation in the east as not so bad, 77; as unreceptive to objections to atrocities, 72, 75, 76, 77

Hamburg, 325, 326, 387

handicapped, killing of the, 184–93, 429, 430, 431

Harster, Wilhelm, 204

Härtel, Herbert, 350

Hartheim, 191

Hartl, Albert, 378

Hassell, Ulrich von, 221

Haupttreuhandstelle Ost (HTO), 23, 53, 117, 139, 140, 154, 155

Hecht, Gerhard, 44–45, 56, 69
Heess, Walter, 355, 356
Heim, Susanne, 461n74
Henrici, Captain, 280
Herf, Jeffrey, 5
Hermann, Günther, 226
Hersmann, Werner, 254
Hewel, Walther, 68, 101
Heyde, Werner, 186
Heydrich, Reinhard: on abstaining from
    drastic measures, 264; activity reports
    sent to Foreign Office by, 399–403; and
    Barbarossa, 216, 217, 224–26, 227,
    228–29, 252–53, 257, 262–63; and the
    Blaskowitz report, 76; and change in
    deportation policy in May 1940, 107;
    on civilian government for Poland,
    440n38; on concentrating Polish Jews
    in cities, 26, 27, 111, 113; on coordi-
    nated effort in the east, 301; daily
    reports of, 312; on deportation of
    Berlin Jews, 327; and deportation of
    German Jews, 301–2, 318, 324–25,
    326, 327, 329, 333–34, 371, 381, 393;
    on deportation of Gypsies, 26, 27, 40,
    181, 182, 441n65; and deportation of
    Jews from Baden and Saarpfalz, 90, 91;
    on deportation of Jews from Stettin,
    64; on deportation of Jews to a place to
    be chosen later, 104, 200; deportation
    of Spanish Jews opposed by, 368; and
    deportations into General Govern-
    ment, 71, 96, 99; on Dutch Jews, 203;
    Eichmann made special assistant to, 52,
    378; and Eichmann's deportation plan
    of January 4, 1940, 53; and Einsatz-
    gruppen leaders, 16, 438n11; on Ein-
    satzgruppen-Wehrmacht cooperation,
    18, 19–20, 493n69; executions dis-
    cussed with Himmler, 303; and exhaust
    gas tests, 355, 356, 372; expanded
    authority for Jewish question on July
    31, 1941, 315–16, 411, 517n34,
    517n36; and extermination camp de-
velopment, 365, 366, 368, 371, 372;
fear of going too far too quickly, 263;
feasibility study for solution of Jewish
question, 277, 315–16, 330, 353, 370,
406, 426; files regarding Final Solution
destroyed, 317; on French anti-Jewish
measures, 199; and Garsden executions, 255, 310; and Himmler discuss
Jewish question in March 1942, 427–
28; integrating bureaucracy into the
Final Solution, 398, 399–403, 406–7;
on Jewish councils, 26, 111, 138; Jewish
emigration as responsibility of, 83, 87;
on Jewish labor, 142; on Jewish question in Slovakia, 208; on liquidation of
Polish leadership, 31–32, 34; and
Madagascar Plan, 83, 87, 88, 316; on
marking of Jews, 105; and Mogilev
camp, 307; Müller request for halt in
executions denied by, 287; and Nisko
plan, 36–37, 39; October 2, 1941,
speech on events of previous year, 300–
301, 307–8; and Ohlendorf, 313; and
Parisian synagogue bombings, 519n76;
and Polish atrocities against Germans,
17; political signals radiating outward
from, 317; at Prague conference of October 10, 1941, 301, 329; on proposals
on the Jewish question, 25–26; at resettlement meeting of January 30, 1940,
59–60; in resettlement schedule agreement for 1940, 93; and Rosenberg, 236;
Schnellbrief of, 26, 27, 111, 113, 138; on
screening Soviet POWs, 277, 501n173;
on self-cleansing efforts, 228, 262, 268,
272; and Serbian Jews, 342, 346, 422;
on settling Jewish question after the
war, 102; on short- and long-range
plans for deporting Poles and Jews, 26,
49; sole responsibility for Jewish question claimed by, 306; and Uebelhoer's
protests over deportations to Lodz,
332; and Volhynian action, 65; and
Wannsee Conference, 406–7, 410–14

ment for 1940, 93; resettling ethnic Germans, 22, 42, 43, 46, 48, 96–97, 139; responding to Hitler's signals, 425; and Rosenberg, 236, 284; and the Selbstschutz, 31; on shooting Polish insurgents, 21, 28, 439n21; speech of October 1943, 263; on spiritual care of executioners, 258, 300; spreading responsibility for murder of the Jews, 263; ss men encouraged to father children out of wedlock by, 451n44; on ss not speaking about mass murders, 391; Stuckart informed about Jewish policy by, 404; turning attention to wider question of European Jewry, 315; and Uebelhoer's protests over deportations to Lodz, 331, 332; unease about the open secret becoming too open, 409–10; visit to Belorussia in mid-August 1941, 283, 312; on the Volhynian action, 67; war economy and deportations of, 56; warning about arbitrariness and violation of guidelines, 305; on women and children, 299, 313, 516n21

Hinghofer, Lt. General Dr., 338

Hinterberg, 115

Hitler, Adolf: on accelerating pacification in mid-July 1941, 313; all necessary measures authorized by, 265, 309, 310; anti-Bolshevism of, 224; anti-Semitism of, 10, 11, 224; on Barbarossa, 215, 216–17, 218, 309; on Blaskowitz report, 75, 451n136; on brutal treatment of Poland, 15, 17, 18–19, 24, 25, 437n8; bureaucratic style of, 242–43, 317; changing goals regarding the Jewish question, 101; civil administration in the east established by, 267; civilian administration for Poland decreed by, 23; coup preparations against, 73, 80; as curbing zeal for deportation, 318, 321; in decision-making process, 320–21, 424–28, 517n44; deportations

postponed by, 319, 321, 323, 325, 352, 371, 424; and deporting Berlin Jews, 104–5; on deporting German Jews, 27, 54, 302, 319, 321, 323, 325, 330, 352–53, 371, 375, 378, 424, 426, 427; and deporting Jews from Baden and Saarpfalz, 90, 91; on deporting Polish Jews, 27, 36, 54, 328, 361, 426; on depriving German Jews of their citizenship, 175, 380; eradication of European Jews approved by, 371; on euthanasia, 185, 189; France defeated by, 79, 80, 81, 426; fundamental observations on eastern situation, 265–66, 309–10; general approval for action on Jewish question, 199; on Germanization as long-term project, 108; Grand Mufti of Jerusalem received by, 406, 539n107; and Gypsies, 181; on the handicapped, 186; and Himmler's racial reorganization plan, 68–70; and Hungary, 209; intentions for European Jews on July 22, 1941, 314–15; Jewish question as obsession of, 424–25; Jewish question discussed by Goebbels and, on August 19, 1941, 319–20; on lack of German manpower in east, 278; legal and moral norms of pre-Nazi society repudiated by, 399; losing faith in population resettlement, 68; and Madagascar Plan, 83, 101, 426; marking German Jews approved by, 371; at meeting of July 16, 1941, 265–66, 309–10; meets with Himmler in March 1942, 427, 428; meets with Himmler on December 18, 1941, 410; military government in Poland continued by, 24; on non-Germans not bearing arms, 273; no paper trail leading to, 317; November 1939 western offensive planned by, 23, 24, 72, 73, 80; optimism about military situation in Soviet Union, 309, 546n1; on partition of Poland, 21–22; on Polish Jews

Hitler, Adolf: (*continued*)
working in the Reich, 178; on Polish
resettlement in General Government,
98, 99; prophecy about Jews of January
1939, 11, 209, 299–300, 319, 320, 321,
370, 391–92, 407, 408, 425–26, 429,
510n295, 517n45, 546n2; proposals on
Jewish question submitted to, 10–11;
Reichenau commended for his zeal,
293; remarks to Nazi leaders on
December 12, 1942, 407–8, 427;
reverses policy on deportations, 325,
330, 352–53, 375, 378, 424, 426, 427;
rhetoric becoming more candid in
October 1941, 370; on Rosenberg, 236;
signals radiating outward from, 317,
425; and Slavic nations, 15; on Slovakia, 207–8; Sportspalast speeches of,
328, 392, 546n2; and Stahlecker's plan
for the east, 286; statements on Jewish
question in early 1942, 546n2; on turning the east into Garden of Eden, 266,
267, 309, 426; unease about the open
secret becoming too open, 409–10; on
the Wehrmacht in the east, 249–50,
264, 265
Hlinka Guard, 207
Hoche, Alfred, 185
Hoepner, Colonel General Erich, 250,
259
Hofbauer, Untersturmführer Dr., 146
Hoffmann, Major General, 343
Hoffmann, Kurt, 150, 151, 163, 164
Hofkartei (farm files), 66
Höfle, Hans, 362, 363
Hofmann, Otto, 411
Holland. *See* Netherlands
Holocaust. *See* Final Solution to the Jew-
ish Question
homosexuals, 45, 454n192
Homyel' (Gomel), 289
Hoppe (Four Year Plan), 199
Höppner, Rolf-Heinz: in extermination
camp development, 321–23, 354, 361,

371, 373; in Polish resettlement, 67,
94, 95, 96
Horodenko, 350
Horthy, Miklos, 209
Höss, Rudolf: on Eichmann's meeting of
Jewish experts, 539n105; on Eichmann's visit to Auschwitz, 544n169;
on gassing tests at Auschwitz, 356–57,
364, 421, 526n207, 526n208, 526n209,
527n210
Hoth, Hermann, 291
HTO (Haupttreuhandstelle Ost), 23, 53,
117, 139, 140, 154, 155
Hungary: as ally of Germany, 194, 207;
anti-Jewish measures in, 208–9; anti-
Semitism in, 208; in Barbarossa, 275;
deportation of Jews of, 197, 382; Jewish population of, 194, 210; Romanian
territory acquired by, 209, 211; treatment of Jews in, 208–10

Iasi, 276–77
ideological war, 250–51
imperialism, racial, 14, 28, 184, 231, 430,
431
Imredy, Bela, 208, 209
Industrial Revolution, 4
infants, deformed, 185–86, 190
Institute for Research into the Jewish
Question, 236
intelligentsia: deportation of Polish, 44,
48, 51, 54, 57; eliminating Soviet, 216,
217, 218, 220, 294; as having priority
over the Jews in Poland, 110; Heydrich
on elimination of, 18; in Hitler's vision
of Poland's future, 24; killing of Galician, 350; liquidation of Polish, 32, 34,
430
intermarriage, 172, 211, 248, 379, 412
International Committee of the Red Cross
(ICRC), 195
International Refugee Committee, 202
internment camps, 47, 50
Iron Guard, 210, 211–12

Italy: as ally of Germany, 194; German Jews emigrating to Palestine through, 196; relatively small Jewish population in, 194; trains deporting Jews from, 382

Jache, Oberregierungsrat, 146, 147
Jäckel, Eberhard, 517n34
Jäger, Karl: and Battalion for the Defense of National Labor, 273; on execution of women, 261; Himmler not meeting with, 505n219; on killing of Jews in Kaunas, 260, 395; on killing of Jews in Lithuania, 287–88, 311; and Lohse's guidelines, 286; as making no reference to instruction from Berlin, 306; sends men to Belorussia, 290; and Stahl-ecker's position paper on Jewish ques-tion, 311; and Streckenbach's alleged killing order, 227
Janetzke, Wilhelm, 394
Jansen, Christian, 443n99
Jastrzebski, Wlodzimierz, 442n83
Jeckeln, Friedrich: in deportation of Ger-man and Polish Jews, 304–5; and execution of Berlin Jews in Riga, 397; experience in administering the Jewish question, 242; and 1st ss Brigade, 261, 279, 281, 310, 311–12; Generalkom-missariat Weissruthenien transferred to, 393; and Himmler on racial purity, 240; and Himmler's "explicit order" to kill Jews, 503n208; Himmler warning about arbitrariness and violation of guidelines, 305; as HSSPF for south front, 234; in Kamenets Podolsky mas-sacre, 291, 312; and liquidation of Riga ghetto, 395–97; in Pripet marshes pacification, 279, 280; radio reports on August, 1941, activities by, 312; repri-manded for murder of Berlin Jews, 307; in Ukrainian killings, 291, 292
Jelgava (Mitau), 274, 400
Jersak, Tobias, 517n44

Jew houses (Judenhäuser), 172
"The Jew in German History" (training brochure), 248
Jewish councils: in Amsterdam, 203, 204, 205; in Cracow ghetto, 132, 133; debate over supervision of, 143; Heydrich on, 26, 111, 138; as indis-pensable to ghetto management, 166; and Jewish labor, 138, 142, 143, 144, 145, 149–50; in Lodz ghetto, 115, 119; in Warsaw ghetto, 121, 126, 127
"Jewish desk" (Judenreferat), 11
"Jewish experts" (Judensachbearbeiter), 11
Jewish labor, 141–51; as becoming dis-pensable, 261–62; demand for rising in spring 1942, 164–65, 167–68; exploit-ing German Jews', 175–78; exploiting in Lodz ghetto, 116–19; Heydrich's Wannsee Conference speech on, 411–12; labor as not precluding murder, 296, 297; labor camps, 145–46, 148, 149–50, 176; in occupied Soviet Union, 295; Rasch on economic effects of killing, 314; as still valued in 1942, 394. See also forced labor
Jewish property: of Belgian Jews, 205; of Dutch Jews, 203, 205; of French Jews, 199, 200, 201; of German Jews, 173, 380–81; of Polish Jews, 139–41; regis-tration in Warsaw district, 138; of Romanian Jews, 211; of Serbian Jews, 335; of Slovak Jews, 208; taxation on confiscated, 155
Jewish question: "education for murder," 251; Hitler and Goebbels discuss on August 19, 1941, 319–20; Hitler as obsessed with, 424–25; Hitler's gen-eral approval for action on, 199; inva-sion of Soviet Union complicating, 110; as key to all other problems for Hitler, 10; Lebensraum requiring solu-tion of, 26; in Lohse's plan for the east, 285; Polish Jews altering, 12; proposals submitted to Hitler on, 10–11, 25–26;

Lammers, Hans: (*continued*)
Jews as "dependents" of the Reich,
175; at meeting of July 16, 1941, 265,
266, 309; at Wannsee Conference, 411
Lange, Herbert: Bach-Zelewski requests
visit from, 312, 354; on construction of
Chelmno, 365–66, 416–17; gas vans
promised for Chelmno, 372; operating
gas van killing mental patients, 188–
89, 365
Lange, Rudolf: on concentration camp for
Riga, 512n316, 512n323; on German
Jews deported to Riga, 332, 333, 367;
on German Jews diverted to Kaunas,
395; in liquidation of Riga ghetto, 396;
at Wannsee Conference, 411
Langhäuser, Rudolf, 18
Langmuir, Gavin, 3, 7
Lasch, Karl, 109, 135, 136, 350
Lattmann, Erich, 222
Latvia: integrating locals into occupation
structure, 274; pogroms in, 268; refugees after Soviet annexation, 269;
Schutzmannschaften in, 499n150. *See
also* Riga
Law for the Defense of the Nation (Bul-
garia), 212
Lebensraum: Barbarossa and, 110, 223,
234; creating as long-term process,
108; eastern European empire for
providing, 14, 245; Nazi racial policy
and, 27, 28; population resettlement
for, 35, 97, 234; solution to Jewish
question required by, 26, 43; victory
and radicalization of, 427; western
Europe and, 194
Lechthaler, Major, 289, 290
Leeb, Wilhelm, Ritter von, 73, 78, 242,
267, 271, 488n137
Leese, Arnold, 81
Lehmann, Rudolf, 219, 220
Leibbrand, Max, 382
Leibbrandt, Georg, 304, 333, 368, 410,
414

Leideritz, Peter, 349–50
Leipzig, 175
Leist, Ludwig, 160
Lemberg. *See* Lwow
Leningrad, 239, 325, 326, 327, 426
Lepecky commission, 82
Levy, Richard, 8
Lewy, Guenter, 473n47
Ley, Robert, 101
libraries, German Jews denied access to,
172
Liepaja, 260, 303, 304
Liepe, Walter, 341
Linden, Herbert, 186, 190, 191
Lindqvist, Sven, 437n6
Lischka, Kurt, 195, 198
List, Wilhelm, 334, 335, 336–37, 339,
344, 440n36
Litauer Aktion, 97–98, 112
Lithuania: civil administration takes over
in, 277–78; ethnic Germans in, 62, 99,
102; German guidelines on treatment
of civilians in, 238; Germans executing
civilians in, 253–55; Jews murdered in
Alytus, 275; killing of Jews, August–
September 1941, 287–88; local in-
formers in, 252; pogroms in, 268;
Polish Jewish refugees in, 196; provisional government in, 273; refugees
after Soviet annexation, 269; regular
execution of Jews in, 285; Saugumas,
269; Vilnius, 272. *See also* Kaunas
Lithuanian Activists Front, 270
Litzmannstadt. *See* Lodz
Litzmannstädter Warenhan-
delsgesellschaft (LWHG), 117, 119, 140
Lodz (Litzmannstadt): Baltic Germans
coming to, 58, 64; Chelmno for reducing ghetto population of, 366, 419; and
Cholmer Aktion, 97; deportation of
German Jews to, 301–2, 303, 325, 326,
329, 330–32, 333, 361, 362, 366, 370,
371, 375, 384, 392–93, 411; deportation of Jews from, 48, 50, 51, 65, 85,

Nedic, Milan, 336, 337, 344
Netherlands: extermination of Jews becomes known in, 405–6; German rule in, 194; new HSSPF created in 1938, 234; relatively small Jewish population in, 194; trains deporting Jews from, 382; treatment of Jews in occupied, 202–5
Neuhausen, Hans, 334, 336
Neumann, Erich, 411, 413
Neumann-Neurode, Karl-Ulrich, 121
newborns, deformed, 185–86, 190
newspapers, German Jews denied access to, 172
Nikolayev, 292
Nisko plan, 36–43, 112, 181, 378
NKVD, 259, 269
Nockemann, Hans, 222, 226
Norway, 194, 234, 253
Nosske, Gustav, 226, 227
Novak, Franz, 381–83
Novinki, 283, 355
Nuremberg, 385
Nuremberg Laws, 180, 183, 211, 248, 379, 405, 414

Oberg, Carl Albrecht, 109
Oberhauser, Josef, 363–64, 419, 420, 543n163
Odessa, 292–93, 508n264
Oebsger-Röder, Franz, 31, 32, 33
Ohlendorf, Otto: in Bukovina and Bessarabia killings, 276, 277; as Einsatzgruppe D commander, 226; Heydrich initiating in Final Solution, 313; on Himmler order to kill Soviet Jews, 292, 508n263; on Jewish labor, 516n29; in Nikolayev killings, 292
old people's ghetto, 412
Opatow, 134, 135
Operation Barbarossa. *See* Barbarossa
Operation 14f13, 192, 357
Operation Reinhard, 131
Operation Typhoon, 328

Order Police, 229–34; in Barbarossa, 224, 225; in Belorussia, 289, 290; in Bialystok killings, 257; British break code of, 263; at Chelmno, 416–17, 418; in deportation of German Jews, 381; in Galicia, 349, 350; Heydrich's orders to, 252; Himmler gains control of, 229; Hitler's prophecy on annihilation of Jews in training journal of, 299–300; ideological training of, 251; in mass murder, 256; no single order for Final Solution to, 313; in Pripet marshes pacification, 279, 280; and Schutzmannschaften, 274, 275; in Ukraine, 291
Ordnungsdienst, 115, 274, 500n153
Organisation Schmelt, 357, 397–98, 421
orphaned children, 293
Orth, Karin, 357, 526n207
Oster, Hans, 73
Ostjuden (eastern European Jews): in German perceptions of "the East," 247; German soldiers encountering in Poland, 13, 420; harsh treatment planned for, 16; pockets of survival of, 206; quadruple jeopardy of, 205–6. *See also* Polish Jews; Soviet Jews
"Ostland," 237, 486n108
Ostrowiec, 135
Ostwall, 27, 60, 145

Paersch, Fritz, 129
Palestine, German Jews emigrating to, 195–96
Palfinger, Alexander: on dying out of the Jews, 119–20, 460n34; in Lodz ghetto, 117–18, 119–20, 152, 153; and Tarnopol ghetto, 348; in Warsaw ghetto, 125, 126, 127, 128, 130, 462n86
partisans: as collaborators, 275; and deportation of Jews to the east, 306; German fixation with, 279; Jews associated with, 288; in Poland, 17; in Serbia, 335, 336, 337, 339, 346; ss Cavalry

Brigade killing, 280; targeted groups described as, 282, 309
Paul, Gerhard, 534n11
Pavlu, Obersturmbannführer, 134
Paxton, Robert, 201
Pearl Harbor, 407
Pelplin, 33
Pelt, Robert Jan van, 357, 421, 544n167, 544n169
Pemsel, Max, 339
Petain, Philippe, 198
Petzel, Walter, 56, 74
Ph.D. dissertations, restricting citation of Jews in, 175
"phony war," 73
Piaski, 464n119
Piotrkow, 459n13
Pithiviers camp, 201
Piwonski, Jan, 365
Pleschtschenitzy, 289
Ploesti oil fields, 210, 211
Poche, Obersturmbannführer, 384
pogroms: in activity reports from the east, 400; during Barbarossa, 268–77; deportation of Jews resulting in, 42; during First Crusade, 3; in Iasi, Romania, 276–77; Kristallnacht, 10, 13, 169, 399, 428; military participation in restricted, 280; in Zloczow, Ukraine, 260–61, 494n76
Pohl, Dieter: on death toll in eastern Galicia, 260; on death toll of Polish Jews in 1939, 442n82; on extermination camp at Belzec, 360; on ghettoization and massacres, 348; on ghettos in Lublin district, 464n119; on Jeckeln and 1st ss Brigade, 503n194; on Katzmann and Lwow ghetto, 351; on killing of women and children, 282; local and regional focus of, 504n217; on Ukrainian Jews at end of 1941, 293–94
Poland: agricultural workers to be sent to Germany, 59, 60, 61, 66; alliance with

Germany rejected by, 15, 206–7; Bialystok, 255–56, 257, 259, 260, 278, 310; Bydgoszcz, 17, 29, 31, 32, 33, 441n69; change in German-Soviet demarcation line, 27, 30; Congress Poles, 32, 44, 47, 54, 55, 60; curbing of Nazi deportation plans, January– February 1940, 54–63; Czestochowa, 30, 135; division into military districts, 21–22; educated Poles trying to pass as ethnic Germans, 55; the General Government, 1939–42, 109; German invasion of, 12, 15, 207; German occupation of eastern in World War I, 247; German terror in, 28–35; Germany's predatory policy toward property in, 139; ghettos in, 111–68; Göring in economic exploitation of, 23, 42, 56; Katowice, 18, 39, 40, 41; Kielce, 135– 36; as laboratory for racial policy, 12– 35, 429–31; Lepecky commission, 82; mass murders begin in occupied, 14– 25; mentally ill killed in, 186–89; Poles suited for Germanization, 44, 55, 70; population resettlement, fall 1940– Spring 1941, 93–101; Reich Jews settled in, 39; resettlement of Jews to Madagascar considered by, 81; *Reststaat* (rump state), 45; shaping of Nazi policy in, 25–28; Soldau, 34, 189, 443n105; transformation from chaotic terror to systematic liquidation, 31– 35; Wehrmacht moves from abdication to complicity, 72–81. *See also* Cracow; Lodz; Lublin; Polish ethnic Germans; Polish Jews; Poznan; Radom; Warsaw; Warthegau
Police Battalion 304, 292
Police Battalion 307, 259–60, 493n65
Police Battalion 309, 232, 233, 255, 257
Police Battalion 314, 292
Police Battalion 320, 291
Police Battalion 322, 233, 257, 312
Police Reserve, 230

Jews," 82, 102; becomes aware of extermination plans, 369, 372; and deportation of Croatian, Slovakian, and Romanian Jews, 379; on deportation of Serbian Jews, 323, 531n281; and halting of Jewish emigration, 369; and the killing of male Jews in Serbia, 341–42, 343, 369; and the killing of Jewish women and children in Serbia, 423; and Madagascar Plan, 82–83, 85–86, 87–88, 92, 415, 453n168; prepares memorandum for Wannsee Conference, 407

radios, confiscation of, 172

Radom: ghettoization in, 131; Police Battalion 309 stationed in, 232

Radom district: ghettoization in, 131, 135, 137; Gypsies deported to, 182; Jewish labor exploitation in, 146, 148; Jewish population in July 1940, 462n87

Raeder, Admiral, 83

Ragger, Major, 132, 133, 134

Rajakowitsch, Erich, 203–4

Rapp, Albert: on deportation of agricultural workers, 59; on Polish resettlement plans, 47–48, 49–50, 51, 55, 56, 63, 93; on politically active Poles, 34; on property seizure, 139; staff for evacuation of Poles and Jews under, 47; on the Volhynian action, 66, 67

Rasch, Otto, 34, 226, 227, 287, 302, 312, 313–14

Ratnitsi, 212

Rauff, Walter, 355–56, 418

Rauter, Hanns, 202, 204

Rediess, Wilhelm, 189

Reeder, Eggert, 205

Reich Commissariat for the Strengthening Germandom, 22–23, 234

Reich Committee for the Scientific Registering of Serious Hereditary and Congenital Illnesses, 185

Reichenau, Walter von, 29, 73, 282, 291, 293, 299

Reichsbahn, 58, 63, 100, 382

Reitlinger, Gerald, 193

Remmers, Hans-Hermann, 393

rental rights, 172

reprisals (retaliation): in Bessarabia and Bukovina, 276; collective, 219, 222; in Drobomil, 259; selecting victims of, 278–79; in Serbia, 335–46, 347, 422

Reserve Police Battalion 11, 289–90, 507n246, 507n247

Reserve Police Battalion 45, 292, 311

Reserve Police Battalion 64, 334, 341, 422, 423, 523n151

Reserve Police Battalion 65, 233

Reserve Police Battalion 101, 251, 297–98

Reserve Police Battalion 105, 260, 261, 314

Reserve Police Battalion 133, 349, 350

resettlement policy. See expulsion policy

residence camps (Wohnlager), 173

retaliation. See reprisals (retaliation)

Retallack, James, 436n9

Retzlaff, Major General Dr., 233

revolution of 1848, 6

Ribbe, Friedrich Wilhelm, 120, 392–93

Ribbentrop, Joachim von: activity reports sent by Heydrich to, 399–403; and decision to invade Poland, 15; and deportation of Baden-Saarpfalz Jews, 91, 92; and deportation of European Jews, 324, 325, 326; and Madagascar Plan, 82, 83, 88; Molotov-Ribbentrop Pact, 15, 27, 211, 249, 347; in Romanian negotiations, 211; and Serbian Jews, 342, 346

Richardt, Wilhelm, 33

Richter (Rapp's representative), 51, 52

Riess, Volker, 188

Riga: in activity reports from the east, 399; auxiliary police actions in, 268, 499n150; concentration camp near, 303, 304, 513n334; execution of German Jews in, 305, 396, 398, 405, 513n339, 538n78; extermination camp

T4, Aktion, 189, 190–92, 264, 304
Thomas, Georg, 215, 218, 235, 236, 332, 486n112
Thomas, Max, 296
three camps system, 66
Three-Ex System (*Drei-A System*), 34
Tighina agreement, 277
Tippelskirch, Kurt von, 76
Tiso, Jozef, 207
Todt, Fritz, 177, 370
Topf & Söhne, 357, 366, 421, 514n349
Topola, 338–39, 340
torturing the Host, 3
Trampedach, Friedrich, 304, 333, 367
transit road IV (Durchgangsstrasse IV), 294, 509n275
Transylvania, 209, 211
Treschkow, Hennig von, 221
Tripartite Pact, 210
Trostinez, 300, 511n300
Trunk, Isaiah, 154, 166, 470n256
Tschierschky, Karl, 286
tuberculosis, 95
Tuka, Vojtech, 207
Tuliszkow, 459n13
Tulp, Sybren, 204
Turner, Harald: gas van acquired by, 422; in killing of Serbian Jews, 334, 336, 337, 339, 340, 341, 342, 343, 344

Uebelhoer, Friedrich: in creation of Lodz ghetto, 114–15; and deportations to Lodz ghetto, 330–31, 332, 392; and food supply for ghetto, 118, 153; on ghetto as transition measure, 116; on marking Jews, 138; on taxing Jewish property, 153, 155; on unauthorized ss interventions in ghetto economy, 140
Ukraine: in activity reports from the east, 400, 401; auxiliary police units in, 274, 310; Babi Yar massacre, 291–92; Berdichev, 292, 297, 510n289; civilians killed in Zborov, 259; German occupa-

tion in World War I, 247; ghettoization in, 294; Jews in workforce of, 296; Kamenets Podolsky, 291, 312; Kiev, 326–27, 371, 402, 403, 426; local collaborators in, 275; local informers in, 252; in Nazi ethnic hierarchy, 269; Odessa, 292–93, 508n264; partially in "Ostland," 486n108; pattern of killing, September–October 1941, 290–92; pogrom in Zloczow, 260–61, 494n76; pogroms in, 268; refugees from, 269; Rosenberg on ghettoization in, 236–37; Rosenberg on governance of, 266; Zhitomir, 291, 292, 400, 401, 403. *See also* Galicia
Ulex, Alexander, 77, 78, 79
Uman, battle of, 277
Umwandererzentrale (Poznan), 378
United Kingdom. *See* Great Britain
United States, Germany declares war on, 407, 410
Upper Silesia: deportation of Jews from, 26, 37, 40, 42, 44, 53, 61; executions in September 1939, 34; Jews gassed at Birkenau, 421; in partition of Poland, 21; Wagner as Gauleiter of, 22
Urkainski, Eustachy, 364
Uzlany-Rudensk, 289

Vallat, Xavier, 201
Varchim, Ernst, 349
Veesenmayer, Edmund, 323, 341
Ventzki, Werner, 158, 330–31
Vichy government: anti-Jewish measures of, 200, 201; Commissariat-General for Jewish Affairs, 201; General Union of French Jews, 201, 205; German policy carried out by, 199; as German puppet government, 194, 198
Vienna: concentration of Jewish population in, 172; deportation of Jews from, 39, 40, 41, 98–99, 100, 104, 105, 108, 112, 327, 328, 329; forced labor by Jews in, 177; Himmler blocking depor-

tation of Jews of, 42; Jewish population of, 383; new HSSPF created in 1938, 234

Vilnius, 272

Vinnitsa, 292

Vitebsk, 289, 401, 402

Volga Germans, 324

Volhynian Germans: deporting Poles to accommodate, 53, 57, 58, 59, 60, 61, 62, 65–67, 93–95, 112; settled at Chelmno, 417

Volkov, Shulamit, 6, 432

Volksdeutsche. *See* ethnic Germans

Vyazma, 328, 329, 371, 426

Wächter, Otto, 109, 134

Waffen-SS: in Barbarossa, 224, 225, 233; First SS Brigade, 233, 256, 261, 279, 282, 310, 312; former mental hospitals taken over by, 187, 188; ideological indoctrination of, 279; in occupation of Poland, 17, 29; random killings in Soviet Union by, 259; Second SS Brigade, 233; in Ukraine, 291. *See also* SS Cavalry Brigade

Wagner, Eduard: attempting to establish military administration of Poland, 22; and Barbarossa, 216–17; and Einsatzgruppen, 16, 18, 19–20, 263; on Hitler's victory in 1940, 79; memorandum to Keitel on army demands in Poland, 24; on partition of Poland, 21; on special powers for third parties, 22, 23

Wagner, Josef, 22, 37, 39, 61

Wagner, Robert, 89, 90, 91, 107

Walbaum, Jost, 122, 161, 162, 359, 360

Walther, Hans-Dietrich, 344–45

Wannsee Conference, 306, 317, 406–7, 410–14, 415, 540n112, 540n113

Warlimont, Walter, 219, 220, 486n109

Warsaw: death penalty for leaving ghetto, 160, 162, 360; death rate in ghetto of, 158; economic self-sufficiency of ghetto of, 105–6, 126–30, 151, 158– 65; epidemics in ghetto of, 159, 160, 161, 360, 469n255; food supply for ghetto of, 124–27, 158–62, 360; General Government rejects deporting Jews to Lublin, 68; ghettoization in, 98, 121–31, 137; ghetto seen as lasting up to five years, 358; imminent clearing of in July 1941, 359; and Madagascar Plan, 84; population density of ghetto of, 124; total population of ghetto of, 124; Transferstelle, 124–25

Warsaw district: ghettoization in, 137; and Jewish labor, 142, 146, 148; Jewish population in July 1940, 462n87; railway travel by Jews restricted in, 138; registration of Jewish property in, 138

Warthegau: agricultural workers sent to Germany from, 59; Baltic Germans immigrating to, 57; center of ethnic German settlement shifting to, 52; chaotic terror in, 34; Cholmer Germans settling in, 96; decline of Jewish population in, 115–16; Frank on government in, 64; ghettoization in, 113, 115, 137; handicapped killed in, 186, 188, 189–90; Lodz's position in, 42, 47; marking of Jews in, 138; new HSSPF created in 1938, 234; resettlement plans for, 43, 44, 47, 48, 49, 50, 53, 54, 61, 64, 84–85, 88, 93–95, 100, 112, 240, 321–23; Volhynian Germans settling in, 59, 65–67, 93–95

water control projects, 146, 148, 149, 150, 151

Weber, Oberkriegsgerichtsrat Dr., 222

Weckbecker, Arno, 443n99

Wehler, Hans-Ulrich, 436n9

Wehrmacht: from abdication to complicity in Poland, 72–81; anti-Jewish measures of, 248; anti-Semitism in, 248; in Barbarossa, 215–24, 426; Blaskowitz, 29, 74–75, 76, 77–78, 79; concerns about antagonizing by excessive zeal, 263; cooperation with Ein-

Wehrmacht: (*continued*)
satzgruppen, 217, 224, 260, 280,
493n69; in crusade against "Jewish-
Bolshevik" enemy, 80–81; as delivering first blows against Soviet Jews, 258;
deportation of Jews to east opposed by,
306; eagerness to support the Nazis,
248; failure to retain executive power
in Poland, 14–24; ghetto-produced
military supplies purchased by, 154,
163; and ideological war, 249–51; in
killing of Soviet Jews, 258, 280, 288,
289, 290–92, 293, 308; letters and photographs from eastern front, 264–65;
mental hospitals taken over by, 187,
189; from passive bystanders to participants, 223; perception and expectations of "the East," 247–50; and
pogroms, 271; Reichenau, 29, 73, 282,
291, 293, 299; Rundstedt, 22, 23, 29,
73, 79, 242, 488n137; Heinrich von
Stülpnagel, 73, 92, 272, 292; Otto von
Stülpnagel, 198, 200, 324; traditional
moral norms of military caste, 80; war
eroding homogeneity of officer corps,
249. *See also* Brauchitsch, Walther
von; Halder, Franz; Jodl, Alfred;
Keitel, Wilhelm
Weichs, General von, 79
Weidmann, Frantisek, 87
Weintz (Himmler's staff), 196
Weirauch, Lothar, 109
Weiss, Aharon, 524n160, 524n165,
525n174, 525n176
Weiss, John, 6
Weiss, Major, 232–33
Weizsäcker, Ernst von, 23, 65, 342, 402,
403, 407
Wentritt, Harry, 355, 356
Wenzel, Franz, 350
West, Werner, 16
Westerkamp, Eberhard, 109
Westermann, Edward B., 484n82
western Europe: anti-Semitism in, 2–4;

treatment of Jews in occupied, 197–
205. *See also* Belgium; France; Great
Britain; Italy; Luxembourg; Nether-
lands; Spain
West Prussia: transformation to system-
atic terror in, 31–34. *See also* Danzig–
West Prussia
Wetzel, Erhard: on euthanasia personnel
in mass executions, 304; and gas vans
for Riga, 372, 393, 416; on *Generalplan
Ost*, 241; on Jewish transports to
the east, 333, 367–68, 531n274; on
Mischlinge, 414; racial policy memo-
randum of, 44–45, 56, 69
Widmann, Albert, 188, 190, 191, 354–55,
356, 372, 525n199
Wielikowski, Dr., 149, 150
Wigand, Arpad, 109
Wilhelm, Hans-Heinrich, 439n21
Wilhelm, Untersturmführer, 33
Wimmer, Friedrich, 202
Winghene, Egon van (Georg de Pottere),
81, 453n168
Winkler (Göring's representative), 70
Wippermann, Wolfgang, 193
Wirth, Christian: in command at Belzec,
420; and Eichmann's visit to Belzec,
363, 364, 371; in euthanasia program,
191, 362; returns to Berlin, 420,
543n163; transfer to Lublin, 362, 371,
372
Wirtschaftsorganisation Ost, Gruppe
Landwirtschaft, 237, 486n112
Wirtschaftsstab Ost, 261, 262, 486n112
Wisliceny, Dieter, 197, 208
Witte, Peter, 518n56
Woermann, Ernst, 207, 402, 403, 415
Wohlthat, Helmuth, 65, 86, 88, 195
Wojack, Irmtrud, 537n66
Wolff, Karl, 422
women and children: euthanasia of chil-
dren, 185–86, 190, 192; first killing of
in July 1941, 260–61; Himmler on
driving out of destroyed villages, 280;

COMPREHENSIVE HISTORY OF THE HOLOCAUST SERIES

The Origins of the Final Solution
The Evolution of Nazi Jewish Policy, September 1939–March 1942
by Christopher R. Browning

The Jews of Bohemia and Moravia
Facing the Holocaust
by Livia Rothkirchen